Italian Art
1900–1945

organized by Pontus Hulten
and Germano Celant

RIZZOLI
NEW YORK

PALAZZOGRASSI

Comitato Amici
di Palazzo Grassi

President
Feliciano Benvenuti

General Manager
Emilio Melli

Artistic Director
Pontus Hulten

First published in 1989 in the
United States of America by
Rizzoli International Publications, Inc.
300 Park Avenue South
New York, NY 10010

First published in 1989 in Italy by
Bompiani

ISBN 0-8478-1134-4

Printed in Italy by Gruppo Editoriale
Fabbri S.p.A., Milan

President
Susanna Agnelli

Palazzo Grassi S.p.A.
San Samuele 3231, Venice

Honorary Committee

*The President of the Council
of Ministers*
On. Ciriaco De Mita

The Vice-President of the Council of Ministers
On. Gianni De Michelis

The Minister of Foreign Affairs
On. Giulio Andreotti

The Minister of Public Instruction
On. Giovanni Galloni

*The Minister of Cultural
and Environmental Assets*
Sen. Vincenza Bono Parrino

The President of the Veneto Region
Prof. Carlo Bernini

The Major of Venice
Avv. Antonio Casellati

The President of the Province of Venice
Arch. Stefano Petris

*The Chancellor of the Università
di Cà Foscari*
Prof. Giovanni Castellani

*The General Director of Environmental,
Architectural, Archaeological, Artistic
and Historical Assets
The Ministry of Cultural
and Environmental Assets*
Prof. Francesco Sisinni

*The Director of the Istituto Universitario
di Architettura di Venezia*
Prof. Paolo Ceccarelli

Advisory Committee

Giulio Carlo Argan
Carlo Bertelli
Giuliano Briganti
Maurizio Calvesi
Giovanni Carandente
Anne d'Harnoncourt
Maurizio Fagiolo dell'Arco
Olle Granath
Wieland Schmied
Nicholas Serota

Lenders to the Exhibition

Museum and Public Institutions

Archivio Centrale dello Stato, Rome
Archivio Centro di Studi
per la Storia Dell'Architettura, Rome
Archivio D'Ascanio,
Sovrintendenza Archivistica, Pescara
Archivio Fondazione Terragni, Como
Archivio Roberto Papini, Biblioteca
di Architettura, Florence
Archivio Piacentini, Biblioteca
di Architettura, Florence
Archivio Storico delle Arti
Contemporanee della Biennale, Venice
Archivio Storico Fondo Gatti, Asti
Archivio del Piccolo Teatro, Milan
Australian National Gallery, Canberra
Biblioteca Centrale di Architettura,
Sistema Bibliotecario Politecnico
of Turin
Camera dei Deputati, Rome
The Carnegie Museum of Art, Pittsburgh
Centro Marino Marini, Pistoia
Centro Studi e Archivio della
Comunicazione - Università degli Studi,
Parma
Civico Museo d'Arte Contemporanea,
Milan
Civico Museo Revoltella, Galleria d'Arte
Moderna, Trieste
Compartimento Ente Ferrovie
dello Stato, Florence
Ente E.U.R., Rome
Fondazione Albert-Birot, Paris
Fondazione Corrente, Milan
Fondazione Palazzo Albizzini, Città
di Castello
Fondazione Primo Conti, Centro
di Documentazione e Ricerche sulle
Avanguardie Storiche, Fiesole-Florence
Fondazione Lucio Fontana, Milan
Fondazione Magnani-Rocca, Corte
di Mamiano, Parma
Fondazione "Il Vittoriale degli Italiani",
Gardone Riviera
Fondo Basile, Università degli Studi,
Palermo
Gabinetto Viesseux, Florence
Galleria d'Arte Moderna, Udine
Galleria d'Arte Moderna di Palazzo Pitti,
Florence
Galleria Comunale d'Arte Moderna,
Rome
Galleria Internazionale d'Arte Moderna,
Ca' Pesaro, Venice
Galleria Nazionale d'Arte Moderna,
Rome
Solomon R. Guggenheim Museum,
New York
Haags Gemeentemuseum, The Hague
Koninklijk Museum voor Schone
Kunsten, Antwerpen

Kunsthaus, Zurich
Kunstmuseum, Basel
The Menil Collection, Houston
The Metropolitan Museum of Art,
New York
Moderna Museet, Stockholm
Musée d'Art Moderne, Villeneuve d'Ascq
Musée national d'art moderne,
Centre Georges Pompidou, Paris
Musée Picasso, Paris
Musée de Peinture et de Sculpture,
Grenoble
Musei Civici, Como
Musei Vaticani, Rome
Museo dell'Accademia Etrusca, Cortona
Museo Civico di Turin, Galleria d'Arte
Moderna, Turin
Hermitage Museum, Leningrad
Museo Marino Marini, San Pancrazio,
Florence
Musco Mcdardo Rosso, Barzio
Museo Provinciale d'Arte Sezione
contemporanea Palazzo delle
Albere, Trento
Museum Boymans-van Beuningen,
Rotterdam
Museum Ludwig, Köln
The Museum of Modern Art, New York
National Gallery of Art, Washington
Pinacoteca di Brera, Milan
Raccolta d'Arte Contemporanea
Alberto Della Ragione, Florence
Regole d'Ampezzo, Galleria
Mario Rimoldi, Cortina d'Ampezzo
Staatsgallerie, Stuttgart
Städelsches Kunstinstitut,
Frankfurt/Main
Triennale of Milan
The Trustees of the Tate Gallery,
London
Wilhelm-Lehmbruch Museum, Duisburg

Private collections and galleries

Paride Accetti, Milan
Carla Menozzi Andreani, Milan
Archivio Patellani, Milan
Archivio Ponti, Milan
Giulio Carlo Argan, Rome
Assitalia Le Assicurazioni d'Italia S.p.A.,
Rome
Banca Commerciale Italiana S.p.A., Milan
Federico Bano, Milan
Lodovico and Alberico B. di Belgiojoso,
Milan
Marco Beltchev, Milan
Anna Boggeri Monguzzi, Milan
Luca Brasini, Orvieto
Angelo Calmarini, Milan
Massimo Carpi, Rome
Cassa di Risparmio della Provincia
di Macerata, Macerata

Cassa di Risparmio di Venice, Venice
Achille Castiglioni, Milan
Giorgio D'Ascanio, Pisa
Salome and Eric Estorick
Angelo Carlo Festa, Vicenza
Mario Finazzi, Bergamo
Teresita Fontana, Milan
Antonio and Marina Forchino, Turin
Fototeca 3M, Milan
Galleria dell'Oca, Rome
Galleria Farsetti, Prato
Galleria Fonte d'Abisso, Modena
Galleria Narciso, Turin
Galleria Palazzo Vecchio, Florence
Galleria dello Scudo, Verona
Italia Assicurazioni, Genoa
Emile Lanc, Bruxelles
Studio Lapadula, Rome
Alain Lesieutre, Paris
Emanuele Levi Montalcini, Turin
Paola Libcra, Romc
Studio Vico Magistretti, Milan
Susi Magnelli, Meudon
Achille and Ida Maramotti, Albinea,
Reggio Emilia
Giorgio Marconi, Milan
Studio Melotti, Milan
Vianella Minoletti, Milan
Beatrice Monti della Corte, Milan
Zita Mosca Baldessari, Milan
Archivio Muzio, Milan
Palino Inc., New York
Carla Panicali, Rome
Pininfarina Studi e Ricerche, Cambiano
Gino Pollini, Milan
Lisa Ponti, Milan
Raccolta Antonella Vigliani Bragaglia,
Centro Studi Anton Giulio Bragaglia,
Rome
Corrado Rava, Rome
Caterina Hellstrom Riccitelli,
Ascoli Piceno
Ricordi, Milan
Massimo Ridolfi, Rome
Laura Rossi Mattioli, Milan
Fabio Sargentini, Rome
Savini Zerboni, Milan
Estate Savinio, Rome
Gina Severini Franchina, Rome
Lica Steiner, Milan
Ennio Tersigni, Rome
Augusto Vallunga, Puos d'Alpago
Emilio Vedova, Venice
Anna and Vittorio Venturini, Savona
Luigi Veronesi, Milan
Zita Vismara, Milan

and many owners who prefer to remain
anonymous

Acknowledgments

I would like to express my gratitude to all those who made this exhibition possibile.

First of all, to the many Italian museums and to their directors for their generous loans, among which I would like to single out Milan's Civico Museo d'Arte Contemporanea, directed by Mercedes Precerutti Garberi, Rome's Galleria Nazionale d'Arte Moderna, directed by Augusta Monferini, Venice's Musei Civici, directed by Giandomenico Romanelli, Turin's Museo Civico, directed by Rosanna Maggio Serra, and Milan's Pinacoteca di Brera, directed by Rosalba Tardito.

There are a number of public institutions, both Italian and international, that offered their support through the loan of important paintings, sculptures, drawings, documents and books, even though this meant their remaining without for a long time — a sacrifice for which we are infinitely grateful: Centro Marino Marini in Pistoia, Centro Studi e Archivio della Comunicazione in Parma, Ente E.U.R. in Rome, Fondazione Palazzo Albizzini in Città di Castello, Fondazione Primo Conti in Fiesole, Fondazione Lucio Fontano in Milan, Koninklijk Museum voor Schone Kunsten in Antwerp, the Menil Collection in Houston and Raccolta d'Arte Contemporanea Alberto Della Ragione in Florence.

It is truly a pleasure to extend my special thanks to those organizations that have sent the Futurist masterpieces to Palazzo Grassi for a second time, so that they may be admired in Venice once again. We recognize this as a gesture of great trust and friendship, and are sincerely appreciative of it; our thanks go to Philip Johnston, director of Pittsburgh's Carnegie Museum of Art, Thomas Krens, director of New York's Solomon R. Guggenheim Museum, Rudi Fuchs, director of the Hague's Gemeentemuseum, Jean-Hubert Martin, director of Paris' Musée national d'arte moderne, Centre Georges Pompidou, Serge Lemoine, director of Grenoble's Musée de Peinture et de Sculpture, Siegfried Gohr, director of Cologne's Museum Ludwig, and Kirk Varnedoe, curator, Painting and Sculpture of New York's Museum of Modern Art.

In order to realize such an ambitious project we turned to a great many colleagues and istitutions the world over, and to them we express our most heartfelt gratitude.

An exhibition of this scale has required the assistance and generosity of many individuals, and we were able to count on the helpfulness of Elica and Luce Balla, Massimo Carrà, Dominique de Menil, Massimo di Carlo, Volker Feierabend, Claudia Gian Ferrari, Teresita Fontana, Marina Marini, Franca Parravicini Marsure, Lisa Ponti, Bianchina Riccio, Angelica Savinio, Ruggero Savinio, Romana Alaya Severini, Massimo Simonetti, Toni Stooss and Silvio Traversa. Furthermore, we had the immense pleasure of working with Alberto Burri, Bruno Munari, Giuseppe Santomaso, Emilio Vedova and Luigi Veronesi whose vital contribution cast light upon our research.

Lastly, space permits only a brief mention of the many individuals who encouraged us along the way to realizing this exhibition.

To all those who have not been named and to all those who wish to remain anonymous, we extend our warmest thanks. (P.H.)

With this exhibition Palazzo Grassi offers to its visitors a panorama of Italian art of the first half of this century.

Examining the past is always difficult, and all the more so because the art of the first half of this century has remained an integral part of our own life and culture. And even if it is contemporary art, in some respects it seems distant, a part of ourselves that we have left behind and that we now experience as a memory, and as something for which we feel a need, similar to the need for our mother.

But a closer look reveals that this art is still an art of today, and this is tanks to its links with the past and its role as a premise to the future.

Every visitor will recognize these links with the past, as he discovers the deep-seated continuity underlying the Italian way of perceiving and conceiving reality.

Already at the turn of the century, art critics related the new forms of expression to a remote past, such as that of Piero della Francesca, and this is a link that can be traced all the way to its roots in the painting and the sculpture of the early Renaissance.

This goes hand in hand with the discovery that the Italian culture is still today based on humanism, which has become an essential value and distinguishing feature of our society.

Such a form of continuity, seen within the context of the whole of the Italian school, cannot but astonish and at the same time hearten us.

Thus, the exhibition that we present here not only permits us to re-examine a course of artistic development, but also to meditate on the deepest roots of our era, an era certainly of change and conquest, along with discoveries and prodigious prospects. But it is also an era of maturation and of apprehension, and we look to the past almost as if searching for the certitudes that a world in movement such as our own tends to leave open to debate, not only in appearance but also in substance.

The visitor to whom we offer the result of our labor in putting together this project will feel compelled to think, and this is what we at Palazzo Grassi are hoping for, because our prime concern is to further the aims of culture and therefore to stimulate reflection and inner enrichment — intellectual and, why not?, spiritual.

Feliciano Benvenuti

Committee of the Exhibition
and of the Catalogue

Artistic Director
Pontus Hulten

Curated by
Pontus Hulten
Germano Celant

Exhibition Coordinator
Ida Gianelli

Secretariat
Clarenza Catullo
Francesca Pattaro

Assistant
Marco Mulazzani

Press Relations
Lauro Bergamo

Project Design
Gae Aulenti
with
Francesca Fenaroli
Vittoria Massa
Chiara Vitali

Lighting Design
Piero Castiglioni

Special Installations
Gipsoteca Mondazzi, Turin

"Painting with Light"
Luminous Dreams from Forty
Years of Italian Cinema
Film anthology, original idea
and text by Gian Piero Brunetta
screenplay by
Gian Piero Brunetta
Roberto Gavioli and
Pier Luigi Radaelli
directed by Roberto Gavioli
production by Gamma Film

Computer-Interactive
Didactic Program
courtesy of IBM Italia
Text by Giorgio Verzotti

Catalogue edited by
Ida Gianelli

Graphic Design
Pierluigi Cerri
with
Andrea Lancellotti

Editorial Director
Mario Andreose

Editorial Staff
Carla Tanzi
with
Doriana Comerlati
Andrew Ellis
Isabelle Harvie-Watt
Giulio Lupieri
Carol Lee Rathman

Iconographic Research
Luisa Violi

Production Staff
Silvano Caldara
Giancarlo Galimberti
Gilberta Stivanin

Contents

The phenomenal cultural regeneration that took place in Italy immediately after the end of the Second World War, from 1945 on, was an example for all of Europe. It placed the country in a leading position in several fields: architecture, design, and filmmaking. This extraordinary recuperation was a typically Italian phenomenon, just as Futurism was a phenomenon that could not have appeared anywhere else in the world. On both occasions, the decisive element was a great appetite for life. If only one word were used to describe the essence of Futurism, that word would have to be *vitality*. The Futurist movement and its affirmative and dynamic attitude impressed the entire cultural world of its time, and had a dominating influence for years. Its early phase had a positive force that was impossible to crush — it was youthful, it was naive and happy.

As no exhibition similar to this one has ever been mounted, it has not been visually obvious that within the Italian cultural setting at the time of early Futurism there existed a current of feelings and dreams totally opposite to Futurism, which led to Metaphysical painting.

The century was new — does that explain the richness and freshness of the ideas that were circulating?

There is an adolescent hypersensitivity in De Chirico's first Metaphysical paintings from 1911. Nothing could be more different from the exuberant vitality of early Futurism. Here the dominant feelings are loneliness and isolation.

It is characteristic of the mysterious and evasive nature of these early works by De Chirico and Carrà, this strong poetic otherness, that they should appear in the same years as Futurism. Only through them can we see the full picture: they represent the other side of what it is to be young in the face of the world.

The Futurist movement was not a factor in the creation of Cubism, it is rather the contrary, but De Chirico and Metaphysical painting certainly played an important part in the conception of Surrealism, the cultural movement that dominated a great part of art and literature in Europe in the two following decades. In the give and take between Paris and Italy that took place in those years, almost all the factors became important.

In one sense, Futurism represents a rationalistic, willful set of options created by the will-energy of one man — Filippo Tommaso Marinetti — a great organizer and manager, but not a poet of profound depth. It is a clearly defined and definable idea-complex. It has certain naive, positivistic aspects that contributed to its international success at the time.

If Futurism belongs to the rational, daytime part of life, Metaphysical painting explores the night-side, the life that wakes with the stars. Futurism is concerned with collectivity, with the masses. Metaphysical painting is a companion for the self. The existential questions that Metaphysical painting was posing were not being asked by the Futurists or the Cubists. While some of the Cubists used a lot of energy analyzing the situation of the artist in the studio, and trying to understand its logic and philosophical content, the loneliness in Metaphysical painting was different and the questions were posed in another manner.

The existential questions that Metaphysical painting posed are strongly related to adolescent attitudes and behavior. (The personality of Giorgio De Chirico may play a role in this context.) One can recognize many characteristic elements — the hypersensitivity to surroundings and space, the extremely emotional relation to objects of affection — taken often directly from childhood experiences. The feeling of loneliness, isolation, and solitude is accompanied by an inner conviction of the need to understand and penetrate the world. This sensation of ambiguity, this complexity of feeling so characteristic of adolescence, is what Metaphysical painting strongly and convincingly presents to our eyes.

De Chirico transmits to us the incurable loneliness of the soul in the face of contradictions: past versus future, being young versus feeling old, melancholy abandon versus nostalgic plenitude, presence versus absence. And also, the presence of absence, the feeling that the void can become tangible. The scene now before the eyes of the artist and the *déjà-vu* scene are transmitted to us in parallel. Melancholy and nostalgia are presented softly, with a directness that only a very young painter can express; there is no need to bridge the conscious and the subconscious.

This concentration on the existential question is to a large extent achieved by the handling of space. It is not a question of the self in opposition to others, or of the individual in relation to one or several other individuals, but of the self and its loneliness.

The definition of space that Alberti and Brunelleschi created when they conceived the rules of the perspective at the beginning of the Renaissance is also related to the self, but in an abstract and mathematical fashion. It is a structure of a totally different kind of beauty. The Renaissance vision is that of the man-god or god-man viewing the world on a clear spring day, ready to dominate it in every aspect, quantitatively and qualitatively.

In De Chirico's paintings the space is often double; the different perspectives correspond to the complexity of conflicting feelings. Rather than the mathematical analysis of a clearly defined problem, there is a medium-like penetration of a mythical environment, a land of shadows and imprecise sources of light.

Metaphysical painting requires the utter concentration of those intense emotional powers related to the self and to space that in most people are available in adolescence only (and very seldom put to any use). It is no wonder that De Chirico could not keep this tension alive throughout his life. It is rather a miracle that he was able to keep it up as long as he did.

The metaphysical search for the self is a yearning that seeks to transcend the human condition. This is the yearning that André Breton saw in De Chirico's portrait of his father, *The Child's Brain*, which gave him the shock and the power to conceive the ideas inherent in Surrealism, to understand the force and capacity of the subconscious.

Of course, the difference between Futurism and Metaphysical painting is not absolute. In theory, a combination of Futurist and Metaphysical ideas should be totally impossible, but art is not concerned with theory. Carlo Carrà painted one work, *The Swimmers*, as early as 1910, which in a magical way combines the search for an understanding of the self with the pictorial gestures of Futurist vitality and aggressivity. If there is one painting that should be returned to its country of origin, it is *The Swimmers*.

Metaphysical painting and De Chirico became an extraordinary influence on the European art scene. No other painter's work, except Picasso's, was such a strong inspirational force. His importance in the conception of Surrealism has been mentioned, but his work also meant a great deal for someone as distant from Surrealism as Malevitch. This great influence is due to the weight of the existential questions that he posed with such power and subtlety.

In Italian art De Chirico's influence is exceptionally strong. In the cases of De Pisis and Sironi it is so strong that one can ask oneself if it is more true to say that Sironi met an environment that matched his own feelings, and thus a general style developed. When he painted the *Periferie* he let himself be penetrated by emotions that were of a similar order and origin.

Such feelings have a long life — maybe they are eternal. We meet them again in *I Vitelloni*, although in Fellini's version they are tinted and altered by his refusal to take them seriously.

Italy was not a major force in the Dada movement. (Modigliani signed the first manifesto, but his interest does not seem have gone much further.) Futurism had already presided over the denial of tradition, the negation of the old that was part of the Dada message. Dada was more radical than Futurism and the critical question of the war was answered in a diametrically opposite fashion. But Futurism nevertheless contributed significantly to the first Dadaists in their denial of the past.

Italian art and literature have never tended toward Expressionism, toward the crying in the wilderness. In a densely populated country where people are generally optimistic and have a tradition of scepticism, and where society is organized in a subtle and complicated way, there is no great purpose in expressing one's feelings with the greatest possible emphasis, except when you are sure that you have your public with you. And in visual arts, that is not the case.

In the Fascist period, and especially in the 1930s, Paris contiuned to play a role as a place where one could recharge the intellectual batteries. Alberto Magnelli had already chosen to leave Italy and live in France. Already in the previous century the renewer of sculpture, Auguste Rodin's competitor, the great Medardo Rosso had spent a part of his life in Paris and De Chirico and Savinio would choose to do the same. *Valori plastici* became a term as much used in Paris as in Italy, and Severini would continue to remain the liason element for a generation of artists.

The message from the great Russians — Kandinsky, Tatlin, Rodchenko and Malevitch — was in Italy received and absorbed very much in relation to architecture. The idea of the *decoratif* (in Matisse's sense) is prominent in the work of Fontana and his contemporaries. A clear understanding of the problems that were posed and a lightness and clearness in their answer and in their work announce the new direction that began in the years immediately after the war.

As we mentioned earlier, Italy was the only country in Europe that at the end of the war, in 1945, was immediately ready to begin creating the new Europe. This may be partly explained by the existence in the early years of the century of a complex and rich culture that could sustain and develop at the same time the great collective movement of Futurism and the introspective exploring of the subconscious that was the essence of Metaphysical painting.

It is the historical co-appearance and co-existence of these two complementary approaches that has given Italy its unique position in 20th-century culture.

The years immediately following 1945 were characterized by a great openness, transparency, and elegance. There was a lightness of creative improvisation. These elements appear in design and architecture, in fashion and perhaps in film, but their strongest expression was in lifestyle. It was a lifestyle dominated by an appetite for a new way of life, a vitality that the rest of Europe did not possess. These are the years when films by Visconti, Rossellini, De Sica, and others totally dominated the movie-houses, when the new openness between the street and the shops and bars was introduced. This is when the light small cars got their success and Vespas and Lambrettas swept through Europe from south to north.

The ideas introduced by Bruno Munari (the new Leonardo, as Picasso called him), Manzoni, and the *arte povera* artists then by the generation that tried to revive psychology, literary references, and the classical tradition, have greatly influenced European art.

One must deeply deplore the lack of a great national collection of Italian 20th-century art. The richness of content and positive conflict that such a collection would contain would have a tremendous effect on creativity by establishing the identity of what has been achieved, and by bringing together the various inspirational forces.

Italy is a country of provinces: it has the advantage of being an agglomeration of many relatively separated elements. This is part of its strength, a structure envied by other nations in a time when decentralization seems to be the solution to some of the administrative and economic problems of, for example, a country like France. It has also the weakness of provincialism, in which a large-scale, long-term, patiently constructed program or project is hard to sustain, the smaller idea often winning over the greater option. Stendhal went into long and loving descriptions of this particular situation more than a century ago, and it has not changed.

The Europe of the late 20th-century, the Europe after the unification of 1992, will probably suit Italy better than any other European country, accustomed as Italy already is to responding to a diversity of groups with different cultural and economic backgrounds.

The 19th century was certainly, in terms of its culture, a French century. Perhaps the 20th century will belong to Italy, once the perspective is established. There could be no better time than now to begin making a general survey of the situation, to begin looking at the failures and successes.

Germano Celant

A Mosaic of Identity

The most noted surveys of modern art, written by such eminent authorities as Ernst H. Gombrich, Giulio Carlo Argan, Arnold Hauser and Herbert Read in Europe, and Robert Rosenblum and Rosalind Krauss in America, all agree in their affirmation of the leading role of French art until around the end of World War II, and after 1946-48 of American art.

This point of view has deep roots and is supported by models of excellence and quality that are accepted by all who interpret history as a logical and linear development of the "new," which in turn is understood as a liberation from the shackles of tradition. The path of selection and of evaluation is blazed by the common "idea of progress" that rapidly took hold following the French revolution and gained definitive acceptance in the American liberal ideal; according to this, the weight of tradition is experienced as a condemnation that requires a violent effort to overturn, or at least to silence. Thus, any culture that shows signs of a relationship with tradition — whether love or hate — is considered tangential, or "unmodern," and hence unworthy of historical consideration. The influential role of the arts with regard to progress is therefore not surprising, as they reflect the optimism and prosperity of the new and are implemented as universal tools of civilization.

Until 1946 Paris and its school, especially the axis formed by Cubism and Surrealism hold the position of leader in the art of the West. After that year, New York "steals" (to paraphrase Serge Guilbaut) the idea of modernity from Europe. It clinches its supremacy with the mass media exuberance of Jackson Pollock and his action painting, whose disruptive energy opens the door to Jasper Johns and Robert Rauschenberg with their "true" American art: Pop art.

In such an analysis, the artistic models influenced by German Expressionism and Italian and Russian Futurism are pushed to the sidelines. These were movements that were absorbed by the regime cultures of the 1920s and 1930s and were not rediscovered until the 1970s, when art historians were ready to rethink the European avant-gardes, transcending any ideological hysteria, and when artists, finding themselves squeezed between the formalist and progressivist poles of French and American art, were able to draw on a tradition that included the Expressionist fervor and the Futurist energy to give new strength and vigor to the present. The fact remains, however that a "history within a history" has been created and maintained through to the present day, where the Franco-American preeminence has eclipsed everything else.

This "image" of modern art should be brought back into discussion, set right and updated so that other identities come forth. The only way to do this is to analyze first the "external" reasons leading to the dismissal of artistic cultures and second, the "internal" reasons for the same, which hindered such cultures from asserting themselves and making themselves indispensable and irrefutable.

In relation to the first set of "external" reasons, art produced during the time of the Nazi and Fascist dictatorships was rejected in full when these regimes were finally toppled, because it was considered to have been at the service of totalitarian communications systems. This overlooks the fact that in general art escapes subjugation since when it agrees to collaborate with the dominant political forces, it lapses into a "realist" monumentalism that denies it a place in history. In any case, underlying this tendency to condemn the reactionary features of Italian and German art is a far more serious affront. What is feared and ultimately rejected in the art of the vanquished is the osmosis between global art and the totalitarian culture, whether the latter is reactionary, as in the case of Germany and Italy, or revolutionary, as in the case of Russia. The American critics have shown a strong preference for a "pure art" imbued with formalistic and apolitical faith over an art that reveals its links with society — whether positive or negative, and regardless of the ideological slant. In Europe, this preference translates into a gradual loss of efficacy and withdrawal into aestheticism on the part of the avant-gardes, which eventually succumb to commercialization.

The "official" version of art history thus dismisses from the international panorama Italian art of 1920 to 1958 because it was directly related to the Fascist regime; whether it was for or against the regime is unimportant. In the opinion of many, it became a form of propaganda, leftist or rightist. In other words, it fell into the trap of social and political rhetoric that is rejected in the somewhat idealized conception of the "free artist" championed by the culture of the winners of World War II.

After 1945 in Italy, many critics seem to have adopted a similar stance, though distinguished by a different intellectual and theoretical bias: for ideological reasons, it was decided to give prominence only to those artists and movements that opposed the contingent reality so as to modify its social order. Seen in this light, Futurism and Metaphysical art, the *Novecento* movement and even Abstract art (which despite its collaboration had demonstrated its opposition to totalitarianism) are untenable, for they lack any revolutionary thrust. Thus linguistic radicalism or visual experimentation were not considered worthy of consideration because they were devoid of overt and banal political significance.

This is not the right place to rehash the developments in art and in cricitism of post-war Italy; it suffices to say that an involuntary alliance between the internal and external visions, which were paradoxically convergent, is what contributed to annul or at least attenuate the historical weight of Italian art of 1900-45. Wherever the French and American influence spread, we find complete ignorance with regard to a half-century of Italian history, while in our own country, despite the praiseworthy efforts of art historians such as Maurizio Calvesi, Paolo Fossati and Maurizio Fagiolo dell'Arco, we can still find pockets of "resistance" to the historical avant-gardes leading to the sacrifice and frenzied excoriation of the avant-gardes of today.

In any case, in the 1960s, once the postwar surge of national and international chauvinism had subsided, contemporary Italian achievements in art acquired a prominent position among the major innovative influences. Meanwhile, critics and art historians directed their efforts toward reinforcing the role of the modern in developments of the contemporary, thus legitimizing the latter. These two factors contributed to altering the Italian visual culture's tendency to seek to neutralize its avant-gardes. Preconceptions became blurred and points of view intersect, permitting contrasting and explicitly free-standing results and outlooks to merge. Thus it was possible to examine several different artistic orientations at once and to offer them a structure without ideological crutches, acknowledging the existence of opposing movements that took nourishment from formal and linguistic controversies and art criticism.

If the opposite poles of the problem are liberation from the ideologically binding formulation of a political aspiration versus the refusal to restrict the scope of art to to mere pleasure and decoration, how are we to reconstruct and treat the weary and fractured body of Italian art so that it regains and reinforces its efficacy on the international front. First of all, we must think of it as a whole, without omitting any of the considerations fundamental to living and thinking in images. This requires a thorough examination of all the events, omitting nothing on account of linguistic or ideological orientations. Exhibitions and publications covering broad geographic areas and periods of time, such as Italian art in the 20th century, can contribute to our understanding of artistic identity and its role in the history of art in the world. The search for an identity is in fact accompanied by a great narrative and by the proposal of a collective and national history (which is not to say a nationalistic history), where the imagination of the artist is offered as a key to interpreting the society and as an expression that stands out from the general cultural contribution. Therefore the cult and the apologia are barred, in order to promote a cumulative overview focusing on the dialectical relationship between artistic forces that have occupied a leading role, even if multidirectional. The artistic foundations must be isolated and brought into focus — maintaining impartiality and avoiding the pitfalls of ruptures and contention — and seeking the unity within the multiplicity of Italian art. Otherwise, it dissolves. Its origins are contradictory: as the work of Giacomo Balla, Carlo Carrà, Giorgio De Chirico and Lucio Fontana is sufficient to show. These artists shunned "blind alleys" of artistic development, each finding a new and different direction and constructing within his own work a complex amalgam of languages. In an analysis of their methods, which are steeped in metamorphosis and multiplicity, all the visual philosophies emerge and we can see how in the evolution of their ideas these artists pass through Futurism and Realism, Metaphysics and the *Novecento*, or figurative formalism and abstract art. And within this heterogeneous spiral of languages, the systems of logic become intertwined in a lively dialogue with one another, maintaining an overall structure of unity, however, that reflects the "nomadic" character of Italian art. This nonlinearity, based on the heterogeneous, and on coherent incoherency, generates conflicting currents that do not fit into a single outline or cumulative image embracing all the nuances. Rather, Italian art comprises vortices of interwoven genres, actions, and reactions, separated by breaks in continuity. A single principle and a single center are therefore lacking — Italy has been united as a nation for little more than a century — and instead, it is heterogeneity that flourishes, and a dynamic of continual movement, driven by social and cultural instability. A typically "modern" spirit takes hold, tied to an awareness of the wild acceleration of styles and fashions, as well as to a sense of historical precariousness. Here, Futurism and Metaphysical art break with tradition (seen as both a condemnation and a support), challenging and belittling old expectations as they make the leap into the void of the present.

When Futurism plunges into the multiplicity of the arts and proposes an aesthetic disordering of life and of the world — or when the protagonists of Metaphysical art, such as De Chirico and Carrà, do not give in to the strict hierarchical system that requires a choice between tradition and innovation — they contradict the prevailing model, which has been influenced by pragmatism and illuminism, and for this reason are "lost." Artistic nomenclature must, in fact, conform to the international prototype, bound by the morality of purity in art, whether moving backward or forward in time, as long as it is not contaminated by the present. The same may be said for the coherence of the artist himself in making his aesthetic choices: any change in orientation brings with it the risk of being accused of linguistic schizophrenia and loss of impact as well as of value and quality.

Moreover, since the turn of the century the world trend in art has favored extroversion and internationalism, and so the future of certain artists was already decided: isolated artists such as Giorgio Morandi and Arturo Martini, eclectics such as Alberto Savinio, the unpredictable Lucio Fontana and Fausto Melotti, or movements focusing on esoteric and provincial areas of inquiry such as the *Valori Plastici* and the *Novecento* artists, are all branded as anachronistic, out of step with their times. As far as Realism is concerned, the reification and fetishization of figuration are not sufficient to deny the positive side of forms of modern art. They are all the interdictions of a praxis that admits only the "strong" meaning in art.

But if we reject this praxis, the ideas of Futurism and Metaphysical art become fundamental — they hold together and signal the Copernican revolution of the 20th century. They open a breach in the humanistic destiny of 19th-century art, which goes as far as Cubism, because they lend importance to the mechanical and to the beyond-the-physical makeup of modern art; they highlight the accomplishments and failures of an art that placed the human being, the human eye, at the center of perception, forgetting his other senses and his intellect, his physical and spiritual energy. They raise a protest that launches human being into the infinity of matter and energy, memories and ideas, tradition and the new.

The subject matter covered by the Futurists and the Metaphysical artists shows their resistance to the humanistic and scientific linearity that pervades art from post-

Impressionism to Cubism. They propel this history of art toward a nihilism that displaces energy in the movement and in the acceleration of time, time of incompletion and of the fragment: the diagnosis of a crisis. All past affirmations are dropped and follow the destiny of the infinite subjects. The era of the "Post" dawns.

In this sense, the premises of 20th-century philosophy are deeply rooted in Italian art. The tide of the modern begins to ebb, and its plan fails. An act of bravado in freeing itself from tradition is aborted when it becomes just as mired in a fascination for speed and dynamism as in the past and memory.

It remains to discuss the final phase of the story, covering from 1922 to 1945, a period that has been considered one of backward evolution, a progressive decay caused by a classical and monumental vision. It is a period of seeking to recover the earliest myths and obscure sanctitudes, when the idealist aesthetic tries to believe in the unity and the tradition of the spirit as the national bond, so as to translate consensus into oppression. In these decades, art concretizes the reigning social tendency in Enrico Prampolini's Second Futurism and Mario Sironi's Realism, unleashing the language of pageantry, working on surface appearances and making itself accomplice to the vague "being in time." Victim of its own endurance, art adapts itself and tries to operate within a sort of "game" between materials and technique, or it confuses research with passing tastes in fashion.

However, in their rejection of the independent world of experimentation and their espousal of the official and reactionary culture, these artists do not succeed in glorifying the obscurantism and the tame new mythology of the petit bourgeois. Indeed, all they manage to create shows them digging even deeper into a rut. While the hidden content of their broken forms and their gloomy funereal colors aims to exalt a "dawning" reality, it actually crystallizes the tragedy of a loss and of defeat. Thus while seeking to project the happiness and magniloquence of an easy and carefree society, they cannot hide the world, which can only appear as it really is.

The swampy scenes of Sironi's cities and the surface fireworks of the Second Futurists hold out against the explosion of the avant-gardes, precisely because Italian art's position was then one of silence and isolation, the null and void. On the outskirts of art, the chromatic tricks produce desolate "plains" imbued with the spellbinding aura of absence. They bear witness to a state of "utter destruction" that offers to the world not an apologetic image of the present, but a grievous one.

The unconscious legacy of Sironi and the *Novecento* is therefore the unwilling memory of a nocturnal and silent itinerary in which the messianic utopias founder and give way to the void. An alternative that serves to fill in and consolidate — in an individual way, and therefore anticonsensus — was offered at the time by Lucio Fontana, with his prismatic and lightninglike writings, and by Osvaldo Licini, whose works reflect the precariousness of his time and the magic formulas of unique experience, divorced from any hint of monumentality or collectivity. They are flashes that uphold their radical and laic origins, which after the war will give rise to various forms of linguistic renewal no longer based on the "sacred" but, rather, on the material and the gesture in the art of Fontana, Alberto Burri, Emilio Vedova.

Such a mesh of currents within the same historical context bears witness to the multifaceted nature of Italian art. It proposes the simultaneity of the street and the interior, the city and the individual, as a solution to continuity. That is, they belong to a single labyrinth: that of aesthetic and social consumption. We have arrived at the complexity of our own times, where the order of the city is in surreptitious dialogue with the disorder of the individual, and everything is transformed into merchandise. This is yet another philosophical contribution of Italian art to the global and unitary outlook of modernity. None of these elements is an irrelevant episode of a half-century of events, because their endresult is to unravel a history that has already been planned, discussed, and theorized. The wanderlust and multiplicity of Italian art, once it has been reinterpreted and reevaluated in full, may make a very explosive contribution to this history. And this is what gives rise to the hypothesis of a century of Italian substantiality in art.

Renato Barilli
Carlo Bertelli
Giuliano Briganti
Gian Piero Brunetta
Maurizio Calvesi
Jean Clair
Enrico Crispolti
Francesco Dal Co
Anna Maria Damigella
Maurizio Fagiolo dell'Arco
Serge Fauchereau
Paolo Fossati
Giuseppe Galasso
Vittorio Gregotti
Donald Kuspit
Silvio Lanaro
Vittorio Magnago Lampugnani
Franco Mancini
Ermanno Migliorini
Mario Perniola
Enzo Siciliano

Giovanni Giolitti

Giuseppe Galasso

Giolitti's Italy

Francesco Crispi

The summer of 1900 in Italy was marked by political events of the utmost national importance. The elections held at the start of June signaled the victory of the more liberal groups of the constitutional line-up. Wins were also recorded by the extreme left-wing parties (which upped their quota of seats from 69 to 97). The right-wing groups had to hand over the government to the country's incoming political leader, Giuseppe Saracco. Scarcely a month later, King Umberto I was assassinated by the anarchist Gaetano Bresci. The new king, Vittorio Emanuele III, ascended to the throne determined not to take advantage of the assassination to abet a reactionary backlash in the elections, and a return of the staunch conservative politics which had dominated the preceding years. Mobilizing themselves along similar lines, the Socialists held their Sixth National Congress and embarked on a prevalently reformist tack.

The new bearing was to last some time, and colored Italian politics until the outbreak of World War I. The change made itself felt immediately when, on 18 December, the Prefect of Genoa dissolved the city's *Camera del Lavoro* (local trade unions) in an initiative that was seen as excessive and headstrong in the eyes of the high-ranking liberal observers of the day. The outcome was an all-out strike in Genoa, which rapidly spread through the entire Ligurian gulf. Three days later, Saracco revoked the Prefect's decree. In February 1901, he too handed in his resignation. The new government was headed by Giuseppe Zanardelli, and included Giovanni Giolitti as Minister of the Interior — a decisive confirmation of the more open and liberal tenor of the country's government at the time. With Giolitti in the Ministry, a climate of tolerance settled in and workers enjoyed a new freedom to strike as a means of making their claims known; however, agitation snowballed at an unprecedented rate among workers in both town and country. Giolitti's rise to government leadership just over two and a half years later in early November 1903 failed to stanch the vehemence of the union struggles. To the contrary, the trend gathered further momentum and incidents of repression grew both frequent and bloody, with dozens of casualties and wounded. For their part, in March 1903 the Socialists opted for head-on confrontation with the government. Giolitti reacted with intransigence, and took advantage of the public's general state of anxiety and weariness to stoke up social tensions further. His gamble paid off, and in September a general strike broke out, instigated by the *Camera del Lavoro* in Milan. The strike had a decidedly political character, and Giolitti seized his opportunity, dissolved the *Camera*, and called an early election. The extremist tendencies were quashed by the electorate and the more moderate political currents were resoundingly confirmed.

However, in March 1905, unable to get his Bill to nationalize the state railways through parliament, Giolitti resigned. After a brief term with Alessandro Fortis (barely a year) as head of the government, followed by Giorgio Sidney Sonnino, Giolitti returned and stayed put until early December 1909. After a new Sonnino government of three months, and one-year with Luigi Luzzatti, by early April 1911 Giolitti was once more sworn in as Prime Minister for further three years. On 10 March 1914, he stepped down again for what most expected to be another brief suspension of his activity as Prime Minister, but nobody at the time could have foreseen the outbreak of a war that was to engulf Europe in the summer of 1914. Italian history books tend to refer to the fifteen years from 1900 to 1915 as the

"Giolitti years," though not simply because Giolitti piloted the government for almost eight of those years, and continued to be a cardinal influence on government matters when not actually in office: the period is justifiably dubbed "Giolittian" because of the fundamental syntony — the importance of which historians have increasingly stressed — between the generally recognized or recognizable flow of Italian history at the time and Giolitti's political approach, both implicit and explicit. This syntony is identifiable in that fact that a) Giolitti's style of government marked the development of a decidedly positive phase in the country's history — more than was realized at the time, and despite the overlapping of a backlog of obstinate problems and new emerging issues; b) though closely tied to events and trends peculiar to that specific period in Europe and other parts of the world, this phase was largely determined by the action of the ruling class; c) thanks to advances made in all sectors of civil life, Italy was decisively launched on the path of modernization and its definitive inclusion among the major industrial countries; and d) this culminated in one of the most dynamic and fecund phases in Italian contemporary history.

The first nationwide strike
Milan, 1904

Italian economic development in those years was both swift and impressive. In 1896, just as world economy was recovering from the severe recession of 1893, Italy enjoyed a spurt of growth that wavered only slightly at the onset of new worldwide economic problems around 1907, continuing, though with less intensity, till the outbreak of war itself. At the time, industry began to play a substantial role in the nation's economy, transforming the country into a full-fledged industrial power, with an 87% rise in the GNP, meaning a two-thirds growth per capita over the European average for 1896 (which had logged a 56% rise in production). Foreign trade also enjoyed a sharp climb (up 118% in Italy, 55% in Great Britain, and 92% in Germany), while the distribution of share capital in 1872 rose from 25% to 66.5% in 1913, in net contrast to the trend in banking (a drop from 57% to 13.2%). And in 1911, employment figures for the new industries — metalworking, machinery, clothing manufacture, and wood production — rose from 22% to 39% compared with 1903. Meanwhile, in the more traditional sectors, such as food production and textiles, figures dropped from 46.2% to 34.7%. This by no means closed the gap between Italy's productivity and that of the other industrial powers in Europe. Furthermore, "the accumulated delay in starting the industrial revolution was too great a handicap," for Italy to catch up with the advances made during the period of "maximum expansion beyond the Alps."[1] Nonetheless, Italy had made a giant step in its own development.

Welcome in Trieste for
eight hundred workers from Milan

What connections exist between this surge in growth and the country's political forces and their actions? It has been observed that "Giolitti's economic program can be broken down as follows: it aimed to stimulate and safeguard industrial expansion; to combat certain private monopolies; to strengthen and defend the State budget against the financial interests representing out-of-date forms of production and foreign finance."[2] The program itself speaks for substantial autonomy of action on Giolitti's part, as both statesman and party man, in spite of the pressure exerted by the old and new economic forces at work in the country. It also bears out the opinion that "he was always alert to avoid getting embroiled with the large private interests, even if they sustained him, but to make the best use of them and tackle them head on."[3] His stance on the official registration of shares in the Stock Market, his difficulties with supposedly sympathetic banks (such as the Commerciale), his frequent anti-monopolistic declarations, his defense of the national budget against all forms of pressure, and his diligence in balancing it, his encouragement of investment in national savings through government securities, his disapproval of Italian investment abroad, and his effort to reduce the foreign debt, his special relationship with the Banca d'Italia, the many special legislative measures he

The first Fabbrica Italiana
Automobili Torino, in the 1900s

Flooded valleys in the Veneto
before land reclamation

pursued, his stand against protectionist and financial circles and his wariness of the indiscriminately liberalist lobbies — all confirm the consummately political figure of Giolitti in Italian history, and his autonomy from the economic forces.

This does not mean that Giolitti refused outright to entertain links with these forces, nor that his stance was without penalties on economic and financial levels. Basically, it means that his political and economic outlook was far from hostile to the idea of assigning an active role to the State: indeed, he envisioned a decidedly interventionist role, guided above all by a keen desire to safeguard the interests of the country at large, while leaving the way open to the dynamics and dialectics of economic cycles — only as long as they did not jeopardize this general intent; furthermore, he encouraged an equal voice for both minor and major interest groups in government debate, irrespective of the various liberalist or interventionist theoretical petitions.

In this respect, Giolitti's economic and fiscal policies dovetailed empirically and organically with his social policy. The kernel of his idea was without doubt to encourage as much as possible the involvement of new social classes in the welfare of the emerging Italian State. At the dawn of the century, this was of historic importance, and of momentous political interest. The initial limitations of the new State as it emerged from the Risorgimento had multiplied with the formation of an industrial proletariat and other classes linked to the capitalist development of the country, and they became more urgent in the light of the strong political and unionist clout that these classes soon began to wield, even if with greater thrust than their numbers or social maturity actually warranted. Whether or not Giolitti was quite aware of the imbalance resulting from this basic discrepancy, it spawned a key and highly problematic aspect of national growth over that period. The marked social contrasts accompanying similar historical periods in other countries (such as in England during the 1830s and 1840s), in Italy acquired radical and dramatic overtones that manifested the social problems, unleashing deep-seated rancors and basic passions and ideas that would have repercussions for many years to come: the governing groups of the subsequent political and social tide were also partly to

Marconi making his first
radio-telegraph transmissions

blame for this as they were not able to fully transcend and buffer an extremist impulse deeply rooted in the events of the country's immediate past.

Most probably all this was the basis for Giolitti's deep feeling for the importance of social peace and his understanding of the more or less spontaneous and free-wheeling composition of class conflicts. The State's stance of neutrality, which Giolitti insisted upon (especially during his early years as Prime Minister) with respect to strikes and worker agitation in both town and country seemed nothing short of scandalous to the traditional front benchers of his own majority. Objectively, this policy favored the emerging forces of Italian society, which thus acquired a new and irreversible mobility previously unimaginable. Furthermore, it launched a message of tacit consent, of recognition of the righteousness of the objectives and claims being made by the working class. Giolitti frowned on the appalling inequality that had arisen during the phase of economic expansion: wages were still anchored to the traditionally low levels of the preceding years of crisis, while the profit levels of enterprise had grown entirely to the advantage of the employers. Furthermore, though his attitude may have been implicit, Giolitti was wholly explicit in his conviction that an increase in the wage dynamics would speed and not hinder, as was traditionally believed, the economy's growth. It was not until later that he changed tack, in the wake of a variety of issues: the escalation of strikes (especially in the public service sector) and their growing connection with extremist groups rather than with the more moderate positions of the socialist movement; the failure of the drive to improve wages to catalyze the economy owing to the glut of available workers; the imbalance between sectors in the effectiveness of their social claims; the increasing reaction of moderate Italians to a government line that was felt to be upsetting social stability and even national values.

The situation led to a labor bill, with clauses affecting contract arbitration, social insurance, and cooperative credit. This bill was a clear declaration of the newly industrialized country's Liberal bearing. Meanwhile, however, Giolitti visibly tightened his grip on the restive masses, intervening with a greater show of force in strikes and other forms of agitation and protest. Though somewhat contradictory, the twofold line of action in no way attenuated the overall impact of his policy. The relative contradiction was, however, indicative of the inherent limitations and penalties of Giolitti's platform, and not just of the political and social situation in general.

At this point it became evident that Giolitti attributed little importance to the *Mezzogiorno* (southern Italy), and to agriculture.

He in fact failed to develop any political philosophy addressing the inequalities of the South. Though neither encouraged nor favored by Giolitti, certain classes in the southern part of the country continued to draw on farm rent and land ownership for social status, prestige, and wealth, not to mention authority. His attitude towards the farmworkers of the South remained, however, quite distinct from his concern for the industrial workers of the North — a bias that he justified in terms of the historical and civil immaturity of the southern countryside, reducing the farmers' struggles to the status of a subversive factor in a libertarian regime. This reasoning was not merely a contrived pretext, but stemmed from a complex, albeit debatable, view of the southern question, demonstrated by the progressive approval and implementation under Giolitti of special legislation and government subsidies for the South. His innovative attitude on social issues had the most immediate repercussions during the first half of the Giolitti period: initiatives included a vast aqueduct for Puglia, new laws affecting Basilicata and Sardinia, the urban renewal and industrialization scheme for Naples, special measures for Calabria (including aid for the earthquake-struck Messina Straits area in 1908) and for the tax exemption of rural buildings, and the State purchase of the southern railways in order to set up a direct line from Rome to Naples.

Giovanni Giolitti

Giovanni Gentile

All this gives an idea of the scope of Giolitti's decision in 1906 to set in motion a grand inquiry in parliament on the real living conditions of peasantry in the South and Sicily ("almost as if compensating for the empirical and fragmentary course of this legislation").[4] The inquiry, as Giolitti later wrote, was intended to "bring the national representatives into direct contact with the neediest classes, and speed a set of social laws."[5] The compromise that led him to give more importance to the increasing support he garnered from the southern deputies came hand-in-hand, however, with a hiatus in dealing with the real social issues of the *Mezzogiorno*; furthermore he also tried to take advantage of a momentary social calm to play out a political and social game with completely different aims. It did not herald a break with the problems affecting the South, nor with the drive toward southern reform. Some of the directives formulated during Giolitti's time were to be applied in later periods (such as the creation of major infrastructure: the railways and aqueducts, and industrialization programs for Naples). Ample demonstration of the validity of these ideas lies in the fact that Francesco Saverio Nitti (a more modern exponent of southern issues) not only found a fertile seedbed for action in Giolitti's policies, but also the springboard that would put him in a position to compete with Giolitti himself for the leadership of the Liberal camp. Nor can we doubt that though this dualism in the Italian economy revealed itself in its most negative aspects during the Giolitti years, it was then that southern issues and the new cultural drive pushed the political movement of the South to an entirely new, central position.

This picture does not match up with the two views traditionally taken of Giolitti's policy for the South: that, first, it was merely part of his general attitude towards the Italian farmland, and that, second, it was the outcome of a underhanded and even cynical scheme to exploit the comparative political and social inferiority (even within the ruling class) of the South, to favor certain advanced and more dynamic sections of the national economy and society. The complex and even contradictory nature of Giolitti's policy has repercussions that go far beyond a crass parliamentary maneuver, and far outside the specific problem of the Italian hinterland.

It is certainly easier to circumscribe Giolitti's attitude towards farming. It was characterized by a long-standing reluctance to intervene with legislative measures — for example, ensuring the juridical recognition of the farmworkers' leagues. His defense and legislative support of industry was more extensive; however, in 1912-13, he turned equal attention to agriculture. But here too we have to be wary of hackneyed assumptions. Almost by way of compensation for his disregard for country affairs, under Giolitti public works and cooperative movements enjoyed a vital boost beyond anything that had gone before, and this somewhat offset the negative effect of his predilection for other social sectors. The public works and cooperatives (an *ad hoc* bank was set up) gave rise to a new political and civil awareness in the countryside, especially in the Po valley, together with economic and administrative know-how; this period also saw the creation of a series of management groups and forms of financial and union organizations that would leave their mark in the country's history. Here too, we can see that the Giolitti years deserve a more positive appraisal, and above all a more in-depth, all-round reassessment.

In this respect, it is worth noting that some Liberals who did not actually voice favor for Giolitti during his years of ascendancy, such as Giustino Fortunato and Benedetto Croce, were to have second thoughts later on. When Fascism set in, significantly it was Giolitti's Piedmont group that continued to uphold the Liberal banner — for as long as political expression remained possible.

As a political figure, Giolitti has been identified with the vibrant and positive phase the country experienced before World War I, symbolized in the conversion of government security yields from 4% to 3.75% at the beginning of 1906 and then, five years later, to 3.5%, for a value of eight billion Lire, without the cut in interest rates causing any withdrawal of investment capital, as the new securities increased in value; meanwhile paper money and currency had a premium over gold. Such developments were not limited to Italy: the same conversion was going on in France, during these same years, though in Italy it had greater impact: during the first years of the *Unità* or national unity, financial problems had seemed to threaten the very foundations of the new State. In this respect, the country had yet to demonstrate its solidity, and the public, indeed the ruling class itself, considered the national budget to be a gauge of values and matters of the utmost importance.

Giolitti's line of action was well-rooted in the Italian right-wing tradition. The yields conversion, carried through by Luigi Luzzatti, seemed more determinant than the balancing of the national budget announced thirty years earlier by the then finance minister Quintino Sella. Giolitti also owed to the right-wing tradition his conception of State, the role of the ruling class, the very essence of politics, as the interpreters, guarantors, and executors of the interests of the general public and of the nation. But there was a basic historical and cultural difference that distinguished him from his predecessors, and that distinguished the politics and the liberalism of his day from those of the earlier right-wing and Liberal tradition up to that point. And the difference did not lie particularly in the fact that "the patently bourgeois concept of industrial relations" common to the right wing and to Giolitti's Liberalism had formerly been an "anachronism inasmuch as it was in contrast to the capitalist trading forces dominating at the time, and to the industrial relations these implied," whereas during Giolitti's time, "the gap had been reduced considerably."[1] The difference in the economic structures was less important than the difference in political formula, which made Giolitti's brand of liberalism more ethically and politically flawed than its predecessors, but far more cogent and sweeping in its historical implications: the difference derived from an acute awareness of the crucial importance, in a developing country, of the questions of consensus, balance and social pluralism, and of the relationship between institutions and civilian life, between political society and civilian society. The withdrawal of the right wing to the stronghold of institutional (and State) roles (understandable in the circumstances in which the Italian unitary State had grown), its top-down oper-

The Czar and the King of Italy
in Racconigi, 1909

ation, and its identification with Unification and national causes, had brought about social immobility and serious political shortcomings. The eventful development of the new State, as it careened between the *jacqueries* and *consorteries*, lack of discipline and ineffectualness, crisis and traumas one after another, could also be interpreted in the light of the role of the right and its demise in 1876 after sixteen years of leadership and deep involvement in the foundation of the State itself. The young Giolitti had been a functionary in the ministry of finance under Quintino Sella before embarking on his political career in 1880. He was in a position therefore to use his personal experience and notions to make a mark on national events, and to change the course of the traditional Liberal line in Italy, toward a liberal-democratic perspective. He did not altogether cross that threshold into full democratic thinking. It is significant that Benedetto Croce and Giustino Fortunato both endorsed Giolitti's Italy at this point; while at the same time, the gap between Giolitti and Nitti was widening. However, the drift towards a liberal-democratic order for Giolitti, which accelerated after World War I, is equally clear, and redoubled the importance of Luigi Luzzatti in his area (public finance and cooperative credit operations).

Benedetto Croce

The weaknesses of Giolitti's politics are more conspicuous on other levels. Above all, there were philosophical flaws: while the atmosphere in Europe and Italy changed critically during the first years of the new century, Giolitti's doctrine remained firmly anchored in a Positivist ethic which neutralized it and undermined its powers of elaboration beyond what the political admixture seemed to suggest. There were shortcomings, historically and politically, to his judgment of the social and cultural complexity of the national territory. These showed up glaringly in his handling of southern Italy, which was somewhat piecemeal compared to his programs for the axis of the developing and dynamic North. There was a lack of coherence on an ethical-political level, reflected in his pursuit of tactical and political objectives within a strategy that was doubtlessly sound and acute in its realism and farsightedness: the State apparatus was maneuvered according to the changing fortune of the government; parliament was understood and administrated as a central aggregation of consensus and support, rather than as an institutional interlocutor with a political-social dialectic consonant with the political strategy being followed; the elections in the Prefectures (and not only those of the South) proved to be equally (or more) vital than the struggle of the various groups and parties on local level; the government's tolerance of the violation of its own rules and those of social liberties made it prone to all sorts of pressure — from the leverage of the more obscure lobbies, to that of the more open "dealers"; local administrators were constantly subjected to the game of the "carrot on the stick," which all too often merely impeded the creation of a fecund and broad-based growth. This is the backcloth Salvemini drew in his definition of Giolitti as a "Minister of the *malavita*."[2]

There were also shortcomings in the Giolitti government's economic policies, which took their cue from the burgeoning social forces, without drawing up a development project like the one Nitti was to blueprint for the hydro-electric industry. The bias toward the emerging economy and the new and old economic forces was seen as a trading of guarantees for social peace obtained through the progressive improvement of working conditions.

Finally, there were failings in the government's conduct of foreign affairs: Giolitti continued to give the impression of shelving them in favor of more pressing issues within the country's intricate political machinery — a mistaken impression, since Italy in fact assumed a growing role within Europe, and determined steps were taken to prevent the country from becoming ensnared in the alliance with Germany and the Austro-Hungarian Empire — steps in line with Italian diplomatic moves since 1882. Meanwhile, the war with Libya enabled Giolitti to absorb a fair amount of the burgeoning nationalist foment, even if he was not in favor of this military involvement.

Another limitation of Giolitti's foreign policy was the scant attention the government seemed to pay to the exodus of millions of Italian workers in search of employment abroad. The vision of an overseas Italy, which some (especially the nationalist factions) spoke of as an Italian market and as part of the nation's sphere of influence, was wholly unrealistic. It was some time before an Emigrations Committee was set up, and emigrants rarely felt that their interests were sufficiently protected. Meanwhile, public opinion on the matter see-sawed: some judged it as a serious impoverishment and dispersion of the country's resources, while others considered it a timely safety valve for an encroaching over-population problem, with positive repercussions on the job market, besides providing a valuable influx of foreign currency, and change of mentality.

Ministers Giolitti and Iswolski leaving Racconigi City Hall, 1909

Most of all, the limitations in Giolitti's working philosophy had serious moral repercussions throughout the country. The monotony, the daily renewal of effort, was a deeply personal affair affecting all of Giolitti's ethos, in utter contrast to the rhetorical spirit of the country, and to the creative impulse in those years. Not only the government, but politics too seemed reduced to pure administration, to a more or less bureaucratic routine. The basic sense of values seemed somewhat blurred or even lost in this demanding, thankless task that was largely spent in frenetic, unscrupulous mediation between small group or class interests and the immoderate appetites of the larger economic and social forces, mediation that failed to produce a viable schedule of reform or progress for the society at large. To the contrary, both morale and social and national discipline suffered a steady decline throughout the country. Parliament (which was typically the focus of Giolitti's mediation) was seen as the emblem of a formalized and hypocritical civil practice, without substantial relationship to the national reality. To both the left and the right of the Giolitti ranks, there was growing urge for a new mentality that would truly rekindle the country's soul and produce a more heartfelt moral and social dimension, leading to a loftier and more binding civil commitment. The moral and/or political opposition to the Giolitti line — whether it involved national or class interests, more complete and rigid Liberalism, or a tighter and more ethically inspired State — presented the regime in power with a whole series of contrasts which cannot be overlooked historically, and which were deeply felt in Italian life at the time.

Gasworkers on strike in Turin 1902

Furthermore, there was an underlying and unshakable restiveness in the Italian Catholic conscience. The "Roman question" (the battle over Rome and the Vatican) persisted, and the Italian State was accused of a prejudicial and damaging lay spirit, contrary to the Catholic tradition, considered the very foundation and the authentic heritage of the nation. Indeed, the reluctance of the Catholics about ceding Rome to the Italian State was compounded by the wariness among lay circles regarding the role of the Freemasons in Giolitti's government (and in the new Italian State since its inception): the Freemason influence was undeniable, though less determinant and pervasive than was claimed at the time, and perhaps more operative in the civil field than in government spheres. To some extent, the Freemasons' basic philosophy was analogous to the confessionalism offered by the clergy, and provided a source of ideals that were on no account base or commonplace.

The Socialist Congress in Rome 1906

Cultural and intellectual life in Italy underwent a wholesale reassessment of values, spurred by the same deep-felt impulse that was affecting much of Europe at the time. The Positivism that had prevailed during previous decades had given way to idealism, spiritualism, Marxism, Futurism, Modernism, pragmatism, and other inspirations, that conspired to overthrow not only this philosophy but also the *ethos* it was based on. In these years of national exuberance, accompanied by growing

Demonstration in Rome over events in Vienna, 1908

material well-being, it was the Italian creative spirit that held sway throughout the country — the perception of a link between culture and moral life was flourishing as it had rarely done in Italian history, and this testifies that Italy was not merely struck by an economic fever or the urge to improve the material conditions of this or that group or class.

As with the debate on Marxism, the comeback of idealistic thinking (especially Hegelian), the activist intuition of modernity expressed in Futurism, the "decadentism" and aestheticism impersonated by Gabriele D'Annunzio, the Catholic reformism sustained by the Modernists — Italian cultural developments were felt on international level. Furthermore, there was an impression that all this was taking place outside, and in many instances, even against the moral world of Giolitti's Italy, which passed for the "official" Italy. Although it admitted to being well administrated (a broad consensus), the country did not feel properly or authentically represented in that administration.

In the more animated areas of national life, this provoked a turmoil that seemed hard to overcome. The prejudicial misgivings of the Catholics and Socialists (which converged despite their opposing principles) were joined by those of the burgeoning nationalist and imperialist camps and those of the Liberals and Democrats who would not give in to the "moral climate" of Giolittian Italy, and who felt it frustrated their values. What is more, in the Catholic camp (Modernism aside) change was in the air. Tendencies that had surfaced during the lengthy pontificate of Pope Leo XIII found their full expression in Romolo Murri and Luigi Sturzo, and were the prelude of a new Catholic involvement in the political and social leadership of the country, unknown in the preceding decades. While this helped dispel the threat of a possible merger of "black" clericals and "red" Socialist-oriented ranks, a merger that had been lurking ever since 1898 (during the years of crisis), it imposed alignment with the Catholics as an essential condition for Liberal continuance — and, anyway, it was the most convenient and tempting means of defending values and order, which were felt to be at the mercy of the classist offensives of socialist extremism. Giolitti too was aware of the merger option, and, through a Catholic-Liberal alliance in 1913, set in motion the change of course of Italian history.

The elections that year also hailed a vital stage in the development of the Giolitti ethic. Universal male suffrage had been instituted; this was a great accomplishment in Giolitti's politics, and welcomed the population as a whole into the sphere of the State. It also signaled the success of petitions forwarded for years by the Socialists, Republicans, Radicals and the pro-southern lobbyists such as Salvemini. Giolitti's hunch was quickly proved right, and conservative apprehensions of a possible subversion of the status quo of political relations proved unfounded: thanks also to his alliance with Catholics, Giolitti achieved a landslide constitutional majority, and it seemed to erect a solid dyke against the growing tide of the left. But he was also paving the way for a new kind of political agent, the "party of the masses," which was totally new to the tradition of the Liberal regime. The effects were soon to make themselves felt. Giolitti's tactical scheme of interrelations between government, parliament, political parties and elections seemed somewhat thwarted. His tactics included calling elections the moment the opposition threatened to make his parliamentary, social or union, formula too heavy-going; pursuing a majority-based democratic line that was more moderate than the line actually sanctioned in parliament; breaching with the majority over projects or issues of vast political or social scope, when the relationship between government and the voting majority seemed undermined by conservative defiance or when the difficulties became too overwhelming; using deputies and lower-profile figures, or giving way to opposition leaders with a meager parliamentary backing in the periods of stalemate to keep things moving while he maintained his position at the head of the government.

The Giolitti government had to reckon with a country that was steadily modernizing and growing more complex in its politics and social composition and increasingly rich in its moral and civil commitment. There was plenty of chaff to be separated from the grain, and many people felt the cheerful calm of the country was threatened by "subversives" of various kinds (imperialists, followers of D'Annunzio, extremists, etc.) who seemed to be bearing down on the hard-earned order with more force than in truth they exerted.

Another aspect that acutely affected Giolitti's Italy was the lack of an opposition capable of offering a viable alternative to the government, both within and without the Liberal camp. One possible alternative was Sonnino's idea of a branch of liberalism anchored in a "fascio" (coalition) of the constitutional and national forces, able to pursue the "lofty" aims of "the national collective," with a vision of the country's problems that was more political and institutional than economic or social. This gave the rivalry between the two leaders a more ethical character — Giolitti's supposed *routinier* and tolerant approach was offset by the Sonninian spirit of severity and coherence, contained in his appeal to the principles of an authentic national constitutionalism. Sonnino's ideas also showed an acute awareness of the true scope of certain problems affecting the country (including the problem of the *Mezzogiorno*) and a more organic aspiration to modernization nationwide and in the public services, and infrastructure. Despite the undoubted ethical-political leverage wielded by Sonnino in many quarters of the Liberal camp, all these features remained essentially abstract and theoretical. Sonnino never quite managed to secure himself a niche in the more concrete business of conducting the country's political and social life, as he lacked the ability to rally support around him both within and without Parliament — as the brevity of his two governments amply proves. The only real opposition to Giolitti and his Liberal line of operation came about through circumstance, with the outbreak of World War I and the subsequent swing towards a modern democracy urged first by Nitti, and then by Giovanni Amendola and others of his generation. A further reversal of direction was brought about by Antonio Salandra's more extemporaneous line of action developed between 1914 and 1915, which heralded a swing back to Sonnino's national constitutionalism, and this was destined to crystallize an unforeseen accord between Liberal lobbies and right-wing forces of entirely different inspiration.

Outside the Liberal camp, by far the most dynamic political force at large in the country's political and social forum was Socialism. Socialism had introduced the dream of sweeping social improvement nationwide, sustained by clear ideals, political commitment, and a well-founded ethical spirit. In the industrialized towns and those where traditional manufacturing methods still prevailed (in the northern Italian plains and central farming areas), the Socialist creed percolated through to broad strata of the working population and petit-bourgeois, like a "civil religion," their first chance at access to the new national State; trade unions, cooperatives, and municipalities offered the Socialists a fertile seedbed for countless initiatives that were to remain forever in the country's heritage. They also provided the means for forming a ruling class capable of assuming a leading role in the nation's welfare. They helped instill discipline and education in matters of ethics and politics, and gave national status to groups and classes which, given the headlong growth of the country in those years, the contradictions and hardships, could have fallen prey to the inconclusive and risky alternatives of extremism, fanaticism, and other impulses. The role these alternatives played can be gauged by the many internal currents of the Socialist party, which influenced and at times stymied or derailed the more organic linear development of the party as a governmental and political force. It can also be seen in the vicissitudes of anarchism, as it careened between noble ideals and direct action (at times criminal). But the limitations of the Socialist par-

Inauguration of the monument to King Vittorio Emanuele II Rome, 4 June 1911

ty's role in the country's development were not only due to the presence of such tendencies in society and the party. Apart from the Giolitti government's Liberal canons, which allowed for a more modern term of comparison with the other social forces, the development of a proper role for the party was hampered also by a doctrinaire outlook, by indecision and divisions between the Socialists, by their cultural backwardness, their rather ambiguous stand somewhere between their philosophical basis in Marxism (which they felt obliged to cling to or lose credibility and the representative hold of the masses loyal to them) and the more concrete and authentic historical and social bedrock of Italian politics, which provided them with their motivations and aspirations. As it stood, Italian Socialism was still a valid mirror of the society. Those who considered it too advanced a hypothesis for the country, and likewise those who felt it to be extraneous and alien to the country's cultural heritage, were all misled, albeit for contrasting reasons. The mainstream of Socialist opinion favored a step-by-step approach to improving the role and lot of the masses, awaiting the final revolutionary dissolution of the capitalist world (of which Italy now felt itself part). But this gradual and reformist approach could not keep pace with the rapidity of the transformations underway, and utterly failed to bring socialism any nearer to national government — only reformist action was able to achieve a consistency sufficient to match the drive behind the socialist movements at work in the country. On the other hand, the reformist line was unable to give compactness to the Socialist camp either. On the right, the "gradualist" approach was stressed, and on the left, the maximalist ethic, both of which jeopardized the more prudent reformist line — more prudent and more deeply rooted, personified at the time by Filippo Turati. In its congresses, the party veered first to one camp then to another, but before the start of World War I the prevalent line seemed to be the maximalist one, although unions and cooperatives continued to buttress the reformist wing. Giolitti's attempts to enlist Turati in his government in 1906, and later Leonida Bissolati in 1911 (following what had taken place in France in 1904), were unsuccessful, but meanwhile, the prospect of socialism as a viable alternative "within" the system and not "agin" it seemed a somewhat inadequate answer.

Now we have seen the conditions and pattern of the Socialist presence in the country, it is understandable how much more difficult it was for major forces within the national tradition, such as the Republicans and Radicals. Their function was not simply one of opposition on principle: in truth, through their frequent coalitions and accords with the Socialists on local and national levels, these groups contributed greatly to the transformation of behavior and political balance, and of legislation and institutions — a transformation that was one of the main fruits of the Giolitti years. Furthermore, while the Republicans had retreated behind their institutional bias (as they were bound to do), the Radicals carried through the reformist conversion that the Socialists had failed to fulfill, and became a constant presence in the governments set up in the Giolitti years.

Maharuga
Submission Parade

As pointed out earlier, the Catholics acquired a new presence in Italian political and social life the moment they stepped into the role accorded them by the electoral pact of 1913. During this period, however, they too failed to take an effective part in governing the country, especially with regard to the "Roman question."

As for the nationalist, imperial and activist currents, which had just made their entrance on the stage, despite the resounding approval they aroused in the public and the suggestion of an argument that was far from limited to Italy at the time, their real political contribution was in fact less than it appeared. What is more, the idea that the war in Libya was a result of pressure exerted by these minor political groups is debatable. There are well-founded reasons for asserting that in fact the war was part of Liberal political design, and that, while Giolitti was not keen on the idea, he was far less pressured into it than is generally made out by nationalist and right-wing ranks; it was more a coherent (albeit prudently very limited) implementation of foreign policy Giolitti had been developing during his preceding governments.

Filippo Turati

At this point, we should ask the fundamental question whether the limitations to the Giolitti philosophy and government are all justly attributable to Giolitti himself — shortcomings inherent to his particular type of leadership and the forces that backed it, as a political reality — or if those limitations are really explained by the conditions affecting the country at the time, and around which the Giolitti philosophy crystallized, taking on the historical form generally attributed to it. The aggregation of political forces Giolitti managed to piece together was stronger than it appeared, and achieved a nationwide consensus that, even admitting the limits discussed above, held terrific sway right to the end, resurfacing after the crisis brought on by the war. This is the confirmation that, while far from being representative of the entire country, "Giolittism" was not a heterogeneous grouping of disparate forces, nor simply an outward manifestation of power, nor the representation of a grand conservative alibi, nor a praiseworthy but contextually inadequate instance of renewal. The basic structure of the country itself was still fragile, and likewise its moral fabric. To a great extent, "Giolittism" was also a race against time, and once the war broke out, time had run out.

The facts show how the accomplishments of Giolitti's Italy were substantial and how the political fortunes of Giolitti's line were long-lasting. After 1918, liberal figures like Giustino Fortunato and Benedetto Croce revised their opinions of Giolitti. In later years, the leader of the opposition party, Palmiro Togliatti (who was destined to play a central position in post-Fascist Italy), made a highly articulate critique of Giolittism — untypically so for the Italian left. And after World War II, the historiographers' critique of the right and the nationalist movement were largely reabsorbed into the *Italia moderna* profiled by Volpe. As regards literature on the subject, the definition of Giolitti passed from "minister of the *malavita*" to "minister of the *buona vita*" or good life.[8] This does not lessen the harsh criticism that Democrats, Socialists, southernists, liberalists, and also nationalists and Catholics in turn leveled at the "regime" or so-called "dictatorship" run by Giolitti. And though each group had its own specific reasons, none of them should be overlooked. This demonstrates how Giolitti managed to translate to institutional and social level his singular "capacity to bring out the progressive thrust of the Italian people and of the more illuminated ranks of the ruling class."[9]

Roman countryside
School directed by Giovanni Cena
1907-08

Notes

[1] Cfr. R.Romeo, *Breve storia della grande industria in Italia*, Bologna, 1972 (4th ed.), p. 114.

[2] Cfr. G. Carocci, *Giolitti e l'età giolittiana*, Turin, 1961, p. 112.

[3] Ibidem.

[4] Cfr. G.Volpe, *Italia moderna*, Florence, 1973 (2nd ed.), Vol. II, p. 442.

[5] Ibidem.

[6] Cfr. G.Carocci, op. cit., p. 46.

[7] The title of a famous book published by Salvemini at the time.

[8] The title of a book published after World War II by G. Ansaldo in open contrast to Salvemini.

[9] Cfr. N. Valeri's introduction to G. Giolitti, *Discorsi extraparlamentari*, Turin, 1952, p. 3.

For an overview of writings on the subject, cfr. *L'Italia giolittiana. La storia e la critica*, edited by E. Gentile, Bari, 1977.

Giuseppe Pellizza da Volpedo
The Fourth Estate, 1901

Giuseppe Pellizza da Volpedo
Spring Idyll, 1896-1901

Giovanni Segantini
Annunciation of the New Word
1896

Anna Maria Damigella

Divisionism and Symbolism

In the December 1890 edition of *La Cronaca d'Arte* Vittore Grubicy de Dragon appealed to artists to abandon the traditional painting forms and adopt new idioms "for the battles that art must fight in the name of everything contemporary and authentic." Then, writing a month later in an essay about a black-and-white exhibition, he made special mention of Gaetano Previati's "shadowy fantasies inspired by Edgar Allan Poe," Giuseppe Mentessi's "menacing architectural flights of fancy," and Luigi Conconi's drawings, hailing them as the return of the "art of the imagination, that branch of art which is rooted in the fertile garden of fantasy, an art that is both stimulating and evocative and which has virtually been driven out of exhibitions by the influence of Realism." Noting that artists appeared unwilling to give free rein to their imaginations, "since it is usually very difficult to reconcile such images with the solid qualities of paint," he urged them to exploit whatever means were at their disposal to convey "the evanescent nature of these conceptions born of the imagination," in the name of the right of the artist to express emotions which only he is able to generate.

The search for a modern and authentic mode of expression found a powerful ally in the art of the imagination. Baudelaire himself had identified the imagination as man's most important faculty, the only one capable of creating a reality that was more authentic and exciting than the visible one. Previati in particular took his inspiration from narrative texts and his drawings convey mental impressions, fantasies, and nightmares through oblique and flexible compositional forms, layers of light, evanescent, chiaroscuro effects, linear movements, and modifications of natural forms to achieve startling, compelling and contemporary-looking results that recall Odilon Redon's so-called *noirs*.

The Divisionist movement marked a turning point for the artistic idiom, whose gradual change also involved the art of the imagination. Divisionism emerged more or less contemporary to the work of Previati, Giovanni Segantini, and Angelo Morbelli exhibited at the First Brera Triennale in 1891, and provided an answer to the central issue raised by Grubicy — the difficulty of matching up images created in the mind with the solid qualities of paint — in terms of both the visible change of language, and the consequent shift towards a new way of perceiving. In fact the Divisionists' adoption of optical mixtures and visible brushstrokes (pure colors applied in layers, threads, or blobs) revealed not only a conscious desire to return art to a foundation of scientific fact in order to achieve a more intense and modern rendering of light, but also their more intellectual approach to the whole creative process, as reflected in their wish to widen the scope of artistic expression to include ideas and emotions, to inject their art with subjective feeling, and to emphasize its communicative potential — all of which was, in fact, in line with late 19th-century spiritual tendencies.

The Divisionists were all born between 1851 and 1858 — Giuseppe Pellizza da Volpedo was ten years younger, however — and reached maturity just as *Verismo*, the Italian form of Realism, lost its impetus and declined into genre painting and technical exhibitionism. Meanwhile, the wealth of ideas and subjects that between 1860 and 1880 had allowed the *Macchiaioli* and the Neapolitan school to use chiaroscuro effects, color and pictorial textures to achieve remarkably original and authentically expressive effects, had played itself out.

The rise of social Realism in the early 1880s had introduced a discordant and disruptive note in an otherwise cohesive period which had seen the middle class become a primary point of reference for ethical and civil values. Social Realism brought into focus a different kind of relationship between the artist and the new aspects of contemporary reality and, especially, social issues, a relationship that was both painful and highly-charged.

Milan, which was to be the cultural and organizational point of reference for Divisionism, did not conform to the national pattern. Examples of *Verismo* were little in evidence, and many clung to the Romantic ideas, thereby linking Divisionism and *Scapigliatura*, which from 1860 to 1880 represented a late-Romantic reaction to a closed and provincial society and to the middle-class mindset, the limits and contradictions of which were being highlighted by the changes taking place in the economic structure and social dictates of industrialization.

The supremacy of subjectivity, the idea of freedom laced with anarchism, and a stand against conformity provided the stimulus for these artists to experiment with different means of expression whose flexibility made it possible to exploit the links between the various art forms with marked subjective, psychological and imaginative effects.

Tranquillo Cremona, Daniele Ranzoni and Giuseppe Grandi took their inspiration from Leonardo, and from the 18th century — both strong influences on the Lombard painting tradition — and continued Federico Faruffini's experiments into light and color and Ferdinando Fontana's and Giovanni Piccio's use of lyricism. Their painting was based on chiaroscuro effects, patches of light and shade, with a strong enigmatic relationship between form and reality. Their preference for using a diagonal layout, repeatedly broken outlines, and flashes of light give their portraits — with their Medieval or 16th-century inspiration — a dream-like, poetic and emotional charge. Their bohemian, anti-middle-class attitudes encouraged them to seek out a more authentic human content for their paintings taking as their subjects the outcasts of lower-class society. This aspect was prominent in the early work of sculptor Medardo Rosso, which combined *Verismo* and Romanticism, rebellious subjectivism and humanitarianism into an awareness of the modern world, and an intuition of the complexity of the relationship between the individual and reality, between object and environment. "In nature there are no limits," he wrote, "and the work of art must encourage us to forget the material used; therefore it is impossible to enclose a sculpture between lines." This statement foreshadowed a perception of the continuous nature of reality and the principle of the interpenetration between the object and its environment, a theme which was later taken up by the Futurists.

Vittore Grubicy, Previati, and Conconi, who early on had been influenced by the *Scapigliatura* painters, kept this trend alive and — thanks to Grubicy's interest in reviving the Lombard school of painting — highlighted the actuality of some of that movement's central themes, the open acceptance of the spirit of modernity, the freedom to experiment subjectively, and examine an expressive art form in a wider, more coordinated context that relates to contemporary society and that society can relate to.

All this gave rise to a movement of change and an ongoing debate about contemporary art involving a variety of inputs: from the expansion of exhibition facilities to the publication of magazines expressing Modernist views, with artists such as Grubicy coming together with a variety of different eclectic people such as Gustavo Macchi to take up positions on issues relating to the crucial problems of Symbolism and Divisionism.

At least until 1894, which was the year of the "Esposizioni Riunite", Milan was the artists' cultural and organizational point of reference.

Vittore Grubicy played an important role in the Divisionist movement and its con-

Giuseppe Pellizza da Volpedo
The Mirror of Life, 1895-98

vergence with Symbolism for a number of reasons: his introduction of the most talented artists on the contemporary art market, his vast culture and refinement of taste, his international contacts established during various sojourns in Paris, London and the Netherlands, and his experience as an art critic.

The extensive knowledge and pictorial preferences he had acquired during his training and which had served him throughout his painting career kept him on the outskirts of Impressionism and neo-Impressionism (movements about which he had a rather indirect and sketchy knowledge), leading him to recognize the innovative force of naturalism, with its special focus on capturing the effects of light, inspired by the work of the Barbizon School, Jean-François Millet and the landscape painters of the Hague School. This was to have a strong influence on his own development as a painter — an influence that would be passed on to Segantini when he was Grubicy's student and can be seen in the first attempts at Divisionism, for example his second version of *Ave Maria a trasbordo (Hail Mary)* of 1886.

Grubicy's influence on other Divisionists was indirect and less powerful, however, and it was primarily Previati, Morbelli, and Pellizza da Volpedo's predilection for experimenting with pictorial technique along with a general atmosphere that favored innovation that were responsible for the development of new artistic expression. In fact, these artists believed in Divisionism and accepted their role as protagonists of a progressive avant-garde working to create an authentic art congruous to its own time. On this basis, numerous affinities, friendships, and exchanges of ideas blossomed, but wary of losing the individuality, freedom and purity of their creative work, the artists rejected the idea of forming a movement as such. The techniques of Divisionism thus came to be interpreted in individual ways, in direct contrast to the scientific and systematic approach of the French neo-Impressionists who, in any event, differed from the Divisionists in their basic premises, environment and aims.

What little pre-ordained and intellectual content there was in optical mixture painting and its related process of synthesizing and simplifying the composition and the object always came to terms with the artist's concept of an ideal world, resulting in a sometimes contradictory mix between individualism and freedom, and humanitarianism and socialism. This in fact corresponded directly to the mood of the time and became an essential part of Divisionist philosophy. For most of these artists, their resistance to breaking with the solid qualities of paint — which Segantini for example identified with the tangible truth of nature and man's link with the natural world — was a major hurdle to be overcome since the Divisionists aimed to replace art as a transcription of the visible reality using pictorial textures, color and chiaroscuro effects, with art as the creation of a reality that runs parallel to nature, through the use of equivalents, in other words, a reductive mode of expression. Previati held a special position in this area, which can be attributed to his late-Romantic *Scapigliatura* training, and his experience as a painter of historical subjects (for which he preferred to use the Cremonese chiaroscuro idiom, with its strong effects of pathos and bold oblique and decorative layouts). His mystical temperament and a strong sense of piety also contributed. The earliest evidence of Previati's Divisionist tendencies can be seen in the drawings inspired by Poe and in his first attempts at using a broken outline (borrowed from Japanese prints, which at that time also interested Grubicy and Conconi) in *Nel prato* (*In the Meadow*) or *Pace* (*Peace*) of 1889.

Previati felt an inner need to free himself from the grip of tangible objects in order to translate ideas, sentiments, and impressions and to recreate — as he himself put it — a far-off world that has either "disappeared or exists only in the imagination," a more beautiful and true world than what contemporary urban reality has to offer us, which, to him, was falsehood and ugliness. His abandonment of a patchy chiaroscuro technique reflected this need. In this sense his *Maternità* (*Motherhood*), which was the first Divisionist painting to be shown at the First Brera Triennale, was an attempt at expressing a powerful human emotion — love for the mother, which is best represented in the iconography of the Madonna and Child surrounded by adoring angels at the foot of the tree of life. This painting also reflects a tendency common amongst the Divisionists to secularize traditional religious scenarios.

The long, thread-like brushstrokes of pure color in shades of gray, green, and light yellow create continuous linear tracks, abbreviating the forms and linking them to each other, imbuing the scene with a feeling of the immaterial and undefined. The loss of solidity and the liberties taken with visible reality and the normal criteria of verisimilitude — misinterpreted by public and critics alike as insufficiently formal — signaled painting's first steps beyond its traditional confines and into the territory traditionally reserved for music, in other words, the realm of ideas and undefined feelings, with their evocative, enthralling idiom.

Grubicy saw in this painting (also shown at the 1892 Salon de la Rose + Croix) the accomplishment of Symbolism's most ambitious aim: "Ideistic art," as theorized by Albert Aurier, and based on Gauguin's religious works. He felt that Previati's attempt to achieve a purer and more elevated expressive level corresponded to the new conception of sacred art propounded by Joséphin Péladan. Aurier's application of Platonic idealism — which confers on art the function of representing ideas, or the true reality over and above appearances, and sees the artist as a clairvoyant and intuitive collector of ideas — appeared to offer a satisfactory solution to the Divisionists' subjective and communicative aspirations.

Gaetano Previati, *Motherhood*, 1891

The artist had the right to select, synthesize, abstract, and even remodel the visible world. He was to extract signs, forms, and colors from the object, to be used as elements of a flexible alphabet with which to create an infinitely vaster, deeper, and more authentic reality: a reality of ideas, impressions, and emotions. Finally the art of ideas signaled a return to what art had meant at the very dawn of civilization, when men first scratched out images on a cave-wall: decorating the human environment with thoughts — not pure illustration but an art of meaning.

Vittore Grubicy de Dragon
Joyous Morning, 1894-1911

For an artist with as refined and aristocratic a taste as Grubicy's, the transformation of the solid and volumetric aspect of forms into immaterial lines using a wide range of pale and luminous colors represented an unequivocal step towards creating analogies and correspondence between lines, colors, and sounds, which echoed the *Scapigliatura* movement's aspiration for a unity between the arts. In addition, Grubicy's theoretical frame of reference enabled him to pick out many of the somewhat subtle links between these expressive possibilities and a major issue kept alive by artists who had become sensitized to the "difficult social question": the communicative, or social, function of art, and the need to safeguard and indeed glorify the freedom of the artist and the aesthetic quality of the work of art, and protect it from the glibness of an art which concentrated solely on social subjects.

Grubicy found the scientific key to transforming art into a means for "social illumination" mainly in the works of Jean-Marie Guyau, such as *Les problèmes de l'esthétique contemporaine* of 1884, *L'art au point de vue sociologique* of 1887, and in Paul Souriau's *La suggestion dans l'art* of 1893. Grubicy was a keen advocate of Guyau's views and published several articles on them in magazines such as *La Riforma* and *Pensiero Italiano.* According to Guyau it was possible to distill aesthetic pleasure into refined and subtle sensations, and to choose associations which are particularly pleasing by following the principle of the relationship between linear directions, compositional layout, geometric plans, and emotions.

Grubicy himself, who abandoned his role as a publicist to devote himself to painting in 1894, tried to apply what could be called the "phenomena of correspondence" between artistic creation and the mechanisms of the nervous system. The theory went thus: at the moment of creation, the intensity of the sensation and of the impressions provoked by reality (which remain in the mind through the memory function) is reactivated as strongly as the first impression through the act of evocation and is transferred into the work of art. Grubicy used a very elaborate and intricate Divisionist technique, in which he identified the "mystery of execution," which, for him, was the essence of evocative painting rich in musical undertones, with a special touch of naturalistic sensitivity. Miazzina's landscapes, simplified by means of the atmospheres and the subtle flow of lines, parallel, isolated or in groups, thus look like little poems or "twilight symphonies," and effectively created an intimist response to the aspiration for an integrated art.

Previati used his considerably greater originality and expressive strength to experiment further with this painting style rich in musical and visionary resonances, until well after the end of the first decade of the new century. The truth and beauty that he could detect in an "ideal but lost world," in the passion of other eras, and in Classical and Christian allegories, become, in his hands, compositions which open beyond the edges of their frame, dense groupings of figures on the diagonal, and perspectives with heroic proportions that are reminiscent of the great Italian painters of the 16th century. Previati specialized in abbreviating and exaggerating forms using line and his own individual and flexible Divisionist painting technique, which was based on complementary colors or tones, violent dissonances, and effects of radiant light between masses of dense and light shadow. Excellent examples are the *Via Crucis (The Way of the Cross* (1901-02), *Paolo e Francesca* (1901), *Il giorno sveglia la notte (Day Wakes Night,* 1905), along with two triptychs, one devoted to the Day

and one to the Age of Heroism, both dating from 1907, *La caduta degli angeli* (*The Fall of the Angels*), and *La creazione della luce* (*The Creation of Light*), from 1912-13 which, to Umberto Boccioni, showed a "wholly modern plastic awareness" applied to the sort of art normally seen in museums.

For Segantini, truth and beauty are to be found in Nature, and the sense of reality and life contained in its colors and shapes reflects the clarity and truth of the idea that the artist wishes to communicate. His more systematic — but not exclusive — use of the visible and Divisionist brushstroke in *Le due madri* (*The Two Mothers*, shown at the Brera Triennale in 1891), a pastoral subject with a daring effect of artificial light, marked his departure from a sentimental view of Naturalism inspired by Millet, and a change in his way of translating natural vision through chromatic and luminous values.

The form is made up of thread-like brushstrokes, side by side or interwoven with thin strands of pure, dense, and solid color, which seem to duplicate the very substance of the real world, while the simultaneous process of simplification, reduction and synthesis of the natural view makes the perception more analytical and acute, and intensifies the effect of the light. The brilliant interweaving of the brushstrokes gives the painting a decorative value, like that of a tapestry.

This sense both of tangible truth and of abstraction also appears in the Symbolist paintings that show Segantini's sympathy for the art of ideas, albeit without Previati's musical undertones. *Il castigo delle lussuriose* (*The Punishment of the Lustful*, 1891), *Le cattive madri* (*The Bad Mothers*, 1894), *L'angelo della vita* (*Angel of Life*, 1894), *L'amore alle fonti della vita* (*Love at the Springs of Life*), and *Vanità* (*Vanity*) are just a few of the paintings that convey literary and pre-Raphaelite references in the creation of a new reality, both actual and imaginary, in which invented figures and the verity of Alpine nature co-exist. In this, his work had much in common with the symbolic decorative painting of the Secessionists, and the fact that his work was better understood and appreciated in those circles than by the Italians is demonstrated by the invitation to attend the 1898 Secession Exhibition, the publication of his work in the journals *Ver Sacrum* and *Pan* in 1895, his participation in numerous exhibitions in Munich and Berlin and his ties with Gustav Klimt and Max Liebermann.

Segantini's liberalism, set against a background of aristocratic and elitist individualism, and his tendency towards a somewhat naïve blend of John Ruskin's aesthetic moralism, Tolstoy's mysticism and social consciousness of art, with the

Angelo Morbelli
The Christmas of Those Left Behind
1903

thought of Friedrich Nietzsche, have more in common with the widespread idealism of the end of the century than with the faith in democratic socialism expounded by the Divisionists. Segantini seems to empathize with the hardships of peasant life as, for example, in his 1895 painting *Ritorno al paese natio* (*Homecoming*), but he tends to shift the human drama onto the universal plane and to find its solution in a cosmic pantheism and a religion based on nature. This attitude comes to fruition fully in the *Trittico della Natura* (*La vita, La natura, La morte*) / (*Triptych of Nature, Life, Nature, and Death*) painted between 1896 and 1899, which was in fact his last work.

Pellizza, who was a great admirer of Segantini's work, shared his ideal of nature as the primary font of beauty and artistic inspiration. But in the former, the call of "solitude" goes hand in hand with an awareness of contemporary human and social issues, with which, he believed, each individual artist must come to terms at the moment of creation in order to try and reconcile the ideal truth to this different concept of natural truth. In 1896, while he was working on *La fiumana* (*The Human Tide*) he wrote, "The reality that we see before our eyes is in constant conflict with the truth in our minds — which is the one we choose to represent. In my paintings I should not be aiming to represent *real* truth but the ideal truth. The conflict created in the mind of the artist between these two truths means that the work of art remains incomplete. If the artist sticks too closely to reality in his search for the truth, he cannot achieve his full potential. The ideal truth can only be reached by sacrificing the real world."

Pellizza started his training in the *Macchiaioli* and Lombard schools of Realism, first studying under Giovanni Fattori (1888) and later under Cesare Tallone, and his early landscapes, with their tightly interlocking planes of dense and luminous color, reveal an extraordinary capacity for synthesis. In terms of expressive technique, his "shift" to Divisionism represented the move most consistent with the broad range of intellectual and cultural influences he had experienced, and was prompted by two specific events: the 1891 Brera exhibition, and his meeting up again in Genoa in 1892 with Plinio Nomellini, whom he already knew from his time studying with Fattori. Nomellini had made the most original and daring innovations in the late-*Macchiaiolo* style, following Impressionist and neo-Impressionist models (which were current in Florence), and an intuitive Divisionism, derived more from Impressionism than from scientific research. His technique was based on the use of free brushstrokes, in flicks, points and dabs, to achieve a more dynamic and intense im-

43

pression of light — *Golfo di Genova* (*Gulf of Genoa*, 1891) and *Il naufrago* (*The Castaway*, 1893) and so on. His enthusiasm for integrating aspects of the new industrial urban reality into his work can be seen in *La diana del lavoro* (*The Hymn to Workers*) of 1893, a period when he had Anarchist sympathies, although he was unable to coordinate these felicitous pictorial intuitions into a consistent expressive style.

It was Pellizza's intensely emotional, sensitive, and reflective personality that enabled him to integrate the technical aspects of Divisionism into the development of a humane and social conscience. His shift from a Bastien-Lepage-influenced luminous *plein air* style to Divisionism is clearly exemplified by comparing his 1892 painting *Le mammine* (*The Little Mothers*) against *Sul fienile* (*In the Hayloft*, 1893) and *Speranze deluse* (*Dashed Hopes*, 1894). And while this shift symbolized his conscious choice of a method more sophisticated than realism for portraying light, and the particular effects of light best suited to communicating "modern ideals," it also showed a move towards a social democratic stance and a form of positive progressivist idealism. Artists and writers who shared his ideas were to prove helpful to him in his research into social issues. Angelo Morbelli, who was also born in the Monferrato area (Piedmont) and was some fifteen years his senior, was an important mentor and sounding board both in terms of developing his Divisionist techniques and in terms of the social issues involved, as testified by their extensive correspondence.

As in the case of Pellizza, Morbelli's shift towards Divisionism — as heralded in his painting *Alba* (*Dawn*), shown at Brera in 1891 — reflected his evolution from a realism dependent on materialism and chiaroscuro, and a personal interest in experimenting with painting techniques. His probing nature later led him to investigate the human condition, and he focused on social outcasts and the oppressed as his artistic themes. He painted minute pinpoints of color using a special paintbrush with three fine, hard points, over a rigorously-detailed design, creating a finespun and compact fabric, with subtle light and shade effects, which offered him the chance to produce concise and balanced compositions. The correct dose of the pre-ordained and scientific in his work creates an objective detachment from the emotional subjects that reflects his reserved and controlled personality. And thus, with his paintings of the elderly inmates of the Pio Albergo Trivulzio institute, or the female workers in the rice-fields in *Per ottanta centesimi* (*For Eighty Cents*, 1895), Morbelli manages to convey the desperate conditions precipitated by changes in the family structure and labor organization provoked by economic change and its psychological repercussions, and the oppression of human vitality and individuality, which are the divine right of every human being. These aspects introduce an idealist and emotive charge, enhancing the communicative potential of an artist who was otherwise little affected by the Symbolists' aspirations.

Divisionism answered Pellizza's need to give priority to the creative side of composition. Through his selection, arrangement, and synthesis, familiar aspects of the countryside and rural reality of Volpedo cease to be accidental and transitory, and become legible and balanced compositions with a calm and harmonious treatment. The points and the fine traces of closely juxtaposed color create a compact but sparkling, light-filled texture, and this natural truth captured in its vital essence is synonymous with beauty and becomes the intermediary of ideal truths, universally accessible ideas and emotions; hence the themes of serene resignation in the face of life's inconstancies, portrayed in *Lo specchio della vita* (*The Mirror of Life*, 1895-98), and the inexorable march of the workers, the vital forces of social progress in *La fiumana* (*The Human Tide*), and the original notion behind *Cammino dei lavoratori* (*The Workers' March*) and the 1901 painting *Il quarto stato* (*The Fourth Estate*) — all these paintings illustrate the commonplace details of life, love, old age, and death.

Leonardo Bistolfi, *The Sphinx*
1890-92

This was Pellizza's "art for humanity," and in the field of natural Symbolism his more modern approach distinguished him from his fellow Divisionists. In terms of symbolic expression, he gives priority to the technical aspects of painting, using geometric layouts, linear rhythms and flows, groupings, massing of forms, according to the principles of correspondence between certain specific shapes and pleasurable sensations. It is important to note his preference for lighting effects, since light is the source of the greatest pleasure and the equivalent of life, as seen in *La processione* (*The Procession*), and for compositions based on radiant forms as in *Idillio primaverile* (*Spring Idyll*). This move towards a type of psycho-physical symbolism led to his estrangement from the *Marzocco* literary circle, and a distancing from his own paintings such as his heavily Symbolist *Self-portrait* and the paintings entitled *Idilli* (*Idylls*) and from subjects which were too closely linked with current social issues. His need for an ongoing intimate contact with nature also led him to reject a too-scientific and pre-established approach to Divisionism, in favor of pure landscape, as interpreted by the Romantics such as Jean Corot and Antonio Fontanesi, a change which came about in and around 1901. This landscape was balanced, and was based on atmospheric and luminous values, which became an intermediary for a musical feeling and the artist's perception. His aim was to "glorify sublime nature which absorbs and annihilates man in the splendor of her own immortal beauty," capturing her eternal qualities and her greatest vitality and exuberance as shown in *Sole nascente* (*Rising Sun*, 1904).

Pellizza's cosmic pantheism relates him in some way to Segantini, but most of all to his friend Giovanni Cena, the Turin-based writer, poet, and critic, with whom he shared ideological viewpoints. His particular interpretation of symbols link him to the Turin-based circle of intellectuals which included the artist Leonardo Bistolfi, writers such as Cena himself, Paola Lombroso, and Guglielmo Ferrero, the historian and theoretician of Symbolism, and Pio Viazzi, all of whom had been influenced to some degree by Cesare Lombroso's Positivism and by the new positive idealism. They all came to support a view of a democratic art, which included architecture and the decorative arts, in line with the new drive to integrate the arts into the hu-

Leonardo Bistolfi
The Beauty of Death, 1895

man environment, and in which an increasingly subjective and complex psychic world dominated by the subtle relationships between the individual and objects comes together with human and social objectives.

Within this group, Symbolism assumed a special importance and value as a modern means of expression. For them, the creation of symbols corresponded to what happens when we experience sensations — that is, we perceive the main features of a given situation — which encourages the process of synthesizing and simplifying, common to the work of the artist. In "seeking to express the interior being, and using artistic means to give an external appearance to the sensation itself," wrote Paola Lombroso, symbols allow unconscious thoughts be experienced by the conscious self, or images to be revealed through associations, all of which have a scientific basis in *synopses* and *dynamogenesis*, and fulfill a need that has always existed in terms of social relations for communication on a psychological level. The symbol is the intermediary for the generalized experience and universal and constant truths, which are comprehensible to all, and Symbolist art is a harmony that runs parallel to nature, presaging an integrated reality, which is freed from the doubts, contradictions and the fragmentary nature of the present.

Bistolfi was acutely aware of the affinity between artistic creation and the mechanisms of the unconscious. This was the reflection of a restless and nervous temperament that sought an outlet in various forms of expression such as sculpture and painting, as well as the written word. Influenced by the *Scapigliatura* artists and Grandi, he sought to extend the expressive scope of sculpture. Using a soft and freehanded sculpting style, which showed an almost pictorial sensibility to light, he rendered romantic themes in tersely blocked-out Realist models to express emotional states. His idealist leanings prompted him to create a greater distance between the "I" (subject) and the object, and to give a higher priority to simplifying and changing the proportions in the visible form — the roots of which he traced to unconscious phenomena, thought, and memory — in order to intensify the communicative power on a symbolic level of the work of art, and its integration into the environment. Bistolfi was also very sensitive to the contemporary issue of the renewal of the decorative arts, and in 1902 he joined the editorial staff of the magazine *L'Arte Decorativa Moderna*.

Because of their focus on the individual and their exaltation of man's intellectual capacities, portraiture, and funerary and commemorative sculpture take on a new importance towards the end of the 19th century. They become leading vehicles for the new symbols, such as the female figure and flowers, which are done with tangible naturalism. *La sfinge* (*The Sphinx*, 1890-92) exemplified man's new conception of the afterlife provoked by the crisis of traditional beliefs: enigma and the impossibility of knowing what the life beyond holds. Nature's constant renewal and the immortality of the products of man's own genius were embodied in the images of female beauty and flowers signifying the beauty of death (*La bellezza della morte*, 1895).

We find in Bistolfi the first signs of the importance that the psychic world will assume in the work of the early Futurists, and particularly in Boccioni's work: the attempt to create an art of synthesis that could project emotions and sensations onto the canvas and into the clay, since, as Domenico Oliva remarked, "Every exterior facial expression, gesture and attitude is an emotion, sensation, or thought made visible."

Though it is true that at the end of the last century no rigid divisions existed between the various artistic tendencies, and indeed the spread of idealism created links between the Divisionist painters and the members of the literary *Marzocco* group as well as the late exponents of the pre-Raphaelite school, there were some differences of opinion, and the Futurist manifestoes' dramatic repudiation of the re-

Giovanni Prini, *Cypress*, c. 1904

Gaetano Previati
Descent of the Maelstrom, 1890

cent history of Italian art and its contemporary developments is fully justified. These differences of opinion refer to the modern choice of means of expression, the democratic and humanitarian stance, and the espousal of the social *credo* (all of which found themselves at odds with the currents of nationalism, aristocracy, and aestheticism of Gabriele D'Annunzio, the Rome-based literary magazine *Il Convito* founded in 1895-96, and the painting of Giulio Aristide Sartorio, who followed the modernist suggestions of the art of ideas, looked back to the great masters of the Renaissance for its inspiration).

The Futurist claim that the only serious and inspired artists were Segantini, Previati, Pellizza and Medardo Rosso — and that they had been unfairly neglected and misunderstood, in favor of "flabby Classicism," the cult of the Museum, and genre realism — was an acknowledgment of the vitality and actuality of these artists' work. Following their initiative, the Futurists "sing the praises of this modern era which is so hated by all artists," as Boccioni noted in his diary in September 1907; this also means establishing the due distances between the creators and the leading figures of Divisionism and the phenomenon of its growing banalization.

Given a more detailed knowledge of Italian art in the early 20th century, we can see how the drastic stance of the early Futurist manifestoes had a predominantly moral value since it touched on questions vital to that particular generation, in other words: the idea content and the integration of art into life. Certainly the themes and intentions were different, but the Futurists' point of departure in terms of expressive technique was not that far from intuitive Divisionism (and its later developments) and the idiom of pure color, as well as the typically post-Impressionist visible brushstroke, which can be traced to various areas of the arts both in Italy and throughout Europe. Boccioni later reported on the experimentation that took place during the Futurists' incubation period, including free-style Divisionism (or congenital complementarism) and a "violated and synthesized impressionism, which was the only form of neo- and post-Impressionism possible since we were so pressed for time." These experiments are reflected in the early exploits of Boccioni, Severini, Carrà, and Russolo, and perhaps only through later Futurist development do they acquire full value as points of reference: we are referring to the late-Romantic style influenced by the *Scapigliatura*, whose lines, colors, and musical resonances spark an echo in the viewer and recreate a state of mind, and to Previati's chromatic dissonances and use of primary and binary colors, as Maurizio Calvesi has remarked, as well as Balla's lesson in objective Divisionism, and the new human and social awareness of art that was born in Rome.

In the first decade of the new century there was a feeling of receptiveness, flexibility and of great potential and promise, much of which was never realized outside of the Futurist avant-garde. Obviously Divisionism and Symbolism were the two major poles but they were both much revised and transformed in respect of what had been produced a decade earlier: finally they were both breaking away from Naturalism, and had a number of features in common with other tendencies. We need only look at two examples: the situation in Florence before the neo-Renaissance period with the *Giovane Etruria* of 1906, and the instance of internationalism at the Palazzo Corsini Secession of 1904, when the experience of intuitive Divisionism came together with the influence of the Belgian Symbolists (such as Henri de Groux, Charles Doudelet and Jan Toorop) and that of the northern artists (with their mix of Expressionism, the fantastic and the grotesque), and the infatuation for Arnold Böcklin and the so-called "ancients," culminating in interesting results in terms of Giovanni Costetti's portraits of "ideal types."

In Liguria, Symbolism and Divisionism manifested special features, thanks to Previati's influence (he had summered at Lavagna, near Genoa, since 1901), and that of Plinio Nomellini, whose allegorical paintings such as *Sinfonia della luna*

(*Moonlight Symphony*, 1899), and *I tesori del mare* (*The Treasures of the Sea*, 1901) drew on the legend of Garibaldi, and featured light masses of filamented color, shadows broken by sudden bursts of color, the whole shot through with classical references. In addition, the individual styles of the younger artists Giuseppe Cominetti and Rubaldo Merello injected some modern developments tending towards expressionism and decoration (the gesture and brushstroke have a value in themselves).

In Rome, the traditional center for Italian artists, the influx of painters from Turin, such as Cena, Pellizza, Balla and the Genoa-born Giovanni Prini, sympathetic to humanitarian socialism and conversant in the Divisionist idiom, provided the elements for an embryonic avant-garde movement with a clear ideological and expressive focus. This was a welcome alternative to the weak tendencies established in the city such as the dominant neo-Renaissance style and the superficial Divisionism of Enrico Lionne, Arturo Noci, Camillo Innocenti and the like — little more than warmed-over naturalism, borrowing from the most conventional aspects of Impressionism. In his autobiography, Severini recalls that this community of artists, writers, and musicians, to which both he and Boccioni belonged, was a lively Bohemian scene which "was never immortalized by the likes of Henri Murger, but should have been." Severini also commented on the tendency for the artists to

Duilio Cambellotti
The False Civilization, 1905

Domenico Baccarini, *Night*, c. 1906

develop a social conscience through their reading of Marx, Engels, Bakunin, and Tolstoy, as well as Schopenhauer, and Nietzsche, combined with an interest in the relationship between art and social issues. He also noted that they were more interested in theory than in its practical application.

Guelfo Civinini was a writer, poet and first-rate critic, an attentive observer of this small Roman avant-garde seeking to capture its special characteristics. It was he who identified a trend inspired by contemporary reality, such as the city, the world of work, and the living conditions of the various social classes, and at the heart of which idealism became tinged with emotional, psychological, social and populist undertones, and a healthy dose of humanitarianism. Following the example of Auguste Rodin, the Belgian sculptor and painter Constantin Meunier, the Scandinavians, and the Belgian Symbolists, these artists sought to inject their work with a powerful charge of idealism and heroic accents keeping man and the world of work at its center. What they were aiming for was an art based on thought and emotion, with links to poetry and music.

"The refined art of black and white," is a primary expressive mode for the artist, offering a more modern and direct expressive freedom than painting. The great international "Bianco e Nero" exhibition of 1902, and new magazines such as *Novissima* (modelled after *Ver Sacrum*), *Fantasio*, *Avanti della Domenica*, and *La Casa* with their modern graphic design and illustrations by the artists themselves, all contributed to the development of this expressive mode. The linear outlines and the freedom of gesture, the areas of delicate and evanescent chiaroscuro, the shadows broken by sudden flashes of white or color in pen and pencil drawings, charcoal sketches, or pastel drawings offer the most concise, stylized and intense translation of reality. Portraits, the themes of work, the emotions, landscapes and the corners of the new Rome become intermediaries in the recreation of a state of mind, emotions, ideas and truth. The human figures, nature and the little every-day details are immersed in shadows, and acquire the status of universal symbols.

The most accomplished results were the Divisionist pastel drawings, and Balla's so-called *notturni* (*nocturnes*), the idealized and socially-conscious charcoal drawings of Duilio Cambellotti, an artist whose ability to create a compact architectural composition of form and sign was much admired by Boccioni, and Prini's drawings whose expressive effects and emotional charge derive from the simplicity of form and conciseness of the line. With his early training based on Bistolfi's Symbolism, and a mild and affable character, Prini became a point of reference for the Roman avant-garde, and a leading light in the new sculpture which was founded on an open-ended concept, sensitive to material and form, and heavily charged with emotional, humanitarian, and psychological content. His portraits, inspired by work, childhood and the outcasts of society are all presented as fragments of life.

Alongside these works, we find those of Boccioni in his Roman period, Severini and Sironi, the sensitive and rigorous works of the Faenza-born sculptor Domenico Baccarini, the graphic design of Umberto Prencipe, and the highly individual Symbolism of Florence-born Raul Ferenzona which resembled Sergio Corazzini's *Crepuscolarismo* and was inspired by the work of the Belgians. Theirs was a receptive and intelligent response both to the cues provided by the leading figures and to the great wave of influences from a variety of sources, such as modern French graphic design, the Secessionists, the Arts and Crafts Movement, and the Belgian scene. While these painters chose to stay on the sidelines, partly due to their anti-conformism, they did, nonetheless, provide fertile ground for both Boccioni's Futurist work and for the later developments towards a stylized or expressionist Abstract art, as well as offering an alternative to the vacuousness of so-called *gigantismo*, and monumental art's historicism.

The Evolution of Photography in Italy

Alessandro Perelli
Melon-Seller
Milan, c. 1915

In the introduction to a book on a hundred years of Italian photography, published by Alinari, Piero Chiara told the story of his father's experience at the battle of Dogali in Ethiopia. He had saved himself by hiding inside the corpse of a mule that had been killed by a shell: "I was small and thin enough to slip into its belly, pulling my feet in after me... inside the mule I quenched my thirst with the liquid from its lungs and stomach. I nibbled at what was within reach of my mouth and took a breath of air every so often by raising a flap of the animal's skin." It is a horrifying story told with complete naturalness, indeed with the sort of disturbing normality that rightly belongs to the mysteries of a fairytale.

Recent accounts of isolation in the Aspromonte mountains of Calabria have described survival techniques which suggest that, as in the case of Chiara's father, the vital secret lies in the absence of those inhibitions that would bar the only possible route to surivival for people far-removed — by reason of their mental habits if not as a result of life experience — from a life of real hardship. Henri-Irené Marrou has observed, in connection with the ascetic practices of the monks of ancient Egypt: "Tout depend du contexte de civilisation... ces rudes paysans coptes partaient d'un niveau de vie si bas que leur ardeur à réprimer la concupiscence les portera souvent à des excès pour nous déconcertants."

It might be disconcerting to encounter this story at the beginning of Piero Chiara's book on photography, and to repeat it here, but the underlying purpose in doing so is to show how difficult it must have been for photography to define its role within the context of Italian life at the end of the last century. Although photography in Italy developed early, as the research of Silvio Negri and others long ago revealed, its social importance remained extremely limited, thus conditioning the attitudes of the photographer towards his own work, or rather perhaps towards his "hobby." Indeed recent research on photography in Umbria from 1855 on (Diego Mormorio and Enzo Eric Toscanelli, *Immagini e fotografi dell'Umbria 1855-1945*, Rome 1984) indicates that photography was a means of "masking reality" in that it depicted "a happy world, which followed the rhythms of the natural cycle," a model which influenced even the honest reformative or humanitarian intentions of the authors.

The photographic career of the painter Francesco Paolo Michetti has been the subject of much study even in the course of his own lifetime. His images of peasant life, which at times were quite uncompromisingly grim, comprise a body of work that began with the passionate verism of *Voto* and drew inspiration from the imaginative genius of his friend Gabriele D'Annunzio. But when his stark photographic studies, accompanied by endless notes in an effort to impose some sort of compositional and thematic structure, culminated in his famous paintings *Le serpi* (*The Snakes*) and *Gli storpi* (*The Cripples*), that era was clearly over. These two great Symbolist works, executed in a style still strongly reminiscent of the brilliance of Mariano Fortuny, and consequently far removed from any formal contemporary trends, betray a moral indifference towards the world of the peasants that he had portrayed in tones of harsh realism. His photographs replaced the sort of life study in which a painter establishes a close rapport with his model. They were not research but pure, unsentimental documentation produced with the sole aim of supplying material for painting. But the conflict between these two separate phases of his working method had dire consequences and in the early years of the 19th century, the discordance was so strong that Michetti found himself faced with a

Mario Nunes Vais
Signorina Ruggeri Laderchi
1890-1900

choice: either pursue formal research in photography more deeply, which meant following the road of "pictorialism" (at that time the only way open), or abandon photography altogether as a short cut to research and return to the dedicated study of his subjects. Michetti, who by then had become a senator, opted for neither: bitterly disillusioned, he resorted to painting little scenes for his own pleasure in an attempt to escape from facile verism and to discover how much the Art Nouveau movement could offer him, while in photography he turned to neutral subjects such as plants, children and portraits, finally taking up color work.

Michetti's story is worth pursuing a little further as it illustrates an important point. Photography was initially intended as a means of documenting a reality which — it should be stressed — was harsh and unpleasant; it was also difficult to portray,

The Lovazzano brothers
Galleria del Lavoro
"Esposizione Nazionale"
Turin, 1898

G. Marchi, *Air*, 1905

Gabriele D'Annunzio in 1938
Istituto Luce

Paris International Exposition
"Floating Pavilion"
for the Italian Navigation
Association, 1937
Projects by Banfi, Belgiojoso
Peressutti, Rogers

almost inaccessible, both because of its own inherent closed character and because the painter-photographer himself was extraneous to its situations and events.

The immediacy of photography made it the only possible means of recording the primitive world of the country. But the painter-photographer was entirely unaware of the special qualities of photography; he did not appreciate the beauty of the images in themselves, and consequently did not bother to print them with any real care, remaining satisfied with poor-quality prints to be viewed through a stereoscope. Meanwhile, the subjects treated by photography at the time of D'Annunzio's *Novelle della Pescara* became inconvenient in the climate of moderation that existed in the Italy of Umberto I. Michetti's political development shared much with that of his friend, the journalist Edoardo Scarfoglio, and he acquired a similar degree of scepticism, protected by his natural predisposition towards isolationism. His case is also of interest because an opportunity to unite photography, painting and literature had been lost, and this was due in part to the fact that photography had exposed a harsh side of reality, stark and immediate, which people preferred to ignore.

Seminal as it was, Medardo Rosso's impact on photography remained an isolated event. It was isolated because it arose from purely personal imperatives on the part of the artist, and thus could never function as a model for imitation. The poor print quality contrasts with the elegant bromide, carbon and gum arabic prints and other visual treats offered by the pictorial photography of the time. But Medardo Rosso, like the pictorialists, felt that the format imposed by the lens and the plate was an unbearable tyranny, and he found it necessary to correct the print by hand. Rosso did this in a way that had neither precursors nor a sequel: he drew over the print in pen, cut out the silhouettes of the figures, and in short turned the images into objects, unique objects without any possibility for reproduction, mass or otherwise. At the same time he captured the photograph's expressive ambiguity of light, giving it a profound and original meaning. Other photographs done by sculptors, for example Constantin Brancusi, to record their own work, act as composers' orchestral instructions: they served to describe the lighting conditions and position in which to exhibit the sculpture. Such photographs were therefore subordinate to the sculptor's main preoccupation: his work of art. Medardo Rosso's case was different, because for him the reality of photographic documentation as a phenomenon bestowed an ulterior existence on the sculptures portrayed, one which could only be photographic inasmuch as a record of an historically real appearance. Here, it is not a matter of stating how others might photograph it, or giving instructions for its exhibition. Since the persons in the sculpture portrayed do exist in those photographs and the historical reality of the photograph is a *thing* that takes shape at a given time, it becomes a return to the initial moment of the work's inspiration, to the omnibus or the little sailboat, to the sudden realization that the light has made the gift of a different reality.

Photography's lack of success in Italy at the beginning of this century is felt all the more keenly when comparing its bleak, unhappy story with the one full of promise and imagination that can be garnered from the collected photographic images of Gabriele D'Annunzio. No matter whether he was photographed by a professional, an amateur or one of the first photo-journalists, in a trench, on a horse or wrapped in a bath robe, the results are always spectacular, marked by an unmistakeable sense of style and conveying a wealth of information on the cultural attitudes and manners of the time. These images display a remarkable awareness of the expressive potential of photography if not always on the part of the photographer, certainly on the part of the subject. The relationship between photography and culture in Italy in the first decades of this century is perfectly illustrated by the diversity between one of these vivid images of D'Annunzio and the look of suspicious surliness to be found in any of the portraits of Benedetto Croce.

The theme of conservation, of recording evidence, was Giuseppe Primoli's primary concern in his elegant series of photographic images done at the end of the 19th century, as it was later on, though with more attention to the documentary aspects and greater detachment, for Francesco Chigi in the pictures he took before the end of World War I. But an examination of collections of photographic material reveals a certain uneasiness on the part of Italian intellectuals with regard to photography. The passing from fashion of the ubiquitous parasol deprived the open-air group of one of its most essential compositional elements, and since the marble busts lining the avenues of Rome's Pincio park remained the model par excellence among parents well up on such matters, young people's attempts to mimick American film stars' photographic poses were generally stymied by mothers' stern glances.

It is not until the end of World War II that we can see any real rapport between intellectuals and photographers starting to form again; this development can be traced to a precise year, 1947, when the magazine sponsored by the film manufacturer Ferrania, under the editorship of writer Guido Bezzola published a manifesto by the group known as La Bussola, which was signed by, among others, Luigi Veronesi. Here, finally, Italian photography endorsed certain statements of intent regarding "direct" or, as it was referred to there, "elementary" photography.

Photography became an industry with its own market, and as a result the related literature was primarily concerned with product awareness and marketing techniques; only rarely did it touch on technical developments in order to help both the professional and the amateur to achieve better results.

An authoritative study of photography should begin with a discussion of cameras and lenses and move on to qualities of paper and methods of developing and printing. In theory, such a program of research would not be impossible to carry out, since the dates of production are readily available, but in Italy it becomes a very difficult task because photographic archives are quite lacking (apart from the collection of Italian-made photographic equipment in Turin's Museo del Cinema). Photography in fact hinges on the choice made from the range of possibilities, and therefore for analysis it is important to know what was available at any given moment.

For the same reason, an area of research that turned out to be less rewarding than it promised was the body of articles that appeared in photographic magazines such as *Corriere Fotografico*, beginning in the 19th century, *Fotografia Artistica Italiana* (Turin 1912-17, edited by Annibale Cominetti) and the annual *Luci e Ombre* (1923 to 1934). Indeed, the main point that emerges from articles on the subject is the extent to which the world of the photographer was detached and separate. The magazines tended not to reject any particular trends but to confine themselves to purely pragmatic discussion. Undoubtedly, the widespread circulation of some of them, especially *Corriere Fotografico*, contributed to improving technical knowledge, and the reproduction of important works by great foreign photographers, especially in the elegant *Fotografia Artistica*, seems to have encouraged a less provincial approach and inspired some interesting new work.

Technical magazines began to flourish with the development of photographic "pictorialism." If elsewhere this trend signified a rapprochement of photography and art and an attempt to correct what was considered the vulgarity of photography and conform with the aesthetics of Symbolism, in Italy it became a means of enclosing photography even more firmly within its own world. If photography was in fact a form of artistic expression, it had no need to compete with the other arts, and the initial problem of gaining acceptance "where the Muses smile," was no longer an issue once it had discovered its own point of reference — its own Muse — and had set up its own structure of exhibitions, competitions and magazines. As a result, these magazines tended to discuss photography within broadly philosophical terms, major works often being accompanied by exactly the same kind of comments as

Anton Giulio Bragaglia
Poly-Physiognomical Portrait
1913

The Paris Grand Prix
in *La Stampa Sportiva*, 1915

were applied to exhibitions of works of art. (It was no accident that the critic Marziano Bernardi's signature was among those that appeared in *Luci e Ombre*.) Thus portraiture, landscapes and genre scenes were talked about, while no mention was made of the work of many photographer-subscribers, which was by no means restricted to portraiture but involved three quite different areas: the documentation of industrial development, works of art and sport.

This last area was by far the most significant in the field of communications of which photography had become a part. It directly involved recording events that were real and unrepeatable. The immediacy of photography was its *raison d'être*: it spoke a forthright language that was instantly understood by the people.

At the turn of the century, sports photography was the only type of magazine illustration demanding a transformation of the layout: it presented the new task of emphasizing the image's contents of actuality and immediacy, rather than subordinating it to old or new graphic design conventions.

One area of photography that has taken on great importance in Italy is the documentation of works of art. There, it has a deeply rooted tradition that can be traced back to the 19th-century arts of the veduta and architectural drawings of monuments. This was a field which Italy, with its long experience of craftsmanship and technical experimentation, made almost exclusively its own. Photography's contribution to the world of contemporary art is incalculable: one has only to think of the number of explicit references to Alinari's photographs that we can find in various painter's works, including still lifes (by Filippo De Pisis, for example) to appreciate the significance of its role. It would be well worth some investigation — and soon, before all the clues have disappeared — to discover what collections of, say, Anderson's, Böhm's and Sommer's photographs inspired certain painters. After all there should be nothing scandalous about the fact that the maestro studied Gentile Bellini from the photographs that he had in his studio rather than make the trip to Milan's Brera gallery to look at the original paintings, or that the same commodity was offered to students of Tintoretto, on the ground floor of the Accademia in Venice.

Photography influenced the artists of the first half of the century in a variety of

Aerial view of the Roman Forum
Rome, 1919

Factory for railway stock
Turin, c. 1920

ways, above all by offering a repertoire of subjects and by directing attention towards what had already been reproduced. In terms of painting and sculpture, it offered guidelines on color values, three-dimensional effects using chiaroscuro effects, and precise information from a range of different viewing points.

Photography thus became an integral part of Italian art and perhaps to a greater extent than is conceded in most analyses of the relationship between the two. Their interdependence became even stronger when the government took on the task of documenting its artistic patrimony. While the great photographic studios worked with certain museums and archaeological and historical building projects in an external, independent capacity, the connection between them being simply that of studio and client, in working for the state they became part of the system. The photographer worked alongside the archaeologist and the restorer, in close collaboration with the project director. Though it would be an exaggeration to regard the relationship between the two groups as one of reciprocal exchange, ignoring the social and hierarchical differences that separated them, there is no doubt that the architect, art historian and archaeologist were dependent upon the photographer; they needed straightforward photography without artistic pretensions. Here too, research into the archives would yield more information on the various names and the developments that were significant in the evolution of the language of photography, which so far it is possible to discuss only in the broadest of terms.

The role of the state official in the circle of intellectuals and artists is also worth consideration; for example, the archaeologist Guido Calza, who married Raissa, later the wife of De Chirico, and the friendship and family link between Giorgio Castelfranco and Alberto Savinio, first in Florence and afterwards in Rome.

Lastly, industrial clients played an important role not only because they required technical excellence from photography but also because of their links with engineering and their keen appreciation of photography as an irreplaceable tool for product documentation. Among the major clients in this area were the state railways, the electrical industry, Ansaldo, Breda and Fiat. Of the important professional studios specialized in industrial photography, we can cite Bombelli of Milan, to whom we owe the extensive and excellent photographic record of Milanese industry, including coverage of companies such as Pirelli and Falck.

Alongside Bencini and Sansoni of Florence, who were responsible for introducing a new method of photographing works of art — using a matter-of-fact but engaging approach and imaginative cropping techniques (Mario Sansoni worked as official photographer at the Frick Gallery in New York for many years) — there were also photographers, such as Vasari of Rome, who worked both in art documentation and in the industrial sector, which in Rome mainly involved construction companies.

Other possibilities for development lay in what might be called "encyclopedic" photography, though its social impact was less immediate than that of those already discussed. The decision to publish a large national encyclopedia, lavishly illustrated with photographs and sponsored by Giovanni Treccani, was a decisive factor in this area's development. The year was 1925, and the man who carried out the project design was Giovanni Gentile. The first volume was issued in 1927 and included the entry "Abruzzo," with photographs by Luciano Morpurgo. His pictures were still painterly in style but already show signs of the new demand for geographical information rather than simply for pictorial evocation. Shortly afterwards Morpurgo, together with Roberto Almagià, professor of geography at Rome University, produced a remarkable book on Palestine (this was at the time of the first Jewish settlements), which is still today the most perceptive survey of that country ever undertaken. (Many of the photographs taken for it have still never been published.) Morpurgo was later commissioned by an IRI (Institute for the Reconstruction of Industry) bank to do a similar book on Albania, where it planned to open a branch;

Enrico Peressutti, *Pantheon*, c. 1935

Tato, *Mechanical Portrait and Transparency of Opaque Bodies* 1940

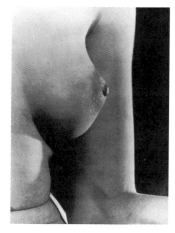

Mario Finazzi, *Volumes*, 1942

56

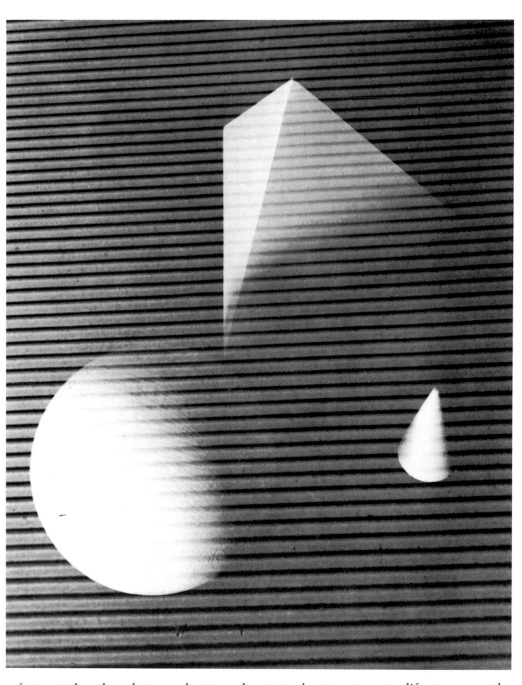

Luigi Veronesi
Superimposition, 1938

unfortunately, the photographs turned out to be too true to life to serve the purposes of publicity.

It was by a rather recondite route that Italian photography succeeded in freeing itself of its aesthetic conditioning. This involved two major breakthroughs, in quite separate camps. The first was sensational: the exhibition of the Fascist Revolution, held in Rome in 1932, for which Aldo Terragni devised an entirely new way of presenting material for exhibition. Using photography he found the key to a brilliant assimilation of the innovations of the entire period spanning Futurism and the Dada movement. The other breakthrough was the transformation of the graphic communications system which now depended upon a style of photography that was journalistic and objective rather than literary and artificial in its approach. The impetuses for this change came from the editor Görlich , the two annuals *Tipografia 1931* and *Tipografia 1932* by Guido Modiano, Aldo Boggeri's new graphics studio in Milan, and lastly, and most importantly, Adriano Olivetti's undertaking to radically alter the style of Italian office life. The "modern office" was a symbol comprising practically all that Italy had achieved in terms of modern design. One of the leading figures of the Bauhaus movement, Xanti Schawinsky, collaborated with Olivetti on this project from 1934 onwards. Around the same time the Milanese photographer Alfredo Ornano, who had made a name for himself in pictorial photography and had taken part in the "Fotografia artistica" movement in the early 1900s, became editor of the German firm Agfa's magazine, which promoted the sort of objective photography that until then few Italian photographers had yet adopted. Working with Ornano were Max Bill and Albe Steiner.

Towards the end of the 1920s and the beginning of the 1930s a rapport of mutual understanding and collaboration arose between the modern current in architecture, design, the European avant-gardes (with which the Milanese Galleria del Milione was founded) and a certain type of photography. In 1931 a book of Atget's photographs was published, with a Preface by Edoardo Persico, which had much in common with De Chirico's dreamlike metropolitan vision. References to Metaphysical painting became a means of identification for all new Italian photography that wished to dissociate itself from the propaganda of the Fascist regime, and that had by now rejected the simplicity of pictorialism. The influence of this trend was so powerful that the first great Italian illustrated weekly, *Oggi*, edited by Leo Longanesi, adopted this striking style of photo-journalism — which aimed to astonish — and it later became the only sort of photography that the magazine would accept.

Medardo Rosso, *Flesh of Others* c. 1883

In 1941 Antonio Lattuada's book *L'occhio quadrato*, published by Corrente, openly declared its support for the idea of the city as purlieu of the inexplicable and of chance meetings or connections bearing some mysterious significance. It is a book of photographs of Milan, yet it is not easy to recognize the city as the same one that Alessandro Perelli had portrayed thirty years before with stark and moving photographs of its people and the conditions in which they lived. Now an air of reticent solitude seemed to reign over a city apparently devoid of human life.

Photo-journalism of a more direct and popular kind now also came to the forefront, following the lead of Adolfo Porry-Pastorel, who, however, remained in a league of his own. Again, it was not the powerful agencies such as Stefani to carry the initiative but freelancers such as the journalist Orio Vergani, with his vivid images of Africa, and from recruits to the new popular weekly *Il Tempo*, which offered a number of innovations, including photo-reportages almost entirely without text.

It is interesting to note the absence here of a co-ordinated program comparable to what the government and the French and American press organized at the same time. But the success of these scattered ventures, largely supported by private funds, was considerable. Their originality was matched by the ineffectiveness of those set up by the regime, even if photography's propagandistic potential was clear to all. And they flourished in spite of the powerful Istituto Luce, founded in September 1924 (nationalized in 1925) and reformed in 1933. This institute's domain extended over both cinema and photography, and through newsreels it disseminated journalistic reports nationwide in a form accessible to all, even to the illiterate.

Medardo Rosso
*Impression de Boulevard
Femme à la voilette*
photography

The "direct" photography of the Fascist regime never really developed a style of its own, unless we can call quotations from Rodchenko and vague references to Leni Riefenstahl a style. "Futurist" photography launched its manifesto in 1930, mainly at F. T. Marinetti's and Tato's initiative. This failed to make any great impression, playing only a relatively minor role when it was not involved in the constructivism disseminated by the Bauhaus movement. By now there was very little evidence of the Futurist or "movimentista" photography invented by the two brothers Anton Giulio and Arturo Ludovico Bragaglia, who had been its sole practitioners. They had engaged for a time in "pictorialism" and had revolutionized it, but they soon abandoned the militancy that they had once embraced with youthful enthusiasm.

Maurizio Calvesi

Futurism and the Avant-Garde Movements

Carlo Carrà
Portrait of Marinetti, 1910-11

Filippo Tommaso Marinetti
and Enrico Prampolini
Poster for the Futurist Movement
dedicated to Larionov

The title of this essay echoes a research paper I was commissioned to write in the 1950s by the late lamented Umbro Apollonio, published in the magazine of the Venice Biennale.[1] Its conclusions were met with incredulity: the role of art in Italy in the first few decades of this century, overshadowed by the Paris movements, was considered marginal at the time. Moreover, Futurism was also regarded as morally suspect, but acquitted due to insufficient evidence.

Futurism's leading figure, Filippo Tommaso Marinetti, was dismissed as "a cretin with flashes of genius"! The movement he led was judged on the basis of its more superficial and negative characteristics, and seen as a weird apologia for machinery, speed, and warmongering, something hovering between the farcical and plain crass. No allowance was given for possible analogies with the aloof European avant-garde currents, which were considered diametrically opposed in poetics and commitment. Still less allowance was given for any contribution by the Futurists — not even in terms of technique — to the formation and development of avant-garde idiom.

Now that the ideological fog has lifted and the many inaccuracies eliminated, we are in a better position to assess my analysis, also drawing on the vast legacy of information gathered in the meantime. Gone too is the veneration for luminaries of the neo-avant-garde such as André Breton. Unlike other important cultural phenomena, his poetics were never sifted for objective clues about their derivation, apart from oblique references to Arthur Rimbaud, Lautréamont, and Alfred Jarry, which were pointed out by Surrealists themselves. Breton's poetics were considered too radically new.

I use Breton as an example, because, as we shall see, one of the cardinal moments (and an outcome of a series of fertile premises) of Futurism's influence on the literary and artistic currents of the avant-garde, and particularly on the Surrealist heritage, is Marinetti's theorizing on automatic writing in his famous *Supplement* to the *Manifesto tecnico della letteratura futurista* (*Technical Manifesto of Futurist Literature*, 1912).

Twelve years later, Breton spoke of "pure psychic automatism" enabling him to "express verbally and in written or other form, the proper functioning of the mind." "The first sentence comes of its own accord, indeed every second there is a sentence quite extraneous to our conscious thinking, that simply needs externalizing... The surreal atmosphere created by mechanical writing... is particularly suitable for producing beautiful imagery. The images appear in a headlong rush, as the only signals of the spirit's orientation. The spirit is gradually convinced by the supreme reality of those images. After a moment of merely submitting itself to them, the spirit soon realizes that they flatter reason, providing an extension of knowledge."[2]

"When I speak of intuition and intelligence," wrote Marinetti, "I'm not referring to two distinct dominions of the mind. Every creative spirit has had occasion to note that during the act of creation, the intuitive process merges with that of logical intelligence. It is therefore impossible to determine precisely where unconscious inspiration ends and lucid will begins. Sometimes the latter provides a spurt of inspiration; other times it merely accompanies it. After some hours of intense and hard work, the creative spirit breaks free from all the restricting obstacles, and somehow becomes prey to a strange spontaneity of conception and execution. The hand that writes seems to detach itself from the body, extending itself freely far from the confines of the brain — also somehow detached from the body — becoming airborne, looking down in awesome lucidity upon the unpredictable sentences issuing from the pen. Does this dominating brain impassively contemplate or direct the spurts of imagination animating the author's hand? It is impossible to say.''

We can see that as far back as 1912 Marinetti was urging artists to indulge in what Breton was later to call "mechanical writing.'' Marinetti was trying to inquire into the links binding unconscious "intuition" with "intelligence" (which Breton was to call "reason"), in order to fathom the "true functioning of the mind.''

The brain, according to Marinetti looked down with "awesome lucidity" on the unpredictable sentences issuing from the author's pen. Meanwhile, according to Breton, his automatic language gave him "supernatural lucidity.''

Breton: "Punctuation destroys the absolute continuity of the flux inside us.'' Marinetti: "When words are freed from punctuation they irradiate one another, their magnetic fields overlap, according to the uninterrupted dynamism of thought.''

Breton: "If silence threatens to impose itself, you have committed an error: an error of distraction perhaps — you must unhesitatingly interrupt a line that is too clear.'' Marinetti: "Blank spaces denote lulls and lapses of intuition.''

In Marinetti's *Immaginazione senza fili* (*Wireless Imagination*, 1913), words-in-freedom are a kind of story related helter-skelter fashion. In turn, Breton recommends writers to "write hurriedly... so hurriedly that you cannot hold yourself back.''

For Breton, "the value of an image depends on the beauty of the intuitive spark obtained; it is therefore a function of the difference in potential between the two conductors" (or "of the two realities placed face to face"). "When this difference is slight, as in resemblances, the spark is not generated.'' This is exactly what Marinetti was pointing to in his *Manifesto tecnico della letteratura futurista*: "Until now,writers have indulged in immediate analogies" (e.g., a "fretful fox terrier" likened to a "small Morse code key"), while "the analogy is a deep-felt love connecting distant things of an apparently different and antagonistic nature. The

Umberto Boccioni
The Laugh, 1911

60

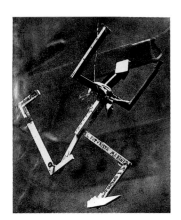

Filippo Tommaso Marinetti
Self-Portrait, 1914, destroyed

Guillaume Apollinaire
L'antitradition futuriste, 1913

broader the leap implied in the comparison, the more astonishing the images become."
In their mechanist manifesto Bruno Corra and Emilio Settimelli (*Pesi, misure e prezzi del genio artistico / Weights, Measures, and Prices of Artistic Genius*, 1914) stressed this point: "Anyone is capable of associating blue with the sky. But there are items of knowledge that are not so readily linked together, as they have never been associated, given the lack of apparent similarities between them... The amount of brain energy required to produce a work of art is directly proportional to the resistance separating the components before its action and the cohesion binding them afterwards."

Breton grasped the Futurist arguments so well that a careful reading of his analysis reveals specific objections directed to them, even though he ostensibly address Pierre Reverdy: "I do not believe it is in man's power to contrive the union of two such distant realities. It goes against the very principle of association of ideas, as things appear. If this is not the case, then we should be getting back to an elliptical art." The accusation of "elliptical art" was meant for Marinetti, who had spoken of an "orchestral style" capable of contriving "vast analogies."

Breton's conclusion, however, harks back to one of Marinetti's pet themes — automatism. "We cannot help admitting that the two terms of the image are not deduced one from the other by the intellect in anticipation of the spark to be produced, but that they are simultaneous products of that activity which we call Surrealist, whereas reason limits itself to noting and assessing the luminous phenomenon."
This does not contradict Marinetti's comment above: "Every creative spirit has had occasion to note that during the act of creation the intuitive process merges with that of the logical intelligence." And as for the "simultaneous" production (note the Futurist adjective) of the equation of two distant terms, it should be mentioned that Severini had already spoken of "plastic affinities or aversions that its [reality's] expansive action simultaneously evokes in us." (*Le analogie plastiche del dinamismo / Plastic Analogies of Dynamism*, 1913).

Breton strikes up a dialogue with Marinetti. With extensive knowledge of the latter's proposals, he adopts them and redirects them toward a systematic application of indubitably more cogent objectives. But we must not overrate the ideological diversity, nor its political implications: in actual fact, if the innovative action of the avant-gardes indeed had any effect at all on the social side of things it was in the emancipation of the prevailing customs and mentality, which came about through the power of language as a bold paradigm of freedom, independently of ideologies, or in parallel to ideological stimulus. Futurism fits in with the same disruptiveness.

The "technical" ingredients of the idiom also served to broaden the horizons of expression (in this case, with automatic writing), tapping the unconscious and the preconscious for its improbable and illogical imagery. The fact remains, of course, that what was only a cue for Marinetti, the start of a spiral of ideas, later became the systematic and global brief of Surrealism, with very engaging results. On a poetic level, the two contexts differ however, and we need to investigate how Marinetti's automatism slots into the Futurist world.

His idea had few repercussions in Futurist visual expression. The principle of "simultaneity," linking moments that are separate in time in our perception and memory (immediate or distant), takes place in the waking consciousness (a Bergsonian consciousness), and not in the unconscious. Only Gino Severini applied the theme of "analogy" to painted form (as dancer-sea-bunch of flowers), theorizing it in the manifesto mentioned above. But he applies it horizontally, without probing vertically into its depths. This betrays the same superficiality (in the sense of a surface psychology) of the archaic Marinettian idea of "inconscience," which the Futurists replaced with the Freudian concept. This was their most singular and authentic breakthrough, and had a possible precursor in De Chirico's Metaphysics. Rather than draw directly on Freud, Metaphysical art drew on one of the first Italians to take interest in Freud, Giovanni Papini (not surprisingly later a militant and dissident Futurist), blended with a pinch of romantic irrationality.

Marinetti and De Chirico accounted for a good half of the Surrealist brew. But Marinetti's Futurism alone provided half the contents of Dadaism, as is clear from *Il Teatro di Varietà* (*The Variety Theater*, 1913): "The whole range of stupidity, imbecility, foolishness and absurdity, that drive the intelligence to the brink of madness... A heap of events hurriedly run through and characters swept from left to right in two minutes... Play a Beethoven symphony backwards... Get actors in sacks up to their necks to recite *Hernani*... Green hair, purple arms, blue plunging décolletage, orange chignons... Outrageous outfits... Suddenly stress the need for audience participation... The *Teatro di Varietà* contributes to the Futurist destruction of immortal masterpieces [of the past], copying them, parodying them. Crossing ourselves with *trrrr trrrr* Elevated *trrr trrr* on our heads trumpetpetpets *fiiiii* ambulance sirens + electric pumps. Horror exit exit hurry hat cane stairs taximeter shoving *kaaay-kaaay-kaaay*."

The shift the Cabaret Voltaire made from Futurism to Dadaism was, in linguistic terms, linked and consequential; but what really changed was the ideology.

This is the context in which Marinetti's idea of automatic writing belongs, in the vibrant nucleus of pre-Dadaist inventions contrived around 1913 by Marinetti himself. (Here also the links with Breton make more sense, as Breton had worked alongside Tristan Tzara.)

Marinetti's "inconscience" was not some profound inner realm but a brimming physiological wellspring of the resources (more physiological energies, in fact, than psychic) to be channeled into the irreverent and biting explosiveness of his force, destined to *rejuvenate* the world: once again, alongside the themes of automatism and the illogical, we find the motifs of surprise, hilarity, humor, mechanics, randomness, and of the life of matter.

Since it did not involve the depths of psychoanalysis, automatism appeared as a manifestation of chance, as a form of absolute freedom of choice. In his *Manifesto tecnico della letteratura futurista*, Marinetti suggests that substantives should be thrown in "randomly, as they emerge." Chance photographically records the dynamism of realism, quickened by irrepressible energy; reality "vibrates confusedly around us and on us, strafing us with fragments of jumbled facts, interlocking, mixed, meshed, chaotic." (*Manifesto del Teatro Futurista Sintetico, Manifesto of Synthetic Futurist Theater*, 1915).

With their *Pesi, misure e prezzi* of March 1914, Corra and Settimelli advised people to "devote themselves to contriving compositions out of pieces of wood, canvas, paper, feathers, and nails, which, dropped from a tower 37.3 meters high, will describe, during their descent, a line of more or less complexity, more or less difficult to obtain, and more or less rare." What matters here is not the plastic form of the new composition, but the line created in the fall, as an energy diagram of *chance* (Lat. *casus*, p.part. of *cadere*, to fall).

Here, Dada was already in full swing, but Corra's and Settimelli's contrivance of 1914 provided a central pivot for the development of the Futurist visual arts, from Umberto Boccioni's "polymaterialism" (1912-13) to Giacomo Balla's and Fortunato Depero's "plastic complexes" (1915).

"Wood, canvas, paper, feathers, and nails" are basically an echo of the "polymaterialism" voiced by Boccioni in his *Manifesto tecnico della scultura futurista* (1912), in which he advocated a more organic utilization of materials, to achieve a more interactive effect — "glass, wood, cardboard, iron, cement, horsehair, leather, fabric, light bulbs, etc." But Corra's and Settimelli's invention leads toward the "plastic complex" (no longer a sculpture but an object), which Balla and

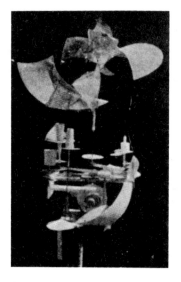

Fortunato Depero
*Colored Plastic Complex
Motorumorist of Equivalents
in Motion*, 1915

Giacomo Balla
*Colored Plastic Complex
of Force-Lines*, 1914-15

Depero expounded in their *Ricostruzione futurista dell'universo* (1915) and which was intended to be "volatile" and "explosive," composed of "wire, cardboard, fabric, tissue paper, etc." The various components will be arranged "according to the caprice of our inspiration," where the word "caprice" echoes the automatism of chance. The aim here is to "reconstruct the universe, making it more joyful, in other words re-creating it entirely."

Balla and Depero recall Marinetti's reaction on seeing the first "plastic complexes": "Before us, art was memory, an anxiety-ridden recollection of a lost Object (happiness, love, landscape)... With Futurism, however, art becomes 'art-action'"! Marinetti had used this term to describe the direct manifestation of a specific energy, and not its representation.

These three stages in the evolution of Futurist thinking on the function and nature of art can be related to Marinetti himself, and affected (though without directly influencing) the entire course of avant-garde developments, through to the 1950s and 1960s.

Boccioni's "polymaterialism" (*polimaterismo*), later developed in an original fashion by Enrico Prampolini, has a parallel in the *Manifesto tecnico della letteratura futu-*

Umberto Boccioni
Head + House + Light
1912, destroyed

rista, which speaks of "lyrical obsession with matter," and theorizes on the use of onomatopoeia, the introduction of "natural" sounds (fragments of reality, from which Russolo's noises were derived) into the mesh of language: "Use all the onomatopoeic expressions, including the more cacaphonic ones, that reproduce the countless noises of matter in movement"; and "abstract onomatopoeia, noisy and spontaneous expression of the most complex and mysterious stirrings of our sensibility," and the "psychic onomatopoeic chord, being a fusion of two or three abstract onomatopoeic expressions." The idea was onomatopoeia as the language of matter, or as the outlet of psychic automatism. The psyche was itself matter, and matter energy. "Substitute the worn-out psychology of man for the lyrical obsession of matter... its different directional impulses, its force of compression, dilation, cohesion and disgregation, its whirling multitude of molecules or its eddy of electrons."

Futurist "polymaterialism" stands out from other parallel avant-garde expedients and collage techniques for its more drastic theoretical basis. Speaking disparagingly of the new trend in a letter of 1912, Robert Delaunay mentions an Italian Futurist (without naming names) who paradoxically "a mis dans un cadre de la mortadelle, des cheveux et toutes sortes d'objets hétéroclites... Les importateurs de ces bluffs," continues Delaunay, are not Frenchmen, they are foreigners: Picasso and Boccioni.

An Italian heir of Futurist "polymaterial extremism" (in a fashion entirely his own) was Alberto Burri, whose materials were later to have a decisive influence on Rauschenberg's *assemblages*. But with the birth of the "plastic complexes," matter and materials were no longer confined to the canvas or sculpture block, and instead created with its own forms a new "object" designed to interact dynamically with space. Alternatively, the artist himself became a colorful, living element which promotes the artistic action in the first person (as with Balla and his "anti-neutral clothing").

In the same year (1915), Marinetti penned the manifesto *Il teatro futurista sintetico*, in which he advocated "eliminating the preconceptions of stage footlights by casting nets of sensations between stage and audience," and by invading the floor and audience with "scenic action," an idea which corresponds to the abolition of the conventional limits of the picture frame. In Marinetti's theater, the stage is unlimited, and the set merges with the intrusive structures of the *Ricostruzione futurista dell'universo*.

Later, Marinetti's imagination broke through yet another convention barrier: *Lo spazio vivente* (*Living Space*), the title of a theater piece based on a character dubbed Ballamar (from Balla + Marinetti). Said Ballamar: "We will remodel the sea with new types of wave! New water springs, new water spirals, with arithmetical and geometrical progression, elliptical trap-doors of see-sawing waters! And above rows of equilateral triangles of water we will have new marine curves hurtling from a hole in their arched backs their green white gassy spirits... A marine keyboard will modulate the forms of the sea and the wind through vertical tubes, openings, graduated elastic trap-doors and tunnels. We will remodel the sky! Buoyant and polymaterial architectures will blend with the clouds, the rain, the snow, the darkness ... We will create sun-traps, huge funnels lined with a thousand rapidly moving mirrors."

This signaled a shift from the work of art or drama as a point or locus circumscribed and labeled for representation, to the world as an enormous, unlimited theater for artistic performance; this logical evolution provided an ideal setting for the *happening*,[3] *environment* and *Land art*. It is the programmatic debut of Futurism, in its extremist consequentiality, that *necessarily* anticipates the entire parabola of the avant-garde and neo-avant-garde movements. Compared with the outstanding theoretical importance of the manifestoes, the actual achievements of the Futurists take second place.

At the core of Futurist theory lay the vastly fertile concept of Modernity, reaching

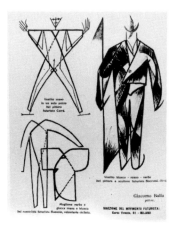

Giacomo Balla
Page from the manifesto
The Anti-Neutral Suit, 1914

beyond the apologia of the machine and capturing instead the sheer novelty of the revolution in communications: "Futurism is founded on the complete transformation of human perception brought about by scientific breakthroughs. Those who today use the telegraph, telephone, or gramophone, the train, bicycle, motorcycle, motorcar, transatlantic liner, dirigible, airplane, cinema, newspaper, are unaware that these forms of communication, transport, and information are exerting a decisive influence on their psyche." (Marinetti, *L'immaginazione senza fili*, 1913).

Flanking this program for the "complete transformation of human perception" is another critical Futurist insight, this transformation's global reach into all sectors of artistic expression (including visual arts, literature, theater and music), bringing each sector into contact with the others to foster greater osmosis and exchange, which would also become hallmarks of Surrealism and then of the neo-avant-garde movements. The words-in-freedom patently mimicked telegraphic communication, invalidating "the Ego in literature, i.e., its psychological content," as opined by Marinetti. Furthermore, the concept of "simultaneity" much exalted by the Futurists ties in with the vision of the world altered by rapid transport and communications, a world affected by a new omnipresence brought about by speed.

Even by 1909, in his founding manifesto, Marinetti had decreed: "Time and Space died yesterday. We already live in the absolute, since we have already created the eternal omnipresent speed!" A few years later, in 1913, Severini commented that "in our epoch of dynamism and simultaneity" there was a rising need to totally destroy the "unity of time and of space," blending "into a single plastic whole all the realities perceived" in various physical points. The scientific and epistemological arguments melded well with this kernel of intuition, anchored in the evolving reality of the communications universe. Art shifted from a question of individual expression to a privileged vehicle in the world of media and machines.

Unlike Fauve and Cubist experimentation, the novelty of Futurism, even in Futurist painting, was spurred by a radical new philosophy, whose flexible principles would irradiate to all fields of expression, and constitute a system of universal application, with concrete links to social spheres. Until Dadaism and Surrealism took over from this system, absorbing some of its urgency and technical cues despite ideological modifications, Futurism reigned practically unchallenged on the horizon of international avant-garde expression from around 1912 to 1915, after the crisis in Cubism and before the first inklings of Dadaism. Probably, a similar Futurist supremacy existed in the field of newspaper and magazine graphics, though a systematic study has yet to be undertaken.

A keen interest in Futurism evolved in Russia, where there was a singular need for total mutation of values in intellectual circles, even before the Revolution.[4] Viktor Sklovskij refers to the thinking of Vladimir Maiakovsky, who joined the Bolshevik Party just as Futurism was being kindled: "He said that the world would be obliterated and then rebuilt from scratch. He spoke of the coming revolt of things, saying that things would turn against mankind. There were just a handful of us, bent on redoing the world. Everyone was waiting for the Revolution, though no one was quite sure what form it would take." Russian Futurism's supposed lack of links to Italian developments is one of the most brazen falsifications thought up by the critics of the second postwar period. In the course of 1912, Larionov, Goncharova, and Malevich executed paintings featuring representations of movement that clearly drew inspiration from Italian Futurism. Larionov himself defined Rayonism as a synthesis of Cubism, Futurism, and Orphisme (or Orphic Cubism), and in his painting *Lights on the Street*, the influence of Boccioni's *Forze di una strada* (*Forces of a Street*) is evident. The *Manifesto of Rayonism* (dated 1913) bears the legend: "We declare: the genius of our times must be: trousers, jackets, shoes, tram, car, bus, airplanes, wonderful ships." The influence of the pictorial texts themselves is bolster-

Umberto Boccioni
Forces of a Street, 1911

Michail Larionov
Lights in the Street, 1912

ed by that of the manifestoes. When in December 1915, Malevich theorized on the "supremacy of pure sensibility in art," it is no surprise that he echoed the words of Carlo Carrà in *Lacerba* of 15 March 1913: "We affirm an art of pure sensibility." Enrico Prampolini too had spoken of "pure sensibility" in March 1915.

In 1914 Olga Rosanova paid a visit to Balla's studio, after which she began to experiment with dynamic and rhythmic abstraction that betrays the influence of the Futurist master; similar influence can be discerned in the paintings of Alexandra Exter and Liubov Popova. And, finally, Nikolaus Pevsner and Naum Gabo were clearly struck by the "plastic complexes" reproduced in the Balla-Depero *Ricostruzione futurista dell'universo* of 1915.

As late as 1924, the magazine *Noi* (nos. 6-9) carried a news item that testifies to the persistence of Futurist poetics, this time in a musical conception on a more popular level: "In Moscow a Futurist symphony was performed in commemoration of the Revolution, played by an orchestra of cannons, rifles, factory sirens, train whistles, and all the noises commonly heard in modern daily life."

Vorticism, invented in England in 1914, has undeniable links with Italian Futurism. That same year, Christopher R. W. Nevinson and Marinetti published a manifesto entitled *Vital English Art*, and at the Vorticist exhibition in 1915 Nevinson presented himself as a "Futurist." On another occasion, Nevinson was joined by Wyndham Lewis, and they declared themselves "Futurists" at the Camden Town Group exhibition held in Brighton between November 1913 and January 1914. Lewis had already aligned himself with Marinetti and the Futurists on their arrival in London in 1912. In autumn 1913, Lewis, Nevinson, Edward Wadsworth, Cuthbert Hamilton and Frederick Etchells put their works on show at the Doré Gallery in an exhibition entitled "Post-Impressionist and Futurist Exhibition."

The term Vorticism itself came from Futurist vernacular, in particular the language used by Carlo Carrà, who, in his manifesto *La pittura dei suoni, rumori e odori* (*The Painting of Sounds, Noises and Smells*, 1913) had spoken in terms of "boiling vortexes of forms and light," stressing that the artist "must offer a vortex — must be a vortex — of sensations."

James Joyce and T. S. Eliot also dallied with Vorticism, which seems to tie in with a declaration made by Ezra Pound before 1930, saying: "The Italian writer who in-

Review of conference on *Tactilism*
held by Marinetti in Paris, 1921

terests me most at present is Marinetti, to whom I must confess I owe and am most grateful. Marinetti and Futurism have given an enormous boost to all European literature. The movement Eliot, Joyce and myself started here in London would not have come to be, were it not for Futurism."

Paris was more miserly with its recognition, and instead boasted its own avant-garde movements' manifest precedence to Futurism. But this does not mean that the Futurist ideas did not penetrate into French artistic experimentation.

Apollinaire's attitude is worth looking at apart; just as he had reached his closest to Futurism, he made an abrupt about-face. This reversal of ideas is conveyed in his manifesto *L'antitradition*, which opens with the names "Marinetti Picasso Boccioni Apollinaire" listing the front-liners of the avant-garde, and was dashed off between 20 and 21 June 1913, during a fateful dinner lasting eight hours, from 7 pm to 3 am the following morning, in the presence of Marinetti and Boccioni themselves.[5]

But the understanding between Apollinaire and the Futurists was eroded by the heated disagreement over Orphisme, and on this score we can only say that, frankly speaking, between Delaunay and Boccioni there was plenty of give-and-take.[6] Generally speaking, the Futurist debt to Cubism is undeniable. However, the Futurist influence may, tentatively, be traced in the work of Fernand Léger (between 1913 and 1917), Henri Laurens, Albert Gleizes, Henri Le Fauconnier, Jacques Villon, Juan Gris, Raymond Duchamp-Villon, Jacques Lipchitz, and perhaps even in that of Marcel Duchamp and Francis Picabia.

In Germany, while Franz Marc mixed Kandinskian motifs and Delaunay's "Orphisme" with Futurist components from Boccioni and Balla, his compatriots Otto Dix, Georg Grosz and Max Ernst were to fall under the spell of Futurism. Kandinsky and Mondrian were also intrigued by Marinetti's movement.

For an exhaustive overview of the spread of Futurism in these and other countries (including Belgium, Denmark, the United States, Japan, Czechoslovakia, Poland, Spain, Mexico, Sweden, and Hungary), see the catalogue of the recent exhibition at Palazzo Grassi, "Futurismo & Futurismi," edited by Pontus Hulten.

Notes

[1] M. Calvesi, "Il Futurismo e l'avanguardia europea," in *La Biennale*, n. 36/37, July-December 1959 (republished with the title "Il Futurismo e l'avanguardia" in M. Calvesi, *Le due avanguardie*, Milan, 1966; successive edition by Laterza, Bari, 1971, 1981, 1984).

[2] A. Breton, *Manifesto del Surrealismo*, 1924.

[3] The birth of the happening in the context of neo-avant-garde movements has a cornerstone in the Japanese performances of Gutai in Osaka and Tokyo (1955) and the playscript published in the magazine *Anthologist* by Allan Kaprow in 1959 (the same year in which I wrote my resumé of Marinetti's manifesto on *Il Teatro di Varietà*, commented in the article cited in Note 1). The influence of Japanese Futurism on Gutai should be reassessed, though it is directly linked to precedents (as yet unexplored) of far-eastern artistic concepts and practice of a "diffuse aesthetic." In his playscript, Kaprow (who at the time taught art history at university) draws on ideas that stem, directly or indirectly, from Futurism. Kaprow envisages planting naked and heavily-dressed actors amongst the audience, so that the spectators find themselves sitting next to un-clothed, clothed, and over-clothed people. This might be compared with Marinetti's manifesto on *Il Teatro di Varietà*: "Introduce surprise and the need to interact among the audience... Offer free places to men and women who are notoriously loony, or argumentative, or eccentric — people who kick up a fuss, commit obscenities, pinch women's behinds, and whose behavior is otherwise bizarre." In 1921 Marinetti wrote that the inventive precedents that theater and music-hall owed to Futurism were "acknowledged by the public in Paris, England, Berlin, America, and recently in a leader article in the Parisian daily *Comoedia*."

[4] For a more circumstantial analysis of the observations on the Futurist influence in Russia and other countries throughout Europe, see *Dinamismo e simultaneità nella poetica futurista*, vol. V of *L'arte moderna*, Milan, 1967, pp. 232-312. See also the catalogue of the Palazzo Grassi exhibition "Futurismo & Futurismi", Venice, Palazzo Grassi 1986, organized by Pontus Hulten, with ample bibliography; see also the article cited in Note 1.

[5] As reconstructed by myself and Ester Coen in *Boccioni. L'opera completa*, Electa, Milan, 1983, pp.124-128; and along the lines of previous studies made by Pasquale A. Jannini (*Lettere a F. T. Marinetti con il manoscritto del manifesto Antitradizione Futurista*, Milan, 1978; *Le avanguardie letterarie nell'idea critica di Apollinaire*, Rome, 1979).

[6] See article cited in Note 1 above, and book cited in Note 4.

Fortunato Depero, Futurist Hall
First International Exhibition of
Decorative Arts, Monza, 1923

Vittorio Magnago
Lampugnani

Architecture, Painting and the Decorative Arts in Italy 1923-1940 from the First Biennale to the Seventh Triennale

Modern Italian architecture's first opportunity to exhibit to the general public was offered by the 1927 Third Monza Triennale where in a small room of the Villa Reale, the newly-formed *Gruppo 7* hung their (still-somewhat unpolished) designs on the walls and displayed their models on a large, specially-constructed plinth. This rather modest accomplishment did not attract much attention, either from the public or from the critics but, nonetheless, it marked the beginning of a relationship between exhibition organizers and the most avant-garde levels of Italian architecture that was to take on great importance in the coming decade.

Italian architects' first contact with international developments in the arts, crafts, and architecture had taken place at the Arts and Crafts Exhibition of 1902 in Turin, to which the Circolo degli Artisti Torinesi had invited the leaders of "every artistic tendency which was not tied to reproducing the art of the past." This exhibition also explored the relationship between the arts, crafts, and industry, which was to lead to the formation of the Deutscher Werkbund five years later. It was no surprise that the exhibition turned out to be a celebration of Art Nouveau, and brought the somewhat bewildered and uninitiated Italian public face-to-face with the works of Victor Horta, Henri Van de Velde, Charles Rennie Mackintosh, Josef Maria Olbrich and Peter Behrens. The main Italian representatives were Domenico Morelli, Raimondo D'Aronco and Giuseppe Sommaruga. The Venice Biennale's re-action was swift and the 1902 event was a resounding vote of confidence for the traditional and the nationalistic. Three years later, the Milan International Exposition quashed any fledgling attempt to make a connection between Italian art and industry, by handing over the event to a display of the most hidebound provincialism.

The issue of the Applied Arts was shelved until 1917 when the Socialist Member of Parliament Guido Marangoni, who was also Superintendent of Milan's municipal museums as well as the leading light of the Art Schools of the Società Umanitaria (established in 1893) wrote an open letter to the then-mayor of Milan, Emilio Caldara, recommending the creation of a biennial exhibition that would, "in the immediate post-war period, revive those decorative arts which once were the pride and distinguishing mark of each Italian region."[1] The first Lombardy Region Exhibition of the Decorative Arts took place in 1919 at the Milan headquarters of the Società Umanitaria. In 1922 Marangoni organized a conference to oversee the establishment of these biennial exhibitions, and in the following year the First International Exhibition of the Decorative Arts[2] was inaugurated at the Villa Reale in Monza, with Marangoni as its Director General.

Each region had its own section, and the resulting pot-pourri of folk crafts, eclecticism and the typically Italian Art Nouveau style called Liberty clearly showed how far behind their European counterparts Italian artistic craftsmen really were. The only bright spots in this otherwise depressing scene were Marcello Nizzoli's decorative panels, Gio Ponti's ironically neo-Classical ceramics, and most of all, Depero's Futurist Hall in which the talented painter and sculptor had arranged an inordinate quantity of paintings, drawings, sculptures, carpets, cushions and toys around a piece entitled. *Glorificazione plastico-luminosa di F.T. Marinetti* (*A Plastico-Luminous Glorification of F.T. Marinetti*), a curious collage-sculpture from whose loud-speakers boomed the voice of the founding father of Futurism.

The Second Biennale held in 1925[3] was not much of an improvement over the first.

While the *Exposition des Arts Décoratifs et Industriels Modernes* in Paris was effecting the shift from the traditional to the avant-garde with consummate nonchalance, its modest Italian rival was still clinging to the picturesque rustic with its implicit *petit bourgeois* rhetoric. Despite this, sixteen nations had been invited to take part. The Belgian, Victor Bourgeois, was responsible for the elegant Salon of Abstract Art and of Pure Plastic Art while the German contribution was a showcase for the work of the Deutscher Werkbund.

Felice Casorati, The Butcher's III Biennale, Monza, 1927

At the Third Biennale[4] in 1927, innovation was finally in the air. The artistic committee consisted of figures such as Carlo Carrà, Gio Ponti, Margherita Sarfatti and Mario Sironi, whose claim to artistic and political authority had been confirmed by the "Novecento Italiano" exhibition of the previous year. The four of them managed to instill the entire event with an anti-folklore and anti-decorative feeling, placing the stress on a "modern classicism" which was only slightly different from the so-called heresies of *Gruppo 7*. The work of the Milanese *Novecento* group had much in common with that of the leading Turin-based artists. At the invitation of the Piedmont region art workshops, the painters Felice Casorati, Emilio Sobrero, Teonesto Deabate, Francesco Menzio and Gigi Chessa donned the role of architects and created a butcher shop, a bar, a telephone exchange, a bakery and a pharmacy. Standing alone in the grounds of the Villa Reale was the Book Pavilion, the brainchild of Fortunato Depero for the publishers Treves and Bestetti Tumminelli: a monument to typography, it highlighted the Futurists' in-built flair for creating unusual publicity vehicles.

The idea of creating model-constructions in the context of an exhibition had been successfully attempted in the early years of the century at the Mathildenhöhe artists' colony in Darmstadt, and then at the Werkbund's 1914 exhibition in Cologne, and at the Stuttgart exhibition where the Werkbund were commissioned to design a model suburb, the Weissenhofsiedlung. This was 1927, the same year as the Third Milan Biennale, and the time was now ripe for the idea to take root in Italy. In 1928, Giuseppe Pagano, a supporter of Rationalist Architecture — and therefore in conflict with the conservative Giovanni Chevallier — was appointed Director of the Turin International Exposition which was held in the Parco del Valentino. Alberto Sartoris designed the Crafts Communities' Pavilion, Gigi Chessa the Photographers', and Umberto Cuzzi and Giuseppe Gyra worked together on the Goldsmiths'. Enrico Prampolini attracted considerable acclaim for his work on the modernist-decorative Futurist Pavilion. Pagano himself designed the Gancia Pavilion and worked with Paolo Perone and Gino Levi Montalcini on the Ceramics Pavilion and the Palazzo delle Feste, respectively.

Emilio Lancia and Gio Ponti Holiday Home IV Triennale, Monza, 1930

The next Monza exhibition (which had by now changed from a biennial to a triennial event)[5] featured three full-scale house-models.[6] Emilio Lancia and Gio Ponti's Holiday Home was a small country house, geared to a British life-style, with Mediterranean neo-Classical overtones. Designed for a middle-class "used to good taste and comfort," it was sponsored by the Rinascente department store and the De Angeli Frua textile company, and furnished by Domus Nova. The "Dopolavorista" (After-Work) home was made for workers and the lower-middle classes. It was designed by Luisa Lovarini and built by the *Opera Nazionale Dopolavoro Fascista* (the special body created by the Fascist government to develop free-time facilities). In reality, the only concessions to its proletarian end-users were that "noble" materials, such as marble, were not used, while the layout betrayed its more opulent intentions by providing for servants' quarters! Meanwhile, *Gruppo 7*, represented by Luigi Figini, Guido Frette, Adalberto Libera and Gino Pollini worked with Piero Bottoni to create the Electric House, an elegant *Novecento*-style interpretation of the *Esprit Nouveau*, sponsored by the Edison Company for the purpose of encouraging the use of electrical appliances in the modern domestic economy.[7]

Luisa Lovarini House of the "Dopolavorista" IV Triennale, Monza, 1930

Piero Bottoni and Gruppo 7 Electric House IV Triennale, Monza, 1930

Giovanni Muzio, Marble Hall
IV Triennale, Monza, 1930

Giuseppe Pizzigoni and Achille Funi
First Floor Atrium
IV Triennale, Monza, 1930

Giuseppe Terragni
Room of Models in Tailor's Shop
Mannequins by Marcello Nizzoli
IV Triennale, Monza, 1930

Painting Gallery
V Triennale, Milan, 1933

The 1930 Triennale, officially entitled the Fourth International Exposition of the Modern Decorative and Industrial Arts, under the auspices of its new directors, Alberto Alpago Novello, Gio Ponti and Mario Sironi, marked the death-knell for the folk-based craftsmanship favored by Marangoni. The introduction of the word "modern" into the exhibition title gave the organizers the chance to abandon the regional layout in favor of a more flexible, thematic approach. The exhibit was arranged around an atrium with a polychrome floor in geometric motifs by Alpago Novello. Five doors led to the *Sala dei Marmi*, a Metaphysical interior design by Giovanni Muzio in which the flooring, the twelve doorways, the fireplaces and the reliefs on the walls, were all made of different kinds of marble and granite, and were in the kind of dissociated classical forms typical of the Italian *Novecento*. The German section, designed by Ludwig Hilberseimer, concentrated on the industrial products from the Deutscher Werkbund and the Dessau Bauhaus. Josef Hoffmann was responsible for the Austrian section and devoted most of its space to the work of the Wiener Werkstätten. Under the auspices of Luigi Maria Caneva and Enrico A. Griffini (Marcello Piacentini having also been involved in their selection), the Architecture Gallery was devoted to "a modern one-family house" — a very topical preoccupation. The exhibition featured designs by, among others, Ottorino Aloisio, Piero Bottoni, and Franco Albini.

On the upper floor, the atrium was taken up with Giuseppe Pizzigoni's rigorous, illusionistic architectural background for Achille Funi's classical figures. Sebastiano Larco and Carlo Enrico Rava showed their sober and rational furniture designs in the setting of an "apartment for a lady." Giuseppe Terragni had designed the austere interior of the "room of models," watched over by Marcello Nizzoli's metal mannequins in a mock-up of a tailor's workshop. Giuseppe Pagano and Gino Levi Montalcini's work was represented by a series of outstanding designs for office interiors. Arturo Martini showed his elegant ceramic sculptures. Meanwhile, in the Graphic Design Gallery, Mario Sironi and Giovanni Muzio used a shocking (if not outright subversive) combination of (mostly classical) architectural motifs to create a spatial sequence which exuded an ecstatic air, and which was destined to become one of the emblems of the Italian *Novecento*. Every element seemed remarkable and "familiar" but the unexpected combination foreshadowed a new way of perceiving things. "The wide and full capitals of the columns as in the Tuscan order are shiny and made of glass; the solid, rich outlines which are unexpectedly broken off and remain so without any further implication appear to have been stopped in their tracks by some unknown and inevitable necessity, while the perspectives that are etched out of the white walls — straight out of the architectural treatises of the Quattrocento — look like the cabalistic symbols of an unexpected, wonder-filled world".[8]

All in all, the Fourth Triennale could be interpreted as a confrontation between the Italian *Novecento* and Rationalism. In any event what at first glance looked like a full-scale clash, turned out to be a contrast in appearance only. As Edoardo Persico quite rightly pointed out, "A room by Ponti, and one by Terragni, for example, seem to reflect the same aims and, over and above aesthetic preferences, are motivated by the common need for a practical and up-to-date result. This means that, at Monza, neo-Classical and Rationalist furniture represent one trend only, in terms of modern theory. These objects do not have different end-uses, nor are they designed for different consumers; they are both intended for furnishing the modern home and are designed with the family of today in mind".[9]

The accuracy of Persico's sympathetic but nonetheless uncompromising analysis was to be confirmed three years later. The 1933 Fifth Triennale, which by now had changed its title to the International Exposition of the Modern Decorative and Industrial Arts, and Modern Architecture,[10] was launched in Milan in its new made-to-order venue: a building on the edge of Parco Sempione, designed by Giovanni

Muzio in a slightly stilted, neo-Classical style with tentative modernist touches. The organizing body had by now achieved autonomous status (Ente Autonomo). Carlo Alberto Felice had replaced Alberto Alpago Novello in the Directorate, and the institution had won recognition in European figurative arts circles.

The ambiguity of its ethical and aesthetic content remained unchanged however. The exhibition was divided into three main sections. The first was devoted to mural painting and, under Sironi's direction, it offered a concrete demonstration of the unity between painting and architecture; this was a theme dear to him, about which he had developed a set of theories. Massimo Campigli, Gino Severini, Giorgio De Chirico, Achille Funi, Carlo Carrà, Gabriele Mucchi, Corrado Cagli, and Sironi painted monumental frescoes on the walls of the Palazzo dell'Arte, while Felice Casorati, Arturo Martini, and Marino Marini carved some very special bas-reliefs.[11] The second section was dedicated to the Applied Arts, and reflected the new middle-class taste which Gio Ponti was promoting in *Domus*, presenting a sophisticated look that mingled neo-Classicism with Modernism. The third, and most momentous section was dedicated to architecture, a field that was new to the exhibition (and important enough to be included in its new name).

The exhibition's main attraction was not situated within the Palazzo dell'Arte,

Mario Sironi, *The Works and the Days*
V Triennale, Milan, 1933

Enrico Prampolini
Station for a Civil Airport
V Triennale, Milan, 1933

Gruppo BBPR, Piero Portaluppi
Umberto Sabbioni
Newly-weds' Weekend Home
V Triennale, Milan, 1933

however, but in the park outside, which had become a sort of extension of the main exhibition area and featured thirty-one small temporary structures grouped around a tower of Dalmine steel tubes, designed by Gio Ponti and Cesare Chiodi.

Ten of these constructions in the park were pavilions to house various events, and included Luciano Baldessari's Press Pavilion, an elegant structure in brick, metal and glass, noticeable for the five slender cylinders that adorned it, and the Futurist Pavilion, designed by Enrico Prampolini and constructed in collaboration with Filippo Tommaso Marinetti and an army of so-called "aero-painters": entitled "Station for a Civil Airport," it celebrated the experience of air travel.

The other twenty-one pavilions made up the Housing Exhibition, and were all full-scale models of experimental housing, as seen at Weissenhofsiedlung. These included a steel-frame house; a bridge-shaped building; and a structural *tour de force* by Franco Albini, Giuseppe Pagano, Renato Camus, Giancarlo Palanti, Giuseppe Mazzoleni, and Giulio Minoletti. The Artist's Lakeside Vacation Home by Mario Cereghini, Adolfo Dell'Acqua, Gabriele Giussani, Pietro Lingeri, Gianni Mantero, Oscar Ortelli, Carlo Ponci, and Giuseppe Terragni was a free interpretation of Le Corbusier's theories. The Newly-weds' Weekend Home by the BBPR partnership (Gian Luigi Banfi, Ludovico Belgiojoso, Enrico Peressutti, and Ernesto Nathan Rogers) and with the (unexpected) collaboration of Piero Portaluppi and Umberto Sabbioni, was a bold attempt at designing the house of the future with gymnasium and mini-swimming pool. Finally, the Artist's Studio-Villa designed by Luigi Figini and Gino Pollini, was a Mediterranean re-interpretation of a Mies van der Rohe-style house with patio, *impluvium*, pool, solarium and space for outdoor physical exercise.

Nearly all the youngest and most enthusiastic members of the Italian architectural avant-garde took part in this expensive and spectacular initiative. The results, however, were not in any way comparable to those attained at the Stuttgart Werkbund exhibition six years earlier. The choice of the individual topics — which in most cases were idiosyncratic holiday homes in exclusive locations, with only one example of public housing and one of utilitarian housing on display — betrayed the indifference of the modern Italian architects to "*Existenzminimum* housing" which had been on the international agenda for at least ten years, particularly in Germany. The various experimental forms on display revealed a lack of stylistic confidence and an excessive dependence on foreign models, especially Le Corbusier's luxury homes: in fact Villa Savoye, with its solarium, its terrace-garden for outdoor exercises and its opulent "bath suite" had been completed little more than twelve months earlier. It was hardly surprising that *Quadrante*, the magazine of the Mediterranean Rationalists, was launched in the same year as the Fifth Triennale, nor should it be that during the exhibition's run, Pietro Maria Bardi, Piero Bottoni, Gino Pollini and Giuseppe Terragni were representing Italy at the *IV Congrès International d'Architecture Moderne* (CIAM), on board a luxurious cruise liner in the Mediterranean, far from the political upheavals that were rocking Europe.

Italian Rational architecture, a late imitator of the modern architecture scene, failed to share the real social impact of the latter. Rather than having its roots in a social democracy committed to addressing the needs of the working classes, Rationalism was created during the Fascist supremacy, having been plucked from the left wing of the party, with Giuseppe Bottai at its head, to represent (not without the odd nationalistic undertone) Mussolini's supposed "revolution." Over and above all else, it found most of its support from the relatively enlightened middle-class *intelligentsia* which was keen to show its progressive cultural ideas through specific forms (rather than mere types) and was prepared to pay for the privilege of doing so — a phenomenon which was also reflected in other European countries. Rationalism, therefore, did not become the style of the Italian proletariat, but that of the Italian middle-classes to which it conferred a "white" cosmopolitan aura in the midst of the mean-spiritedness of the period of the Black Shirts.

Edoardo Persico, Giancarlo Palanti
Marcello Nizzoli, Lucio Fontana
Hall of Victory
VI Triennale, Milan, 1936

Marcello Nizzoli and Edoardo Persico designed the *Sala delle Medaglie d'Oro* at the 1934 Salon of Air Travel. The structure's rigorous and extremely rarified design, which offered a successful and totally novel re-interpretation of the use of space, was one of the most harmonious end-results of Italian modern architecture.

The Sixth Triennale took place in 1936 under the auspices of Carlo Alberto Felice, Mario Sironi and Giuseppe Pagano. It was mainly through the latter's influence that the exhibition was overwhelmingly dominated by Rationalism. The foreign contributions were on the ground floor of the Palazzo dell'Arte. The Swiss exhibit was designed by Max Bill, the French by Auguste Perret, with Pierre Vago, and Alvar Aalto's furniture was featured at the Finnish stand. The German contribution demonstrated that the Germans had lost their previously inviolable ascendancy, which was hardly surprising given their political and cultural situation. On the upper floor, Edoardo Persico, Giancarlo Palanti, Marcello Nizzoli, and Lucio Fontana turned the pompous *Salone d'Onore* into the monumental *Sala della Vittoria*, which was destined to become one of the finest Italian Rationalist interior designs.

Giovanni Muzio, Palazzo dell'Arte
V Triennale, Milan, 1933

A children's playground and an open-air theater had been built in the park in which the *Torre Littoria* and the Press Pavilion still stood. Carlo Cattaneo and Mario Radice had also built the abstract fountain in reinforced-concrete blocks which would eventually be permanently sited in Brunate, near Como. Finally Pagano had built a new, two-storey pavilion, with a simple tower in concrete and glass rising above it and linked by a gallery to the main building.

This main building also housed a number of urban planning and architecture exhibitions. Overall, the exhibits were well-planned and comprehensive, despite a few problems provoked by the political situation — such as excluding Walter Gropius, Erich Mendelsohn and Ludwig Mies van der Rohe from the German section in the International Architecture section. The most remarkable contribution was the least orthodox: the relatively small exhibition by Pagano and Guarniero Daniel entitled "Rural Architecture in the Mediterranean Basin".[13]

Carlo Cattaneo and Mario Radice
Fountain
VI Triennale, Milan, 1936

The exhibition and catalogue primarily examined Italian rural architecture as it currently looked, and according to region and type. Underlying the ostensibly scientific non-judgmental approach, was a challenge. The exhibition concentrated on the simplest architecture, rather than any "stylistic" tendencies — in other words the architecture of peasants' homes rather than those of the great landowners. Sober forms and specific types were interpreted as the logical conclusion of an historical process based on optimizing function and building practices — precisely what the Rationalists were doing, and the design approach propounded in the pages of *Casabella* during that period.

The atmosphere at the Seventh Triennale, which opened in 1940, a few months before Italy entered World War II,[14] was quite different. The new Executive Committee was made up of Giuseppe Bianchini, Raffaele Calzini, Marcello Piacentini, and Gio Ponti. The Rationalists were not absent, as Pagano and a number of others had been commissioned to organize the International Mass-Production Exhibition, while Bottoni and Albini contributed to the work of a group responsible for formulating design criteria for the contemporary house. Banfi, Belgiojoso and Peressutti organized the acclaimed "Il Verde nella Città" ("Green About Town") exhibit as part of the Architecture Exhibition, which was directed personally by Marcello Piacentini. Fausto Melotti, Achille Funi, Lucio Fontana, and Massimo Campigli had also been invited to display their work in Palazzo dell'Arte.

However, after visitors crossed the *impluvium*, the first exhibition they saw was an imposing model of the main square of "E42," a chilly urban scenography conceived by Marcello Piacentini and Ludovico Quaroni. In the "Major Contemporary Italian Architecture" section, visitors could see the project for Via della Conciliazione in

Rome, by Piacentini and Attilio Spaccarelli, albeit alongside Luigi Carlo Daneri's modernist ideas for the redesign of Piazza della Foce in Genoa. The cities created by the Fascists could be seen in the "New Cities of the Regime" section, which was pure propaganda. The *Salone d'Onore*, which had been renamed the *Aula Massima*, or Great Hall, featured Agnoldomenico Pica's clumsily pompous decorations.

The Italian Rationalists' power of invention seemed to have been played out. Despite the odd unconscious concession to Internationalism and some hesitation brought about by the true advocates of quality, Fascist provincialism had finally managed to invade, and bring to its knees, even this great Milanese stronghold.

Marcello Piacentini
and Ludovico Quaroni
Scale Model of E42
VII Triennale, Milan, 1940

Notes
[1] Guido Marangoni, *Lettera aperta a Emilio Caldara*, in "Bollettino municipale di Milano", January 1918.
[2] *Catalogo della prima Mostra internazionale della arti decorative, maggio-ottobre 1923*, Milan, Rome, 1923. For the history of the Triennale, see Anty Pansera, *Storia e cronaca della Triennale*, Milan, 1978.
[3] *Catalogo seconda Mostra internazionale della arti decorative, maggio-ottobre 1925*, Consorzio Milano-Monza-Umanitaria, Milan, 1925.
[4] *Catalogo ufficiale della III Mostra internazionale delle arti decorative, maggio-ottobre 1927*, Consorzio Milano-Monza-Umanitaria, Milan, 1927.
[5] *Catalogo ufficiale della IV Esposizione triennale delle arti decorative ed industriali moderne, maggio-ottobre 1930*, Milan, 1930.
[6] Gio Ponti, Enrico A. Griffini, Luigi Maria Caneva, *Progetti di ville di architetti italiani all'Esposizione triennale della arti decorative e industriali moderne alla Villa Reale di Monza*, Milan, 1930-1931.
[7] Giacomo Polin, *La Casa Elettrica di Figini e Pollini. 1930*, Rome, 1982.
[8] Quoted in Agnoldomenico Pica, *La mostra grafica a Monza*, in "La Casa Bella," May 1930, p. 23.
[9] Quoted in Leader (Edoardo Persico), *Tendenze e realizzazioni*, in "La Casa Bella", May 1930, now in *Edoardo Persico. Tutte le opere 1923-1935*, edited by Giulia Veronesi, Milan, 1964, p. 12.
[10] Agnoldomenico Pica, *V Triennale di Milano. Catalogo ufficiale*, Milan, 1933.
[11] Mario Sironi, *Pittura e Scultura nell'architettura moderna*, in "Domus", May 1932. Gio. Ponti, *Serafini e i pittori*, in "Domus", February 1932. Lamberto Vitali, *Noi e l'affresco*, in "Domus", October 1932 and Lamberto Vitali, *La pittura murale alla Triennale*, in "Domus", June 1933.
[12] Agnoldomenico Pica, *Guida alla VI Triennale*, Milan, 1936.
[13] Giuseppe Pagano, Guarnerio Daniel, *Architettura rurale italiana* (Quaderni della Triennale), Milan, 1936.
[14] Agnoldomenico Pica, *Catalogo della VII Triennale*, Milan, 1940. And Agnoldomenico Pica, *Guida alla VII Triennale di Milano*, Milan, 1940.

The Valori Plastici Years

The drive to reinstate formal values in painting was the issue that most concerned the boldest currents in Italian art and art criticism immediately following World War I. Born of a number of cultural stimuli and shot through with a range of aesthetic implications, this movement found an outlet for discussion and development in the pages of *Valori Plastici*, a magazine founded and run by Mario Broglio from 1918 to 1922.

The *Valori Plastici* years (in fact, the period became known as such, so influential was the publication) spanned the interval between Metaphysical art's consummation and the birth of the *Novecento* proper. There is no doubt that the successful magazine offered the maximum expression of the common artistic inspiration of the time, and of an intellectual climate wholly of Italian making. From the very first issue its contributors were artists and critics often at odds with one another — indeed, it is probable that it was a hotbed more of controversy and animosity than of fraternity. And the "made in Italy" intellectual climate generated by the publication stood out from its European counterparts, with their *rappel à l'ordre* raging through the continent, thanks to its solid foundation in critical reflection and its focus on defining "the nature of art." Similarly, the classicism — or better, "artistic Italianism" — called for by the magazine's contributors (men who had been through the din of Futurism and the silence of Metaphysical art) differed from that of Pablo Picasso's Mediterranean idylls or Paul Valéry's *Ode aux colonnes*.

The contributors to *Valori Plastici* had in common their essentially Italian experience. Many of them had participated in the recent national developments in art — most as prime movers. Their desire was to engender a positive art form, unencumbered by Romantic and Symbolist residues, free of sentimental and lyrical affectations; to focus their energies on achieving a style and an idiom that respected formal rules considered eternal but infinitely variable ("the liberally adopted rule of the eternal Italian formal spirit"); to spurn all forms of unresolvable dramatic tension, and achieve a formal consistency that would be specific to painting alone — these were the ideas that in this delicate period of transition following the dissolution of the avant-garde experiences, rallied a group of artists, critics, and literary figures, coordinated by Mario Broglio — with Carlo Carrà, Giorgio De Chirico, and Alberto Savinio at its hub, soon flanked by Ardengo Soffici, Filippo De Pisis, Emilio Cecchi, Giuseppe Raimondi, and a host of others.

Inevitably, each member of the group liberally interpreted these ideas, which were still under the disquieting dominion of the silent Muse of Metaphysical art, according to his own personality, origin, and temperament. But the first impulse to respond to the call and consider those aspirations and their contents necessary, vital, non-reactionary, was not born just then in the *Valori Plastici* years. Put another way, it was not simply the fruit of the interwar period. Both before and during the war there had been moments during which, in the work or ideas expressed in the works of the artists, the burgeoning need for a specific "discipline," for a return to principle, for an art form that was only art, found its complement in a vital impulse, a piercing intuition that behind the object of that need there was something immense, something *terribile*, awesome. This was the expression Umberto Boccioni pronounced in a letter to Herwarth Walden, written in August 1916, shortly before his death, when the war was at its height. "I will come out of this experience with a contempt for everything that is not art. Nothing is more *terribile* than art.

Everything that I am seeing now is nothing compared with a fine brushstroke, a well-balanced verse, a harmonious chord. Compared with this, everything is just a question of mechanics, of habit, patience, memory. Only art exists."

These thoughts surface in some of Boccioni's earlier writings. On this point, Paolo Fossati quotes from a note pad dating back to 1915, a phrase relating to "discipline," one of the basic themes of those years: "Style is the negation of liberty, the daughter of materialism. The more liberty is held in check, the more style there is — just as a liquid takes the form of the vessel that contains it, or it would spill and scatter everywhere, and be absorbed, disappear." Carrà wrote many similar statements over the same period.

Carlo Carrà
The Builder's Son, 1921

This all goes to show how *Valori Plastici*'s themes had germinated in a cultural seed-bed prepared before the war. To some extent they were rooted in the avant-garde and post-avant-garde developments, or at least provided a sequel to them. And this is also the reason why it is incorrect to consider the "return to craftsmanship" heralded by De Chirico (in the November-December 1919 issue of *Valori Plastici*), and the "artistic Italianism" formulated by Carrà (in the April-May issue of the same year), merely as reaction to the extremism of the avant-garde calling, like the need for a return to normality after the trauma of war. "We believe in a law coordinating visual reality," wrote Carrà, "without which pictures remain nothing but naturalistic fragments, vainly aspiring to a unitary center." At the heart of this new quest for a more exacting idiom there was a specific, positive outlook that originated before 1918 and followed a scheme of ideas quite separate from the tragic events that had scored the lives of at least two generations. The path of development was a long one, and might also be seen as an identity crisis that had lived on unaffected through the war. Renato Serra, one of the first to die in the war, had accurately sensed this separateness: "War is a fact of life, like so many other things in this world," he wrote in his *Esame di coscienza di un letterato* (*Confessions of a Man of Letters*, 1915). "It is something momentous, but nothing more. Alongside the others that have been, and those to come, this war will add nothing, nor take anything away. It will change absolutely nothing in the world. Not even literature." Later he added, "And at the end of it all, everything falls more or less back into place; the war will have wound up the situation that existed, without creating a new one... Literature will not change. There may be some temporary interruption in it, but in terms of spiritual breakthrough or conscience or insight, it will remain where the work of the previous generations had left off: whatever may survive of it will set out again from there, and from there only will it go on."

These were prophetic words, and reading them now makes it easier to appreciate the mood of the excerpts above from Boccioni's letter to Herwarth Walden and his notebooks. Their thoughts are like a mental bridge suspended high above the war, and high above a vision inflamed by the tragedy of a drama that was both human and very real, but quite alien to the development of art; their thoughts are an expression of their anxiousness to reach a more solid terrain, something more specific and more suitable with which to "reinstate," through the discipline of a specific style, the principles of the sovereign autonomy of art itself. "Work will resume from there." What better way to put it? *La Ronda*, the literary magazine which was in a similar position to *Valori Plastici* and first came out in the same year, took over (as correctly noted by Alberto Asor Rosa) the role of "eyewitness" from Giuseppe De Robertis' journal *La Voce*, which, during the years preceding the war, had represented the front line in the literary avant-garde; and in fact the new journal "resumed" work from where *La Voce* had left off, asserting the specific nature of literature, its centrality, and not least its autonomy. In the same way, the parallel quest for specifics and formalization underpinning Broglio's magazine was echoed by the upheavals in the minds of Boccioni and Carrà (albeit differently), provoked

Gino Severini
Portrait of Jeanne, 1916

by the crisis in Futurism. But there were also other episodes in contemporary developments in the avant-garde that bear witness to those links: Gino Severini's well-known painting *Maternità* (*Motherhood*) and his beautiful luminous *Ritratto di Jeanne* (*Portrait of Jeanne*), both dated 1916, are like experimental inversions of the path taken by the Cubists. Far from being academic exercises or displays of skill, they are the fruit of a careful project, a rigorous pursuit of style, in keeping with the foremost Cubist-Futurist research in those years. Here, however, that inquiry is expressed with keen inner logic, respecting the fundamental rules specific to painting down through the ages.

Furthermore, Severini's own statements about his intention in these paintings to find "a simple form that harks back to the work of the Tuscan Primitive artists" are consonant with that particular drive towards style which, once the Futurist flame had begun to gutter, veered sharply towards Primitivism and Archaism. "The modern element [in my work] will emerge," wrote Carrà to Ardengo Soffici in September 1916, "if and when my spirit has rid itself of its many Futuristic prejudices. Simplicity in tonal and linear relations has become my obsession." Also in 1916, Carrà's essays "Parlata su Giotto" (A Talk about Giotto) and "Paolo Uccello costruttore" (Paolo Uccello, Builder) appeared in the magazine *La Voce*, just when he began to investigate the relationship between old and modern aesthetics.

The rediscovery of Giotto and the reappraisal of the Primitive painters led Carrà on the trail of "rediscovering our rhythm, returning to OUR spiritual consistency"; a path linked to the intensification of the Piedmontese artist's contacts with Tuscan circles, and in particular with Ardengo Soffici and Giovanni Papini — and soon after, with Roberto Longhi. Indeed, Longhi's first essay on Piero della Francesca dates from 1914, and was undoubtedly seminal to the emerging awareness among the artists of the vital connection between painting and a good knowledge of art history. This new understanding was to spread quickly during the 1920s in Rome in what is known as the early *Scuola Romana*, superseding the reigning concept of creativity, which preached art as something instinctive and romantic. Ardengo Soffici himself had already commented that "art proper begins with critical analysis"; and on various occasions in *Valori Plastici*, Soffici had insisted on the importance of combining art practice with a good grasp of its development, of pairing painting with its history.

Carlo Carrà, *Antigraceful*, 1916

But returning to Carrà, his preoccupation with Giotto — tantamount to a rejection of the Futurists' vaunted "dynamism" ("I am studying the 'body' of form and I'm not interested in dynamism any more, nor in other theoretical ideas for that matter") — was a necessary prelude to his brief, intense encounter with Metaphysical art "because the magical silence of Giotto's forms," which had so attracted him even back in 1915, presumed a perception which, though not different exactly, was certainly richer and more spiritual than the syllabized primitivism of his *Antigrazioso* (*Antigraceful*), or than the bitter spelling-out of "essentials" that had transpired in his *Fanciullo prodigio* (*Boy Prodigy*) of 1914. But Carrà's fascination for Giotto and Masaccio really comes to the fore, broadening into more complex themes and freer, articulated forms, in the paintings he completed between 1919 and 1924, namely *Le figlie di Loth* (*Lot's Daughters*), the series of landscapes on the lines of *La Crevola* (Jesi Collection), or those spare views across Lake Maggiore — all works from the *Valori Plastici* period. Some interesting parallels can also be found here in the works of Ottone Rosai of the same period.

The nature of this "reinstatement" of style unfolding in Carrà's heart (which gives us clues as to the door through which he entered that magical world of the *pittura metafisica* — quite a different door than the one through which Giorgio De Chirico entered) shows how beneath the converging stream of ideas regarding the need to change course and by "reinstating" the principles of art, there were rising currents of deep dissent, of differences that would make themselves felt later on, and that can be traced back as far as the brief period the two artists shared in Ferrara.

Even from this point of view, everything "will set out again from there, and from there only will it go on." Although De Chirico and Carrà labeled both themselves and their works "metaphysical" during the *Valori Plastici* period, in reality they differed highly from each other, more than one might suspect. Quite dissimilar in temperament, origin, mood, and habit, the two artists were also divided by greatly differing cultural backgrounds. On the one hand, there was the earthy Lombard character, the tumults of Futurism, the violence of *Antigraceful*; on the other, the climes of Greece, the Academy in Munich, Böcklin, Nietzsche, Schopenhauer. It was therefore quite logical that their creative objectives should also differ considerably. And yet, for a brief period, they found a point of contact, here amid the magical perspectives of the silent city, where the war had brought them together. Each of them decanted his ambition to grasp Weininger's "sense of things" — in itself a somewhat vague aspiration — into two quite differently-shaped vessels. In the case of De Chirico, this meant melancholy and pensiveness — or rather the literary specter of melancholy, under the emblematic banner of the "enigma." This seed brought forth nostalgic scenarios, desolate, enigmatic spaces that were undefinable because his mind sought other means. And so that "mysterious sense of things" dissolved in his uneasiness with the unquantifiable, rematerializing in myths without time, in symbols of absence, and silence. Carrà on the other hand projected that "sense of things" in his solid spatial imprint of the antique Italian sense of form, in those solidly-built cells of tight perspective, inspired by Giotto, this too a magical, enchanted world, in which he could enclose his romantic sensibility (without quelling it), faced with the mysterious epiphany of physical objects.

When the eagerly-awaited first issue of *Valori Plastici* came out in November 1918, barely a year had passed since the two artists' first meeting in Ferrara, but already Metaphysical art — that moment of convergence that saw a handful of "companions in solitude" united around De Chirico in Ferrara, Milan, and Bologna — was drawing to an end. The opening illustration, which served as a frontispiece to the magazine, was *L'ovale delle apparizioni* (*The Oval of the Apparitions*), dated 1918, the last work of purely Metaphysical iconography Carrà was to paint. The same issue carried De Chirico's *Il grande Metafisico* (*The Great Metaphysician*, dated 1917), while other Metaphysical works by De Chirico, Carrà, and Giorgio Morandi were reproduced in the third and fifth issues. The magazine seemed to come into being under this enigmatic constellation, and in fact the essays of Carrà, Alberto Savinio, and De Chirico (seemingly converging around a common objective) in the third issue (April-May 1919) represent the first attempt to invest the term 'Metaphysical art' with a conceptual base, though less with reference to the poetics of the Ferrara interval, preparing the basis of a renewal of art as something Italian, and new. This was the crux of the matter, because this "receptacle," "Metaphysical art," had become a depository for too many diverging ideas. After all, Filippo De Pisis had written that Metaphysical art existed quite independently of the various painting techniques, temperaments, individual passions and aversions of its proponents. And this was certainly so. It existed as an emanation, as a mute symbol that symbolized nothing, but which presented itself anyhow and everywhere with the authority of a symbol. *Incessu patuit Dea*. But when *Valori Plastici* started to come out, that poetic and ineffable mental inclination was already beginning to lose its original profile, its "Ferrara" character: it had been deviated and coerced (despite its being so alien to the concrete pattern of history) by that drive for "reinstatement," by that urge for stylistic discipline and reconstruction which seemed so imperative in 1918. It was also deflected by the artists' recourse to the expressive essentiality of the Primitives, by the peculiar "Giottesque" weight of things, which, like the issue of

Giorgio De Chirico
The Great Metaphysician, 1917

80

Giorgio Morandi
Portrait, 1917, destroyed

Giorgio Morandi
Still Life, 1918

"heritage," so excited Carrà's imagination. It is no coincidence that right from the first issue of the magazine, in open contrast to Carrà's enthusiasm, Alberto Savinio declared himself openly averse to this love for the "Primitives," who, he stated, "were simply artists who had difficulty painting," and who, owing to their lack of mastery, "became stylists by force of circumstance."

It is clear from this that when De Chirico and Savinio spoke of "mastery" and "return to craftsmanship" and Carrà spoke of the "Italianism of art" and "renewal of Italian painting," they meant two different things. Similarly, De Chirico, who having praised the hundred or more perfectly washed and stacked paint-brushes used by Jean-Auguste-Dominique Ingres, sealed his "return" with the words "*pictor classicus sum*" (I am a classical painter) and inveighed against the shoddiness of "today's avant-garde" (and yesterday's Futurists) — the same De Chirico, who, a year later wrote beneath his self-portrait "*et quid amabo nisi quod rerum metaphisica est?*" (and what will I love, if not the metaphysical?) — was also putting distance between himself and the arcane sorcery of the Disquieting Muses, adding to the literary specter of melancholy and meditation a further one: the specter of Classicism. This was his contribution to the call for "reinstatement" in an interwar period full of pitfalls. And with this contribution, he only accentuated his solitude, a solitude that was really only a particular phase of the isolation he had always experienced.

Talk of Metaphysical art continued in 1918 and 1919, but to Broglio's way of thinking, *Valori Plastici* was not supposed to be a forum for current trends: it had no precise program. Nor was it a springboard for manifestoes. Instead, it was to be a thought-provoking publication providing a stage for "inside" debate, representing an awakening to the situation as it stood, and encouraging the scrutiny of possible new avenues. It was no coincidence therefore — nor simply indicative of the urge to keep abreast of things — that between the first and third "Metaphysical" issues (with their texts and illustration by De Chirico, Carrà, and Morandi), the second issue was illustrated throughout with exclusively Cubist works of Pablo Picasso, Georges Braque, Fernand Léger, Juan Gris, and others. This is not simply an indication that, at the outset of the 1920s, they still refused to lock themselves into solely national perspectives (which would in fact turn out to be merely provincial); what is more important to note about this alliance — and also sheds some light on what I stated above on the aspirations towards new values of form that gave the initial impetus to the magazine — is that from the very outset the *Valori Plastici* group propounded both Cubism and Metaphysical art (if not on the same level, certainly on a plane that favored their convergence), excluding Futurism. This is because, unlike Futurism, even from as early as 1908 Cubism had shown its adherence to a program of pure research into form, shunning all extra symbolic and social side-issues; that is, it had dismissed Symbolist residues and psychological and "vitalistic" fallout. In this, the Metaphysical painters offered a parallel outlook. However, during their *Valori Plastici* "post-Ferrara" phase of the 1920s, while aware of working on the very "body of form," the Metaphysical artists refused to renege on the spirit of its origins and forsake their adopted "Muse." They were not prepared to abandon the quest for that indefinable ingredient of form, that something which lay outside the outward appearance of the form itself. The supposedly gratifying beauty of truly classical origin in the signs of Braque's or Picasso's "collage" works, failed to gratify the Metaphysical artists. And while for De Chirico "going further" into the nature of objects was synonymous with "enigma," the lure of the unknowable, or the delusion of an impossible knowledge, brought to the threshold of poetry — for Carrà it meant the marriage of plasticity and Primitivism (or, "Giottism" as it was known), which made possible the retrieval of a "primal" spirituality that was wholly specific to Italy. It was like an astral conjunction in which both formal and spiritual fluxes, falling from the sky of a hypothetical

Italian history for Carrà, and of a timeless Classicism for De Chirico, helped give birth to the modern-day reinstatement of values forecast by Broglio and by the diverse, discordant party of artists contributing to his magazine.

But in the first half of the 1920s, that Metaphysical tide began to ebb, even in De Chirico's output, because although he maintained his stance against painting devoted to "the apparent meaning of things" (the work of Armando Spadini, for one), De Chirico no longer abandoned himself uncritically to that sense of the "unknowable," as he had done in the Ferrara years. The "Grande Metafisico" was also seized by the drive for change, by the utopia of discipline, by the urge to unmask the false prophets and discover the universe of "master" painting, of ancient art, of classical sculpture, and the eternal nobility of forms. This was De Chirico's moment of revelation, as he beheld one of Titian's canvases in the Galleria Borghese, one spring morning in 1919 — an awakening he himself likened to Saul's enlightenment on the road to Damascus. And from that morning on perhaps, during his sojourn in Rome, from the studio on the Gianicolo hillside where he worked in solitude between bouts of depression and misanthropy, but constantly dipping his cup into the stream of his brimming unconscious, De Chirico heard the bells peal in that sky and scatter in a thousand echoes among the woods and garden plots of the Roman hillside, the vibrant trumpets of his personal "Rinascimento." During these years he turned to the masters: Raphael, Michelangelo, Lorenzo Lotto. His pictures were freighted with a statuary academicism, with stiffened figures set in a motionless space, one that remains essentially the *Piazze d'Italia*, though now subject to the rules of Renaissance perspective. This group includes *La partenza degli Argonauti* (*The Departure of the Argonauts*), *La statua si è mossa* (*The Statue Moved*), *Mercurio e i Metafisici* (*Mercury and the Metaphysicians*), and *San Giorgio e Lucrezia* (*St. George and Lucretia*), all painted between 1920 and 1922. It was hardly De Chirico's most cheerful period, but he soon pulled himself together. The first signs of a "neo-Metaphysical" departure, so to speak, appear in *Paesaggio romano* (*Roman Landscape*) and *Pagliai* (*Haystacks*) in 1922, and later in the series of landscapes and romantic "imaginary views" (the so-called *Ville Romane* series) of 1923, thanks to a sudden return of youthful love for Böcklin, which now enriched his painting, salvaging it from that statuary and academic rigidity, injecting the landscapes with a new and undefinable sense of "suspension." This shows how the "celestial portent" that struck him in the Galleria Borghese, rather than bear him towards Florence or Venice and Renaissance splendor, had sped him towards Basel and the ambiguous, Nordic light of the classical "idyll" illuminating the twilight of the 19th century.

Giorgio De Chirico, *Lucretia*, 1922

Carlo Carrà's parting from the Metaphysical spirit was predictably more decisive. In the brief period from *Lot's Daughters* of 1919 (the year of De Chirico's "conversion"), to *Il pino sul mare* (*The Pine Tree by the Sea*) and *Mulino di Sant'Anna* (*Windmill at Sant'Anna*, both from 1921), Carrà visibly pitted all his energies into an intense quest for spatial delineation, with a concerted determination to simplify things, to pare them down to the bone in a bid to attain the primary essence of the poetic imagination: these two landscapes, with their lack of human figures, esoteric furnishings, and of statuary reminders, seem (to use one of Longhi's expressions), "trimmed to four words spelled out and luminous like one of [Giuseppe] Ungaretti's 'illuminations'." But Carrà's real conversion to "mental impressionism, as opposed to phenomenal impressionism" (Longhi again) — which was yet in some way a "return to order" — his real escape from the ascetic, metaphysical isolation that had borne him to the unadorned poetry of the two 1921 landscapes (perhaps his greatest works of all) started in 1923, with the paintings of the Camogli countryside.

Giorgio Morandi
Still Life, 1920

As for Giorgio Morandi, by nature far removed from the "enigmatic poetics" of his colleague and immune to the allure of those imaginary scenarios, he approached De Chirico's world through the interpretation Carrà had supplied of it. Morandi ac-

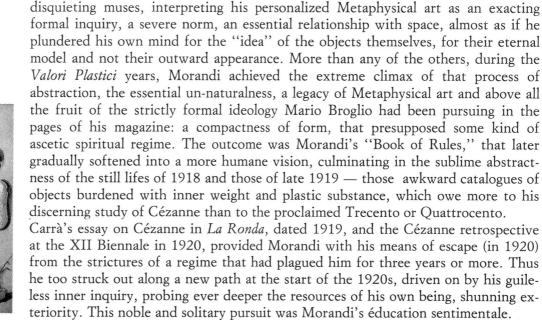

Giorgio Morandi
Still Life, 1918

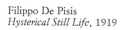

Filippo De Pisis
Hysterical Still Life, 1919

ceded to the realm of Metaphysical art as if entering a religious order, apprehending it as a "moral tension," as a quest for the absolute. His works from 1917 to 1919, some of which were reproduced in the first, fifth, and penultimate issues of *Valori Plastici*, show him even more immured than Carrà to the silent beckoning of the disquieting muses, interpreting his personalized Metaphysical art as an exacting formal inquiry, a severe norm, an essential relationship with space, almost as if he plundered his own mind for the "idea" of the objects themselves, for their eternal model and not their outward appearance. More than any of the others, during the *Valori Plastici* years, Morandi achieved the extreme climax of that process of abstraction, the essential un-naturalness, a legacy of Metaphysical art and above all the fruit of the strictly formal ideology Mario Broglio had been pursuing in the pages of his magazine: a compactness of form, that presupposed some kind of ascetic spiritual regime. The outcome was Morandi's "Book of Rules," that later gradually softened into a more humane vision, culminating in the sublime abstractness of the still lifes of 1918 and those of late 1919 — those awkward catalogues of objects burdened with inner weight and plastic substance, which owe more to his discerning study of Cézanne than to the proclaimed Trecento or Quattrocento.

Carrà's essay on Cézanne in *La Ronda*, dated 1919, and the Cézanne retrospective at the XII Biennale in 1920, provided Morandi with his means of escape (in 1920) from the strictures of a regime that had plagued him for three years or more. Thus he too struck out along a new path at the start of the 1920s, driven on by his guileless inner inquiry, probing ever deeper the resources of his own being, shunning exteriority. This noble and solitary pursuit was Morandi's *éducation sentimentale*.

The presence of Filippo De Pisis, which is limited to a single article in the first issue, may seem somewhat out-of-line with the cultural tenor of *Valori Plastici*, especially if we set his temperament and personal approach to painting against the moods and intentions of the other headlines of the magazine, not least of its editor.

And yet the youthful De Pisis — who in 1918 had proclaimed himself De Chirico's and Savinio's "herald," passionately embracing (from a literary point of view) their ideology and poesy throughout the *Valori Plastici* years — also felt himself to be a "metaphysical" artist. But this label could hardly be applied to his youthful "collages"; they are closer to the wordplay and nonsense of the Dadaists. But in 1919, in a painting entitled *Poeta folle* (*Mad Poet*) just a few months after his debut article, De Pisis virtually "plundered" one of De Chirico's paintings, and in 1923 he painted that "Metaphysical landscape" which tends toward the spatial spareness and formal simplification of Carrà, through not without a certain poetic heedlessness of its own. After his dalliance with Broglio's magazine, born undoubtedly of the close friendship the artist had with Savinio and De Chirico during the Ferrara years, in 1923 De Pisis pulled away from the avant-garde bridgehead and embarked on the road to "order," prompted perhaps by Ardengo Soffici. It was a clean break from the *neo-Quattrocentismo* and De Chirico's Classicism — and in particular from the rising *Novecento* current. This was the period of his Rome and Cave still lifes, before his departure for Paris, the period of his first "marine" paintings. Shortly before 1925, with an ever-quickening pace throughout his Parisian period, De Pisis found his element in strident shades of color, in the joy of breathing life into objects through painting. However, "that vivid quivering of objects in the light, that continuous invention of color alongside color, seem a far cry from the silent immobility of the metaphysical hour, when the sky is green and the shadows long on the deserted Italian piazzas. And yet in some of the still lifes De Pisis completed in the 1920s, and in the first marine still lifes, the objects — scattered along an infinite plane of airborn perspective that seems to garner the vibrant air and distant sound of waves, as if heard in a seashell — have a looming, ponderous presence that eludes De Chirico's definition of 'metaphysical'." Here — through the eager ferment of ideas, through that crop of stringent intentions and idealistic yearning for classical shores animating the *Valori Plastici* group, through their utopian aspirations for a radical reinstatement of artistic canons — the finest currents of Italian painting rose out of the ashes of Futurism, even before the onset of war.

Francesco Dal Co

Italian Cities and Architecture in the First Half of the 1900s

The debate about the links between the younger members of the Milan-based *Nuove tendenze* group in 1914 and the *Manifesto dell'architettura futurista* (published later) is still alive today, at least for historians of architecture. In a famous interview with Giulia Veronesi in 1952, Mario Chiattone spoke of his own past and shed some light on this debate, when he said, "Sant'Elia was not a Futurist... The proposal was to move away from the Wagnerschule... The ideological confrontation between *Nuove tendenze* and Futurism really only took place on a political level or, more precisely, on an 'interventionist' level." This comment of Chiattone's tends to substantiate Antonio Sant'Elia's status in the history of 20th-century Italian architecture, and also bears out the belief that, despite the ambiguities and shortcomings of his contribution in strictly artistic and design terms, Sant'Elia has had a lasting influence on architecture as a discipline. The fact remains that Otto Wagner's teaching and the output of the more talented exponents of the Wagnerschule were the preferred reference points for the incoming generation of Milanese architects at the beginning of this century, including Sant'Elia and Chiattone himself. Both studied at the Brera Accademia di Belle Arti in Milan, and matured in an intellectual sphere whose outspoken magazine *Emporium* provided a learned and far from provincial mouthpiece for their ideas. Sant'Elia and Chiattone were also the (somewhat frustrated) heirs of Liberty style (Italian Art Nouveau), and of the illustrative style practiced by Raimondo D'Aronco, Ernesto Basile, Giuseppe Sommaruga, and Giulio Arata, although initially the Academy was under the spell of luminaries like Camillo Boito, and later that of teachers such as Luca Beltrami, Adolfo Zecchi, and Gaetano Moretti.

The "Futurist" works of Sant'Elia attest to the complex weave of formative currents making up his background. The "ideal city" the young architect designed in 1914 in a set of plates and drawings with dramatic perspectives earned Sant'Elia immediate acclaim; this scenario, drawn with an as yet indeterminate idiom, explored the themes being tackled by Viennese Secession architects at the time, and only marginally brushed with Marinetti's poetics, rather than adhering to them. However, as Sant'Elia's compositions clearly reveal, these influences did not determine a complete break from the taste and tradition of Liberty style, however generic this definition may sound today.

But there is another, no less significant area of questions prompted by the statement quoted above. According to Chiattone, the young Lombard architects' adhesion to Futurism had more to do with politics than with aesthetic preconceptions; given the climate in 1914 these impulses found their most logical outlet in the rationale of "interventionism."

Whatever the basic motives behind Fascist "interventionism," it was this political option (which has been investigated in depth by historians) that provided the ideological basis for the gravitation of Marinetti's movement toward Fascism. Written by Marinetti in 1918, just a few years after the publication of Sant'Elia's schemes — though separated by the decisive years of World War I — the *Manifesto del partito futurista* displays the links between the political alternatives summed up by Fascism and the principles developed by the Futurists in their search to be an all-pervasive movement — principles which can in no way be broken down into the individual experiences of the leading interpreters of the Futurist poetic.

After 1919, the Futurist appeals, and a people intoxicated by the new awareness of national cohesion that the war had given them, contributed to translate time-worn tensions in the nation's political and cultural arenas into incisive slogans. As pointed out by Alberto Asor Rosa, the intellectuals gathered around the magazine *La Voce*, which was not only important in literary circles — eminent figures such as Benedetto Croce and Gaetano Salvemini — found themselves advocating opinions that differed little in structure from those fueling the Futurist propaganda, in spite of Croce's considerable misgivings about Marinetti's aesthetics. These opinions were representative of the ideology that had developed inside the burgeoning anti-Giolitti faction, and which was later to exert a decisive influence on the Fascist movement, whereas the political focus of Futurism was an immediate and vital link in this chain of developments.

Raimondo D'Aronco
Casa D'Aronco, Turin, 1903

Given this stance, Mussolini's rise to power and the subsequent consolidation of the Regime occasioned no decisive breach. While the paradoxical nature of Marinetti's political choices, which were motivated by a radical dislike for the political class, helped to guarantee the continuity of the ideological foundations Fascism had made its own (and by paradox I mean Marinetti's wavering vision of history, which led him to imagine that politics could be somehow separated from the political class that upheld it), the fertility of this ideological terrain owed much to personalities that had been prominent in pre-war culture. As Giuseppe Prezzolini stated, "Fascism has not managed to destroy with violence that which has taken us twenty years to destroy with thought, through criticism — namely, Italian democracy."

This sketch of the background events brings us closer to the main subject of this essay, and can now be slotted into the broader debate to give a clearer idea of the arguments discussed below. However worthy of attention and rich in implications the work of the architects from the turn of the century to just after World War I, it was not until after the first phase of Fascism that architecture finally began to thrive and to keep pace with the developments in the more advanced countries of the West. Of course, this is not to contradict the established historical perspective, but rather to confirm its findings that contradictions were rife and developments followed a highly erratic course. In the 1920s, and particularly during the ensuing decade, the polemics, research and experiment all enjoyed a flurry of intensity without precedent in Italian architecture. The proof of this is the remarkable quality of the designs, which can be ranked alongside the major architectural achievements on an international scale.

Alberto Alpago Novello
Giuseppe De Finetti
Giovanni Muzio, Tommaso Buzzi
Ottavio Cabiati, Guido Ferrazza
Emilio Lancia, Michele Marelli
Gio Ponti, Ambrogio Gadola
Antonio Minali, Piero Palumbo
Ferdinando Reggiori
Competition for Master Plan
and Expansion Scheme
Milan, 1927 (II Prize)

Because of the variety of the offering in architecture at the end of the 1920s, Giorgio Ciucci has rightly pointed out that the year 1928 signaled a turning point that merits the special attention of historians of architecture. That year, critical political decisions were made which defined important institutional components of the Fascist regime. Other events that specifically affected the architectural profession include the founding of the magazine *Domus* by Gio Ponti, *La Casa Bella* by Guido Marangoni, the Turin Exhibition on Futurist architecture, and not least the first Italian Exhibition of Rationalist Architecture, held in Rome in March and April.

Due to the sheer complexity of the developments in the design field in the 1920s, it is impossible to trace a linear path describing the structural links between the Regime's ploys to establish social and political stability, and the developments in architecture over the same period.

Between the end of the 1920s and 1936, once the Regime had proclaimed the Italian Empire and soared to mass popularity, the Futurists opposition was first crystallized, then developed, with all its various cultural ramifications. Broadly speaking, this is when the Futurists began their divorce from Fascism, opening a debate that became increasingly virulent in the course of the 1930s. As Ciucci observed, on one side were those architects who were pursuing individual projects and committed to defending artistic and intellectual autonomy in their field; on the

Ottorino Oloisio
Project for the Terme Littorie
1926

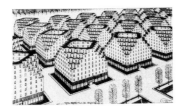

Piero Portaluppi
Project for the Neighborhood
"Alabanuel", 1920

Innocenzo Sabbatini
Suburban hotel in Garbatella
Rome, 1927

other were those who were reluctant to make any value judgments about the prevailing political setup, and, stressing the radical change that had occurred in political and social spheres with Mussolini's rise to power, were bent on making architecture part of a broader program already underway to define a new and all-encompassing art form that the Regime could call its own.

This contraposition was not spurred by ideological and aesthetic differences alone, but by changes that had occurred over the years relative to commissions and professional roles. In the 1930s there was a marked increase in the range of demands made on the architectural sector from all directions; and it was notably from the beginning of the preceding decade that new forms of schooling for architects were set up: 1919 marked the foundation of a Scuola Superiore di Architettura in Rome, and shortly afterward new architectural faculties were opened with the intention of merging the tradition of the Accademia di Belle Arti with that of the engineering faculties. In this way, a new set of professions were profiled to meet the need for specialization brought on by the new tasks and functions that the design field was now expected to fulfill. So while various elements of the Milanese *Novecento* group (Giovanni Muzio, Gigiotti Zanini, and Giuseppe De Finetti) are intent on addressing the upper middle class demands for quality, mindful of tradition and able to blend neo-Classical nostalgia with hints of the Metaphysical, it was the young minds graduating from the new faculties of architecture which provided the more incisive examples of innovative design, and took the floor in the debate that had formerly served as their reference point. These new projects coincided with the steady consolidation of Mussolini's politics, which had become fairly clear by 1925, and increasingly so as the decade wore on. The tenor of the situation is clear from Mussolini's famous "discorso dell'Ascensione" (Ascension speech, 26 May 1927), in which he outlined new guidelines for planning policy — typified by his slogans for the depopulation of the urban centers, "lo sfollamento delle città."

Marcello Piacentini's 1928 master plan for the town of Brescia gave an identity to the new policy, and heralded the start of a series of large-scale urban clearance schemes implemented throughout the country over the ensuing years. The schemes laid bare the inner-cities to vast speculative operations and radical substitution operations that cast aside old or simply different concepts of urban design that had presided since the late 19th century, such as those established by Gustavo Giovannoni, who, operating in Rome, had been an exponent of the cultural tradition of Camillo Sitte.

The building programs instituted by the Regime were only part of the income of the more established professionals, who were well-integrated with the old bureaucratic

Giacomo Mattè-Trucco
Stabilimento Lingotto, Turin
1916-28

system, the city management apparatus of the new political regime, and the financial and industrial establishments. The Regime showed a certain dexterity as it maneuvered amid the polemics raging in the world of architecture. With a singular display of pragmatism, the Fascists managed to garner the support of the intellectual class by pledging to definitively unite the nation on a cultural level also; on the architectural front, this commitment was competently handled by Piacentini. In the meantime, the professional appointments for the realization of the social renovation program (which the Fascists fostered for propaganda reasons, with the building program serving as a pragmatic spearhead for revitalizing the country's economy) were deftly rationed out among the various components of architecture, and the young designers increasingly had occasion to showcase their talent and further their personal research, especially through the numerous competitions the Regime set up. The competition for a new railway station in Florence (1933) was won by a group of ardent and enterprising young Tuscan architects led by Giovanni Michelucci, whose style was marked by its boldness and coherence. This is one of the more remarkable examples of Fascist handling of cultural initiatives, not least for the repercussions and debate incurred by the way the consultations were run. The results of the Florence competition boosted the aspirations of those among the new-generation architects who were more open to developments abroad, and more sensitive to the vanguard of radical architecture in Europe.

In the "opposition" camp, with the formation of *Gruppo 7* in 1927 (which comprised such young architects as Figini, Frette, Larco, Castagnoli, later replaced by Libera, Pollini, Rava, and Terragni), a new wave of incidents seemed to strengthen the status of the more radical architects. In 1928 came the first exhibition of Rationalist architecture, promoted by the MIAR, whose second session in 1931 was sanctioned by the presence of Mussolini himself, and rekindled the expectations of the leading exponents of Rationalist architecture, as revealed by the sudden change of tack made by Giuseppe Pagano and Pier Maria Bardi. The year 1932 saw a special exhibition celebrating the ten year anniversary of the Fascist revolution. The installations were designed by Libera, De Renzi, Terragni, Prampolini, Nizzoli, Sironi, and others, testifying to the trust accorded to the prime movers of some of the more advanced modern experimentation. In the meantime, the Milan Triennales, from 1930 (at the time still staged in Monza), to the more renowned ones of 1933 and 1936, provided the young architects with an exclusive arena for airing their ideas; some of the more enterprising members had managed to take over the more prestigious architectural magazines, which were to publish works by Raffaello

Giuseppe Pagano Pogatschnig
Umberto Cuzzi
Gino Levi Montalcini
Ottorino Aloisio, Ettore Sottsass
Competition for the redevelopment
of Via Roma, Turin, 1933

Giuseppe De Finetti
Study for the redevelopment
of the Arena, Milan, 1933

Giolli, Persico and Pagano, Bardi and Ponti. The dispute over what was defined as "academic monumentalism" and the empty *passéist* celebrative works of the Regime grew more and more bitter. In spite of the apparent cohesion binding the work of the younger generation of designers whose services were called on every time the Fascist regime wanted to give a modern edge to its image and impress its willingness to innovate, research into architectural form and expression in the 1930s was highly varied. For example, in Turin Pagano (one of the most outspoken in the debate and polemics of the decade) led a fairly assorted group of designers (including Levi-Montalcini and Sottsass) on the clearance project for Via Roma (1933), and drew up a plan that shows him in favor of a more balanced approach and against the more sweeping proposals of radical architecture. Meanwhile in Rome new and perhaps more significant centrifugal forces began to appear, attesting to the autonomy Italian architecture was capable of summoning when faced with the stylistic koine of international Rationalism. The post office buildings constructed by Giuseppe Samonà, Adalberto Libera, and Mario Ridolfi in the early 1930s are also prime examples of this chain of developments. The outstanding results achieved in this area, and by Libera and Ridolfi in particular, earned their authors a position on a par with their more celebrated European counterparts. A further example of the pragmatic approach taken by the regime, availing itself of Piacentini's mediating abilities, is the construction of the Città Universitaria, a university "campus" or neighborhood in Rome (1932). This scheme is for many reasons outstanding, as well as a demonstration of the dynamism of the Fascist Regime's public works policies. The presence of Piacentini and Pagano at the helm, and contributing architects such as Michelucci, Ponti, Minnucci, and Aschieri guaranteed (at least until new polemics broke out over the project for the E42 district) a balanced evolution of architecture through the first half of the decade.

While discussions over the need for a specific form of architecture for the Regime, a distinct Fascist style and a national art secured the involvement of the leading figures in the design field, experimentation continued in a climate of considerable autonomy, with the occasional unexpected spin-offs resulting from the ideological clashes that colored developments in other sectors of the country's culture. In the

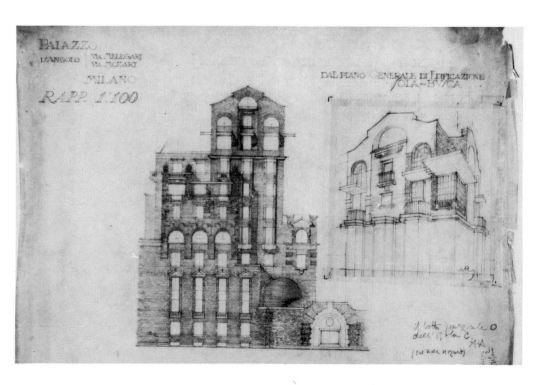

Aldo Andreani
Project studies for
Palazzo Fidia, Milan, 1930

field of architecture, the bickering between the various factions was suddenly directed on what was perhaps the most far-reaching of all the competitions set up during the 1930s — the competition for the construction of the Littorio Palace on Via dell'Impero in Rome (1934). Although the winners of the competition belonged to the group led by academic luminaries such as Del Debbio, Foschini, and Morpurgo, the projects submitted by the younger generation of architects provided a remarkable show of vitality.

Of particular interest are the projects entered by Mario Ridolfi and by the Milanese group BBPR (Gian Luigi Banfi, Ludovico Belgiojoso, Enrico Peressutti, Ernesto Nathan Rogers), and above all the entry submitted by Giuseppe Terragni's group composed of Carminati, Lingeri, Nizzoli, Saliva, Vietti, and Sironi, which (especially the first two versions of 1934) represented a lyrical celebration of the Regime using geometrical abstractions and severe order to express strong moral cohesion. They suggested a new urban order, a "new city" designed according to the criteria of an essential language and a radical formal purity. Terragni's experience with the residential complex in Como, "Novocomun" (1927-28), and later with the Casa del Fascio (Como, 1932-36) were highly coherent examples of his vision, whereas the ideas behind his project for Rome foreshadowed schemes he completed in the second half of the 1930s, such as the "Danteum" (1938) and the Palazzo dei Congressi in the E42 district (1938-39).

In the meantime, the architects continued their inquiry into specific problems of history and tradition, exploring new hypotheses aimed at defining a new "national architecture." Sometimes the issues were analyzed in the terms favored by the Rationalists, who devised their own form of rhetoric that starkly opposed the Mediterranean tradition and spontaneous and rural building types; other times the issues were expressed in the more academic terms adopted by the likes of Ugo Ojetti, a noted polemicist, or in the less antagonistic tones of Piacentini and his kind.

While the magazine *Casabella* run by Pagano offered an open forum for Rationalist

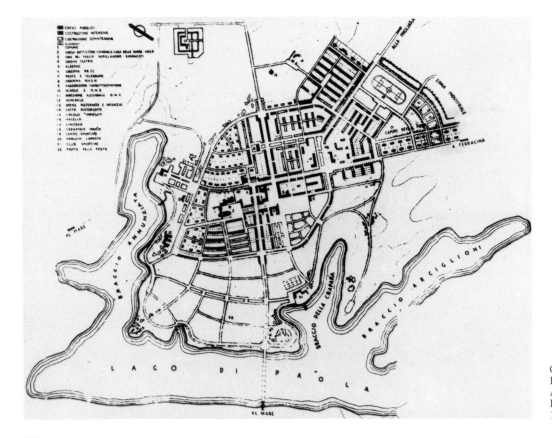

Gino Cancellotti
Eugenio Montuori, Luigi Piccinato
Alfredo Scalpelli
Plan for the town of Sabaudia,
1933-34

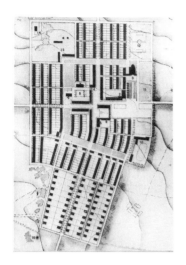

Eugenio Montuori
Luigi Piccinato, Alfredo Scalpelli
Location plan of the town of Aprilia
1936

architects — hosting contributions by Edoardo Persico, which were inspired by Catholic values and radical liberalism, and set out to acknowledge ethical valencies of formal research in Rationalist architecture — it was in a more marginal sphere that the radical architects found a unique occasion to carry through their ideas, for both geographical and ideological reasons: in the intellectual oasis that Adriano Olivetti created in the family business in the town of Ivrea. By appointing members of the rising generation of young designers to key positions in his company, Olivetti initiated an innovative production policy focused on the formal quality of the product design. Olivetti's policy gave vital impetus to the development of a truly Italian design style. Figini and Pollini designed the new ICO factories (1934 and after), and a residential area; later they were teamed together with the BBPR group and Piero Bottoni to draw up the master plan for the Valle d'Aosta, a plan that attempted to create a new ideology for city and territory, modeled on the sociological inclinations of Olivetti himself, with a purely architectural language of Rationalist stamp.

The ongoing debate in the pages of *Casabella* and the new openings by Olivetti brought to maturity new themes that have no direct links with official lines of design practice and architectural or planning philosophy promoted by the Regime. It was no coincidence that the problems tackled in *Casabella* and at Ivrea provided a crucial bridge between pre-war culture and the new culture that emerged after the fall of Fascism. No less significant, however, were the new opportunities promoted by the Regime. In the area of territorial planning, for instance, the creation of new towns in the Agro Pontino as part of land reclamation schemes in the late 1920s was a concrete test of new ideas in planning. The scheme was accorded the utmost importance, and was funded by the Opera Nazionale Combattenti, involving the mobilization of vast resources.

The entire project took on a specifically architectural character. The regime showed astuteness in its use of the competition system to award commissions. While the

Giorgio Calza Bini
Buildings in Guidonia, 1938

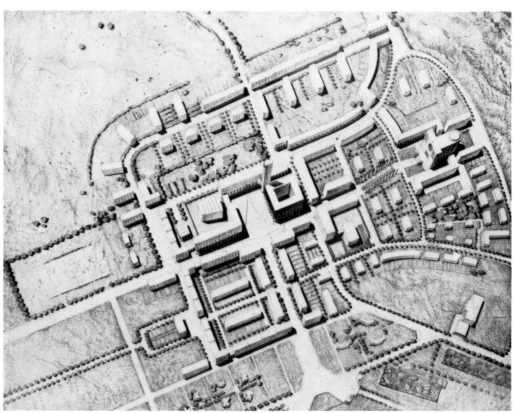

Giorgio Calza Bini
Gino Cancellotti, Giuseppe Nicolosi
Project for Guidonia downtown
1937-38

town of Littoria (1932) was designed outright by Orio Frezzotti, the construction of Sabaudia was decided through competition, which gave Piccinato, Cancellotti, Montuori and Scalpelli the chance to draw up a Master Plan that served as a blueprint for later projects of the kind. A competition was also set up for the construction of Aprilia, whereas the Opera Nazionale Combattenti was entirely responsibile for seeing to the completion of the urbanization scheme for Pomezia (1938) and other similar cases.

The construction of the "reclamation towns" and rural communities in Sardinia was a further expression of the anti-urban leanings of Fascist ideology. But despite this, and despite the campaign for the depopulation of the urban areas, from the late 1920s on, a great deal of attention was paid to urban renewal schemes, which illustrates the innate contradictions of the Regime's policies in planning. The massive clearance operations mentioned above (together with Piacentini's intervention in Brescia, and similar schemes in both Turin and Genoa) were accompanied by a string of competitions for master plans for a variety of major towns and cities. Other cities earmarked for a new master plan were Arezzo and Foggia in 1929, Bolzano in 1930, Genoa in 1931, Perugia in 1932, Pavia in 1933, Como in 1934, Mantua in 1935, and Aosta in the following year. Meanwhile, a great many consultancies were set up for rehabilitating large inner-city areas throughout the country. The shortage of living space prompted a wide-scale building boom and the creation of several imposing suburban residential schemes, including the Garbatella, a "model neighborhood" designed by Aschieri and De Renzi in 1929. In 1931, a new master plan was approved for Rome, sanctioning the outward spreading of residential areas and the monumental redevelopment of the outskirts, plus the demarcation of a theoretical city-to-coast development axis. This new corridor road served as the site for the special exposition district known as E42, commenced in 1935, to commemorate the first twenty years of Fascist rule. The Regime set up the scheme with scrupulous care, entrusting the drafting of the master plan to a specially appointed team which included Piacentini, Piccinato, Pagano, and Vietti; during the implementation phase, from 1937 on, work was directed by Piacentini alone, however. The designs for the most important buildings for the E42 precinct were chosen through competitions. Among the first architects to receive assignments were Quaroni, Fariello, and Muratori, who designed the Palazzo dei Congressi (Congress Hall), while Figini, Pollini, and De Renzi were assigned the Palazzo delle Comunicazioni (Communications Hall); the BBPR Group competed against a team composed of Gardella, Albini, Romano, and Palanti, for the commission to do the Palazzo della Civiltà Italiana (Italian Civilization Hall). Between June 1937 and March 1939, five competitions in all were publicized for the E42 precinct. The Vice-Commissioner for the independent body set up to arbitrate over the precinct's construction was Cipriano Efisio Oppo, who presided on all the jury boards. Occasionally taking part on these boards were Piacentini, Pagano, Minnucci, Piccinato, and Vietti, and a variety of other architect-designers. Involvement was almost total, and the architects assigned to the E42 district alternated between being judges and being judged; the scheme drew on the contribution of the country's architect class *en bloc* — Libera, Terragni, Vietti, Albini, Quaroni, Vaccaro, Figini, Pollini, Moretti, La Padula, Palanti, BBPR, Minnucci. With few exceptions, the leading minds of architecture were brought to bear on the Regime's most prestigious scheme in its twenty years of power, to create that complex of "classical monumentality," which, after several adjustments and compromises Piacentini pledged to complete. The objective was not merely to compile a sort of inventory of architectural form through which a true "Regime style" could be profiled, but to achieve the maximum cohesion around this, the Regime's most celebrative venture. It was to be a resounding demonstration of stability and efficiency, and was coupled

Luigi Figini, Gino Pollini
Master Plan for Courmayeur
1936

Marcello Piacentini
Attilio Spaccarelli, Project
for Via della Conciliazione
Rome, 1937-50

Giuseppe De Finetti
Project for restructuring
Piazza Cavour, Milan, 1942

with a concerted propaganda campaign. But the kaleidoscope of works and projects conceived for the E42 district merely confirms that Italian architecture at the time was highly divided. As a whole, the scheme lacks homogeneity of form or idiom, and also shows the hesitancy and incompetence of the young architects involved when faced with schemes of this caliber. Pagano's vehement attack on Piacentini in 1937, in which he accused the latter of subverting the original program for the E42 district in favor of "lies and appearances," testifies to an imminent change of climate. This change was amply reflected in the sheer variety of the schemes submitted to the competitions for the various sections of the Rome exposition venue. But the magazine *Casabella* had announced the change in even more explicit terms. The aggressive Rationalist stamp of the projects discussed, such as the "Milano verde" project elaborated by Albini, Gardella, Minoletti, Pagano, Palanti, Predaval, and Romano, and the characteristics of the city neighborhood in Milan's Viale Argonne (built by Albini, Camus, and Palanti), attest to how the models inspiring these architects were no longer ideologically reconcilable with the aims that projects like the E42 set out to celebrate. Commenting on the outcome of this joint enterprise, Pagano wrote "Thus Academe has won, and on the flattened Acropolis of the Three Fountains, the two and a half million Lire so far spent simply monumentalize the void." Later he was to comment on the sudden collapse of illusions nurtured in the 1930s: "We are, unfortunately, quite alien to the art of the State, and we look on it with open dismay and despair. We do not feel responsible for it, and it does not interest us." The projects of the Rationalist architects in the late 1930s seem to

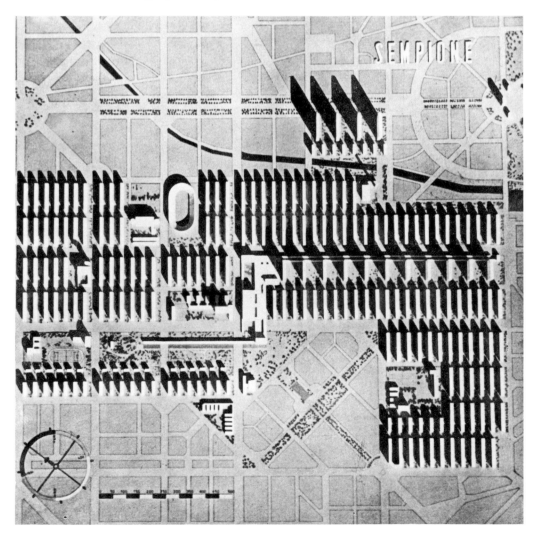

Franco Albini, Ignazio Gardella
Giulio Minoletti
Giuseppe Pagano Pogatschnig
Giancarlo Palanti
Giangiacomo Predaval
Giovanni Romano
"Milano Verde"
Plan for Sempione area
Milan, 1938

convey this withdrawal, and display a desire to distance themselves from the events around them, striving to achieve a kind of cathartic purity after the compromises, clashes and expectations that took place during the years in which the Regime established its hegemony. In December 1940, Pagano held a conference at the Centro delle Arti in Milan on the theme of *Defeats and Victories of Modern Architecture*, and hashed over the events of the previous busy fifteen years. He declared that the time for compromise was over, and pointed out gloomily that, despite the efforts made by architects in that period, they had failed to construct what he significantly termed a "urbanistic civilization." He felt that the time had come to realize that "at this point, every artistic judgment can only be a moral one."

But in spite of the rather negative picture from the point of view of the leading figures in the cultural spheres at the start of World War II, the defeats these architects suffered, though grave, were not in vain. It was the pragmatic ambiguity of the Regime itself that paved the way for the renewal that was to take place in Italian architecture in the postwar years; at the same time, the persistent disillusionment of the more talented architects through the late 1930s provided the ideological reasons for a solid new approach which, though traumatically interrupted by the war, outlasted it. In 1937, the first Congress of Planning was held in Rome, and was the first stage in a process that, under Bottai's guidance, led to a government bill on planning regulations (1942). The new bill sanctioned a set of norms that enabled postwar architects to aspire once more to the ideal of a "urbanistic civilization," though not without some grievous setbacks. But at the same time, it was the implicit critical revisionism, "intimistic" attitudes, and populist tendencies (which made for an irregular architectural panorama between the Rationalist idiom and the work of young designers in this twenty-year period) that would give birth to neo-Realism and the dominant reductive outlook and sobriety that emerged after the war in the same architects who had been the (albeit flawed) advance guard in the peak of Fascism. And it is here that we find the fertile ground for what Pagano in 1934 called "a free and modern architecture — courageous, spontaneous, without compromise, with room to move and speak out."

Serge Fauchereau

Italian Artists in Paris

Le dôme de Florence se mirait dans la Seine
André Salmon, _Carreaux_

Ardengo Soffici
Autumn Fields
1907

The 1900 Exposition Universelle held in Paris revealed the unforeseen impact that Italian artists were making on the French cultural scene — from the fashionable painter Giovanni Boldini, to the audacious sculptor Medardo Rosso, via Leonetto Cappiello and his drawings and posters. The Italian section of the exhibition at the Grand Palais attracted a lot of attention, thanks to the works of Giovanni Segantini, Angelo Morbelli, and Giuseppe Pellizza da Volpedo, who was awarded a prize. The exhibition also gave a number of young artists an excellent pretext for visiting Paris. While Carlo Carrà was already working there as a decorator, Giacomo Balla's visit extended to seven months, and Ardengo Soffici remained there for several years.

Soffici was probably the most important of the Italian artists in Paris. He earned a living working for publications such as the Symbolist magazine _La Plume_, and the weekly humorist magazine _Le Rire_, as well as the anarchist _L'Assiette au Beurre_. This work offered him the opportunity to meet the older, as well as the younger, generation of artists and writers from Jean Moréas, the French Symbolist poet, to Frantisek Kupka, the Czech painter, engraver, and illustrator. Apollinaire, who wrote in praise of Soffici on a number of occasions, had every reason to believe that he was "a talented artist, and one of the finest writers on Italian art. He is not unknown in Paris, and he is as knowledgeable as anybody else about the latest developments on the French art scene" (_Anecdotiques_, new ed., Paris, 1955). The fact that Soffici divided his time between Paris and Florence, moving constantly between the two, meant that, up until the outbreak of World War I, he was probably the best-informed of anyone on the artistic scene regarding developments in both France and Italy. He aimed to present everything that appeared genuinely innovative in both countries, and was among the first to recognize the merits of Medardo Rosso, or Picasso and Braque's Cubist experiments. Equally fluent in French and Italian, he highlighted the originality of the Futurists' experiments in Milan and Florence, and in articles appearing in the Italian reviews _La Voce_ and _Lacerba_ offered an impartial comparison of the relative merits of the Cubists and the Futurists.

Ricciotto Canudo was another Italian who had moved to Paris at the turn of the century, who as early as 1901 had established links with artists and writers, and after World War I, with filmmakers. His outstanding magazine _Montjoie_ (1913-14) provided a vital platform for artists. Canudo's role as a prime mover in the attempts to bring together the different art media, maximizing their strengths and techniques, is often quite unjustifiably forgotten. He was responsible, for example, for the original story line of the _Skating Rink_, Honegger's well-known ballet performed by the Ballets Suédois, the sets for which were designed by Léger. Canudo's role was eventually eclipsed to a large extent by Marinetti, who was already commuting between Milan and Paris even before the Futurist manifesto's publication in _Le Figaro_ on 20 February 1909. From the very earliest years of the new century Marinetti's willingness to talk to the press was rewarded by extensive coverage of the bombastic pieces he produced for their benefit. It was, however, Futurism which for many years revealed Marinetti's consummate skill as an impresario. Without his enterprising spirit, the signatories to the Futurist manifesto of 1910 would never have been led to join forces. Thanks to Marinetti's persuasive nature, and the fact that the painters had regained their voices, the 1912 Futurist Exhibition attracted considerable attention — not only in Paris but also in other capital cities. This outspoken attitude did have its

Rembrandt Bugatti, _Elefante_
c. 1904

negative repercussions and the Futurists' relationship with Apollinaire suffered some ups and downs, but we will return to this topic later.

Of the Italian artists who moved to Paris in the first decade of the new century the first to find fame was Rembrandt Bugatti. In 1904, the very year he moved to Paris with his family, the nineteen-year-old sculptor organized a one-man show at the Galerie Hébrard, which was so successful that it became an annual event. Modigliani and Severini moved to Paris in 1906. Fifty years later, Severini was to confess: "When we were young, when Modigliani and I landed in Paris, no-one was entirely sure what was going on" (*Ecrits sur l'art*, Paris, 1987). The two young artists each set to work getting rid of their own post-Impressionist tendencies, each developing his own style. However, while Severini produced a whole series of Divisionist paintings from 1907 onward, Modigliani's highly individual portrait-painting style did not emerge until 1909. If life for both of them was hard, their French friends, André Salmon, Max Jacob, Francis Carco, Maurice de Vlaminck, Pablo Picasso and Diego Rivera and the like, were not much better off. This was the heyday of Futurism, however. When the time came to ratify the 1910 manifesto, Umberto Boccioni, who had remained in Italy, immediately thought of Severini who was delighted to lend his name to the document, since it corresponded perfectly to his own views at the time. Though urged by Severini to sign, Modigliani refused. Speed, *macchinismo*, activism and violent action were at the opposite extremes of his introverted and meditative style.

Gino Severini, *Listening to Music* 1907

Initially Paris looked as if it would not take the loud slogans of Futurism seriously, and even Apollinaire — always ready to latch on to any innovation — kept a cautiously ironic distance. The opinions of the most finely-tuned critics did not change until the exhibition of Futurist painting in 1912. Some of the Cubists considered these new arrivals to be rivals. Delaunay, Léger, and Duchamp could in fact see them as experiments which duplicated much of their own work. And it is undoubtedly true that Severini and Carrà (who visited Paris several times between 1911 and 1914) must have been aware of the Cubists' work. The aesthetic linking the Cubists and the Futurists created confusion. Conservative critics made little effort to differentiate between them, although they were slightly more bewildered by the latter. Gustave Coquiot, a very open-handed man, devoted two chapters to them in his book *Cubistes, Futuristes, Passéistes*, but restricted himself to reproducing only a part of the first 1909 manifesto, the 1910 manifesto on painting, and Boccioni's manifesto on sculpture, without adding any critical comment whatever.

Amedeo Modigliani, *The Hebrew* 1907

There was no *rapprochement* between Cubists and Futurists. Despite their keenness to recruit new members, the Futurists secured only one French convert, the painter Félix Delmarle — who made his mark by picking a public quarrel with Severini in the magazine *Comoedia* in July 1915. In 1913, hostility was to become open war over the issue of Simultaneity and its origins. Apollinaire's affirmation that it originated with Delaunay was countered by Boccioni's claim favoring the Futurists. Both *Lacerba* and *Der Sturm* became involved in the dispute and, in addition to the above-mentioned, Marinetti, Léger, and Blaise Cendrars soon became embroiled in the argument. When hostilities had ceased, the publication of Apollinaire's witty piece "L'antitradition futuriste" appeared in *Lacerba* at the start of the summer and marked the resumption of peace.

In February 1915, when Giovanni Papini, Ardengo Soffici, and Aldo Palazzeschi of the *Lacerba* group abandoned "Marinettismo," dragging Carrà and Severini with them, Apollinaire took the side of the Marinetti clan also. In December 1916, he published three harshly-worded articles in his column in *Mercure de France*. In "La science futuriste," he branded the new manifesto on Futurist science, among other things, "uninformed," "totally absurd," and "devoid of common sense." Despite the fact that at the request of Soffici he was writing "Umberto Boccioni," an article

Amedeo Modigliani, *Diego Rivera*
1914

announcing the artist's death, Apollinaire appeared to be somewhat reticent about
the artist's beginnings and his contribution to the Galerie Bernheim exhibition ("the
only artists with any flair were Severini and Carrà") even though he did conclude
that Boccioni was "undoubtedly one of the most innovative of the new sculptors."
Finally, in "Futurisme italien" he finally acknowledged that the best of the Futurists,
that is the *Lacerba* group, had escaped the influence of Marinetti who, while "not
lacking in talent," had nonetheless failed to make "a significant contribution." Carrà
opted for "Metaphysical painting" during World War I, while Severini moved away
from Futurism and carved out a niche for himself in the Parisian Cubist environment.
Italian art in Paris did not, in any event, define itself in terms of Futurism. We need

97

only recall that Arturo Martini had been studying with Aristide Maillol prior to 1914, and he had no intention of pursuing his career within Futurism.

There is of course also the case of the De Chirico brothers. The younger of the two, Andrea, a musician and writer who had already dabbled with the figurative arts, arrived in Paris in February 1911, while Giorgio the painter followed five months later. Both lived in Paris with their mother for four years until they were called up for war service. Possibly through Soffici they soon came into contact with Apollinaire and his friends on the periodical *Les Soirées de Paris*, who were all enchanted by the brothers' originality. Apollinaire continued to defend both of them personally or through the intermediary of others, such as André Salmon and Guillaume-Thomas Raynal. Meanwhile Andrea, who had changed his name to Alberto Savinio in order to avoid confusion with his older brother, organized a series of noisy concerts as well as publishing poems in French in *Les Soirées de Paris*. As far as Giorgio De Chirico was concerned, Apollinaire was immediately struck by the originality of his

Gino Severini
Plastic Synthesis of the Concept of War, 1915

98

Ardengo Soffici and Medardo Rosso
Paris, 1910

Medardo Rosso Hall
at the "Salon d'Automne"
Paris, 1904

painting style, and from 1913 he never ceased showering praise on the painter's "curious landscapes full of new intentions" (*Chroniques d'Art*, Paris, 1960). For his part De Chirico painted several portraits of Apollinaire from 1914 onwards, and when the latter started preparing his collection of *calligrammes* entitled *Et moi aussi je suis peintre*, published in the summer of 1914, De Chirico designed the frontispiece, which was later engraved by Pierre Roy. During the same period, Apollinaire was also developing the ideas for a mime show, *A quelle heure un train partira-t-il pour Paris?*, with music by Savinio, and sets by Picabia and Marius de Zayas. But the outbreak of war brought these projects to a halt.

Italy's entry into World War I in 1915 forced the De Chirico brothers, Soffici, Magnelli and the others to return to Italy, where they became liable to be called up. In fact only Modigliani and Severini escaped service, due to ill health, and during this period Modigliani's exceptional talents were recognized. His aesthetic demands and somewhat unorthodox behavior made him a high-profile personality in artistic circles, and he knew all the artists and writers ranging from Léopold Survage, to Diego Rivera, Francis Carco, and Pierre Reverdy. But, despite widespread admiration for Modigliani, articles on his work were few and far between, and came late in the day, apart from a mention of his presence at the Salon des Indépendants in a review written by Apollinaire in 1910. This was due to one of Modigliani's fundamental demands according to André Salmon — perhaps his most enthusiastic admirer — who tells us, "For some time, this great artist had been courteously brushing off my every attempt to write something about him in a magazine. 'Art cannot be explained; people write about everything; and all they write is rubbish!' he used to exclaim" (*L'Art Vivant*, Paris, 1920). He was only acclaimed after his death, after the memorial-writers and legend had taken him over.

A few weeks before his death, Apollinaire was puzzling over what had prevented the recognition of the talents of Medardo Rosso. He said, "The critics have not taken Rodin's death as an invitation to talk about Medardo Rosso, who is now the greatest living sculptor. It seems unlikely that the unjust treatment this highly-talented sculptor has always suffered will now be redressed" (*Chroniques d'Art*). Apollinaire's words were prophetic as, in 1925, the journalist Charles Fegdal was wondering, "Will we ever know why Rodin is considered to be one of the greatest of geniuses, while in France, Rosso — who led the way for Rodin — is immured in an obscurity from which not even the critics have been able to rescue him, however hard they tried?" (*Ateliers d'artistes*, Paris, 1925).

Gino Severini's Paris career took a different turn. After having acclaimed him as one of the brightest of the Futurists, the French critics were delighted when he left the movement in about 1915 in favor of Cubism. In fact, Severini justified this move in a series of articles published in *Mercure de France* (in which he claims that Mallarmé was the true father of Cubism). He undertook an intensive study of mathematics to back up his theories and, with his friend Diego Rivera (who made himself out to be an expert), he startled the members of Henri Matisse's weekly salons with some of his new ideas. In any event, this was how he managed to assert himself as an authoritative figure.

While adopting a Cubist approach, Severini was one of the first to conceive of the "rappel à l'ordre" that was about to take hold in the figurative arts. In 1916, for example, when he was in the full of his Cubist period, he exhibited a completely Realist *Maternità* (*Motherhood*), which respected all the principles of classical perspective. "Even a member of the Institut would have been taken aback," wrote Pierre Albert-Birot (*Sic*, February 1917). This was hardly an accident. Severini was about to dedicate himself to what some critics had already called the "rappel à l'ordre," in the face of what he himself referred to as "artistic anarchy," and he wrote, "It is easy to see why: artists in this day and age do not know how to use compasses, slide-rules and numbers" (*Ecrits sur l'art*). Severini offered a summary of his research work and his thoughts in *Dal cubismo al classicismo* (1922). While stressing the fundamental geometrical foundations of the Cubism of Juan Gris and others, Severini made it clear that he had a strong preference for a new kind of art — an art that is both rigorously structured but nonetheless figurative. The author himself was on the threshold of a period in which he would paint scenes featuring *commedia dell'arte* figures and stunningly accurate still lifes.

In these immediate postwar years which were encouraging a "return to order," with De Chirico as an example and a *maître à penser*, the magazine *Valori Plastici* was also being read in Paris; André Salmon recalls that here it was jokingly dubbed *Valori Place Clichy*. In any case it published Salmon's "Peindre", a poetic composition that celebrated the period when "Florence cathedral was reflected in the Seine" (*Carreaux*, new ed., Paris 1986). The Italians played a fundamental role in the Realist "rappel à l'ordre" that was spreading outwards from France and Italy. The journalist and correspondent Massimo Campigli started painting in Paris during this period, adopting a style inspired by the figurative tradition. Filippo De Pisis, who lived in Paris from 1925 to 1939, also underwent the same sort of change in his painting style. Last and anything but least, De Chirico and Savinio were the leading figures of the Paris artistic scene from 1925 to the beginning of the 1930s.

Initially De Chirico was warmly welcomed by the Surrealists of L'Effort Moderne, Léonce Rosenberg's gallery. The younger generation, represented by André Breton and his friends on the magazine *Littérature*, took over from Apollinaire and Salmon in their undisguised admiration of De Chirico. De Chirico's arrival in Paris in the autumn of 1924 for the performance of the Ballets Suédois' *La Jarre*, for which he had designed the sets, coincided with the publication of the *Manifeste du Surréalisme*. De Chirico settled in Paris in the following year, but his relationship with the Surrealists soon soured as a result of the misunderstandings provoked by his most recent works. The Surrealists in fact were very keen on his pre-war and Metaphysical painting, whose oniric qualities they appreciated, and in which they saw a confirmation of their theories on the unconscious. Somewhat out of touch with De Chirico's ideas during the *Valori Plastici* years, they felt that he now wanted to be seen as a "classical" painter. All the Surrealists, with the exception of Roger Vitrac, denounced De Chirico's new approach as a fraud and as a betrayal, and in 1928 they even went so far as to organize a counter-exhibition of his earlier work. In the preface to the catalogue *Le feuilleton change d'auteur*, Louis Aragon described De Chirico's latest paintings as "the jokes of an idiot."

In the meantime, De Chirico had found a new patron in Jean Cocteau, who was always prepared to take a chance on a new style and who published *Le mystère laïc* in 1928, an aesthetic meditation that used De Chirico as the pretext. In the following year, De Chirico was to design the sets and costumes for Vittorio Rieti's *Bal* for the Ballets Russes, as well as publishing *Hebdomeros*, a novel which surprised even the Surrealists. During this period he also designed the decor for the Hôtel Rothschild and for Léonce Rosenberg's apartment, projects in which painters such as Savinio and Severini were also involved. De Chirico, by now firmly established in Paris, found his success was spreading abroad. And yet in 1931 he left Paris, to return only for brief periods during the 1930s. Alberto Savinio, who had also left Apollinaire's coterie, benefited by his good reputation in avant-garde circles, and particularly among the Surrealists. Despite their clash with De Chirico, or possibly because of it, they always maintained "a soft spot for Alberto Savinio" as Philippe Soupault said in *Vingt mille et un jours* (Paris, 1980). Thus keeping in close contact with the Surrealists, he often contributed to their publications, right up to 1933 when he too left Paris. It is worth pointing out that it was more his writing than his painting that attracted the Surrealists, although his highly unusual talents as a paint-

From left: De Chirico Vitrac, and Eluard Paris, 1927

Giorgio De Chirico sketch for *La Jarre*, Paris, 1924

Giorgio De Chirico *The Departure of the Argonauts* 1921

From left
De Pisis, the Conte di Castelbarco
Funi, Broglio, Barbaroux
Maria Savinio, Tozzi, Peroni
Aniante, Savinio
at the Galerie Bernheim, Paris, 1932

Poster for Luigi Russolo's Paris
concerts, 1921

er were confirmed at his first one-man show at the Galerie Bernheim in 1927. But again it was his skills as a writer that earned him a place in Breton's *Anthologie de l'humour noir* published in 1940.

Next to, and in spite of this wave of Italian Realists and Surrealists that had swept Paris, Abstract painters also sought to carve out a niche for themselves. After World War I, Marinetti resumed his active role and revived his manifestoes, despite a large part of the early exponents of Futurism had either defected or died in the Great War. However, in 1920 the Parisian Dadaists — in contrast to their Zurich-based colleagues some years earlier — showed their scarce liking for the Italian Futurists. During the following year they actually sabotaged two Futurist events, drowning out with their heckling and otherwise kicking up a row at Marinetti's lecture about Tactilism and one of Luigi Russolo's noise concerts. Denying that they owed any debt to the Futurists — which in fact they did — the Dadaists' only aim seemed to be to deride and laugh at their expense, refusing to take any interest in Russolo's research or in Marinetti's latest ideas, claiming that similar experiments had already taken place in New York, the invective flying in the pages of *Comoedia* and *L'Esprit Nouveau*.

After the truce of 1922, the Dadaists' hostility was taken up by the Surrealists, who never missed a chance to attack the Futurists, concentrating their efforts mainly on their political differences and the pretext offered by their association with the Fascists. Not content with ironizing on Marinetti's nationalist braggadocio, in the pages of their magazine *La Révolution Surréaliste* the group went so far as to loudly picket Prampolini's Futurist mime experiments at the Théâtre de la Madeleine in 1927. In 1931, the periodical *Le Surréalisme au service de la Révolution* reprinted a survey by Marinetti, satirizing it with added handwritten ironies and insults such as, "flies in black shirts on words-in-freedom... anti-tradition passéist swastika... skulls..."

The general hostility towards Futurism, which was made official upon Marinetti's nomination to the Accademia Italiana in 1929, was in direct proportion to the curiosity and the sympathy the movement attracted at the start. And this hostility was to increase throughout the 1930s as a result of Marinetti's declarations which journalists such as Roger Vailland delighted in publishing, "I am one of the originators of Fascism; I was the first to infuse it with many of its fundamental criteria" (*Paris Midi*, 5 January 1930). From that point on, Prampolini and Fillia and their manifestoes on sacred art and cooking would serve as pretexts for condemning all Italian art, which had been unfairly reduced in the magazines to aeropainting or publicity art: "One painting by Enrico Prampolini was even entitled *Believe, Obey, Fight*. This piece, to be lodged in a Casa del Fascio, a meeting place for young Fascists in their spare time, as was *Book and Rifle*," as René Crevel points out in his *Discours aux peintres* (later reissued in *La querelle du réalisme*, new ed. Paris, 1987, a book that echoed the whole tone of the year 1936). On the other hand Prampolini, Fillia, and Russolo were the only Italians represented at the "Cercle et Carré" exhibition held at the Galerie 23 in 1936, and the exhibition "Enrico Prampolini e gli aeropittori futuristi italiani" in 1932 held at the Galerie de la Renaissance (presented again in Lyons three years later) was widely publicized. First and second generation Futurists were often active in equal measure in initiatives for the reorganization of Italian art, even if doing so they were forced to align themselves with artists of opposing tendencies. This explains how the *Manifesto della pittura murale* published in *La Colonna* in December 1933, which aimed at defining the so-called "style of Fascist painting," could have been signed by such a disparate group: Sironi, Carrà, Campigli, and Funi. While in Italy it was possible to take circumstances into account and make the distinction between those militantly committed to the Fascist cause, and those who were merely paying lip-service, in France it was not.

Filippo Tommaso Marinetti in Paris
In the background: the *Futurist Manifesto* published in *Le Figaro*

Most artists and journalists tended to make no distinction between the regime they disliked and the artists who were forced to live under it, thereby grouping all the Italian artists into a single category and ignoring the existence of a whole outfit of opponents to the regime who were severely persecuted. This situation was exacerbated by the fact that the economic crisis of the early 1930s had forced most Italian artists, including Savinio, De Chirico, and Severini, to leave Paris and their absence created a void. Apart from official and prestigious events, such as the 1937 exhibition, Italian art no longer had a place at the forefront of the Parisian scene. The publications and exhibitions organized by *Abstraction-Création*, which eschewed national boundaries, were the only outlets for the work of the younger and less well-known Italian artists such as Lucio Fontana, Virginio Ghiringhelli, Osvaldo Licini, Fausto Melotti, the ubiquitous Prampolini, Mauro Reggiani, Anastasio Soldati and Luigi Veronesi. Many of the above-mentioned also took part in the Salon des Realités Nouvelles at the Galerie Charpentier in 1939 in which Alberto Magnelli was also involved.

Magnelli's situation was quite unusual. Unlike the more well-known artists discussed up to now, this old friend of Apollinaire had been somewhat tardy in arriving to Paris, not getting there until 1931, just as the others were returning to Italy, and he came to stay. Magnelli's first Paris exhibition was held in 1934 at the Galerie Pierre. This occasion gave him the chance to meet Kandinsky, Arp, Hélin, and other members of *Abstraction-Création* even though he eventually decided not to join up with them. At the outbreak of war, Magnelli stayed in France, going into hiding near Grasse, where he worked assiduously, sometimes with Arp, Sophie Tauber, and Sonia Delaunay, who had also fled the Occupation. In 1944 he returned secretly to Paris where he took part in the exhibition "Peintures abstraites, compositions de matières" at the Galerie L'Esquisse with César Domela, Kandinsky, and Nicholas de Staël. While Magnelli's contribution was relatively modest, it was nonetheless the first public appearance of an independent Italian painter in occupied Paris. This was a good omen — for both France and Italy.

Enzo Siciliano   **Dream of Literature, Dream of Painting**

Giorgio De Chirico
Mystery and Melancholy of a Street
1914

Italian Novecento painting sprang fully-formed from the metaphysical mind of Giorgio De Chirico, and at the time appeared to blot out the whole of the 19th century. De Chirico's so-called "severe melancholy" and "lyrical geometry of the piazza" became the raw material of a powerfully oniric painting style. Open spaces, tailors' dummies, theater flats used as floors, mysterious oppressive shadows: a little girl chases her hoop towards a carriage with its door left open, in the outstanding 1914 painting entitled _The Mystery and Melancholy of a Street_ where the backlit foreground creates a nearly unfathomable rush of emotion, while in the background, behind the porticoes, we espy the shadow of a giant's arm brandishing a stick...

What sort of intense alchemy did this painter work on his canvases to make them look as if they were the products more of the workings of the mind than the senses? An intellectual style of painting encroached on one based on pure sensibility. It framed the images within an abstraction in which perspective took on a stilted, theatrical role, and was applied with a swift, but sweeping and forceful hand.

A free-ranging anthropomorphism asserted its own transgressive presence over these canvases. Billiard balls, fish, and biscuits, devoid of any trace of naturalism, reaffirmed their impeccable and essential nature, revealed a disquieting linearity, as well as a certain weight, or "depth," accessible only to minds receptive to ideas rather than the flickering of light.

De Chirico wrote that on Cretan vases the profile of the figure is established by the eye — the eye is all-important, it seeks out, and establishes proportions. This description is also applicable to De Chirico's gaze, which initially appears to be fixed, but a closer look reveals it to be alert to every move — the eye of a god who has just returned from a disappointing visit to Hades. This eye rediscovers the motionless surfaces of noon-day spaces. As the painter himself wrote, "In my opinion, I believe that there is much more mystery in a 'fossilized' village square in the afternoon sunlight than in a darkened room, in the dead of night."

And, like an archaeologist of sight and imagination, De Chirico worked in that "fossilized" light, never losing sight of the present in which he was living and suffering, until he managed to bring to light never-before-seen vistas, vistas which as it turns out could have been the most famous as well as the most commonplace — such as the piazzas of the city of Ferrara on the eve of World War I, or even the piazzas of Rome, or the porticoed streets of Turin, Bologna, Florence or Venice. His visit to Paris infected him with a special pride — that of being the legitimate heir of the great painting of the 16th century while stranded in the world of industrial conflict, in landscapes ravaged by smoke-stacks, trains, machinery, and workshops. He strove to grasp both those universes, that of the great and noble past, and that of the "white heat" of the present.

The past and present could come face to face unhindered in the metaphysical vision, and merge into an unobstructed lyrical flow. De Chirico's work was the equivalent of the most welcoming inn for Italian literature — an inn which could offer private accommodation to a vast range of often bad-tempered travelers, many of whom could not bear the sight of each other.

Gabriele D'Annunzio's 1912 poems "La stanchezza dell'infinito" ("The Tedium of the Infinite") or "Melanconia" ("Melancholy") epitomize the poet's most tormented and modern emotions, which for us today still burn with poetic ardor and move us. The anthropomorphism in his poem "Alcyone" is pure De Chirico: the relics of the

103

poetic tradition tower amongst the lights of the present — "fossilized" relics in the mystery of the noon-day sun. The god Pan has cast his sorrowful gaze on these forms and they stand before us, enveloped in words, like magnificent ruins.

D'Annunzio too sought this "fossilized" light, in language, and enjoyed making plaster casts of all the fossils he recovered. The never-ending game of making a copy for the *glyptotheca*, a copy which the color of lyricism mysteriously transforms and deflects from the original, runs parallel to the figurative quotations in De Chirico's canvases, the statues from the museums at Olympia and the Acropolis (childhood memories) which the *esprit moderne* interpreted as thoughtful, melancholy, and shrouded in shadows. D'Annunzio said in the "Poema paradisiaco":

Everything will be as it was long ago.
The soul will be as simple as it was;
and it will come to you, when you want it
as light as water flowing into your cupped hand.

Giorgio De Chirico
Roman Villa with Horseman, 1921

The assorted clutter in D'Annunzio's homes at Capponcina and Il Vittoriale is nothing more than a surfeit of quotations — the so-called *Comandante* collected copies and plaster casts in addition to degrading and degraded artefacts. This collection is clearly the result of the work of an acquisitive eye, which ranged languorously over the infinity of a History unbounded by philological restraints. This was, in other words, a metaphysical eye. And surely the image we see in "Leda without the Swan" — a story that loses itself in a burst of anguished and immaterial autobiographical quotations — is nothing but pure metaphysical painting:

We can imagine that the relationship between the author of "Alcyone" and the painter of the piazzas of Italy was complex and intense. Rather than establish an historical relationship, however, we would like to point up the affinities that exist among artists, which provide a sort of backdrop that simultaneously unites them and highlights their differences.

Could the unassuming Guido Gozzano, who wrote about Signorina Felicita, not see traces of his anguished modernity in the two biscuits which are the focus of De Chirico's 1915-16 painting, *Death of a Spirit*? Here also, the relationship has spread from the poet to the painter. But, again, we are not discussing philological affinities but common attributes. Which came first is immaterial. What matters is the correspondence between certain materials — the "long ago" which has been transformed into explicit signs — a range of materials that existed in the empty space of an unsullied modernity.

A slim, fine chrysalis	*I occasionally go up to the attic*
jewel-like	*to look at it,*
hangs from the coping	*and I admire and address this tiny creature*
of my house.	*that does not speak to me.*

Gozzano, whose collected poems are published in the volume entitled *Colloqui*, saw the profile of "Pinocchio and (his) destiny" in the flames of the fire, just as De Chirico could discern a wooden toy train in the squares of Italian towns and cities. This is a pure diachronic and phenomenological experience, that speaks of the relationship between Italian painting and literature, but it is the only relationship possible if we want to exploit references, echoes, and thought-provoking anomalies to the full.

Thus in Italo Svevo's novel *The Confessions of Zeno*, Zeno's obsession with cigarettes stands as tall as the smoke-stack in De Chirico's 1913-14 painting *The Anguish of Departure*. In this painting, the small male figures in the background are leaning against the wall in the sunshine, evidently discussing ways of escaping from this towering, tormenting presence, but, frozen by the ironic and merciless brush-stroke, they will never make the move — just as, in fact, Zeno never gets round to quitting smoking.

Metaphysical painting (that hospitable inn) was prodigious in its welcome. The so-called "fossil" — that violent noon-day silence of the imagination with its towers,

Giorgio De Chirico
The Enigma of the Hour, 1911

parapets, and empty doorways, is the most daring sign that the Italian mind has ever been able to offer the world. Giuseppe Ungaretti's "balustrade of breeze" meets up with De Chirico's enigma of the hour, and we see that the so-called "man of suffering" also harbored an equally painful melancholy.

De Chirico spoke of the "beautiful prophetic dream dreamt with open eyes." His personal "vein of gold" was the Classical Era. Ungaretti was to retrace the same "vein" in his poem "Sentimento del tempo" ("Sentiment of Time") — which once again matches up with *The Enigma of the Hour* — in which he says: "The fables are returning to burn brightly on high," and his was a beautiful metaphysical dream. Ungaretti, with Stéphane Mallarmé as his guide, sought the *esprit moderne* in Racine and Góngora. He discovered it himself by uniting it with an "ancient" and traditional poetic form just as De Chirico discovered it in the traditional side of his painting. De Chirico had great technical skill, and Ungaretti's reasons for adopting "ancient" forms were equally technical. The 20th century offered the arts the possibility of expressing their desperate desire for objects. The power with which objects burst onto the scene was quite stunning. Set free from the context of ordinary usefulness, objects became elements of a mysterious alphabet. The world does not speak in them but through them. These objects are on the same wave-length as a Stravinskian rhythm — illusionist "Petrushka" — and describe a wild *ronde* whose aim is to re-establish a Platonic paradise of ideas.

Other Italian Metaphysical paintings, such as the early works of Carlo Carrà, Filippo De Pisis or Giorgio Morandi which stood out for their Giottoesque or primitive purity, set out to crystallize this paradise. This radical purity can also be seen as a disruptive literary proposition — the search for an essential language to which reality would be forced to find an accommodation.

The Futurist experience was now a thing of the past. Its pictorial results, in Boccioni as well as in Balla's early work, had been dazzling, and of such a high quality as to eclipse Marinetti's theories and precepts. Over and above a relationship with painting, Futurism was offering graphic solutions. It stripped down the excessive Art

Nouveau style, dragging it towards the dry and linear decorative solutions that would be so much in demand in the 1920s. The simultaneity of Boccioni or Futur-Balla involved taking a tangible fact to its extreme — which was quite the contrary of De Chirico's aim for an interior crystallization. The Futurists' angle of perception was optical and, to a lesser degree, mental. For De Chirico, however, it had been mythopoeic — and this explains the many links between his work and literature.

But pictorial Futurism encouraged the search for objects mentioned earlier, and their fragmentation. Meanwhile, for some artists, a detour from the Futurist idiom led to the discovery of a new and different essence of objects.

It was, however, the acute sensual awareness of De Pisis that led him and the other Ferrara-based Metaphysical painters to find a new way of coming to terms with objects, which was different from De Chirico's but just as accommodating. It was a cheerful approach, a flash of happiness, the reverse side of which was unlimited sorrow, and enigmatic and ephemeral feeling. When the poet Eugenio Montale wrote his *Motets*, he was interested in details and objects bathed in the same seaside, or wind-swept light that pervaded De Pisis' many (magnificent) still lifes, and early traces can, in fact, already be detected in his 1925 work, *Cuttlefish Bones*. There is a clear connection between Montale and De Pisis, which goes beyond mere connection to become an acute and highly-specific parallelism.

Montale could see "a life that offered inklings," where, "years flew by as quickly as days," as he wrote in "Fine dell'infanzia" ("The End of Childhood"). The "cicada's hard body" was lost in this flight, shrugged off by the "wounded acacia" in the "first mire of November"; the reed languidly plucked "its red flabellum in the Spring"; perhaps a Bedlington terrier, "a blue-colored lambkin," would then have disconsolately looked over at the bombed-out remains of the Santa Trinità bridge in Florence. Every detail appears to be enhanced by an enigma — this was a day-time enigma however, one that life does not reveal but merely hints at. Coffee pots, pipes abandoned on tablecloths by half-empty glasses, and a bunch of *radicchio*, an ocellated plate, a pear, a yellow squash, veined seashells, a small nude fixed to the wall as a quotation of itself, a palette, a woodcock, or a sheet of music all gathered together in a perspective lacking proportion, which appears to clash with reality (but how knowingly, how realistically and how irrepressibly rich in the poetic richness of the image it really is!). In De Pisis they would have evoked exactly the same kind of enigmatic thoughts, and allusive mystery in the light of day.

De Pisis was no stranger to the written word and wrote: "Two birds on high, the black thrill of flight is sufficient to single out the atmosphere: a line of Prussian blue in the background beneath the palpitating sky will create a seascape. I am seized with a kind of frenzy when, having decided on the colors for the seashells in the foreground, I have to do the background. It is the air pressing down on me..."

The air is the point, and De Pisis offers a lavish welcome to writers who concentrate on the air. This welcome includes the sea for the Trieste-based Umberto Saba, or the earth, and the urban environment for Sandro Penna, and even Aldo Palazzeschi, not to mention Carlo Emilio Gadda, with his dense tapestry of Lombard memories that echoed the world of the painters Giovan Gerolamo Savoldo and Pitocchetto.

De Pisis portrayed a bony and angular reality, which is sometimes playfully hinted at while at others it is almost obliterated, and pushed to its extremes with a sorrowful hand — some of his Roman paintings being excellent examples. De Pisis was diverse, and so he offered hospitality to a vast range of writers, and floated through time like a chimera. His "link" with the writer Giovanni Comisso, author of *People of the Sea* and *War Days*, testifies to a brilliant "Venetian" sensibility in which his genius seemed to culminate. His flexibility and his cultural background, his trips to Paris and his espousal of the best aspects of Impressionism have contributed to making him considerably more important than was first thought.

Filippo De Pisis
Sacred-Profane Still Life, 1926

Filippo De Pisis
Pink Nude, 1931

It is said that literature limits painting. If painting is steeped in literature, it takes on a content-heavy, intentional snobbishness that annihilates any expressivity. In De Pisis, literature or writing became the testing ground for a polished pictorial quality, and conversely, painting became the confirmation of an attempt to achieve a highly ephemeral and distinct style. In his 1916 work *Emporium*, De Pisis drew up a catalogue of "sweet things" in which he listed:
A multitude of longboat and bragozzi *masts in port under the blazing sun*
... A handsome raw silk cloth in yellow, orange and blue stripes
... A flock of white doves winging their way towards a purple-hued sunset.
If *Emporium* is a hand-book of images specifically sought out for their sensuality, useful for establishing a chromatic scale of emotions, so to speak, the style used to express this scale rids it of every trace of implicit literalness, placing it against the airy sky of the canvas to be painted.
After the end of World War I, the advent of a new and powerful mind was to make an indelible mark on the relationship between art and literature, and was to create a critical ideal upon which contemporary Italian art would reflect for many years. Roberto Longhi understood that the next line of innovative painters would follow in the great tradition which extends from Piero della Francesca and Caravaggio and thence to the great French painters such as Gustave Courbet and Edouard Manet. These were the years of *Valori Plastici* and *La Ronda*. Longhi's influence — which affected established figures such as Emilio Cecchi, or younger writers like Anna Banti, and would, after World War II, extend to figures like Giorgio Bassani, Attilio Bertolucci, and Pier Paolo Pasolini — effectively became a literary teaching: his writing encouraged a vibrant and diverse view of the world. Longhi developed his own fragmented and highly-charged, pluri-linguistic approach, superimposing a cultured lexical concreteness on the minute dispersal of objects, or the craft and technical idiom. The result was an almost unparalleled pictorial splendor.
Longhi probed the history of Italian art outside the traditional canons. In my opinion, Longhi invites us to enjoy Botticelli's *Venus and Mars* as if it were a Japanese *surimono* (or print), while at the same time identifying the development of the surface forms and colors, by means of which he explains composition and dialectic.
He says the following about Piero della Francesca's *Defeat of Maxentius*:
"Emphasized foreshortening, flattened chests, broken knees, smoothly turned clogs, black and white in a silent chess game. Circular wells stagnate, clean-mown and mottled hills form a patchwork. To the left, lances and spears cast liquid amber and ebony hues on the blue expanse of the sky, which is overhung with clouds laced in light, while to the right the endless ruddy petal of the victory banner of the defeated is being hung out to dry, and the indestructible spheres of pale ivory move forward, balanced on metallic helmets until, in the dazzling light, against the breast of the azure sky, they become medals — for coloristic value!"
Longhi's words — with their clear echoes of both D'Annunzio and the Futurists — recapture the painter's inventive rhythm, and the words and syntax recreate the technique and rhythm of brushstrokes. His involvement in art criticism entailed a similar imaginative fervor, which aimed at defining an art history which was neither influenced by nationalistic rhetoric nor was merely a literary projection of painting. This was Longhi's great achievement, and so with his modern spirit he was able to rediscover the road to expressive quality, a road which opened up for the solitary Morandi, Mario Mafai and Scipione and for those minor artists who made up the various factions of the immensely fertile *Scuola Romana*.
Between the 1920s and 1930s, this fertility extended to both literature and painting. Painters included: Mario Mafai, Scipione (Gino Bonichi) and Antonietta Raphaël, the neo-Romantic, inventive, wizards of color; Classicists such as Riccardo Francalancia or Francesco Trombadori, Virgilio Guidi, Antonio Donghi, and

Fausto Pirandello
Crowded Beach, c. 1939

Guglielmo Janni whose work was marked by bold and incisive brushstrokes; Alberto Ziveri and Fausto Pirandello (son of playwright Luigi), through to Corrado Cagli and Renato Guttuso who, at the outbreak of World War II, were the youngest of all the Roman artists.

Rather than finding its counterpart in the decorative literature of writers such as Antonio Baldini and Lorenzo Montano, the fetid eroticism of certain oil paintings and the depiction of interiors redolent of painful existentialist *ennui*, reminds us of the poky apartments and small boarding houses probed by Luigi Pirandello, Corrado Alvaro and Massimo Bontempelli in his Roman period. These paintings also recall the faint heartbeat underlying the arched lyrical rhythm of Vincenzo Cardarelli, or the harsh face of the Alberto Moravia of *Time of Indifference* or his short stories from the 1930s. This was a disturbed frenzy in which sensuality tippled from contradictory stimuli. While there was, perhaps, an attempt to take refuge behind the fictitious bulkheads of an arid and parsimonious reasonableness, the overwhelming feeling was one of bewilderment, a pervasive bewilderment which had struck like a disease. This feeling provided a common poetic destiny for the artists and painters nurtured by "Roman" air.

Giorgio Morandi, *Landscape*, 1925

Osvaldo Licini's "errant, erotic and heretical" experience appears in stark contrast to this endemic feeling. It had its roots in Bologna, in the same atmosphere that had nurtured the talents of Morandi, and which had absorbed, distilled, and selected the very best of Futurism. In addition to painting, Licini also used words to depict a Bohemian milieu, which prefigured what would later be defined as Surrealist. This Bohemia was portrayed in his *Tales of Brutus*. Brutus is a thinly-disguised alter-ego of the painter/author and is effectively his active projection, achieved through written words and signs: "Brutus was lying down but was getting bored. So, plunging his hand into his chest, he pulled out his heart, placed it on a cushion and watched it beat. Then he put his heart in the palm of his hand and admired God's work. And he was delighted to see the hole through which the soul passes in and out and the little blue veins where the emotions nestle..."

Mario Mafai
Street with Red House, c. 1928

There is a feeling of rebellion in Licini's words, and this rebellion was to be manifested in skies, flying angels, dead birds of various kinds in a far-away paradise, and in abstract geometric shapes. "He attached his heart to a piece of string and flung it

108

Scipione
Men Turning Round, 1930

up onto the telegraph wires. But he had second thoughts and hauled it down again.''

This irony, mixed with a certain testy enjoyment, turn the painting into a feather-light but visceral creamy surface. Licini's literary efforts have a tendency towards becoming tormented, insulting, and harrowing. He relates that Brutus has a lover called Dodò, who ''is a whore, or *cocotte* even...'' One evening he goes to her house where he smashes her mirror and then: ''He strode over to her wardrobe and her chest of drawers and turned everything upside down, threw everything all over the place. Then he flung himself down on the mess on the floor and rolled around, wound himself in it, ensnarled, gnashed, crushed, crumpled, smashed, slashed, raped, ripped, and stripped, and sniped; then, grabbing hold of Dodò, he threw her down, kissed her, bit her, licked her, buggered her. And then he said, 'Let's go to bed.'''

This revolt has a physiological tone, and sex is used here — as elsewhere in his sto-

Osvaldo Licini
Landscape with Man, 1925

ries — to accentuate the hurt and man's uncontrollable urge to assert his identity.

This assertion finds echoes in the *Crepuscolarismo* movement, as well as in pre-Sur-realism. It luxuriates in its defiance of conventions, and transgressions: excess is the order of the day. These were the years preceding World War I; for Licini they were pre-historic years. And yet the use of that excessive, harsh word highlights his links with European artistic experiences, and shows he had an instinctive intuition of a climate that was prejudicing the health of poetry while simultaneously making it purer than ever before, infecting it with a dazzling and celestial light.

Rimbaud and Baudelaire — France, the essential crossroads for exchange — are the prophets of a whole range of Italian *Novecento* painting. They are the poets of a gospel which breathed new life into an art that had had little to show for itself since Antonio Canova's funerary visions one hundred years earlier. The *Novecento* re-turned Italian art to the international arena; but this return was entirely due to transfusions from unlikely sources, and by cultural syntheses carried out at feverish caprice, but also with strange detachment, or a feeling of arcane distance. Baudelaire's memories forgotten in a drawer could become Morandi's bottles re-produced *ad infinitum*, their metaphysical urgency becoming an irrevocable, exis-tentialist *malaise*: their pictorial beauty seems to exclude any literary reference.

Therefore in the poems of Luigi Bartolini, a talented etcher, the words seem to be free from any kind of painting influence, and imply a negation of everything that is not purely verbal. Perhaps Campana experiences the same kind of exclusiveness, ardor and pain in a savage rage that would be petty-minded, misplaced and even vul-gar, were it not for its raw elegance which is an echo of enduring peasant tradition:

Let no-one be my witness any longer! This is all I want.
Let the farmer with his cattle take another route.
Let him not raise his eyes towards the shadow of my house;
And may I, locked inside myself, waiting for a return
Stop myself, dear Anna, from desiring another face.

There is an element of the gross and the over-charged in Bartolini's poetry, and his

Renato Guttuso
Mimise with Red Hat, 1940

Renato Guttuso
Execution in Countryside, 1939

Renato Guttuso, *Salomè*, 1940

prose and short stories also seem exaggerated. But everything is interpreted in the key of a full-bodied and vigorously plastic style. What appears to be bloated is in fact lean: he is neither mannered nor Baroque; he has a swollen heart and an irascible incubation of his imagery.

A steadying rapport with the cosmos exists no more, there is only a deep vibration, which continues to switch on and off, swerves off course and then returns to normal, seems to suffer a seizure and then regains its health. The importance of human action becomes more flexible, and the concept of nature has never been more internalized. Writing and painting are consumed by the need for brevity and the lightning flash. And for those who refuse to adopt this rapid tonic sol-fa, the alternative is a state of ecstatic expectancy: the Metaphysical as expressed by De Chirico and Licini.

Bartolini belongs to Jacopone's group of revolutionaries — on the side of those who were unable to find an identity apart form the changing of the seasons and the cultural goings-on that took place on the slopes of the Apennines. Bartolini the poet and engraver has a rural vision which contains the intransigence of the peasant's life, the feeling of being alive and in despair, lucid and in the thrall of the unconscious, full of joy and sorrow.

The younger literary and artistic generation in the 1930s felt an affinity with nature, which wavered between enthusiasm and despondency. This was Rosai's Florence period, with the writers of the Giubbe Rosse, Mario Luzi, Alfonso Gatto, Tommaso Landolfi, Carlo Bo, Piero Bigongiari, and Alessandro Parronchi. Their contemporaries Attilio Bertolucci, Vittorio Sereni, Sandro Penna, and Giorgio Caproni kept their council and isolated themselves within their own incisive vision. Their words maintain a trace of a reality that has just disappeared, an everyday reality teased out, in a gentle dying dazzling light, as if by a second Chardin.

Soft marks on yellow paper, with their own glare, or faintly etched profiles, a leaf, a straw basket, a half-empty bottle, or an old coffee-pot — these are traces left behind by Mario Marcucci's dry paint-brush. Marcucci is an artist who frees painting in myriad ways, sometimes lissom and airy, sometimes compact, or rugged as if it were desperately keen to take its place on the canvas or a sheet of newspaper; it lingers on the poorest surfaces, exploiting that poverty to the full.

Florence's gradually fading civilization breathed through Marcucci's strange flashes of light with an arcane sentimental glow. Neither Caproni, Penna, Sereni nor Bertolucci are Tuscan — but Marcucci's direct way of touching objects brings him close to these poets, and enables him to bring together other Tuscan writers such as Romano Bilenchi and Vasco Pratolini in his yellow papers, which are the same as the ones used by bakers, butchers, grocers and greengrocers. This brings us to the inviolable vitality that was be christened neo-Realism in the postwar period, the apogee of the Milanese group *Corrente*. Cesare Pavese's painfully carved out youthful verse or Elio Vittorini's charming, almost Cubist caprice in his *Red Carnation* find their home in Guttuso's whirling, quick-tempered, intensely creative anxiety.

I feel as if I can really sense the full expression of the youth of these new writers — trapped between "Letteratura" and a covert rejection of Fascism, while the rest of Europe was over-run by the first harbingers of imminent war — in Marcucci and Guttuso's harsh and luminous colors.

Guttuso in 1939 was already depicting the executions, and if his model was Goya, the full tragic force, the red earth, the olives in the background, tell us of Mafia-style executions and of a criminal madness that was to become institutionalized. Guttuso was heading for the great epic of the *Crucifixion* — but his novel, as well as Marcucci's, was already finding expression in self-portraits, where humanism was a feeling of sustained anxiety, life studied and lost and great moral intensity.

And these were, in fact, the novels of the time: where the hero was sought out by

Osvaldo Licini
Composition on Red Background
1935

suffering or a blaze of inner passion that tempered the form and made the soul rejoice. And here we meet Moravia once more, in his short stories, as well as Corrado Alvaro and Carlo Emilio Gadda who, in *The Knowledge of Suffering*, was coming to terms with sorrow. This was the novel of the still lives with lamps (*Still Life with Lamp*), and of Guttuso's boys on the balcony (*The Boys on the Balcony*), where the dense and dragged color disrupts the design and translates it into a human heartbeat, in tune with concrete fantasy and intellectual significance.

The *Flight from Etna* brings together the movement of Sicilian narrative — the very same *epos* as Giovanni Verga's. But there is, everywhere in Guttuso, a range of vision which makes him resemble De Chirico — style notwithstanding. De Chirico opened up one era and Guttuso in his turn opened another, on the very eve of World War II. Guttuso pointed in a new direction — not Metaphysics but Realism, objects and their special tragic features. Guttuso was able to express the revulsions of the war, and of the postwar period, as well as the heat of hope. His supremely fluid brushstroke, which could also be tense and concrete, linked him to other young painters of the day, such as Carlo Levi, Renato Birolli, and even to the delicate touch of Giacomo Manzù. But in his wide-ranging expansiveness, his involvement in the themes such as that of existence, and the later images of middle-class life such as *The Swimming Pool* or the *Caffè Greco*, imbued as they are with the Metaphysical and the feel of reality, Guttuso resembles De Chirico — who was in fact portrayed in Guttuso's *Permanence of the Metaphysical* — in that his painting contains the essence of a whole host of literary innovations. While the full extent of his influence is perhaps yet to be assessed, we can be sure that he is the greatest, the most dynamic, and the most talked-about of Italy's artists of the middle of the century. The literature of life was to follow, and that life was to paint its own pictures with a great and fertile passion, which is the rich Italian literature of recent years.

Italian Artists and Western Magazines and Periodicals

L'Assiette au Beurre
issue illustrated by Ardengo Soffici
Paris, 1904

It was not until the 1890s — just when Symbolism was emerging — that European avant-garde magazines and periodicals started to devote space to painting. In addition to articles about the painters' work, the magazines published drawings, illustrations, reproductions and, occasionally, texts by the painters themselves. These additions contributed in no small measure to the success of many magazines published before the turn of the century, such as the Parisian *La Plume* and *La Revue Blanche*, the London-based *Yellow Book*, *Pan* in Berlin, and *Ver Sacrum* in Vienna. The satirical magazines, the leading representatives of which were probably *Simplicissimus* established in Munich in 1896, and *L'Assiette au Beurre*, which appeared from 1901 to 1912, also played their part. More politically mordant than the Parisian *Charivari*, or the London *Punch*, these publications offered artists the opportunity to exploit their talents in a lighter vein by providing illustrations. Italian painters contributed to the whole range of these publications.

The first Italian avant-garde painter to become involved with these magazines was probably Ardengo Soffici who, in addition to painting, also produced a considerable amount of fiction, poetry, and essays. Italian artists were well-known for being as talented with the pen as with the paint-brush during this period. Soffici arrived in Paris at the turn of the century, and was very soon contributing drawings to *La Plume*, and to the humorous magazine *Le Rire*, before moving on to the much more radical *L'Assiette au Beurre*, with its distinctly anarchist leanings. Commentators, such as Carlo Carrà writing on Soffici, no doubt exaggerated when they reminisced about how hard it was for artists such as Frantisek Kupka, Jacques Villon, Kees Van Dongen, and Soffici to have to devote so much time to these kinds of illustrations. As it happened, the work was reasonably well-paid — besides, relatively unknown painters saw their work being published alongside that of established names in the art world. In 1901, the drawings of the twenty-two-year-old Soffici first appeared in *L'Assiette au Beurre*, in the same issue as works by Théophile-Alexandre Steinlen, Adolphe Léon Willette, Félix Vallotton and other leading artists. Moreover, the publication's intemperate tones and the Censor's constant surveillance of the magazine certainly appealed to the budding Futurist. While lacking the expressive strength of the work of Vallotton, or Kupka, Soffici's drawings were more or less on a par with Villon's. In any event he undoubtedly had more contact with artists with revolutionary ideas here, than he would have done at Marinetti's *Poesia* (1905-09). This magazine was still very much geared to Symbolism although it provided an important link between Paris and Milan, since it was published in both French and Italian.

Up to the time he published the Futurist manifesto, Marinetti was wholly taken with literary Symbolism and gave no thought to the possibility of creating any links with other artistic movements. This explains *Poesia*'s lack of artistic verve, visible even in Arturo Martini's cover design, which wavered between the so-called "style nouille" and "Symbolistic" ghosts. Since he divided his time between the two countries, and because he was both a writer and a painter, Soffici was the most important bridgehead between Italy and France up to the start of World War I, producing drawings, poems and articles for the French magazines *La Plume*, *La Revue Blanche*, *L'Assiette au Beurre* as well as the Italian *Leonardo* and *La Voce*. It has sometimes been suggested that Soffici was only keen on French art. He was, however, also capable of focusing on the latest innovations in Italian art, including

Medardo Rosso for example. In 1914, moreover, he published *Cubismo e futurismo* in Florence, a comparative study of developments in the plastic arts in Italy and France.

The most important periodical of the avant-garde — according to the 20th-century definition of this term — was probably *Der Sturm*, founded by Herwarth Walden in 1910 in Berlin. Its only literary competitor was *Die Aktion*, launched a few months later by Franz Pfemfert. Though both these magazines concentrated on German Expressionism, they gave ample space to international contributions. This became all the more important for *Der Sturm*, as it soon opened a gallery of the same name, which later organized the exhibition of Futurist paintings that toured Europe. Meanwhile, translations of several of the Futurist manifestoes, and articles about them, appeared in the magazine. At the invitation of Walden, Marinetti himself went to Berlin to give a presentation on Futurism. Without taking sides in the debate over Simultaneity that was to break out between the Futurists and the Cubists in 1913, *Der Sturm* showed its interest by giving equal space to Umberto Boccioni, Robert Delaunay and Fernand Léger. The reverse of the coin was the Munich-based almanac of *Der Blaue Reiter*, published in 1912, which never mentioned the Italian Futurist movement at all.

Les Soirées de Paris, no. 26-27
Paris, July-August 1914
Frontispiece

Despite the fact that its secretary was André Salmon, the periodical *Vers et Prose*, established by Paul Fort in 1905, paid relatively little heed to the latest developments in the art world. Seven more years would go by before a voice for the avant-garde emerged: *Les Soirées de Paris* established by Guillaume Apollinaire and a group of friends, including Salmon. A journalist and art critic, Apollinaire was anything but indulgent with the early manifestations of Futurism — his review of the first exhibition of Futurist painting held in February 1912 was, in fact, quite critical.

An article by Robert Delaunay on Simultaneity published in *Der Sturm* in early 1913 sparked a stormy debate, which ranged Apollinaire, Léger, Delaunay and *Les Soirées de Paris* against Boccioni, Marinetti and the magazine *Lacerba* (1913-15) founded by the Florentine Ardengo Soffici, Giovanni Papini, and Aldo Palazzeschi, all recent converts to Futurism. The two camps soon reached a peace. But, although *Lacerba* published "L'antitradition futuriste," a self-ironic piece by Apollinaire written to humor the Futurists, *Les Soirées de Paris* did not reciprocate, with the exception of Soffici who was, after all, only a Futurist in passing, and had earned a place for himself on the magazine as a poet, rather than as a painter and art critic.

Guillaume Apollinaire
L'Antitradition futuriste, 1913

When Apollinaire did introduce the subject of Italian art in *Les Soirées de Paris* it was to present the De Chirico brothers, with whom he had a close friendship at the time. Apollinaire was among the first to champion Giorgio De Chirico's unusual style of painting and his younger brother Alberto Savinio's music. In addition to praising his prowess as a pianist, the magazine also published his first writings in French. With the backing of Apollinaire and Marius de Zayas, Savinio was able to publish two musical scores in the New York magazine *291* (1915-16).

Ricciotto Canudo was another major figure in Franco-Italian relations, and had been living in Paris since 1901. He had become so well-established in French intellectual circles that, like Marinetti, he wrote in French and, in February 1914, even went as far as putting forward his own aesthetic of *cérébrisme* — to no great avail, however. This *cérébrisme* turned out to be little more than a mediocre variation on Marinetti's idiom: "The hurricane of Life, whose heart-beat, cries, and trembling Nietzsche could sense all around his proud soul, inspires the new generations" (*Montjoie*, no. 2, February 1913). Canudo edited *Montjoie* between 1913 and 1914, publishing the work of writers and painters who were his friends. He did not give any special preference to Italian painters — and, certainly less than to painters such as Mikhail Larionov, Fernand Léger, or Robert and Sonia Delaunay.

Lacerba, year II, no. 22
Florence, November 1914

The last of the major artistic and literary avant-garde magazines to appear before the outbreak of World War I was *Blast*, published in London in 1914. The second issue came out a year later, but the war prevented the publication of the third. Though unashamedly borrowing its lay-out style from Futurist publications, especially in terms of typography, this dense British magazine was not necessarily ready to acknowledge the Italians' talents. Editor Percy Wyndham Lewis, the painter and writer, was very condescending and ironic about Marinetti: "His *automobilismo* is only Impressionist sophistry. His nostalgia for war has a parochial and limited aggressiveness to it, which is both romantic and rhetorical." Wyndham Lewis was, however, prepared to concede that "Futurism has three major artists in Balla, Severini, and Boccioni, in that order, I believe."

The advent of the war sealed the fate of a number of magazines — such as *Les Soirées de Paris*, and *Lacerba* which ceased publication in 1914 and *Blast*, which closed in 1915 — since many of their contributors were called up for service. However they were soon replaced by other new periodicals, produced by young men invalided or demobilized from the army. Among the magazines that provided a platform for the art world were *L'Italia Futurista*, *Noi*, *Roma Futurista*, in Italy; *L'Elan*, *Sic*, *Nord-Sud*, and *Les Trois Roses*, in France; *Résurrection* in Belgium; *Cabaret Voltaire*, *Dada*, and *L'Eventail*, in Switzerland; *Orpheu* in Portugal; *291* in the United States; *L'Instant*, *Troços*, and *391* in Catalonia; and *Zdroj* in Poland. In Italy the main theme was Futurism, in France Cubism, while in Central Europe it was Expressionism or Dada — a new trend which had emerged in neutral countries, such as Switzerland and Catalonia, where many artists and writers fled to escape the war.

With the outbreak of war, Italian artists disappeared from the pages of the magazines of "enemy" countries such as Germany and Austria, while communication difficulties and mobilization made it hard for them to get publicity in the allied countries. In Britain, moreover, Wyndham Lewis and his fellow Vorticists maintained their low opinion of the Futurists and ignored the rest of the Italian efforts. The same fate awaited the Italians in *Résurrection*, edited by the Belgian Clément Pansaers, which devoted all its attention to the German Expressionists. While Pierre Reverdy's magazine *Nord-Sud* was too exclusively focused on Cubism to pay any attention to the Italians — except for Alberto Savinio, in his function as a poet — *Sic*, edited by Pierre Albert-Birot, was always generous in allocating space to them, thanks to Gino Severini. Not only did Albert-Birot and Severini live in the same building, but the latter had also established close links with French poetry circles. In 1916 and 1917, through the good offices of his father-in-law Paul Fort, Severini published theoretical studies in *Le Mercure de France*, a mainstream magazine which devoted limited space to articles on art. In his memoirs about *Sic* (published in *Les Lettres Nouvelles*, no. 7, 1953), Albert-Birot gave a most eloquent summary of Severini's contribution to the development of *Sic*'s editorial policy, following the first issue's publication in January 1916. "Obviously he found the first issue of my magazine rather meek; however, after we spoke he realized that I was willing to fight for a just cause and I can still hear him say, 'You must seize the high ground of the avant-garde.' And he added, 'I will introduce you to Apollinaire.' And so, in the second issue, I published a reproduction of his painting *Train arrivant à Paris*, and then two pages later, I launched into an all-stops-pulled aesthetic dissertation in a response to an exhibition of his work. This magnificent modern world which I had instinctively sensed, and ruminated on, for a long time, opened up before me, and I dived in headlong..." Even though Severini did not become a long-term collaborator, the publication's enthusiasm for Italy was to endure right through to its final issue in December 1919. Enrico Prampolini, Fortunato Depero, and Giacomo Balla were just a few of the artists who contributed to *Sic*, which published a handsome text on Boccioni following his untimely death. Shortly afterwards, *Troços* followed suit by publishing the Catalan J. M. Junoy's tribute to him.

Dada sprouted up in a number of places between 1915 and 1918 and focused on a number of people and places: in New York with Marcel Duchamp in the lead, at the Cabaret Voltaire in Zurich, and in Barcelona around the figure of Francis Picabia. Italian artists hardly had any exposure in New York, despite the exhibition of Severini's work at Alfred Stieglitz's Gallery 291 in March 1917, and articles on Savinio which had been appearing in *291* since 1915. Moreover, they never got a single mention in Picabia's magazine *391*, despite its extraordinary longevity for an avant-garde magazine — it was published in Barcelona from January to March 1917, New York from June 1917 to April 1918, Zurich in February 1919, and then in Paris until October 1924.

In recompense, the Italians were often considered to be fellow-travelers by the Zurich-based Dadaists. In addition to two examples of "words-in-freedom" by Francesco Cangiullo and Marinetti, *Cabaret Voltaire* — published in June 1916 by Hugo Ball in French, German, and Italian — also featured a portrait of Hans Arp by Modigliani. The first two issues of *Dada*, published in 1917 by Tristan Tzara, included contributions from various Italian artists, such as Francesco Meriano, Nicola Moscardelli, and Gino Cantarelli, and the ubiquitous Alberto Savinio. The magazine also included a woodcut by Prampolini, and a reproduction of De Chirico's *Le mauvais génie d'un roi*. As Dada gradually evolved its own aesthetics, it moved away from whatever did not conform to its own spirit, and thus, from the third issue of *Dada* (1918), Italian contributions started to be phased out. Savinio and Prampolini survived, and it is worth noting that Tzara and his friend the painter Marcel Janco both contributed to Prampolini's magazine *Noi*. The hostility manifested towards Futurism may be explained by the many new Parisian additions to the *Dada* staff, including Picabia, Reverdy, and Soupault, who were decidedly cool towards Futurism. A short poem by Julius Evola was the total Italian contribution in the seventh edition which appeared in March 1920.

In the immediate postwar period, the absence of Italian involvement was common to all the magazines which had either declared their espousal of Dada or entertained Dada sympathies, such as *391*, Raoul Hausmann's *Der Dada* (published in Berlin from 1919 to 1920), *Cannibale* (Paris, 1920), *Ça Ira* (Antwerp, 1920-23), and even *Manomètre* (Lyons, 1922-28). The most remarkable instance is the magazine *Littérature*, whose thirty-three editions from 1919 to 1924 mention Marinetti once in December 1919 — not for any aesthetic reasons, but to protest against his arrest — and once in May 1922 when they published some of his play summaries. The only other Italian artist mentioned is Giorgio De Chirico, who was honored — it must be granted — by an essay written by André Breton in as early as January 1920, and two years later (March 1922) Roger Vitrac wrote another review which included a reproduction of the painting *Le cerveau de l'enfant* and a transcription of one of his letters.

While Futurism had dominated the immediate pre-war scene, the deaths of Boccioni and Antonio Sant'Elia marked a turning point for the movement. Severini broke away from Futurism in 1917, and Carrà left to seek common ground with De Chirico and establish Metaphysical painting. The Futurists' increased output of manifestoes and reviews, published in *Noi*, and *Il Futurismo* in Italy, and Ruggero Vasari's *Der Futurismus* in Berlin in 1922 was in vain — their original verve had gone. Even extra-European countries which could have shown some interest in Futurism rejected it, mainly for political reasons. Thus, in *Horizonte*, the Stridentist Mexican magazine we read: "We have lost all our sympathy for Marinetti since he joined forces with that charlatan Mussolini" (no. 6, 1926).

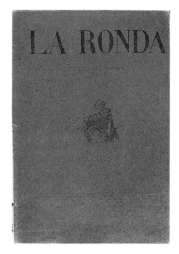

La Ronda, no. 1, Rome, 1919

Noi, no. 1, Rome, June 1917

Der Futurismus, no. 2-3
Berlin, June-July 1922

So it was that De Chirico came to be the top name in Italian painting — it is worth remembering that Amedeo Modigliani received very little attention from the magazines in his life-time with one of the few exceptions being an article by Francis Carco in the Geneva-based magazine *L'Eventail* in July 1919. De Chirico would prove very important in attracting certain painters, such as Ardengo Soffici, Ottone Rosai, Mario Sironi, and Primo Conti, who had erred towards Futurism, back towards Realism. Italian magazines such as *La Raccolta*, but above all, *Valori Plastici*, both established in 1918, and *La Ronda* which appeared a year later, were the first to hail this change of direction by praising De Chirico, Carlo Carrà, Filippo De Pisis, and Giorgio Morandi's painting. Savinio was also at his peak as a writer during this period. The success of *Valori Plastici* (1918-22) was boosted by editor Mario Broglio's decision to publish a series of brief monographs in France and Italy — which in fact continued to appear even after the magazine's demise. The majority of these monographs were, inevitably, written by Italian authors, and their sympathy for figurative art is undisguised. Carrà was responsible for one work on André Derain, one on Soffici (excluding his Futurist works), and one on Georg Schrimpf, while Severini and De Chirico wrote on Edouard Manet and Gustave Courbet respectively.

An attempt was even made to publish *Valori Plastici* in French, and three editions did in fact appear, between 1919 and 1920, in which De Chirico, Carrà, Soffici, Savinio, and the sculptor Arturo Martini featured prominently.

Zenit, Belgrade, 1920

Looking at these magazines gives us the chance to trace the development of the misunderstanding between the Surrealists and De Chirico, originally revealed by Apollinaire. Even before the Surrealists had set up their movement, they had praised De Chirico's work in *Littérature* and elsewhere, as had René Crevel in the Brussels-based magazine *Le Disque Vert* in December 1923. De Chirico appreciated their praise, and contributed poems, prose works, and reproductions of his paintings to *La Révolution Surréaliste* between 1924 and 1925. However, all these reproductions, not to mention the praise being heaped on him, related to a chapter of his work that was now closed, as several years had already passed since he turned his talents to neo-Classicism. Conflict became inevitable. In the March and June 1926 editions of *La Révolution Surréaliste* André Breton denounced De Chirico's "abdication and apostasy," illustrating his articles with reproductions of De Chirico's recent painting *Oreste et Electre* covered with offensive graffiti. Only Roger Vitrac who, in any event, had been expelled from the Surrealist group that year, kept the faith. Before being published as a book, his appreciation of De Chirico appeared in the May-June 1926 issue of *Les Feuilles libres* illustrated by several drawings and paintings.

Throughout the 1920s, a number of art magazines sympathetic to De Chirico sprang up. These included *L'Esprit Nouveau* (1920-25) published by Ozenfant and Le Corbusier in Paris, *7 Arts* (1922-29) in Brussels, *Sélection* (1920-27), an Antwerp-based magazine which published a special supplement on De Chirico in 1929, with fifty-six reproductions and, last but not least, *Bulletin de l'Effort Moderne* published by the Galerie Rosenberg from 1924. A number of first and second wave Cubists contributed to this magazine, but figurative artists such as De Chirico, Savinio and Severini were equally welcomed. Outside Paris, thanks to an active network of correspondents, De Chirico's fame spread abroad. One example of the network's power was an enthusiastic article which appeared in the January 1932 edition of the Cuban magazine *Social* published by Alejo Carpentier, entitled "The Classical and Singular Art of Giorgio De Chirico," which also provided Carpentier with an excellent opportunity for redressing the balance as far as Italian art was concerned — a few months earlier he had discussed the *Manifesto of Futurist Cooking* by Marinetti, and the celebration of Fascism.

Severini was often in the news in the magazines of the period, all the more so because he proved to be quite provocative in his writings — his article "Cézanne and Cézannisme" published in *L'Esprit Nouveau* in November 1921 was not to everyone's taste. For Modigliani, posthumous success was to be the order of the day in magazines such as *Sélection* and *L'Amour de l'Art*, while, as far as the younger generation of Realists were concerned, Felice Casorati probably received the most exposure, with articles appearing as far afield as Barcelona (*La Ma' Trencada*, January 1925), and Antwerp, where a study of him (and Massimo Campigli) appeared in *Sélection*.

The Futurists seemed to attract considerable attention in Central and Eastern Europe, since, unlike other Italian painters, they had a highly-organized publicity machine for disseminating their ideas, under the careful leadership of Marinetti. Several of the Futurist manifestoes were translated in Russia, and Marinetti himself paid a visit there at the start of 1914. By then, the Russians had developed their own form of Futurism so the Italian variety remained little known. On the other hand, Prague and Budapest were able to judge Futurism at first-hand since many of the works were exhibited there.

Het Overzicht, no. 13
Antwerp, 1922

It was only after World War I that Futurism started to make its mark as subject matter for the periodicals, all of which welcomed it as warmly as they did other movements connected with Modernism. The first to do so was *Ma*, published by the Hungarian Lajos Kassak. Other noteworthy publications were *Zwrotnica* in Poland, *Zenit* in Yugoslavia, *Contimporanul* in Rumania, and *ReD* in Czechoslovakia. There were also some special — somewhat late — issues devoted to Italian Futurism, by magazines such as *Integral* (Bucharest, 1925) and *ReD* (Prague, 1925). However, none of these publications restricted themselves to Futurism. In 1922, for example, *The New Artists' Book*, an offshoot of *Ma*, published reproductions of the work of Boccioni, Russolo, De Chirico and Prampolini in a piece on the latest developments in the arts in Italy.

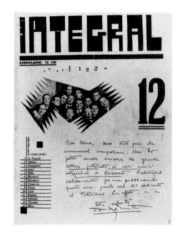

Integral, no. 12, Bucharest

While they showed an interest in every artistic movement, these central European magazines were all strongly affected by the instability of Constructivism, which hovered between Theo Van Doesburg and Piet Mondrian's *De Stijl* and Vladimir Maiakovsky's *Lef*, and their feelings that either Futurism had nothing to teach them, or that they had no use whatever for either De Chirico and Casorati's so-called "rappel à l'ordre" or Surrealism which would gain ground after 1924. Surrealism, the "rappel à l'ordre," and Constructivism represent the three aesthetic tendencies the magazines of the 1920s had to reckon with. While the smaller avant-garde magazines gleaned material from wherever they could find it, those with a wider circulation, such as *Der Querschnitt*, maintained a position of neutrality, and did not favor one tendency over another.

Constructivism was a very important trend in Western art in the 1920s and 1930s. Its main mouthpieces in Western Europe were *De Stijl* and *L'Esprit Nouveau*, *Lef* and *Novy Lef* in the Soviet Union. The Central European magazines, which had closer contacts with the Russian Constructivists, had little time for Italian art. The Ukrainian Constructivists tended to be more eclectic and featured Picasso as well as De Chirico in their magazine *Nova Generatsia*, while the Polish magazines *Blok* (1924-26), *Praesens* (1926-30), *Dzwignia* (1927-28) and *Forma* (1933-38), all descendants of *Zwortnica*, were particularly neglectful of the Italians. On the other hand, Polish magazines such as *Muba* and *L'Art Contemporain* published in Paris during the same period mentioned only Prampolini and (occasionally) Balla. Magazines oriented towards Western European developments included *Het Overzicht* (Antwerp, 1921-25), *7 Arts* (Brussels, 1922-29), *Der Driehoek* (Antwerp, 1925-26), *Documents Internationaux de l'Esprit Nouveau* (Paris, 1927), *Cercle et Carré* (Paris, 1929-30), and also *Les Cahiers d'Abstraction-Création* (Paris, 1932-36) and *Axis* (London, 1935-37). What all these magazines had in common was that Enrico

Les Feuilles libres, no. 45
Paris, May-June 1926

ReD, no. 6, Prague, 1929

Prampolini was involved with them all in some capacity. Such a widespread — if not somewhat excessive — fame was due to the prestige of Prampolini's magazine *Noi* which from 1917 to 1925 was one of the leading proponents of the "rappel à l'ordre" style of Realism. Meanwhile other artists were making appearances here and there. Russolo and Depero for example were featured in *Het Overzicht*, while *Cercle et Carré* gave space to Russolo, Fillia and the architect Alberto Sartoris, who also featured in *7 Arts*. It fell to *Abstraction-Création* to present — in addition to the ubiquitous Prampolini — artists such as Lucio Fontana and Fausto Melotti who could show that Italian art could be more than an extension of Futurism, or a return to Realism. This excellent example was not followed however, as witnessed by the fact that Sartoris was the only Italian featured in *Circle*, the major directory published in London in 1937, while even he was excluded from *Plastique*, published in Paris from 1937 to 1939.

As far as the Surrealists were concerned, Italian artists did not exist, apart from De Chirico and his brother Alberto Savinio, and we have seen that, from 1926 onwards, the orthodox Surrealists rejected De Chirico's recent output, and their attitude did not change. While De Chirico was frequently quoted in the movement's official organ, *Le Surréalisme au Service de la Révolution* (1930-33) and one of his earlier paintings was the subject of a study in 1933, he was effectively considered "dead." His brother, on the other hand, continued to be on good terms with the Parisian Surrealists, and published a short story in *Le Surréalisme* in 1933.

The only periodicals featuring De Chirico's latest work were those whose staff included defectors from Breton's movement, such as *Les Feuilles Libres* (1926), *Bifur* (Paris, 1929), or *Variétés* (Brussels, 1928). The Surrealist movements in other countries did not feel obliged to follow the edicts of the Parisian group, and so the Prague-based *ReD* (1927-31) was largely favorable to both De Chirico and the Futurists, while *Art* (Barcelona, 1933-34) published reproductions from De Chirico, Balla, and Prampolini, as well as a number of other painters unconnected with Surrealism.

Despite a number of Surrealist contributors, the artistic and literary *Minotaure* (1933-38) was not dominated by them and so felt free to feature De Chirico in its fifth edition which appeared in 1934. *Les Cahiers d'Art* was another important magazine of the second half of the 1930s. Less attached to the Surrealists, it started to feature Alberto Magnelli's work from 1934. *XX Siècle*, which was launched in 1938 but whose publication was interrupted by the outbreak of World War II, showed interest in all tendencies but particularly in Italian art — unusual for the time — including De Chirico, Magnelli, and Severini in equal measure.

It has been noted that, as international tension rose during the 1930s, the magazines tended to snub Italian art, almost as if they believed that Italian art as a whole came into the same category as the Fascist regime they despised. On the eve of the war, there was a dichotomy of views in Western Europe regarding Italian art: confidence in its ability to survive, and concern for its current situation. This attitude was illustrated by the American *Partisan Review*, a magazine committed in its opposition to Fascism. In 1939, the same year that Clément Greenberg commented that Mussolini had finally managed "to relegate Marinetti and De Chirico to the ranks" in order to humor the tastes of the "Italian general public," the *Partisan Review* included Magnelli among "The Latest European Tendencies" worthy of note. This was surely a reassuring paradox for an art that appeared to be in decline.

Vittorio Vaser in *Sole*, 1929
by Alessandro Blasetti

Silvio Lanaro

A Regime in the Interwar Years

How and Why

"Too many people for such a fragile and thread-bare spiritual framework," was Gioacchino Volpe's typically aggressive and abrasive comment on the 1923 crisis in Italy's liberal government.[1] Clearly he was not saying that numerically there were too many people — the war and the Spanish flu epidemic of 1918 had wiped out nearly one million Italians (the population had dropped from 38,142,000 in 1916 to 37,250,000 three years later). By "too many" he meant that they were making their presence felt too much, they were making too much noise, they were taking to the streets, in a word: they were *mobilizing*. The factory workers were in dispute, either to "imitate what was happening in Russia," or to take control of their factories or, more modestly, to gain control of some of their companies' profits. Women burst on on the scene strong from their experience as leaders of the pacifist demonstrations of 1917 and feeling emancipated in the wake of their wartime involvement in the labor force. At long last in a position to vent their feelings, the veterans of the trenches protested to the faceless authorities on the sluggish pace of the demobilization — by 1919, one year after the end of the war, just under half of the 3,000,000 men were still officially under arms. The press was a vital mouthpiece for their complaints about the numerous violations of so-called military justice that they had put up with for more than three years. The middle classes who had been in favor of interventionist action were seething at the amnesty offered to deserters in 1919 by the Nitti government. With between 60 and 70 per cent of officers killed — a record unequaled in any of the other European armies, they felt they had paid too high a price. There was unrest among the farmers, who were being economically penalized by the ceiling imposed on the prices of staples. Trouble stirred in the ranks of the poverty-stricken peasants, who had been taken in by the myth of land redistribution. Industrialists were fuming because of the rash of strikes, many of which were directed against the government but for which they paid the price in material terms. Four years of war had taught people that in fighting for a "just" cause, it is permissible — and perhaps necessary — to violate the sovereignty, territory, and property of others. Taking hold in the psychology of subordinate classes, blending with scraps of ideology, and the stresses of poverty, this vague awareness of the legitimacy of the "rightful claim" had given birth to a new form of social conflict: the occupation of the factories in September 1920, with the red flag flying over the workshops of Turin, which was preceded by the occupation of uncultivated land in Puglia, Sicily, Lazio, and Calabria — between 40,000 and 50,000 hectares, according to Arrigo Serpieri.[2]

Whatever their political alignment, the protectors of the faith of the "Italy of Vittorio Veneto" found it difficult to hide their anxiety in the face of such an unexpected collapse of the "virtues" of war: obedience, order, discipline, spirit of sacrifice, and altruism. Nationalist Francesco Ercole was unable to understand how city and country folk alike could be "so quick to forget" what had come so naturally for more than three years, and how they had let themselves be "overwhelmed by a monumental repudiation of the values in the name of which they had suffered, and won."[3]

Giovanni Amendola, the Democrat member of parliament, claimed that it was "unimaginable" for a nation to emerge from such a successful enterprise "having lost what it had when it first started," but declined to try and unravel the rights and wrongs, preferring to call for "harmony, tenacity, and silence."

"We must aspire to a time when politics stop stirring up people's souls, and when the disruptions of public life give way to the interests and preoccupations of private life, and when work provides the unspoken and wholesome lead for national life."[4]

His diagnosis was completely wrong, almost as wrong as that of Emilio Bodrero, who wrote in his *Manifesto alla borghesia* that, "Politics, in the traditional sense of the word, is a thing of the past," because, "for some time now they have been replaced by a spirit of labor unionism."[5] In fact, political struggle was precisely what Italy needed — in other words the struggle for power between elites, where the victor would be able to impose a strict regime on economic self-interest. This was something Italy had never had before, except perhaps during the crisis years at the end of the century, and in the months preceding the war in Libya. But then it had only been manifested in the unsophisticated forms and half-measures of the peasants' revolts, oligarchic power struggles, palace intrigues, the the so-called "*settimane rosse*," or the struggle between different factions for control of a town or provincial council. A whole generation had been called to arms. It had been required to throw itself heart and soul into the attack. It had grown used to hating the enemy without, and to considering him undeniably "different." It was now professed that these same men should not have learned to recognize the potential of conflict as a form of social interaction.

Between 1918 and 1921 there was an undeniable void in terms of political initiative at both the national and the local level, a void that yawned ever wider as the economic crisis worsened. The deficit in the foreign balance of payments stood at 5,591,000 Lire in 1919 — five times higher than six years earlier. The gap between income and expenditure was widening — 7,885,000 Lire in 1919-20 had soared to 17,409,000 Lire a year later. The National Debt rose from 60,213,000 Lire in 1918-19 to 74,496,000 Lire in 1919-20, reaching 86,482,000 in 1920-21. An industrial recession was increasing the unemployment figures: 102,000 were out of work on 31 December 1920, but within a year this figure had soared to 542,000. The inflation index (based on prices for 1901-05) stood at 637 in January 1920, had jumped to 774 by June, and reached 832 by September.[6]

The problem was not merely that of instituting economic reform, but of ensuring the succession of a strong political force, which would be able to gather support without having to cede too much in the bargaining, and would govern according *to its own* assessment of what was good for the country. The danger, or as Gioacchino Volpe put it, the "spiritual worm in the apple" was that the Italian political parties flourished on compromise (the old "transformist liberalism"), or entailed — on pain of extinction — a situation of economic growth (Nitti's and Giolitti's "democracy"), or sat and drew up elegant combinations of labor unions and corporations that, however, postulated a prior return to normalcy whose implementation was delegated to someone else (the Nationalists), or acted as surrogates, providing social services in place of the State (the Socialists and the Movimento Cattolico).

Now, while the absence of a Jacobin tradition was a major handicap to the traditional ruling classes (and by Jacobin, I mean the idea that the majority should push ahead with their own policies and not make compromises with minority groups in the hope of softening the opposition), an even more dangerous condition was the Partito Popolare and the Socialists' insistence on representing or protecting specific groups, sectors and factions in society, and their consequent unwillingness to take responsibility for the government of the country as a whole.

Luigi Sturzo's Partito Popolare was set up to give a democratic say to the southern Italian middle classes, with its anti-protectionist agricultural policy concentrated on the Mediterranean, as well as to satisfy some of the long standing demands of the Italian Catholics, such as the "freedom to teach." When members of the party ac-

Torviscosa, the dock
and the industrial buildings

Reclaimed Marshlands

cepted cabinet posts they did so unwillingly, or only in the hope of achieving certain specific aims — to the extent that as late as 20 October 1922, when they addressed an "appeal to the nation," they claimed that they were in ministerial positions only because "parliament and the institutions required it," while it was clear that, "our own interests dictate that we keep our distance."[7]

The reforming Socialists, who were hampered by an excessively talkative and inconclusive maximalist majority, showed little inclination for nationwide reform, being much more interested in their cooperatives, their labor unions, their consortia, and their model-town councils. Anna Kuliscioff, the most acute intellectual of the Italian Socialist Party (PSI), was well aware of what we could call a fervid torpor, as demonstrated by her belief that only a "program to reconstruct and renew the whole country" would be able to save certain sectors of society. Writing to Filippo Turati, on 18 May 1920, to encourage him to speak out in parliament on the subject of Italy's reconstruction, the "Remaking Italy" speech he did finally deliver on 26 June, she said that she hoped his suggestions would provoke a split in the party, with the best of the middle class members moving towards a socialist-democratic party of government." She was well aware that the "red" parliamentary group would never have allowed their old leader "to speak on their behalf."[8]

The most eloquent demonstration of the urgency of political mediation in the postwar class struggle was the unexpected emergence of Veterans' movements which sprang up all over Italy, and which were all linked in some way with the National Association of Combattants. In some cases these were somewhat haphazard groupings with tenuous ideological and organizational links, such as intellectuals with officers, and peasants with soldiers — hypnotized by the charisma of characters such as Giuseppe Lombardo Radice and Vittorio Emanuele Orlando — which in the 1919 elections ensured that Sicily was shared out between Republicans, Liberals and Social Reformers.[9] Another group, based around Salerno, fell foul of the blandishments of the old rogue *notabile* Pietro Capasso.[10] In the Friuli, for example, groups of middle-class *señoritos* set up organizations with a worldly production-oriented and forward-looking outlook, such as the Piero Pisenti's Partito del Lavoro which rapidly became the nucleus of the local Fascist party.[11] Elsewhere, as in the Sannio area (Abruzzo), which was pulled apart by clans and rival interest groups even after the March on Rome, and the formation of the ANC (National Association of Combattants), the situation became an instrument in the hands of Raffaele De Caro, a corrupt social democratic politician, who used it for wearing down the resistance of the prefect-backed Fascists and to protect his own interests against the newcomers.[12]

In relatively important areas, however, the veterans managed to set up coherent and politically vital pressure groups, such as Camillo Bellieni and Lionello De Lisi's Partito Sardo d'Azione which at the Congresso di Macomer of August-September 1920 supported a program of policies that were clearly inspired by democracy and the ideas of Gaetano Salvemini.[13] Despite internal disagreements and ruptures, the Partito di Rinnovamento Abruzzese was for a number of years the "only peasant movement to be organized like a mass movement,"[14] in an area known for its poverty. These factions were usually motivated by a reformist and radical philosophy, and they usually ended up being absorbed into the Fascist party — even though they did not give up without a struggle and the conclusion was anything but foregone. It was not true that the disorderly unrest of the war veterans or the pervasive social malaise of the middle classes were responsible for the rise of Fascism in Italy. In fact the party also attracted and reshaped breakaway political groups which had suffered the disillusionment of having failed to achieve reform and to take an active lead such as, the Democrazia Sociale Veneziana, or the Socialismo Rivoluzionario Ferrarese. This goes to show that Fascism was a symptom

The March on Rome
24 October 1922

of a political system in crisis, rather than the product of a generalized and widespread social malaise.

The broad lines of the Fascist doctrine can be sketched out as follows: the patriotic myth of a "mutilated victory," an essential tool for a movement that aimed to address interventionist inter-class collaboration; a rallying mechanism that had some affinity for the ideas of Sorel — at least as far as Mussolini was concerned — an exaltation of the "values" of dynamism and preparedness for action ("Fascism is not a church: it is a gymnasium."); an undisguised (even provocative) pragmatism ("We reserve the right to be aristocrats, democrats, conservatives, or progressivists, reactionaries or revolutionaries... according to time, place and mood, in a word, according to "history.");[15] finally, a kind of sober political Futurism, backed by people like Giuseppe Bottai, who used constant references to the idea of "competence" to back the call for the establishment of a new national managerial class.

The progress, success, and certain aspects of the "modernity" of Fascism may well be due to the oft-repeated prophecy of the coming of an elite that would oust the superannuated liberal politicians — which was another way of saying that there would be a ruthless battle to seize power itself. Another reason may have been Mussolini and his followers' skill in crushing the veterans' movement, which was a potential *Sammelpartei* made up of the democratic middle class which had always lacked credibility and influence.

It is undoubtedly true that the "troubled season" which reached a peak on 22 October 1922 — or perhaps more precisely on 3 January of the following year — was instrumentalized by people who thought they could benefit from a "revolution." These included a bloc of bureaucrats, entrepreneurs, and military men, all born around 1908 (the Giolitti crisis), who had gained valuable experience from the committees of industrial mobilization during the war years. They were joined by a certain part of the land-owning class which neither minced words nor counted costs when they saw an opportunity to undermine the class war. Also involved were a group of conservatives who were totally unable to grasp that the Fascists' ultimate aim was to create para-military structures and a government based on arms in a country which by then was completely out of practice with their use.

Fascism would not have survived long without the backing of a "determination for power" — albeit softened by a tactical *phrónesis*, in addition to a recognition of the need to update the structures of a country that had not been exploiting its potential

The Corn Wheat Exhibition

to the full. And the exile Francesco Saverio Nitti, who never ceased to predict its collapse, would have been more than pleased.

Underlying and Notwithstanding

After 1924-25, the Fascists, under the influence of Alfredo Rocco's theories of organic unity and neo-Absolutism, quickly set about creating a totalitarian state which would subordinate the individual's rights to the state's, abolishing any distinction between the citizen's public and private life. What actually happened was that the demolition of the old order created by the Statuto Albertino (established by King Carlo Alberto of Sardinia in the 19th century) was incomplete and was undertaken in three rather hardhitting) stages. First came Law 100, of 31 January 1926 on the executive's power to legislate, which did away with the venerated principle of the separation of power. This was followed by Law 2693 of 9 December 1928 which laid out the powers of the Gran Consiglio del Fascismo. As these included the power of consultation over the royal succession this meant that the Crown was, to all intents and purposes, subject to the whim of the regime. Finally, Law 129 of 19 January 1939, establishing the Camera dei Fasci and the Camera delle Corporazioni which completed the process of amalgamating state institutions with those of the Fascist Party.

There was of course a whole range of other measures testifying to the regime's illiberal and dictatorial nature. The Consolidation Act regarding public security laws (Regio Decreto 6, Number 1848, 6 November, 1926) which introduced internal exile for penal, as well as political, offenses, and also gave the prefects the power to disband all associations whose activities were against the "national interest" — the political parties first in line as victims. A special Court to protect the state was established by Law 25, November 1926, No. 2008. Consisting of officers from the armed forces, it dealt with "crimes" against the state such as anti-government propaganda, and the re-instatement of the disbanded parties. Other measures included the replacement of the elected town mayor with a *podestà* nominated by Royal Decree (Regio Decreto 3 September, 1926, no. 10). On 31 July 1931 a new Penal code came into force, dealing severely with "crimes against the state," widening the scope of the crime of "subversive association," as well as reinstating the "ancient concept of punishment as a deterrent."[16]

All this notwithstanding, Fascism only achieved the status of an "authoritarian regime with limited political pluralism,'' in the words of Karl Dietrich Bracher. According to Alberto Aquarone, writing many years ago, this was because of ''Mussolini's insufficiently strong totalitarian aspirations, and his often displayed inability to address with the necessary firmness and totalitarian efficaciousness the fundamental issue of Fascism's relationship with the Monarchy on the one hand, and the Church on the other.'' Ultimately, ''the Fascist state repeatedly and very confidently proclaimed itself to be totalitarian, but right to the end it was also a Monarchy and a Catholic state so it was not totalitarian according to the Fascists' definition of the word.''[17] In fact, no amount of verbal acrobatics could define as ''totalitarian'' a state whose symbol of national unity was, by definition, alien to the aims of that regime, and which delegated the politically sensitive role of controlling the individual conscience and the development of the family to the confessional power of the Church — as even Giovanni Gentile was forced to admit in 1929 at the signing of the Lateran Treaties.[18]

Alfredo Rocco, ''Guardasigilli della Rivoluzione''

There was another more fundamental reason why the Fascist regime could not be considered totalitarian: it claimed to harness society, while simultaneously making it vibrate in unison like a mystic body, through the use of *the law*. Before 1931-32 when Mussolini took over, a phenomenal number of regulations, decrees and consolidation acts were enacted at the behest of Rocco, the Keeper of the Seals of the Revolution. It was almost as if Rocco, who claimed to see the law as something majestic and sacred and thought of a collection of laws more in terms of a Papal edict than as the result of the modern deliberative process, saw the liberal state as a huge empty room, which had been sacked by individualism and asocial behavior, while the totalitarian state was a warehouse of precepts, whose every compartment had to be stuffed full.

Max Weber has pointed out the incompatibility between the legal legitimization and charismatic legitimization of a state, and that an obsession with legislation — even if it is outside the state's immediate scope — does not allow for the spiritual, moral, and socio-cultural cloning processes based on the idea of *acclamatio* and *Führerprinzip*. It is worth considering what was happening in Germany, where Hitler ruled for twelve years using Imperial Acts in the wake of the Decree for the Protection of the People and the State, of 28 February 1933, which suspended civil rights, and of the proxy-law of 23 March 1934 giving him full powers. The ''unlimited power of the regime'' which led from the ''absolute coercive authority'' of its leader was not solely a question of ''political praxis'' since its ''integral'' and ''exclusive'' nature implied that Hitler had also assumed every pre-, extra- and suprastate prerogative. From 1934 onwards, the *Wehrmacht* swore a ''sacred oath'' and its ''unconditional obedience''[19] to Hitler as a high-priest of the historical mission of National Socialism, rather than just as the *Führer*.

The ''Carro dei Tespi'' taking the joys of theater all over Italy

In Italy therefore, the myth of the leader could not avoid being influenced both by the regime's polycratic nature, and the opaque religious halo imposed by the mediation of a ''rational'' institution such as the law.

Concordat between Italy and the Vatican

In fact Mussolini was loved and obeyed as the *Duce*, or leader, guide, ''father of the people,'' but he never came to be the physical embodiment of a supreme charismatic and inaccessible transcendence. In fact, much of his popularity depended on the fact that the average Italian, and the lower middle-classes in particular, could identify with him, taking pride in his achievements, and seeing him as the affectionate father taking a holiday with his children, and a gallant and successful ''man about town,'' with a slightly kitsch taste in books and theater.

The Foro Mussolini

The clutter of laws and decrees aimed at inculcating the idea of ''national harmony'' inevitably reflected on the forms of the so-called ''consensus'' making it intermittent, partial, uncertain and fragmentary, ultimately turning it into more of a pragmatic acceptance than a pro-active and positive involvement. Assessing public opinion became impossible in a country where the principle of representation had been suppressed, and where surveys of public opinion consisted of reports written specifically to humor the authorities by the prefects, or articles written by a muzzled and self-censuring press. While it was possible to deduce that there was probably a general consensus in favor of the land reclamation project for the Agro Pontino area, which promised a livelihood and homes for the farmers of the Veneto and Emilia regions, it is difficult to imagine a similar reaction towards the enforced exchange rate on the pound sterling, as attested by the fateful "Quota 90," which led to a deflationary spiral that seemed to be designed specifically to force the rural classes into ever greater financial straits. While workers surely were not disappointed with the legal benefits achieved by the Fascist labor unions following the enactment of Law 3, of 3 April 1926, no. 563, such as paid holidays, family allowances, job security in the event of illness, freedom from dismissal, and the establishment of company health insurance schemes, they no doubt felt differently about the unexpected and frequent fluctuations in real income caused by the government's tinkering with monetary policy, or the privileges accorded to the Confindustria in relation to collective bargaining.

Having taken power in order to mastermind a systematic modernization of the

Balilla and Giovani Italiane

country, to include the relaunch of industrialization, financial reform, completion of infrastructures, and urban renewal, Mussolini's party was forced to admit defeat on its most cherished aim: the creation of a technically and professionally trained elite managerial class capable of addressing all aspects of the management of the economy and the local political system, and helped by the streamlining of decision-making processes, and the elimination of formal obstacles.

However paradoxical it may seem, eliminating the election process revealed the inexperience and gaucheness of the Fascist *Faidocrazia*, which was forced to jockey for position with the traditional leaders of society. Unable to benefit from the backing of a prestigious government, and the merit that winning an election would have conferred on them, the smooth-operating *ras* and the federal secretaries, the militia consuls, and the "first-hour" leaders had a hard time getting the better of the great landowners, the priesthood, the bankers, the "wheeler-dealers," and the administrators who had been the nerve-center of the "public spirit" for decades. In Tuscany, "if the creation of the *podestà* 'favored the restoration of the influence of the natural leaders of the community,' the aristocratic *podestà* whose number... was destined to multiply during the course of the 1950s did not restrict themselves to using their hereditary titles to reinforce 'the inherently inviolable nature of an established social hierarchy,' based on the share-cropping system, but they also 'turned their political positions to their own advantage,' running the local administration ostensibly independently of the 'in-fighting and conflicts' typical of the more private sectors of municipal government, which were often exacerbated by the excessive capriciousness of the local fascist squads."[20]

In the "white" or heavily Catholic Veneto region, where the Opera Nazionale Dopolavoro and the Opera Nazionale Balilla never managed to compete with the youth, recreational and sporting associations sponsored by the Azione Cattolica or parish priests; if there was a showdown between the bishops, who were backed by a number of industrialists, and the Fascist party leaders, the latter were often merely repudiated, transferred or summarily dismissed by Rome.[21] But the most remarkable example of the Fascists' failure occurred in Sicily, where the campaign to dismantle the municipal parties and the Mafia "families" had been particularly ruthless and had a genuine moralistic streak to it. In Ragusa, Caltagirone and elsewhere, the prefects disbanded dozens of *"circoli di galantuomini"* which controlled the island's meager resources. Fired by a "determination that borders on paranoia" the "totalitarian system undertook something like the task of Sisyphus. In their attempt to squeeze the society into an ever smaller cage, they ended up by giving fresh impetus to the more informal aspects of the local power mechanisms. While they smashed the Mafia networks, they were unable to replace them with anything else, so that corruption merely filtered downward into the lower echelons."[22]

It might have been possible to overcome the difficulties inherent in making appointments from the top, however much they may have been dictated by interests, if the various "scuole di gerarchi" had been more than "talking shops," and especially if, after 1928, the party had not rapidly degenerated into an accumulation of veterans of the march on Rome all chasing a salary or a position for themselves, and had acted as a filter for attitudes and merits. Perhaps time was short, or perhaps it was the great depression, which demanded men skilled in taking bold decisions, that kept the experts and the young intellectuals out after 1922, the first year of the "Fascist recruitment trawl."

Despite the shrill protests of Italo Balbo and many others like him, it is undoubtedly true that even at the very heart of the state, the fundamental instruments of power were delegated to *commis d'état* with many years of experience in liberal government behind them, and who combined coolness or suspicion of the regime with a highly professional attitude, and an ill-disguised desire to show their worth

The campaign for agricultural promotion

Life at the Campeggio Mussolini

without having to submit to pleas, blackmail or political fetters.

Thus, Arrigo Serpieri, the Undersecretary for Agriculture, who had been an active Nitti supporter right from the turn of the century, was responsible for what little success the 1925 law on land reform had — the regulations relating to expropriation were mitigated and even abolished. The two authentic major economic reforms achieved by the Fascists, the establishment of the IRI (Institute for National Reconstruction) and the 1936 Banking Act were planned and put together by the ex-Socialriformista Alberto Beneduce, and the ex-Liberal Donato Menichella, whose only links with Fascist philosophy were a contempt for ministerial bureaucracy and the idea that parallel public bodies were needed to make up for their inefficiency. But the "true" Fascists, the pre-"March on Rome" members, the party faithfuls or the crowds of opportunists and climbers, who congregated around the Fascist party sections were probably none too pleased when the *Istituto per il credito al lavoro italiano all'estero* (Credit Institute for Italian work abroad) was delegated to Giuseppe De Michelis, the ex-Minister for Emigration, or when a fervent Nittian like Bernardo Attolico was appointed Ambassador to Moscow in 1930. Equally galling must have been the appointment as the first head of the Court of Cassation of Mariano d'Amelio, an expert on colonial law, who had started his career under Francesco Crispi and had been head of the Cabinet under Orlando and Scialoja; the appointment of Luigi Rava the Minister of Agriculture, Education, and Finance in the pre-war governments as head of the Italian Tourist Office; or the presence of Carlo Schanzer, the ex-director General and probably the most fervent Giolittian in the prestigious State Secretariat; the appointment to the Consiglio di Stato, one of Italy's most important consultative and legal administration bodies, of the "pure" academic Santi Romano, author in 1918 of *L'ordinamento legale*, an influential book on legal organization; and finally the presence among the ranks of the Gran Consiglio of Guido Jung, the Minister of Finance, a cultured Jewish figure who was ex-President of the *Istituto per il commercio con l'estero* (Institute for Foreign Trade) and had joined the party as late as 1924. In addition to the shrewd logic of this broad parcelling out of posts, another reason was the unexpected collapse of the Fascist lobby of wheeler-dealers, such as Costanzo Ciano's legendary Livorno faction. Whenever sectors that were crucial to the nation's economy such as industrial policy were in the hands of the party, the results were normally unsatisfactory or even negative. The famous law giving government authorization for the installation of new factories ended up being a protective measure for the large monopolies — only 414 of the 5114 plans authorized were eventually realized. Apart from Venice-Mestre, the other six zones selected for intensive expansion by other special laws never took off even though the locations had been chosen either for political reasons or by out and out favoritism. In Bolzano, for example, the need for immigrant workers created by the new factories to be built was intended to accelerate the "Italianization" of the province; in Ferrara the aim was to placate Italo Balbo; in Palermo, cosmetic surgery was planned to cover over the worst aspects of the island's economy; in Rome, a smattering of industrial development would have disguised the capital's "assisted" status; in Livorno and Apuania the idea was to satisfy the greed of the Ciano family and their associates.

While on a financial and administrative level the revolution was functioning well, with the help of the nationalist, apolitical, and conservative technical experts, maintain its impetus required a certain ideological input, not to mention ritual, ceremony, collective gestures, and mass involvement.

As far as propaganda was concerned, results were more than satisfactory, and often quite spectacular. In addition to the massive rallies, the "Birth of Rome," the parades of the *avanguardisti* and the *piccole italiane*, there was also the minutely-detailed planning of the elementary school text-books, broadcasts by the rural radio

129

service, the competition held in 1924 to find the "Bible of the Italian language," the exhibition to celebrate ten years of the Fascist revolution, the "Thespian carrige" of the Opera Nazionale Dopolavoro that trundled all over the country bringing theater to the people, the *agones* and the cultural *littorale* games, the excited tones of the bulletins issued by the press in uniform, and the exhilarating apologist films such as *Camicia nera*, *Cavalleria*, and *Luciano Serra Pilota*.

What the regime gained in breadth it lost in depth. Apart from the militarism and the war-like figures of speech which peppered the language ("the plough makes the furrow, but the sword defends it," and, "cinema is the most powerful weapon,") Fascist ideology came down to three main points. Firstly, the idea of Nationalism, which fluctuated between a desire for revenge, that of being "number one," and of Italy's "mission"; secondly, a theory of strength in numbers, referred to by Mussolini in his Ascension Day speech on 26 May 1927 ("If Italy is to be important, it must face the second half of the century with a population of not less than 60,000,000 people").[23] His ideas echoed Corrado Gini and Giorgio Mortara's call for a policy of "kinetic" population increase, an idea that had already fallen into disrepute before the war. Thirdly, there was "corporativism" which predicted the overthrow of the class struggle, and the opening up of a "third way" based on the self-determination of producers, that would eschew the shortcomings of individualistic liberalism, and the Bolsheviks' calls for egalitarianism. Each of these points was a cog in the Fascist machinery, and confirmed a strategy. The idea of being "number one," expansion in the Balkans, in the first instance, and then in Eastern Africa; the theory of strength in numbers led to a development plan based more on labor than on capital investment, while over and above talk of "communism" the idea of corporativism justified the government's intervention in the economy.

The spiritual and initiation side was not provided for by Fascist ideology. It lacked existentialist passion, the zeal needed for creating the "new man," and the determination to translate a vision of the world into a moral code and life style. Zeev Sternhall may be correct in his view that a *Bildung* only hovers in a pure state when the movements it generates do not take over and thus are not subject to attenuations and the transactions that the exercise of power inevitably brings about.[24]

Because Fascism had not reacted in a culturally suitable fashion to the problems for which it was born, Mussolini's dedicated, and slightly sceptical followers were not in the slightest affected by the anthropological pessimism, the rejection of rationalism and progress in the name of a "barbaric" vitality inherent in the impossibility of changing human nature and the gratuitousness of the cosmos, anti-puritanical moralism and the cult of *hubris* as the only antidote to contemporary man's biological and intellectual decadence, anti-egalitarianism and the hierarchical mentality borrowed from society's traditional habits, the hope for the establishment of a tragic civilization in which joy and suffering where one and the same thing. And yet these were the very myths that, according to Tarmo Kunnas, "tantalized" writers like Robert Brasillach, Pierre Drieu La Rochelle, Louis-Ferdinand Céline, Ezra Pound, Gottfried Benn, Alphonse de Châteaubriant, and Ernst Jünger, who were the most attracted to Fascism.[25]

There was no chance of Italy's producing a literary *Kultur* figure like Hanns Johst or Erwin Kolbenheyer who fluctuated between excesses of lyricism and telegraphic conciseness. Equally impossible would have been a novel about an emotional education as cynical, rebellious, insolent and cruel as Drieu La Rochelle's *Gilles*. Set against a backdrop of war-torn Spain, this is the story of a "hero in the making" — the resigned heroism of someone who lets his companions be killed in his place because the superior person must survive at all costs. Thanks to Mussolini's capricious personal dictatorship in the 1930s and his unwitting loss of hold on the population, it was occasionally possible for people to live *despite* Fascism as illustrated in

Mussolini placing the first stone
for the city of Sabaudia
5 August 1933

The Land Reclamation Exhibition

Ettore Scola's film *A Special Day*, where the main characters manage to establish a desperate dialogue while the sound of military marches filtered through the closed windows to remind them that Rome was celebrating Hitler's visit to Mussolini.

The push towards Ruralism and laws, such as that of 9 April 1931, aimed at restricting and controlling internal emigration and diverting it toward the Roman Campagna, and the exotic "Paradisiacal" locations of Fertilia and Arborea in Sardinia, remained dead letters. While adroit administrators turned a blind eye, kept silent, and falsified figures, Italy's country dwellers flocked to Milan, Turin, and Rome, even preferring to settle in derelict suburban slums to avoid being deported to the new cities of Sabaudia, Littoria, Pontinia, Aprilia, and Pomezia which had been so carefully planned by the Rationalist architects.

"The anti-immigration policy and above all measures to prevent urban expansion proved to be inconsistent. Aimed at responding to basic economic and territorial planning principles which did not reflect the aspirations and needs of the civilian society, they were still-born. Rather than say they were not fulfilled, it is fairer to say they were not even attempted. "Reduced to an ideological frame for police operations aimed at keeping control and using brutal methods over the unemployed and the lower classes, the Fascist policy of anti-urbanism played a negligible role in the demographic and migratory patterns of the period... During those two decades internal emigration matched that of the past, and was certainly not dwarfed by the massive post-war migratory movements."[26]

The intellectuals were often best equipped to benefit from the carelessness, laxity, and stupidity of the authorities. Benedetto Croce was able to publish *La Critica* on a regular basis without too many problems; Luigi Einaudi was less fortunate as *La riforma sociale* was closed down in 1936, but he was still able to work relatively undisturbed on his essays like "Miti e paradossi della giustizia tributaria" ("Myths and Paradoxes of Fiscal Justice") of 1938; in 1942, when a feeling of disintegration was already in the air, and regardless of the fact that Roberto Rossellini was accepting contracts to direct films such as *L'uomo dalla croce*, Luchino Visconti made *Ossessione*, a film with a strongly anticonformist sentiment. Nothing could have been further from the official stance of optimism than certain narrative texts then in circulation: not just and not only Alberto Moravia's 1929 novel *Gli indifferenti*, which, despite its harsh tone was ultimately a classical novel with a clearly defined plot, but novels such as Tommaso Landolfi's *Dialogo dei massimi sistemi* (1937) and Carlo Emilio Gadda's *La cognizione del dolore* (1939-40) which were intemperate, irreverent, and disquieting in quite a different way.

During and After

"Dear Balbo, In your concluding report of the 7th, you told me that you were leaving me 3125 planes, This figure is also recorded in the ledger signed by Valle and yourself. I have looked into the matter and find that there are only 911 planes fit for service to date. I would point out that I am satisfied with this situation. Best wishes. Mussolini."[27] This gloss to the request for the resignation of the Minister of Aeronautics, dated 12 November 1933, is an ample illustration of the irresponsible cunning the Duce used as head of the armed forces, and no further comment is needed on the reasons for Italy's defeat in World War II. A dictator who speculated on military stockpiles to blackmail adversaries and competitors was clearly not someone who would concentrate seriously on plans of attack, the effectiveness of the officers, the conditions of equipment and supplies, or potential theaters of war, even after Italy's arrogant attack on Ethiopia, or the humiliating defeat of General Roatta at Guadalajara. Italy's entry into World War II came about as a result of a hurried and badly thought-out alliance treaty, ill-starred from the start in terms of internal "morale" and public consensus regarding the declared objectives, which remained strangely at odds with each other and absurdly vague despite an active campaign over the years stressing the need for military preparedness and the inevitability of war. Historian Carlo Morandi's penetrating articles (published in 1941 in *Primato*, Giuseppe Bottai's somewhat iconoclastic journal) the rather cryptic and ambiguous tones of the intellectuals "in quarantine" who wanted to distance themselves from the regime, give a clear idea that no one had the slightest desire to die for the European "new order" since no one was motivated in the slightest by such a "new order."

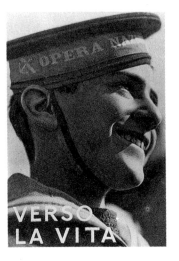

Member of the Maternity and Child Welfare Organization

Because it was being fought far from home, in places few people had heard of because they were not on the map of the countries people normally emigrated to, for many Italians, World War II was seen as unreal, something like a story-book expedition, a highly-colored swashbuckling affair. However, the air-raids — that bizarre novelty of war technology — soon ensured that the war became a constant reality, in time and place, of everyday life.

"What a sad war this is. It is more like a destruction of houses, old people, and children than anything else, it's pure butchery, not a war. It would have been better if the inventor of the airplane had been struck dead, and yet people talk of civilization,"[28] wrote a soldier to his mother in the Piedmont. And yet the number killed in the air-raids was not what devastated the cities most. The evacuations were much more damaging, throwing the transport system into disarray, and creating a new relationship between the city and the countryside. The curfew, disrupted timetables, routines, the way of life, travel arrangements, and personal relationships. And then there was insomnia, fear, insecurity, and nightmares.

It was inevitable that in such conditions it became unclear as to who the enemy really was. Who was responsible for such anguish and destruction?

Clearly the British and the Americans, who were raining destruction from the skies, and also the Italian civil and military authorities who had been incapable of organizing an effective anti-aircraft defense in the time of greatest need. But it was above all, Mussolini, Il Duce, whose passion for power meant that the generals, leaders, soldiers and *podestà*, ministers, and railroadmen were stripped of theirs.

While the "national front" was crumbling, and consensus for the regime was diminishing at lightning speed, the troops on the front line often noticed they were not facing a "real enemy," an inexorable and historic enemy, as they had done in 1915 with the Austrians. During the Russian campaign, Mario Rigoni Stern, the "sergeant of the snows" succumbed to the generosity and the hospitality of the truculent "Bolsheviks."

Also, as the 1954 film *L'armata s'agapò* (which provoked a major storm of censorship) showed, after the Italians' treacherous attack in Greece on 28 October 1940, the soldiers flisted happily with the local girls.

The aggressive march of the provincials who wanted to be world leaders became the long tormented voyage of a people who were achieving a painful urbanity shot through with guilt complexes. Even among the staunchest Fascists who had volunteered more out of an abstract sense of duty than a conviction that the war was just and their position was strong, often felt "insignificant" and abandoned, in the face of a drama that seemed increasingly absurd and meaningless. Thirty-year-old Giuseppe Berto who was captured and interned in a concentration camp after the brave defense of Tunisia concluded his book *Guerra in camicia nera* bitterly confused: "Before evening set in, we found ourselves in a compound, under the surveillance of blacks, near Enfidaville. We got nothing to eat but they promised us water to drink. We are surrounded by many other compounds. There are thousands and thousands of Italians and German soldiers. I never thought there could be so many. Something must have gone wrong. In any event, it is all over."[29]

The young intellectuals, the bright and cossetted faithfuls of the GUF who were babies or in short trousers in 1922 eventually understood that if they wanted to realize the revolutionary transformation they had dreamed of in their days on the *fronde*, they would need to operate from without the regime.

When everything fell apart, between the Allied landings and 8 September 1943, Italy ceased to exist. Three governments and two armies of occupation had turned it into a no man's land, where the only local representative of power was the church, the righter of wrongs and the solacer of the suffering, with maternal care feeding the starving and dressing the naked. Even if this organization, with its universal appeal, had no soldiers or tanks, as Stalin contemptuously remarked, it could assert itself on a par with all the other military powers on earth.

Over the next twenty months, the war increased the divide between the north and the south. In the south, hostilities ceased immediately, and officially, in 1943. In an atmosphere of ever-increasing contempt for uniforms and rifles (the "We won't join up" movement was symptomatic), the post-war period started immediately — with all its hardships and degradations, but also with its vibrant and dignified desire for survival, outstandingly portrayed in Eduardo De Filippo's *Napoli milionaria*.

In the north, however, which had been invaded by the Germans, a bloody civil war broke out between the Fascists and the Anti-Fascists, which became superimposed on the national war of liberation, influencing the revival of ideas, studies, plans, and political debates which had been exiled or sent into internal exile for the past 20 years. The Democrazia Cristiana tried its best to update a clearly ancient social Catholicism, while the Partito d'Azione developed the idea of "liberal socialism" which aimed at an equitable distribution of wealth in terms of civil rights and private property. The communists meanwhile worked to assert themselves as a loyally nationalistic and democratic force, and all of them struggled to overcome the

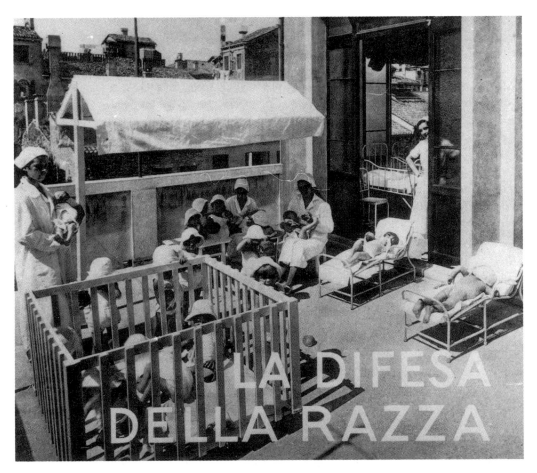

Maternity and Child
Welfare Organization

deficiencies of a political culture atrophied by the distant, summary, and fleeting gaze to which the opposition had been condemned. It was not just the usual militants who took to the hills with the Brigate Garibaldi and the GL; motivated by their beliefs, their instincts, a romantic urge or even youthful student impulses, there was the man in the street, the young (and even the *very* young) students from the Fascist schools who had acted out war in funny uniforms in the *Ventitré giorni della città di Alba* by Beppe Fenoglio, or played the rugged Castagna who meted out violent but good-natured reprisals on the grown-ups of the village in Luigi Meneghello's *Piccoli maestri*. The democratic republic that was "born of the Resistance" was achieved also thanks to them. Italy's "honor" was also regained with the help of their "republican" colleagues — without confusing them with the more gloomy and rowdy followers of Fascism — and who hardly ever gave up their pursuit of that honor even if they were on the wrong path.

Notes
[1] Gioacchino Volpe, "Giovane Italia", (1923) in *Fra storia e politica*, Rome 1924, pp. 396-397.
[2] Arrigo Serpieri, *La guerra e le classi rurali italiane*, Bari 1929, p. 210.
[3] Francesco Ercole, "Miti del dopoguerra" (1922) in *Dal nazionalismo al fascismo - saggi e discorsi*, Rome 1928, p. 95.
[4] Giovanni Amendola, *Una battaglia liberale - discorsi politici (1919-1923)*, Turin 1924, pp. 15, 34.
[5] Emilio Bodrero, *Manifesto alla borghesia*, Rome 1921, p. 29.
[6] Felice Guarneri, *Battaglie economiche tra le due grandi guerre*, vol. I (1918-1935), Milan 1953, pp. 39-45.
[7] Luigi Sturzo, *Popolarismo e fascismo*, Turin 1924, p. 90.
[8] In Filippo Turati, *Socialismo e riformismo nella storia d'Italia - scritti politici 1878-1932*, ed. F. Livorsi, Milan 1979, p. 360.
[9] Giuseppe Miccichè, *Dopoguerra e fascismo in Sicilia*, Rome 1976, p. 60.
[10] Giovanni Bruno, Rosario Lembo, *Politica e società nel Salernitano (1919-1925)*, (with a preface by F. Barbagallo), Salerno 1981, pp. 67-73.
[11] Anna-Maria Preziosi, *Borghesia e fascismo in Friuli negli anni 1920-22*, Rome 1980, pp. 23-33.
[12] Marco Bernabei, *Fascismo e nazionalismo in Campania (1919-1925)*, with introduction by G. De Rosa, Rome 1975, pp. 243-256.
[13] Salvatore Sechi, *Dopoguerra e fascismo in Sardegna*, Turin 1969, pp. 210-223.
[14] L. Ponziani, *Notabili, combattenti e nazionalisti - L'Abruzzo verso il fascismo*, Milan 1988, p. 13.
[15] Quoted in Adrian Lyttelton, *La conquista del potere - il fascismo dal 1919 al 1929*, Bari 1974, p. 71.
[16] Alberto Aquarone, *L'organizzazione dello Stato totalitario*, Turin 1965, p. 237: the texts of the regime's main laws are listed in the appendix to this volume and can also be found in Claudio Schwartzenerg's *Diritto e giustizia nell'Italia fascista*, Milan 1977, pp. 221-296.
[17] Alberto Aquarone, *L'organizzazione dello stato totalitario*, Turin 1965, p. 291.
[18] Paolo Ungari, "Ideologie giuridiche e strategie istituzionali del fascismo", in *Il problema storico del fascismo*, Florence 1970, p. 75.
[19] Karl D. Bracher, *La dittatura tedesca - origini, strutture, conseguenze dal nazionalsocialismo in Germania*, Italian transition, Bologna 1983, 2nd ed., p. 457.
[20] Marco Palla, "I fascisti toscani" in *Storia d'Italia - le regioni dall'unità a oggi*, *Tuscany* ed. G. Mori, Turin 1986, p. 490.
[21] Silvio Lanaro, "Genealogia di un modello", *ibid*, "The Veneto" ed S. Lanaro, Turin 1987, 2nd ed., pp. 39-40, 66.
[22] Salvatore Lupo, "L'utopia totalitaria del fascismo (1918-42), *ibid*, *Sicily* edited by G. Giarrizzo and M. Aymard, Turin, 1987, pp. 456-7; see also *Blocco agrario e crisi in Sicilia tra le due guerre*, Naples 1981.
[23] Benito Mussolini, "Il discorso dell'Ascensione", in *Scritti e discorsi*, vol. VI, 1927-1928, p. 42.
[24] Zeev Sternhell, *Ni droite ni gauche - l'idéologie fasciste en Francell*, Paris 1983.
[25] Tarmo Kunnas, *Drieu, Céline, Brasillach et la tentation fasciste*, Paris 1972.
[26] Anna Treves, *Le migrazioni interne nell'Italia fascista - politica e realtà demografica*, Turin 1976, pp. 160-161.
[27] Quoted by Giorgio Rochat, in "Mussolini e le forze armate", in *Il regime fascista*, ed A. Aquarone and M. Vernassa, Bologna 1974, p. 126.
[28] Quoted by N. Gallerano in "Gli italiani in guerra 1940-1943 - Appunti per la ricerca" in *L'Italia nella seconda guerra mondiale e nella resistenza*, ed. F. Ferrantini Tosi, G. Grassi, and M. Legnani, Milan p. 309.
[29] Giuseppe Berto, *Guerra in camicia nera* (1955), Venice 1985, p. 221.

Maurizio Fagiolo
dell'Arco

De Chirico and Savinio: From Metafisica to Surrealism

The Development of a Myth

"Tout le mythe moderne encore en formation s'appuie à son origine sur les deux œuvres, dans leur esprit presque indiscernable, d'Alberto Savinio et de son frère Giorgio De Chirico, œuvres qui atteignent leur point culminant à la veille de la guerre. Les ressources du visuel et de l'auditif se trouvent par eux simultanément mises à contribution pour la création d'un langage symbolique, concret, universellement intelligible du fait qu'il prétend rendre compte au plus haut degré de la réalité spécifique de l'époque (l'artiste s'offrant à être victime de son temps) et de l'interrogation métaphysique propre à cette époque (le rapport des objets nouveaux dont elle est amenée à se servir et des objets anciens, abandonnés ou non, est des plus bouleversants en ce qu'il exaspère le sentiment de fatalité)". (All modern myth that is still in phase of development relies at its origin on the two nearly inseparable bodies of work of Alberto Savinio and his brother Giorgio De Chirico, work which achieves its high point just before the war. The sources of sight and sound are simultaneously utilized in the creation of a language which is symbolic, concrete, and universally understands the role of the specific reality of the period [the artist offers himself as martyr of his time] and the metaphysical preoccupation characteristic of the period [the relationship between the use of new objects and old, abandoned or not, is the most shattering in that it increases the feeling of fatality].)

In this little known quote from his fundamental book *Anthologie de l'humour noir* (1939), André Breton, the father of Surrealism, attributes the two intellectuals with an almost mythical role, a common spirit "presque indiscernable," the positive and negative charge of an electrical current. Savinio adds in his introduction to *Tutta la vita*: "We two brothers are the unknowing instigators of Surrealism, children of the same mother and father, brothers in spirit and in flesh. How can we contradict the affirmations of the leader of Surrealism and his most noted theory?"

While continuing research on the origins of De Chirico's second Metaphysical period, when, returning to Paris in 1924 he is both witness and accomplice to the birth of Surrealism, this author interviewed several members of the movement regarding the personality of the less fortunate Savinio. Philippe Soupault, one of the founders of the group, wrote in 1980 as follows: "J'ai toujours regretté, et le regrette encore, qu'on ait pas accordé à Alberto Savinio toute l'attention que méritait son œuvre. Je sais l'estime qu'avait pour lui le poète-prophète, mon ami Guillaume Apollinaire. J'espère et je crois qu'il n'est pas trop tard pour qu'on rende justice à l'homme, à l'écrivain et au peintre, qui fut d'une modestie exemplaire, et l'on sait que la modestie est le signe éclatant de la valeur" ("I have always regretted and still regret that the works of Alberto Savinio did not receive all the attention that they deserved. I know that the poet-prophet, my friend Guillaume Apollinaire, held him in great esteem. I hope and believe that it is not too late to give justice to the man, to the author and to the painter who was of such exemplary modesty, a striking sign of his worth.")

"Modern myth." Giorgio and Andrea begin to construct the first myth of their career as adolescents, in their Athens, a bit Bavarian and a bit Turkish, where all their certainties but also all their complexes are born. From time to time the myth of the Dioscuri, the inseparable Castor and Pollux, or that of Orestes and Pylades (with the help of the Furies, or better yet of the Argonauts, whose search for the golden fleece left right from their small port city of Volos) will provide their source of inspiration. The brothers are joined by that tight childhood bond of "indirect birth," of being Italians born outside Italy, by a turbulent childhood (De Chirico speaks of "dark years" while Savinio refers to the "tragedy of infancy"), by their common studies, at the same desk (Italian and Greek, mythology and European culture).

De Chirico remembers his first years in the following way: "I painted works inspired by Böcklin, and my brother also painted and drew; furthermore, we read and studied a great deal." In 1943 Savinio adds: "It is there [in death] that my brother and I will be again what we were twenty or so years ago, when nothing separated us yet and together we had only one thought." Eventually life separates them, but De Chirico honors his brother on the day of his death by placing a laurel crown on his head and dedicating the Italian version of *Hebdomeros* "to the sacred memory of my brother Alberto Savinio."

But how was the idea of *metafisica* born? Its definition is "beyond the physical," just as Surrealism (Apollinaire's term, taken from André Breton) means "above reality." And yet, the etymology of the term adds something and omits something. The true concern of De Chirico and Savinio is the investigation of the hidden meaning of things (Nietzsche's enigma or the demon of Heraclitus). They never refer to a supernatural world of ideas, but they work around a simple mystery: common objects, if observed from a different angle, can become the real source of the enigma.

There is no need to disturb the "spiritual" (as Wassily Kandinsky was doing in the same period in Munich) or to focus on the dream as the double of human life (as Sigmund Freud was suggesting in Vienna). In short, the metaphysical enigma is concealed in any type of architecture or musical event, even one easily approachable, such as a deep arcade or a toy, a statue or a flute, the hymn to Garibaldi or a hiccup, a Greek hero or a mannequin, silence or a shadow... The spectral and the eternal moment, the philosophical knot of "metafisica," can coexist anywhere.

In this way past and future merge in De Chirico's works. Those that he defines as "eternal signs" hide their geometry and esotericism, vision and irony (in the Greek sense of the word). From that autumn afternoon in 1910, when he sees a new world in Piazza Santa Croce in Florence (immortalized in the painting *Enigma di un pomeriggio d'autunno - Enigma of an Autumn Afternoon*), the prophetic painter states that sight should transform itself into vision, and the visionary into prophecy.

Their sources are few, and all are carefully recorded by the Dioscuri: Nietzsche and Weininger, Schopenhauer, Böcklin and Klinger. The ideas are those of "revelation" and of the "eternal return" (as Weininger stated, "All things are but appearance, they reflect to me always and only my subjectivity").

The writings of the twenty-three year old painter (this author found the originals in the Picasso collection and published them philologically), even more than the explicit philosophy present in the paintings, are essential to understanding the brothers' works. The poetic flights of Pindar chase one another like an abstract montage: Nietzsche is related to Van Gogh who is related to Picasso, and even to Pinocchio, and to Böcklin and Poussin, who succeed in going "beyond all paintings" (the circle closes since it is enough to translate "beyond" with the Greek word "meta" in order to have a Metaphysical painting).

Paris 1911-1915: Metaphysical Painting and Music

Giorgio De Chirico arrives in Paris on 14 July 1911. His brother Alberto (who had been living in the *Ville Lumière* for more than a year) and his mother are waiting at the Gare de Lyon. He arrives dazed by the trip to the city bustling with festivities for the anniversary of the Revolution. He first resides on the Rive Droite, but moves in quick succession to three different studios in Montparnasse. He remains in Paris with his brother for four years. Giorgio exhibits his first works at the age of 24, and

Giorgio De Chirico
Self-portrait, 1908-11

Portrait of Nietzsche

Giorgio De Chirico
Portrait of Andrea De Chirico
1909-10

Giorgio De Chirico
Portrait of Apollinaire
1914, engraving

Alberto Savinio, *Death of Niobe*
1914, musical score

enjoys the mounting esteem of Guillaume Apollinaire (and also of Salmon, Raynal, Vauxcelles and Roger-Marx); he also signs his first contract (with Paul Guillaume). Andrea changes his name to Alberto Savinio and holds his first concert in May 1914 in Apollinaire's club.

"Modernity, that great mystery, lives everywhere in Paris," De Chirico writes ten years later. And thus he is able to view the city as a new Athens: the Pallas Athena at the corner of the Bourbon Palace parallels the Athenian propylaea. "Like Athens at the time of Pericles, Paris is today the city of art and intellect in absolute. It is here that every man worthy of the title artist must take awareness of his worth."

Chronology

1911-1912. The artist passes a year of reflection: he becomes acquainted with the museums, the new city suggests new spatial ideas which merge with those of the mythical Italian city, evident also in the painters before Raphael. In the summer of 1912 the ailing De Chirico is in Vichy; in the autumn he is again at his easel. He again takes up his earlier ideas inspired by Nietzsche, completes the works started in Florence and begins others. Michele Demetrio Calvocoressi, a musicologist of Greek origin who worked with his brother Alberto Savinio on a short opera set in Egypt, introduces him at the Salon d'Automne. De Chirico submits three paintings which are exhibited in the room of Spanish painters: a melancholic self-portrait (ET QUID AMABO NISI QUOD AENIGMA EST?), *Enigma dell'oracolo (Enigma of the Oracle)* and *Enigma di un pomeriggio d'autunno (Enigma of an Autumn Afternoon)*, the painting of the metaphysical "revelation" in Piazza Santa Croce in Florence. He signs his name Giorgio in the catalogue and states that he was "né a Florence." There is much talk about the Douanier Rousseau, and about a fiery group of Italians, the Futurists; Sergei Diaghilev's Ballets Russes are a great success; the works of Marc Chagall and Henri Matisse are exhibited in the Salon d'Automne, along with the sculptures of Amedeo Modigliani and the orphic paintings of Picabia.

1913. The artist works a great deal during the winter. The melancholic *Stimmung* of the *Piazze d'Italia* series begins to appear. He meets the poet Apollinaire at the Salon des Indépendants (according to Savinio, "Pablo Picasso introduced the new painter to Apollinaire as 'le peintre des gares'.") A painting such as *Enigma dell'ora (Enigma of the Hour)* shocks the spectator with its double perspective, a space-time quite different from that of the Cubists, rendered in a delicate, almost naïf, painting style. Apollinaire compares him to Chagall and to Rousseau. In October he has his first exhibition in his studio (115 Notre-Dame-des-Champs) with all his latest works, *La tristesse du départ (Melancholy at Departure)*, *L'énigme de l'heure (Enigma of the Hour)*, *La solitude (Solitude)*, *Le sifflement de la locomotive (The Whistle of the Locomotive)*, and Apollinaire writes an enthusiastic review.

In the spring Savinio attends the opening of *Le Sacre du Printemps*, and is impressed by Stravinski's orientalizing citations and dissonances, which alter somewhat his melodramatic idea of music.

De Chirico exhibits three works at the Salon d'Automne: two piazzas (*La tour rouge* or *The Red Tower* is the first to sell), a portrait and a nude (almost suggesting that he is a fully developed artist). The academic painter Léon Bonnart pauses before the nude entitled *Etude* and offers his compliments. This marks the beginning of De Chirico's cyclical method: he produces many towers (the Greek version of the Eiffel Tower), with the elements of an exotic banquet in the foreground (pineapples, artichokes, bananas). Greek sculpture is placed in an increasingly compressed space, with an absurd perspective, interrupted by sharp shadows (Nietzsche's "high noon"). He expands upon the theme of Ariadne in the Italian piazza, and the presence of the Gare Montparnasse (enigma of the voyage) in his paintings becomes an obsession.

1914. Meanwhile, the two brothers (Dioscuri) are admitted into Apollinaire's circle, headquarters of the journal *Les Soirées de Paris*, published by the Baronesse d'Oettingen and Serge Ferat. They meet poets, painters and many residents of Montparnasse. In the spring Giorgio exhibits three more paintings at the Salon des Indépendants, *La nostalgie de l'infini (Nostalgia of the Infinite), Joies et énigmes d'une heure étrange (Joy and Enigma of a Strange Hour), L'énigme d'une journée (Enigma of a day)*.

Apollinaire states: "Giorgio De Chirico construit dans la calme et la méditation des compositions harmonieuses et mystèrieuses. Conception plastique de la politique du temps." But not everyone has the same opinion. De Chirico feels compelled to respond to the critic of *Paris Midi* in the following way:

"Monsieur le directeur,

Je m'adresse à vous et à vostre amabilité, pour protester contre un malentendu qui a couru à propos de mes tableaux parmi les critiques qui parlèrent des 'Indépendants.' Sauf M. Apollinaire presque tous parlèrent de *décors de théâtre*. Or je voudrais que ces messieurs sachent que mes peintures n'ont rien à voir avec des décors ce qui d'ailleurs est suffisamment prouvé par leurs titres."

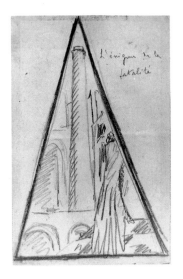

Giorgio De Chirico
L'énigme de la fatalité
drawing

Now begins his future of success, but also one fraught with misunderstanding and struggle (he called himself a "monomaniac," a solitary warrior). In this year he paints the portrait of Apollinaire and introduces a new image into his repertoire, the mannequin. And in this same year he is introduced by Apollinaire to the young art dealer Paul Guillaume, who includes him in his group along with Picabia, Derain, Picasso, Matisse and Negro sculpture.

On 24 May Alberto Savinio has his debut. His *musique métaphysique* is met with applause at a concert in the hall of *Les Soirées de Paris*; it is an alternation of sounds and dissonances, of passages from popular songs or other music and inserted into the melody like a foreign object in a painting by De Chirico. The 23-year-old Andrea declares himself "artisan dionysiaque," and on that occasion changes his name in order not to be confused with the Metaphysical painter. Ardengo Soffici, a collaborator on the journal *Lacerba*, is present at the concert and writes enthusiastically about the two brothers. He visits the studio on 9 Rue Campagne-Première, where he is the first to see such groundbreaking works as the triangular *L'énigme de la fatalité (The Enigma of Fatality)*.

Giorgio De Chirico
The Large Mysterious Square
1913-14, drawing

Savinio also collaborates with Apollinaire and Marius de Zayas in a pantomime which was commissioned by Alfred Stieglitz, the photographer and propagator of the avantgarde, for presentation in America.

In early August the "distant and fatal" war becomes a reality. Apollinaire enlists, and sets off for the front, and the salons and clubs become deserted. The Dioscuri consider a possible move to Italy.

1915. During the winter Giorgio produces a series of dramatic works while Alberto continues to compose. They both send material to Alfred Stieglitz in New York for publication in his journal *291*, and Giorgio paints two portraits of his "patron" Paul Guillaume, excused from military service, but like the artist melancholic. Giorgio's works become increasingly troubled, indicated by such titles as *La pureté d'un rêve (The Purity of a Dream), La lumière fatale (The Fatal Light), Les mannequins à la tour rose (Mannequins at the Pink Tower), Le vaticinateur (The Seer), La contrariété du penseur (The Thinker's Vexation)*. The mannequins placed within the dramatic perspectives demonstrate that their inventor had lost his wise sense of separation.

Savinio also speaks of mannequins and faceless men with too much memory. His pantomime *Les chants de la mi-mort*, published in the last issue of Apollinaire's journal, comes very close to the Metaphysical paintings of his brother, Giorgio, noted also by critics such as Roberto Longhi, upon their return to Italy.

And then Italy declares war. The Dioscuri feeling themselves very much Italian,

Giorgio De Chirico, *The Victor* preparatory sketch for the *Conquest of the Philosopher*

Giorgio De Chirico preparatory drawing for *Mystery and Melancholy of a Road* 1914

enlist and in June are assigned their location in Florence. They are ultimately sent to Ferrara, "city of geometric luxury": a new voyage for the Argonauts begins.

De Chirico exhibits 13 works at the Salons and 30 in his studio in late 1913. By contract many are given to his dealer Paul Guillaume, several remain in his studio on Rue Campagne-Première (strangely enough, the poet Giuseppe Ungaretti will be responsible for their recovery). About 70 works date to the period in Paris.

Scenario

"Esprit Nouveau." In this simple formula Guillaume Apollinaire synthesized the fervent climate of the pre-war period. Through Apollinaire Cubism arrives at a confrontation with Futurism, and when in 1913 his book *Les peintres cubistes* is published, Apollinaire appears more as the historiographer of a movement than as a militant critic. After the presentation of the Fauves and the Cubists in the Salons, there follow the Russians (Kandinsky and Chagall) and the Dutch (Mondrian). Meanwhile Brancusi kills and revives sculpture, contacts with Germany (*Der Sturm*) and Italy (*Lacerba*) strengthen, and the American Armory Show exhibition (February 1913) appears as the first manifestation of this lively environment.

In his "Projet d'histoire littéraire contemporaine" published in the Dada journal *Littérature* in 1922, Louis Aragon summarizes this period. In the "époque des Soirées de Paris," the names of Giorgio De Chirico and Alberto Savinio appear beside that of Apollinaire.

The Dioscuri immediately establish contact with Guillaume Apollinaire. The poet, friend of the artists, is director of the journal *Les Soirées de Paris* from 1912, which in 1913 assumes a new format and addresses current events. In the same year the journal is mailed by subscription, underwritten by Giorgio De Chirico. Leafing through its pages is enough to become familiar with the many people who frequent the club financed by the Baroness d'Oettingen (to whom Savinio will dedicate memorable words): artists such as Picasso and Derain, Braque and Matisse, Picabia, Léger and Archipenko, poets such as Jacob and Cendrars, Salmon and Raynal (De Chirico's critics), Soffici and Papini. The review of Savinio's concert and the text of *Les chants de la mi-mort* are published in the last issue of the journal.

In Apollinaire's club and at *Les Soirées de Paris* the Dioscuri meet the Orphic artist Picabia (the first painter to join De Chirico in Paul Guillaume's gallery), André Derain, much loved by critics and dealers, Brancusi (his polished heads dialogue with De Chirico's mannequins), Larionov and Goncharova (protagonists of a lively story by Savinio), Picasso (De Chirico sketches him in caricature, together with the Baroness), and finally, Pierre Roy, a young painter who becomes their friend (he produces the xylograph of De Chirico's portrait of Apollinaire). They also meet the young Jean Cocteau who will be the new Apollinaire for the Dioscuri during their second Paris period.

"M. Savinio, qui est poète, peintre et dramaturge, ressemble en cela aux génies multiformes de la Renaissance toscane": in this way Apollinaire presents Alberto Savinio to his readers, giving us a further indication of his activity as a painter (Savinio recalls designing the small figurines for the ballets in Paris).

Indeed, the portrait of Apollinaire, an enigmatic composition by De Chirico, remained for many decades the most sublime enigma. The "angel of modern times" as Savinio defines him, appears in the background, like the outline of a moving target in a game at an amusement park, and here the memories of the Dioscuri coincide because De Chirico remembers that Apollinaire and his friends, "as was the fashion of the times, smoked plaster pipes similar to those seen at amusement parks in the moving target games," while Savinio notes that he and Apollinaire "smoked those plaster pipes known as 'Jacobs' which are used as targets in amusement park games." A very simple element assumes a visionary meaning when it is "accompanied" by a classical bust (complete with black glasses) and the perspective of a *camera obscura* with a diagonal frieze (with fish and shell). Suffice it to point out that the bust recalls the blind seer and that Apollinaire enjoyed comparing himself to Orpheus (Dufy represented him as Orpheus with the fish of initiation), and the game is over. The painting, an idealized portrait of a classical, Orphic poet, a seer, a prophetic target, always remained in Apollinaire's possession (it is currently in the Centre Pompidou). And one last enigmatic touch, to further add to the personal myth: Orpheus was the protector of the Argonauts' mission.

This portrait is instantly made into a xylograph by Pierre Roy and becomes the myth of the Surrealists: Apollinaire plans to publish it as the frontispiece of *Et moi aussi je suis peintre*, the book in which he most closely approaches the method of his painter friends, composing words into images, known as *calligrammes*. De Chirico states in the eulogy of his friend who died so young: "He fell under the influence of those same people he defended; he lauded the new painters and they offered new seeds." Savinio too has a close working relationship with Apollinaire. On the eve of the war he prepares the music for a pantomime which is intended to be presented in America along with the stage sets of Marius de Zayas. Apollinaire writes *A quelle heure un train partira-t-il pour Paris?*, a recently discovered text which is strikingly close to the contemporary writings of Savinio. The authorship of several poems and *calligrammes* which the poet-prophet gave to the young Italian intellectual have been identified by this author and by Jannini.

Apollinaire's alter-ego during this period is Paul Guillaume, the great art dealer who is just at the beginning of his career. His beardless face was painted by Modigliani and Derain, and three times by Giorgio De Chirico. In a contract which dates to early 1914, De Chirico agreees to produce six paintings a month for a sum of 120 francs. Paul Guillaume is a melanophile, a friend of Negroes. In 1917 he publishes an important album with a preface by Apollinaire but already as early as 1914 he asks Savinio to give a conference on Negro sculpture which is recorded on tape and transmitted soon after in New York in the gallery of Alfred Stieglitz. A group of paintings by De Chirico is sent by Paul Guillaume to the great photographer in New York for a temporary exhibition. Guillaume remains a point of reference for De Chirico in Ferrara during the war (he continues to send him works according to contract until spring 1917) and after (Guillaume organizes a De Chirico exhibition in 1922, presented by André Breton, and gives him a regular contract upon his return to Paris in 1926).

Themes

The brothers work together and develop their subject matter, comparing their ideas with those of their friends, above all with Apollinaire, but also with Paul Guillaume and the choreographer Michail Fokine, the Greek Calvocoressi and the American de Zayas. They look at Nietzsche as their first idol, inspired by his idea of melancholy and his myths (that of Ariadne for example), but above all his formation of an idea which is at the same time distant and present, that of Italy which is almost foreign to them.

The myth of Nietzsche permeates the first works. There is never a reference to Zarathustra, but instead a faithful adhesion to a *Stimmung* which communicates to the Dioscuri "the sense of lyrical illumination," the need to "transcend the literal meaning," the "free and lyrical game." Already with his first self-portrait which includes the phrase ET QUID AMABO NISI QUOD AENIGMA EST? the artist delves into the depths (the enigma is that of Oedipus before the Sphinx) and investigates the theme of melancholy. The painter depicts himself with his arm resting on his cheek, in the classical gesture of Dürer and of those "born under Saturn," and also of Nietzsche, as revealed in a photograph and a print. Nietzsche wrote: "The fundamental differ-

140

Giorgio De Chirico
untitled drawing
(*Piazza d'Italia*)

Giorgio De Chirico
untitled drawing
Metaphysical composition
with book, eggs, and arrow

ence between sadness and melancholy is that sadness excludes thought while melancholy thrives on it."

From Nietzsche derive several of his states of being, such as the sense of "convalescence" (the philosopher defined it as "drunkenness") which leads to his first paintings; and from Nietzsche comes his passion for time, the "great midday" shadows. Savinio also develops this passion as illustrated by the following quote: "Et ils sont deux maintenant / à cheminer sous le soleil de l'ombre," thus succeeding in combining the philosophical idea of the "wayfarer and his shadow" with the Piazzas of his brother. Nietzsche is the source of his passion for a city, Turin, with its "severe and solemn piazzas," "the arcades which seem to meet a need," "the wonderful light," a city deemed "beyond the good and the bad." The city in which the philosopher received the enlightenment of folly appears in many works of that period, representing a backdrop for monuments of the Risorgimento period, or for the "gay science" (Ariadne is related to the minotaur and the bull is the emblem of Turin), and as an idea of "unbounded perfection."

The importance of the game derives also from Nietzsche: "Vivre dans le monde comme dans un immense musée d'étrangeté, plein de jouets curieux, bariolés, qui changent d'aspect, que quelquefois comme des petits enfants nous cassons pour voir comment ils étaient faits dedans — et décus, nous nous apercevons qu'ils étaient vides."

And finally, they follow the enigma of the eternal return in search of lost time, even with the risk of discovering that childhood is always a tragedy.

The paintings of 1913 always include the figure of Ariadne in the Italian piazza. This myth appears in seven canvases, always juxtaposed with the ocean background and the lighthouse (departure), the tower (nostalgia for infinity), the train (the voyage), and in the paintings in which he includes the word MELANCONIA under the statue, revealing the true aim of his search. Ariadne, like the painter, is melancholic. And Nietzsche too was drawn to Ariadne, declaring himself her Dionysus and her labyrinth... Ariadne is science (when she helps Theseus enter the labyrinth and defeat the Minotaur), she is melancholy (when she is abandoned by Theseus), she is rapture (when she is won over by Dionysus); she is the personification of the Nietzschean "gay science."

During this period Savinio writes his most illuminated works, essays and musical compositions. He, too, is imbued with the German culture and diffident of the weakness and monotony of the French (Debussy and Ravel, Satie and Franck). He seeks a music in which space and time, and harmony and disharmony are overlapping: "La musique est l'émanation d'une métaphysique nouvelle." This Dionysiac spirit wins over Apollinaire. On 24 May 1914 Andrea De Chirico, now known as Alberto Savinio, holds his first concert in the hall of *Les Soirées de Paris*.

Savinio's themes are similar to those of De Chirico. His music is also a visual experience, with leaps of imagination found in De Chirico's paintings, a music which is neither harmonious nor pure, but "désharmonisée." He includes folk tunes and burlesque rhythms, the hymn to Garibaldi and the drum roll, sounds, and above all (as Nietzsche would have liked) dances.

His music theory appears in *291*, the avant-garde journal published in New York by Alfred Stieglitz, and his script for *Les chants de la mi-mort* appears in the last issue of Apollinaire's journal. From Savinio's imagination emerge the piazzas with the statues of the Risorgimento, the fruits of a sacred banquet, the human targets and the disquieting mannequins, the ships on the horizon and anxiety over the aesthetic of the machine age, the cannon and the stage-curtain, Giuseppe Verdi and Victor Emmanuel, the palm leaf which decorates the Samaritaine department store, and the fountains — indeed, the overlapping of memory and dreams, in that state of halfconsciousness which is too often buried along with childhood.

It is not inappropriate to recall a statement by Savinio regarding the mannequins:

"*Les chants de la mi-mort* is Alberto Savinio's first literary work, considered by the Surrealists to be one of the first examples of Surrealism... The sketches of the scenery and the characters of this dramatic production were painted by the author in 1914. These sketches (the Bald Man, the Yellow Man) are the sources of the 'mannequins' of the so-called 'Metaphysical' painting."

The two brothers were born in Greece of Italian parents, and were educated in an Athens that much resembled Munich. They passed fleetingly through Italy on their way to Munich, and returned briefly to Milan and Florence; they are Greek by their childhood memories, German by culture, Italian by origin and aspiration. In the Salon catalogues De Chirico states that he was "né a Florence", and declares himself "florentinus" in the frontispiece of his translation of Schopenhauer, and Soffici also defines the two brothers as "Florentine." Florence, their father's native city, and Turin, the city of the Savoy and of Unity, combine.

Thus, the myth of the Risorgimento is evoked by both artists: Camillo Benso di Cavour, Vittorio Emanuele, Giuseppe Verdi and Emanuele Filiberto represent the Risorgimento and Turin and Italy. *Scènes dramatiques d'après des épisodes du Risorgimento* is the subtitle of Savinio's *Les chants de la mi-mort*.

Equestrian statues appear in the piazzas of the "ville carrée" in De Chirico's paintings of 1914, but fundamentally they are not so different from the statues he saw as a child in the piazza of the Stadium or in the Academy of Athens. In one painting the flapping banners bear the letters "To." In the painting *Le vaticinateur (The Seer)*, considered by the artist his masterpiece, the word TORINO is concealed on the blackboard bearing traces of the cabala.

Giorgio De Chirico
drawing for *Still Life*

Methodology

The Dioscuri practice more a philosophy than a painting style; theirs is more an *ars memoriae* than a search for new images. In his writings of 1913, De Chirico confirms that it is not the thing painted which is important, but the new angle from which it is viewed (a belief shared by Nietzsche). Thus, in his mind's eye Italy and France are juxtaposed using a photographic technique which takes over where the imagination stops. The chimney which he discovers one day in Montparnasse, the signs stencilled on the shop windows, and the Chinese shadows co-exist with the equestrian monuments of Turin and the porticoes of the city of the Savoy. And later in Ferrara he will juxtapose military maps with the pastries copied from the windows of confectionary shops in the Jewish ghetto with the anatomical charts from the clinic for nervous disorders where the brothers were patients.

As Savinio states in his contemporary texts, several of their images derive from images of the modern city. The large red hand in his masterpiece *L'énigme de la fatalité (The Enigma of Fatality)* was suggested by the image in glove-shop windows, the giant-sized eyeglasses of the trapezoidal painting *La sérénité du savant (The Serenity of the Wiseman)* were taken from the signs of an oculist's shop. Their search for the double and the void logically leads them to derive their inspiration and their themes from shop windows. Furthermore, their careful attention to the vestiges of the city of the future is evident: the tower (the Mole Antonelliana, the tall projection of the Turin synagogue, is joined by the Eiffel Tower, that masterpiece of engineering), the chimneys of the factories, or the train station. One of the most splendid works of that time, formerly in the Soby collection and currently in the New York Museum of Modern Art, represents none other than the Gare Montparnasse, surrounded by the lateral portico which is now destroyed and only known in photographs of the time. It seems surprising that this artist, considered by the Surrealists a painter of fantasy, should be so concerned with the actual sights (which he transforms into vision). It is even more surprising that at this time De Chirico is working in the manner of the ancient painters. Through a study of the drawings in the collection of Paul Eluard

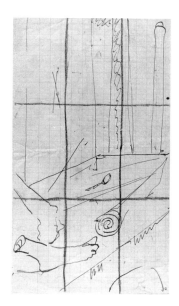

Giorgio De Chirico
drawing for Metaphysical
composition

and later in the Picasso collection, this author was able to recreate the working process of the Metaphysical painter. These drawings reveal his ability to adapt his technique to the theme and its variations (the arcade, Ariadne, the child with the hoop, the wagon) and above all his traditional use of the preparatory drawing, outlined and squared off for transfer on canvas. This is the technique he uses in *Joies et énigmes d'une heure étrange (Joys and Enigmas of a Strange Hour)*, where the blue pencil-marks of the grid are evident, used again in the preparatory drawing for the painting with feet and the chimney. Indeed, traces of this process can be detected on the finished canvas. Already at this time De Chirico is not spontaneous in his "nostalgia of the infinite," but follows a clear and ordered methodology.

Paris 1926-1930: The Surrealist Revolution

The Dioscuri spend seven years in Italy. Between 1919 and 1925, Giorgio De Chirico moves from a Classical to a Romantic phase, while Savinio is occupied with literature and the theater. De Chirico is a major figure in the group headed by Mario Broglio, publisher of the journal *Valori Plastici*, and paints at this time in a strange, romantic fashion (somewhere between Böcklin and Courbet). A self-portrait of the artist with his brother painted in 1924 depicts the Argonauts with a melancholic but confident air — invited to Paris, they are about to be launched separately in the *Ville Lumière*. They have not lost their contacts in Paris. In 1922 Paul Guillaume organizes a one-man show, with an introduction by André Breton, Apollinaire's heir, and in late 1923 Paul Eluard and his wife Gala (later the wife of Dalí) come to Rome to buy a number of his paintings.

The brothers meet again in Paris in July 1926, accompanied by their ever-present mother, Gemma. Giorgio is thirty-eight; Alberto is thirty-five. Both had passed a brief period in Paris in late 1924. Also Savinio had come through Paris at the end of that year. Giorgio saw firsthand the formation of the Surrealist movement, under the guidance of André Breton. The photographs by Man Ray on the cover of *La Révolution Surréaliste* include De Chirico at the center of the group and seem to introduce a new phase.

In these years De Chirico develops a new and disquieting painting style; neither the subject matter nor the "gray matter" have suffered a drop in quality since the first Metaphysical period. Savinio, also, devotes himself completely to painting, becoming more surrealist than the Surrealists. This new period coincides with the debut of Breton's very boisterous group. De Chirico is declared the father of the new movement, but his imaginative disciples quickly reject him, considering him no more advanced than them.

De Chirico produces about 300 works during this period for his dealers Paul Guillaume and Léonce Rosenberg, and for European and American collectors. Savinio paints about 200 canvases and quickly acquires a large market in Paris (Jeanne Castel, Mme Pomaret and Léonce Rosenberg). The world crisis triggered by the Wall Street crash in 1929 does not interrupt their activity. They work together on the decoration of Rosenberg's house, while De Chirico tries his hand in theater, producing the sets for the penultimate performance of Serge Diaghilev's Ballets Russes. At the same time he is preparing for his return to Italy — a new sad voyage for the Argonauts.

Chronology

1926. De Chirico exhibits in Milan (the "Novecento Italiano"), in Europe (Dresden and Brighton) and also in the United States (New York and Boston). In an exhibition at Paul Guillaume's gallery he presents forty-one paintings equally divided between Metaphysical and recent works (the enigma continues). He is supported by several of the dissidents of Surrealism such as Georges Ribemont-Dessaignes and Jean Cocteau, but Marcel Duchamp writes the most enlightened comment on De Chirico's work in the exhibition catalogue of the *Société Anonyme* in Brooklyn: "In about 1926 De Chirico abandoned his Metaphysical conception and turned to a less disciplined brushstroke. His admirers could not follow him and decided that De Chirico of the second manner had lost the flame of the first. Bur posterity may have a word to say." Meanwhile Savinio joins his brother, taking up residence nearby in the Rue Jacob. His first paintings, almost suggesting revelation, are produced in his hotel room. Savinio states: "Art has no point of contact with dreams. Thus should an art ever become one with dreams, and respect the peculiar character of dreams, that is the lack of memory, it would become not only useless but also immoral: no less immoral than the dreams themselves. Thanks to memory we, in looking at images, see what those images were and what they will become: it is the poetry of the glance."

1927. De Chirico is at the height of his new creative phase. The exhibitions overlap: from Zurich to Amsterdam, Berlin to Hamburg. He exhibits at the gallery of Jeanne Bucher in Paris, introduced by Waldemar George, who states: "Deux faits dominent l'art du XX siècle: le fait Picasso et le fait De Chirico." Savinio is introduced to the public for the first time in October at the Bernheim gallery. The catalogue is a cabalistic image by Jean Cocteau: the letters of the name Savinio form the phrase "Son Art Vexe Ingénieusement Nos Imaginations Occidentales" and "Sans Artifices Votre Instrument Nouveau Intrigue Orphée." In a biographical note Savinio recalls that eighteen paintings were sold immediately and cites a comment from the *Bulletin des Arts*: "Savinio is to De Chirico what Cocteau is to Apollinaire."

1928. Savinio is now self-confident as a painter; his works are a calligraphy of dreams which in their imagery owe a great deal to the enigma of his brother, but which are developed with an individual technique (dark and heavy like the unconscious they represent). His daughter Angelica is born while the Surrealist editions Au Sans Pareil announces the book *Angélique ou la nuit de mai*, a text accompanied by lithographs. De Chirico's themes are precise and focused (nostalgic of the Greece of his childhood), and his first one-man shows open in New York (Valentine Gallery) and in London (Tooth and Sons Gallery).
The Surrealists respond aggressively to De Chirico's two solo exhibitions in Paris (Rosenberg gallery) and Brussels with two exhibitions of works (from their collection) dating from his first period. While André Breton's bible of Surrealism, *Le surréalisme et la peinture*, achieves international fame, three books dedicated to the painting of De Chirico appear: a small monograph by the Russian critic Boris Ternovetz, the splendid book by Waldemar George, published in Paris, and a pamphlet by his new Orpheus, Jean Cocteau, entitled *Le mystère laïc - Essai de critique indirecte*.

1929. Many things take place in this year. The most important is certainly De Chirico's work on Diaghilev's *Le bal*, for the Ballets Russes presented in Montecarlo in the spring. The artist's paintings become a stageset of *tableaux vivants*, a scenic and colorful apology to invention. The same renewed inventiveness is seen in the illustrations for Apollinaire's *Calligrammes* and above all in the hermetic novel *Hebdomeros*. When it appears in bookstores at the end of the year, the novel is acclaimed as a masterpiece even by his enemies Breton and Aragon ("un outrage interminablement beau") and by his friends Max Jacob and Michel Leiris (who reviews it in *Documents*), and even by Henry Miller. Meanwhile, Savinio continues working on his paintings, rife with deep mythical significance, in his characteristic plastic style, focusing on the whims of metamorphosis. The two brothers meet in the house of Rosenberg: De Chirico decorates a room with gladiators taken from mosaics of the Late Empire, while Savinio paints a room with monuments to toys, geometric cathedrals dedicated to childhood and to the imagination.

Man Ray, the Surrealist group
Center: Breton, Eluard
De Chirico

Paris of the 1920s sees the triumph of Art Déco, the scandals of Surrealism, the disharmonious harmonies of the Ballets Russes, the death of Marcel Proust, the exotic nudity of Josephine Baker, Coco Chanel and the legend of Montparnasse. Modernity, reflects De Chirico, this strange mystery lives everywhere in Paris, and this seems the ideal stage for someone who has just disguised himself as classical and romantic. All the Surrealists herald the arrival of De Chirico: not only Breton and Paul Eluard, but also René Crevel (who dedicates an important article to the artist), Louis Aragon and Jacques Baron (both purchase his works), Philippe Soupault (who admires both De Chirico and Savinio). The heated dispute which will soon arise is caused by practical matters. The Surrealists cannot entirely accept the new style of painting, so fantastic and strange, attentive to technique but also to the original mystery, to the continuous enigma. In short, they find his new style too surrealist. The Surrealists, collectors of his early works, organize one-man shows of these paintings; however, the artist De Chirico objects to seeing his works of ten years earlier exhibited.

The Surrealists are responsible for the successful acceptance of his early works (and for his debut in the United States), but also for the devaluation of his current paintings. The problem is not one of aesthetics, but perhaps can be traced to commercial reasons and even, ironically, a neurotic state of mind.

During these years of heightened activity, several dissidents of Surrealism continue to believe in Metaphysical painting and follow closely Savinio's artistic debut. Georges Ribemont-Dessaignes and Antonin Artaud are very interested in their work, Roger Vitrac includes two small portraits by the Dioscuri in the frontispieces of two books of poetry. But their true prophet is Jean Cocteau, who recognizes De Chirico's "mystère laïc" ("Chirico, né en Grèce, n'a plus besoin de peindre Pégase. Un cheval devant la mer, par sa couleur, ses yeux, sa bouche, prend l'importance d'un mythe"), and recognizes Savinio's fascination with metamorphosis.

Waldemar George, already a fan of Picasso, backs the *Italiens de Paris* by writing a monograph on De Chirico and several handsome articles on Savinio, the "nouvel Esope." Waldemar sees in the works of Savinio a fantasy of inspiration which is not nordic and puritanical, but which rather preserves the Mediterranean mood. His love

Paintings by Giorgio De Chirico
in Léonce Rosenberg's
Paris apartment

for the Late Empire results in his deep appreciation of De Chirico's *Gladiators* in Rosenberg's house, where the theme of the myth is celebrated.

Another friend, Nino Frank, secretary to Massimo Bontempelli for the journal *900*, writes the only article relating the works of the two brothers (in *Cahiers de Belgique*, 1929). A passage from this article reveals the closeness of the two brothers and their shared style: "The two brothers lived in the same building, one apartment above the other. If I remember correctly, Savinio was on the second floor, De Chirico on the third. And they shared the marvelous Baroness, their mother, who slept at Savinio's apartment and ate almost all her meals with De Chirico, who was then married to his first wife, a quick-witted and cultured Russian. The two brothers responded to their mother quite differently: Savinio did not hesitate to tease her and in a certain sense to flee from her rule, which she exercised as if the two boys were children, while De Chirico was respectful and docile and tried to imitate the perpetual Olympian bearing of the Baroness... While Savinio was communicative and talkative — speaking was more important to him than writing or painting — De Chirico was laconic and assumed a mask of ambiguity and removal... We must not forget the ever-present sense of mystery of the Dioscuri's double inspiration, their more than fraternal shared lifestyle, almost carnal and infinitely profound, in which the mother, the famous and powerful Baroness, played an integral part, the mother who remains in every sense the creator of the Dioscuri."

The participants of the Roaring Twenties are lauded in the essays that Savinio publishes in the Italian newspapers (and which will be published together twenty years later in the book *Souvenirs*): he speaks of Cocteau and Max Jacob, of René Clair and his Surrealist cinema, and of the paunchy ghost, Guillaume Apollinaire, of Paul Guillaume, the brothers' dealer. He refers to Léonce Rosenberg, another of their great protectors and dealers, as follows: "Among the many art dealers who exercised such an important role in the development of the so-called modern art, he was the most worthy, the purest of soul. He understood and appreciated the imagination and poetry of my painting. For several years he bought my paintings regularly."

Between 1928 and 1929 the Dioscuri work together in the house of Rosenberg at 75 Rue de Longchamp. Their paintings are adjacent to those of Picabia and Léger, Max Ernst and Georges Valmier, Jean Metzinger and Gino Severini. The *Hall of Severini*,

146

Alberto Savinio
The Advisers, 1927

Alberto Savinio
L'île des charmes, 1928

a dance in costume held in the Roman forum, suggests a romantic vision of Italy, perhaps the same vision that De Chirico celebrates in the Pompeiian enigma of the *Gladiators* (juxtaposed with real Empire furniture, they carry on an intentionally kitsch dialogue). Savinio, with his *Monuments to Toys*, presents "landscapes of air" and cathedrals of clouds, works which he was unable to write about. And finally, the two rooms painted by De Chirico and Savinio both celebrate a Metaphysical idea: the tragedy of postponed death and the Elysian fields of the hereafter.

Themes

In this period De Chirico involves himself seriously in his work: his *Piccolo trattato di tecnica pittorica* is published in Milan in 1928. While the followers of Breton declare that he is dead, the artist makes a public appearance wearing his less modern mask: this painter of imaginary subjects presents himself as the alchemist of technique. Several of his disciples, such as Dalí, Magritte and Tanguy, will also be concerned with the techniques of antiquity and, in some cases, of the Flemish or Dutch. Savinio's painting develops between 1927 and 1930 as the inverse of the De Chirico coin. His works of 1927 depict a world of statues and childhood photographs rendered in a linear fashion. In 1928 he assumes a heavily coloristic style, as thick as his paintings are crowded (De Chirico is more removed and Olympian).

The heavy impasto used during these years creates a disturbing effect. The image is dark, and even the style assumes the tormented and insidious movements of the Unconscious. The male figures become the muscular types of Michelangelo (whose heads are replaced by buds containing only thought); the Greek heros are placed in compressed or expanded interiors. The rooms are decorated with blowing curtains worthy of the oracle, and the sea appears with the symbols and history of primitive times. The painting is not a daydream but (according to one of the titles) a "souvenir d'un monde disparu."

Savinio seems to have a stronger need to express literary meanings than to devise a real style, and indeed it is this very quality that defines his style, which now reaches its height. During this time De Chirico develops his relationship with the phantoms of the past: he uses the technique and the subjects of Zeuxis, Parrasios, Douris and Apelles. He strives for a surface which resembles encaustic ("a smooth painting") and proposes a linear ("the demon of classicism is the demon of linearity"), graphic style ("the brushstrokes can be very fine, like lines drawn with a sharp pencil or with a pen"). He seeks an effect which is at the same time "opaque and luminous" (like Apelles) and accepts Pliny's idea that painting should include only four colors (even risking the monocromatic). Like Apelles, he seeks the "splendor" of material: "the perfect way of creating interior luminosity." He longs to paint with luminous colors in order to rival fresco painting. And it is in fact this sophisticated search which distinguishes him from the aggressive Surrealists.

De Chirico's themes assume a clear precision. When Jean Cocteau asks him to illustrate the pamphlet in his honor *Le mystère laïc*, the artist submits examples of all his types. The year is 1928. His painting *Cavalli in riva al mare (Horses on the Seashore)* suggests a Greek subject (the horses of the Dioscuri or of Achilles in Thessaly), modernized by the often exotic colors (green adjacent to blue, pink to purple), like those of the components of a rocking horse or a merry-go-round. The *Trofei (Trophies)* are a curious mixture of weapons and faces, architectural fragments and armors, based on the prototype of the *Grande Metafisico (Great Metaphysician)* painted in Ferrara, nearly a parody of Surrealist collage. His *Archeologi (Archaeologists)* are seated mannequins with exaggeratedly large limbs, who remove colored toys or ancient landscapes from their bellies. These philosophers are a transposition of the "gay science" but also a psychoanalytic depiction of the Profound. The *Mobili nella valle (Furniture in the Valley)* suggests the same disorientation of the *Piazze d'Italia* series, with their shifts in time (the mobile becomes immobile) and place (placed outdoors they are the scene of a strange tragedy). *Paesaggi in una stanza (Landscapes in a Room)* develop the opposite theme: the temples and the waterfalls are tamed and decorate the night-table like presences of memory. The last theme is that of the *Gladiators*, which appears also in the novel *Hebdomeros*. Here, the ancient characters have only one destiny, death, yet they do not compete in the arena but rather in a comfortable bourgeois living room which seems to crush them.

Giorgio De Chirico
La joie soudaine, 1926

When the publisher Scheiwiller sends Savinio a questionnaire in 1929 asking him to respond to the question "What is your preferred subject?" Savinio answers: "The absence of subject." Is this not the same idea of enigma that De Chirico was searching for? Or rather, is it not understood that every subject (birds, mythological heroes, identifiable objects) is in reality only superficial and his real concern is perhaps "the tragedy of childhood," the search in one's own soul, paralleling Freud's theories? Many of De Chirico's themes parallel those of his brother. In *Interni-esterni (Interiors-Exteriors)* strange apparitions (a landscape or the ocean) are included inside a normal room, or figures are placed before a window, suspended between "l'être et le néant." The brothers share mannequins and statues and new faceless robots. One of the artists' favorite themes is the *Primordial*: Savinio is inspired by the animals in the science museum (and maintains that the antediluvian period was the most creative and important) and in children's book illustrations. And there is the eternal theme of the *Toys*, sturdy and brightly colored evocations of childhood, that dark but creative period which all have experienced. The theme of Metamorphosis is increasingly present, in which men with animal's heads (does the animal become human or the man return to his primitive state of bestiality?) are represented without the *humour noir* of Max Ernst and the other Surrealists, but are instead constructed like the frescoes of a new Renaissance. A predominant theme is that of *Flight*, a psychoanalytic idea of liberation and active dream, yet another reference to the Voyage and to the Unknown.

Alberto Savinio, *Atlante*, 1927

In 1929 and 1930 the idea of searching for prehistory behind history, of tragic childhood behind bourgeois maturity, the history of a soul beyond the specificity of painting, becomes increasingly important.

"In my case, one does not ask oneself what painting is, but what am I. I will tell you instantly, I am a painter beyond painting. For painters, painting is an end, for some it is a means. Few." Thus Savinio clarifies (with Max Ernst's slogan) the essence of his works. He tries to retrieve a lost totality and defines himself as a "creative power plant." Painting is born from literature and is measured against music or ballet to then return to painting. His process is under the sign of "mystery" but not that of the Surrealists. Breton seeks illumination from the savage or from children, Savinio finds it in his Greece, the continent where the Apollonian and the Dionysiac irrationality and reason, prophecy and revelation, dream and life co-exist. According to Savinio if Surrealism is the "representation of the formless," his painting gives "form to the formless and consciousness to the unconscious."

Methodology

As usual, the Dioscuri are inspired by scenes of the city, behind-the-stage of childhood and the realm of culture. Their paintings are composed according to an indirect, reflexive image, a double: a street sign or an adventure book, a family picture or an archaeological manual. De Chirico is attracted by the images of advertising; indeed he reflects that he was deeply impressed by the poster by Leonetto Cappiello for Poulain chocolate, and in fact that very plumed horse and zebra are soon after included in his paintings.

And then there is the influence of Classical antiquity, which his wife Raissa is studying at the Sorbonne. We are fortunate to have a brief passage by De Chirico's assist-

Alberto Savinio
Self-portrait as Child, 1927

Page of Reinach's *Répertoire*

Labyrinthodon
(prehistoric animal)

Alberto Savinio as a child

ants Salvatore Fornari regarding this: "In Paris during 1926 we assisted De Chirico for several months. We prepared his canvases according to a specific process, washed his brushes, cleaned his palettes... De Chirico lived at that time with his wife Raissa at 30 Rue Bonaparte, in an intimate apartment where a large room was used as a studio. We entered the studio on a cool spring day to find on the easel a painting that did not represent the usual painful togaed mannequins. Instead, there was a thin white horse with a thick mane, a luscious curled tail, galloping along the shore of a grey and sugary ocean. An open book was placed on the Master's chair. With that curiosity about the employer's secrets common to all men, we stuck our noses into the book as if it could reveal the meaning of the new painting. The book was none other than Salomon Reinach's *Répertoire de la statuaire grecque et romaine*, open to the page where the horses of Classical Greek sculpture were quickly sketched. It was the book which his wife used in her class with Prof. Picard at the Sorbonne."

Indeed, Reinach's book provides unlimited sources for the Dioscuri. From it Savinio reproduces Pompeiian paintings and Coptic portraits, in addition to fragments of Greek art, while De Chirico adopts the horses and gladiators. For their "indirect" vision it is important that someone should have already catalogued a world as unbounded as the Classical one, translating it into a linear diagram, almost a stereotype. Reinach's methodology becomes a filter of the German Romantic tradition and of historical archaeology. De Chirico and Savinio are not plagiarists, but rather seek the "double image" (like Dalí will do later on), a linear drawing to transfer, without variation, onto the canvas, and indeed it is this very precision that evokes the metaphysical enigma. Through these manuals they rediscover the reflection of antiquity, just like their Athens that they saw reinvented by the Bavarian architects: Athens and Florence re-created in Munich. Since the ancient world cannot be retrieved entirely, the Dioscuri seek it in the pages of books. They are not interested in "originality" but as always in the "original," the eternal return and the continuous circle.

Savinio's interest in photography must be mentioned (today this would be referred to as the "pop" methodology). His paintings at this time derive from the yellowed family photographs, such as *Autoritratto (Self-portrait)*, one of his first works in which he appears as a fat puppet, his mother resembles a marine monster, his father a threatening figure standing beside his train.

In a brief essay dedicated to the Venice Biennale of 1907, which Savinio saw as a youth, the artist recalls the accusations against Sartorio's reproduction of photographs. Indeed, his discredit lay not in the reproduction of photographs, but in the fact that he did so without imagination. "The more intelligent an artist is, the more he uses indirect methods," states Savinio. He goes on to explain the "lyrical" value of photography which in its anonymous contrast of light and dark produces a "reduction of nature," with the result of revealing the different and the artificial (the first step of art). The modern magician of the image discovers that he must look at reality with the glasses of a "double" because only in this way can the unfocused truth of memory be retrieved.

And finally, the artists use children's books as sources. One of De Chirico drawings in the Picasso collection, a sketch for a famous painting, includes on the book in the foreground the words *Le avventure di Pinocchio*. In 1920 De Chirico states: "I remember as a child the strange and deep impression made by a picture in an old book entitled *The Earth Before the Deluge*. The image reproduced a landscape of the Tertiary period. Man did not yet exist: I have often wondered about this strange phenomenon of the absence of man in metaphysical thought." Indeed, the book by Louis Figuier, a classic of childhood reading, like their adored Jules Verne, influenced Savinio's forests (as demonstrated by Jean Clair). The toys are included in the foreground and the photographs of forests in the background reveal that man's childhood relates to the childhood of the world (*La terre avant le déluge*). Like a librarian of

Babel, Savinio carefully retraces in his paintings of 1927 the world of prehistoric animals found in that book lovingly devoured thirty years earlier.

And finally, their own work provides one of the Dioscuri's most important sources: the probable end of their continuous circle. Thus, De Chirico takes directly from the mannequins of Ferrara or the estranged still lifes of his early Paris period. In their art (which invokes the "disquieting muses") the fundamental role of their mother Mnemosine, the goddess of memory, is evident.

Giorgio De Chirico
Self-portrait with His Brother
(The Dioscuri), 1924

Note

Just ten years ago few people spoke well of Giorgio De Chirico, and his brother Savinio was almost unknown. Today, on the contrary, the two artists are being studied by critics and historians. I feel that in order to clarify their close relationship, we must take a moment to reflect. This study, by choice simple and sketchy, proposes to identify the two Parisian periods in order to correctly analyze two exemplary, parallel lives ("Together we had a single thought," stated Savinio). I wish to refer the reader to several of my other works of the past ten years for additional information.

For biographical data: *La vita di Giorgio De Chirico*, Turin, 1988. For their writings: *Il meccanismo del pensiero, critica polemica autobiografia 1911-1943*, Turin, 1985. Regarding the Metaphysical period: *L'opera completa di De Chirico 1908-1924*, Milan, 1984; *Il tempo di Apollinaire, Paris 1911-1915*, Rome, 1981; *Giorgio De Chirico, i temi della metafisica*, Milan, 1985; "Le carnet de Giorgio De Chirico / Musée Picasso," in *Cahiers du Musée National d'Art Moderne*, Centre Pompidou, Paris, 1984, n. 13, pp. 47-73. Regarding their activity during the 1920s: *Giorgio De Chirico, Parigi 1924-1929*, Milan, 1982; *De Chirico, gli anni venti*, Galleria dello Scudo, Verona (and later Palazzo Reale, Milan), 1987-88, pp. 33-247.

Franco Mancini

La scena è bella: Objectivity and Transfiguration in Gabriele D'Annunzio's Set Designs

In late 19th-century Italy, the stock in trade of the numerous "spot-light chaser" and "touring" companies were productions by the leading French playwrights or their Italian emulators, along with a handful of perennially-popular classics. These productions boasted little in the way of scenery — make-shift cloth backdrops or painted paper *trompe l'œil* effects were considered sufficient — and, irrespective of the varying financial positions of the companies, there was a tendency for a fixed number of backdrops to be used over and over again, with little regard for fidelity to style or the play's specific requirements. The actors each had their own set of costumes, which consisted of: several modern outfits, one "ancient" costume for Greek and Roman tragedies or comedies, one "medieval" outfit (which was worn even for Baroque plays), and one *velada* or *crinolina* for performances of Goldoni's plays. Between 1898 and 1900, the Teatro d'Arte in Turin and the Casa Goldoni in Rome amongst others tried to rebel against such a make-shift approach to stage sets and costumes. Although still-born, these attempts did smooth the way for the advent of Italy's first stock theater companies, the Teatro Argentina in Rome, and the Teatro Manzoni in Milan, established in 1904 and 1912 respectively.

During the period immediately before and after World War I, however, the most vocal attacks on the out-dated practices of Italian theater came from artists who nearly all had a figurative arts background and were involved in the Futurist movement. Recent interest in the revolutionary role of these artists has produced a number of exhibitions and monographic studies[1] that have done much to improve our understanding of their multifaceted contribution to, amongst other things, the renewal of the Italian theater. We will limit our discussion here to a few salient points of the intense debate that flared up around the charismatic figure of Filippo Tommaso Marinetti. In a manifesto dated 1913, Marinetti outlined the basic objectives, putting up for consideration the contrast between the antiquated nature of the traditional "serious" theater and the dynamism and spontaneity of the *Teatro di varietà*. The latter form of production, it was claimed, brought action onto the floor, into the audience, as well as allowing the traditional rules regarding perspective, proportion, time and space to be broken.[2]

The major exponents of the Futurist movement developed these concepts. Giacomo Balla had appeared in a number of memorable productions by the Cabaret Sprovieri,[3] and developed the idea of the *Teatro sintetico*,[4] a series of quickfire sketches, in which the actors used their voices and gestures to imitate machinery. After a series of other projects,[5] Balla set about the production of *Feu d'artifice*[6] at the invitation of Diaghilev. Focused on a series of diverse crystalline forms surrounding a single silver-lamé element, this ballet without dancers provided a chromatic representation of Stravinsky's music by means of a complex interplay of lighting effects.

Fortunato Depero's initial research followed along the same lines. For example, in his piece *Mimismagia*, the main actor was replaced by a sort of "costume-machine" based on the idea of the *uomo-motore* or "man-engine," the mechanical inhabitant of a new world. This idea was similar to the *artificial human being* he put forward in a manifesto published in 1916 about the Futurist reconstruction of the universe.[7] The costume designs he produced in 1916 for Diaghilev's *Le chant du rossignol*[8] also derived from the same source, but they never reached the stage; the choreographer instead asked him to realize the designs for *Parade*, which had been painted by Picasso.[9]

The Cubist influence was evident in Depero's geometric designs for the *Balli plastici* (*Plastic Dances*)[10] a production that also introduced him to the work of Gordon Craig, suggesting the use of marionette theater techniques to create a robot-like character free of the influence of the actor's subjective responses, which had hampered the *uomo-motore* up to then.

The presence of the human figure was also one of the recurring themes in Enrico Prampolini's work. Of the Futurist painters, Prampolini was probably the one who devoted most attention to the theater. Unsatisfied with the two-dimensional *scenosintesi* (synthetic set) and the three-dimensional *scenoplastica* (modelled set), he introduced the idea of four-dimensional *scenodinamica* (dynamic set), which was dominated by an architectural and spatial element, and the play of rhythmic movement. He proposed the contrast between the multi-dimensional theatrical space, or the *absolute* element of theatrical expression, and the *relative* element represented by the actor, a harmful presence to be used as a machine, while the latter was to be used as an actor. *Santa Velocità* (*Holy Speed*)[11] was the practical demonstration of these ideas, and was staged by Prampolini in 1927. This pantomime, without characters or dramatic action, used a plain, neutral backcloth on which chromatic architectures were created with projectors — replacing the *scena illuminata* or illuminated set with a *scena illuminante* or illuminating set, an idea theorized by Prampolini himself as early as 1915 in his manifesto on Futurist scenography.

It was largely thanks to his experiments in 1920 with Achille Ricciardi that Prampolini was able to gradually refine his ideas on the expressive potential of lighting. Ricciardi saw the set as the only visual component of the play, based on the principles of abstraction and dynamism explored by the Futurists, the Russians and the Germans. However, despite D'Annunzio's influential support, Ricciardi's ideas, published in the essay *Il teatro del colore*[12] were only realized in a handful of performances, which ran late and in such ramshackle conditions that they proved a disappointment to the audiences and provided grist for the critics' mill.[13]

Much more fruitful was the long and pioneering career of Anton Giulio Bragaglia, another respected champion of set design's role as both scenery and character and not merely a space-environment framing the dramatic action. Like Ricciardi he operated outside the ambit of the Futurist movement and, like Ricciardi, he based his set designs on the emotive possibilities of the "localized atmospheres created by the use of moving colored lights." Right from his early productions,[14] Bragaglia replaced painted scenery with *luce psicologica* (psychological light), as set out in a manifesto published in 1919.[15] While arousing considerable attention abroad, his experiments fueled a spirited debate in Italy since, according to some, they were redolent not only of Ricciardi's work but also of Balla's *Feu d'artifice*. Bragaglia's merits remain firmly connected to the many scenographic innovations he introduced, his prolific output as an essayist, and above all to his creation of the Teatro degli Indipendenti where, by trial-and-error experiment, he hit on the way to modify dramatic atmospheres according to the script's requirements, with the various possibilities offered by the plastic volumes of the so-called *scenografia ritmica* (rhythmic set design). But, over and above the novelty value of these schematic installations, the tiny theater in Rome's Via degli Avignonesi gained a reputation for specializing in productions which touring companies would have been unlikely to stage.

Rosso di San Secondo, Marinetti, Sebastiano Arturo Luciani, Massimo Bontempelli, Luciano Folgore, Ardengo Soffici, Orio Vergani, and Achille Campanile (Gino Cornabò) are just a few of the writers who found refuge at the "Indipendenti." Luigi Pirandello was another, and Bragaglia presented his *L'uomo dal fiore in bocca* (*The Man with the Flower in his Mouth*)[16] with a stark stage set consisting of a shabby café against a backdrop of a tree-lined avenue. This is one of Pirandello's few plays to require exteriors,[17] as the others are usually set in sophisticated middle-class drawing rooms, austere studies, or opulent ball-rooms, with antique furniture, sofas, divans, writing desks and book shelves. Apart from a few exceptions such as *Sei personaggi in cerca d'autore* (*Six Characters in Search of an Author*), where the action takes place on a bare stage, *Questa sera si recita a soggetto* (*Tonight We Improvise*), which incorporated the theater and the foyer, and *Ciascuno a suo modo* (*To Each His Own*) to a certain extent, Pirandello's plots did not require much variation on the theme of the intimist stage set.[18] Pirandello's stage directions primarily aimed at rounding out the psychology and the physical appearance of the characters, making them come alive, yielding to the forces of their tragic destiny; but they offer little in the way of indications for the setting, leaving it to the discretion of the set designer. One of Pirandello's first set designers was the painter Cipriano Efisio Oppo, who designed the sets for *La sagra del signore della nave*, the opening production of the Teatro d'Arte in April 1925. The play was directed by Luigi Pirandello himself, with the assistance of Mario Pompei[19] and Guido Salvini,[20] who were later involved with other productions of his.[21] Their contribution did not venture beyond the workman-like, and later revivals presented by Maria Signorelli,[22] Pietro Aschieri's 1937 set design for *I giganti della montagna* (*The Mountain Giants*),[23] or even Giorgio De Chirico's first work in the theater (the costumes and sets for the 1924 production of *La Jarre*) did not show much improvement.

Gabriele D'Annunzio's set designs were another matter altogether, even though — with exception of Mario Corsi's and Valerio Mariani's essays,[24] and the exhibition that opened in December 1988 (following theatrical presentations) with installations by Luca Ronconi, commemorating the fiftieth anniversary of the poet's death[25] — his contribution has almost entirely been overlooked.

This neglect is quite unjustified considering that, at the turn of the century, D'Annunzio not only restored the dignity of the dramatic idiom through his treatment of ancient myths and fables in a modern key, but he was also the first person in Italy to suggest a new approach to scenic design. In contrast to the slip-shodness of the producers who were out to make a "fast buck," he proposed three-dimensional sets, based on the dual principle of historic verisimilitude, and close correlation between what we could call the "dramatic environment" and the action. In his own plays, D'Annunzio left nothing to chance or individual interpretation, and he gave the set designer minutely-detailed instructions on every aspect, however negligible, of how the set should look — almost always producing a clear and rational vision. These analytical and elaborate stage directions were the result of patient research; D'Annunzio delved into ancient chronicles, military and naval treatises, scientific and archaeological manuals, and tracts on the history of art and costumes. They also bear witness to the experiences "lived" by the writer himself in his frequent travels to different cities, museums, temples and monuments.

D'Annunzio's desire to provide the audience with a visual backdrop based on the most solid historic documentation possible is clearly evident in almost each of the plays he wrote over a span of fifteen years[26] even if, as Silvio D'Amico has pointed out, the facile symbolism of some of the earlier attempts[27] makes it difficult "to ignore the exaggerated prominence given to the spoken word, over and above the proud and painfully amateur quality of the stage sets."[28] But the production of *La Gioconda*[29] prompted Edoardo Boutet to write that its star, Eleonora Duse, deserved special mention for having ensured that the scenery was created with an unusual unity of vision. "She chose not to rifle through the often garish stock of the theatrical suppliers for the fabrics and the furniture. She made sure furniture and fabrics were all coordinated within the setting, and, never losing her eye for refinement, she applied her mind to choosing exactly the right smaller props, turning her back on the colored cardboard, painted wood, and assorted, often cheap, junk of the props department."[30] In the Italian production of *La città morta* (*The Dead City*)[31]

G. D'Annunzio, *The Dead City*
Featuring Eleonora Duse
and Ines Cristina
Teatro Lirico, Milan, 1901

the attention to the formal detail was matched by an unusually strong link between the setting for the action and the mood of the piece. The classical theme of incestuous obsession, which was the central motif of the drama, was foreshadowed by the stage set: an interior of a *loggia* overlooking the "ancient city of the Pelopides," where, as described in the stage directions, "there are moldings of statues, bas reliefs, inscriptions and fragments of statues: all of them testimony of an isolated life, vestiges of a lost beauty. The mass of these white objects gives the room a clear, sharp effect, almost tomb-like, in the immobility of the morning sunlight."

If this work was the culmination of the impressions gained during his long journey through Greece, the strong link that bound the poet to the so-called cities of silence (*città del silenzio*) inspired him to write *Francesca da Rimini*,[32] an historical tragedy, based on the story of Francesca's tragic love affair with her nephew, which Dante had included in Canto V of the *Inferno*. In this work, the scenery played a more complex and integral part than in his previous plays. Preparations for the production — which, after a number of setbacks, finally opened in 1901 — were extraordinarily complex. D'Annunzio, with his comprehensive knowledge of Medieval Italy, wanted to achieve an absolutely accurate reconstruction of the Romagna region, where Dante wrote much of the *Divine Comedy*. Consequently he insisted on supervising every single detail of the set design; he personally scrutinized the fabrics chosen for the costumes designed by Caramba,[33] the wigs produced by Edouard Doudel (the Honorary President of the Académie-Ecole Française de Coiffure de Paris), the props and furnishings carved by Andrea Baccetti, the arms provided by the Florentine Tani, and the details of how the crowd-scenes, coordinated by Luigi Rasi, would be staged. The scenery was constructed by Odoardo Antonio Rovescalli,[34] and the painter Adolfo De Carolis[35] — who had been in the employ of D'Annunzio for some time as an illustrator — was responsible for the decorations, and probably much more, considering D'Annunzio wrote him a long letter describing costumes and scenery, down to the finest detail.[36] His sketches, which were carefully executed according to the poet's lengthy instructions, and D'Annunzio's trust in De Carolis' judgment, demonstrated by his request for details regarding a new scene in the play just a few days before a revival of *Francesca da Rimini*, and his request for the artist to be present at the stage setting and the lighting rehearsals[37] illustrate the climate of harmony and understanding in which these two worked.

Adolfo De Carolis and Odoardo Antonio Rovescalli were, therefore, the master craftsmen behind this spectacular set; in it they achieved a formal sophistication —

Sets by A. De Carolis
and A. Rovescalli
for G. D'Annunzio's play
La Francesca da Rimini
Featuring Eleonora Duse
Teatro Costanzi, Rome, 1901

Sets by F.P. Michetti
for Act I of G. D'Annunzio's play
Iorio's Daughter
Teatro Lirico, Milan, 1904

Sets by F.P. Michetti
for Act II of G. D'Annunzio's play
Iorio's Daughter
Teatro Lirico, Milan, 1904

Sets by F.P. Michetti
for Act III of G. D'Annunzio's play
Iorio's Daughter
Teatro Lirico, Milan, 1904

in the case of the Rocca dei Polentani based on studies of Ferrarese paintings, and impressions from on-the-spot observations — and helped to create a feeling of historical realism unprecedented in Italian theater. The second act featured the bastions of the Malatesta castle; this time the author had asked the property manager Bergonzi to ensure that the Medieval weapons — which included cross-bows, cauldrons of boiling pitch, and even a vast mangonel weighing several tons — were all in perfect working order. While some critics felt that this vast array of props overwhelmed the action, others believed that it formed an integral part of the play and corresponded to the psychological grounds of the drama, and that the characters "would not have been what they were, and they would not have acted the way they did, had it not been for the presence of all these appurtenances to their every-day life."[38] Far from being passive presences, and simply decorative details, these objects were playing a specific "dramatic" role as conceived by D'Annunzio, who insisted that during the battle scenes the action was to be enhanced by the shouts of the warriors, smoke, and flames.

But the first night, which only came about thanks to the intervention of Eleonora Duse[39] herself — was marred when the carefully-planned special effects exceeded their creator's expectations, provoking a series of incidents which offered considerable grist to the mill of the poet's many critics. During the second act, the actors' voices were drowned by the cries of the extras who had thrown themselves heart and soul into their role of creating fight scenes, and the whole collapsed into a farce when an (authentic) rock, fired by the mangonel on the Malatesta ramparts, hit a set and brought it crashing down. The worst incident occurred when the smoke from the vat of boiling pitch and the "Greek fire" created by the chemist Helberg spilled into the audience, causing many of them to rush for the door, blinded and gasping for breath, amidst the sound of coughing, shouting and derisory whistles.

The director, whom it was said had "let himself get carried away by the desire to overwhelm the audience's senses,"[40] found himself the target of numerous accusations, even though Domenico Oliva, normally a harsh critic of D'Annunzio, said of the show's visual appeal, "This was truly a work of art: each scene is a painting, and the costumes could have been created by the greatest Italian painters: the overall effect is of a truly aesthetic grandeur."[41]

Another review commented on the fact that, although the action was set in the 13th century, the architecture of the Da Polenta palace was, in fact, 16th-century, the towers were not the same shape as those of the Malatesta castle, and the Flemish organ and the windows with three lights in Francesca's room were all further anachronisms. Isidoro Del Lungo came to the poet's defense by suggesting that the historians should be the ones to judge the production's historical veracity or otherwise, and passing on to a lengthy discussion of the effects produced by D'Annunzio's stage sets, which "form part of his whole poetic vision, convey the Medieval atmosphere as he conceived it, studied it, and made it his own, giving expression to it in terms both of people and things."[42]

The style introduced in *Francesca da Rimini* was further refined in *La figlia di Iorio* (*Iorio's Daughter*),[43] a pastoral tragedy inspired by the painting of the same name by Francesco Paolo Michetti. The painter, who like D'Annunzio was born in Pescara, helped design the sets and costumes for the play. In a letter dated 31 August 1903, D'Annunzio seemed to have taken to heart Lugné-Poe's ironical challenge that true champions of realism should use only authentic furniture in their stage sets, for he wrote to his friend, "We must at all cost *avoid any theatrical falsehoods*: we must search out utensils, objects, and furnishings that breathe life." In a later text, he returns to the themes dear to his heart and asks that "the costumes look *archaic*, and have a touch of the *barbarian* and the *long-ago* about them, so they can immediately transport the audience back in time, almost into the land of legend."[44]

A production of this sort created considerable difficulties since, in addition to the search for authentic props and furnishings, about 150 costumes for the leading actors, the extras, and the choruses of reapers and mourners needed to be sketched. According to the documentation available, Francesco Paolo Michetti made every effort to overcome difficulties and, assisted by one of his students, the painter Arnoldo Ferraguti, he set about scouring the Abruzzo region for period clothes, headgear and necklaces. The search was fruitless however, and the few old clothes found in Ferraguti's house, or in the market at Chieti, had to be complemented by costumes made up in Milan under the supervision of Ferraguti, who had been entrusted with Michetti's sketches, the *maestro* himself having just been taken ill.[45]

The search for props was more successful however: the rustic finds included vats, barrels, pots, spinning wheels, ploughs, babies' cradles, carpets, leather bags, majolica tiles, and even a massive weaving loom, all used to great effect on the three sets all of which Michetti had sketched out at the hermitage at Francavilla (the Grotta del Cavallone was used as model for the cave of Aligi). While Edoardo Antonio Rovescalli's scenery might look dated to the modern eye, it was not only a faithful reproduction of the stage directions, but it also offered a metahistoric and crudely realistic representation of the Abruzzo region. As Mario Corsi has pointed out, it reflected "the mystical and sensual destiny that weighed down on the powerful and dynamic characters of pastoral tragedy."[46]

The triumphal success of this production was followed by the failure of the second Abruzzi tragedy, *La fiaccola sotto il moggio* (*The Torch under the Bushel*).[47] While lacking the dramatic tension of its predecessor, this piece did confirm the poet's extraordinary capacity for linking environment and action: the plot, set "amongst the wild gorges of the Sagittario" in the area of Anversa degli Abruzzi, called for a single set depicting, as described in the stage directions, "a huge hall in the ancestral home of the Sangro family, built on the uneven summit of a hill. The Norman building bears the weight of stone and terracotta additions, the marks left by each successive generation from the Angevins to the reign of the Bourbons." The buttressed arches, the wooden scaffolding, the sacks lying around, and the rough wooden ladders propped up against the walls created the impression of the desolation and ruin of an old stately home, and the decline of an aristocratic Bourbon family, the symbol of an entire social system. The set, which was carried out by Rovescalli to the sketches of Adolfo De Carolis, highlighted D'Annunzio's commit-

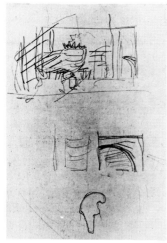

G. D'Annunzio, *The Ship*
autographed sketch

Sketch by D. Cambellotti
for G. D'Annunzio's play *The Ship*
Teatro Argentina, Rome, 1908

Sketch by D. Cambellotti
for G. D'Annunzio's play *The Ship*
Teatro Argentina, Rome, 1908

ment, but its sophistication did little to change the largely negative tone of the reviews. Similarly, a year later, the copy of a statue from the Parthenon — which had been moved onto the stage of the Teatro Costanzi by permission of Corrado Ricci and Ettore Ferrari — could not alter the fate of *Più che l'amore* (*More than Love*)[48] which was received with undisguised hostility by critics and public alike.

Undaunted by these two failures, D'Annunzio went on to offer one of the most potent and convincing displays of the expressive power of his style of scenography in *La nave* (*The Ship*),[49] which was staged by the Compagnia Stabile Romana in 1908. The scenes and costumes for this "Adriatic tragedy" — which was, as the author wrote, "molded by the mud of the Lagoon, the gold of Byzantium, and the life force of my most ardent passion for Italy"[50] — confirmed the merits of the multitalented artist, Duilio Cambellotti,[51] who had only recently become involved in the theater. The suggestion to use Cambellotti probably came from the Baron Rudolf Kanzler, an authoritative figure in the Stabile company and a consultant for the production. (The poet often turned to him for advice on various problems, such as how to style the beams to impart "an enormous expressive force in their roughhewn simplicity."[52]) Cambellotti proved to be ideally suited to tackling such problems right from the start, when he showed that he had many of the attributes D'Annunzio considered essential, such as a natural predilection for archaeology, a distinct preference for a plastic set, a marked manual dexterity, as well as an enthusiasm for exploiting new scenographic possibilities.

According to the dedication written by D'Annunzio, Cambellotti had been "prodigiously successful in transforming the humble materials," to "make the richness of that dream a reality,"[53] in the complex stage set which "was designed to enhance the sonorous flow of the words, with the massive frame of the ship under construction, and the Church of the Arengo."[54] Acting on the suggestion of the author, Cambellotti visited the small port of Lussimpiccolo to capture the gestures of the Istrian fishermen, and the exact shape of the boats built at the Lido at first hand. Thus learned references to the mosaics at Ravenna and St. Mark's in Venice, as well scenes from books of nautical art, were integrated with personal observations of the attire and traditions of the sea-going people.

On the left hand side of the massive stage set, most of which was painted by Leonida Liverani, was the third, and final, "episode," which consisted of an entire arsenal with the gigantic hull of the ship *Totus Mundus*. It proved necessary to call

upon the services of a master ship-builder, a certain Cupellini, who was able to guarantee not only the realism of the boat but who also solved the difficult problem of the ship's launch which takes place at the end of the play. Unlike the performance of *Francesca da Rimini*, this time things went smoothly and the first night, termed by some "a prophetic announcement of Italy's destiny in the Adriatic," guaranteed the play's success. This unexpected triumph was due in no small measure to the current political climate, but also to the superb scenery, whose influence would be reflected in Cambellotti's later set designs for the Greek theater at Syracuse in Sicily, and has remained one of the high-points of modern Italian scenography.

A year later, *Fedra* (*Phaedra*)[55] offered the by-now veteran team of De Carolis and Rovescalli a chance to create a stage set fit for an operatic production, with a wealth of powerful effects — from the dramatic lighting effects in the first act that traced the rhythm of a magnificent peristyle's columns, half-buried in the shadows, to the sensational device of six stallions (borrowed from the Sidoli circus) to draw the main character's chariot. The actors' performance was markedly below expectations and contributed to the show's failure, though it had been blighted from the start by the author's inattention; D'Annunzio was absorbed in the affairs of his own tumultuous private life, that would shortly force him to take refuge in France.

This voluntary exile did, however, give him the opportunity to confirm the potential of his vision, a type of theater based on the value of scenography. This was, in fact, the main thrust of the two spectacular shows that he offered to Parisian audiences, acquainting them with "the magnificence of his Byzantinism."[56]

In his introduction to *Le martyre de Saint Sébastien* (*The Martyrdom of Saint Sebastian*),[57] a religious play in which the decline of paganism is seen in counterpoint to the rise of Christianity, D'Annunzio claimed to have been inspired by the stained glass artists: "I have divided my theatrical stained glass window into four large segments, filling them with multitudes of figures, and I have placed the image of the transfigured saint at the very top. The whole of the action seems to take place in transparency, between the gloom of the church and the light of day. Strong, clean lines, like the window leading, surround the characters. Clear bright colors, like those used in stained glass, reveal them, together and separately, in large groups."[58]

For the show's scenery and costumes D'Annunzio found another talent whose aggressive domineering spirit was much like his own. This artist, Léon Bakst,[59]

158

Sets by L. Bakst for
G. D'Annunzio's play *La Pisanelle*
Théâtre du Châtelet, Paris, 1913

Costume by L. Bakst for
G. D'Annunzio's play *La Pisanelle*
Théâtre du Châtelet, Paris, 1913

produced vibrant compositions with a chromatic exuberance that nearly eclipsed the stylized pattern of the original design. Bakst was also an expert in oriental illuminated texts, and the Minoan civilization. The *Martyre* could not but fire the enthusiasm of this typical exponent of oriental-style figurative art, and Bakst united elements of the Byzantine decorative arts with the special skills of the Cosmati families of marble workers from the Rome area to create a spectacular set, which is still considered one of the best in his long career as a set designer. Most acclaimed were the sets for the Third Act, entitled *Le concile des faux dieux*, with their double rows of "heavy and voluptuous" twisted columns in which some saw a representation of D'Annunzio's "sensuality in the round,"[60] permeating the whole of the play. Ida Rubinstein's interpretation of the saint was the crowning touch to an exceptionally high-level figurative performance as it opened in Paris in 1911, her study of the paintings of Mantegna, Pollaiolo, and Sodoma having contributed greatly to the plasticity of the movements.

Visual aspects were no less important in the play *La Pisanelle ou la mort parfumée*,[61] a profoundly pagan piece, which provided another personal triumph for the Russian-born Bakst two years later. The set design was inspired by illuminated missals, and D'Annunzio decided that, in order for the set to provide a key to the drama, each scene was to have its own color. For the Prologue, set in Cyprus in a hall of the palace of the Prince of Tyre, the color blue was chosen; a blood-red curtain opened onto the scene in the port of Famagosta, and the cloister of the monastery of Sainte Claire was done in white. In the Third Act, the vast Gothic hall, featuring the throne of the Queen of Cyprus and two enormous doorways, one opening onto a marble staircase and the other onto a flower-filled garden, was light green, as was the curtain with its wide diagonal stripes. Stars, crests, fleurs de lis, lions rampant, heraldic symbols, tapestries, and damasks enhanced the grandeur of these scenes, which looked like paintings on parchments, framed by two Gothic columns on either side of the stage, between which hung a curtain decorated with gold circles, surmounted by a canopy. While decidedly cool towards the play itself, both critics and public agreed on the sophistication and beauty of the sets. This sentiment was echoed in Roberto De Flers's review in *Le Figaro*, in which he claimed never before to have seen a play where "harmony between the sounds and colors has been so successfully achieved."[62]

Opulence and splendor gave way to sobriety — of outstanding beauty nonetheless — chosen for the next play, a modern drama called *Le Chèvrefeuille*.[63] The last of the three acts, each of which created a different atmosphere, was the most striking: a vast terrace — where the three characters stand immobile throughout — half-covered by an arch, and bordered on one side by a stone parapet over which could be seen a tragic sky and the dark profiles of a stand of cypress trees. The same play, translated as *Il Ferro*, was later seen in Italy, with a set design by Odoardo Antonio Rovescalli who, even without the author's direct intervention, successfully confirmed D'Annunzio's ability to use sets to define a play's dramatic atmosphere. Fausto M. Martini's review of the play included the acute comment that, "once again we have seen how a great poet is capable of giving substance and life to the immaterial. Gabriele D'Annunzio has created a character called Nightmare, Shadow, and Death. We sense this character as strongly in the first act of *Il Ferro*[64] as we did the unctuous unwelcome guest in Maurice Maeterlinck's *L'intruse* (*The Intruder*). This is an amazing achievement on the part of Gabriele D'Annunzio. He makes the air, trees, walls, objects, and furniture more eloquent than the words of men and women, At certain points it is almost as though he has established a dialogue with our most subliminal conscience, who replies direct. The other amazing thing is the deep correlation between things and people: this is the power of atmosphere."[65]

The play *Il Ferro* was D'Annunzio's last piece either for the Parisian, or the Italian, theater.[66] However his talents as a man of the theater came to the fore once again in 1927 with a revival of *La figlia di Iorio* at Gardone Riviera. This formed part of a long-standing project for an open-air theater on the shores of Lake Albano, first planned over thirty years earlier by the poet and Eleonora Duse.[67] In a letter to the play's director, Giovacchino Forzano, D'Annunzio included these words, "You will undoubtedly find, and invent — in the true sense of the word — the actors and actresses. You will be able to overcome the falsehood of bombastic declamation which disfigured my best-constructed plays for many years. You will be able to reduce the stage sets to the barest essentials."[68] Such suggestions — which were in fact entirely appropriate to the specific needs of open-air theater — were, quite wrongly, assumed by some critics to imply a complete break from the emphatic grandiloquence of his earlier work.[69]

While the myriad fragments that document this story — reviews, chronicles, sketches, and photographs — can give little more than a general idea of the objective value of those historic "first nights", they do reveal enough to help us appreciate the influence their creator had on the future of the Italian theater. In the first place, it is clear that very few other playwrights have understood as clearly as D'Annunzio did the importance of the stage set to the entire production, while even fewer have been able to create stage sets as "learned" and detailed as his. It is no coincidence that, while he always had the choice of the best actors, D'Annunzio was often content to accept changes in the cast list, but steadfastly refused to accept any compromises that might jeopardize the success of his meticulously-supervised stage sets, as Stanislavski had done before him. The formal aspects of the production took on such importance for him that they became the catalyst for his poetic vision, and in many cases, contrary to normal progression, it was the evocative force of certain settings that provided the creative stimulus for his dramas. *La città morta* was prompted by his voyage to Greece and King Minos' Crete, while Italy's ancient cities spawned *Francesca da Rimini*. It is no surprise therefore to find that, while in some plays such as *La figlia di Iorio* and to a lesser extent *Francesca da Rimini*, *La Gioconda*, and *Più che l'amore*, the visual environment and script were perfectly balanced, in others, where the poetic input was weaker, the scenography stole the show, relegating the performance to second place.

It is undoubtedly true that D'Annunzio's aspiration to "supreme beauty," which he

Il Parentado

Costumes by Caramba (Luigi Sapelli) for G. D'Annunzio's play *Iorio's Daughter* Vittoriale, 1927

Lazaro di Rojo

Costume by Caramba (Luigi Sapelli) for G. D'Annunzio's play *Iorio's Daughter*, Vittoriale, 1927

pursued with almost maniac intensity and scant regard for cost, often caused the role of the scenography to be amplified even beyond his intentions; this provided a royal opportunity for all those who sought, right or wrong, to attach labels to a difficult and larger-than-life character who, for reasons often related to his artistic work, was simultaneously loved and hated, worshipped and ignored, praised and reviled. But his aesthetic excesses were insufficient to justify the hard-hitting criticism of Gino Gori, who included D'Annunzio among those who "demand an erudite architecture of scenery, music, song, and dance; but these elements do not arise from the dramatic structure, they are merely a garnish that he may attempt to pin to part of the dramatic structure, but he will never succeed in causing their full integration or creating dialogue between the two. The *quid dicendum novi* does not appear, because it is missing. These pervasive extraneous elements should be subordinate to the spoken phrase. Since the spoken word — with its lyricism, its sweeping range, its ardor and its flights — predominates, it becomes a song. And thus it is able to conceal the absolute existence of the very weakest, or totally absent, tragic content."[70]

Whatever his real contribution as a playwright, we must acknowledge that D'Annunzio, dubbed *L'Immaginifico*, did succeed in blending an innate ability as a manipulator of words, with a no less instinctive skill in manipulating theatrical devices. Over and above an objective and well-documented reconstruction, it is quite clear that D'Annunzio's efforts were to create an atmosphere in harmony with the text's dramatic climate, the result of which is a kind of lyrical transformation. Fausto M. Martini, as quoted earlier, clearly understood this, as did Isidoro Del Lungo, who remarked on the "audacious inaccuracy" in various "shifts and assimilations" in the stylistic liberties taken in *Francesca da Rimini*, leading Camilleri to comment that, "we already have an insight of how the show as a whole can be considered a critical interpretation of the text: other productions, however acclaimed, had never opened up such bold horizons."[71]

The many innovations introduced by D'Annunzio's stage sets, such as the highly complex scenes involving crowds of people, heralded the advent of a "dynamic" style of stage set. This new characteristic, along with other "special effects," was widely exploited — albeit for quite different reasons — by the Futurists in their irreverent and iconoclastic attacks on the official theater. Even though not entirely intentional, we should not neglect audience participation in the smoke-scenes in *Francesca da Rimini* — the idea of having been the first to experiment with "poison gas" amused D'Annunzio considerably — and the smell of the pitch used to coat the shell of the ship that wafted through the theater during performances of *La nave*.

In addition, Achille Ricciardi, who like the poet was from Pescara, provides first-hand evidence of how closely D'Annunzio followed the experiments taking place during that period, and remarks on the "intriguing results" achieved in Florence together with Gordon Craig in the attempt to "create an overall luminous atmosphere which would eliminate the violence and harshness of the light and shade from the projectors."[72]

Over and above the formal implications peculiar to a specific era, it is not difficult to recognize a number of ideas in his work which would be adapted and developed in the years following World War II. It would be easy to underestimate the extent of D'Annunzio's influence in the light of the scant recognition accorded his work today — a stark contrast to the tumultuous acclaim it received in the first decades of the century — and the massive weight of preconceptions that still reflect negatively on his contribution, not the least of which involves his collaboration with the Fascist regime. New productions of his plays by such people as Giorgio De Chirico, Antonio Valenti, Virgilio Marchi, Aldo Calvo, Guido Marussig, Cesare Maria

Cristini, and in more recent years Renato Guttuso, Pier Luigi Pizzi, and Enrico Job — albeit based on different degrees of commitment and varied results — have been insufficient to sweep away such preconceptions. There has been a recent claim that the only way to restore D'Annunzio's work to its proper place in our time is to let go of the myth of *Dannunzianismo* that surrounds him and his *opus* and concentrating on a textual re-interpretation of the words he wrote.[73] To this, we would add that if, once and for all, we want to eliminate the doubts that still persist on the value of his work as a director *ante litteram*, we will need to undertake a more in-depth analysis of the productions created by this unique man of the theater who rightly deserves recognition as a leading figure in the history of contemporary theatrical scenography.

Sets by G. De Chirico
for G. D'Annunzio's play
Iorio's Daughter, 1934

Notes

[1] For bibliographical information, see F. Mancini, *L'evoluzione dello spazio scenico dal naturalismo al teatro epico*, Bari, 1975, pp. 108-114.

[2] *Teatro di Varietà*, Milan, 23 September 1913.

[3] *Il funerale del filosofo passatista* by Francesco Cangiullo, 13 April 1914; *Piedigrotta*, by Francesco Cangiullo and *Discussioni di due critici sudanesi sul Futurismo*, 29 March 1915.

[4] *Synthetic Theatre* (*teatro sintetico*) was launched in 1915 in a manifesto signed by, among others, Marinetti, Settimelli, and Corra.

[5] *Sconcertazione di stati d'animo, Per comprendere il pianto*, 1916.

[6] *Feu d'artifice*, music by Igor Stravinsky, Teatro Costanzi, Rome, 12 April 1917.

[7] *Complessità plastica, Gioco libero futurista, L'essere vivente artificiale*, handwritten manifesto, 1916.

[8] *Le Chant du rossignol*, commissioned from Depero in 1916 but unrealized, since Diaghilev canceled the performance, perhaps at the instigation of Cocteau.

[9] *Parade*, choreography by Léonide Massine, music by Erich Satie, set and costumes by Pablo Picasso, Paris, Théâtre du Châtelet, May 1917.

[10] The *Balli plastici* (or *Plastic Dances*) were performed on 14 April 1918 at the Teatro dei Piccoli, by the Gorni dell'Acqua marionette company.

[11] *Santa Velocità*, a mime show by Enrico Prampolini was staged in 1927 at the Théâtre de la Madeleine, in Paris, with sets and costumes by Prampolini himself, and musical score by Luigi Russolo.

[12] Achille Ricciardi set out his ideas in an article published in the 8 May 1906 edition of *Secolo XIX*, and in later essays which were collected in 1913 under the title of *Il Teatro del colore*, at the suggestion of Gabriele D'Annunzio, but not published until 1919.

[13] Performances of *Teatro del colore* were held at the Teatro Argentina from 20 to 30 March, 1920, with sets and costumes by Enrico Prampolini and Ugo Giannattasio, included a variety of heterogeneous plays many of which were by Symbolist authors, such as *Il velo della felicità* by G. Clemenceau, *Ditirambo III* and *Novilunio* from Gabriele D'Annunzio's *Laudi*, *La nuit d'octobre* by Alfred de Musset, *Rose di carta* by Luciano Folgore, *L'intruse* by Maeterlinck, *L'après-midi d'un faune* by Stéphane Mallarmé, *Lo schiavo* by Achille Ricciardi, *Kitra* by Rabindranath Tagore, *Salomé* by Oscar Wilde, *Le bâteau ivre* by Arthur Rimbaud, and, *Simun* by August Strindberg.

[14] *La bella addormentata* by Rosso di San Secondo, Teatro Olimpia, Milan, 1919.

[15] *Sinopsie e trasposizioni visive della musica*, manifesto signed by Anton Giulio Bragaglia, S.A. Luciani, and Franco Casavola.

[16] *L'uomo dal fiore in bocca* was performed at the *Indipendenti* on 21 February 1921 along with *All'uscita*, another one-act play by Pirandello.

[17] Some of the few Pirandello pieces that involve exteriors are: *Non si sa come* (terrace), *Quando si è qualcuno* (garden), *All'uscita* (country landscape with cemetery), *La nuova colonia* (rocky island promontory), *Lazzaro* (hanging garden and atrium), *La signora Morlì, uno e due* (garden), *La giara* (grassy clearing), *L'altro figlio* (path), *Liolà* (Argrigento countryside with shed), and *L'innesto* (open space in front of a villa).

[18] Variations on the theme of classical middle-class sets include: the interior of a derelict house (*La nuova colonia*), the editorial offices of a political newspaper (*La ragione degli altri*), a sculpture studio (*Diana e la Tuda*), a room in a boarding-house (*Come prima, meglio di prima*), an editorial office (*Quando si è qualcuno*), and a corridor in a gymnasium (*Pensaci Giacomino*).

[19] Mario Pompei was responsible for the sets to *Ma non è una cosa seria* (1926) and *Come prima, meglio di prima* (1927).

[20] Guido Salvini, who was also involved in directing from 1925 to 1927, was responsible for the stage sets for a number of Pirandello's plays (almost all of which were world premieres), staged at the Teatro d'Arte, including *Sei personaggi in cerca d'autore*, *Così è (se vi pare)*, *Il piacere dell'onestà*, *Vestire gli ignudi*, *Due in una*, *La vita che ti diedi*, *Il giuoco delle parti*, *L'uomo, la bestia e la virtù*, *Il berretto a sonagli*, *Tutto per bene* and *L'uomo dal fiore in bocca*.

[21] Pompei's noteworthy set designs include a 1936 production of *Liolà* by the De Filippo Company. Salvini was director and set designer of *Questa sera si recita a soggetto*, presented as a world premiere in 1930 by his own company which included Renzo Ricci and Carlo Ninchi.

[22] In 1937, Maria Signorelli presented *L'imbecille*, *L'uomo dal fiore in bocca*, and *Il berretto a sonagli* for the Guf Experimental theater, and in 1940 she presented *Non si sa come* for the Teatro dell'Artistica Operaia.

[23] *I giganti della montagna*, directed by Renato Simoni and Girogio Venturini, sets by Pietro Aschieri, costumes by Mattia De Matteis, was performed as a world premiere at the Boboli Gardens, Florence, on 5 June 1937.

[24] Cf. M. Corsi, *Le prime rappresentazioni dannunziane*, Milan, 1928 and "D'Annunzio regista e scenotecnico," in *Rivista italiana del dramma*, II, 1940; V. Mariani, "Scenografia dannunziana," in *Scenario*, 4 April 1938.

[25] Cf. "D'Annunzio. La scena del Vate," exhibition organized by Luca Ronconi, Milan, Museo Teatrale alla Scala, 6 December 1988 - 4 February 1989.

[26] Between 1897 and 1912, D'Annunzio wrote sixteen dramas and tragedies, eight each in verse and in prose, all except the first two having more than three acts.

[27] *Sogno di una notte di primavera*, Théâtre de la Renaissance, Paris, 15 June 1897, Eleonora Duse Company. This first production was followed by *Sogno d'un tramonto d'autunno*, which was published in 1899, but was not staged until 2 December 1905 at the Teatro Rossini in Livorno by the Fumagalli-Franchini Company.

[28] S. D'Amico, *Storia del teatro drammatico*, vol. IV, Milan, 1940, p. 273.

[29] *La Gioconda*, Teatro Bellini, Palermo, 15 April 1899, Eleonora Duse-Ermete Zacconi Company. On 27 April, the same company staged *La Gloria* at the Teatro Mercadante in Naples, with sets designed by Piero Stroppa. The play failed mainly for political reasons.

[30] The excerpt from Eduardo Boutet's article "Allestimento scenico" which appeared in *Le cronache drammatiche* of 14 May 1899, is reproduced in A. Camilleri, *I teatri stabili in Italia (1898-1918)*, Bologna, 1959, pp. 32-33.

[31] *La città morta* was presented by Eleonora Duse at the Teatro Lirico in Milan on 20 March 1901, having previously been performed in French, as *La ville morte* at the Théâtre de la Renaissance in Paris on 21 January 1898, starring Sarah Bernhardt.

[32] *Francesca da Rimini*, Teatro Costanzi, Rome, 9 December 1901, Eleonora Duse Company, set design by Odoardo Antonio Rovescalli, decorations by Adolfo De Carolis, furnishings by Andrea Baccetti, costumes by Caramba, arms by Tani, crowd scenes choreographed by Luigi Rasi. According to S. D'Amico, IV, p. 274, this was the first time Duse saw one of D'Annunzio's plays through to success, despite protests and controversy.

[33] The journalist and caricaturist Luigi Sapelli (1865-1936) adopted the pseudonym *Caramba* and became a successful set and — especially — costume, designer. His first project, in 1887, was to design the set and direct two operettas *D'Artagnan* and *La cicala e la formica*, for the Ciro Scognamillo company. The success of these projects enabled him to set up his own company, with which he worked until 1898, when he was invited to join the newly-formed Teatro d'Arte in Turin as set designer. A prolific designer, he produced thousands of costumes for the leading Italian theater companies in the early decades of this century. Some of his sketches, most of which are in black-and-white, with techni-

cal notes and swatches attached, are still extant. He was appointed director of set installations for the Scala Theater in Milan in 1921 — a post he held until his death. He also worked in the cinema, where his most memorable work was for a film based on Dante's *Vita Nova*, in which he was able to exploit his taste for the pre-Raphaelites.

[34] Odoardo Antonio Rovescalli (1864-1936) was only twelve years old when he was apprenticed to his uncle Luigi Dell'Era, the set designer for the Teatro Manzoni in Milan. He later studied perspective at the Brera Academy, where one of his teachers was Carlo Ferrario, whose philosophy he was to remain faithful to, even after he was influenced by the Modernist movements. As Maria Muraro (1961, p. 1286) points out, despite the fact that he spent time working abroad with the leading actors of the day, including Sarah Bernhardt, Coquelin Ainé, and Juditte in France, and Maria Guerrero in Spain, his name is always associated with shows starring Eleonora Duse. A particularly fruitful project was his collaboration with Francesco Garzes (who committed suicide in 1894) as these were the first shows in Italy to use specially built scenery, with real furnishings and lights. He later set up a company with Caramba, which supplied scenery and costumes to, among others, La Scala (Milan), the Teatro Costanzi (Rome), La Fenice (Venice), the Regio (Turin), and even the Metropolitan in New York.

[35] After graduating from the Accademia in Bologna, and the Museo Artistico Industriale in Rome, where he studied under Alessandro Morani, and Nino Costa, the painter Adolfo De Carolis (1874-1928) rapidly made a name for himself with his pre-Raphaelite style paintings, such as *La donna della fontana*, as well as for his decorative work for public buildings, including the large fresco painted in 1907 in the Salone of the Palazzo del Podestà in Bologna. He was also in the forefront of the attempt to relaunch wood-engraving, a medium he used for illustrating a number of D'Annunzio's first editions, such as *Le Laudi*, *Il Notturno*, *Francesca da Rimini*, *La figlia di Iorio*, *La fiaccola sotto il moggio*, *La nave*, and *Fedra*.

[36] The letter, dated 21 November 1901, is reproduced in C. Di Marzio, "Lettere di D'Annunzio a De Carolis per le illustrazioni delle tragedie," in *Rivista italiana del dramma*, II, 1940, p. 3), who describes it as being "as meticulous as stage set instructions and as analytical as a dictionary definition."

[37] "At the end of February, when he was still in Genoa, while discussing the sets for *Francesca da Rimini*, and the poor theater facilities, he asked De Carolis for news about a *new scene* with the column, the chair and the chest. He also asked him to go to Milan *to help with the set construction and lighting*," ibid., p. 5.

[38] M. Corsi, 1940, p. 180.

[39] D'Annunzio and Eleonora's Duse's somewhat rocky relationship ended with *Francesca da Rimini*. Duse, who had made a major contribution, financial as well as artistic, to these productions, went on with her pioneering work in the Italian theater by working with Lugné-Poe and Gordon Craig.

[40] M. Corsi, "D'Annunzio regista e scenotecnico," cit., p. 181.

[41] The extract of Domenico Oliva's review, written for the *Giornale d'Italia*, is reproduced in A. Camilleri, *I teatri stabili in Italia (1898-1918)*, cit., p. 34-35).

[42] Isidoro Del Lungo in *Nuova Antologia*, 11 March 1903, ibid., p. 34.

[43] *La figlia di Iorio*, Teatro Lirico, Milan, 2 March 1904, Talli-Grammatica-Calabresi Company, sets by Odoardo Antonio Rovescalli, to designs by Francesco Paolo Michetti, costumes by Arnaldo Ferraguti.

[44] The extract of this letter, dated 31 August, 1903, is reproduced in M. Corsi, *op. cit.*, p. 183.

[45] Cf. A. Ferraguti, "La figlia di Iorio, tragedia pastorale di G. D'A.," in *Il Dramma*, nn. 187-188, 1 September 1953, p. 61.

[46] M. Corsi, *op. cit.*, p. 184.

[47] *La fiaccola sotto il moggio*, Teatro Manzoni, Milan, 27 March 1905, sets by Odoardo Antonio Rovescalli, to designs by Adolfo De Carolis, costumes by Caramba.

[48] "After a successful excursion into the realms of history and legend," *Più che l'amore*, an experiment in prose theater presented by the Ermete Zacconi Company at the Teatro Costanzi in Rome, on 29 October 1906 was a failure.

[49] *La nave*, was presented at the Teatro Argentina, Rome, on 11 January 1908, by the Compagnia Stabile under the artistic direction of Ferruccio Garavaglia, with scenery, costumes, and props in the style of Duilio Romano (Cambellotti), scenery built by Leonida Liverani, and music by Ildebrando Pizzetti.

[50] D'Annunzio, *Le faville del maglio*, I, p. 628.

[51] A versatile actor, whose work as a sculptor attracted Boccioni, Duilio Cambellotti (1876-1960) also made a name for himself as an illustrator of classical texts, and as a painter. His works included the stained glass windows for the Chapel of the Flagellation in Jerusalem, mosaics, and large canvases on bucolic subjects for a number of schools in the Roman hinterland. He also worked as a designer, producing drawings for lamps and gold jewelery, and had been particularly interested in poster design at the beginning of his career, because this medium "speaks directly to the people, and offers more space and scope for artistic expression." He felt the same about wood-engraving, which he considered more accessible, since it could be reproduced, and also the theater, where he started working in 1905, with set design for *Julius Caesar* and *King Lear* at the Teatro Argentina for the Compagnia Stabile Romana, while in 1910 and then in 1910, he designed Fausto Salvatori's *Furia dormente*. However, his name is mainly associated with the open-air theater productions at the Greek theater in Syracuse (Sicily), which, as E. Povoledo (*Enciclopedia dello spettacolo*, vol. II, 1954, p. 1548) has pointed out, illustrate two stages in the artist's style. In the first (c. 1914 to 1926) his style was already plastic and stylized, but still linked to the current taste for archaeology. His architectural, and archaic and evocative elements alluding to Greek myth worked well with ancient ruins, and the relationship between the landscape and the stage, though seemingly spontaneous, operated in the restricted area of histori-

cal recollection. During the second stage, he seemed freer in his creative approach, eschewing the pitfalls of archaeological reconstruction in favor of integrating the sets into the play's overall environment through the use of large-scale, mostly horizontal, stylized pieces of scenery.

[52] D'Annunzio's letter, dated 21 November 1906, is reproduced in E. Bona, "La prima della 'Nave' in quattro lettere inedite di G. D'Annunzio," in *Rivista italiana del dramma*, I, 1939, p. 62. A man with a wide range of cultural interests, extending from music and Christian archaeology, to theater, and the history of costume, Baron Rudolf Kanzler acted as historical consultant for the set design for *La nave*, providing original documents to help reproduce places and clothes.

[53] The text of the dedication, written by D'Annunzio in a copy of the play which he presented to Cambellotti, is reproduced in M. Corsi, *op. cit.*, p. 187.

[54] Ibid.

[55] *Fedra*, Teatro Lirico, Milan, 10 April 1909, set design by Odoardo Antonio Rovescalli, to designs by Adolfo De Carolis, costumes by Caramba.

[56] E. Scarfoglio, *Il libro di Don Chisciotte*, Naples, 1911, p. XV.

[57] *Le martyre de Saint Sébastien*, Théâtre du Châtelet, Paris, 21 May 1911, directed by Armand Bour, music by Claude Debussy, choreography by Fokine, performed by Ida Rubinstein, set and costumes by Léon Bakst. The Paris production was later used for a performance at La Scala in Milan on 4 March 1926, directed by Arturo Toscanini.

[58] The extract appears in M. Corsi, *op. cit.*, p. 193.

[59] A painter, graphic designer, set and costume designer, Léon Bakst (1866-1924), with Diaghilev, played a major part in the success of the Ballets Russes whose performance seemed to achieve a fusion of all the arts. Despite the influence of Italian culture, filtered through the masters of Baroque set design, Bakst's designs are noticeable for their violent contrasts, evocative of barbaric assonances — albeit tempered by the refined choice of tonal relationships. His sets, like those of the Russian school, emphasized the pictorial, and were remarkable for an almost total lack of historical references in their architecture. In addition, the costume designs used strong color contrast and stylized designs, which seemed to offer the actor even greater freedom of expression. While he does not fit into the category of the artists who were fighting to free the theater from the shackles of tradition, Bakst is, nonetheless, one of the greatest contemporary set designers.

[60] M. Corsi, *op. cit.*, p. 194.

[61] *La Pisanelle ou la mort parfumée*, Théâtre du Châtelet, Paris, 12 June 1913, music by Ildebrando Pizzetti, directed by Mejer'chold, choreography by Fokine, dancer Ida Rubinstein, sets by Bakst.

[62] The extract, taken from an article by Roberto De Flers, published in *Le Figaro*, is quoted in M. Corsi, *op. cit.*, p. 197.

[63] *Le Chèvrefeuille*, Théâtre de la Porte Saint-Martin, Paris, 14 December 1913.

[64] On 27 January 1914, *Il Ferro* was performed at the Teatro Carignano in Turin, the Teatro Manzoni in Milan, and the Teatro Valle in Rome.

[65] F.M. Martini, quoted in M. Corsi, *Le prime rappresentazioni dannunziane*, cit., p. 142.

[66] D'Annunzio wrote the libretto for *Parisina*, which was performed at La Scala in Milan on 15 December 1913, with music by Pietro Mascagni, sets by Odoardo Antonio Rovescalli, and costumes by Caramba. This work was later performed at the Teatro Argentina on 12 December 1921 as a verse tragedy by the Compagnia Nazionale directed by Virgilio Talli, with sets by Donatello Bianchini, to designs by Previati, and costumes by C. Del Debbio. Conversely, a number of D'Annunzio's prose pieces were adopted as operas, including *La figlia di Iorio*, music by Franchetti, directed by Mugnone, scenery by Angelo Parravicini, Rota, Sala, and Songia, costumes by the Sartoria Teatrale Chiappa, Milan, presented at La Scala, Milan, on 29 March 1906; *La nave*, adapted by Tito Ricordi, music by Italo Montemezzi, directed by Tullio Serafin, with sets and costumes by Guido Marussig, presented at La Scala in Milan on 3 November 1918; *Fedra*, music by Ildebrando Pizzetti, scenery by Léon Bakst, performed at the Paris Opéra in 1923; *Francesca da Rimini*, adapted by Tito Ricordi, music by Riccardo Zandonai, sets by Edoardo Marchioro, costumes by Caramba, performed at La Scala in Milan on 18 April 1929; *Le martyre de Saint Sébastien*, music by Claude Debussy, conductor Victor De Sabata, directed by Bronislaw Horowicz, sets by Nicola Benois, costumes by Ebe Colciaghi, performed at La Scala in Milan on 23 May 1951; *La figlia di Iorio*, music by Ildebrando Pizzetti, conductor Giannandrea Gavazzeni, directed by Margherita Wallmann, scenery and costumes by Renato Guttuso, performed at La Scala in Milan, 24 March 1956.

[67] After seeing a performance of the *Eumenides* in French at the Roman Theater in Orange in 1898, D'Annunzio conceived the idea of an open-air theater on Lake Albano, in response to Wagner's Festspielhaus. He had promised Eleonora Duse, who was his partner in the enterprise, that the theater would be inaugurated on 21 March 1899 with a performance of his new work *Persefone*. The project was, however, never realized.

[68] This letter is reproduced in M. Corsi, *op. cit.*, p. 199. *La figlia di Iorio*, performed on the hillside of Il Vittoriale, D'Annunzio's home, in September 1927, was directed by Giovacchino Forzano, with sets by Gian Carlo Maroni, and later performed at the Teatro Argentina on 10 October, 1934, under the direction of Luigi Pirandello and Guido Salvini, with sets by Giorgio De Chirico.

[69] Ibid., p. 200.

[70] G. Gori, *Il teatro contemporaneo e le sue correnti caratteristiche di pensiero e di vita nelle varie nazioni*, Torino, 1924, p. 61.

[71] A. Camilleri, *op. cit.*, 1959, p. 35.

[72] A. Ricciardi, *Il Teatro del colore. Estetica del dopoguerra*, Milan, 1919, p. 24.

[73] Giuseppe Pontiggia, quoted by D. Trotta, "Il trionfo del testo," in *Il Mattino*, 17 November 1988.

Mario Sironi
Urban Landscape with Truck, 1920

Jean Clair

The Blind Kittens

Fausto Pirandello, *The Stair*, c. 1934

Achille Funi
One Person and Two Ages, 1924

In 1957, Prince Giuseppe Tomasi di Lampedusa wrote a short story entitled *Il mattino di un mezzadro* (*The Morning of a Sharecropper*). Lampedusa intended this to be the first chapter of a sequel to his earlier novel *The Leopard*, and he had planned to call it *The Blind Kittens*, but his death in the same year forestalled completion of the project. Set at the end of 1901, the story takes up where *The Leopard* left off. It too contrasts the *nouveaux riches*, represented by the aggressive and coarse Ibba family, to the old landed gentry, who are increasingly at odds with the world and unable to cope. The key character is Ferrara the lawyer, the son of the accountant Ferrara, a liberal *petit bourgeois* who appeared in *The Leopard*. His boss, Salina, is none other than the grandson of Prince Don Fabrizio.

This is therefore a saga which traces one generation after another, changing its tone with the passage of time. By the turn of the century, life had become increasingly unyielding and complicated. The decline of a class whose splendor dated from the Renaissance gathers speed, while plebeian vulgarity finds strength in its arrogance. The young liberal Ferrara has none of his father's vigor while the young aristocrat Salina lacks his grandfather's brio. At the other extreme, the Ibba family, which is still firmly grounded in the soil, having only recently risen above its illiterate, peasant origins, demonstrates a greed that goes far beyond what the benign Naturalism of the Risorgimento had dared portray.

In this story then, as harsh as the parched Sicilian land that bore it, told with a mordancy matched only in certain passages from Honoré de Balzac, Guy de Maupassant or Emile Zola's *La Terre*, we observe the death throes of a class that is witnessing, along with the break-up of its landholding supremacy, the eclipse of its very *raison d'être* and social continuity.

"A deep-buried current of disquiet" rippled through the consciousness of the Palermitan nobility, as they became aware that in that epoch, at the dawn of the 20th century, it was possible to build up a great fortune based on land-ownership, a form of wealth which, as each one of these people knew from his own bitter experience, was fit only for demolition and not suitable for building elegant new buildings. In seeing the Ibba family as the modern incarnation of the Chiaromonte and Ventimiglia families of earlier centuries with their boundless holdings of wheat fields these same land owners felt that it was all so irrational, and for them, dangerous."[1] "Irrational" and "dangerous": in just two words, the Prince of Lampedusa sums up the social revolution in which the descendants of the Ibba family were to play a prominent role. If in 1901 they wore chaste-looking sailor suits, twenty years on these would be replaced by the black shirts of Fascism.

The vastness of the Ibba family's land holdings (more than 14,000 hectares), the lust for ownership, a remarkable fertility which would ensure the perpetuation of the race (Ibba had eight children), an amazing capacity for work (Ibba got up at four every morning), a plebeian vulgarity mingled with a predilection for ostentation, and a passion (common to all peasants who have made good) for everything that was new and for whatever delights the modern world could offer (Baldassare Ibba apparently commissioned the painter *à la mode* Rochegrosse to fresco every room in his new house, just as Mussolini — who was always in step with the latest trends — was to engender a plethora of bombastic scenographies): these are the ingredients of Lampedusa's short story. He managed to portray, in a nutshell, all the elements of the future Fascist hierarchy: the foundation of the great estates, the hunger for new land to cultivate, a policy of demographic growth, an impassioned agrarianism, teamed with, paradoxically, a powerful attraction towards the fruits of technology and "modern" art, an almost monastic exaltation of commitment and effort, and finally, the pompous rhetoric and the trumped-up splendor of people desperate to forget their humble origins.

The extent to which the agrarian theme dominated the Italian painting of the 1920s is striking, while in the same period, painters in England, Germany, the United States, and to a lesser extent, France, were turning their attention to the city, or in fact the metropolis. This was the Golden Age of the streetscape with its stunningly tall buildings and its dazzling advertisements — the German painters Otto Dix and Rudolf Schlichter of the *Neue Sachlichkeit*, or the American Precisionist artists Charles Demuth and Charles Sheeler, the Belgian Frans Masereel who produced the series entitled *La città*, or Fernand Léger's *Le remorqueur* (*The Tugboat*) and *Formes dans la ville* (*Forms in the City*) are good examples. The city will also be exhaustively treated by the Surrealists, from Louis Aragon in *Le paysan de Paris* to Max Ernst in *Vision nocturne de la Porte Saint-Denis* (*Nocturne: Porte Saint-Denis*). The 1920s proved to be one long celebration of the new "urban culture," its apotheosis and its attractions. It matters little that by the 1930s these trends, which grew out of the Expressionism of Ernst Ludwig Kirchner and Caligari, would have foundered on the deserted and barren road of the Great Depression — at the time, they represented the hopes and pride of all those who had made the City their natural habitat.

Antonio Donghi
Equestrian Circus, 1927

In this period in Italy, however, the city was conspicuously absent from painting. The Novecento remained firmly attached to its representations of a rural world, which may well have changed hands, but was still alive and well, its unchanging landscape seeming to symbolize the identity of the nation.[2]

Whether we look at the magical and cold Realism of Antonio Donghi, Achille Funi and Antonio Nardi or the warm Baroque of Fausto Pirandello and Mario Mafai, whether in the North or South of Italy, we see endless representations of harvests, country scenes, peasants and county-folk, albeit a far cry from the elegant landed gentry or the good-natured rural middle classes painted by Giovanni Fattori, Silvestro Lega and Telemaco Signorini. We get the idea that, from Giuseppe Garibaldi's heroic "Spedizione dei Mille" of 1860, right up to the end of the 1920s, Italy remained an agrarian society. This implies that the Fascist "Revolution" only served to ensure the continuity of a social order based on land-ownership and that the aesthetics of the Novecento merely extended the bucolic and melancholy poetics of the Macchiaioli Movement into the 1930s.

Giorgio De Chirico
The Painter's Family, 1926

Few artists escape from this generalization. The Metaphysical painters, and Giorgio De Chirico himself, took refuge in an imaginary antiquity. The *Archeologi* (*Archaelogists*), which De Chirico painted during this period — figures constructed in Arcimboldo style, their bodies made up of fragments of ancient ruins — are none other than a fantastical representation of the feelings experienced by the dispossessed aristocrats described by Lampedusa, the same aristocrats who are only too keenly aware, from personal experience, that "this form of wealth... is fit only for demolition and is not suited to constructing elegant new buildings."[3]

De Chirico's figures, too, are constructed from stones taken from ancient buildings, just as in reality fragments of ruins were used to build up the new.

Artists such as Felice Casorati and Giorgio Morandi found an even more radical solution. Caught up in the whirlwind of widespread social unrest, they both chose to cut themselves off, under the protection, as it were, of the *genius loci* of where they lived. The countryside exists in Casorati's painting — the hills around Turin later to be described by Cesare Pavese — just as Grizzana exists in Morandi's work. But this countryside is empty, uninhabited, dateless and timeless. Urban reality is re-

Mario Mafai
Mannequin with Fan, 1940

168

Mario Sironi, *The Architect*, 1922

Mario Sironi, *Solitude*, 1926

Felice Casorati
Double Portrait
(with the Artist's Sister), 1924

presented in equal measure in these painters' work but in the form of the small town, unchanging and fixed in the modesty and rigor of its *petit bourgeois* order — precisely as it was depicted by the Renaissance painters.

There remains the awkward problem of the Futurists and their enthusiasm for the world of modern technology. Attracted and at the same time repelled by technology and science, Fascism adopted the same ambivalent and unexpected stance towards it as Gabriele D'Annunzio, the loyal and close friend of Mussolini, took at the turn of the century.

On the one hand, lacking a real past, the new social order that was to form the Fascist squads created one of its own. From its humble origins, it invented a nobility with its own attributes. In fact it appropriated the past, plundering the universal heritage and reducing it to a vast storehouse of assorted anachronism, of which D'Annunzio's house, "Il Vittoriale," is the supreme example. The Fascist regime's construction projects, such as the EUR and the new towns (taking their cue from antiquity) only perpetuated this process. On the other hand, these plebeian masses were to be the heralds of the brand-new. The hunter fighter, the machine gun, the MAS 96 with its two torpedoes, the plane propeller and the winged wheels of the railways would all come together, as they did at the "Vittoriale", with the sheaf of corn, the sickle and the stone capitals of antiquity to form the new symbols of the regime, both puerile and dangerous.

One painter stands out though, and he was the only one to openly declare his allegiance to the regime. This was Mario Sironi who, alone among painters depicted urban life, the new metropolis, and the modern world lived in all its day-to-day mundanity and horror. As well as portraying the demoralized suburbs, the deserted outskirts, and the chaos of electrification, he was to paint the ghostly apparitions of trams at dawn, killers' lorries on their dusk missions, Piranesi-inspired Battles of the Titans, the sordid alleyways, scenes of unbounded acts of heroism and the brutal excesses of desire — Sironi was the only artist who knew how to praise the regime in his writings while denouncing it in his paintings. This state of affairs continued until 1933.[4] Then the city, which had been glaringly absent from the Italian painting scene for many years, returned to the forefront, like some nagging remorse which eats away at the soul.

The worthy heir of Alberto Martini's so-called black symbolism, of Lorenzo Viani's hopeless Expressionism, and Umberto Boccioni's doleful suburbs of the early industrialization process, Sironi made the modern city a legitimate theme for Italian art in the 20th century. His art spoke with lucid and bitter Nietzscheanism, that urged contemporary society towards nihilism. To the new plebeian class which had just attained power, Sironi was what Lampedusa had been for the old and fallen aristocracy: a bold and incisive chronicler.

In France too, Louis-Ferdinand Céline, a man of the people, arisen from the back alleys of the city or, more precisely, one of those *passages* so admired by Walter Benjamin, would pay homage to Fascism. With his *choses vues* or "things seen" he too would unwittingly become its most acute critic.

In German or American paintings of the same period, the city was nearly always shown either as a utopia — an abstract technological megalopolis — or as a realistic city teeming with trivial detail: the city in its every-day incarnation, often sordid and over-crowded, versus the city of tomorrow, deserted and sterile. This separation of the city into present and future scenarios can be equated to the city's role as a stage for society. Overlaying it is another separation which, this time, corresponds to a function: the city as a *political instrument*. This second separation gives voice to history and mythology. Alternately, the city returns to a more or less imaginary foundation (for example *Lutetia*, who was often portrayed by the French painters of poetic reality) or is projected as a sublime objective and a conclusion for

Mario Sironi
Corporative Italy, 1936

history. These four tendencies find expression in the four contradictory styles of Futurism, *Neue Sachlichkeit*, Archaism and neo-Classicism.

The aesthetics of totalitarianism, and in particular of National Socialism, exasperated the variance between these four tendencies. In Hitler's Germany, artists painted new subjects (such as motorways) in the style of Wilhelm Leibl or Hans Thoma, as well as painting the neo-Doric buildings of the future Reich in Biedermeier style, though they offset this with representations of traditional and vernacular architecture in the dry, bare, "modern" style of the *Neue Sachlichkeit*. But no divide between role, function and style has ever been greater than that of the depraved aesthetic of German fascism.[5]

Sironi escaped such a fate. His tragic greatness, which cannot be reduced to his political compromise, lay in his invention of an idiom which was able to merge Futurism, Archaism, neo-Classicism and Realism into a new unity, a powerful synthesis, the same one as that offered by the modern city. Thus, his cities acquire a vital presence which no other contemporary painting style has matched. They are steeped in a sense of Greek tragedy, and yet they are never bombastic. Despite the columns and porticoes, these are still cities of the 1920s, condemned and abandoned to a sorry fate. Single-handedly Sironi redeemed the omissions and the deceit of the Italian painting of this period.

Notes
[1] G. Tomasi di Lampedusa, *I racconti*, Milan, 1972, p. 19.
[2] Gino Severini did in fact deal with urban poetics; but he was an exile, living in Paris, and in the 1920s he did not hesitate to turn for inspiration to pastoral fantasies, spurning the innovations of the first decade of the century.
[3] Loc. cit.
[4] 1933 was to mark the climax of his debate with Roberto Farinacci, and in the same year Sironi stopped working for *Il Popolo d'Italia*.
[5] For a more detailed treatment, see author's "Retour, renaissance et restauration", in *Nouvelle Revue de Psychanalyse*, no. 26, autumn 1982, pp. 105-120.

Mario Perniola

Philosophy and Italian Painting Between the Wars

The Anti-Humanism of Italian Painting

The first thing that the scholar of philosophy discovers when inquiring into Italian interwar painting and its poetics is the acutely critical attitude many painters had towards "neo-idealism." In the heyday of the periodical *Valori Plastici* (1918-22), Savinio (Alberto De Chirico), Carlo Carrà, and Filippo De Pisis felt that their art was quite removed from the concepts of Benedetto Croce,[1] and about fifteen years later, Carlo Belli did not hesitate to define Giovanni Gentile's ideas as "foolish and clumsy."[2] These hostilities were not aimed at philosophy in general, but more specifically at a school of thought that had taken root in Italy — in fact, Arthur Schopenhauer, Friedrich Nietzsche, and Otto Weininger had provided various points of departure for the poetics of Metaphysical art, while Antonio Rosmini and ontology had contributed to the poetics of Abstract art. However, the philosophical interest of Italian interwar artistic developments lies less in the possible links to be drawn between a given painter and a given philosopher, than in the value and autonomously philosophical meaning of the experience of certain specific artists who billed themselves as "new philosophers."[3] Besides, art's claim of autonomy with regard to aesthetics was nothing new — ever since the end of the 18th century, both poetry and the arts had refused to ascribe a normative value to aesthetics, and had introduced a new way of conceiving the essence of art that saw the basic source of art theory in the actual experience of creating.

The difference between philosophical aesthetics and poetic-artistic experience during the 19th and 20th centuries hinges on the question of the *subject*. Philosophical aesthetics was created and developed with the idea of basing the experience of beauty and art on subjective perception — it builds on René Descartes' *cogito*, extending it to include sensory awareness through the elaboration of the concepts of emotion, taste, and genius. As a result, its orientation is essentially humanistic, one which ascribes a paradigmatic role to conciliation. Strictly speaking, the whole of modern aesthetics is a philosophical scheme aimed at the conciliation of opposites through sensibility and feeling. In contrast to philosophical aesthetics, the poetic-artistic experience — rather than focus on the subject — pivoted on the work of art itself, seen with all its objectivity, as something extraneous and radically different to the ego, the subject, the human being. The activity of the artist therefore assumed the character of an adventure that was quite separate from any design rationale — poets and artists were bearers of a knowledge that could not be reduced to an absolute knowledge of which the consciousness, the spirit, the man was master. This knowledge was by definition something *else*, something unsettling, perturbing — it was linked to a perception of objects not as means or tools at man's disposal, but as things whose impenetrable essence constantly confronts us with an unanswered question, an enigma. The artistic experience, it was claimed, was thus structured on this contrast between subject and object, on the conflict between man and things, on the difference between author and work of art — it gains in cogency the more the humanity of the artist is dominated by a disturbing and savage extrinsicality of the thing, the work of art.

It is within the framework of this centuries-old conflict between the artistic adventure and aesthetics that the issue of Italian interwar painting's philosophical import should be discussed. The fact that art and aesthetics on the one hand, and neo-idealism on the other are separated by a long-standing and reciprocal incomprehension is hardly surprising, considering both Croce and Gentile are the logical heirs of the "aesthetics of the subject" so firmly contested by the poetic and artistic experience of Mallarmé, Rilke, Rodin, and Kandinsky, among others.

The point of departure for Metaphysical art really lies in the refusal to place *man*, *ego*, and *subject* at the center of the world. This radical, anti-humanist stance exalted the thing itself as the wellspring of all meaningful experience. The Metaphysical artist dismissed the subjectivity of Man, and instead viewed him as a thing, a statue, an architectural element, a dummy, a simulacrum, a "hermaphrodite idol." This reification did not imply impoverishment, depreciation, or reduction, an offense to dignity — to the contrary: it was a liberation from the obvious, the banal, an emancipation from the merely psychological, like the opening up of a more spacious and essential horizon.

We can understand the *necessity* of this anti-humanist drive only in the light of its cultural context, one that saw no continuity but only a gaping chasm between the human and the divine, the utilitarian and the poetic, the medium and the work of art. The achievement of true artistic experience, it was alleged, depends on the extent to which the subject can be suppressed; therefore it is the complete opposite of *expression*. As Wilhelm Worringer pointed out, it is an urge towards abstraction, self-destruction, and the utter abandonment of all traces of naturalism and vitalism.[4] "The ability to extinguish every last flicker of life," wrote Giorgio De Chirico, "that ordinary and explicable life shown in painted figures, and to cloak them with that solemn immobility, a severe and disquieting appearance, like impressions that contain the secrets of sleep and death — this is the privilege of Art."[5]

Carlo Belli, *Kn*, 1935, cover

Despite the initial similarities, however, this anti-humanist philosophy differs considerably from nihilism. While nihilism ratifies everything on one level only, the anti-humanist outlook sets up ineluctable contrasts. On one side we have man with all his weakness, his idiosyncrasies, his "animal orgasm" — and on the other, we have the thing, the "serene beauty of matter," the metaphysical aspect of the world. For De Chirico, the metaphysical dimension of things could only be revealed when the continuity of past life, the "rosary of memories" that makes it all familiar, was interrupted.[6] This interruption, this sudden blank in our relationship with the things, makes them seem senseless, disturbing, different. The very basis of De Chirico's Metaphysical art was the absence of Man as subject, the exclusion of all acts of expression and all forms of empathy. When we observe people in their homes, for instance, from the street, through uncurtained windows, we perceive them in metaphysical terms: "You will never be able to speak to them, nor will they ever hear your voice and answer your questions... They do not know where they are, nor where you are from."[7] Their only lesson was their exhortation to listen to the voice of things, in silence. The emergence of this otherness is linked to a suspension of the process of becoming over time, the abolition of the past and future, the assertion of an absolute present, a spatial dimension of experience, the transition "from the same, to the same."[8]

This radical theory of anti-humanism, set forth with great lucidity by De Chirico just after World War I, was largely responsible for the ensuing climate, and consequently the tone of painting in Italy throughout the 1920s and 1930s. Another equally active figure at the time was Carlo Carrà, who held that the task of painting was to unveil the meaning of "ordinary things"[9] — and it was no coincidence that the only monograph Worringer ever devoted to a living artist was to Carrà and his painting *Il pino sul mare* (*The Pine Tree by the Sea*, 1921). The work of Giorgio Morandi was likewise focused on the *thingness* of things[10] and a similar theme can be found in many other artists of the period, all of whom show the influence of the Metaphysical artists.[11]

In 1935, the same anti-humanist stance is energetically upheld by Carlo Belli in his

Nietzsche, *Geburt der Tragödie aus dem Geiste der Musik (The Birth of Tragedy)*, 1872, frontispiece

Kn, a work that is now considered the manifesto of Italian abstract art. For Belli, art was not a human issue — it was just the opposite of expression, of psychologism, of naturalism, of identification. "The more art is understood," he wrote, "the less it deals with humanity"; artistic emotion cannot be "psychological"; "mistaking art for oneself would be an act of the utmost distraction, if not the height of presumption." Belli harked back to the anti-humanism of Metaphysical art "in whose frosty grandeur, Man is absent, and Nature has left behind only his skeleton"; he accused what he termed the *Novecento* tendency of reintroducing "half-measures," of watering down and distorting with idle eclecticism the radical drive of the artistic experience expressed in the works of Wassily Kandinsky, or Piet Mondrian. Taking up where Worringer left off, Belli wrote: "Art is liberation from the human condition." He too saw anti-humanism as being quite the opposite to nihilism; artistic experience was considered fundamentally similar to the experience of being, of God, of otherness. Art, he considered, was an encouragement towards attentiveness and humility: "Art is when the artist humiliates himself and not art." But there was also humiliation and cheapening of art, each time it was reduced to being a pretext for the expression of the subject, for an anthropomorphic or naturalistic representation.

Nonetheless, the anti-humanistic premise that provides the backcloth to Italian painting can also lead to quite contrasting outcomes, the *Apollonian* in the case of Metaphysical art, or the *Dionysian* in the case of Abstract art. These two notions, which show up repeatedly in discussions on the artistic production of the last two centuries, find one of their most cogent expressions in Nietzsche's *Birth of Tragedy*. It is important to note that for Nietzsche, neither the one nor the other have anything to do with the subject. He believed that the idea of art as an expression of the ego is the product of a conciliatory idealism that is incapable of conceiving and experiencing conflict and struggle, and as such is far removed from the real experience of art, and its otherness.

The Apollonian Outlook and Metaphysical Art

When the Apollonian outlook is considered synonymous with neo-classicist decorativism, it becomes incomprehensible. Even in Johann Winckelmann, the notion acquires a complexity that goes far beyond external beauty. Its noble simplicity and serene grandeur offer an unfathomable and enigmatic dimension; they imply an inner fervour and joyful impulse beyond mere ornament, and maintain an intrinsic ambiguity that can be expressed, for instance, in the comparison of beauty to water: like water, beauty assumes the color of any liquid mixed with it. It is in this *Stimmung* that Metaphysical art has its roots — its *Stille* and *Gelassenheit* never mean desolation, but presuppose a fervid spirituality, enthusiasm, and possession. The Metaphysical picture, according to De Chirico, generates a sense of joy and serenity — the new art, is truly a "jocund art."[12]

However, this flagrant act of perceiving is by no means evanescent or extramaterial. Metaphysical art does not liquefy the universe — on the contrary, it makes it solid. Rather than de-materializing it, it "super-materializes" it. It therefore articulates the penetrating intuition expressed by Hölderlin and Schelling, who held that Greek mythology belonged to the realm of the existing, and not the spiritual. Schelling in particular emphasized the material nature of the Olympian gods, as opposed to the spiritual nature of the Eleusinian gods (Demeter, Dionysus). They are less comprehensible, and more estranged from mankind, from consciousness and spirit; as such they are more concrete, arousing amazement, confusion, and paralysis. What man needs, according to Schelling, is not to retreat inside himself, but to reach outwards; the mythological experience gives rise to a state of annihilation and torpor because of its utter lack of conceptual footholds, its sheer opacity

173

— it requires no consent, and simply demands recognition, almost imposing or inflicting itself, inescapable.[13] It is precisely here that the Apollonian enigma lies — this intellectual daze or ecstasy is not an abdication of thought but an intensification of its possibilities, an opening to a simple, bare existence, and as such it is unutterable, something that defies being tied down to a word or a concept.

The Apollonian outlook involves the combined presence of both hot and cold elements, and processes of petrifaction and ecstatic transport. One of the seminal interpreters of this state was Heinrich Heine, who was in fact one of the main inspirers of Metaphysical art.[14] The obsessive presence of classical marble statues of gods, the enigmatic dimension of the women in stone that embrace the poet, the confusion of men and simulacra in Italian piazzas (something Schopenhauer had also noted) are all themes linking the cultural world of Heine and the realm of Metaphysical art. When De Chirico advised painters to draw statues and not hu-

Arturo Martini, *Lovers*, 1920

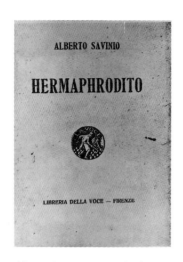

Alberto Savinio, *Hermaphrodito*
1918, cover

Arturo Martini, *Ophelia*, 1922

man bodies, so that, if a miracle should bring them alive, they would have "bones, muscles, nerves and tendons in working order,"[15] we find a direct parallel in Heine and his comparisons between the hollow eyes of the classical statues and the dark eyes of Italian men and women, apparently opposite but substantially identical. For Heine, the ancient gods did not die out with the end of paganism, but have been living a secret existence in Italy, mingling with the living beings. The resulting image is of an Italy that hovers between life and death, capable of delirium one moment and total stasis the next, and for that reason strange and disquieting, a kind of *mi-mort* or half-death (to use the expression that opens Savinio's novel *Hermaphrodito*), in which "les statues s'acheminent à pas cadencés."[16]

A link between the Apollonian aesthetic and the process of petrifaction had also been pointed out by Johann Jakob Bachofen in reference to Lycia, the matriarchal land which he held to be under the guardianship of the Delphic god. In Lycia, a feeling of the perishability of life drove the inhabitants to build themselves vast stone necropolises. They believed that a sarcophagus could turn either corpses or living people to stone in a mere forty days. Certain works of Arturo Martini in the early 1920s, such as *Fecondità* (*Fecundity*), *Amanti* (*Lovers*), or *Orfeo* (*Orpheus*) seem to be inspired by the myths of the Lycian Apollo, and similarly the verses of De Chirico in which he evokes the sarcophagus that would contain his remains, wishing that some new magic might hold him in a big, maternal, "stone embrace."[17]

Throughout the 1900s, the question of the Apollonian aesthetic — from Walter Friedrich Otto, who dubbed Apollo the god of distance, to Luce Irigaray, who defined him as the "being of fire and ice," the moment of coincidence between what is too hot and what is too cold, the will to survive all suffering — reinforced the mythological and poetic experience that the Italian Metaphysical artists had been trying to render visible. The importance De Chirico attributed to the framing of his works, and which Carrà was to attribute to the picture's composition in terms of the figurative values of form and color stems from an Apollonian point of view that tends to distance the object. This distancing creates a metaphysical effect because it gives the object solidity, isolating it from the surrounding space; the arches, the windows, the columns found in Metaphysical art have this function. The landscapes lose their naturalness and become things, according to a process that Rilke had grasped earlier on when he observed that people had begun to understand nature only when it was no longer understood, when it was felt as something utterly indifferent. It often happens that a picture represents another picture. The weight given to the picture frame in Metaphysical paintings is not meant to detract from the *ergon* in favor of the *parergon*, that is, from the work of art in favor of the decoration. If anything, it has just the opposite intention, namely to lend a solemn atmosphere to the *work*, placing it at an infinite distance from daily reality, in which both past and future are suspended. The realm into which Metaphysical art introduces us is not eternity, but the present, a moment in the sense of something that offers itself, that comes towards us, but which we cannot govern.

The essential enigmatic nature of the Apollonian experience consists in the paradox of a "non-participative" state of being possessed, in the oxymoron of a *sobria ebrietas*. Apollo, the god of calm, of self-control, of moderation, of "self-knowledge," of "no excess," of "repent if you have sinned," somehow excites a state of delirium whose vehemence has been evoked down through the ages, by Marcus Annaeus Lucanus and by Paul Valéry alike. This oxymoron is the foundation of the poetics of Metaphysical art, which on the one hand confers a fundamental importance to technique, skill, and discipline, while on the other it assigns no less importance to inspiration, ecstasy, and surprise.

Few painters of the Italian *Novecento* gave such importance to academic training and expertise as De Chirico did. For De Chirico, the act of painting was a means for

Giorgio De Chirico
Self-Portrait, 1924

deepening his understanding of his materials, his brushes, paints, colors, canvases, and other technical means. "No respectable painter that I am aware of, whether old or new," he wrote in his *Piccolo trattato di tecnica pittorica*, "lacked or lacks knowledge of painting technique."[18] The painter, he claimed, is first and foremost an artisan who constructs his canvases and colors on his own, who works for months and years on the same painting. "I grace myself with these three words, which I would like to be the seal of every work I have produced: namely *Pictor classicus sum*."[19]

For De Chirico, the painter was not just a technician, he was someone possessed — the world, he claimed, is full of demons and we must "discover the demon in all things."[20] The Metaphysical painters considered themselves the heirs of a timeless tradition that saw poets and artists as the bearers of a privileged experience of which they could never be masters. The divine madness animating the painters

Giorgio Morandi
Still Life, c. 1923

came from without — they were merely its instruments, a channel for words, drawings, and works that originated from somewhere outside of them, somewhere different. They felt that the artist's condition differed little from that of the viewers, as he too was passive in the process that removed him from his subjectivity, and because the creation of a work of art was a kind of "seizure," a form of ecstasy. According to De Chirico, the viewer of a Metaphysical painting entered a "completely different existence," "something very intense, very concentrated and therefore almost *more real* than his usual life."[21]

It is not easy to understand what internal links there are in the Apollonian state that bind technique and "being possessed" together. Both of them are intermediate forms of knowledge standing midway between science and ignorance, between absolute knowledge and utter madness. The value of a technique is assessed on the basis of its practical results: the fact that the ultimate criterion for judgment is stark effectuality means that the learning of a technique implies a process of alienation similar to a state of possession. In the second place, the chances of being inspired depend in turn on techniques, on the set of practical conditions that Nietzsche called the hygiene of the thinker and artist. The Apollonian dimension is much more bound to the perception of practical, daily realities than it may at first appear. It should not be surprising that De Chirico himself, the leading theoretician of Metaphysical art, was also the author of *Considerazioni sulla pittura moderna* (1942), an essay aimed at dispelling the myths, a wary and severe critique of the social transformations that had taken place in the circle of artists during the 1930s and 1940s.[22] De Chirico's thoughts are not far from the radical analysis that Theodor Adorno and Max Horkheimer were beginning to formulate in *The Dialectic of Illuminism* regarding the art market and the cultural industry.

The Dionysiac Outlook and Abstract Art

While the Metaphysical artists had felt that painting was akin to architecture, the Abstract artists equated it with music, the quintessential form of Dionysiac expression. Carlo Belli had already discussed this link, stating his opinion that music is the art form that painting should take as its example. The title of his manifesto *Kn* originated from the convention of numbering musical compositions — Belli was aspiring for "an exhibition of works that are untitled, unsigned, without dates, and without any human reference, distinct from each other by simple algebraic clues, such as K, K_1, K_2... K_n."[23] The same relationship between painting and music is claimed by Lucio Fontana, who together with Osvaldo Licini, Fausto Melotti, and others formed a group of Italian Abstract artists gathered round the Milanese Galleria del Milione. Fontana's idea of music anticipates the fundamental line of modern art, which "marches towards movement developed through time and space."[24]

Fausto Melotti, *Drawing*, c. 1934

What characterizes most of the exponents of Italian Abstract art in the 1930s compared with their counterparts elsewhere in Europe was, in the eyes of Paolo Fossati, their anti-constructivist orientation, the tendency towards a "real and virtual disintegration of geometry,"[25] the exultation of movement, of energy, power, the compulsion to dissolve matter into rhythmic form. In this drive to liberate themselves from material things, Schelling had divined the essence of a Dionysiac urge, the origin of its delirium — feeling itself unexpectedly free from the dominion of real matter, the consciousness becomes inebriated. "Creating a work of art," wrote Belli, "consists in forcing one's intuition... becoming unhinged, out of one's mind."[26] This rejection of Self is quite opposite to the mental processes involved in Metaphysical art — it is not the transformation of body into thing, into a dummy, or statue, but the opposite dissolution and negation of every visible reality, a departure from materiality, the metamorphosis of man into angel or into demon, as in the works of Licini — or the dismemberment of every object into parts, as in Melotti,

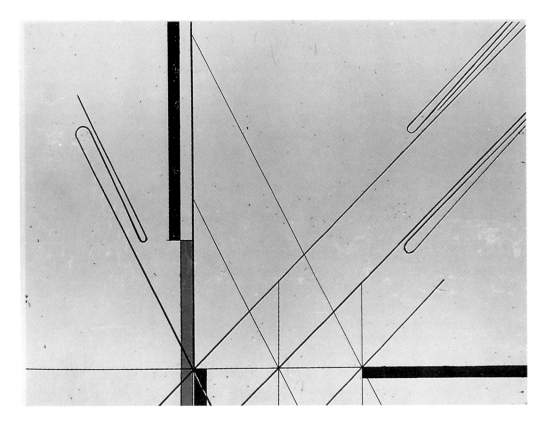

Osvaldo Licini
Abstract Wires on White Background
1931-34

or the paring down and "de-realization" pushed to their utmost limits, as in Fontana. Once again, Fossati observes that these artists lacked a functional and modular orientation, the idea of an elementary model that could be multiplied.[27] What prevails is an accentuated rejection of sensory data that is essentially anti-geometric and anti-architectural. This orientation seems to stem from a Dionysiac urge towards the *sparagmós*, i.e., the laceration and dissolution of reality.

The works themselves are no more than the remains, the traces, the reliquary of an impulse to destruction, of an iconoclastic urge, which in critical theory finds its proper point of reference and illumination in the Dionysian aesthetic. "Any form of modern art that was not iconoclastic," writes Belli, "would be nonsense."[28] Bruto, one of the main characters in the short stories of Osvaldo Licini, embodies all the exaggeration, excesses, and cruelty of Dionysus, but also the torment, an anguish pushed to its very limits, an intense yearning for the redemption and palingenesis or rebirth that are intrinsic to Dionysian religion. The tale, in which Licini's character tears out his heart to give it to someone else, and after offering it in vain to a child, a beggar, and a priest, has to cast it into a latrine,[29] seems to hark back to the passion of Dionysus, the ancient myths recounting how he was butchered at the hands of the Titans and subsequently the sudden mutations (*peripeteia*) of what remained of his body, and especially of his heart, which was carried from place to place until it was finally transformed into a reliquary.

According to a recent and very erudite study of the figure of Dionysus,[30] the essence of this god lies in the sphere of movement, transition. This is the fundamental concept behind Lucio Fontana's *Manifiesto blanco*, in which the activity of the artist found a very incisive poetic formulation. For Fontana, it is not form that is vital, but force and its dominion over matter and space. "We take the energy inherent in matter, its necessity to be and develop. We postulate an art that is free of all aesthetic devices."[31] Friedrich Hegel's theory that art is no longer the highest means by which truth is expressed, since religion has appropriated this function, has always seemed a little bizarre in Italy because it does not correspond to the

Lucio Fontana
Manifiesto blanco, 1946

178

Lucio Fontana
Study for Iron Sculpture, 1934

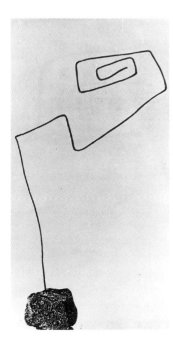

Lucio Fontana, *Sculpture*, 1934

country's collective historical memory, which pivots on the crucial passage from the Middle Ages to the Renaissance, and hence considers art as something that comes *after* religion, and not the other way round. Instead, Hegel, in maintaining that art had ceased to be our supreme need is really thinking of the transition from Renaissance to the Reformation, of which he felt he was a direct heir. His conclusion that the spirit inherently needs only its own interior satisfaction is explained historically in the iconoclastic explosion that accompanied the Reformation, and in the constant diffidence that Protestantism has always nurtured for the visual arts.

Two further issues arise at this point: is there any relation between Italian Abstract art and Hegel's thesis on the death of art? And secondly, how does Abstract art fit in with the Italian cultural tradition, which seems to enjoy more positive attitudes (even exaltation) towards the visual image, and as such, is fundamentally more Apollonian than Dionysian?

It is interesting to note that at the close of the 1930s, the question of the death of art was central to Antonio Banfi's theoretical discourse in *Motivi dell'estetica contemporanea* (*The Basis of Contemporary Aesthetics*, 1939), thoughts he matured in his *Esperienza estetica e vita dell'arte* (*Aesthetic Experience and the Life of Art*, 1940). In limiting the range of Hegel's affirmation to the realm of "beautiful art" alone, Banfi expresses some ideas on the situation affecting the art contemporary to him, not in disagreement with the poetics of Abstract art. "Today, the artist is more than ever his own critic," writes Banfi in his first essay. "He recognizes, or wishes to recognize, his problem or the problem of his generation, and his fidelity to this idea is indicative of his nobility and honesty — even when this compromises his own creative skill and fortune. Spontaneity in art seems only capable of generating banal and unconscious imitations which, although they excite a commonplace and superficial appreciation, lack any effective meaning or seriousness."[32] And here, art is finally attributed a meaning that goes beyond mere aesthetics; according to Banfi, art is a highly complex spiritual reality that cannot be reduced to the merely aesthetic. In his second essay, Banfi observes, "Never before has art so boldly tested its strengths, revealed so deeply the secrets of its workings, so radically and universally tackled its issues. There is a mingling of primitivism and deep self-reflection, irregularity of contents and discipline of form; a fresh awareness and a grave sense of dark and complex experience — and all this is set in a precarious equilibrium, an unbroken dynamism. Perhaps we have not yet reached the end of this process. However, the enthusiasm seems to be waning, the breakthroughs diminishing, and suspicions of the pointlessness of the exercise are finding their way in, as all the compromises, the sudden halts, reversals, begin to seem false and worthless."[33]

It is far more difficult, however, to make a short reply to the second question. It raises various other issues that concern the very foundations of our current historical situation and our relationship with Italy's national tradition. Can we accept this "idea of Italy" as the country in which the visual image came into its own through the appreciation of the "grand spectacle of the world" and its visual representation? Has it really escaped in past centuries damaging Dionysian influence, the furor of iconoclasm, the passion of radical spiritualism?

A series of recent studies has just begun to shed light on aspects that have been obscured for a long time, removed from the collective memory and the attention of scholars.[34] Perhaps the attitude towards visual images has never been quite as naive and unprepared as certain apologists of realism have led us to believe. Perhaps the "worm" of aniconism has been secretly eating away more than we imagined. Perhaps the roots of Baroque are founded in a deep-seated distrust of images, of appearance and spectacle.[35] If this were the case, Italian Abstract art would seem less isolated and eccentric.

Benedetto Croce, Luigi Albertini
and Francesco Ruffini, Milan, 1924

Notes

[1] P. Fossati, *"Valori Plastici" 1918-22*, Turin, 1981, p. 213; P. Fossati, *La pittura metafisica*, Turin, 1986, p. 92.

[2] C. Belli, *Kn* (1935), Milan, 1972, p. 66.

[3] G. De Chirico, *Sull'arte metafisica* (1919), in *Il meccanismo del pensiero. Critica, polemica, autobiografia. 1911-43*, edited by M. Fagiolo, Turin, 1985, p. 88.

[4] W. Worringer, *Astrazione e empatia* (1908), Italian trans. by E. De Angeli, Turin, 1975.

[5] G. De Chirico, *Raffaello Sanzio* (1920), in op. cit., p. 160.

[6] G. De Chirico, *Sull'arte metafisica* (1919), cit., p. 85.

[7] G. De Chirico, *Metafisica dell'America* (1938), in op. cit., p. 351.

[8] M. Perniola, *Transiti*, Bologna, 1985.

[9] C. Carrà, *Tutti gli scritti*, edited by V. Fagone, Milan 1978.

[10] Various, *Morandi e il suo tempo*, Milan, 1985.

[11] R. Barilli, *L'arte contemporanea. Da Cézanne alle ultime tendenze*, Milan, 1984, p. 226.

[12] G. De Chirico, *Noi metafisici* (1919), in op. cit., p. 68. On the Apollonian aesthetic in Metaphysical art, cfr. M. Calvesi, *La metafisica schiarita*, Milan, 1982, p. 50.

[13] L. Pareyson, *Lo stupore della ragione in Schelling*, in *Romanticismo. Esistenzialismo. Ontologia della libertà*, Milan, 1979.

[14] P. Fossati, *"Valori Plastici" 1918-22*, cit., p. 97.

[15] G. De Chirico, *Il ritorno al mestiere* (1919), in op. cit., p. 87.

[16] A. Savinio, *Hermaphrodito* (1918), Turin, 1982, p. 38.

[17] G. De Chirico, *Arte metafisica e scienze occulte*, cit., p. 65.

[18] G. De Chirico, *Piccolo trattato di tecnica pittorica* (1928), in op. cit., p. 284.

[19] G. De Chirico, *Il ritorno al mestiere*, cit., p. 99.

[20] G. De Chirico, *Zeusi l'esploratore* (1918), in op. cit., p. 81.

[21] G. De Chirico, *Discorso sul cinematografo* (1942), in op. cit., p. 415.

[22] G. De Chirico, *Considerazioni sulla pittura moderna* (1942), cit., p. 391 ff.

[23] C. Belli, *Kn*, cit., p. 30.

[24] L. Fontana, *Manifiesto blanco* (1946), in *Concetti spaziali*, edited by P. Fossati, Turin, 1970.

[25] P. Fossati, *L'immagine sospesa*, Turin, 1971, p. 176.

[26] C. Belli, *Kn*, cit., p. 49.

[27] P. Fossati, *L'immagine sospesa*, cit., p. 162.

[28] C. Belli, *Kn*, cit., p. 60.

[29] O. Licini, *Racconti di Bruto* (1913), in *Errante, erotico, eretico*, edited by G. Baratta, F. Bartoli, Z. Birolli, Milan, 1974, p. 63 ff.

[30] M. Daraki, *Dionysos*, Paris, 1985.

[31] L. Fontana, *Manifiesto blanco*, in *op. cit.*.

[32] A. Banfi, *Motivi dell'estetica contemporana* (1939), in *I problemi di un'estetica filosofica*, edited by L. Anceschi, Florence, 1961, p. 65.

[33] A. Banfi, *L'esperienza estetica e la vita dell'arte* (1940), in op. cit., pp. 137-138. On the question of the death of art in Italian aesthetic thought, cfr. D. Formaggio, *La "morte dell'arte" e l'estetica*, Bologna, 1983.

[34] Here I am refering to the works *Il sacco di Roma 1527*, Turin, 1983, by A. Chastel; *La sessualità di Cristo nell'arte rinascimentale e il suo oblio dell'epoca moderna*, Milan, 1986, by L. Steinberg; and *Rome 1630*, by Y. Bonnefoy, Milan, 1970.

[35] M. Perniola, *La società dei simulacri*, Bologna, 1980, p. 115 ff.

A Theoretical Note on Modern Italian Sculpture

Umberto Boccioni
Antigraceful, 1912-13

Giacomo Balla
Boccioni's Fist, 1916-17

More than any other work, Umberto Boccioni's *Antigraceful* (1912-13) capsulates the problematic of modern Italian sculpture: how to overcome the gracefulness — "that sweet and facile grace which hovers midway between the seen and the unseen," as Vasari described it[1] — that is every Italian artist's inheritance. *Antigraceful* can be read as anti-mother, for Boccioni's mother is its subject matter. Indeed, a large number of his works thematize her.[2] They can be viewed as secular Madonna images — idealized Mother imagoes realistically rendered — suggestive of the continuing unconscious hold of all that the mother represents on Italian art. Thus, the problematic can be re-stated: modern Italian art is unconsciously motivated by the wish to be free of the mother, at once a "hidden god... constantly present through occult fantasy" and a "paradise lost but seemingly close at hand."[3] Modern Italian art rebels against the fantasy of the Madonna, that illusory paradise of reassurance and narcissistic consolation, signified by grace. The rebellion serves a new, would-be heroic masculinity. The well-known fighting spirit — destructiveness — of Futurism is perhaps its most obvious expression.[4] Sculpture, by reason of its dramatic projection into space — its dramatization of space, as it were — can be a particularly effective medium in which to make a "heroic" statement of virility, as Auguste Rodin's *Balzac* indicates. Boccioni's hyper-dramatic *Anti-graceful* suggests that sculpture may be the major instrument in the Italian "battle for deliverance from the mother," as Carl Gustav Jung called it.[5] The battle is a determined effort to be realistic in the face of the cloying fantasy of the mother — to liberate Italian imagination from the claustrophobic grip she has on it.

This militant pursuit of masculinity is pervasive in modern Italian art. More precisely, it is the struggle between the strong desire to be masculine — realistic, modern, mature — and the difficult-to-escape emotional power of the feminine, epitomized by the mother, who instantly infantilizes whatever she touches, that is, returns it to the childhood condition that is the tradition we all inwardly share. This struggle between will and grace seems most evident in modern Italian sculpture, in part because sculpture thrusts the fictional space of art — the "potential space" of "the zone of illusion", in the words of the psychoanalyst Donald Winnicott[6] — into the literal space of the world. Modern sculpture goes further, ambitiously superimposing the subjective space of art on the world.

In general, the ideological and stylistic interests communicated by art are secondary to its power to create and assert subjective space. (The task of art is to show that subjective space is more fundamental than stylistic and ideological concerns.) In sculpture, art's subjective space is made more insistent by reason of the projective character of the medium. That is, subjective space is more likely to be experienced as though it was literal — a world in its own right — when it is projected three-dimensionally. In a sense, modern sculpture appropriates real space rather than simply projects into or onto it. This makes potential space — the imaginative zone in which the battle for deliverance from the mother occurs — seem omnipresent, and thus irreducible and irresistible.

If sculpture is the direct intervention of the potential space of art into the actual space of life, then modern sculpture attempts to overwhelm actual space, and completely blur the boundary between art and life, that is, between the subjective and objective. The subjective creation is no longer placed in the objective world, but seems of a piece with it. In contrast to traditional sculpture, which assumes that

Umberto Boccioni
Synthesis of Human Dynamism
1912, destroyed

Amedeo Modigliani, *Head*, 1911-12

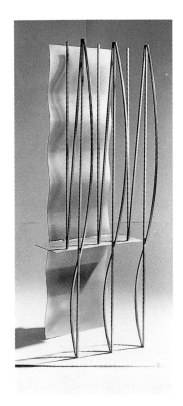

Fausto Melotti, *Sculpture 14*, 1935

every sculptural fiction takes its place in actual space, conforming or submitting to it (and thus being objectified by it), modern sculpture rejects the idea of simple placement in the world. For it there is no such things as clear and distinct space, a denial that begins the transformation of objective actual into subjective potential space. Modern sculpture stretches static place until it seems moving space — until it is impossible to speak of simple location in space. The denial of simple space seems self-evident in Boccioni's *Antigraceful.* Stated another way, where traditional sculpture presupposed fixed, absolute space, modern sculpture relativizes space. It invents dynamic spatial fictions that irrealize space. Actual space is, of course, never abolished; it is transformed, along with experience of it. Modern sculpture reduces it to the afterimage of potential space: actual space comes to seem fictional as potential space comes to seem actual.

Italian sculpture makes an important contribution to the modern reconceptualization of sculptural space, which is inseparable from the overthrowal of the mother — who must be identified with absolute space. Some modern Italian sculpture is on the side of the mother — most notably Amedeo Modigliani's manneristic, totemic females, who are Virgin Madonnas re-idealized in modern, quasi-primitivist terms — but most of it, whether in the form of the abstract "concrete art" of Fausto Melotti or the expressionistic figures of Marino Marini, is on the side of the father's masculinity. Art oriented to the mother emphasizes placement or containment in space, confirming the sense of it as absolute, rather the "displacement" of it, suggesting its flexibility. When Modigliani places his "absolute" objects — phallic women all — in absolute space, he is in effect confirming the femaleness of space, that is, its existence as a womb-like receptacle. He is acknowledging the mother as the absolute space in which all things are placed; they originate in her, and return to her, as in the Nativity and Pietà. Indeed, all beings are subtly immobilized in the ideal mother. It is an illusion that they move on their own; they move only by her grace: they do not really have a dynamic will of their own. It is because every being implicitly belongs to her that it comes to seem graceful, as in traditional Italian art, with its inimitable unity of grace and fate — its seemingly miraculous articulation of the gracefulness that both inanimate and animate beings have when they are fated to live in and through the mother. In contrast, the vehement concreteness of Melotti and Marini refutes the fixity that belongs to the mother, and with that refutation liberates matter from a gracefulness that increasingly seemed forced, artificial, and absurd in the modern world of practical matter.

In 1901, Boccioni began the new century with a gesture of autonomy — not truly realized until his 1913 Futurist works — by inventing himself as an "atheistical-skeptical-materialistical philosopher."[7] His first act in his new role was to declare — with a hyperbole suggestive of the intensity of his (erratically realized) rebellion against transcendental Italian gracefulness — that "in Rome, in the other cities of Italy, and Abroad, public meetings are being held requesting permission to throw into the Tiber and into the similar rivers of other cities all of the Madonnas existing in the museums and churches."[8] The basic mission of Futurism — the pace-setting movement of 20th-century Italian art — was the dissolution of Italian grace, represented by the absolute mother. The articulation of that grace — implying the seamless fusion of the spiritual and the material, the sublime and the concrete — was once the whole ambition of Italian art. The question for modern Italian art is whether there is anything beyond or as significant as gracefulness, which had seemed all-consuming, self-justifying, and the only proper "theme" of art. In fact, gracefulness had been realized in Italian art with an artistic subtlety and brilliance that has never been surpassed, and has been justly acclaimed by the world. In other words, the question of modern Italian art is: is there an artistic future after Renaissance grace? Did modern Italian art in fact accomplish its heroic, supposedly

183

historically necessary task, namely, the destruction of the idealism associated with the mother and the creation of a new "realism"?

Both answers must be equivocal: a residual unconscious obsession with gracefulness remains in modern Italian art, in the form of a persistent interest in design. Italian design can be regarded as the ironical return of repressed gracefulness, and Italian sculpture must finally be comprehended as design in disguise — gracefulness re-designed, as it were. Indeed, such sculptors as Rembrandt Bugatti and Bruno Munari are overtly designers. Their work shows a seamless integration of high style and design — which is not the same as the modern attempt to integrate high style and socially useful popular art. Design absorbs and displaces both; it does not reconcile them, but bends both to new purpose. Unexpectedly, modern Italian sculpture tends to be design reified. It neither destroys nor transcends the Madonna's grace, but abstracts and reconceives it, giving it a new embodiment, a complex new lease on life as secular design. *Il pugno di Boccioni* (*Boccioni's Fist*), as Giacomo Balla's 1916-17 sculpture is called, has not so much smashed traditional Italian gracefulness, as transformed it, becoming graceful itself. Futurism gives gracefulness a new hardness, a fresh formulation. *Boccioni's Fist* is not a more powerful fist, but a re-designed fist.

On March 11, 1915, in Milan, Balla and Fortunato Depero published the *Futurist Reconstruction of the Universe*. As has been pointed out, the ideology of reconstruction is "the indispensable key to interpretation of the Futurist experience as a whole." Interestingly, Aldo Tanchis argues that the idea of art in this manifesto "reveals [Bruno] Munari in a nutshell," suggesting an astonishing continuity between early and late 20th-century Italian sculpture. Tanchis points out: "The use of lowly materials: 'Metal wires, cotton threads... coloured glass, onionskin paper... transparent wire meshes of all kinds... mechanical and electrical devices, etc.' The longing to achieve movement! 'Three-dimensional groups that turn on a pivot... on several pivots, etc.' The interest in toys, which should no longer 'bewilder and dis-hearten the child' but get him used to 'laughing quite openly... to the greatest elasticity... to the leap of imagination... to reaching out infinitely and making sup-ple his sensitivity.'"[9] Il should be noted that these "qualities" are also those of *arte povera*, which with its stylized arrangements of everyday materials attempts to "set out from reality," as Tanchis says Munari does, and "draw attention to its un-familiar aspects."[10] It is only possible to do so under the auspices of the ideal of design. That is, in the Balla/Depero manifesto the outlook of design is already im-plicit: the conception of design as idealization of the everyday, that is, visual re-habilitation of everyday materiality. Indeed, design is a kind of therapy on the use-ful objects of everyday life. Il does not dismiss practicality, as style does, but re-shapes it in terms of the demands of a vision of the good enough life.

The Balla/Depero manifesto makes something else clear: that there is no stylistic center to Italian scupture. The liberation from stylistic absolutism opens the way to design. Modern Italian art in general is not interested in style as such; it tends to appropriate style for design purposes. Style tends to exist as a disinterested end in itself. In contrast, design is always "interested"; it is a way of articulating the hu-man interest invested in ordinary things. Design disseminates style through every-day objects, counteracting style's tendency to set up a world of its own objects. Where style claims to be pure gracefulness, design regards gracefulness as meaning-less unless it is a quality of everyday life.

Thus, in Italian art the turnover of styles — inseparable from modern art — leads away from style, that is, self-centered art, towards design, or art decentered to serve everyday life. Perpetual "revolutionariness" involves (among other things) in-venting new styles of artistic detachment, in response to the fact that in the modern world every style tends to rapidly become aesthetically banal, that is, reified as a

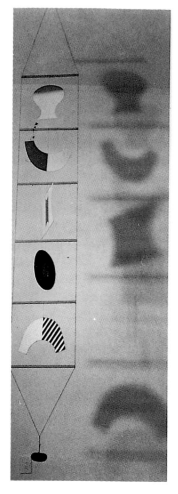

Bruno Munari
Useless Machine, 1934

Bruno Munari
Aerial Machine, 1930, destroyed

formula. (In the modern world, style is grace, but grace is an elusive, easily lost quality because of modern materialism and practicality. The rapid consumption of styles in the modern world is a futile attempt to have and sustain grace in a psycho-social situation inimical to it.) Italian art attempts to avoid the apparently self-emptying character of style in the modern situation by rearticulating style in a design context. Style is re-attached to the everyday lifeworld; it in effect gains a new lease on life by giving new life to the everyday world.

The Italians implicitly assume it is one of their important qualities — that the everyday lifeworld is a major space. Indeed, it is the space which subsumes all other spaces; we are all embedded and live our lives in it. So the everyday lifeworld must be cared for. It must not be neglected, or trivialized, or brutalized, for it is the primary space of existence: it is design's task to make the best of the concrete space of the lifeworld. The paradoxical purpose of modern Italian art, and particularly modern Italian sculpture, is to make antigraceful modern styles serve the everyday lifeworld. They give a new meaning to design's ideal of gracefulness.

The anti-stylism of modern Italian sculpture, particularly Futurism and *arte povera*, is a way of asserting that art is a form of war against the world. The question from the point of view of design is whether war can be a means to a new kind of grace — a seemingly absurd question on the face of it, but one that implies recognition of the shopwornness of old forms of grace, and the banality of everyday life in the modern world. This question was in fact implicit in Futurism itself, with its aggressive dissatisfaction, which still echoes in *arte povera*.

F.T. Marinetti's celebration of war is well-known. It seems all the more inhumane today, in the aftermath of the fascism and the world war it is more than innocently related to. Balla and Depero, as contemptuous of human life as Marinetti, have written: "We Futurists, Balla and Depero, will construct millions of metallic animals for the vastest war (conflagration of all the creative forces of Europe, Asia, Africa and America, which will undoubtedly follow the current marvellous little human conflagrations."[11] But the Futurist elevation of war as a perverse panacea was not entirely what it seems to be. The violence of war was a metaphor for what Carlo Carrà, in his 1918 manifesto *Warpainting*, called "dynamic distortion." It "will be used to fight: Any tendency towards the 'pretty,' the 'tender,' the 'sentimental' (Botticelli, Watteau). Any tendency towards 'literary heroicism' (Delacroix). Any tendency towards the 'bourgeois' or 'academic' (Raphael, Leonardo da Vinci). Any tendency towards 'harmony,' 'equilibrium,' 'symmetry,' the 'decorative,' 'pure illustrationism' (Veronese). Any tendency towards the 'analytical,' towards 'scientific or rationalist perspective,' towards 'objectivism and natural probability' (Seurat, Signac, Gros)."[12] As Carrà said, modern "fragmentariness" inaugurates "*a rebellion* against all gangrenous, millenarian, artistic traditionalism."[13]

Fortunato Depero
Construction of Pinocchietto, 1917

This rebellion — the fragmentariness and dynamic distortion that are the instruments of antigracefulness and antistyle — has now itself become traditional. What was once revolutionary war has, with mocking irony, become an everyday dynamic — everyday aesthetic. In the process, it has lost its pathological character — the pathology inherent in any pursuit of total revolution and a totally new (utopian) future. It has submitted to the inertial force of everyday life, which it infiltrates but does not overcome: instead, it becomes the good design of the everyday world. It makes the everyday lifeworld seem sensually and emotionally nourishing — a good enough world, if still not the best one. But in fact design intends to suggest the abandonment of utopian dreams, and the attempt to make the best of the world, if not to think it is the best of all possible worlds. Like total stylistic revolution, design blurs the boundary between art and life, but now constructively rather than destructively.

Fortunato Depero
Chinese Dancer, 1917

One might say that the Futurist sense of art and life as total war is replaced by the fusion of art and life in total design. In a sense, it is easier to make revolutionary war than to redesign the everyday world. It takes more care to do the latter. The importance of Italian sculpture is that it enlists the revolutionary aggression of modern art in the service of the subtle task of re-designing reality. It is no doubt a lesser task to re-design than to revolutionize, but it is a saner task, and one more likely to be successful. The ideal of the graceful mother unexpectedly returns through design, with its sense of mission in and responsibility to everyday life. The mother serves to make the seemingly willfully revolutionary power of masculinity, and the rotten world to which it has given rise, more graceful — to "reform" it. In design, the mother's gracefulness, which attempts to regenerate the lifeworld so that it seems both virginal and secure, struggles with the vanity and vulgarity of the father's machismo, masking the insecurity of his masculinity.

To me, the ambiguity of Italian art — its paradoxical position as both stylistic revolution and regenerative design — is epitomized by Lucio Fontana, in the numerous 1960s works titled *Concetto spaziale, Natura* (*Spatial Concept, Nature*). In these sculptures a receptacle with a more or less crude, amorphic texture is split or forced

Marino Marini, *Horseman
(The Angel of the City)*, 1949

186

Mino Rosso, *Skier*, 1927

open, as though something was hatching in it. Or it may be offering itself as a refuge or sanctuary — a sacred space in which every being can be inviolate. This uncanny space of rebirth seems styleless yet it is full of the special grace that only style can give. It is at once masculine and feminine, active and passive, aloof and inviting, axiomatic (fated) and incompletely formed ("free"). It is an absolute object but also a germinal natural force. A new sense of life is implicit in it, yet it also transcends life, to accomplish what only the highest art can, the apparent reconciliation of opposites, with deceptive ease. Fontana's sculptural objects are clearly of the mother — they achieve a new kind of graceful "objectivity" — but they also have the father's willfull intransigence. Being of both, they let each live in and through the other. They bring us to an awareness of what Italian sculpture at its best has always offered: the sense of the immanence of spiritual grace in graceless reality, that is, of the mothering nature in even the most raw matter. It is the recognition and recovery of the strange grace that is at the core of life — the first step in its transposition to the everyday world — that is the real revolution of modern Italian sculpture.

Notes
[1] Quoted in R. Klein and H. Zerner, *Italian Art 1500-1600*, Prentice-Hall, Englewood Cliffs, N. J., 1966, Sources and Documents in the History of Art Series, p. 75.
[2] See my article "Umberto Boccioni: The Creative Dilemma of a Mother's Boy," to appear in *C Magazine*.
[3] J. Kristeva, "Motherhood According to Giovanni Bellini," in *Desire in Language*, Columbia University Press, New York, 1980. p. 240.
[4] The Futurist love of a good fight is epitomized by F. T. Marinetti's famous statement, in *The Foundation and Manifesto of Futurism* (1908), that the Futurists "will glorify war — to only true hygiene of the world — militarism, patriotism, the destructive gesture of the anarchist." There is "no masterpiece," he insisted, "without the stamp of aggressiveness." Quoted in Herschel B. Chipp, *Theories of Modern Art*, University of California Press, Berkeley, 1984, p. 286.
[5] C. G. Jung, *Psychology of the Unconscious*, Dodd, Mead, New York, 1944, p. 307 ff.
[6] For a discussion of Winnicott's concept of potential space as the zone of illusion in which subjective and objective reality are simultaneous, with neither having priority over the other — in no hierarchical relationship — see M. Davis and D. Wallbridge, *Boundary and Space: An Introduction to the Work of D. W. Winnicott*, Brunner/Maxel, New York, 1981, esp. p. 63 ff.
[7] Quoted in E. Coen, *Umberto Boccioni*, exhibition catalogue, Metropolitan Museum of Art, New York, 1988, p. xii.
[8] Ibid., p. xiii.
[9] A. Tanchis, *Bruno Munari: Design As Art*, MIT Press, Cambridge, Mass., 1987, p. 11.
[10] Ibid., p. 12.
[11] Quoted in *Futurist Manifestos*, ed. Umbro Apollonio, Documents of Modern Art, Viking Press, New York, 1973, p. 200.
[12] Ibid., p. 205.
[13] Ibid.

Poster for *Cabiria*, 1914

Gian Piero Brunetta

Comets and Fireflies: the Shining Dreams Great and Small of Forty Years of Italian Cinema

La presa di Roma
by Filoteo Alberini, 1905

Sets at the Cines studios, 1907

Barone Franchetti in Uganda
by Luca Comerio, 1911

Rina De Liguoro in *Messalina*
by Enrico Guazzoni, 1923

Italian cinema was born a decade late with respect to that of other countries, and from the start was marked by a financial and organizational situation that was frail and lacking in vigor. The thousands of people who flocked to the Via Nomentana in Rome on the evening of 20 September 1905 to witness the maiden screening of the first film, *La presa di Roma*, produced and directed by Filoteo Alberini, did not seem at all concerned about this, however.

The press recorded "enthusiastic applause" and "emotional involvement" on the part of the audience as it viewed events that thirty-five years previously "had made the hearts of all Italians skip a beat." To judge from these reactions, it was as if the people were oblivious of the screen stretched in front of them, opposite Porta Pia; so caught up were they in the events they were viewing that they seemed ready at a moment's notice to join the *bersaglieri* and celebrate the birth of a nation.

It was certainly no accident that for the inauguration of Italian cinema Alberini chose an episode in which the symbols of national identity were instantly recognizable, and a setting for the projection that coincided with the reality of the incidents it portrayed. In 250 metres of celluloid, the original events are accurately reconstructed, with minute attention to detail in uniforms and in recreating the military actions and bearing of the time; all this contributes to making the film seem a declaration of intent, clearly indicating the road cinema should take in the future.

Between 1905 and 1912 Italian film production gained its independence and began to define its own particular character, identifying its literary and visual references, its sources of inspiration and its genres; it compared its own qualities with the narrative styles and forms of expression adopted by others countries, and it concentrated a great deal of its efforts on reaffirming its natural claim to a great literary and artistic tradition.

From its very first steps the newborn film industry sought to establish its heritage and to define its legitimate role in the fullest artistic and cultural sense. Without showing the slightest sign of an inferiority complex with respect to the other art forms, it succeeded in assimilating, adapting, transforming and translating the parallel and related worlds of literature, history and the humanities.

The fact that in just a few *tableaux vivants* it was possible to convey the essence of a Homeric poem or a theatrical masterpiece, or to bring to life the subject of a cycle of medieval frescoes or a Renaissance painting — or even those of prints or popular illustration — demonstrated that cinema had an infinite potential; it could go in almost any direction and it chose to do so in style, adopting "the grand manner," a phrase used by Heinrich Wölfflin in talking of the Renaissance.

Unlike American cinema, Italian films did not set out to celebrate and explore the rhythms of modern life but they ranged over a much broader timespan. Without seeking to upset the basic classifications immediately adopted internationally, Italian cinema succeeded in bringing to the fore and giving expression, within a relatively complex structure, to the major areas of artistic endeavour. Epic narrative, fiction, drama, poetry, scenography, architecture and the visual arts, including photography, were all points of reference against which the cinema measured itself on equal terms, rapidly establishing itself as a new art form.

The notion that films could be the easiest and most economical means to provide the sort of people's university that socialist intellectuals and positivist teachers dreamed of did not last long: cinema aimed a good deal higher than that. By the end of the first decade of the 1900s the major "film factories'" planning directors in Rome, Turin and Milan had already set their sights on the great middle-class, a public which until then had been little attracted by the cinema's broad-based appeal, and the social mix of the audiences filling the first film halls.

Indeed, the bosses of such studios as Cines, Milano Films, Ambrosio, and Itala felt more akin to Renaissance patrons of the arts than to their contemporaries in the rapidly expanding motor industry, with whom many of them had occasion to rub elbows.

Gli ultimi giorni di Pompei
by Carmine Gallone
and Amleto Palermi, 1926

For the rising middle classes the cinema became the quickest means of acquiring a certain cultural sophistication; it was also a sort of universal meeting place, where the trade in pretty images put on prominent display the symbols of the national identity and seemed to fire a spirit of patriotism.

One of the cinema's many objectives was to capture foreign audiences by making use of the vast cultural heritage at its disposal: the works of the greatest painters and writers of all time. In short order, a film archive had been produced which could claim the contributions, to a greater or lesser extent, of such masters as Homer and Manzoni, Shakespeare and De Amicis, Dante and D'Annunzio, Titian and Canova, Raffael and Dante Gabriel Rossetti, Doré and Bartolomeo Pinelli, Hans Makart and Francesco Paolo Michetti. Italian cinema stood precisely at the point where the creative streams of literature and the figurative arts converged, and it developed very quickly, due mainly to the conviction that so much of its cultural inheritance could be adapted for the screen. For Italian film producers the cinematic image was the prime result of a synthesis in which every sort of encounter, hybridization and metamorphosis was legitimate and acceptable.

Il granatiere Roland
by Luigi Maggi, 1911

A careful study of the sources of inspiration behind the images used in the first films to express the will to conquer space and time — from *Nerone* by Arrigo Frusta (1909) to *La caduta di Troia* by Giovanni Pastrone, and *Odissea*, *Il granatiere Roland* and *Nozze d'oro* by Luigi Maggi (all 1911) — reveals the cinema's desire to place itself on an equal footing with all the great figurative arts movements of the past, from the Medieval to the more recent Gothic Revivalist school.

In principio fuit traductio: in the early years the screen was used as a mirror to reflect and multiply the cultural patrimony that the cinema had inherited by direct and legitimate descent.

In 1911 Milano Films produced *Inferno*, the first major full-length production to have the honor of being shown at the Sorbonne and other international centres. Its two artistic directors, Francesco Bertolini and Adolfo Padovan, had put Gustave Doré's illustrations of Dante's writings onto the screen bringing to life not only the text, but especially Doré's well-known figurative interpretation of it. Intellectuals around the world — among them Benedetto Croce — viewed every scene with enormous respect, admiration and emotion.

Inferno by Francesco Bertolini and Adolfo Padovan, 1911

The fixed desire of cameramen such as Roberto Omegna, Giovanni Vitrotti and Luca Comerio was to widen the scope of the camera lens and it did not seem that they would be satisfied until they could take in the entire surface of the earth in one shot. Meanwhile, the producers and creative teams at the great studios of Cines, Ambrosio, Itala, and Milano Films were ever more determined to conquer time and space, and they continued to break barriers of scale and extend the perspectives of their images. They packed their films with literary and artistic references set in historical contexts to compensate for any constitutional weaknesses. Total immersion in history seems to have been an essential factor in the development of the entire industry. Within a few years in a continuous process of transformation historical energy was converted into financial profit. Born to educate the people, historical films became mirrors and magnifying glasses through which to view the aspirations of the present day.

Cabiria by Giovanni Pastrone, 1914

The films produced in Turin, Rome and Milan shared a vision of massive proportions: their subject matter ranged over the entire span of history, set in all corners of the world; the costumes, styles and events of every age came under the eye of the camera sooner or later. Techniques of representation were borrowed from landscape painters, neo-Classical court artists, popular weeklies illustrators, theater and opera designers... Every element was broken down and transformed, condensed or expanded in order to give life to a unique invention capable of conjuring up cities and far-away places.

This obsession with visual forms that dominated the early Italian cinema was almost immediately rewarded with unanimous international recognition and approval and with economic success. By 1911 the Frenchman Victor Jasset, in a seminal essay on film directing, was writing of "artists of the cinema," of "exclusive rights to history" and of the "Italian school."

The triumph of the dramatized history film genre in Italy between 1910 and 1915 contrasts sharply with its dismissal by the film historians and critics who from the Thirties on brushed it off with an air of annoyance as an "endless carnival." Examples of such films come to mind, willy-nilly: *Quo Vadis?* and *Gli ultimi giorni di Pompei*, *Cajus Julius Caesar* and *Marcantonio e Cleopatra*, *Spartacus* and *Il granatiere Roland*, *Gerusalemme liberata* and *Scuola di eroi*, *Otello* and *Cabiria* — films that evoked the glory of the past and the great days of Rome and Venice. They stirred the hopes and ambitions of their contemporary generation, serving as a sort of bloodless manifestation of the frenzied desire to take up arms that then affected enormous numbers of young nationalists. Cinema enlarged upon and illuminated the ideas these people believed in, giving new meaning to the rallying calls of the leaders of the nationalist factions and inspiring new hope in those who cried out for a revival of the power of Rome.

As far as stylistic aspects of cinematography were concerned, the discovery of the fundamental dynamics of editing — its syntax and its rhythms — is not as striking as the wish to confirm cinema as one of the "figurative arts," raising it above its

Amleto Novelli in
Cajus Julius Caesar
by Enrico Guazzoni, 1914

Quo vadis?
by Gabriellino D'Annunzio
and Georg Jacoby, 1925

status as mere entertainment and representation. Suddenly there seemed no limit to the power of the movie camera: endless possibilities opened up before the cameramen's eyes, and the vast spectrum that presented itself to him could be broken down into as many small centers of action and focus as he chose. The breadth of these new perspectives was matched by the extent to which they were exploited, above all in terms of scenic imagination, and by the reaction of cinema audiences. The international success of *Quo Vadis?* and *Cabiria* illustrated the Italian film industry's single-minded pursuit of its cultural and economic aims in the period under discussion.

If Guazzoni, Antamoro and Pastrone — to varying degrees — were the apostles of the loftiest new creed, and of cinema in the "grand manner," Gabriele D'Annunzio was its prophet, having come to cinema to administer the highest celebration of the rite of the Creation, offering inspiration and guidance to Giovanni Pastrone in the making of *Cabiria*. Although it has long been considered that D'Annunzio's brief interest in the cinema was solely financial, in reality he went through the experience in a state of great exaltation, as if he believed that he could achieve certain aims only through the medium of film. If he could fill the screen with the great mythological themes and historical events, the past could be revived as a symbol of the present and future aspirations of an entire people. D'Annunzio regarded film as the perfect medium through which to tell a modern epic and to present the Total Work of Art, as theorized by Richard Wagner and Friedrich Nietzsche.

Cabiria is a "film monstre," one of the wonders of early cinema, and through it shone the brilliance of D'Annunzio's personality, as he spread his creed. In terms of technical and visual effects (its visual make-up, compositional and structural rhythms, the movements of the characters among the architectural and scenic elements of the film), however, it was Pastrone who masterminded this great work. The alter ego of Marco Gratico — the hero of D'Annunzio's *La nave* — he "armed the prow [of *Cabiria*] and set sail for the world."

The stormy upheaval of the war soon put an end to this great dream of conquest and caused the Italian *homo cinematographicus* to reassess his role, in accordance with the more modest and human proportions of the Art Nouveau drawing rooms and urban environment of European cities of the early 1900s.

These were the years of the triumphal rise of the "star system". Between 1915 and 1920 the average filmgoer became aware of interchange of ideas between cinema and the applied arts, poetry, the theatre, architecture and urban design. Besides D'Annunzio, the most important influences were Arnold Böcklin, Alphonse Mucha, Hugo von Hofmannsthal, James Whistler, Gustave Moreau, the poetry of symbolism, *Crepuscolarismo*, and the sculpture of Auguste Rodin and the historical works of the pre-Raphaelites. In an intermarriage of the arts that was unique to Italy, writers, poets, painters, illustrators, architects and scenographers — Guido Gozzano, Nino Oxilia, Giovanni Verga, Salvatore Di Giacomo, Duilio Cambellotti, Aristide Sartorio, Enrico Prampolini, Pietro Mascagni and Ildebrando Pizzetti — were very much a creative part of the film industry. Fragments, just the muscle from the works of dozens of artists, nourished the "bodies beautiful" of the stars of the day, such as Francesca Bertini, Lyda Borelli, Pina Menichelli, Hesperia, Leda Gys and Eleonora Duse.

An army of Eves, Pandoras, Lucretias, tigresses, serpent-women, predatory bird-women, ladies of the camellias, and tree-like figures with bodies as supple as a convolvulus and with prehensile arms like a carnivorous plant, drifted between poetry and painting, sculpture and the silver screen as if no barriers existed between one medium and another. The hair of Lyda Borelli seemed to have been borrowed from a painting by Dante Gabriele Rossetti, and the movements of her hands have been likened to the "sinuous twists of wrought-ironwork that decorate the Paris metro

Poster for *Za la Mort*, 1915 directed by and starring Emilio Ghione

entrances." There are scenes in *Ma l'amor mio non muore* (1913) and *Rapsodia satanica* (1917) that seem to be perfect interpretations of the paintings of Gustav Klimt, Aristide Sartorio or Adolfo De Carolis. The second of these two films, directed by Nino Oxilia, is a sort of visual and poetic synthesis of the ideals of Art Nouveau and Symbolism. The *femmes fatales* of Italian cinema were bringers of death and ruin, but audiences around the world made it clear that they much preferred a sweet demise at the hands of these ladies to one for glory and honour.

Il fuoco, Tigre reale, La falena, L'ombra, La sfinge, Odette and *La signora delle camelie* made up a solid defensive front put up by Art Nouveau and Symbolism against attack from the Futurist avant-garde.

Lyda Borelli

The clash never really occurred in the cinema, however, as the Futurists confined themselves to launching in 1916 the *Manifesto of the Futurist Cinema*, which was more influential in terms of ideas and potential than on a practical level, though we are still a long way from evaluating clearly the nature of its contribution. It appeared as Futurism was entering its final phase, but in a certain sense it also marked the point of its fullest development and assimilation, encapsulating the Futurist ideals which were to form the basis of a new cinema and a new world. In practice the *Manifesto* triggered off a series of chain reactions, and though the quality of the results it produced was not comparable with other areas of the arts, it helped to bring about changes in the cinema on an international scale which in turn affected poetry, painting and music. The dazzling pyrotechnics anticipated by Giacomo Balla and Fortunato Depero in their *Futurist Reconstruction of the Universe*, conjuring up an abstract artificial world in which the arts and sciences intermingled and physics and chemistry collaborated in order to achieve greater expressiveness, reappear in a more complete and visionary form in the *Manifesto*. Its signatories, Balla, Marinetti, Bruno Corra, Emilio Settimelli, Arnaldo Ginna and Remo Chiti, claimed the cinema's right to unrestricted self-expression, and attributed to the medium a greater potential than any other art form: "The cinema must be allowed free expression," says the manifesto, "in order to become the perfect instrument of a new artistic medium, one that is farther reaching and more versatile than any already in existence... Futurist cinema today is creating an infinite range of expression... We shall invent a medium with complete freedom of speech, which can break down the barriers between literature, painting and music and can create a bridge between the spoken word and reality... We shall take the universe apart and rebuild it in whatever way we wish." The *Manifesto* was the creator and inspirational force behind all cinema of the period except in Italy. If one compares the various points of the *Manifesto* with the work of the French, German and Russian avant-garde directors of the 1920s, it becomes apparent, or at least it seems to be the case, that everything had been predicted and planned, and that the ethics of Futurism influenced, for example, Hans Richter and Dziga Vertov, Viking Eggeling and Man Ray, René Clair and Germaine Dulac in the same way.

Pina Menichelli, 1916

As far as Italy was concerned, however, Futurism found its ideal interpreters in cameramen such as Luca Comerio who from 1911 onwards devoted themselves to recording images of the war in Libya, photographing it from the air, as Paul Virilio has described, in order to view the world from a new angle and discover some new means of representing it in visual terms. In 1914-15 Comerio was the only civilian film-maker to be given permission to work at the front; the armed car from which he filmed is identical to the one described by Marinetti in *Alcova d'acciaio*.

There are certain affinities between the poems of Marinetti, such as "Il monoplano del papa" (The Pope's Monoplane) of 1910 and "Bombardamento di Adrianopoli" (The Bombing of Adrianopolis), and the first aerial shots taken by Comerio and other cameramen who recorded the war in Libya, and who responded with perfect timing to the demands of the Futurist cinema. Before it turned to the lights and

Francesca Bertini in *Assunta Spina* by Gustavo Serena, 1915

rhythms of the city, the cinema revealed the beauty of the night-time spectacle of machine-gun fire and cannon flares, and when Marinetti made his first flight over the Libyan front in 1912, the images of his own imagination must have accorded perfectly with those of Comerio, whose first shots were taken from the skies over Libya in the same period.

As is well known, the results of the Futurist declaration yielded very little in terms of the number of films produced — the only officially recognized work being *Vita Futurista* of 1916 (but it appears that it was not projected in the cinemas until the beginning of 1917) — and its influence on the later development of the cinema in general was minimal.

The only film that could with any justification be considered Futurist was *Thaïs* by Anton Giulio Bragaglia, with scenography in the second part by Enrico Prampolini. The geometrical rigour of the imagery and symbolism representing the dreams of the main character do not, however, suggest a total assimilation of Futurist ideals, and the scenography itself consists merely of stylistic variations on work being carried out at the same time by Duilio Cambellotti, Camillo Innocenti and Aristide Sartorio. The failure of the Futurist program was due not to any lack of technical competence on the part of Marinetti, Settimelli and the others, but to the impossibility of reconciling the commercial demands of the film industry, which were linked to production and distribution methods, with those of Futurism, to which chaos and disorder, and the destruction and free reconstruction of the very world of the cinema itself, were fundamental principles.

Hard though it may be to identify any real relationship between cause and effect in terms of Italian cinema of the following decades, it is possible to trace the influence of a few important themes and characteristics of Futurism which reappeared from time to time — like a river running through limestone, which disappears underground and every so often resurfaces — in the work of scenographers and directors of the early 1930s, such as Gastone Medin, Virgilio Marchi, Vinicio Paladini, Antonio Valente, Carlo Ludovico Bragaglia and Italo Cremona.

Several years of a leading role in the international scene were followed by a long period of silence for the Italian cinema. Then, towards the end of the 1920s, it made a major come-back. A new generation of directors, led by Alessandro Blasetti and Mario Camerini, decided to cut every remaining link with the silent movies of the past and to try to open the way to a new Italian cinema, up to linguistic, expressive and narrative standards achieved by other countries.

Paradoxically, the hiatus in film-making that occurred in the second half of the 1920s resulted in a sort of parting of the ways between the actual geography, language and attitudes of Italy itself — for which Fascism was trying to provide a common denominator — and the imaginary world of the movie screen which showed objects, places, houses and settings reflecting the more modern French and German lifestyles. For about fifteen years the screen became a shop window and traveling showcase for all the products of modern, progressive European industrial design.

30 secondi d'amore
by Mario Bonnard, 1936

196

Thaïs by Anton Giulio Bragaglia
1916

Blasetti and Camerini aimed at realism, concentrating on the depiction of ordinary everyday situations in the lives of country and working people, and trying to act as interpreters of the proletarian and lower middle class ideologies. But their approach differed from that of the mainstream directors whose primary objective was to identify themselves with the characteristics, vocabulary and aims of Art Déco and Bauhaus architecture and design.

In sound films, it is above all the objects — the sets and props — that speak, and theirs is a universal language that is entirely at odds with the ideals and commandments of the Fascist creed.

The *homines novi* of the Italian cinema believed that they could move freely in a full 360-degree circle to go in search of the thousand-and-one new Italies, that they were entitled to film everything. In fact, however, and from the very start, their way was far from clear: every turn was marked by yet another restriction. Effectively what happened was comparable yet contrary in certain ways to what had occurred just before the First World War; but, instead of its initial aim of conquering time and space, now cinema seemed to operate within a space that little by little was being reduced, choked off. In the hundreds of films made between 1930 and the Second World War, there is not a single moment in which one feels overwhelmed by an immensity of space, as one does for example in the films of John Ford. Not once does one experience the thrill of recognition as one does with Josef von Sternberg's close-ups: studies of faces that become almost landscapes. Everything takes place in a confined space and is observed by the camera from a distance that remains virtually constant.

This small area, however, contained all the symbols that were most precious to the people of Mussolini's Italy. The first to try to let these symbols speak out for themselves and to look at Italy and the Italians as they really were, ignoring the propaganda of the regime, were set designers and painters such as Gastone Medin and Carlo Levi and architects such as Enrico Paulucci and Giuseppe Capponi. They collaborated on such films as *La voce lontana*, directed by Guido Brignone in 1931

Emma Baron in *Anonima Roylott*
by Raffaello Matarazzo, 1936

and 1933 respectively, on *Patatrac*, made by Gennaro Righelli in 1931, and on *Due cuori felici* by Baldassarre Negroni in 1932.

The representation of new environments for living, which seemed to have been created under the eyes of Le Corbusier, Mies van der Rohe or Marcel Breuer, were met with fierce protests on the part of the critics but, on the part of the public gave rise to an unforeseen number of dreams and hopes in conflict with the ideals of the Fascist regime.

The architect Giuseppe Capponi, writing in the magazine *Architettura*, discussed the primary role of these objects: "The set designer's task is not simply to devise the backdrops but to control the silent elements of the set (the inanimate objects, lights, furniture which should express themselves in their own concise language and perform in the same way as the actors do." The great architectural and design magazines of the 1930s published important articles on modern interior design in the cinema. While interior design acknowledged — though to a fairly limited extent — the influence of the paintings of Mario Sironi, Massimo Campigli and the followers of the *Novecento* movement, it displayed a very clear and well-timed capacity for interaction with industrial design (or the decorative arts, as they were still known) and rationalist architecture.

Contrary to what one might imagine, Rome and its imperial glories were not a recurrent subject in cinema between the two wars. *Scipione l'Africano* by Carmine Gallone (1937) is in fact unique in this respect, and its reception disappointed the political regime's expectations.

The set designers and painters who followed an international style (in addition to those already cited, we might add Guido Fiorini, who worked with Le Corbusier, Piero Filippone, Antonio Valente, Maria De Matteis and Virgilio Marchi) sought to give expression not so much to the actors and the sets as to the dreams of the Italians, who yearned for something more than the one thousand lire a month that had been fixed by a popular tune as the average Italian's maximum aspiration. The closer the war came, the more the cinema celebrated the life of extravagance and

Scipione l'Africano
by Carmine Gallone, 1937

Sergio Tofano in *Cenerentola e il signor Bonaventura*, 1942

Fulvia Lanzi in *Squadrone Bianco*
by Augusto Genina, 1936

198

waste, with huge sums of money and every imaginable type of luxury object in free circulation on the screens.

Examination of the films popularly known as *telefoni bianchi* (the "white telephone" being a symbol of the ultimate in luxury) makes it clear how over a few years' time the attitudes and desires of millions of people were radically transformed, thanks to a compact and well-integrated network of film distribution. This new mentality gives no space to Fascism and its dreams of expansion. Ironically, the cinema city which Mussolini had wanted to establish "so that Fascist Italy can spread the light of the Roman civilization more rapidly around the world" ended up by inspiring the private hopes and dreams of people throughout the nation, thanks to those *telefoni bianchi*, so abhorrent to the regime. Cinecittà gained importance less as a locations site in which to recreate Harlem and the Malayan jungle, the interiors of the Kremlin and the Ducal Palace in Venice, than as a gigantic emporium in which, in film after film, thousands of objects and symbols of collective desire were put on display.

This was a far cry from the frugality and self-sacrifice preached by the State! Within a few months of its birth in 1937, Cinecittà had taken hold in the popular imagination as a sort of Grand Hotel with red carpets rolled out to welcome the dreams of a lower middle classes that firmly resisted the idea of being forced to set out on the warpath in order to ensure the worldwide victory of the *pax mussoliniana*.

It would be interesting to examine the sets of the films made in the years leading up to the war — *Mille lire al mese, Voglio vivere con Letizia, La dama bianca, Validità giorni dieci, Eravamo sette sorelle, Ore 9 lezione di chimica, A che servono questi quattrini, Miliardi che follia, Assenza ingiustificata...* — and to simply compile a catalogue of items such as cars, jewellery, clothes and furnishings that appeared in them. The interiors shown in these films seem right off the pages of the latest issues of the classiest Italian interior design magazines, *Casabella* and *Domus*.

In dozens of films the leading roles were ostensibly the engineers, surgeons, students, journalists, shop-assistants and "the unemployed of good society," but in reality they were the cars made by Maserati and Isotta Fraschini or the furniture designed by Gio Ponti, Piero Portaluppi, Giuseppe Pagano, Ignazio Gardella, Franco Albini, Giuseppe Mazzoleni and Pietro Aschieri. In luxury apartments the Frau or Colombo armchairs, the radios designed by the Castiglione brothers, the Lenci ceramics, the Venini or Barovier glass and the Pietro Chiesa and Luciano Baldessari lamps all captured the audience's imagination in a way that was far more powerful than that of the autocratic stars.

In the same period, alongside these productions, films of a very different nature — which hovered somewhere between the figurative arts and literature — were being made by a group of directors that included Mario Soldati, Luigi Chiarini, Alberto Lattuada, Renato Castellani and Ferdinando Maria Poggioli. They chose to go back in time and explore the possibilities of the legacy of art and their own capacity to translate it onto the screen. The pictorial influences in films such as *Malombra, Piccolo mondo antico, Via delle cinque lune, La bella addormentata, Un colpo di pistola* and *Giacomo l'idealista* ranged from the impressionist paintings of the Italian *Macchiaioli* group to great works by European masters from Rembrandt to Courbet. The lighting — above all the sources of light in interior scenes — played a vital role in terms of drama and expressiveness. These directors' skill in using light as a means of artistic expression grew in response to their desire to get as for away as possible from related contemporary events in the fields of art and literature, and to sever all links with them. The present, in their view, was dark and only the past emanated powerful beams of light.

Any expanding industry shows, with increasing clarity over time, its points of tension and of thrust as its boundaries and lines of development take on definition.

Luchino Visconti in 1942
on the set of *Ossessione*

Nothing seemed to unite the conventional directors, grouped together under the label of "calligraphers" with the critics, intellectual artists and up-and-coming directors who gravitated for a few years around the magazine *Cinema* and then trooped off in the wake of Luchino Visconti to the area around Ferrara and the Po delta, to film *Ossessione* in 1942. Some have readily perceived in the images of *Ossessione* the vestiges of a "genetic" inheritance handed down from Renaissance art, through Caravaggio, to 19th-century literature and early Italian cinema of naturalist inspiration. Umberto Barbaro, who for years has predicted and promoted the birth of a new age in the cinema, has re-examined Visconti's images of Ferrara, and come to the conclusion that the lessons of Cosmé Tura and the Ferrarese group of painters of the (recently the subject of an excellent study by Roberto Longhi) are now — having undergone a series of changes and a process of synthesis — being revived in a rising new school of cinematography. It seems that in Ferrara the way to a new movement in the cinema is finally being opened, one which is firmly rooted in a tradition that is "truly ours, and ours alone, that of the figurative arts." In an article entitled "Neorealismo," published in the magazine *Film*, on the eve of 25 July 1943, Barbaro announced the advent of a new era of Italian cinema. In the pages that followed, he took up and orchestrated like a musical symphony a number of Longhi's themes, applying them to Visconti's *Ossessione*: "It is a horrifying story set in the sweetest and gentlest landscape in Italy. It is not a well-ordered landscape redolent of classicism... but that of the Po valley, damp, fertile, steaming... a part of Italy that had not been seen before in our films..."

Visconti challenged the conventions and established a new order, with a new approach to the handling of space and the relationship between "man and his surroundings" (as Longhi would have said). *Ossessione* was the spark that kindled the fire of a new cinema that will conquer the world.

Enrico Crispolti   **Futurism and Plastic Expression Between the Wars**

Today, any historically up-to-date assessment of the impact of Futurism in Italian culture between the wars, at least in artistic spheres, must take certain basic facts for granted, facts that are best summarized straight away, albeit schematically.

The arguments and sequence of events of Futurism itself, as an influential creative movement, were formerly considered by critics to be over and done by the mid-1910s (with the death of Boccioni and Sant'Elia in 1916 marking its outer limit). This chronology has been definitively disproved, and was based on an essentially "painting-centric" (or more specifically Boccioni-centric) assessment of the Futurist experience. The date corresponds more closely to the phenomenon of the *Novecento* — i.e., to the works of Carrà, Sironi, and Soffici, after their dalliance with Futurism — and is anyway inconsistent with the developments in Balla's pictorial inquiry (which in the early 1910s provided a cogent counterpoint to the work of Boccioni); nor does it tally with the development of the Futurist oeuvre in general (including their literature).[1]

Unlike other avant-garde movements termed "historical" (and not improperly), Futurism effected a widespread influence on daily life in its time, and sought to initiate a creative renaissance in all aspects of reality, behavior, and social intercourse — all in the name of a "Futurist reconstruction of the universe" (the highly significant title of the Manifesto dated 11 March 1915, signed by Balla and Depero). Today, this particular commitment is perhaps the key to understanding the Futurist phenomenon as a whole, and to assessing the implications of its various individual creative positions.[2] The "Futurist reconstruction of the universe" was announced midway through the 1910s and immediately put into practice, with Balla, Depero, and Prampolini in the front line, as they appeared at the international exposition of decorative arts and modern industry in Paris in 1925. Their proposition only really came to full fruition during the period now generally referred to as "Second Futurism" (an expression I myself coined thirty years ago), which spanned from the highly intense 1920s to the not-repetitive 1930s.[3] This ambition (often limited to the works of the artist himself, or otherwise in a sort of complementary contiguity) involved creatively intervening to remodel every possible aspect of reality: the image of a city and its architecture, stage sets, artificial nature, exhibition installations, painting and sculpture geared to plastic dynamism, "plastic complexes," "tactilism," furniture, clothes, everyday objects and appliances, advertising, typography, books, aesthetic objects, narrative prose, works for the theater, poetry, "words-in-freedom," the visualization of "free-word tableaux," photography and photomontage, cine films, mass communications (radio), postal art, criticism and the practice of science, politics, customs, and behavior.[4]

The idea of a hypothetical "Second Futurism" was discussed in its day to account for the existence of further developments that went far beyond the acclaimed initial exploits; by the first half of the 1910s, Futurist painting and sculpture had really only lived out the first chapter of a more complex and involved development. Various distinct "phases" can be detected in the course of this development, which, although certainly not equally valid in qualitative terms, represent the true innovative course of the Futurists' creative interests.[5] And while the initial sensational phase (which affected painting and sculpture in particular) in the first half of the 1910s was mainly led by Boccioni and Balla, then the second phase saw Balla projected even more to the fore, joined by Depero and Prampolini. This trio piloted the last experimental spurt of Futurism through the second half of the 1910s and into the 1920s, channeling their efforts into putting their "Futurist reconstruction of the universe" into practice on a broader front. Balla was constantly serving up his formal analogies in thrilling combinations of consistently pure and vivid color. Depero was more inclined to a world of fable, first almost "metaphysical," then asserting a mechanical "primitive" re-invention of his view of the world (including natural and rural). Prampolini, more concrete, explored possible new plastic expressions, following the analogical suggestions of the mechanical world. He was also more committed to developing theories and to keeping up a multi-faceted and intense exchange with the emerging European avant-garde. In the 1930s, it was Prampolini who effectively shepherded the last experiments in Futurism.

The development of Futurist painting can be divided up into various phases, the first of which is best defined as "analytical," largely centered on Milan and spanning from 1910-1911 to 1914; this was followed by a phase we might define as "synthetic," this time centered on Rome and taking form around 1914 to 1915. After gravitating toward a mechanical vision around 1918, first on a linguistic level and then in terms of the visual content, Futurist painting shifted into a final phase, which ten years later matured into the aeropainting and "cosmic" phase.

However debatable and arbitrary the idea of a clean break is, the events up to the "Second Futurism" can safely be said to start with the work of Balla, Depero, and Prampolini in Rome in the second half of the 1910s, and correspond to the "synthetic" phase of Futurist painting. The preceding or "analytical" phase, initiated in 1910-11 and evolving in two stages, began to show signs of decline toward 1913-14, a decline that starts with Boccioni's studies and their almost abstract volumetric synthesis (1913 and 1914), culminating in a marked return to figurative plasticity of Cézannian stamp (1914); Balla's pursuit of a dynamic synthesis of "force-lines" of an increasingly abstract nature in 1913-14, working on themes of "abstract speed," "speed lines," and "speed lines + landscape"; Carrà's use of the collage technique (1914); the new synthesis of plastic analogies abstracted by Severini (1913-14); the broader plastic creations of Sironi; and even in the more confident narrative plasticity of the exponents of the "para-Futurist" Milan-based group *Nuove Tendenze*, composed of Funi, Dudreville, Erba, and Nizzoli; and finally, hints of "synthetic" Cubism in Soffici and Rosai's work.

But the real turning-point heralding the new synthetic phase is evident in Balla's cycle of *Demostrazioni interventiste* (*Interventionist Demonstrations*, 1915) and in his "plastic complexes," completed in league with Depero between 1914 and 1915 (though another artist who pursued this idea was Prampolini, whose paintings and set designs betray a similar orientation between 1915 and 1916).

At this point, the general ambition was to achieve "plastic complexity," a kind of "abstract Futurist style," in the form of an inventive formal analogism that shunned the normal pursuit of representative synthesis; it was achieved particularly through the "plastic complex," an entirely new mixed plastic-pictorial object with an analogic value that offered the formal basis for the "Futurist reconstruction of the universe."[6] In Balla and Depero (and also Prampolini, though with less linguistic clarity) this resulted in highly condensed pictorial constructions of dynamic outlines and solid fields of color.[7] Balla increasingly used color to achieve "an explosive art, a surprise art," as he wrote in his *Manifesto del colore* (*Manifesto on Color*, 1918).[8]

The main outcome of this synthetic phase in Futurist painting, besides Balla's "interventionist" cycle (1915), is found in his intense work from 1916 onward (*Velo di vedova, The Widow's Veil*, 1916; *Il taglio del bosco, Tree Felling*, 1918; his "season" cycle, 1917-18; *Colpo di fucile domenicale, Sunday Gunshot*, 1918; *Trasformazione forme-spiriti, Form-Spirit Transformation*, 1918-20), in Depero's paintings completed between 1915 and 1918 (*Rom-kraskri — Esplosione di granata, Rom-kraskri — Gre-*

Fortunato Depero
Sun Giving Birth to Train, 1924

nade Explosion, 1915; *Movimento di uccelli, Bird Movement*, 1916; *Ballerina idolo, Idol Dancer*, 1917; *Rotazione di ballerina e pappagalli, Rotation of Ballerina and Parrots*, 1917-18), up to the "Balli Plastici" (Plastic Dances) cycle of 1917-18. And while Prampolini was piecing together his own plastic synthetic idiom, on very similar precepts (*Danzatrice, Dancer*, c. 1916), Gerardo Dottori had begun his highly personal spiritual vision from above (*Forze ascensionali, Rising Forces*, 1919), and Julius Evola was engaged in a new reverberant plastic synthesis of his own (*Fucina, Studio di rumori, At the Forge, Study in Noise*, 1917-18).

Tato, *Oblique Urbanisms*, c. 1935

At the end of the 1910s, this synthetic phase was gradually superseded by mechanical themes. The analogical plastic synthesis that had characterized the synthetic phase, though drawing on the same type of language, took on increasing substance in terms of "mechanical" formal analogy.[9] Machines offered an example of formal coherence, a clean, exact vision. Working in Rome, Vinicio Paladini, Ivo Pannaggi, and Prampolini speculated on this approach defining it in a manifesto entitled *L'arte meccanica* (*Mechanical Art*), which was published in May 1923 in *Noi*, a Rome-based journal run by Prampolini himself; in its second series (1923-35) the magazine became the main outlet for this particular area of research, and a bridge for the new "purist" and "constructivist" avant-gardes in Europe.[10] In 1922-23 however, on the initiative of Fillia (who was not even twenty at the time), a new "mechanical" sub-group emerged in Turin, one of the three cities of the so-called northern "industrial triangle," where the movement started with a marked proletarian bias,[11] just as Paladini's "proletkult" movement in Rome had already done in 1922 in the interests of communist political commitment.[12]

Enrico Prampolini
Spatial-Country Polychrome, 1917

However, as I suggested thirty years ago, this mechanical phase seems to comprise two internal stages. In the first, the prevalent mechanical analogy is expressed through flat plastic shapes, more or less geometrically arranged, and resonant, uniform color schemes.[13] This approach is particularly noticeable in the work of Prampolini between 1919 and 1923-24 (*Costruzione spaziale — paesaggio, Spatial Construction — Landscape*, 1919; *La geometria della voluttà, The Geometry of Delight*, 1922; *La palestra dei sensi, The Palaestra of the Senses*, 1923), and also in the evolution of Paladini, Pannaggi (who also translated it into sculpture) and De Pistoris at the beginning of the 1920s; a similar stamp can be seen in the work of Fillia from 1925-26. Some traces of this approach, can also be detected in Balla's works in the same period, though he also makes a free-ranging use of analogy (abstract landscape themes, or in paintings such as *Non rompere le scatole, Buzz Off....*, c. 1923), or in Depero (*Bagnante, Bather*, 1919; *Città meccanizzata dalle ombre, City Mechanized by Shadows*, 1920), or in Dottori (*Il Lago, The Lake*, 1920; *Primavera Umbra, Umbrian Spring*, 1923; *Flora*, 1923), or in Benedetta (Marinetti's wife), or some time later, in the works of Mario Guido Dal Monte, and in the sculpture of Ernesto Thayaht and Mino Rosso. In his own way, even Severini participated in this exercise from his studio in Paris, though he was well into the mature "synthetic" Cubist stage he had embarked on in the mid-1910s.

Fortunato Depero
Grenade Explosion, 1915

The second stage of this mechanical phase sharpened the geometrical focus, with plastic volumes forming complex articulated structures, especially when portraying the human body; this demonstrated an open dialogue with the European camps of Purism and *Esprit Nouveau* led by Le Corbusier and Ozenfant (Archipenko and Herbin in France, Schlemmer, Baumeister and Belling in Germany, Servranckx Peeters and Floquet in Belgium, for instance).[14] Good examples of this can be found the canvases of Prampolini dating from around 1924-28 (*Architettura femminile — Scomposizione di nudo, Female Architecture — Analysis of Nude*, c. 1924), Pannaggi, Fillia, Nicolay Diulgheroff, Ugo Pozzo, and Fedele Azari. But some traces are also evident in in Balla's accentuated plastic purism (*S'è rotto l'incanto, The Spell Is Broken; Numeri innamorati, Numbers in Love*, and *Pessimismo e ottimismo, Pessimism and Optimism*, 1923), and in Depero, who was deeply involved in his highly personalized, colorful fantasy narrative with its essential plastic rendering (*Marinetti temporale patriottico, Marinetti Patriotic Storm*, 1924; *Fulmine compositore, Lightning Composer*, 1926). Dottori too participated (*Forme-colori, Color-Forms*, 1925; *Trittico della velocità, Triptych of Speed*, 1925-26; *Vele-onde-monti, Sails-Waves-Hills*, 1927); and later recurrences can be seen in the ideas of Antonio Marasco, Tullio Crali and Osvaldo Peruzzi.[15]

At the end of the 1920s, this mechanical phase gradually gave way to another phase of aeropainting and cosmic art, formulated in the manifesto *Aeropittura futurista*, written in 1929 and signed by Balla, Benedetta, Depero, Dottori, Fillia, Marinetti, Prampolini, Somenzi, and Tato. The manifesto was a conceptual point of reference for the several later re-interpretations issued by individuals and local groups on the occasion of the Futurist exhibition at the Galleria Pesaro in Milan in 1931.[16] This phase of aeropainting and cosmic art (which comprises the second or later stage of Second Futurism), continued through the 1930s and into the early 1940s.

Aeropainting, which also involved sculpture and spilled over into the field of poetry and literature, moved on two distinct fronts — the first, which contains the more originally creative exploits, is exemplified chiefly by the work of Prampolini, who had at the time become the leading figure in Futurist painting (which he was to make more complicated by exploring "polymaterialism"), and who worked chiefly in Paris from the mid-1920s on (*Superamento extraterrestre, Extra-terrestrial Supersession*, 1930-31; *Forme forze nello spazio, Force Forms in Space*, 1932); further examples can be found in the works of Fillia, Pippo Oriani, Diulgheroff, Pozzo, and Franco Costa in Turin, and Munari in Milan. Meanwhile, in the field of sculpture, instances include Rosso (Turin), Munari and Regina (Milan), Domenico Belli and Mino Delle Site (Rome), Tano and Sante Monachesi (Macerata), and the itinerant artist Arturo Ciacelli (who had also gravitated to Paris). This front developed the theme of flight as a cosmic projection expressed in highly fantastical terms, at times even "para-surreal," and tying in with with analogous research going on elsewhere in Europe, such as in the *Cercle e Carrè* (where both Prampolini and Fillia were present) and the *Abstraction-Création* group in Paris in the early 1930s (which included Baumeister, Molzahn, Servranckx, Hiller, Pressig, Sima, Styrsky, Toyen, and Strzeminsky). Links between Futurist painting and Metaphysical art had already been foreshadowed in the area of "mechanical" art as early as the start of the 1920s, and now a certain "neo-Metaphysical" inflection was discernible in the emphatically colored, amorphous volumes clustered in neutral tonal areas of spatial symbolism with "cosmic" inflections.[17] The same idea can also be seen in the work of Dottori, though translated to his highly individual lyrical-landscape-cosmic projection (*Volo sull'oceano, Flight over the Ocean*, 1932; *Aurora sul golfo, Dawn over the Gulf*, 1935; *Isole vulcani, Volcano Islands*, 1938). To some extent, these tendencies also showed through in Depero's more down-to-earth visions (*Inaffiatori a New York, Waterers in New York*, 1934); or in the related fantasy landscapes of the independent painter Marasco (*Silagrande*, 1930).

The other line of development is represented by, among others, Tato, Renato Di Bosso, Alfredo G. Ambrosi, Tullio Crali, and Sante Monachesi.

They, on the other hand, interpreted flight as the occasion for aerial views and ecstatic description of flying machines (including warplanes, as in the African war and World War II).[18] Meanwhile, standing somewhat apart, was Balla's extreme Futurism, a narrative style steeped in the dynamic synthesis of plastic and chromatic expressiveness (*Forse!, Perhaps!*, 1930), or elaborations of plastic structures of a distinctly non-figurative nature, frequently focusing on psychological themes, which at the end of the 1920s verged on the surreal (*Le frecce della vita, The Arrows of Life*, 1928; *Il vortice della vita, The Whirlwind of Life*, 1929).

Such were the various and distinct "phases" of Futurist pictorial and sculptual research between the end of the 1910s, through the 1930s and up to the early 1940s, when the movement's cohesion was waning as a result of Marinetti's death in 1944, and the events surrounding the war.[19] They make up part of the vast program of research toward the "Futurist reconstruction of the universe," covering all developments in plastic expression, literature and behavior.[20] The most important of these activities need a very quick mention, with particular reference to the visual works: the architectural imagery of the metropolis (Virgilio Marchi, Prampolini, Sartoris, Crali, Cesare Augusto Poggi, Diulgheroff, Angiolo Mazzoni, Guido Fiorini),[21] and the related work of environmental painting and sculpture, and interiors (Balla, Depero, Pannaggi, Dottori, Fillia, Ciacelli, Monachesi, and Tato), and installations for exhibitions and fairs (Dottori, Prampolini, Diulgheroff);[22] "mural sculpture," "fotoplastica" and murals (Prampolini, Dottori, Fillia, Oriani, Mino Rosso, Benedetta, Tato);[23] interior, object, and fashion design (Prampolini, Tato, Balla, Depero, Rizzo, Corona, Tullio d'Albisola, Fillia, Diulgheroff, Munari, Farfa, Dal Monte, Di Bosso, and Crali);[24] graphics and advertising (Depero, Prampolini, Pozzo, Diulgheroff, Pannaggi, Tullio d'Albisola, Farfa, and Munari);[25] theater and entertainment (Depero, Prampolini, Pannaggi, Crali, and Benedetta);[26] photography and photomontage (Tato, Thayaht, Paladini, Pannaggi, and Munari);[27] and, not least, visual poetry and literature (Depero, Benedetta, Giuseppe Steiner, Pietro Illari, Pino Masnata, Bruno G. Sanzin).[28]

Tullio Crali
Nose-Dive onto the Airport, 1939

This highly diversified activity was furthermore scattered far and wide over the country, and in fact, Futurist development in Italy in the 1920s and 1930s was characterized by a multitude of eminently individual pockets of activity, almost as proof of the sheer diversity the movement offered. This multiplicity and decentralization of the avant-garde was significant to the development of other modern artistic currents, irrespective of the fate met by Futurism, and this can be seen (though not exclusively) in cases where artists began with Futurism and set off in separate directions, such as Bruno Munari in Milan between the 1920s and 1930s; and also Franco Grignani for instance in the 1930s; at the end of the 1920s both Vittorio Corona and Pippo Rizzo in their Futurist phase had a hand in orienting the budding artist Renato Guttuso, at work in Sicily, or M.G. Dal Monte in Emilia Romagna, Luigi Spazzapan in northeast Italy, and even in Guido Strazza's youthful participation in the movement, for instance.

Nicolay Diulgheroff
The Rational Man, 1928

This shows that developments took place well outside the main Futurist centers of the 1910s (first Milan and then Rome), along widely divergent lines, reflecting specific groups or individual problems. These scattered pockets of activity gathered weight in the 1920s, becoming even stronger in the 1930s, when even more isolated groups sprang up. The larger hubs of activity included the Turin group gathered around Fillia (Ugo Pozzo, Diulgheroff, Rosso, Oriani, Paolo Alcide Saladin, Franco Costa, Enrico Alimandi, Mario Zucco, Mario Sturani, and others); the group in Liguria, which crystallized around the activity of the potter and sculptor Tullio d'Albisola, and was closely linked to its Turin counterpart; then there was Milan, with Munari, Regina, Cesare Andreoni, Riccardo Ricas, Ivanoe Gambini, Osvaldo Peruzzi, Mario Duse, and the Emilian artist Osvaldo Bot; while in Emilia Romagna itself, developments focused around Tato, Bot, Angelo Caviglioni and M.G. Dal Monte; further to the northeast, artists from the regions of Veneto, Trento, and Venezia Giulia, aggregated around the person of Depero, and included the young Spazzapan, Crali, Di Bosso, Ambrosi, Nello Voltolina, Carlo Maria Dormàl, Augusto Cernigoj (a professed "Constructivist"), Giorgio Carmelich, Sofronio Pocarini, and Wanda Wulz (a Surrealist photographer), among others; in Florence, a group had formed around Marasco, Thayaht, Marisa Mori (who was also closely linked with the Turin group), and Peruzzi; in Umbria, Dottori was the leading figure in a group that also featured Alessandro Bruschetti; in the Marches, Pannaggi presided during the 1920s, and later Tano, Monachesi, Peschi, and the younger artist Wladimiro Tulli in the 1930s and early 1940s. Lastly, of course, there was Rome, clustered around Balla during the 1910s and 1920s, with Prampolini gradually taking ascendance, together with Evola, Paladini, Pannaggi, De Pistoris; when Prampolini came back from Paris in the 1930s, he presided definitively over the group, which had now attracted the likes of Domenico Belli, August Favilli, Mino Delle Site, and Sebastiano Carta, eventually joining forces with the Futurists operating in the Marches. Meanwhile, in Naples, in the wake of Cangiullo came the "circumvisionists," including Mario Lepore, Pepe Diaz, Carlo Cocchia, Gildo De Rosa, Guglielmo Peirce, and Paolo Ricci; and both Puglia and Sicily had their Futurist nuclei, which included Rizzo, Corona, and Giovanni Varvaro, and Giulio D'Anna in particular.[29]

Gerardo Dottori
Rising Forces, 1920

On comparing the initial — or if you will, "heroic" — phase of Futurism of the early 1910s and the second phase, it is important to realize that the latter is not a reluctant winding-down of the creative tensions of the first with analogous methodologies and motivations. On the contrary, it reflects a sharp swerve in cultural interests and stimuli, creative aims and approaches. The period involved spans the events following World War I through to the crucial years of World War II, and in effect marks the advent of a more "advanced" reality in the technological sense, and likewise in social and individual behavior (and not only in Italian society). The progress made in the 1920s (and even more markedly so in the 1930s) closed the critical gap that had given Futurism its ideological distance, a distance based on the utopian and futuristic leanings it sported in the 1910s; now Futurism suddenly found itself running out of inventive steam, not least because of the lack of contrast between Futurism and the new social reality.[30]

Furthermore, the Futurists were affected by new political limitations, as their "revolutionary" activity was relegated to a specifically "artistic" field only, owing to the inevitable political monopoly exercised by the Fascists. Collusion was a tempting alternative, as it meant being able to realize one's work. The progressive dwindling of that initial creative force of protest did not only take place on this physiological, as it were, plane. It was also provoked by the ongoing absorption of the Futurist schemes into current public tastes and "consumption."

The new Futurists (in a direct line of descendence legitimized by the creative presence of front-line figures such as Depero and Prampolini — and Balla himself, until he quit Futurism at the start of the 1930s) were forced to take stock of the new era, where their predecessors had swept it aside with their utopian polemics; they were obliged to come to terms with other interventions and competitions that addressed the issues raised by the new reality. In some way, while the Futurism of the 1910s (and also of the early 1920s) was able to challenge its contemporary world (which was considered largely *passéist* and conservative, especially in Italy) through an authentic "futuristic" projection of the future, this future they had presented as something "realizable" during the 1920s and even more so in the 1930s had suddenly been caught up by the new present, by the new reality (which, as it turned out, was by no means as distant as the Futurist had claimed). This situation was a serious test to the operative viability and inventive of the new Futurists.

And it was due to this challenge that the Futurism of the 1930s failed its long-standing revolutionary aspiration, with a consequent reduction in imagination and real effectiveness on the reality and demands of the contemporary world — demands which included the celebration of the reigning Fascist ethic; alternatively, the new demands came from the new privileged and influential class, which the Regime catered to, not always wittingly. The fideist imagery that the Futurists developed, particularly in the 1930s, was tuned to a realizable present rather than a realizable future. The creative impulse of their art was no longer aimed at challenging the "passéist" present with the "Futurist" imagination, but at fashioning a tenable image of the present world, a world that had already been updated. The new imagery was a hymn to the machine age, and catered to the public's new perception of speed. The reality of the present was no longer fodder for confrontation. The earlier utopian excuse was gone. In its place was a concrete integration of aspects of everyday tastes and, to put it bluntly, of "consumption."

In the 1930s this situation generated a brand of Futurist architecture closely engaged with Rationalism, which had been largely assimilated (and not only in Europe). Likewise, Futurist painting and sculpture either internalized the present in cosmic (or escapist) imagery, or illustrated it directly, thereby impairing its potential as protest and provocation. However, one area in which the challenge was well met was in interior and large-scale exhibition design. The exhibitions offered an occasion for the Futurists to show their flair, producing communicative and compelling solutions to the rising demand for a new role for "public" art, which, because of

Fillia, *Heavier Than Air*, 1933-34

their engaging ideas, brief life-span and immediate emotional and imaginative hold, nimbly eluded the rhetorical cadences typical to the sculpture and painting destined for public consumption as prescribed by the Regime (and which were largely a source of income for the artists of *Novecento* inspiration).

On the other hand, in relation to the Futurism of the 1910s, the new Futurist "tradition" of the 1920s and 1930s was an idealistic pledge for continuity, rather than a close descendant in terms of inquiry and purely linguistic expedients. The "Second Futurism" of the 1920s and 1930s was not a mere "revival" of "early Futurism," but defined a new and articulate position of its own, with different historical referents; it was only linked to its predecessor by its ideals, as it continued to defend its cultural heritage. This heritage was otherwise increasingly ignored and brushed aside by the Italian critics of the day — and not only by the more traditionalist minds (those subscribing to the *Novecento* mentality)[31] but also by some members of the "avant-garde," for example Edoardo Persico, even if the latter were involved in the defense of the new breed of architecture — Rationalist architecture — and of new figurative proposals in stark contrast to the *Novecento* movement. (In any case, this excludes Sartoris who together with Paladini had been mediating between Futurism and Rationalist architecture ever since the 1920s.) Meanwhile Carlo Belli was deeply committed to defending abstract "Concretist" painting, and his avant-garde criticism frequently exploded into open polemics with the Futurist camp.[32]

Of a different historical value was Futurism's attitude towards artistic research elsewhere in Europe, which may be described as *horizontal*, or open-minded. Conversely, it entertained, autocratic links with its own tradition; its rapport with its past was a problem-ridden one, limited in scope, and mainly consisted in similarities in rhetoric. In brief, the position of the Futurists in the 1920s and especially in the 1930s took a "horizontal" form, and crystallized into the following: a) a categorical rejection of the Italian *Novecento* culture for its permanent archaisms and for its unabashed neo-Naturalist overtones;[33] b) a purely internal debate over the issue of modernism in art, parting from a cohesive stance against the non-figurative solutions of the *Concretismo* movement centered around Milan's Galleria del Milione and of parallel movements on a European level, as well as against neo-Plasticism;[34] c) close attention to, though deeply critical of, the activity of the Surrealists, resulting in a formal dispute with André Breton's group, and coupled with their own experimentation in a sphere of marked accentuation on the imaginary (which I have dubbed "para-Surrealist";[35] d) a critical attitude, at the same time collaborative, towards Rationalist architecture, especially, with Italian Rationalism, participating in the polemics against a return to Classical canons, as Rationalism parried the assault of the architectural traditionalism of the *Novecento*.[36]

There remains the question about Second Futurism's relationship with the Fascist Regime (which had been in power since 1922). The facts demonstrate that this relationship was neither exclusive, nor pre-eminent. The Futurist position in relation to the Regime from the 1920s through to the early 1940s does not appear to be a great compromise — either in the individual cases or on the whole. The Regime itself had no set cultural policy, and kept its options open, as can be seen from the developments within the *Novecento* tradition (starting with Sironi) and within Rationalism, which had its own "political difficulties."[37] By contrast individual cases of anti-Fascist stances are recorded among the Futurists.

The relationship between early Futurism and what was to become full-fledged Fascism can only be mentioned in limited terms, as a distant precedent to the convergence between the Futurists and Mussolini (who by then had withdrawn from the Socialist party) during 1914 and the first half of 1915 on "interventionist" matters, and with regard to Italy's involvement in World War I; by the time Fascism first appeared, in 1919 early Futurism was over (the Futurists' concern over whether to have an explicit political stance dates back to 1909, almost ten years prior to the *Manifesto del partito politico futurista* February 1918).[38] A brief and intense period of collaboration had taken place in late 1918 to 1919 between Futurism and Fascism which was abruptly broken off following the Second Fascist Congress of 24-25 May 1920 (Milan). Relations were resumed a few years later,[39] and we may speak in certain terms of a bond developing in the mid-1920s to 1930s, though the rupture of 1920 had left a permanent mark. The moment of greatest collusion had come with the Futurists' contribution (headed up by Marinetti) to the formation of Mussolini's *Fasci di Combattimento* in Milan on 23 March 1919. Mussolini had clearly taken some pointers from the Futurist political program of the previous year; similar influence had been noticed with regard to the program announced by the Fascist party's Milan faction and discussed in Mussolini's daily paper *Il Popolo d'Italia* on 6 June 1919. Meanwhile, the incompatibility between the Futurists' ideological maximalism and Mussolini's pragmatic "possibilism" soon became apparent, and the divorce became official in the following year, when the Futurists took their stand of revolutionary "Fideism," in net opposition to the political opportunism of the Fascists — who meanwhile were busy turning heel in a crucial maneuver towards reaction and conservatism (which all became clear in 1921). The split manifested itself in a direct confrontation between Marinetti and Mussolini: the former spoke with renewed fervor to the Second Fascist Congress in favor of the claims of the working class, and of social justice, warning that a wave of reaction could never stem from the Carso (the famous site of bloody battles between Italian and Austro-Hungarian troops between 1915 and 1917). The latter claimed that the real political issue at hand was "restoration," and sustained the need for a pact between the productive proletariat and productive bourgeoisie. A few days after the clash, Marinetti and a clutch of other Futurists quit the *Fasci di Combattimento*. The following year, it was Antonio Gramsci who gave the Futurists their new label of "revolutionaries."[40]

The lingering idea that sustained Futurist interest in the Fascists (who had since climbed to power) from the mid-1920s and 1930s was the Futurists' heartfelt nostalgia for the "revolutionary" Fascism of 1919. Moreover, they were deeply distrustful, and occasionally openly critical, of the "regime" style of Fascism being put into practice. The resumption of relations in 1924 occasioned by Marinetti's "national honors," and the Futurist Congress, held in Milan, culminated on 23 November with a declaration addressed to Mussolini.

The declaration, phrased by Marinetti and the "interventionist" Futurists was an appeal to their "old companion Benito Mussolini" to restore to Fascism "that marvelous 1919 spirit, which was so unselfish, bold, anti-socialist, anti-clerical, anti-monarchical," and to imitate "the inimitable Giolitti," whom they considered the "Mussolini of 1919."[41]

That same year, in his book *Futurism and Fascism*, Marinetti announced a change of roles, explaining first that Fascism was in fact born "of Interventionism and Futurism," and had drawn on "Futurist principles." Furthermore, he considered that Fascism's rise to power was none other than "the realization of the Futurist minimal program." Be that as it may, while Fascism operated on political level, Futurism's work unfolded "in the infinite dominions of the imagination," forging ahead "ever more dauntlessly," and therefore acting as the "avant-garde of Italian sensibility, [...] by definition always ahead of the sluggish sensibility of the people," thereby always risking incomprehension. In this declaration, Marinetti confirmed that Futurism would no longer undertake overt political action, in favor of an artistic working front. "Futurism is an artistic and ideological movement. It may intervene only in moments of acute national peril."[42]

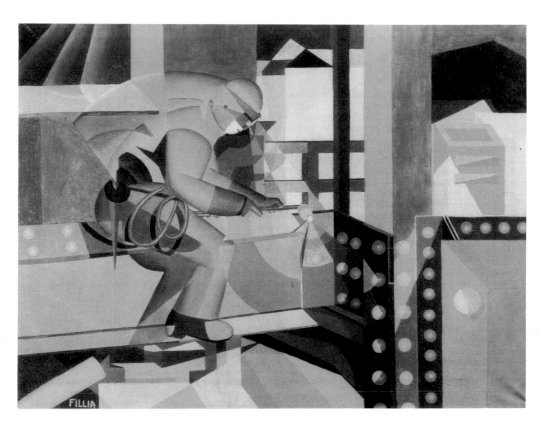

Fillia, *The Welder of Speed*, 1927

One such moment of peril was presaged by Mino Somenzi (and by Marinetti also) fifteen years later, in late 1938, when a "right-wing" Fascist branch made an attempt to institute an Italian version of Nazi Germany's "degenerate art" campaign. The attempt (fortunately abortive) was directed above all against the Italian avant-garde and all of its tendencies (from Metaphysical art to the *Novecento*, from Futurist developments to "Concretist" abstract art or the new figurative inventions of the young Expressionists), and was part of a broader anti-Semitic drive sponsored by the Nazis.[43]

Nonetheless, in the 1920s and 1930s, the prevailing political climate forced the Futurists to drastically reduce their so-called "revolutionary" campaigning and keep to purely "artistic" matters, abandoning political involvement altogether. In this sense, the position of this "Second" Futurism under the Fascist regime in the 1920s and 1930s is one of extremism, culturally (and, implicitly, also politically) oriented toward irreducible revolutionary ideals, i.e., against all forms of bureaucracy, hesitation, stasis, passivity, or speculation.[44]

Their position left them under the constant threat of emargination. Furthermore, they were also ignored by the supposedly illuminated "Fascist left," one of whose leading figures was Giuseppe Bottai, the then-Minister of National Education (who had been involved with the Futurists in 1918-20). His initiatives had included backing for the young Expressionists (who were allotted their own forum, particularly in the form of the Premio Bergamo, which was awarded between 1939 and 1942), and represented the more advanced cultural front of the Fascist movement, aware of and responsive to the brooding unrest among the country's artistic generation.[45]

This somewhat hazardous position of "Second" Futurism in the 1920s and 1930s in relation to Fascism can be gauged by looking at the regime's tolerance toward other areas of artistic research, avant-garde or otherwise, in the overall strategy of consensus.[46] The degree of acceptance or approval can be measured in the amount of commissions for large-scale mural work on the regime's new buildings, and the Futurist presence in the major exposition events of international standing, such as the Venice Biennale, the Milan Triennale, and — on national level — the Quadriennale in Rome, besides the intense exhibition activity of the Sindaco Artisti (Artist's union), which operated both locally and nationwide. Other available outlets were the large exhibition initiatives of ideological, technological, or merceological orientation (which include the 1923-33 Mostra della Rivoluzione Fascista held in Rome, the 1939 Mostra del Minerale also held in Rome, the Triennale d'Oltremare held in Naples in 1940, and lastly the E42, a commemorative exhibition venue programmed for Rome in 1942).

Giacomo Balla, *Plastic Complex Colored with Force-Lines*, 1915

A close look at the level of acceptance of Futurism on the part of the Regime compared with other ongoing fronts of artistic research in Italy, whether avant-garde or not, reveals that while the Futurist movement was certainly accepted (even officially acknowledged), and received direct commissions, this acceptance and the resulting appointments were in fact very limited indeed. Their situation is in no way comparable for instance with the contracts awarded to members of the *Novecento* Italiano. The *Novecento* and its offshoots were the beneficiaries of a marked favoritism, and enjoyed most of the official commissions in both the 1920s and 1930s. Among those particularly privileged were Marcello Piacentini in the realm of architecture, and Mario Sironi in mural design, painting and sculpture. The Futurists received very few commissions indeed, nor did the abstract "Concretists" for that matter. Even some of the rising Expressionist exponents who had emerged at the close of the 1920s and early 1930s enjoyed considerably more attention from the Regime that did the Futurists or the "Concretists" (commissions included mural works in the 1933 Milan Triennale, and later murals — sometimes immediately contested by the authorities — by Cagli, Afro, Mafai, Guttuso, and others).[47]

In reality, the Futurists were obliged to continually re-assert their claim to political legitimacy, reminding the now-established and conservative Fascist regime of its originally revolutionary and subversive spirit (long-since disowned). In vain were the Futurist efforts to gain recognition as the "Art of the State."[48]

Enrico Prampolini
Female Architecture, c. 1925

Official appointments for the Futurists were marginal. And yet the Futurists were outwardly favorable to the Fascists, inasmuch as they recognized a regime that in any case was in power, with whom they shared some origins, albeit remote. It was to these "revolutionary" origins that they were nostalgically tied, rather than to the idea of a rigid and conservative Regime from which the Futurists demanded full rights to artistic freedom. Despite their claims, the Futurists had relatively little leeway to practice such freedom, and their operations remained marginal, compared with other areas of artistic research going on in the country at the time, which enjoyed highly remunerative commissions. The Futurists did however take on commitments that were in some way complicitly celebrative of the Regime, but these were largely geared to heroic-mechanist mythologizing of their own particular stamp. Those Futurist works that can be said to be linked to a celebration of the Regime are, in effect, connected only on a thematic level, and not in terms of style. The principal intention of Futurist artists was to take the theme material (in this case Fascist) and reinterpret it in their own synthetic-dynamic idiom, rather than transform their own style to suit the propaganda needs of the Regime, as normally tended to happen.

Gerardo Dottori
Volcanoes Island, 1938

All this would seem to imply that the Futurists managed to conserve a remarkable degree of autonomy, though in situations which from the outside may seem a compromise. The examples multiply if we include works by Prampolini, Mino Rosso, Thayaht, Di Bosso, and many others.[49] Paradoxically, this "Second" Futurism in Italy might be grouped together as set of artistic events that continued basically *despite* the country's being under Fascist rule, though not entirely unconnected with it. In fact it never really coincided with Fascist art, although in certain circumstances the Fascists borrowed Futurist themes. Such episodes of collusion with the Regime must be weighed against other father-reaching cases of collaboration on the part of avant-garde movements, and they are compensated by the many positive initiatives of the Futurists in defense of the modern avant-garde movements throughout the 1920s and 1930s. This activity was in fact an ongoing struggle not only against the constant threat of their own emargination at the hands of the official Fascist culture, but was also as a gesture that went beyond the scope of Futurism itself, initiatives directed aimed at the entire spectrum of Italian avant-garde currents, and in particular the new horizons of visual arts.

This Futurist stance was not only mounted throughout the 1930s in defense of the emerging Rationalist architecture, but emerged in violent and, in the long run, victorious ideological battles against the institution of an Italian version of Nazi Germany's "degenerate art" campaign, a move attempted by the right-wing Fascists toward the end of 1938, in the wake of the ongoing Nazi racial campaigns. Even back in 1934, on the occasion of the Italian Futurist aeropainters in Hamburg and Berlin, Marinetti and Ruggero Vasari had wrangled with the Nazi censors in outspoken defense of avant-garde tradition, seeking out contacts among the rising generation of non-figurative German artists, which Nazism seemed bent on nipping in the bud. Meanwhile, from the pages of *Stile Futurista*, Prampolini spoke out against the reactionary cultural ethic being preached by Hitler at the Congress in Nuremberg.[50]

Dissent reached a peak between October and December 1938 with the debate over the Roman weekly *Quadrivio*, run by Telesio Interlandi, and an early champion of racist viewpoints in the field of culture. On 24-25 November 1938 he published an article in the journal *Il Tevere*[51] attacking all modern art as Jewish and Bolshevik; naming Marinetti and a crop of other Italian examples of "degenerate art" (De Chirico, Carrà, Cagli, Birolli, Reggiani, Fontana, Ghiringhelli, Soldati, Lingeri, and Terragni). This culminated in a large-scale demonstration called by Marinetti and Somenzi in the Teatro delle Arti in Rome on 3 December 1938, accompanied by a harshly critical pamphlet by Somenzi, entitled *Artecrazia* (no. 117) of 3 December, followed up by a second on 11 January 1939 (no. 118), vehement enough to incur the political suppression of the journal; the same pamphlet published a poll conducted by Somenzi in which popular opinion resulted in favor of modern art.[52] This was just one example of the climate of open contrast that described relations between Fascism and Futurism throughout the 1930s,[53] despite sporadic episodes of apparent collaboration. A further explanation of the reasons for this can be found in Giuseppe Prezzolini's cogent analysis of the regime, published in *Il Secolo* on 3 July 1923. All in all, between the 1920s and 1930s (and the start of the 1940s), the Italian Futurists managed to evolve a very broad spectrum of expression with outstanding results that frequently showed extraordinary inventiveness, ranging from imaginary architectural projects to painting and sculpture, to *plastica murale* or mural sculpture, from the design of theater sets, exhibition installations, fashion, objects, to visual poetry, prose and drama. The Futurists successfully established their own broad margins of expression in each field they ventured into, often infiltrating the mechanisms of production and consumption, in which, despite their verbal nationalistic flag-waving, they managed to achieve an international level of dialogue (from Purism and "mechanical style" to Rationalism, and others areas of research verging on Surrealism). They never, however, really succeeded in pushing beyond their limitations to a truly revolutionary artistic position, as they did not pose any real contrast or challenge to their contemporary social and economic situation, which had basically already been "emancipated" by spreading industrialization and modernization. Thus their position was ostensibly one of agreement (as can be seen in the Futurist reaction to World War II, in the works of the aeropainters, as also with certain aero-poets). In spite of their professed thematic "heroism," in truth their expression was lyrical — varying between the new lyricism of flight and landscape (Dottori), to the fantasy reconstructions of the cosmos and the formation of matter (Prampolini), which were enhanced and developed by the psychological insights of Fillia.

Notes

[1] Cfr. E. Crispolti, *Storia e critica del futurismo*, Laterza publishers, Bari 1986 pp. V-XXI. This work sheds new light on Balla's œuvre, exposing his role as an alternative creative pole to Boccioni's dramatically conflicting vision; cfr. M. Drudi Gambillo, in *Il Futurismo*, Rome 1959 (introduction by A. Palazzeschi, texts by G. Castelfranco and J. Recupero), M. Drudi Gambillo, T. Fiori, *Archivi del futurismo*, vol. II, De Luca, Rome 1962; and E. Crispolti, M. Drudi Gambillo, *Giacomo Balla*, Galleria Civica d'Arte Moderna, Turin, 4 April 1963. Despite the advances made in the historiography of the Futurists, there is still a rather nostalgic emphasis on the Futurist output of the early 1910s; cfr., for instance, E. Coen in *Arte italiana del XX secolo, Pittura e scultura 1900-1988*, Royal Academy of Arts, London, 14 January - 9 April 1989, Leonardo, Milan, p. 56.

[2] Cfr. E. Crispolti, *Storia...*, cit. , pp. V-XXI.

[3] Cfr. E. Crispolti, "Appunti sul problema del secondo futurismo nella cultura italiana fra le due guerre," in *Notizie*, year II, no. 8, Turin, April 1958, pp. 34-51; republished in E. Crispolti, *Il mito della macchina e altri temi del futurismo*, Celebes, Trapani 1969, pp. 245-267.

[4] E. Crispolti, ed., *Ricostruzione futurista dell'universo*, Mole Antonelliana, Turin, June-October 1980; and E. Crispolti, *Storia...*, cit., pp. 46-103.

[5] This distinction is expounded in my text for the catalogue *Futurismo*, Break Club, Rome, April 1988, and discussed further in "Appunti su Depero 'astrattista futurista' romano," in *Depero*, Rovereto, 12 November 1988 - 14 January 1989 (Exhibition curated by G. Belli, catalogue edited by M. Fagiolo dell'Arco and N. Boschiero), Electa, Milan, pp. 183-203; and in "Il secondo futurismo," in *Arte italiana...*, cit., pp. 165-172, a text that inevitably covers similar ground to this essay.

Enrico Prampolini
Project for a theater in the E42 district in Rome, 1939-40

[6] E. Crispolti, "Il 'nodo' romano 1914-1915: Balla, Depero, Prampolini e Boccioni," in *Futurismo futurismi*, supplement to the journal *Alfabeta*, year VIII, no. 84, Milan, May 1985, p. 44-45; and "Appunti su Depero...," cit.

[7] Boccioni himself realized the novelty in this development during his visit to Rome in 1916, when he saw the works of Balla and Depero (cfr. E. Crispolti, "Il 'nodo'...," cit.). It was indeed a radically different chapter of great creative intensity for Futurist painting and sculpture, and its beginnings are comparable with the first signs in Europe of a non-figurative formal Structuralism, and likewise with Russian and German Suprematism and Constructivism, and neo-Plasticism in the Netherlands (cfr.: E. Crispolti, "Appunti su Depero...," cit., p. 199). Although "abstract" Futurism was to take a different path, as the formulation of "analogism" paved the way for the use of synthetic figurative elements, based (analogically) on references to the real emotive event. These references are inseparable because of their underlying Futurist dialectical positivism (by the mid-1910s, Boccioni and Prampolini's debate against Kandinsky's abstraction of the mere "interior necessity"; and the mistrust they showed in the 1920s and 1930s toward intransigently non-figurative attitudes, such as "Concretism"). While the first hints of non-figurative work in Italian art in this century undoubtedly came from the Futurists (especially Balla's cycle of "iridescent interpenetrations" from 1912-1914, and the later cycle of 1914-15, and then in Boccioni himself in 1913, and the ideas of Depero in 1915-16, and of Prampolini; and later Pannaggi's central-European Constructivism), Italian "Concretism" of the 1930s, which matured in Milan at the Galleria del Milione, was not a filiation, but linked to a path of development that spanned from late French Cubism to contemporary "Concrete art", particular that of French and German extraction.

Giacomo Balla
Project for Salon Interior, 1918

[8] Published in the catalogue *Le più recenti opere del pittore futurista Giacomo Balla*, Casa d'Art Bragaglia, Rome, 4-31 October 1918 (reprinted in *26 esposizioni futuriste 1912-1918*, edited by P. Pacini, SPES, Florence, 1978).

[9] Set design played a prominent role in the transition from the peak of the *synthetic* phase to the *mechanical* phase and particularly in the development of the latter. At the start of 1917 Balla designed a series of dynamic and brightly colored abstract sets for the Ballets Russes performance of Stravinsky's *Feu d'artifices* directed by Diaghilev. In 1916-17, Depero designed both sets and costumes for a Ballets Russes production of Stravinsky's *Le chant du rossignol*, and for Francesco Cangiullo's work *Il giardino zoologico*, which was to be set to music by Ravel. Depero's designs comprised a markedly synthetic use of color and form to match the narrative, an expedient he explored further, in 1917-18 in the *Balli plastici* he did for Gilbert Clavel, carrying the artist's *Teatro magico* toward a fantastic enunciation of autonomous forms. Depero's costumes for *Anhiccam del 3000*, performed for the first time in 1924, were clearly mechanistic, though hovering between fairytale and irony. Taking a different angle, was Prampolini, who theorized on an entirely new, dynamically colored form of set design in his manifesto *Scenografie e coreografie futurista*, published in *La Balza* no. 3, Messina, 12 May 1915), and envisages stage entertainments as a "mechanical rite of the eternal transcendence of matter" in his later manifesto *L'atmosfera scenica futurista*, published in *Noi*, year II, nos. 6-7-8-9, Rome); his ideas are expressed in intense chromatic and plastic synthesis in his creations for the Podrecca's marionnette theater, the "Teatro dei Piccoli" in 1919, and for the "Teatro del colore" set up by Achille Ricciardi in 1920, again in Rome, and then for the Teatro Svandovo and the National Theater in Prague between 1921 and 1924, and Bragaglia's "Teatro degli Indipendenti" in Rome in 1923; till it was

transformed into a more searching plastic and full-fledged "mechanical" Constructivism, in his "Teatro Magico" in 1924, and then in the performances for the "Compagnia della pantomima futurista" in Paris and Turin in 1927 and 1928. In 1922, for the circle called "Cronache d'Attualità" in Bragaglia's theater, Paladini and Pannaggi put on a performance of *Ballo meccanico futurista*, one of their own creations with a marked content of dynamic plasticism and "mechanical" analogy; whereas Pannaggi's costume for *L'angoscia delle macchine* by Ruggero Vasari in 1926-27 was decidedly Constructivist, with strong "mechanical" stereometric overtones.

[10] Cfr. *Noi*, SPES, Florence (Reprint, with a critical comment by B. Sani). The 1923 manifesto combined the two manifestoes of the previous year: *L'arte meccanica futurista* by Paladini and Pannaggi (published in *La Nuova Lacerba*, no. 1, Rome, 20 June 1922), and *L'estetica della macchina e l'introspezione meccanica nell'arte*, by Prampolini (published in *De Stijl*, V, No. 7, July 1922; in *L'Impero*, Rome 16 March 1923; and in the article "Směry italské ho malířství 'Avantgardy' a nové malířství absolutní," in *Veraikon*, Prague, August 1922, pp. 44-48). Cfr. G. Lista, *Dal futurismo all'immaginismo: Vinicio Paladini*, Il Cavaliere Azzurro, Salerno, 1988, pp. 14 27. In its first series (1917-19), *Noi* became the means for Italian participation in Dadaism, in whose early stages Prampolini, at the time engrossed in his "proto-mecchanical" phase, was a leading figure; later, at the beginning of the 1920s, its prime mover became Julius Evola, also based in Rome (cfr. E. Crispolti, "Dada a Roma - Contributo alla partecipazione al dadaismo," in *Palatino*, year X, nos. 3-4, Rome 1966; year XI, nos. 1-4, 1967, and year XII, nos. 1-3, 1968).

[11] Cfr. *Fillia e l'avanguardia futurista negli anni del fascismo*, edited by S. Evangelisti, texts by P. Baldacci, S. Evangelisti, M. Pinottini, published by A. Mondadori, Milan 1986; and *Fillia, fra immaginario meccanico e primordio cosmico*, edited by E. Crispolti, Cuneo, San Francesco, 14 May - 30 June 1988, Mazzotta, Milano.

[12] Cfr. G. Lista, *Arte e politica: il futurismo di sinistra in Italia*, Multhipla, Milan 1980; U. Carpi, *Bolscevico immaginista - Comunismo e avanguardie nell'Italia degli anni Venti*, Liguori, Naples 1981; U. Carpi, *L'estrema avanguardia del Novecento*, Editori Riuniti, Rome 1985; G. Lista, *Dal futurismo...*, cit.

[13] The manifesto *L'arte meccanica*, published in May 1923 in *Noi* (II s., year I, no. 2, Rome) though "back-dated" to October 1922, urges artists to portray "the spirit and not the outward form of the machine, creating compositions that draw on all kinds of expressive means, and even on real mechanical parts," coordinated however, "by an original lyrical rationale order. " Meanwhile, in a text accompanying the publication of the manifesto in *Noi*, Paladini talks of the "geometrization and solidification toward a unique and indestructible form of architecture. Limpid dream beyond all time! Thought and calculation, anti-sensorialism and antigraciousness, rigid and metallic art, *Classical* art!" (*Estetica meccanica*, in *Noi*, II s., year I, no. 2, Rome May 1923). E. Fillia (with Tullio Alpinolo Bracci) attempts to use psychological analogy to define the values of pure color, stating that he wanted to "create a form of painting composed essentially of color, in which the subject is the simple definition of the colors themselves, which are divided and modeled into different forms to stimulate our sensibility the senses." ("Creazione Bracci-Fillia," in *Futurismo* [single issue], Sindacati Artistici del Movimento Futurista Torinese, Turin, 9 March 1924). A further stage (with Bracci and Angelo Maino) was to use this system of analogy to compose a kind of "spiritual alphabet" ("Alfabeto spirituale," in *Sale futuriste*, Palazzo Madama, Turin, catalogue, exhibition organized by the Sindacati artistici futuristi [January 1925]). Again with Bracci, Fillia dreamed up a new mechanical "spiritualism": "Aesthetic comprehension is achieved through the creation of 'plastic planes' [...] natural objects lose their primitive form in favor of a plastic construction; becoming an indispensible whole, achieving a new architecture [...] the picture tends toward an original situation state of mechanical existence, in which the spatial and chromatic construction eventually anchors the sense of this new plastic comprehension [...]. The possibility of an entirely materialistic work, with all its importance and technical conception, allows for a much greater spiritual development, toward the luminous horizons of a future sensibility." ("La pittura spirituale," in *L'Impero*, Rome 15 March 1925). See also Fillia's "L'idolo meccanico," also in *L'Impero*, Rome 19-20 July 1925, and the manifesto that followed it, signed jointly by Caligaris and Pino Curtoni, published in *La Fiamma*, no. 6, Turin, 2 May 1926. Additionally, there is also Prampolini's text, "Architetture spirituali," in *L'Impero*, Rome 26 June 1924. Cfr. *Fillia, fra immaginario...*, cat. cit.

[14] Writing on the work of Prampolini in 1940, F. Pfister (De Pistoris) makes a distinction between the early mechanical phase of his work, as a "chromatic spatial abstraction" (in which "the analysis of the object in space through an architecture of colored planes has the chief effect of geometrizing the design, and reducing the plastic elements to two dimensions, in favor of a uniform body of color"), and the second phase, as a full-fledged "mechanical period," which, writes Pfister, "is not in contrast with the spatial and chromatic style, but rather fleshes it out and complements it, because it retains the same characteristics. Only a certain few plastic elements are brought out, allowing the subject, which is more in harmony with the style adopted, to become a central nucleus around which the composition clusters. The plasticity of these central elements clearly echoes chiaroscuro technique, and the forms are thus freed from the rigid theory through the spiritual content of the work. " (*Enrico Prampolini*, Scheiwiller, Milan 1940, pp. 14-15). Fillia spoke of a "constructive pictorial system," "Pittura futurista da cavalletto," in *Il Nazionale*, Turin, 8 December 1928).

[15] On the "mechanical" phase of Futurist painting and sculpture, see E. Crispolti, *Il mito...*, cit., pp. 436-489; and *Ricostruzione...*, cit., pp. 149-175.

[16] *Mostra futurista di aeropittura e di scenografia*, Galleria Pesaro, Milan October-November 1931 (reprint in *26 Esposizioni Futuriste 1918-1931 + 1913-1914*, edited by P. Pacini, SPES, Florence, s. a. [1979]).

[17] For Prampolini, "aero-sensibility" meant a form of "extra-terrestrial spirituality." "We have to go beyond the *transfiguration of apparent reality* [...] and launch ourselves toward the absolute equilibrium of the infinite, and infuse it with the latent images of a new world of cosmic reality." Prampolini was aiming for a form of "plastic analogy, i. e., for a metamorphosis into mystery, between concrete reality and abstract reality." He appeals for "a *pictorial-indefinite*, in which the color-tone element and the force-form reinforce each other." He felt that aeropainting was the key to "the total supersession of the boundaries of terrestrial reality, triggering inside us inextinguishable pilots of new plastic reality, and the latent desire to live the occult forces of cosmic idealism." Meanwhile, Fillia and the Turin Futurists were striving to achieve "new symbols" of the modern epoch in their painting, translated in plastic images, in "cosmic landscapes which are revealed to us once we have broken free of terrestrial restrictions; the 'spiritual aerial organisms' whose plasticity represents the new divinities and new mysteries created by the 'machines'" (*Mostra futurista...*, cit., pp. 12-13, 15-17).

[18] Ambrosi described one of his "non-documentary" aeropaintings thus: "*Cinquemilametri* - A chromatic fusion of landscape-sky and atmosphere-matter, in which, from the dizzy heights of flight, the gleaming luminosity of space annihilates the earthly conventionalism of the horizon-limit. On the gray screen of the ground, the silhouette of a cloud, inebriated by the sun's glory" (*Mostra futurista...*, cit., p. 18). For more on this *aero and cosmic* phase of Futurist painting, see *Ricostruzione...*, cit., pp. 490-516; E. Crispolti, *Aeropittura futurist aeropittori*, Galleria Fonte d'Abisso Edizioni, Modena, May-June 1985.

[19] On the evolution of the movement, see G. Salaris, *Storia del Futurismo*, Rome Editori Riuniti 1985. Sources can be found in the bibliography for the same volume: *Bibliografia del Futurismo 1909-1944*, Rome Biblioteca del Vascello, 1988.

[20] For an overview, see *Ricostruzione...*, cit.

[21] Worth noting are Marchi's *Manifesto dell'architettura futurist dinamica, stato d'animo, drammatica*, dated 1920 (in *Roma Futurista*, year III, no. 72, Rome 29 February 1920); and Mazzoni's *Manifesto Futurista dell'architettura aerea*, dated 1934, signed jointly with Marinetti and Mino Somenzi (in *Sant'Elia*, year II, no. 3, Rome 1 February 1934); and Poggi's manifesto *Architettura futurista Poggi*, dated 1933 (drafted by the *Gruppi Futuristi d'Iniziativa*, under the direction of Antonio Marasco, Florence). Also worth noting is *Architettura Futurista. Prima Mostra* at the Esposizione del Decennale, Turin, Parco del Valentino, April-October 1928. For more on Futurist architecture, see E. Godoli, *Guida all'architettura moderna. Il Futurismo*, Bari, Laterza 1983.

[22] Cfr. *Ricostruzione...*, cit., pp. 264-291, 522-543; and E. Crispolti, "Gli allestimenti dei futuristi," in *Modo*, no. 34, Milan November 1980, pp. 35-40; republished in *Storia...*, pp. 270-279.

[23] I refer to the *I Mostra di Plastica murale per l'Edilizia Fascista*, Palazzo Ducale, Genoa, November 1934 — January 1935, and a second edition of the same at the Mercati Traianei, Rome, October-November 1936; and Prampolini's manifesto *Al di là della pittura verso i polimaterici*, of 1934 (in *Stile Futurista*, year I, no. 2, Turin, August 1934, pp. 8-10), and his booklet entitled *Arte polimaterica (verso un'arte collettiva?)*, Rome O.E.T., and *Architettura futurista* published in 1924 (Campitelli, Foligno), Edizioni del Secolo, 1944. On the question of "mural plastic art" and Futurist Muralism, see *Ricostruzione...*, cit., pp. 534-538; E. Pirani, "La prima mostra di plastica murale," in S. Lux, *Avanguardia, tradizione, ideologia. Itinerario sironiano attraverso un ventennio di dibattito*, Cattedra di Storia dell'Arte Contemporanea II, Rome University *La Sapienza*, Academic year 1985-86, pp. 283-288, 290-295, 310-324.

[24] Worth referring to are the following manifestoes: A. Ginna's *Il primo mobilio italiano futurista* of 1916 (published in *L'Italia Futurista*, year II, no. 12, Florence, 15 December 1916); F. Cangiullo's *Il mobilio futurista* of 1920 (published in *Roma Futurista*, year III, no. 71, Rome, 22 February 1920); Tullio d'Albisola and Marinetti's *Manifesto della ceramica futurista*, of 1938 (published in *La Gazzetta del Popolo*, Turin, 7 September 1938); Balla's *Le vêtement masculin futuriste* (20 May 1914), and *Il vestito "antineutrale"* (11 September 1914); Volt's *Manifesto della moda femminile futurista* of 1920 (published in *Roma Futurista*, year III, no. 72, Rome, 29 February 1920); and that of Thayaht and R. Michahelles *Manifesto per la trasformazione dell'abbigliamento maschile* of 1932. On furniture, accessories, and Futurist fashion, see *Ricostruzione...*, cit., pp. 295-332; A. M. Ruta, *Arredi Futuristi*, with preface by E. Crispolti, Edizioni Novecento, Palermo 1985; *La ceramica futurista da Balla a Tullio d'Albisola*, edited by E. Crispolti, Florence, Centro DI 1982; E. Crispolti, *Il Futurismo e la moda. Balla e gli altri*, Marsilio, Venice 1986; M. Scudiero, *Depero. Casa d'Arte Futurista*, Cantini, Florence 1988.

[25] I refer to Depero's *Manifesto dell'arte pubblicitaria futurista* (1932), and its earlier version dated 1929 (published in *Futurismo*, year II, no. 2, Rome, 15-30 June 1932). On Futurist graphics and advertising, see G. Lista, *Le livre futuriste, de la libération du mot au poème tactile*, Panini, Modena 1984; C. Salaris, *Il futurismo e la pubblicità*, Lupetti, Milan 1986; G. Lista, *L'art postal futuriste*, J. -M. Place, Paris 1979; M. Scudiero, *Futurismi postali. Balla, Depero e la comunicazione postale futurista*, Longo, Rovereto 1986; G. Fanelli, E. Godoli, *Il Futurismo e la grafica*, Comunità, Milan 1988; *Depero per Campari*, Fabbri, Milan 1988.

[26] I refer to: Azari's manifesto *Il teatro aereo futurista* of 1919; Depero's manifesto *Il teatro plastico Depero. Principi ed applicazioni* of 1919 (published in *Il Mondo*, 27 April 1919); Marinetti and Cangiullo's manifesto *Il Teatro della Sorpresa* of 1921 (published in *Il Futurismo*, no. 11, Rome 11 January 1922); Prampolini's manifesto *L'atmosfera scenica futurista* of 1924 (published in *Noi*, year II, nos. 6-7-8-9, Rome 1924); Marinetti's manifesto *Il teatro totale futurista* of 1933 (published in *Futurismo*, year II, no. 19, Rome 15 January 1933). On Futurist performances, see *Sipario*, year XXII, no. 260, Milan 1967 (whole report devoted to Futurist works); M. Kirby, *Futurist Performance*, Dutton, New

York 1971; G. Lista, *Théâtre futuriste italien, anthologie critique*, La Cité, L'Age d'Homme, Lausanne 1976; L. Lapini, *Il teatro futurista italiano*, Mursia, Milan 1977; P. Fossati, *La realtà attrezzata. Scena e spettacolo dei futuristi*, Einaudi, Turin 1977; A. C. Alberti, S. Bevere, P. Di Giulio, *Il Teatro Sperimentale degli Indipendenti (1923-1936)*, Bulzoni, Rome 1984.

[27] Worth noting is Tato and Marinetti's manifesto *La fotografia futurista* of 1930 (published in *Il Futurismo*, no. 22, Rome, 11 January 1931). For more on Futurist photography, see G. Lista, *Futurismo e Fotografia*, Multhipla, Milan, 1980; *Photographie futuriste italienne 1911 1939*, Musée d'Art Moderne de la Ville de Paris, Paris, 28 October 1981, 3 January 1982 (text by G. Lista); *I futuristi e la fotografia. Creazione fotografica e immagine quotidiana*, edited by G. Lista, Galleria Civica, Milan, Galleria Museo Depero, Rovereto, Edizioni Panini, Modena 1985; G. Lista, *Futurist Photography*, Hyogo Prefectural Museum of Modern Art, Hyogo, May 30 — June 28, 1987.

[28] Cfr. *Tavole parolibere futuriste (1912-1944)*, anthology edited by L. Caruso and S. M. Martini, Liguori, Naples 1974; II vol., ivi, 1977; and *Ricostruzione...*, cit. , pp. 336-386.

[29] Cfr. especially, *I luoghi del futurismo*, with a foreword by F. Barbieri, Multigrafica Editrice, Rome 1986; and especially E. Crispolti, *Il secondo futurismo: 5 pittori + 1 scultore, Torino, 1923-1938*, Pozzo, Turin 1962; C. Bendetti, *Il futurismo in Liguria*, Sabatelli, Savona 1976; B. Passamani, U. Carpi (ed.), *Frontiere d'avanguardia. Gli anni del futurism nella Venezia Giulia*, Musei Provinciali, Palazzo Atems, Gorizia February-April 1985; G. Meneghetti (ed.), *Futurismo a Firenze 1911-1921*, Bi e Gi, Verona 1984; A. C. Ponti, M. Duranti (ed.), *Futurismo in Umbria*, Corciano, Chiesa di San Francesco, 2 August-7 September 1986; A. C. Toni, *Futuristi nelle Marche*, De Luca, Rome 1982; U. Piscopo, *Questioni e aspetti del futurismo*, Ferraro, Naples 1976; U. Piscopo, *Futuristi a Napoli — Una mappa da riconoscere*, Cassitto, Naples 1983.

[30] Cfr. *Ricostruzione...*, cit., pp. 456-458; and E. Crispolti, *Storia...*, cit., pp. 283-288.

[31] As in the case of Carrà, acting as art critic in the pages of the Milanese daily *L'Ambrosiano*.

[32] I refer especially to Persico and Marinetti's exchange in 1930 through the pages of *Belvedere*, and the debate between Persico and Fillia in 1933 conducted through *L'Italia Letteraria* (see E. Persico, *Tutte le opere (1923-1935)* edited by G. Veronesi, Comunità, Milan 1964, vol. I, pp. 86-88, vol. II, pp. 338-342).

[33] I make particular reference to the polemics between Marinetti, Prampolini, Dottori, and Fillia. Prampolini also accused the Futurists of internationalism, and indicted the *Novecentisti* of being vassals of the "dregs of French romanticism" (*Spiritualità italiana dei nostri artisti all'estero*, published in *Futurismo*, year I, no. 6, Rome, 16 October 1932). Meawhile, Dottori wrote: "We Futurists have stood up against Novecentism since its conception: we have opposed its deforming and ugly inclinations in the name of *beauty* and *transfiguration*, in the name of inquiry into the *subject*, and against their indifference to it [...] and we have struggled in the name of the *Italianità* (Italian-ness) and *Tradition* [...] against the importing of Nordic tastes and their earthy, bituminous and funereal colors. " (*Addio "900"!*, published in *Futurismo*, year II, no. 56, 15 October 1933).

[34] The dispute was over an art that the Futurist claimed was inadmissable and limiting "a totally abstract art, without human, animal or vegetable subjects. An art based on elementary forms and pure colors, aimed at creating a uniquely pictoric effect," as Fillia, for example, stated about "Mondrian, Arp and the Dutch Constructivists." ("Pittura atmosferica," *Oggi e Domani*, Rome, 12 January 1932) Prampolini himself explained the different development of abstraction "beyond Alps," which was dominated by the positivist aesthetic "and technical speculation," versus the "new spiritual values" of the Futurists, who were then exploring "cosmic" horizons ("Conquiste della plastica Futurista," *L'Impero*, Rome, 8 July 1932). In some respects they echoed some points raised by Boccioni himself and a very young Prampolini about Kandinsky and also some orientations taken by Balla and Depero. All the same, already in the mid-1910s the term abstract had been used in reference to Balla, Depero, Prampolini, Dudreville and, later, Evola, in his involvement with the Dadaists at the start of the 1920s (cfr. "Appunti su Depero...," cit.).

[35] In 1931, Fillia contested Carrà by drawing comparisons (deliberately limited) Prampolini's Cosmic period with Surrealism (in *L'Ambrosiano*, Milan, 22 and 28 October 1931). But the question was not raised just by chance — Fillia had looked into it regarding Prampolini and the Turin group ("It is important to point out that 'none' among these Futurists believes in the Freudian inflections so dear to the Surrealists, and no one has aesthetic links with Mirό, Masson, or Max Ernst, and that everyone upholds those non-existent solid qualities typical to the fragmentary literary-based works of the young French avant-garde members"; "La pittura di Marasco alla Quadriennale di Roma," in *Il Giornale dell'Arte*, Rome, 1 March 1931), and likewise, Marasco had looked into the question of the Turin Futurist group (their works, he considered, "even when they issue from the depths of the subconscious, strive to achieve their objective with a marked awareness of research"; "La mostra futurista di Firenze," in *L'Eclettica*, Florence, 15 March-15 April 1931).

[36] The main occasions for a battle of wits were the large-scale competitions at the beginning of the 1930s, including the one for Via dell'Impero and the Casa del Fascio in Rome, for Via Roma in Turin, for the town of Sabaudia, and for the new railway station and new stadium in Florence. But the Futurists opposed the predominant Rationalist functionalism with a form of sculptural lyricism which they considered an essential prerequisite ("That's enough of Rationalism!" wrote Dottori. "[...] a new Italian architecture for Italy implies turning to lyricism, warmth, color, whose basis was laid twenty years ago by Sant'Elia;" *Architetti pittori arte decorativa*, in *Futurismo*, year II, no. 29, Rome, 19 February 1933).

[37] Proof of this can be found in the studies of the iconography of the period, such as those carried out by Umberto Silva, entitled *Ideologia e arte del fascismo*, Mazzotta, Milan 1975, Second Edition.; by

Fernando Tempesti, *Arte dell'Italia fascista*, Feltrinelli, Milan 1975; by Guido Armellini, *Le immagini del fascismo nelle arti figurative*, Fabbri, Milan 1980. But a correct definition of the place Futurism holds in the context of Italian culture in the times of the Fascist Regime is explained in full in my essay "La politica culturale del fascismo, le avanguardie e il problema del futurismo," published in *Futurismo, Cultura e Politica*, edited by Renzo De Felice, Fondazione Giovanni Agnelli, Turin 1988, pp. 247-283; and likewise in Susanne Falkenhausen's *Der Zweite Futurismus und die Kunstpolitik des Faschismus in Italien von 1922-1943*, Frankfurt am Main, Haag & Herchen 1979.

[38] Published in issue no. 1 of *Rome Futurista*, 20 September 1918.

[39] Cfr. E.Crispolti, *Storia e critica...*, cit., pp. 183-224; and E.Gentile, "Il futurismo e la politica. Dal nazionalismo modernista al fascismo (1909-1920)," published in *Futurismo, cultura...*, cit., pp. 105-159.

[40] Cfr. A. Gramsci, "Marinetti rivoluzionario?," published in *Ordine Nuovo*, Turin, 5 January 1921.

[41] Cfr. F.T.Marinetti, *I diritti artistici propugnati dai futuristi italiani — Manifesto al governo fascista*, in *Il Futurismo*, Rome, 1 March 1923, and in *Noi*, II s., year I, no. 1, Rome, April 1923. And on the Milan Futurist Congress, see M.Somenzi, *Difendo il futurismo*, A.R.T.E., Rome 1937, pp. 117-124; and C.Salaris, *Storia...*, cit., pp. 136-141.

[42] Campitelli, Foligno, 1924; now in F.T.Marinetti, *Teoria e invenzione futurista*, A. Mondadori, Milan 1968, p. 430.

[43] Cfr. M.Somenzi, "Italianità dell'arte moderna," in *Artecrazia*, no. 117, Rome, 3 December 1938.

[44] In 1933, one of the exponents of the First Futurism, poet Paolo Buzzi, said "there is only one real Futurism, that of the extreme left wing" ("Estrema sinistra," in *Futurismo*, year II, no. 29, Rome, 29 March 1933). For an example of Marinetti's open criticism of the Fascist party, see G. Manacorda, "Marinetti, l'E.I.A.R. e Th. Wilder," in *Rapporti*, no. 1, 1974.

[45] Cfr. G.B. Guerri, *Giuseppe Bottai, un fascista critico*, Feltrinelli, Milan 1976; and also G.B. Guerri, "Bottai: da intellettuale futurista a leader fascista," in *Futurismo, cultura...*, cit., pp. 221-245.

[46] On this topic, see Ph. V. Cannistraro, *La fabbrica del consenso. Fascismo e mass-media*, preface by R. De Felice, Laterza, Bari 1975.

[47] This was affirmed by Bottai in 1941, who promoted the 2% law in favor of installing works of art in public buildings, a law that was passed in 1942: "The State, instead of promulgating abstract canons for an official art, can give official proclamation to — or better still, recognize the historical validity and compatibility with its own line of action — the art which is currently being created in Italy by Italian artists" in *Le Arti*, year I, no. 4, Rome, April-May 1941.

[48] This hypothesis is advanced by Fillia at various points througout the book, which is provokingly entitled *Arte fascista*, published in 1927 in Turin by Edizioni Sindacati Artistici; and is further upheld by Somenzi in the Second Futurist Congress in Milan, 1933. Actually, the question of State Art was a means, if not an expedient, which the various currents in Italian art turned to from time to time, especially at the start of the 1930s, sometimes even desparately. Pier Maria Bardi raised the issue for architectural Rationalism in 1931, and the following year Anton Giulio Bragaglia, this time in favor of experimental theater. But the Novecento itself pushed the issue in 1934. See E. Crispolti, "La politica culturale...," cit.

[49] Cfr. U. Silva, *Ideologia...*, cit.; and G.Armellini, *Le immagini...*, cit.

[50] E. Prampolini, "Il Futurismo, Hitler e le nuove tendenze," *Stile Futurista*, year I, no. 3, Turin, September 1934, p. 7 (republished in E. Crispolti, "Il secondo Futurismo," cit., pp. 300-301.

[51] T. Interlandi, "Straniera bolscevizzante e giudaica," in *Il Tevere*, Rome, 24-25 November 1938.

[52] Cfr. E.Crispolti, *Il mito...*, cit., pp. 695-843.

[53] Prezzolini concluded, "How can Futurist art possibly agree with Italian Fascism? There is a misunderstanding, which arises from the proximity of certain persons, from the accidental nature of the meeting, from their fervent energy, and has brought Marinetti alongside Mussolini. This was understandable during the period of revolution. But it is out of place in a period of government. Italian Fascism cannot accept the destructive program of Futurism, and it should — by dint of its Italian logic — restore the very values that Futurism stands against. Political discipline and hierarchy, are also literary discipline and hierarchy. Words are scattered by the wind when political hierarchies are scattered by the wind. If it is to truly win its struggle, Fascism can only consider Futurism assimilated into what Futurism found exciting, and repress everything in it that is still revolutionary, anti-classical, undisciplined from an artistic point of view." ("Fascismo e futurismo," in *Il Secolo*, 3 July 1923; republished in L.De Maria, *Marinetti e il futurismo*, Mondadori, Milan 1979 (1981.4), pp. 286-291.

The Critical Readings

Romolo Romani
Vittore Grubicy de Dragon, 1905

Poesia no. 7-8-9, Milan, 1909

The year was gently drawing to a close, and with it, the century. In a climate of relative composure, Gabriele D'Annunzio penned a tribute to Botticelli in the pages of *Tribuna* in 1887, describing the artist as "certainly the most original painter of the 1400s — the most subtle and passionate, the most elegant." Later, in 1892 in the review *Nuova Antologia*, Adolfo Venturi hailed Botticelli as "the painter of spring in the pure Renaissance." This was quite in contrast with Vittore Grubicy de Dragon's nearly contemporary critical attack on Realism, in favor of the "ideaists" and the new technique of painting in "divided colors." Our brief examination of Italian art criticism begins here, with these parallel but utterly opposing appraisals — one celebrating past glories, with its innumerable appeals to the "Italian tradition," and the other with its special poetics and programs which caused unrest to spread rapidly throughout the art world, injecting it with unexpected ferment. In this same period, Vittorio Pica had begun to pillory the tastes of the "upper classes of modern society," which, he declared, were rife with "spiritual malaise and neurosis, with an abhorrence of all things commonplace, and a marked preference for all that is rare, for the artificial as opposed to the natural, for uniquely individual sensual delights, misunderstood and spurned by the general crowd." In his eyes then, this art was destined for appreciation by only a restricted number of highbrow minds, and as such was utterly reprehensible — it was a reaction against the democratization of art favored by the market, and basically tended towards Symbolism. This Symbolism was more literary than pictorial in character; it was steeped in ideology and rejected all that was modern; it was closed in subjectivism and pessimistic in its outlook towards the scientific and social progress of "our" century. "To protest," continued Grubicy de Dragon, "in the name of heaven knows what histrionic need of the picturesque, against the telegraph lines, against the railways, or the newspapers, is utterly puerile, since by wantonly flying in the face of the progressive contemporary scientific spirit, one can only risk of being mercilessly trodden underfoot."

Spiritual malaise, neurosis, a preference for the artificial — a lexicon extrinsic to the world of art — were words evoked by Vittorio Pica to champion a kind of "benign populism" that repudiates the urbane preferences of characters like *Des Esseintes*, and looks kindly on all things new, on a modern, progressive world firmly grounded in a sense of reality. These were sensible observations at the time, and are remarkably prophetic, but were later taken up with somewhat less good sense during the Futurist furor (which in this improbable setting of provincial calm seems somehow foreshadowed). But with its literary inception, Futurism was not entirely exempt from that spiritual malaise — considering that Filippo Tommaso Marinetti burned the midnight oil "of bronze Mosque lamps with domes of filigreed brass" and enjoyed the feel of "opulent oriental carpets" underfoot. The supersession of the mystical ideal was at odds with the "flight of the Angels," and with the cleansing rage of madness. Given these limitations, the first flames of art criticism were kindled with the touchwood of moods and sensations, rather than any professionalism. The ranks of critics included painters, museum curators, and historians, who momentarily set aside their documentary and philological research to cast a critical eye on the evolving cultural environment.

One such critic was the painter and literary man Enrico Thovez, who, commenting on the first Venice Biennale in 1895 and itching to enter the fray, launched an attack on the pre-Raphaelites. "Soon we too will have Gothic-style furniture," he snorted, "and carpets and curtains embellished with all those spindly lilies, and symmetrical tulips, and water-lilies without a single leaf or root fiber out of place... Soon our eyes will linger over the long, wizened figures of the Knights of the Round Table, since, together with its stunted graphic sensibility, the Middle Ages transmits its grim poetic subject matter — and suddenly witches are back in fashion, along with the dance of death, skeletons, and the return of symbolism, that parasite of ideality... Already this new style has begun to show through in the field most liable to succumb, that of Italian illustration..." Two years later, the same author resumed his lament: "We ask for poetry, and the pre-Raphaelites have given us nothing but their rachitic artificiality. We ask for ideality, and modern art fobs us off with allegory and symbolism. We ask Art to convey the indefinable quality of Nature, and we are given mysticism wrapped in riddles. We appeal for more dynamic techniques, and we are offered the degenerate fantasies of Divisionism..." It was a case of *bellum omnium contra omnes*. There was little room for finer reflection, and for want of historical insight, personal taste came strongly to the fore.

Giovanni Papini
and Ardengo Soffici, 1910

This rather bleak panorama found a vibrant antidote in the Futurist movement, which advanced its revolutionary ideas through a series of "manifestoes," through its new "programmatic" poetics and literature. Along its tempestuous path, the Futurist movement had the great fortune to encounter a critic of unequaled caliber, Roberto Longhi. In an exacting critique of the trends affecting the country at the time (published in the journal *La Voce* in 1913), Longhi wrote: "Let us imagine that the reader — having first swept aside the prejudices and preconceptions (especially those regarding the misfired 'national aesthetic') that kept him from appreciating pure painting — is actually willing to look at paintings without searching for motifs that should not be there in the first place, i.e., extra-pictorial motifs: ideals of all kinds, literature, interpretations of an inner psychological world, sensual beauty, and so forth... and get straight to the point, and speak of Futurist painters in pictorial terms." Longhi concluded incisively: "In their assertion of this lyrical and pictorial expression of their movement, the Futurists have embarked with determination along the principal avenue of the Art of Painting..."

Filippo Tommaso Marinetti
D'Annunzio intimo, cover

In parallel with this illuminating appraisal, Longhi also suggested the need to reflect a moment on the "worn-out symbolist pretensions" advanced "in works that are quite obsolete," and on "the growing return of interest in the subject-matter, which is to say a recognition of the need to depart from the more immediate and lively reality that surrounds us, rather than from traditional memories which then shed their original pictorial value only to acquire a poetic one."

This statement of Longhi's contains a number of interesting concepts. First of all, he brings the reading public into focus; that is, he demands that the readership rid itself of prejudices and preconceptions (brushing aside all accumulated poetics, not least the poetics of that "misfired national aesthetic," which to avoid misunderstanding Longhi would later redefine as "Parthenopean aesthetics," the "aesthetics of intuition"). Then come his comments on pure painting, which he places in opposition to "certain extra-pictorial motifs" such as the various ideals of literature, of psychological interiority, sensual beauty. He thereby dismisses in a single judgment all the stock canons of interpretation and assessment — and not only the more common, or "obvious," popular ones such as literary, psychological and sensual values, but also the more highbrow canons typified by the "misfired national aesthetic," which jar against the rudiments of the Art of Painting. This Art turns out to be essentially architectural in nature, and in terms of geometry and perception is understood as space, a composition of planes and volumes, lines and chiaroscuro, as formulated in the eternal intuition of Benedetto Croce's philosophy. Longhi's appraisal concludes with a decisive verdict of Futurism's superiority over

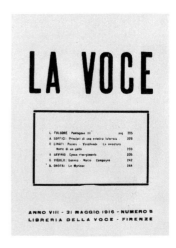

La Voce no. 5
Florence, May 1916

Filippo Tommaso Marinetti
in his study at his home in Milan

Cubism. It was an altogether unexpected declaration of the movement's legitimacy, in the climate of tumultuous debate that had raged over this new art (sometimes instigated by the Futurists themselves), and with it, Longhi frankly declares his adhesion to the new poetics, which saw in Cubism the dismemberment and tumefaction of forms compared with the movement that Futurism had injected into them. In conclusion, it is important to observe how Longhi focuses on the outmoded symbolist content, and how he appeals to a return to subject-matter and to traditional memories, which take on literary value rather than pictorial. Equally important is his repeated emphasis on the need to discuss painting in pictorial terms, rather than to seek extra-pictorial motifs which distract the viewer from the purity of painting technique. He is inviting the reader to look at painting with an uncluttered mind, and concentrate on what is strictly proper to painting.

Criticism of the Futurists' works — contemporary criticism, that is — did not penetrate much deeper than these incisive remarks of Longhi's. For the rest, the Futurists themselves (Filippo Tommaso Marinetti, Umberto Boccioni, Carlo Carrà, Ardengo Soffici, Giovanni Papini, Gino Severini, and others) were quite prepared to take up their pens and provide critical praise of their own making, along with arguments against form and color in traditional painting. In their ruthless advocation of the desecration of monuments and the history of art, they drafted aggressive manifestoes "as a forward guard against the ranks of the enemy." When seen in retrospect, art criticism contemporary to the art itself is necessarily shallow; it does not dally with broad perspectives and shades of meaning. All this makes it difficult to reconstruct events and fully appreciate their implications at the time. Hence, in 1924, *Metafisica* or Metaphysical art, and especially Giorgio De Chirico, appeared to Emilio Cecchi as "a twilight piazza with a cemetery gate; an acropolis with an oracular statue placed behind a curtain, and a woman gazing out on a deserted city. But also those acrid, bewitched still lifes with their verdigris fruits, and wine that could be cut with a knife, with their backgrounds of somnambulant and mortuary landscapes decked with theatrical hangings... Giorgio De Chirico paints nature to suggest destruction and putrefaction. His figs remind one of the lazaretto." He is an "eccentric, a visionary, a 'type,' and somehow or other, an artist. His subject-matter often verges on the hideous, his expedients are trivial, and they betray their derivation from Arnold Böcklin... the squalor of the funeral palls, the pestilent swellings of the flesh and other equally repugnant details, nonetheless do not detract from their occult allure, which hovers somewhere between the legendary and the provincial." This acute reading of Emilio Cecchi's does not highlight the mood of absence, the desire to flee reality, which characterizes De Chirico's work, nor his sense of omission, of incongruity and stasis, and his detachment from his earlier attitudes of militancy and immersion in the world and in life, which had been the very crux of the Futurist mien.

The criticism instead limits itself to a rather "surrealist" description of the subject-matter — or what this could have been — in some of De Chirico's works, dwelling on the squalid and repugnant aspects, on the trivial and distasteful, the sinister and provincial, the theatrical and the illustrative details. And by way of conclusion, Cecchi turns this description into a definition. But even Roberto Longhi's famous essay *Al dio ortopedico* (*To the Orthopedic God*) of 1919, bore a similar tone: "Spurred by his cruel, mechanist hand, humanity — pitilessly mutilated and inexorably made mannequin — emerges amidst shrieking and groaning sounds on vast deserted settings, monitored by cumbersome box-like tenements gorged with stifling darkness. Here, *homo orthopedicus*, in a grating voice, recites his nonsensical lines to the disinherited statues of ancient Greece."

Taking a somewhat different line, however, is Carlo Carrà in his article dated 1925, in which he dauntlessly asserts that "the need to seek some kind of backing was, in a way, what dominated the post-war period, and the 'return to tradition' slogan was born. But exactly what tradition this referred to was only later understood when paintings and sculptures with a patent neo-Classical stamp began to turn up at the exhibitions. Jean-Auguste-Dominique Ingres suddenly came into fashion. The motto became *calm instead of passion, essence instead of chance*. Fine words which no one was prepared to controvert. But when they spoke of tradition, this merely meant the tradition least rooted in our country. For some Italian artists, was it not better to hark back to the very origins — to Giotto, to Masaccio? And since there was no artistic tendency more explicitly serene than neo-Classicism, after a spate of insalubrious individualistic experiments, the Italian critics swallowed the bait and unanimously applauded the new evangelists. Everyone, or nearly everyone, believed that the restlessness of our young artists would finally be quieted."

In fact, the *Valori Plastici* movement attempted to redirect art to the roots of tradition, back to Giotto and Masaccio, to the construction of solid, plastic, and volumetric forms, to absolutes and archetypes. Almost in parallel with *Valori Plastici*, the first group of Italian *Astrattisti* or Abstract artists emerged. The group was largely overlooked by the critics who were busy with the *Novecentisti*, and their work was only revisited after the second postwar period, after many years of silence. "Abstract painting," wrote Atanasio Soldati, one of the movement's advocates, "loves analysis, order, the harmonious proportions of geometry, the clarity of every work of art," emphasizing lines, colors, surfaces, i.e., all the traditional means at the disposal of painting. This appeal to technical meticulousness announced the close of a chapter of art criticism, several episodes of which I have tentatively sketched out here. One final point of interest — the banner under which this last movement operated, *Valori primordiali* (Primordial Values), was clearly intended as a counterpoint to *Valori Plastici*. Here too, lies a subtle and coy polemic intended to annul — to drive back to its distant and almost dreamed origin — the hidden meaning of things.

Carlo Carrà and Roberto Longhi
Forte dei Marmi, 1935

Valori Plastici, no. IX-XII
Rome, 1920

Paolo Fossati

Abstract (and Non-Figurative) Art of the 1930s

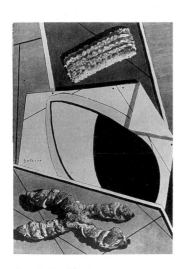

Giorgio De Chirico
Greetings from a Distant Friend, 1916

Giorgio De Chirico
The Temperate Afternoon, 1916

The key events surrounding the development of Abstract art in Italy took place between 1932-34 and World War II. This development was both an explosion and an answer to specific questions of idiom and style. The relative compactness of the explosion was largely decided by the outlets the Abstract artists had for exhibiting their work, though the phenomenon would have been more unitary had it not been for the widely varying conditions and motives of the individual members of the small group; while their departures were relatively similar in cultural and professional terms, each of these artists evolved in his own quite separate way.

To understand exactly what the new non-figurative idiom meant at the height of the 1930s, three crucial factors have to be considered (in Italy's case the term "non-figurative" is generally preferable to the more committed term "Abstract"). The first factor is the absence of any real "tradition" behind the inquiry into non-figurative expression prior to this date. There are, of course, various isolated examples and presages of non-figurative art, and also some individual artists, such as Arnaldo Ginna, who could be described as precursors. Dating from the end of the first decade and through the 1910s, however, Ginna's "non-figurative" work is somewhat weighted with "Liberty" (Italian Art Nouveau) and Symbolist vernacular. At a pinch, Giacomo Balla's various *Compenetrazioni iridescenti* (*Iridescent Compenetrations*) fall into the "non-figurative" category. Strictly speaking, these aspire to a kind of "para-scientific" method bent on stylizing forms of natural energy phenomena; of this series, *Mercurio passa davanti al sole* (*Mercury Passing in front of the Sun*, mid-1910s) is a prime example. Other possible candidates alongside the schematic works of E. Jules Marey and Eadweard Muybridge, are *Sole nascente* (*Rising Sun*, 1904) by Giuseppe Pellizza da Volpedo, with its symbolisms and visionary sparks, the works of Enrico Prampolini, and the mixed "mechanist" and spiritualist paintings of the Futurist continuance. But these scattered instances in no way interrupted the consistent realism with precise pictorial referents nor weakened the dominion of figurative *Verismo*. At most, they punctuated the course of development, without however providing landmarks for those who were keen to get away from the figurative canons. Once or twice, there was someone who strayed into what could be termed expressions of "Italian Dada," as in the case of Julius Evola and his pamphlet on *Arte astratta*, with relative drawings and canvases. But basically, there was no legacy whatsoever in the non-figurative direction for artists working during the 1930s.

The second essential factor is that, owing to the situation outlined above, it is impossible to draw parallels with other experiments with Abstract art in the rest of Europe. Certain similarities in iconographic terms (use of geometrical idiom, color muting, spatial suspension) are of more interest here than instances of actual contact with artists such as Kandinsky, Klee, Kupka, or Vantongerloo; at any rate, Cézanne and Archipenko were more decisive influences. This means that any ongoing development of "abstraction" with relative programs or developments (including crises and eclipses), is wholly absent from the Italian art scene, and in the case of *Astrattismo*, or Abstract art, it was really a question of variants occurring within a compact national system following the *Novecento* experience and much of the formalistic and academic art prevalent in the 1920s. Two basic landmarks stand out, however — first and foremost, Giorgio De Chirico and his "metaphysical" scenarios; and secondly, the Futurist legacy, which was soon to fall under De Chirico's spell of magical and pointedly suspended reality.

223

The third factor, and a highly significant one, is that there was much talk of abstract and "indeterminate" art between the mid-1920s and early 1930s in the gazettes and journals. Here, "abstract" and "surreal" practically coincided as forms of negation: any repudiation of forms and objects as palpable and definitive reality, was considered "abstract"; and likewise any accentuation of detail relative to the painted whole, any stroke of color not firmly anchored to the conceptual feeling of the canvas. In other words, the term embraced all decorative suggestion, emotive "meddling" or other subtle narrative resources. It is a curious paradox that Classicism, hailed as the modern destiny of Italian painting (with its arches and pillars, and bucolic settings), should have turned out to be the most faithful to the logic of harmonic masses, forms and spatial rhythms. Any defection from this principle was labeled "abstract," and therefore prey to surreal interference, be it from the gut or from the brain. Basically, individual intervention was being classified as abstract, where ten years earlier it had enjoyed the status of *sentiment*. Similarly, in the language of the day, those ardent cataloguers of reality were also to turn to "abstract" — the "Turin Six" and their lot, the Milanese artists from the Caffè Craia group, and the young Roman "Tonalists."

Osvaldo Licini, *Tasting*, 1933

Two things can be inferred: that there was an attempt to capture emotions and rationales that could not be immediately externalized; and that the term "abstraction" was in itself rather overused. As we will gradually see, the former (i.e., that surrealist-inclined "wizardry") was never really part of the poetics and praxis of the Italian "abstract" artists, nor did the solution reside in the term "abstract," as understood by the critics. Indeed, if such a thing as Abstract art truly existed in Italy, it was largely due to the sustained rejection in the gazettes and magazines of formal plastic abstraction, or "distraction."

Osvaldo Licini, *Bird*, c. 1936

Milan, the Architects, the Painters

The developments referred to here are specific to the 1930s. Their focus was in Milan in a few scattered venues, with their hub at the Galleria del Milione. Events were influenced by another important factor: while our heroes took interest in themes outside the field of painting (such as graphic design, photography, architecture, set design), one of the chief characteristics of "abstract" art was its resolute aim to achieve autonomy for painting and for themselves as painters. The artists steered clear of the muralist trend — or "walls for painters," as the cry went — and its relative integration with architecture. They criticized it, and not just because they spurned its inherent "subjectivism" (exasperated, indeed "ersatz") through the ethical claim of murals as a form of "social art."

It is worth looking closely at the affinities (especially in terms of the spoken and written language) between the "abstract" current and the forms, formulas, and precedents of the Rationalist architects, and graphic designers and typographers. All these areas were in ferment in Milan during the 1930s. Their common ground (in an affirmative sense) involved them in a common artistic climate, and led them to work with common expectations, though each kept to its individual field of operation. The situation can be summed up another way: the call for change after World War I voiced on various sides (the urge for modern Classicism, "Metaphysics," the *rappel à l'ordre*, "magical realism," purism) had turned to architecture as a coherent system, so as to give precedence to an ordered form of narrative, and to highlight the individual features of the composition, whether plastic or chromatic. Actually, they did not focus on architecture alone; it was a peculiar "visionary" architecture, seen as both metaphor and painted "datum" or as the architecture of physical buildings, and they also studied sculpture and monuments, as modular plastic forms or spatial resources — something the critics have been mistakenly silent about. All this fits neatly into the Italian artistic grid, and was preached by almost everyone

involved (despite the broad divergence between the gospels of Ugo Ojetti, Margherita Sarfatti or Somaré, or Carlo Belli's peculiar strain of Rosminian integralism). Abstract art was one offshoot of this interplay of ideas and events. The few exceptions — Osvaldo Licini, Lucio Fontana, and Luigi Veronesi — were all the more remarkable as their work stemmed from the selfsame artistic premises. The reasons for this overwhelming consensus (which was to break apart in the 1930s with the contribution of the "non-figurative" artists to the state-organized Quadriennales) are quite straightforward: even before the dawn of the 20th century, Italian art was permeated by a deep-felt need for public exposure and for the possibility to be interpreted collectively, a need at times with scientific allusions and at others times a question of social resource, but always chary of individualism and romantic solipsism. If this (shall we say historical?) vocation could be coupled with the formal resources and psychology of form with which Futurism met the European wave of the *Einfühlung* (empathy), then the game was won. The outcome was inevitable — the situation led painters back to the issues of painting proper, while keeping them aware of the wide range of possibilities offered by painting before venturing into other areas of visual inquiry.

It is a fact that, in the 1930s, what I defined as a "common artistic climate" imposed "new aesthetic problems" geared towards a "clearly-defined orientation," such as *proportion, clarity,* and *simplicity,* or *stability, rhythm,* and *method* — motifs that crop up both in the statements of the architects and in the *Dichiarazione degli espositori* (*Exhibitors' Declaration*), published for the first exhibition of Abstract art at the end of 1934. But it is also true that these resolutions and explanations (all formal and figural) do not touch factual issues.

Thus, care should be taken not to confuse climate with words, words with language, and spoken (or written) language with the works themselves. Indeed, this idea of a "tradition of the new" founded on architectural constructs was, in the 1930s, frankly speaking, hackneyed. It can come as no surprise then, that the friendships between artists and architects failed to bear common constructive fruits. In fact,

225

when it came to the crunch, the architects overlooked the work of those painters closest to them (those who now appear to have the closest links, that is). Alternatively, they opted for variants of these artists' works, with an abundance of the non-figurative painters' figurative works.

Before discussing the events and works, we need to clear the field of something that can easily mislead anyone looking into the Italian Abstract artists of the 1930s. As it happened, our heroes had no critical outlook or theoretical approach. This must be true, since the interwar period (from 1918 to 1922-23 or thereabouts) saw a complete redefinition of the status of the artist, and now, in the 1930s, being an artist on a level with the times meant incorporating an awareness of the ends of art itself into one's work. Generally speaking, the "common ground" that was to describe the climate of the time betrays a kind of disassociation: a strong conceptual emblematic content (proportion, clarity, harmony, stability, rhythm, simplicity, method) that did not particularly aid the profession, or more specifically, the idiom. We have reached a kind of breakwater. On this side we have the fabled "tradition of the new" with its companion conceptual legacy; and on the other side we find linguistic pragmatism, the commitment to one's own work as a real horizon.

However, it is traditionally claimed that the Abstract artists did have their own theoretical text, a text that Kandinsky (who had barely skimmed through it, if at all) described as the "gospel of Abstract art." Moreover, it is said that its author, Carlo Belli, was the prophet and mentor of Abstract art as a way of life, through the publication of this and other texts, and through various initiatives. Belli's treatise, *Kn*, was published in Milan in 1935 (a dense and crucial year for the Abstract artists), but it had already existed in a definitive draft as early as 1930, ahead of its time, therefore. But rather than being prophetic, the text provided a striking parallel to the Abstract painters' development toward non-figurative conclusions, if it

Lucio Fontana
Scratched Tablet, 1932

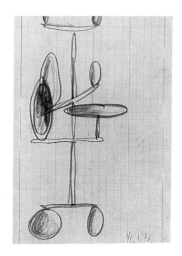

Fausto Melotti
Drawing for Sculpture no.13, c. 1935

Fausto Melotti
Sculpture no. 21, 1935

is true that so far no one has managed to identify in the Abstract works clear echoes of things that could be explained by *Kn*. As mentioned above, in our analysis of these years we must proceed with a policy of not confusing catchwords with a love of the "climate"; here even greater care is needed. To say that the climate had changed, and that it was marked by the need for art to come to the fore and not be confused with other things, that it imposed clear ideas, strong affirmations, readily legible features, a commonly-used language, and that all this was transposed into formulas, aphorisms, and stylistic subtleties — all these combined factors attest more to a literary incursion than to specific attention to contents: and in *Kn* Belli tends more to bespeak the thinking of his contemporaries than to establish a dialogue with them.

Carlo Belli was a journalist of strong Catholic inclinations, bent on establishing a transcendental objectivity to which he could sacrifice everything; a good Fascist who saw in Mussolini the creator of an ethical and anti-materialist clean-up, and as such the artificer of a revolution that would carry its mission to divine conclusions, confident that the time was ripe (1930-32) for rebirth. "Art is. It has no adjectives or addenda," he wrote. "It transcends psychology, profession, and history. It is the contemplation of being." He suggested that if artists could discard imitation and not make technique a sovereign issue but look to loftier matters, with method, commitment and faith, then art would reveal itself in its Platonic essence. At a certain point, Belli's booklet reels off a series of disconcerting tautologies (aphorisms or metaphysics in pill-form, depending on personal taste) such as: "What is art if not Humanity? — Art"; or, "A musical idea is more easily imagined than a pictorial idea. A pictorial idea, i.e., the pure imagination intervening in painting." The "K" of this merry-go-round of reasoning stands for the absolute invariable "Art is," a constant which, in its various manifestations — the number "n" — reasserts itself unfailingly each time. This rash of suppositions was garnished with the mythology of Revolution: palingenesis, Greek perfection, the rejection of the "too-human human," the new (and fated) future awaiting Europe.

All things considered, Belli's *Kn* was an extraordinary feat, mainly because it has no slot among contemporary events — and not simply because it carries its argument to the extreme and brings to the boil issues and ideas that had been brewing for some time. It stands out for its utter lack of any useful application, yet it was important in this impracticality to those very artists it failed to address; it was, according to Cerritelli, "a highly personal way of shedding light on art while obscuring artists." It was a thorough-going system of complete abstraction, a basically abstract form of "concretism," and was too highbrow for Italian arts.

The Galleria del Milione and the Abstract Artists

The setting for all these developments was Milan, with its focus at the Galleria del Milione in Via Brera, right in front of the national Academy and picture gallery. Previously, the place had served as the stronghold of P.M. Bardi, and then, from 1930 it was run by Virginio Ghiringhelli and his brother Gino, who was a non-figurative artist. Their predecessor Bardi had worked with Edoardo Persico on both the *Bollettino della Galleria* (1928-29) and the *Belvedere*, journals of ideas and stimuli for discussion which also frequently served as exhibition catalogues. The Ghiringhelli brothers resumed the initiative in September 1932 by publishing *Il Milione: Bollettino della Galleria del Milione*. Meanwhile, the new gallery included Persico among its contributors, but he was to enjoy scarcely a month of exhibitions before being dismissed in February 1932. The next important stage in the life of the Galleria del Milione comes with the trio Bogliardi-Ghiringhelli-Reggiani in 1934 and their display of non-figurative works, besides the publication of a programmatic *Dichiarazione degli espositori*. We might also mention an exhibition held in 1933 of

Atanasio Soldati's works, with an uproarious lead-in by Carlo Belli, though the works themselves were not non-figurative; plus a couple of presentations in Florence at an interregional exhibition, of highly stylized works by Soldati and Bogliardi). In any case, all this gave rise to the first round of serious debate. The 1934 self-introductory text speaks of aesthetic issues invoked by a modern, "revolutionarily new" life, issues that had to be met with a clear taking of position. The aspiration to order, the call for a common benchmark, the need for Classicism — all appeals that had been much hackneyed in the preceding fifteen years in a bid to give a style to the epoch.

Virginio Ghiringhelli
Composition 5, 1934

In the midst of this (1930-1934), the gallery staged a blitz of exhibitions, including shows of works by Ottone Rosai, Di Terlizzi, and Ubaldo Oppi; while on the "anti-Novecento" front there were exhibitions of works by Carlo Levi, Enrico Paulucci, the budding groups from Verona, Milan, and Naples, as well as foreign groups with various tendencies, the post-Cubists and the so-called "Parisian" school, followed by Kandinsky, Albers, Vordemberg-Gildewart, and Baumeister: a hard-to-define chain of events that saw the comingling of architects, interior designers, graphic artists, set designers, and costume designers. But the outlook and policy of the gallery was not entirely untried — it had showrooms, a library and bookshop for specialist books and magazines, which also provided space for conferences and discussions (in the bookshop the walls were put at the disposal of graphic artists and designers) — and as such repeated the old formula of the *casa d'arte* (art studio) or *bottega di poesie* (poetry workshop) already experimented in Milan.

As for the three-man show of autumn 1934 of works by Bogliardi, Ghiringhelli and Reggiani (who were to remain at the bottom end of the Abstract group), some intriguing problems came to light: first, their attempts to bring forms and colors to the surface, that is to a plane of perception closer to the viewer; second, the constructive coherence of the parts; third, the highlighting of composition so that it virtually becomes figuration; and last, the relation between real composition — the formal grid — and the space and light. In other words, theirs was a way of picking out reality, stylizing it, and offering it as something conceptual or intellectual, something to be read as an expression of intellectual will. The paradigm was not unusual — it was a scheme that De Chirico had accustomed the public to: careful organization of planes and perspectives, scenarios of forms, with a palette of somewhat sluggish tones (Carrà was also to play his part), and occasional recurring ellipses, squares, lozenges, rhombuses, as if they were outlines of deflated volumes, Cubist echoes without three-dimensional value. With his *Composizione 3* (1933), and *Composizione 5* (1934), Ghiringhelli stuck to these rules. In the latter, a diagonal line adds a hint of animation to the scene, and the latent Picasso underpinnings are evidenced by a somewhat "rubbery" palette. In various works including *Ritmo geometrico* (*Geometric Rhythm*, dated 1932) and *Composizione R.1* (of two years later, assuming the accuracy of the date of the former), Mauro Reggiani outruns his colleagues, by displaying two striking aspects of the going tendency, transferred onto an abstract plane. The clear colors, the yellowish hues, greens and blues in general, supplant the blacks, earthen tones and grays. It signaled a general attenuation (and the gradual cleansing of the initially cumbersome material forms), but also a need for more porous open spaces to work in — not through the use of perspective, but through the gentler immediacy of the colors, which in the paintings of Osvaldo Licini and Luigi Veronesi were to take on depth and lead outward, along a broad horizon, a horizon that had shed the encumbrances of form, becoming more defined (the forms and geometrical figures would later cease to be means for enclosure and spatial syntax but stand within the space, light, or depth, accordingly). The other key aspect is the transition from a leaden sense of equilibrium and burdensome presence, towards suggestions of movement, signs of the precariousness

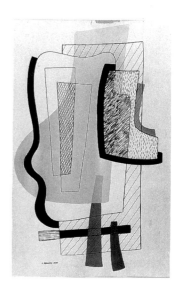

Luigi Veronesi, *Composition*, 1935

of balance, not only noticeable in the transverse lines and ellipses, but also in the subtle imbalances, instability and potential motion (a theme, this "precarious balance," central to the work of Osvaldo Licini, who was to create an extraordinary visual grammar of his own made of inconsistency, perilous balance, and windmills).

Barely a month later, in December 1934, the Galleria del Milione staged an exhibition of woodcuts by Josef Albers and Luigi Veronesi. For Veronesi, Italian-born (in 1908) and the youngest of the entire group, it was his second-ever exhibition, and afterwards he was to show his works only in group or collective exhibitions, isolated from the developments of the Galleria del Milione. The impact of his suspension of rectangular or elliptical forms in space, of his focus on the place in which they are contemplated and interpreted, of the distance they are allotted, was a fundamental feature of his work. With this discovery, Veronesi provided a symbolic cornerstone, because each work, whether graphic or pictorial, photographic collage or tempera-work, opened new vistas on a vast and unbiased dimension, articulating complex movements and shifts of register. They were not still-life compositions or assemblages, but a sort of aligning and framing of evolutions whose figures enunciated paths, dimensions, and intellectual definitions — an interplay of transparency and depth, of light rather than color (the sources are Laszló Moholy-Nagy, obviously, and experimental photography, photomontage in particular, with its seamless overlapping of images and material). Veronesi's work is the fruit of a long, steady development over time. His was not an abstract space, nor his objects mere naturalistic interruptions of the vision. He created a kind of "photogram," compiling objects on light-sensitive paper, and exposing them to light: "The image obtained is never a document, but the transformation of an object into a pure play of light and shade." This dematerialization of objects was coupled with a striking sense of time: "In 1932, Fernand Léger told me to never stop at the individual canvas, but to develop it in all possible variations and transformations."

1935 was an all-important year. It saw exhibitions of works by Lucio Fontana, Atanasio Soldati, Osvaldo Licini, and Fausto Melotti (with Giuseppe Cesetti and Carlo Carrà; and then Fiorenzo Tomea and Aligi Sassu, Renato Guttuso, and Renato Birolli in group exhibitions). Fontana (born 1899) had had works on show in 1931, 1932, and 1934. Now he was proposing a set of "sculptures" in iron and concrete, plaques in concrete scored with a bradawl, surfaces braced by metallic arms; fringed forms, juxtapositions of fields of color interlocking with black and white. Rather than belong to the field of sculpture, these works represent Fontana's personal research into fragments and pictorial use of fields of color with striking tonal intensity to catalyze the attention in a distracted vision of the form — though this is secondary to the pictorial basis. The exhibition coincided with the announcement of a monograph by Edoardo Persico (it came out later in 1936, after the critic's death). It described Fontana as being open to a broad range of influences (influences based on emotivity and impression, not style), with a wealth of "soul and passion" which Persico termed as a "token of a highly representative and acute critical awareness." With the sculptural form as pretext his works conveyed an arbitrary plastic solution that contrasted with the artisan coherence of the object itself.

Of particular interest are his concrete "tablets," brief spaces in which a broken, discontinuous drawing runs, both sensitive and indifferent to the beauty of signs, with the result that the pictorial space into which the lines are sunk is "unstable, liquid, tangent to the figures, always participating and yet quite beyond our grasp," wrote Giulio Carlo Argan shortly afterwards.

These works betray a great immediacy of form that lies in the gesture, the unseen thrust of forces extrinsic to the substrata which nonetheless externalizes them and offers them to the viewer. With a similar lack of premeditation (or perhaps in the premeditated lack of premeditation), psychological mobility plays an important part, as if wanting to separate the doing from the thing done. Now this mobility was not merely action or gesture (although it was to provide an interesting preview of postwar trends, likewise to many other experiments in tension involving informality, material and signs throughout the 1950s).

It represented a way of calibrating and defining something within a space: the sculpture (or pictorial fragment presented in the tablet) entertained a complex reciprocal relationship with its site (a wall or other space). The other artists at the Galleria del Milione were fully aware of the import of Fontana's work, and in their collective presentation of the exhibition wrote: "The sculptures Fontana is exhibiting today will give meaning to the naked space of the rationalist house that will hold them tomorrow." The sculptures displayed pragmatism and mobility, even pathetic in the "arbitrariness" with which they offer themselves. Once again, the theme was instability, precarious balance, potential motion; this embraces the gesturality of the sign and the sense of wonder at seeing it suspended there. The difference between this and the outlines of Giorgio Morandi's bottles and vases is minimal.

Equally significant were Fontana's full sculptural works — the plaques and fragments suspended in a void, like huge leaves deployed in space — an experiment in the arrangement of plastic forms, freely ranging over a variety of suggestions, that goes beyond all formalism or preordained architectural rules (i.e., the absence of magical references, as pointed out by Argan).

The Fontana exhibition was followed by a one-man show devoted to Atanasio Soldati (born 1896), whose works had appeared regularly at the Galleria del Milione (first in 1931, then the following year with Bogliardi and Ghiringhelli, and again in 1933). For Soldati, the reference to architectural precepts and images (and his later "machines for living") were a necessity: the structure of his imagination derived directly from architecture. His pictures provided a selection of images, references, allusions (often willingly figurative, though decontextualized, like mental flotsam or jotted impressions: a row of houses, a veranda, a violin, a torso), linked together on the canvas by lines and scrawls, conceptual ornaments or signs. "Lines love space," wrote Soldati. "They create rhythm and, logically, functions too." It is worth reflecting on this declaration of love between signs and spaces (Melotti used the word "enchantment"), as the relationships between elements, also existing outside the work, which painting is supposed to resolve. It was also a way of holding on to the threads of the "Metaphysical" tradition, though not without a shift in tone: memory, the mysterious clarity of individual objects against the flux that contained them, the joyful dance of assemblage with which they are arranged — Soldati injected Italian painting with a new awareness of harmony, including formal balance, in a series of synoptic, kaleidoscopic expressions. His aim was to reconstitute contemporary painting in some way (writing to a friend, he commented "we are the primitives of a new spirituality," imitating and modifying the Futurist formula of the "primitives of a new sensibility"; but the twist is by no means casual). His was a vocabulary of essential terms and personal figures, or figures borrowed from his contemporaries (a cogent admixture of Picasso, Braque, and Kandinsky), commanded by a spiritual logic (and here "spirit" lies midway between emotivity and intellectualism) that indulged in linking up different moments and situations on the canvas. Its success, once again as with the early De Chirico, lies beyond the canvas itself. "In the trees, stones, the primitives of secret color, in the windows, the streets," he wrote later, "in this emporium of values or 'alphabet' — the mysterious key-word of my work — and in the countryside I find a green that evinces a yellow I couldn't find on the palette." And in this rediscovery of nature outside the scope of his palette, Soldati paved the way for the development of Informal art in Italy.

Osvaldo Licini (born 1894) had first encountered the Milanese faction in the halls of the Second Quadriennale in Rome in spring 1935: Bogliardi, Ghiringhelli,

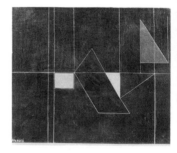

Atanasio Soldati
Composition in Black, 1935

Atanasio Soldati, *Drawing*, c. 1933

Luigi Veronesi
Composition XI, 1938

Alberto Magnelli, Cristoforo De Amicis, Reggiani, Soldati and Fontana were all there. Licini presented *Il bilico* (*Balance*), *Castello in aria* (*Castle in the Air*), and *Stratosfera* (*Stratosphere*) — three extraordinary works which stand apart from the others for their sheer invention and handling of poetics. He was fully aware of having a different poetic motivation, and intended to keep his involvement with the artists at the Galleria del Milione within certain bounds. When shortly after that first encounter in Rome he was invited to exhibit in Milan — the gallery's *Bollettino* ran a headline: *Osvaldo Licini presents his work for the first time in Italy: the Galleria del Milione to host a one-man show with 37 oil paintings, a review of his output from 1925 to 1934*, under a reproduction of his *Uccello n. 2* (*Bird no. 2*) — Licini intervened, displaying great caution. "We do not know each other," he admonished in an open letter to the Galleria del Milione group, explaining, both reluctantly and diplomatically, that his work was still inchoate, and that his masterworks were yet to be committed to canvas. In actual fact, he was not convinced by the self-confident proclamations of the "Abstract" artists. "To doubt is not a weakness," he said. "It is an act of strength, like forging metal." Licini did not believe in a premeditated architectural register for painting. To his mind, painting was distinct from architecture, it was the art of color and form. For him it involved an *irrational* act of creation — something purely poetic, guided predominantly by his imagination.
There are many indications that Licini differed from his contemporaries in terms of background, spirit, and intention. His fascination for colors and forms, for his own poetry, stripped of ideology, free of schemes, formulas, confirms this. His unmitigating slogan "segni non sogni" (signs not dreams) shows an extraordinary departure from the rampant ideology of his time. Free lines and colors: poetry. "We will show," he wrote, "that geometry can become feeling... a respite for the spirit." Sensing impending polemics, the gallery's members answer Licini in the *Bollettino* defending Belli and his pamphlet *Kn* as an indispensable reference point, and reduce the issue to a need for a "morality of the abstract painter," with all the heuristic passion recognizable, not without impropriety and limits, nor ambiguity.

Carlo Carrà wrote a review of the exhibition, and, in his own way, tried to pin down the artist, who had irked him, and place him in a context; he cited Morandi in particular. (Licini's nervous graphic style invited comparisons with Kokoschka). The answer was quick in coming: where Morandi drew on Chardin, Corot, and Cézanne, Licini drew inspiration from Cézanne, Van Gogh, and Matisse.

In Licini's work, that elusive beauty ("which for us painters is all that matters," wrote Licini in reference to Matisse) was elicited through the use of color, through glimpses of figuration, and arcane harmonies — particularly, unusual forms of visual balance, sudden changes of horizon and a unique use of color, both transparent and open. Each component of this kind of painting — the strokes, fields of color and glossy tones used — was indicative: "The signs express volition, strength, ideas; the colors express magic." These works manifest Licini's sensuality and vitality, a feeling of lightness (with respect to the means and material employed) — qualities without parallel in Italian painting, except perhaps in De Pisis, whose extraordinary light-handed and delicate works create a vivid sensation of rapid transition from physical tension to a rambling flow of ideas and attitudes; significantly, comparisons to Licini generally reach out beyond the orbit of his non-figurative work. To define Licini as an "Abstract" artist has little sense. Nor has reducing his work to "figurative formulism." Here too, as with his interlocking of high and low, sky and earth, interior and exterior, Licini's painting cannot be classed as either abstract or figural, but moves in a nervous, middle path, with magical penetrations of different horizons. Rather than bracket him with the non-figurative group, in this kind of multi-faceted exhibition it would be more logical to allocate Licini a room of his own, not to stress the presence of a distinctive personality, but to underline the complexity of the artist's work, which was not so much a one-dimensional visual inquiry as a revelation of states of mind and experiences.

The "Abstract" season came to a close in May 1935 with the one-man exhibition devoted to works by Fausto Melotti (born 1901; in 1934 he had presented a "course on modeling at the school of furniture craft in Cantù, run by sculptor Fausto Melotti," during which he had suggested that the attention of art critics turn "from geometrical laws to physical laws of the composition of forces, statics and kinetics"). But what about art? An "angelic" state of mind of a geometrical nature, while geometry itself was harmony and counterpoint, akin to musical form; furthermore, art was an activity involving the intellect and not the senses, and therefore techniques and materials were less important. His was a form of sculpture without modeling, because it was "modulation, not modeling" that was important — "modeling comes from 'model,' i.e., nature, disorder; and modulation from 'module,' i.e., canons, and hence, order. A crystal holds nature transfixed."

Fausto Melotti was the first of the group who could rightfully be attributed the title of sculptor, since Lucio Fontana hovered between painting and sculpture. Melotti's works are three-dimensional organisms that project into space; indeed they explore the problem of just how to occupy the space and unfold within it. Traditional materials and weight held little attraction for Melotti. "The way Doric columns occupy space does not change when the marble is replaced with painted plaster." Plaster, clay, painted and chromium-plated metals were the main materials he used (their monochrome unity and polished cleanness offered pictorial resonance), as in *Scultura 15* and *Scultura 21*, which is perhaps the most complex piece Melotti completed during the 1930s. It consists of a framework of twelve compartments holding nine spheres and three flattened forms — a dual exercise in the representation of the sphere and circle. Other exemplary pieces are *Scultura 17*, and then a series of bas-reliefs (the closest he came to achieving a plastic variation of painting), and then *Scultura 16, Scultura 23*, and *Scultura 24*. The underlying "themes" of these "sculpture-energy accumulators" are the uncertain balance and vibration of metallic

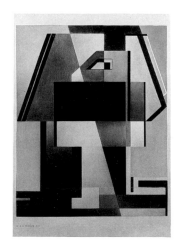

Mario Radice
Secret Portrait, 1936

filaments, clear surfaces, and slight spatial contortions — as if the few features scored into the object acted out in space the rhythms transmitted by the object's color and metallic properties, extending it in time: this accumulator of energy was also a "commutator" of images.

This brings us to one of the more recurrent arguments regarding most of the painting and sculpture of this period, namely, the sensibility and intensity of colors, tones and textures (nearly always sumptuous and loaded), which are protracted by the forms and figures, giving them suggestiveness and magnetism. For the Abstract artists it was a point of interest that came closest to the common experience. It was also an area in which the quest for simplification and lightness of form prompted some of their most incisive solutions. This was especially true for Melotti's sculptures, and underlines his relationship with time. Interestingly, the bulk of the Abstract artists shunned the timeless Platonist outlook Belli was so fond of, preferring instead to tackle the question of form-space relationships as concrete invasions, extensions, durations, whether mental or tactile.

Other Artists and Areas of Inquiry

Before investigating the work of artists outside the Milanese hub, it is worth taking a quick look at the situation in Como, with its central figure, architect Giuseppe Terragni. What is remarkable about Como is the rapport — albeit precarious — that was established between the artists (painters as well as sculptors) and the architects, leading to surprising and successful results. One of Terragni's fellow townsmen, Cesare Cattaneo, was to write that painting (and the same goes for sculpture) could come into harmony with architecture only as the interpretation in a different language of the same spiritual message. In this context, the most immediately striking feature of the work of the two painters Mario Radice and Manlio Rho is their common sense of decoration and the ritualism they felt in the act of painting — their understanding of decoration as the ability to harness a climate or taste, shifting and stylizing it to make it reflect the interior plan — either to be incorporated into architecture (Radice contributed to the Casa del Fascio, an emblematic attempt at clarity on the part of Terragni, grafted onto Como's urban fabric), or as a stand-alone work. It goes without saying that the Catholic spirit made itself felt — especially in Radice's output. It was no coincidence that his preoccupation with form led him back to Nature. "Everything exists in the infinite field of Nature," he himself observed. "Each form, each color, has already been created by God."

Manlio Rho (born 1901) tended, rather mechanically, to compose sets of rectangles of varying colors and intensity to lend a sense of spatial succession and restore depth to the painting's surface: this peculiar extrusion of the surface is achieved through the systematic use of oblongs (perhaps the least resolved and harmonious of rectangular figures) and diagonals, defining the limits of the viewer's perception. Rho's encounter with Kandinsky and his study of color as a form of transparency, which was broadcast among the Abstract artists in 1935 (coinciding with a general shift in the younger artist's handling of the palette), led him to more complex compositions, packed with patterns, both horizontal and diagonal, cramming the visual field in which colors are used to bring out different superimpositions and atmospheres. The sense of atmosphere, typical to the Lombard tradition of naturalism, seems to gather more weight here than in the "intellectualistic" abstraction of color.

This "color-light" formula and its related natural effects surface in the work of Mario Radice (born 1898), except that Radice's painting pivots more on a sentimental, intimate axis. Once again, it was a highly perceptive Cattaneo who intuited the real crux of painting in Como. He realized that more important that the questions of harmony, clarity, and architecture was "the search for the *organic* origins of these systems." In other words, it made the sense of light and color a kind of principle and

Aldo Galli, *Sculpture*, 1938

Bice Lazzeri, *The Black Sign*, 1929

beginning to organic development, which unfolded through figures and patterns, often in the form of something "breaking out," as in *Composizione in arancio* (*Composition in Orange*, 1938), or in a circular development, as in *Composizione SPICF* (1935).Other important figures include painters Carla Badiali and Carla Prina, but one of the least predictable personalities to emerge at this juncture in Como was the sculptor Aldo Galli (born 1906). Galli too clung to the idea of protracting the plastic effects beyond the limits of the form itself, and adopted precise dynamic schemes, using scored circles, or brief plastic tracts with colorized contouring.

Since the continuation and ulterior developments in Futurism in the 1920s and 1930s will be treated in a separate chapter of this catalogue, just a passing mention will be made here of Bruno Munari, with his collection of free-floating devices dubbed *Macchine inutili* (*Useless Machines*). These objects, stirred by chance currents of air, liberated sculpture from the strictures of plinth and weight. Munari's real contribution here was to shift the stress on lighter material and forms from the object itself to its design and its mode of use, exploiting the factors of play and chance as a means for imbuing the work with levity and an openness that was wholly uncharted in Italy at the time. Meanwhile, in his paintings, such as *Anche la cornice* (*The Frame Too*, 1935), all the elements (the back-, fore-, and mid-grounds) are brought onto a single plane, toppling the normal sense of hierarchy. Two other artists need mentioning here, Piero Rambaudi (born 1906) and Bice Lazzeri (1900).

Rambaudi worked in Turin, and in 1932 exhibited a series of paintings focusing on the pure continuity of the line, creating a structure free of any clear-cut references whatsoever. Later, in 1938, he exhibited a set of sculptures, painted cardboard trunks from which sprouted blocks of monochrome plastic; the works shun any attempt at naturalism, and show his keen interest in Paul Klee's ventures. Bice Lazzeri's works draw on her activity in the field of applied arts. They include embroidery, cushions, and other handicraft items. The interlinear patterns, which are never orthogonal, and the symmetry of motifs, mirror-images multiplied in various directions, create a striking, novel sense of spatial values.

Vittorio Gregotti

Manufactured Product Design 1900-1945

To explain the development of Italian craft and manufactured product design in the first half of the 20th century and its relationship with the contemporary world of the visual arts, involves examining two sets of premises.

The first set relates to Italy's economic and productive development, and this may be divided into three separate phases. The first covers the period from the turn of the century to 1914; the second comprises the boom in industrial output brought about by the war and which lasted to the end of the 1920s, while the third relates to the ambitious program undertaken by the Fascists to modernize the country's structures, with all the ambiguous political objectives that implies. The impact of these circumstances was that products developed according to relatively original and independent national criteria, forcing gradual modifications to be made to traditional craft models inherited from pre-industrial peasant culture.

The second set of premises relates to the rapid development of the decorative or applied arts that had occurred during the second half of the 19th century. The subject of intense debate in all of Europe, the applied and decorative arts made major strides which ultimately also influenced contemporary visual arts and architecture. The applied arts had, moreover, developed unusually close links with architecture, each exerting an influence on the other. In Italy, and perhaps throughout Europe, architecture was the main area through which painting and sculpture could influence the applied and industrial arts and crafts, architecture being, according to William Morris and his followers, the prime mover of a given culture and the aesthetics of environment, and the one which could bring together as well as individually influence industrial philosophy, the traditional crafts, and the debate on the decorative arts.

On occasion, in fact, the urban environment or the hinterland, along with the manufactured goods that were part of them, became the subject and the special domain of the visual arts in Italy — a country which had a very strong international outlook at least until the advent of the Fascist regime. This choice of subject matter was sometimes sufficiently powerful to influence the actual composition of the image in painting.

There is almost unanimous agreement that, in its many guises, Futurism was more successful than Art Nouveau in introducing production as a "new nature" and source of inspiration for the visual arts. Less attention has been given to the influence of this "new nature" on the various forms of the *rappel à l'ordre* and the re-interpretations of traditional styles, typical of the trends that succeeded Futurism in the inter-war years, or even the Metaphysical transfiguration of history in a poetic confrontation with the objects of the modern world. The immediate assimilation of the world of machines and industrial production on the part of neo-Futurists and the Abstract painters often shows through in the optimism and enthusiasm of their painting, whereas the more intimist artistic currents seemed less responsive to the spirit of modernity conveyed by objects for industrial use.

Over and above the different subjects represented by painters, the relationship between art, production, and reproduction became a major issue for contemporary painting.

Even though Italy was lagging way behind other developed countries in terms of production potential and technological developments until 1945, this does not in any way imply that the role of manufactured goods was any less important in the inter-war period in Italy. Manufactured goods were only available to the well-to-do urban classes and reflected their ideals. For examples we need only look to the series of so-called "White telephone" series of Italian films (the white telephone being considered the ultimate in luxury) or the aerodynamic design of trains and cars. We see it best of all, however, in furniture design and in the Modernists' impassioned revolt against traditional and "mythical" styles. Until the end of World War II, when they started to become the symbol for general well-being, manufactured goods represented progress and modernity.

Until the early 1940s, it was difficult to gauge the influence of painting and sculptural forms on the design of industrial products.

It appeared though that the nearer one got to craft and decorative production, the more products were influenced by transformations in taste.

With the "First International Exhibition of Modern Decorative Art" (*Prima esposizione internazionale d'arte decorativa moderna*) held in Turin in 1902 Italy suddenly lifted its gaze to international horizons, and consequently this represented the first official move toward the renewal of the applied arts in Italy. Nonetheless, the issue of linguistic renewal still remained: that is where the use of the new industrial materials formed part of a renewal on a stylistic level, rather addressing production methods to new social problems. In Italy, the major critics, such as Emilio Thovez, Agnoldomenico Pica, and Alfredo Melani, who wrote for the leading magazines such as *Emporium*, *Arte decorativa moderna*, and *Ambiente Moderno* (to name the more important ones) concentrated more on the aesthetic and symbolic aspects of International Art Nouveau than its potential for transformation.

Italian artists, including Galileo Chini, Vittorio Zecchin, Ernesto Basile, Raimondo D'Aronco, Ximenes, Giacomo Cometti, Eugenio Quarti, Carlo Bugatti, Federico Tesio, Gaetano Moretti, and Alessandro Mazzuccotelli, who were well-known throughout Europe, were producing designs for furniture and objects. By throwing off the shackles of stylistic rules they were finally able to work with a greater freedom of expression.

In the immediate pre-war years, the complex phenomena of *Dannunzianesimo* and *Crepuscolarismo* both played a major role as interpretative keys and models of aesthetic life and freedom of thought. The idea of the "oggetto rustico" celebrated by Pascoli was challenged on the one hand by D'Annunzio's *decadentismo* with its underlying philosophy of the "inimitable life," which was aesthetic, sensual, and

Richard Ginori
porcelain ware, c. 1903

Ernesto Basile, table and chair
on show at the V Exposition of Art
Venice, 1903

Vittorio Zecchin, Veronese vase
for Cappellin Venini & C., 1922

Giacomo Balla, small table, 1914

Giacomo Balla, sideboard, 1914

above normal morality, and on the other, by the nostalgic melancholy of the *Crepuscolarismo* group with their aversion to rhetoric and their love of the countryside. A contrast was thus created between D'Annunzio's almost obsessively cluttered interiors, in which formal technicality and aesthetic internationalism were transformed into a collage of multifarious objects — that were unusual in as much as they bore witness to unusual situations — and the dusty atmosphere of "good objects in the worst taste," which the poetry of Guido Gozzano and Marino Moretti made into a paradigm for the silent majority of the lower middle-classes during the reign of King Umberto I.

It is interesting to highlight the unexpected rise in interest in the decorative arts — due in part to a general increase in income levels and consequently in purchasing power — and their refinement into one trend which became emblematic of the lifestyle of the new industrial and bureaucratic classes. Nonetheless, Liberty, as the Italian style of Art Nouveau came to be known, remained by and large an avant-garde movement, never impinging to any great extent on industrial philosophy.

In place of the aspirations behind the Socialist Arts & Crafts movement, or the ideals of the Viennese Seccession, Italian Liberty was fired by little more than a desire to join in the European cultural debate. This proved to be an important example for the Futurists, who were the next Italian avant-garde movement, and it is no coincidence that after World War I, both Liberty and Futurism were accused of romantic internationalism by proponents of the *rappel à l'ordre* and *italianità*.

"A white metallic electric iron, smooth, gleaming, and spotlessly clean, delights the eye more than a nude statuette on a nondescript pedestal painted for the occasion. The typewriter is more architecturally pure than building designs awarded prizes or hailed by the Academies." These were Giacomo Balla's words in 1918 — the year when interest in the decorative arts in Italy reached a peak. Three years earlier he had published his own appeal for the "futurist reconstruction of the universe" but, back in the first decade of the century, when he was setting up his studio-home in Via Paisiello in Rome, he designed his own furniture which included fold-away units, in addition to his well-known character-furniture for the nursery. Expanding the frontiers of painting into all walks of life including graphics, music, theater, and product design was integral to the philosophy of Futurism. The links between art and life, the so-called "inimitable life" mentioned above in connection with Dannunzianesimo, are clearly visible.

The Futurists talked of *complessi plastici* and of an artificial passage and nearly all of them were interested in extending the boundaries of the applied arts — even if only on a theoretical level. In his interior designs, Balla tends to give a predominant role to the color that help the walls, furniture, and objects describe the room, but he was mainly interested in relationships and creating a coordinated environment.

What he was trying to do was to bring together the various artistic functions so as to construct a modern environment, which is the practical demonstration of that "new, completely transformed sensibility," first preached by the Futurists in 1910 with their first technical manifesto.

While this tendency was to have a fundamental effect on the development of design philosophy, it was to be indirect. There is no trace of it in the work or the writings of the Futurists, the aims of William Morris, or the progressivist ideology of the Werkbund tradition.

The Futurists' interest in the applied arts was particularly noticeable in areas where they had contact with Central European culture, and became more ideological and implicit where it was most closely linked with Italian culture. Giacomo Balla and Enrico Prampolini were the most sensitive to this issue. Later converts included Arnaldo Ginna, who wrote a text on futurist furniture in 1916, of magazine *Noi*, and Alfredo Gargiulo. They were all active in the field of applied art, both in the

Gianni Caproni
Idronoviplano Ca 60, 1918-19

Secessione romana, where Prampolini studied under Duilio Cambellotti at the Accademia (Balla formed part of the movement itself) and through their contacts with Germany — Balla realized his first interior design project in Düsseldorf in 1912. In addition, Fortunato Depero, born in Fondo in the South Tyrol and so technically an Austrian citizen, studied at the Scuola Reale Elisabettiana, the school of the Decorative Arts established in 1919 in Rovereto, where his fellow-students included Luciano Baldessari, Gino Pollini, and Adalberto Libera, who later became the leading lights of 1930s Italian Rationalism.

All these factors led the Futurists' philosophy regarding the construction of the object towards the paradigm or model, so that later, in post-war Italy, a large part of Italian avant-garde design made technology and science, mechanization, and rationalization of production the principal contents of the objects: they became demonstration, rather than a production model. On the eve of World War I, even the contrast between the so-called *linea fantastica* and the *linea funzionale* within the Futurist philosophy was more a taking up of positions within the movement rather than an indication of any form of contact with the theories of the European avant-garde in the field of the applied arts.

As far as the Futurists were concerned, the war, which accelerated and changed the destiny of the country's entire production structure, reinforced the relationship with the object — for them, nothing summed up the modern and dynamic world better than armaments.

After the war, the schools became the most influential places for shaping the tastes of designers and exponents of the applied arts. With the eclipse of the art academies' monopoly on artistic training, a greater range of options became available: Faculties of Engineering and Architecture, the painting and sculpture academies to a certain degree, but above all the schools of applied arts, school-workshops, and professional training colleges.

In 1919, the Milan-based *Scuola Umanitaria* promoted and was the venue for the first *Esposizione regionale lombarda di arte decorativa*, which was the result of a survey conducted on the professional conditions of the market. This exhibition was the forerunner of the Monza, and later Milan Triennale exhibitions which provided a major platform for the debate on the decorative arts in the inter-war period. The organizing committee of the 1919 exhibition was made up of leading figures from the world of the applied arts, such as Mazzuccotelli, Guido Marangoni, Melani and Moretti as well as young art critics who were interested in the issue of industrialization, such as Margherita Sarfatti, and Raffaello Giolli.

The ISIA (Istituto Statale Industrie Artistiche) in Monza developed according to more modern and ambitious criteria. Advertising design and painting were taught there from the outset. Depero was the first to work there and he was followed soon afterwards by Marcello Nizzoli, Mario Sironi, and Edoardo Persico, and then Mario Pagano, Marino Marini, as well as craftsmen like Vercellini, Nicolatti, and

Conoletti, who worked in iron, gold, and tin respectively. Guido Balsamo Stella was the School's first director, and the first generation of students included Bramante Buffoni, Mirko, Nivola, and Fancello. While its orientations were somewhat contradictory, the school showed a clear intention to get involved and innovate, and it soon became a center of influence for launching new initiatives in the industrial arts.

We now need to look at developments regarding product design within the context of the maufacturing industry. This is a difficult task and, by and large, comes down to a process of induction from the products themselves. While small-scale inventions soon gave way to large-scale patented products, it is not true to say that there was a universal trend towards factory production, and therefore in the design process.

During this period, many companies became aware of the importance of publicizing their products and their potential uses. For example, both individuals and businesses had to be persuaded of the feasibility and convenience of switching from handwriting to type-writing, and potential buyers had to be educated about the advantages of labor-saving devices for the home. After one electrical appliances company decided to promote its electric iron for home use, production leapt from 500 to 14,000 units in just one year. At this stage publicity was largely a question of conveying information. The market for such publicity campaigns was, however, still restricted to a very narrow social grouping who had the available income or whose life-styles could incorporate such innovations.

Once again the modernization of taste was important but socially restricted. The same thing happened to that somewhat amorphous area surrounding Art Deco, which was a major movement but whose spread was considerably limited. After 1930, the American "streamlined look" with its emphasis on industrial technology and appeal to modernity, youth, and speed was to have a considerable effect on the style of manufactured goods. Meanwhile, the upper echelons of society, and the industrial and professional classes, who had an acute sense of restraint and decorum, and preferred a less ostentatious look turned almost exclusively to the highly-skilled Viennese craftsmen and the more traditional exponents of French Art Deco for their furniture. What becomes evident is a desire to give the object its own identity, amending it according to different (and contrasting) cultural viewpoints, in other words, using style to express life-style.

Fiat Omnibus 18 BL
for Public Transport, 1914-21

In the post-1919 period, which was both post-Futurist and post-Metaphysical, there was a concerted move towards what came to be known as the *rappel à l'ordre* throughout the moderate wings of the avant-garde, the Milan-based neo-Classicist architects taking the lead.

While this group appeared at times to be united, their backgrounds were quite different. Muzio was in tune with the *Novecento* painting movement while his idiom made him the heir of certain aspects of Metaphysical painting; Gigiotti Zanini adopted an ironical angle on Palladio's idiom; then there was Annibale Fiocchi and Giuseppe Pizzigoni's somewhat "fey" Milanese Neo-Classicism with which they aimed to restore the links between the highest levels of the post-war middle classes and its stylistic traditions; finally, there were Greppi, Gio Ponti, and Emilio Lancia, who looked towards the Viennese Seccession for inspiration.

Giuseppe De Finetti was a special case. It was he who was responsible for bringing to Italy certain of the revolutionary values inherent in Adolf Loos' uncompromising message of simplification. Also involved in this debate were the first Italian Rationalist architects of *Gruppo 7* (Sebastiano Larco, Guido Frette, Carlo Enrico Rava, Luigi Figini, Gino Pollini, Giuseppe Terragni, and Adalberto Libera) and in 1926 and 1927 their views were published in the magazine *La Rassegna Italiana*, "We do not want to break with a tradition that is evolving and is changing appearance, which makes it hard to recognize. The new, and true, architecture must evolve from a close attention to logic and rationalism." For at least the next ten years, the *Novecento* and Rationalism vied for the role of the true art of Fascism which was the symbol of a young and dynamic nation, with a complex interplay of influences and ideas. As it turned out, the *Novecento* concentrated especially on the Northern-Italian industrial middle-class which in general collaborated with Fascism, while maintaining its own criteria of taste and tradition. Meanwhile Rationalism claimed to see the new, the revolutionary, and the anti-middle-class in Fascist ideology, while simultaneously maintaining strong links with the international avant-garde, whose underlying philosophy was clearly in contrast to these ideals.

In the 1920s and 30s, the Monza and Milan Triennale exhibitions were an outstanding platform for the decorative arts debate in Italy, providing a faithful reflection of the popularity and the theoretical ideas put forward by the various Italian avant-garde movements of the time.

Giovanni Muzio
ceremonial armchairs
IV Triennale, Monza, 1930

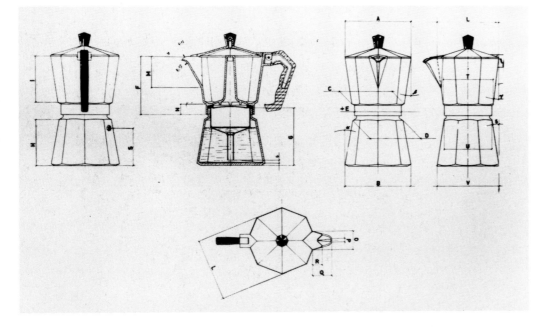

Alfonso and Renato Bialetti
Moka Express, 1930
Definition and prospects

In the eyes of the *Novecento* artists, the object was a luxury item, its quality lay in the workmanship, the notion of the one-off piece of furniture, and single rather than mass production.

For the exhibition commemorating ten years of the Fascist revolution held in 1932, Giuseppe Terragni and Mario Sironi created a flawless expressive balance between Rationalism, the *Novecento* and Futurism.

In the so-called "cultura maggiore," all the elements necessary for the debate that followed were laid in place between 1919 and 1929. In addition to a general trend towards stylistic and decorative simplification, and a more formal order that looked to the basics and an unfailing appeal to the idea of *italianità*, either by harking back to regional folklore, or the Italian tradition at the junction between Classicism and

Fiat 1500, 1935

241

Primitivism. In this context Rationalism was a contradiction, which started out tentatively and then, gaining in confidence, became a characteristic of the Italian Modern movement. Above all else, the plan for the decorative and industrial applied arts represented an unresolved theoretical issue for art criticism which was still dominated by Benedetto Croce. A great many issues came to the fore during this period, from Lionello Venturi's discussion of those connected with the "Taste for Primitivism" to the theoretical thrust of the younger critics, such as Giulio Carlo Argan, who were closest to the contemporary architectural issues generated by the Modern movement in architecture. The typical idealist opinions regarding the significance and unique qualities of the work of art all militated against the idea of duplication, and against its having a structural utilitarian context. However, the

Olivetti Technical Department office in Ivrea with metal furniture from Synthetis range, 1935

Aldo Magnelli
MPI Olivetti typewriter, 1932

Luigi Figini, Gino Pollini
Xanti Schawinsky
Ottavio Luzzati
Studio 42 Olivetti
typewriter, 1935

youngest critics claimed that functionality and assembly techniques were essential features of contemporary objects, and were not incompatible with the work of art.

Taking a major part in the debate were the cultural circles of Turin, which spawned some of the most enlightened critics and enthusiastic supporters of the modern architecture debate in Italy, including Edoardo Persico and Giuseppe Pagano, along with the painter Felice Casorati. There was no mistaking Gustav Klimt's influence on Casorati — not only in terms of taste but also in terms of an interest in the applied arts and architecture — which were exceptional among Italian painters, and which Casorati promptly transmitted to the *Gruppo dei Sei*. This group of six architects, whose theorist was Edoardo Persico, played a major role in asserting an overtly European position for themselves, by re-establishing links with French culture. What followed was an unequivocal opposition to the principles of the Novecento movement.

Apart from a few exceptions, what we could call the new "factory" culture developed according to purely national lines. While not claiming to be political as such, figures such as Gualino, Agnelli, Pirelli, Olivetti, Volpi, Falck, Donegani, Cini, Conti and others, for better or worse, became authentic protagonists not only in Italy's national industrial life, but also in its economic, political and social arenas, with Gualino exerting considerable influence on visual culture, and Olivetti even more so.

The two leading car designers at FIAT [Fabbrica italiana automobili Torino] were strikingly different from each other in terms of character, interests, training and temperament.

In 1935, just a year after the launch of the Chrysler Airflow, Mario Revelli di Baumont designed the FIAT 1500, the first European car with a streamlined profile — and of a much higher standard than its American counterpart. In addition he undertook pioneering research work on taxi cabs. Dante Giacosa was with FIAT from the outset and in 1934, along with the FIAT design team, produced the Zero A car, which was the forerunner of the world-renowned "Topolino" 500.

Like Olivetti, FIAT successfully converted from being a crafts-led business to a modern industrial set-up, not just in terms of massive concentrations of capital and manpower (which was also typical of enterprises sponsored by the public sector) but mainly in terms of systematic operations planning, research, technical updating of products, and the creation of an efficient distribution network.

Designed by Aldo Magnelli, a technical designer with an exceptional aesthetic flair, (perhaps influenced by his brother, the painter Alberto Magnelli), the MP1 was Olivetti's first portable typewriter, and the first example of the horizontal development of a product.

New markets needed to be opened up, ones which could be won over with flexible and versatile machines, coupled with a clear corporate image identity message to be achieved through publicity, buildings, display and sales points.

This highly sophisticated notion of coordinated corporate identity planning was promoted above all by Giovanni Pintori, Xanti Schawinsky, and Costantino Nivola in the area of graphic design, with Luigi Figini and Gino Pollini handling the architectural end, and Nizzoli overseeing industrial design.

In 1935 Adriano Olivetti brought in the architects Figini and Pollini and the painter Schawinsky, along with a team of factory technicians in charge of monitoring production schedules and methods, to help the engineer Ottavio Luzzati in the planning of Studio 42. This first practical, and somewhat isolated example of industrial design conceived of as a joint project between artists, technicians, and public relations people was one of Olivetti's most outstanding achievements. In 1941, Marcello Nizzoli, (who was to become the leading light of Italian design for the next ten years), was involved in the design project for Olivetti's first calculator, the

Multisumma. Nizzoli, a graduate of the Monza school, started as a painter before moving to advertising design, and his posters for Campari were highly acclaimed. He then progressed to the decorative arts where, in addition to detailed technical and distributive research, the formal aspects of his work achieved an importance of their own.

It was no coincidence that the Olivetti company's strong bond with international architectural culture attracted Italian abstract painters, such as Manlio Rho, Mario Radice, Luigi Veronesi, Atanasio Soldati, and even Fausto Melotti came to be associated with Olivetti.

It was only after World War II, however, that this bond found widespread affirmation in public taste and established many new contacts with the world of the figurative arts. This was a more outgoing, internationalist figurative culture, which until the close of the 1950s would remain aloof from the hesitant and introspective canons of contemporary Italian art.

Fiat ATR 100
Locomotive, 1936

Renato Barilli

The "Wild" Realists of the 1930s

Contemporary art is an expression of aversion towards the use of realism, and indeed it is born in defiance of this concept. The term "realism" is used here in reference to the faithful reproduction of visual data, in which the painting is akin to the surface of a mirror, or a window framing the field of view. Furthermore, the artist's interference with the forms was not considered enough to redeem the work from being labeled "realist." In the long run, Impressionism merely sanctioned this idea of mirror-representation, though in the case of the Impressionists, filtered through the personal sensibility of the individual painter, it gave rise to astounding results. Thus the finest interpreters of contemporary art were quick to point out that absolute realism (understood in this traditional sense) coincided with absolute illusion and the renunciation of all the other qualities of the real objects, such as weight, movement, or odor. Animals, with their acute senses of smell and sight, are not in fact fooled by paintings executed with the most scrupulous realism; they remain quite indifferent. The anecdote about the gulls trying to peck at the grapes in a painting by Apelles was probably invented by some theoretician of the day, keen to defend the early forms of *trompe l'œil*, which first emerged in the Graeco-Roman era, and has since remained a thorn in the side of western culture, making itself felt from time to time. It is also a known fact that Pierre Restany, a reliable critic of postwar times re-introduced the concept of "realism" based on the formula of *Nouveau Réalisme*, following it to the letter, a label he used in reference to certain European artists at the end of the 1950s who depicted objects "just as they were," excluding any form of illusory transcription techniques.

In our own times, it is certainly not worth considering art forms that still honor the mimetic-specular conception, i.e., the heredity of the august Impressionist lesson; these art forms are irrevocably hackneyed and nostalgic. Nonetheless, the authority of mimesis in art was such that (without directly cultivating it) the 20th century was forced to deal with some of its sibling residues, adopting some opportune corrective measures, and wary of the risks involved in abandoning oneself to mimesis and illusion. One way of stanching the flood lay in the awareness that one is outside the present, and one is dealing with the past, with museum-pieces. A similar attitude was fostered in Metaphysical artists, by *Valori Plastici*, and by those gathered under the *Novecento* banner, a movement that began with only seven adherents before spilling out in all directions. Such was the lead-up to the 1920s in particular, and it characterized developments throughout the decade, and not only in Italy. Their great importance was also felt in other chapters of development. It goes without saying that artistic phenomena do not simply expire, and the influence of magical-metaphysical realism continued to have effect after the 1930s, though it certainly lost the force of the origins and persuasion that had piloted it through its heyday. Perhaps its swan-song came with the advent of "muralism" or mural art, which to some extent had already been in the offing, ever since the seven of the germinal *Novecento* group — Mario Sironi, Achille Funi, Ubaldo Oppi, Leonardo Dudreville, Pietro Marussig, Anselmo Bucci, Luigi Malerba — had first assembled. Their program had included an appeal to quit easel painting; such works, they opined, were only fit for the salon walls of the bloated bourgeoisie. It was time to turn back to large-scale decorative ventures, even to fresco painting, which had expanded greatly during the "golden years" of the 14th and 15th centuries, before the corruption of naturalism and Baroque. Furthermore, the group felt it was crucial to draw inspiration from the full-bodied, monumental, plastic forms that characterized the proto-Renaissance, and were later atrophied by the harsh treatment of archaism. Such ideas seemed to find a fertile seedbed in Italy, which was geared to launch itself into a new wave of Imperial Roman splendor, portraying the workers in the factories, fields, builder's yards, with sturdy, muscular frames. But the regime of the 1920s had not yet built the kind of architectural support to receive such adventurous decoration.

When the monuments and buildings did begin to appear, the impetus of this magical-metaphysical archaism was already waning, which explains the delayed arrival of "muralists" like Sironi, who were obliged to await first the Milan Triennale of 1933, then the creation of the city's Palazzo di Giustizia (Law Courts) a few years later. Many other opportunities followed, with the construction of post offices, town halls, railway stations, university buildings. Among the initial *Novecento* members of the mural movement were its pilot Sironi (who became its outspoken and highly lucid theoretical champion) and Funi, who earned distinction through various special civic building projects in his native town, Ferrara. Many other leading figures also showed keen interest in the movement offshoot: Giorgio De Chirico, Massimo Campigli, Ottone Rosai, Ferruccio Ferrazzi, and especially Gino Severini, who in the 1920s had been cultivating a variant on muralism styled to Christian *mores*, and filtered through the teachings of the French philosopher Jacques Maritain. When he returned to Italy from Paris in the 1940s, Severini joined in the civic and popular vein of this mural campaign, becoming one of its mainstays.

Antonietta Raphaël
Still Life with Guitar, 1928

His work was largely based on mosaic technique, in place of the classical system of applying paint directly to walls, usually carried out *a secco* (dry wall), rather than *a fresco* (wet). Severini's venture earned the enthusiastic support of the movement's sculptors, headed by Arturo Martini. Another member who had shown great promise, Adolfo Wildt, met an untimely death while still very young.

All in all, the "muralism" of the 1930s has come full circle and is more appreciated today, in the light of the recent spread of the "visual quoting" (*citazionista*) fashion. Mario Sironi, and perhaps even more so Achille Funi, Massimo Campigli, and Pompeo Borra, now seem like the forerunners of Salvo (Mangione) and Carlo Maria Mariani, whose use of realist schemes was conducted in an ostentatious, exaggerated fashion, charged with a sense of paradox, which aimed to ally itself with the "taste of the primitives," or infancy. In comparison, the work that this group of artists (and those colleagues who were even less keen on muralism) continued to produce on canvas is unconvincing. This particular area of their production showed an inevitable reiteration of the scorned "easel painting" destined for the bourgeois salons and market circuits. On canvas, the artists got bogged down in somewhat stereotyped and repetitive forms that overstretch the imagery. This happened to Carlo Carrà, and likewise to Campigli, Borra, Severini, and the member of the so-called "Parisian" group, Mario Tozzi, the Tuscans Rosai and Primo Conti, and certain minor figures in the *Novecento* movement, such as Marussig and Bucci. Generally speaking, all of them suffered a progressive loss of "magic," yielding more and more to the softness and tonalism of the resurgent naturalist tide. This is even true of the work of the "Nordic" artist, Felice Casorati, or of the refined mastery of Giorgio Morandi, who in fact during this decade turned out some of his most fleshy renderings of physical matter, in dense arrangements on the canvas surface. As for De Chirico, he continued unrelenting along his "promenade through the halls of the museum," except that now, in the 1930s, he had reached the more arduous rooms, those which conserved the monuments to high Renaissance and the Baroque mystique of Pieter Paul Rubens and his like, or even to the French naturalism of the 1800s. Throughout his career, De Chirico was to maintain a constant irony, an underlying streak of self-parody. But who, in those years, was able

Antonietta Raphaël
Flight from Sodom, 1935
(1968 cast)

246

to detect this? Most people would have readily sworn that the *pictor optimus* took himself seriously, and that he had surrendered unconditionally to traditionalism, in outright rejection of all the precepts of contemporary progress. Happily, his brother Alberto Savinio managed to salvage some of the dream-like nocturnal aura of his own work, unwaveringly conjuring landscapes of apparitions, which his brother Giorgio had begun to make too "normal." Filippo De Pisis also tenaciously held on to his seemingly facile post-Impressionism, executing works graced with a kind of momentary poise, but which were heroic and insightful owing to the almost stenographic quickness of the agile linework.

It was therefore clear at the start of the 1940s that the *Novecento*, with its excess of cargo, was lying dangerously low in the water, and that those who could, had best flee to safety. In their flight, some daringly embarked on the road to Abstraction, such as Osvaldo Licini, who until that moment had seemed to share De Pisis's fascination for post-Impressionism. Other defectors to Abstract art included two pupils of the bulky monumentalism of Adolfo Wildt, Lucio Fontana and Fausto Melotti, and Atanasio Soldati, a late arrival on the Metaphysical scene. As far as this essay is concerned, we must turn straight back to developments in Realism, and observe that most of the young artists at the time took up a different path altogether, this too in some way linked to the old concept of realism, but following a different solution, so to speak, carrying out a sort of last will and testament. In fact, while magical-metaphysical realism had tended to indulge in "quoting" and returning to the roots, reinstating classical imagery with its "archaic" architectural forms, this particular solution I am referring to chose instead to scramble those same images, reinterpreting them in a quick and cursive hand, almost like something scratched into rock, or scribbles jotted on a schoolbook by a distracted, albeit gifted student. This was yet another way of recycling the "primitive taste," but in a different direction. The new solutions were diametrically opposite to the previous ones: these were spare and superficial, while their predecessors had been swollen and plastic; these were loaded with color, and deformed graphic signs, while the others had been dark, dominated by a solemn chiaroscuro, and a play of shadowy, earthy, colors.

Naturally, the sharp shift in register corresponded to the generation gap, always a significant factor. The artists who developed Realism in the 1900s were all born between 1880 and 1890. Their "wild" descendants — "angry young men" — generally follow on about twenty years later, separated by a generation, and were born from 1898 onward, with the last born in 1910. They too suffered a gradual diminishing of effectiveness. As they became aware of the weakness of their expressions of this "scrambled" and sketchy Realism, they attempted to strengthen it with bracing injections of post-Cubist geometrism. This new stage carried them through to 1945, which marks another of the limits of this essay.

As often happens, the change in generation, or simply the passing of time, was more influential on developments than the geographical setting where the artists gathered. As usual, activity in Italy was shared among various scattered artistic capitals. This fact makes it impossible to sum up developments by concentrating on one city alone, as the productive centers were in fact three — Rome, Milan, and Turin. This tripartite supremacy would later crop up again, in confirmation of the link between economic potential (not least political and cultural potential in general) of the cities and artistic productivity. Thus it is pointless to make comparisons between these cities, and a mistake to overlook their many cultural links, hidden or otherwise. Substantially, what took place was a single, sweeping tide of expressionist Realism (with infantile, "naïf," or primitive leanings) based in the three major centers. Each city, of course, had its own distinct character, though without diluting the phenomenon. Similar processes were evolving elsewhere in the country, but these would require a much more detailed investigation.

Antonietta Raphaël
Portrait of Mafai, 1928

The inquiry in this essay begins in Milan, where some of the earlier exponents first voiced their violent reaction to the *Novecento* tendency. More specifically, it was a reaction to the post-Metaphysical "magical" realism. The counter-movement that emerged carried its own label, eloquent enough and charged with meaning: *Chiarismo*. The term *Chiarismo* seems to have been coined by the writer Guido Piovene to denote the work of Angelo Del Bon, Umberto Lilloni, Francesco De Rocchi, and Cristoforo De Amicis. The light, clear backdrops used by these artists were an attempt to offset the gloomy visual schemes adopted by the *Novecento* artists — witness the work of Mario Sironi, with his figures extrapolated from a wall of obscurity, only to be reinstalled, like statues, in a set of niches. This peculiar darkness symbolized the world of the factory, the patina of history, or — on an even more removed plane — the dogged determination of adult minds in the final stages of their maturity.

In contrast, with their "return to white," the *Chiarismo* artists aimed to return to childhood, to a kind of earthly "paradise regained." A similar palette can be found among other Lombard artists of the same age working in the vein of Abstract art, proof that this chromatic range was the expression of a deep-felt need shared by an entire generation, though its individual members were ready to explore it in two apparently opposite directions — one figurative and the other aniconic. Basically, the two paths shared a common accentuation of the painted surface itself, and a reduction of depth (as opposed to the revival of perspective that had characterized much of the *Novecento* tendency).

The artists named above used these areas of bright color as a support for their flattened and meager figures, blending their outlines with the graininess of the canvas itself and the colored surface areas. This approach produced a series of fluid, trembling, precarious outlines, just like those of a child's painting. The technique was almost a precursor to the *Art brut* of Jean Dubuffet, who had fallen silent during the 1930s, not having yet found a convincing path to counter the reigning tendencies from which he felt isolated. While Dubuffet's *Art brut*, when it finally came into being at the end of the decade, was a staunch and radical voice, the *Chiarismo* group failed to marshal its forces and consolidate its techniques into a stable and consistent tool that would revolutionize art. To the contrary, they succumbed to an ongoing process of "normalization" and their wild and naïve figurative expression reverted to the secure harbor of post-Impressionism. The sturdiest and "wildest" of the bunch, Angelo Del Bon, met an early death, while the others softened their art, rendering it too snug and hedonistic. Umberto Lilloni for instance began churning out small stereotyped landscapes in which the stylized rendering of plant life, reduced to bristly scratchings steeped in a bath of green, soon became repetitive and shallow. The same might be said for Spilimbergo's landscape paintings. Meanwhile, Francesco De Rocchi plunged into a kind of "intimistic" tonalism of French stamp, remotely similar to the work of Henri Matisse or Pierre Bonnard. The same syndrome overtook other exponents active in the two other major centers — Mario Mafai in Rome, and Francesco Menzio in Turin — proof that the risk was common to the entire trend.

While the *Chiarismo* group, despite their effective and precocious beginning (though this may be the very reason), were prone to all kinds of relapses and regressions, a successor group fared somewhat better — Renato Birolli, Aligi Sassu, and Giacomo Manzù (all Milanese by adoption). Once again, there was a generation factor, as all three were a few years younger than their colleagues, which enabled them to get a more radical start in their almost glyphic version of *Art brut*, that fed on impulse and eccentricity. An emblematic work is Renato Birolli's *San Zeno*, with its weary, capricious outlines, like the projection of someone mentally ill, or, as we prefer to say nowadays, of an "uncultured" mind. We cannot appreciate the *Trans-*

Pericle Fazzini, *Execution*, 1945

Aligi Sassu, *Argonauts*, 1931

avanguardia, the most celebrated movement of the 1980s, without fully acknowledging these works of half a century earlier, which are like a foretaste of what was to come, with the same freshness of approach, and an air of protest against all forms of seriousness and austerity. As mentioned earlier, the "angry young men" of Lombardy (and Rome and Turin) were contesting the overly sapient post-Metaphysical aura. Those who followed in their tracks many years later tried to add a note of joyful disorder to the rigid order of Conceptual art, and to the "non-art" of the alternative media.

The same sense expressed in the "de-boned" figures of Renato Birolli applies to the Aligi Sassu's *Uomini rossi* (*Red Men*) series. This same base red, displayed like battle colors right from the outset of this outstanding series of paintings, acts a little like the *chiaro* or luminous patches explored by Angelo Del Bon and the *Chiarismo* group. Sassu sought, in his own way, to contrast the sooty palette of Mario Sironi and his ilk, to apply a more fiery, youthful chromatic note to the painted surface, as also reflected in the youthful, adolescent figures he depicts, delineated in red: figures like tender larvae traced out with the point of the brush. With quite similar results, Giacomo Manzù may well have adopted a finger-painting technique, rather than using a brush, to achieve his very plastic modeling effects. Here too, the work is populated with an analogous array of bare, elementary hominids and "extra-terrestrials"; other figures are plucked from the realm of *romance* and fable. Moreover, Manzù was agile at alternating his modeling work with pure painting technique, as can be seen in the fine series of twelve panels he made for the Villa Ardaini, at the very start of the 1930s.

Unfortunately, though younger and more "angry" than their *Chiarismo* forerunners, these artists were also prey to relapses and regressions into more facile stylistic methods of post-Impressionist flavor. This process shows up in the work of Sassu and Manzù towards the end of the decade, with the disappearance of their more

Renato Birolli, *The Poets*, 1935

249

whimsical, daring figures, and an increased bias for more detailed work, shrouding the compositions with softness and subtlety. Birolli, on the other hand, was to turn to post-Cubist grammar, though not until 1945. But that year was a great divide, a critical juncture that all the artists of this whole generational mix had to face, wherever they were working — Rome, Milan, or Turin. Some were to abide by elementary, expressionist forms of figuration, at the ever-present risk of being sucked back into Impressionism; others, however, sought to consolidate their thematic material through radical revision, using forceful geometrical forms before immersing themselves in the tide of Informal art. Unfortunately, the Italians overlooked the insights of Jean Dubuffet's *Art brut*, which could have provided a valid solution, as it made the expressionist choice irreversible, driving it to the utter limits of reductive rigor, while avoiding the intellectual pitfalls of Cubist decomposition, or, more generally, "concrete," neo-plastic formulas that Informal art and Abstract Expressionism later encountered.

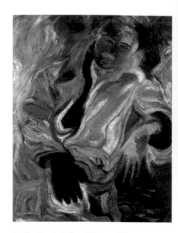

Carlo Levi, *The Chinese Hero* 1930-31

The indecision of Renato Birolli and his crowd whether to stick to rough-hewn, primordial figurative types, or to assume the geometrical "Modernist" vernacular, was shared by another, younger group of artists in Lombardy: Ennio Morlotti, Bruno Cassinari, Ernesto Treccani, and Giuseppe Migneco, who towards the end of the decade generated the new artistic movement *Corrente* and mouthpiece of the same name. A similar diagnosis could be made for other individuals, such as Arnaldo Badodi, Luigi Broggini, Italo Valenti, Gabriele Mucchi, Sandro Cherchi, and a new young talent from Venice, Emilio Vedova, who in fact achieved resounding success. As soon as time permitted, Vedova proved to be the most coherent and bold in espousing the idiom of geometric reconstruction of the universe, "transposing" into this new, more dynamic key the highly-strung style that had animated his work from the outset, albeit with the excuse of emphasizing certain normal figurative motifs.

The second (though no less important) center of activity was Turin, with its celebrated group of six artists who spurred developments in the 1940s. Two of these, Gigi Chessa and Nicola Galante, were the nearest equivalent to Milan's *Chiarismo* group (and closest in terms of age, having been born the previous century). It was almost inevitable that in their whiplash offensive on the *Novecento* tendency they should also make use of post-Impressionism (though a rather blunted weapon), not without a dash of the infantile and pseudo-naïf idioms, so as not to go against the drift of this cultural wave in general. The only woman artist in the group, Jessie Boswell, never strayed beyond her distilled and sensitive "intimism." The two leading figures, counterparts to the Birolli-Sassu-Manzù trio, were Carlo Levi and Francesco Menzio, both pupils of Felice Casorati and therefore raised under the shadow of his "precisionism" with its enchanted and magical play of volumes. In reaction, the two artists devised their own idiom of dry, flattened figures, which they animated with a twist of eccentricity. In his early works, Carlo Levi turned to the disturbing elongated forms of Amedeo Modigliani, and — omitting, however, the plasticity of the sculptor's expression — transcribed them to the canvas in clipped, stenographic form. In the heyday of the 1930s, Francesco Menzio had also shown himself capable of these "savage" reductions, transposed through energetic *à plat* coloring. Unfortunately, both artists fell prey to involutions — a fate common to most of those involved in this particular wave. As with certain others of the *Chiarismo* group (such as Mafai and Sassu) Menzio also succumbed to the "normalization" process, noticeable in his use of inlay-like effect, and flat expanses of color in the "French" manner true to Henri Matisse. Carlo Levi on the other hand remained faithful to Realism to the last, carrying it to uncharted, vibrantly popularesque excesses, and becoming in the process one of the mainstays of postwar neo-Realism, a "committed" left-wing figure. He could have explored more the *Art brut*

Giacomo Manzù, *Guitarist*, 1931

250

aspects of his earlier activity, and achieved some syntony with Jean Dubuffet, but chose not to. Instead he plunged into an overly dense and weighted form of pictorial expression. And lastly, the sixth member of the group, Enrico Paulucci, bravely headed into a post-Cubist phase.

The next center of activity was Rome, where the country's major figures had gathered between 1930 and 1945, making up the *Scuola Romana*. The *Scuola* harbored a rather broad range of artistic tendencies, and so it is worth looking more closely at its various subgroups. Here too we find a trio of artists readily contesting the cultural establishment, and who provided the *Scuola Romana* with its perhaps most compact and vital nucleus: Gino Bonichi (known as Scipione), Mario Mafai, and Antonietta Raphaël (married to Mafai). They also felt the need to take a stand against the reigning *Novecento* climate, though in Rome it had not assumed the same "sovereign" air as it had with Sironi, or with the magical realism of Casorati. An earlier group and possible precursor to the *Scuola Romana*, composed of Antonio Donghi, Riccardo Francalancia, Francesco Trombadori, Carlo Socrate, Gisberto Ceracchini, Virgilio Guidi, and Roberto Melli, had already begun loading their work with heavier figures, incarnations of the same "precisionist" zeal, ready for the wax museum. The tools and methods of this threesome, Bonichi, Mafai, and Raphaël, likewise displayed features common to their entire artistic generation: the flattened, spindly, sketchy figures in the throes of a cultural regression that was to lead back to the realm of infantile expression, or to what might be termed "psychic primitivism." Their grammar was permeated by a blurred sense of color augmented by the inconsistent, smudged outlines. The delirious tentacle-like images of Scipione have been glibly classed as Baroque, but this owes as much to the environment in which the artists worked as to anything else: though a native of the Marches region he remained in Rome throughout his brief, frenetic career. His works are more validly termed Expressionist. Of course the monuments to which Scipione applied his "wild" reductive brushwork are indeed Baroque, and therefore the term is best used to describe the subject matter rather than the treatment. Scipione had the "fortune" to die young (in 1933 of tuberculosis), and was thus spared the process of involution that blighted so many others, like his colleague Mario Mafai. Mafai's images were equally bold, and his early 1930s self-portraits equally jumbled, oblique, as if executed with the left hand. But he too was coaxed (along with Francesco Menzio in Turin, and Giacomo Manzù during the period he was in Milan, and when he experimented in modeling effects before leaving for Rome) into a tempered phase of tonal, post-Impressionist flavor, resulting in paintings of rubble, flowers, and butcher's shops, typical of his late 1930s style. Recently, interest has been rekindled in Mafai's wife, Antonietta Raphaël, who was may parhaps mistakenly accused of an excess of deformation, lapses of visual grammar, and jarring discordance. These criticisms may have stemmed from misgivings about her "irregular" background, a feeling that she was a "dilettante"; or worse still, from an attitude of suspicion toward "women's art." However, if we accept the idea that in those years Realism was considered most effective when at its most disorderly, accelerated, and cursive, then how can we deny that the works of Antonietta Raphaël were the very extreme of daring? It is impossible not to admire the sheer resolution of her painting, with its irregular *à plat* patchwork-like effects, and her sculptures, with their incisive, forceful imagery. During her sojourn in London (before her arrival in Rome), she had studied under a sculptor of remarkable talent, Jacob Epstein, a fact that would seem to refute her alleged dilettantism. Her method was a calculated way of "painting badly," and in the case of sculpture, of modeling her figures aggressively, with excessive, heavy and awkward forms. In this, Raphaël can be seen as a forerunner of the postwar Expressionists. The same might be said for two other sculptors of the *Scuola Romana*, Pericle Fazzini and

Marino Mazzacurati. In stark contrast with this trio of talents is the placid, even-handed Corrado Cagli, though he too was fated to pare down and flatten out his figures. Cagli avoided smudgy flares of color, preferring to lighten his palette, using colors of Disney-like clarity. It was Cagli who really took Sironi's bull of muralism by the horns, providing the *Scuola Romana* with his "mural," the *Battaglia di San Martino* (*The Battle of San Martino*, 1936), an enormous patchwork or jigsaw puzzle, composed of a series of lively outlined shapes in striking colors, like the *cloisonnisme* forms of Gothic stained glasswork, or cartoon films.

Corrado Cagli, *Warriors*, 1933

Another figure from the *Scuola Romana* who has come in for recent reappraisal is Fausto Pirandello (son of Italian playwright Luigi Pirandello). The chronic delay of post-Impressionism perhaps afforded Pirandello a reasonably conventional start — his still lifes and scenes of figures inserted into vast landscapes are not particularly striking in terms of composition, nor can we discern any traces of the daringly stylized reductive urge that had got the better of other "angry young men" during those years. Instead, Pirandello compensates through his dense colors, more often applied with his thumb, to minimize the unwanted display of spatial perspective, and achieving the *à plat* effect courted by others of his age-group. His canvases seem to be coated with an emulsion that accentuates the surface features, spreading a dense, heavy membrane over everything. After the war, the artist experimented with geometrical decomposition, but in a vein that was rather extrinsic and non-essential to the overall concept of the painting. Like some of his contemporary confederates, Pirandello was faced with the thorny task of blending Expressionist sensuality with post-Cubist intellectual rigor.

Ennio Morlotti
The Women of Warsaw, 1946

One group member, of Roman origin, suffered no doubts of this kind: Alberto Ziveri was completely satisfied with using a representative language, which he animated with a rugged, viscous coating. Despite recent attempts to reassess their contribution, two others, Emanuele Cavalli and Giovanni Stradone, trail somewhat behind in importance. However, there are a few curious cases of artists who were "in transit" through the *Scuola Romana*'s area of expression, before settling into more hardy, pragmatic languages: such was Giuseppe Capogrossi, who at the moment seemed a long way from what critic Michel Tapié called *art autre*, which would take hold during the coming *Informel* season. But his anecdotal scenarios already showed the flattening typical to all the valid members of the *Scuola Romana*, and the artist had started toying with graphic decorative motifs wherever and whenever the theme suggested. Another two high-caliber figures "passing through" were the Basaldella brothers from Friuli, known as Afro and Mirko. The former, a painter, progressed on similar lines to those of Giuseppe Capogrossi: he too dallied with crammed, anecdotal compositions, but he was already arranging them in select frontal planes and curbing his use of abstract motifs, which in the successive stage of abstract-concrete experimentation would unfold free and confident in space. With his stylized and twisted figures Mirko, a sculptor, espoused the Expressionist mainstream, arming his sculptures with points and sharp edges in a foretaste of the lively dialectic between mass and void that would characterize his later abstract-informal phase.

Leoncillo, *Self-Portrait*, 1942

Among the youngest associates of the *Scuola Romana* were Renato Guttuso and Leoncillo Leonardi (better known by his first name only). The first was born in Sicily, but moved to Rome in 1933, and is the natural heir of that "sensibilism" peculiar to Pirandello and Mafai. In his early works, Guttuso too occasionally lapses into Expressionist gesture, but in the years to come he was to become the main instigator of the "normalization" process, merging Expressionism and post-Impressionism. In this fusion, the charge of the former galvanizes the latter with a continuous, interweaving of sensations. Shortly afterwards, this dynamism was passed through the multi-faceted prism of post-Cubism, but this retained its singular

Emilio Vedova
Combat, 1942

"plated" surface look. Guttuso successfully achieved a fecund mixture of personal vernacular and traditional idiom, commuting between intelligence and the senses.

Leoncillo, given to extremes and excesses, created outstanding manifestations of Expressionism. His predisposition led him to discard neutral materials like bronze, preferring to entrust his visions of carnal torment to clay. In some respects, he managed to align his work with "Baroque" ceramics that his colleague Lucio Fontana was turning out in Milan, and provide a counterpoint to his usual theme of abstract-geometrical expression. Later, Leoncillo found a means of converting his wilful Expressionism from its original figurative outlook to a more advanced stage of Abstract art parallel to the Abstract Expressionism of Willem De Kooning, or alternatively slipping into the Informal stream prevalent in Italy and Europe. This direction also betrays the signs of the change of generation, with some smaller internal gaps visible between those who were born slightly later. Leoncillo was born in 1915, and is almost the same age as the Lombard painter Ennio Morlotti and the Venetian Emilio Vedova, and like them, he would slip more easily into the Informal mainstream than some of his contemporaries. But this carries us beyond the scope of this essay, to an entirely different series of developments.

Parallel Views
Painting and Sculpture

Photographic Notes

Carlo Bertelli

The product and a tool of modernity, photography is both a stimulus and a testimony to the progress of modern Italy, where it is also present at the industrial level, with the manufacture of plates, films, equipment and accessories.
Small and large industrial enterprises, with Alinari of Florence in the lead, perfected impeccable criteria for reproducing works of art, re-establishing the visual prospect in architecture and propagating new icons: the Egyptians, the Etruscans...
The photographs assembled here do not presume to offer a summary of the already complicated history of Italian photography before 1945; they are meant only to underline certain distinct characteristics. The Bragaglia brothers' "photodynamics" are the most original Italian contribution to artistic photography at the beginning of the century, in which they introduce the themes of the new iconographical Futurist movement. Medardo Rosso's photographs of his sculptures became renown for their unusual effects; even if it was already common practice throughout the world to photograph sculptures, the effects he achieved by cutting them, drawing over them, and intervening in the entire photographic process highlights the sensation of a sudden apparition that he sought to convey in all of his works. The relationship with the modern is also seen as the link between the subjects (of portraits of artists) and photography; special attention is given to Gabriele D'Annunzio, renown personality, who showed an exquisite understanding of photography as a means and instrument of communication. On the other side, Mario Pagano's stark sequence of photographs portraying the offices of the *Popolo d'Italia* in Milan is a photographic account itself in which only the objects speak, conveying the sense of ambiguous fascination exercised by the revolutionary age of Fascism on the new generations.
Finally, towards the 1930s, expanding markets for industry and the rise in weekly publications and almanacs promoted an area of formal research which made Italian photography seem completely isolated from what was taking place in the nation's figurative arts — with the exception of some points in common with the abstract current — orienting itself more towards the Bauhaus ideas, but with clearly original results.

2. Mario Nunes Vais
Group of Futurists. From left:
Palazzeschi, Carrà, Papini, Boccioni,
Marinetti, Florence 1914
b/w photograph, 19 × 15.5 cm - reprint
Rome, i.c.c.d., Gabinetto Fotografico Nazionale
Nunes Vais Fund

3. Gabriele D'Annunzio before
the airplane "Caproni," 1917
b/w photograph, 28.7 × 19.2 cm
Gardone Riviera
Fondazione "Il Vittoriale degli Italiani"

4. Mario Nunes Vais
Gabriele D'Annunzio in his "upper
studio," La Capponcina, Florence 1906
b/w photograph, 12.4 × 17.5 cm - reprint
Rome, i.c.c.d., Gabinetto Fotografico Nazionale
Nunes Vais Fund

5. Anton Giulio Bragaglia
Figure on the Staircase (self-portrait)
1911
photodynamic, 17 × 12 cm
Rome, Antonella Vigliani Bragaglia Collection
Centro Studi Anton Giulio Bragaglia

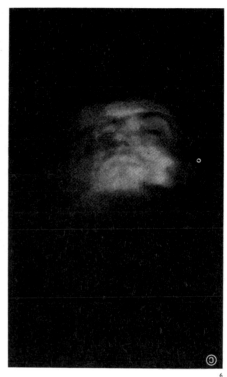

6

5

7

6. Anton Giulio Bragaglia
A Nod
1911
photodynamic, 14 × 9.5 cm
Rome, Antonella Vigliani Bragaglia Collection
Centro Studi Anton Giulio Bragaglia

7. Medardo Rosso
Chair autrui
photograph, 10.2 × 13.5 cm
Barzio, Museo Medardo Rosso

8. Medardo Rosso
Impression d'omnibus
photograph, 14 × 22 cm
Barzio, Museo Medardo Rosso

8

9

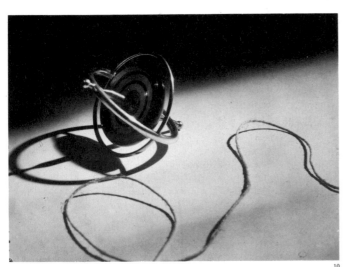

10

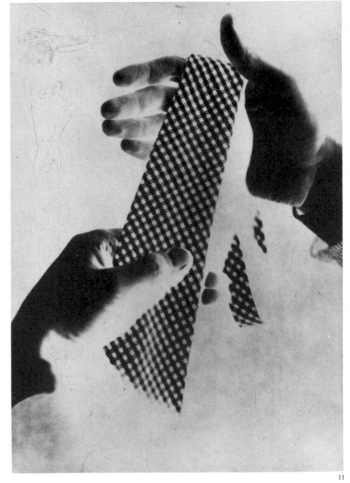

11

12

13

13. Albe Steiner
Photo made by shifting the negative
1940
b/w photograph, 17.4 × 28.4 cm
Milan, Lica Steiner Collection

14. Albe Steiner
Thonet with Shadow
1939
b/w photograph, 23.5 × 17.5 cm
Milan, Lica Steiner Collection

15. Albe Steiner
Cobblestones
1942
b/w photograph, 18 × 24.2 cm
Milan, Lica Steiner Collection

14   15

Italian Artists in Paris

Serge Fauchereau

Some artists such as the sculptor Medardo Rosso or the designer Leonetto Cappiello first gained acclaim in France as they were living in Paris at the end of the last century. With the "Exposition Universelle" of 1900, a large group of Italian artists settled in Paris to form a well-known colony, where, despite the fact that they were amiably integrated in the Parisian life-style, they remained in close contact with the artistic movements of their native country. In this way, Paris became for several decades one of the capitals of Italian art, rivalling and at tunes surpassing Rome, Florence or Milan in importance. Amedeo Modigliani, Ardengo Soffici, Gino Severini, Giorgio De Chirico and his brother Alberto Savinio, and many others, all spent several years in this city.

These artists were all to be influenced by their surroundings, but in turn their works would leave a deep and profound mark on the art of Paris. One cannot begin to understand the artistic developments of this period without the presence of Futurism, and at the same time, it would be impossible to imagine the Surrealist movement without De Chirico. From hereon in, the Italian artists are a constant presence in French avant-garde publications before and after World War I: *Les Soirées de Paris*, *Sic*, *Montjoie* (run by the Italian Canudo), *L'Esprit nouveau*, *Le Bulletin de l'Effort moderne*, not to mention the Surrealist reviews and their rivals who alternated between praising and attacking De Chirico. These contacts were so close, that (as had already occurred with Marinetti's *Poesia*) the Roman review *Valori Plastici*, mouthpiece for a new aesthetic, would eventually publish a French edition together with a collection of monographs.

Because of the overall tensions in Italy during the 1930s, a number of Italian artists left France; however, some of them, most notably Alberto Magnelli, managed to prolong their "golden" exile.

1

2

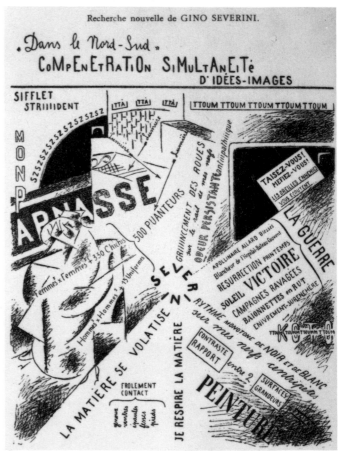

3

4. La Révolution surréaliste, n. 1,
Paris, December 1924
cover

5. André Breton, Le surréalisme et la peinture in
La Révolution surréaliste, n. 6, Paris 1926
Below the article, De Chirico's painting Oreste et
Electre covered with Breton's scribbling.

6. Amedeo Modigliani
Portrait of Blaise Cendrars from the book by
Cendrars Dix-neuf poèmes élastiques, Paris 1919

7. Gino Severini
Nature morte à la revue littéraire Nord-Sud
(Hommage à Reverdy)
1917
collage on cardboard, cm 56 × 67
Private collection

8. Amedeo Modigliani
André Derain
1918 c.
pencil on paper, cm 32 × 23
Grenoble, Musée de Peinture et de Sculpture

9. Les feuilles libres, n. 43, Paris, May-June 1926
cover

10. Primo Conti, Alberto Magnelli
pencil on paper, cm 15 × 11.5
Florence, Museo Primo Conti
Fondazione Primo Conti

9

10

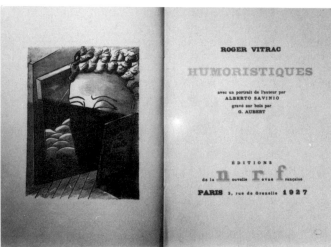

11

11. Roger Vitrac, Humoristiques, Paris 1927
with a portrait of the author by Alberto Savinio

12. From left: Alberto Magnelli, Nelly van Doesburg
Susi Magnelli, Sourow and Sophie Tauber-Arp, 1942

12

13. Alberto Magnelli and Jean Arp, Meudon
June 1938

13

14. Giorgio De Chirico, Le Trophée, 1926
drawing for the review Les feuilles libres, n. 43
Paris, May-June 1926

15. Gino Severini, Souvenirs de Montparnasse in
Présence, weekly magazine for French soldiers in
Italy, August 1944

14

15

Italian Artists and Western Magazines

Serge Fauchereau

1. Primo Conti, Giovanni Papini
pencil on paper, cm 19 × 11
Fiesole-Florence, Museo Primo Conti
Fondazione Primo Conti

It is not until after the Symbolist period at the turn of the century with the new methods of reproduction that magazines began to publish designs and illustrations permitting a larger diffusion of information about art. Literary or satirical, these attractive publications multiplied in the western world attesting to a thick complicity between poets and artists. The Italian artists take an active role: Leonetto Cappiello and Ardengo Soffici contributed drawings to the Symbolist review *La Plume*, and to *L'Assiette au beurre*, a publication of noted anarchichal tendency. The 1910s saw the birth, finally, of the great chronicles of the avant-garde: *Der Sturm* in Berlin, *Les Soirées de Paris*, and *Lacerba* in Florence, where Italian Futurists were met either with enthusiasm or suspicion.

At the end of World War I, the Futurists continued their activity through their reviews (*L'Italia Futurista*, *Roma Futurista*, *Noi...*) or in direct collaboration with foreign magazines. *Dada* in Zurich, *Sic* in Paris, and *Red* in Prague frequently published the contributions of Gino Severini, Enrico Prampolini, and Fortunato Depero. In the Surrealist milieux, the brothers Giorgio De Chirico and Alberto Savinio were nearly omnipresent, contributing to *La Révolution surréaliste* and *Les Feuilles libres* and to *Sélection* (Anvers) and *Minotaure*, among others. Thanks to international Constructivism and especially to its antithesis in the Realist camp — represented in Italy by *Valori Plastici*, *La Raccolta* and *La Ronda* — many new artists achieved notariety: Alberto Magnelli, Felice Casorati, and Giorgio Morandi to name just a few.

1

2

3

2. Primo Conti
Marinetti in bathrobe
1920
pencil and wax on paper glued
to cardboard
Fiesole-Florence, Museo Primo Conti
Fondazione Primo Conti

3. Carlo Carrà, Soffici, Rome 1922
cover

264

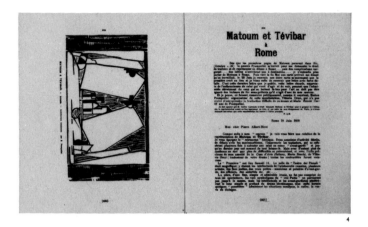

6. Ardengo Soffici
BIF 2F + 18 Simultaneità e Chimismi lirici,
Florence 1916
Fiesole-Florence, Fondazione Primo Conti

7. Giorgio De Chirico, Alberto Magnelli
pencil on paper, cm 36.5 × 28.5
Private collection

9

8

8. Carlo Carrà, Soffici, 1926
pencil on paper, cm 24 × 17
Milan, Private collection

10. Carlo Carrà, The Zither Player, 1945
ink on paper, cm 25.7 × 19
Milan, Private collection

11. Carlo Carrà, Transport of a Wounded Person II
1945, charcoal and pencil on paper
cm 25.8 × 19, Milan, Private collection

267

10

11

12

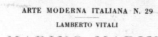

13

14

12. La mà trencada, Barcelona 1933 (?)
cover with reproduction of Felice Casorati's
Lo Studio

13. Lamberto Vitali, Marino Marini, Milan 1937
cover

14. Guillaume Apollinaire, Calligrammes, Paris 1930
Lithograph by Giorgio De Chirico

Images of Architecture and Cities 1900-45

Francesco Dal Co

1. Antonio Sant'Elia
The New City, stepped building on two street levels
1914
inks and pencil on paper, 27.5 × 11.5 cm
Milan, Paride Accetti Collection

However articulate and worthy of attention are the events of Italian architecture in the first two decades of the 20th Century, when exchange was blocked between the academic tendency and the trend representing the "new spirit" — of which one expression is the Liberty style, and to which is linked the ambiguous experience of the first Futurist experiments in architecture — it was not until the political stabilization of Fascism in the late 1920s that the field underwent a phase of growth comparable to what was happening in the most advanced of European countries.

After 1925, the Fascist regime establishes a political project based on a vast program of public works and urban renewal. Presented with such opportunities, the architects react with an enthusiasm that, however, would fade into bitter disillusionment as the years passed. With different currents of thought contributing to an irregular and controversial outline of architectural culture until the second half of the 1930s, an intense debate develops, whose course should be seen in relation to the regime's pragmatism in weighing the pros and cons of the different components of a professional world. Furthermore, although the anti-urbanistic outlook of Fascist ideology is reinforced by the propaganda slogans and is at the base of spectacular enterprises which tend to expand the public assent, the regime, when faced with operations aimed at the evacuation of entire cities, does not hesitate to adopt measures designed to have opposite effects.

During the 1930s, while the numerous competitions promoted by the regime offer the architectural field ample occasion to express the variety of hypothesis intended to contribute to the formation of an original "Fascist style," in the historical towns heavy demolition takes place, in Rome, Brescia, Genoa and Turin, for example, clearly demonstrating the aim to celebrate the regime, but also motivated by precise economic calculations (the advantages in terms of real estate investment are clear). The strategy of demolition is not the only one adopted in these twenty years, however, as can be seen in the numerous projects with a far gentler approach to the future of the city; the urban plans drawn up in the late 1920s to early 1930s for new settlements also demonstrate this. The vast landfill project of the Pontine swamp area is an important testing ground for the urban theories being developed at this time. Besides, the vast project of recoverage of Paludi Pontine, is the significant proof of urbanistic culture during the first few years of the 1930s.

In the Agro Pontino in fact, in just a few years, five new towns are settled; these are the most interesting examples of the urbanistic conceptions of the time. Equally crucial to the development of the ideological debate accompanying the formation of what one of the protagonists of the period, Giuseppe Pagano, defines as the new urban society, are on one hand the episodes tied to the building of the University City in Rome, and E42. These gave Marcello Piacentini, the most powerful representative of orthodoxy in the field of architecture, the opportunity to demonstrate his talent at mediating. On the other hand there are the less spectacular but no less important experiments carried out by Adriano Olivetti to create his fortunate cultural oasis in Ivrea, constructed around the family's industry.

Given the complexity of the total picture offered over these twenty years, it is practically impossible to draw up a register of the works that in such a brief span of time profoundly changed the appearance of both town and country in Italy.

But, it is possible to get an idea of the intellectual fervor that accompanies these initiatives by looking at the richness of theoretical debate that is developed in reviews, industrial publications, and on the occasion of conventions, congresses, and exhibitions, and by thinking about the specific works of the best architects active in this period, including Mario Ridolfi, Giuseppe Terragni, BBPR, Alberto Libera, Figini and Pollini, Ludovico Quaroni, Ignazio Gardella and Franco Albini. Also worth remembering in terms of the culture of architecture is the

fact that from the second half of the 1930s hope was rapidly waning as the threat of war approached. Its definitive collapse was inevitable.

Even now, the architectural patrimony that Italy accumulates during the years 1925-1927 is not in vain, as proven by the fact that these very same architects were called upon after 1945 to make their contribution to Italy's reconstruction.

2. Mario Sironi
The Architect
1922
oil on canvas, 70 × 60 cm
Private Collection

3. Armando Brasini
View from the top of the Urbe Massima
Rome 1916
pen on paper, 70 × 210 cm
Orvieto, Luca Brasini Collection

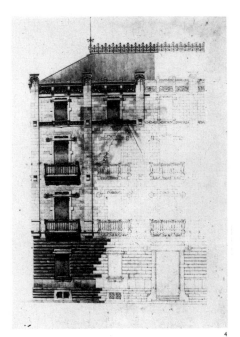

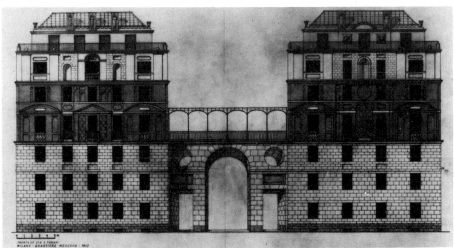

4. Ernesto Basile
Casa Utveggio
Palermo 1901
pencil, ink and watercolor on cardboard
91.5 × 60.8 cm
Palermo, Gift of Basile, Università degli Studi

5. Giovanni Muzio
Ca' Brüta
Milan 1922
India ink on tracing paper, 70 × 125 cm
Milan, Archivio Muzio

6. Gruppo Miar, Pagano, Cuzzi
Levi Montalcini, Aloisio, Sottsass
Project for the renovation of via Roma
Turin 1931
pencil and carbon on cardboard, 87 × 183 cm
Turin, Emanuele Levi Montalcini Collection

7. Plinio Marconi, Giuseppe Samonà, Guido Viola
Project for the Museo dell'Agricoltura
e delle bonifiche all'E42
Rome 1938
photograph of the model
Rome, Archivio Centrale dello Stato

8. Adalberto Libera
Palazzo dei Ricevimenti e Congressi all'E42
Rome 1937
photograph of the model
Rome, Archivio Centrale dello Stato

6

7

9

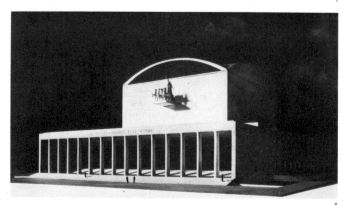

8

9. Città Universitaria
Rome 1933
photograph of the model
Florence, Archivio Roberto Papini - Biblioteca
di Architettura

10. Marcello Piacentini
Palazzo del Rettorato, Città Universitaria, Rome
Study for the first project
1933 (?)
pencil and colored pastels on paper, 29 × 21 cm
Florence, Archivio Piacentini - Biblioteca
di Architettura

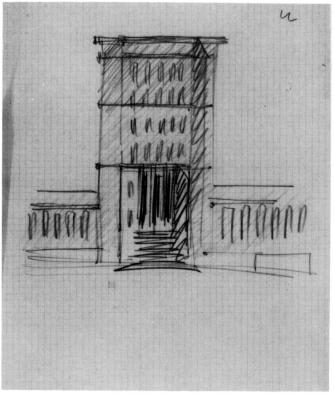

10

11. Studio Architetti BBPR:
Banfi, Belgiojoso, Peressutti, Rogers
Masterplan of the Valle d'Aosta
1936 destroyed

11

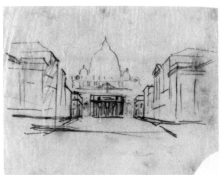

12

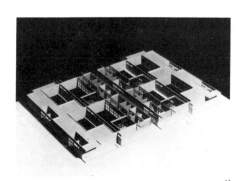

13

15

12. Marcello Piacentini and Attilio Spaccarelli
Via della Conciliazione, study of perspective
Rome c. 1939
pencil on tracing paper, 19.8 × 25.3 cm
Florence, Archivio Piacentini - Biblioteca
di Architettura

13. Irenio Diotallevi, Franco Marescotti
Giuseppe Pagano
Neighborhood of horizontal city
Milan 1940
model 7 × 50 × 35 cm
Venice, Archivio Storico delle Arti Contemporanee
della Biennale

14. Giuseppe De Finetti
Project for the renovation of piazza Cavour
Milan 1942
India ink and pencil on tracing paper, 65 × 77 cm
Parma, Centro Studi e Archivio della Comunicazione
Università degli Studi - Sezione Progetto

15. Aerial view of Littoria

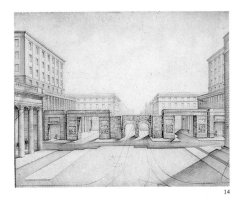

14

271

Italian Architecture 1900

Vittorio Gregotti

In brief, Italian architecture at the beginning of the century can be divided into two main lines of parallel development: one which looks to the modern European style in a radical and international way, as in the case of D'Aronco, Basile and Michelazzi; the second is a mixture of the above with the "official tradition," an updated version of the eclectic tradition which evolved out of Boitani's attempts to establish a national-popular architecture. In this second category, prominent proponents are Sommaruga, Stacchini, Magistretti, and in a more unusual and independent manner, Ulisse Arata and Aldo Andreani. The subversive activity of Antonio Sant'Elia and Chiattone can also be placed in this context. After a clash of opinions, "the return to order" is the password shared by very different and contrasting currents: it is shot through with a metaphysical restlessness fueled by a desire to build and work on a common language of civil architecture, or driven by the rhetoric of memories or the winds of the international Functionalism. In Milan, the *Novecento* and neo-Classical groups (Muzio, Greppi, Fiocchi, Ponti) and the young Rationalist *gruppo 7* (including Figini, Pollini, Baldessari, Terragni), contrasted and influenced each other. In Turin, Pagano and Levi Montalcini, Perona, Aloisio, Sartoris, Diulgheroff, Chessa and above all Edoardo Persico (who will later move to Milan together with Pagano to re-open the review *Casabella*) belong to the Rationalist group, which includes in Florence Michelucci, in Bologna Vaccaro and Bega, in Naples Cosenza, in Rome (with the M.I.A.R., movement for national architecture) Libera, De Renzi, Ridolfi and the irresolute Aschieri and Capponi. After the 1930s, a cultural battle starts over who would best interpret the architecture of the Fascist regime: a clash of opinions which was still alive at the Triennale of 1936, but which was finally won by Piacentini's the neo-monumental group and the Roman architects, who were closer to the power centers of the regime. At the end of the 1930s, among the Rationalists and under pressure from the new generation (B.B.P.R., Quaroni, Albini, Mollino, Gardella), a sort of internal criticism develops regarding internationalist principles from the perspective of regional values; meanwhile the generation of exponents of rationalism develops a real ideological crisis (accelerated by the victory of the academics in the national exposition project of 1942), which would lead a large number of Italian rationalists to jorn the Resistance.

5. Luigi Figini, Pietro Lingeri, Gino Pollini
Giuseppe Terragni
Project for the new Accademia di Brera
Milan 1935-36
Model, plexiglass and painted wood and cardboard
51 × 126 × 33 cm
Venice, Archivio Storico delle Arti Contemporanee
della Biennale

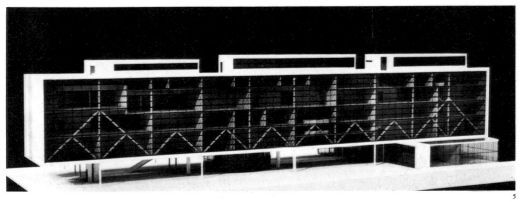

5

6

7

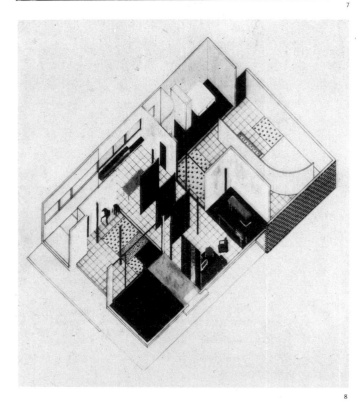

8

6. Antonio Sant'Elia
Studies of buildings
1913
colored inks and pencil on tracing paper
51.5 × 28.7 cm
Milan, Paride Accetti Collection

7. Ottorino Aloisio
Project for the Sports university
Amsterdam 1928
charcoal on cardboard, 61 × 81 cm
Udine, Galleria d'Arte Moderna dei Civici Musei

8. Luigi Figini and Gino Pollini
Home-studio for an artist, at the V Triennale
Milan 1933
ink and tempera on tracing paper, 35 × 35 cm
Milan, Gino Pollini Collection

9. Mario Ridolfi
Project for a church with a circular plan
presented at the fifth competition for the churches
of Messina 1932
tempera on canvas, 68 × 113.5 cm

9

10. Giuseppe Terragni
La casa del Fascio, Como 1932
black and colored pencil on paper,
18.3 × 19.3 cm
Como, Archivio Fondazione Terragni

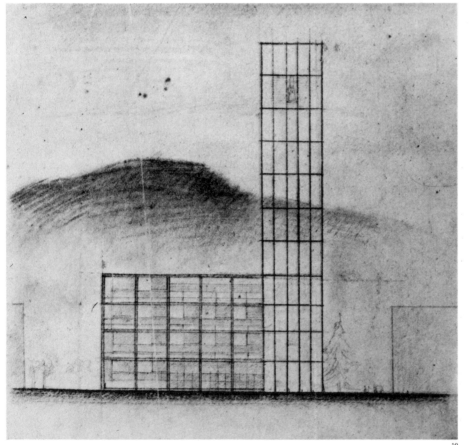

11

12

10

11. Giuseppe Terragni
Profile of the Duce and Italy
Sketch for the ''Rivoluzione Fascista''
exhibition, Rome 1932
charcoal, pastels, collage, foil on paper
mounted on cardboard, 57 × 76 cm
Como, Archivio Fondazione Terragni

12. Giuseppe Terragni
Teatro di Montecitorio
Sketch for the ''Rivoluzione Fascista''
exhibition, Rome 1932
charcoal, pastels, collage, newspaper clippings
on paper mounted on cardboard 55 × 77 cm
Como, Archivio Fondazione Terragni

13. Luciano Baldessari
Metal mannequin for the Italian textiles show
at the international exposition
Barcelona 1929
wax, pencil and tempera on paper, 36.4 × 46.4 cm
Milan, Archivio Mosca Baldessari

13

14. Adalberto Libera
Jetty project for Castelfusano coast, 1933
tempera on paper, 36 × 140 cm
Rome, Paola Libera Collection

15. Studio Architetti BBPR: Banfi, Belgiojoso
Peressutti, Rogers
Post office building at the E42, Rome 1940
charcoal on tracing paper, 73 × 90 cm
Milan, Ludovico and Alberto B. di Belgiojoso Collection

Dioscuri

by Maurizio Fagiolo dell'Arco

A documentary section has been provided to illustrate a fundamental in the history of the avant-garde; as André Breton, founder of the Surrealist movement, had already perceived at the time: "The whole modern myth, just as it was taking form, found its origins in the works of Alberto Savinio and his brother, Giorgio De Chirico, indivisible in spirit."
This angle has been chosen also to illustrate the relationship between Italian artists of different periods with Europe, ranging from the Paris school, to Metaphysics, "magic Realism," the *Novecento* and the *Italiens de Paris*.

1) The Tragedy of Childhood
"The dark years of childhood" are those recalled by Giorgio De Chirico in his memoirs. And Andrea (later Alberto Savinio) dedicates a book to this period, *La tragedia dell'infanzia*; "Not Commedia dell'Infanzia," — comedy (Dante), comédie humaine (Balzac) — not 'Drama dell'Infanzia' which, however drastic implies an 'outcome,' but 'Tragedia'; that is, sacrifice and frustration. The part of the bull is played by children."
Here is their severe 19th-century family: the Baroness Gemma, their mother, of Genoese origin. Their father Evaristo, an engineer by profession, of Florentine origin.
The mother depicted in a romantic oval with her children, Giorgio and Andrea. The small Andrea with his lace collar and hairstyle in the manner of the Roi Soleil, and little Giorgio with his hoop.
The two brothers standing side by side with the Garibaldians who landed on the shores of Volos in 1897.
For an art which is based on recollection, childhood is the most authentic material to work from: a sort of psycho-analytical parallel. The mother is an idol and tyrant: a legend. We see her in a portrait by De Chirico in 1920 and in another by Savinio painted around 1932.
Their origins are already mythological: Volos in Thessaly where Giorgio was born, Athens where Andrea was born (nicknamed Bettì in his family). De Chirico writes, "I used to amuse myself by the seaside where the Argonauts set sail in their ship, at the foot of the mountain which witnessed the childhood of Achille, the swift foot and the sage warnings of the pedagogue centaur."
Athens was an ancient and very lively western centre: poor but proud. Volos was enriched by the station constructed at the time by the engineer Evaristo, watched over by the statue of Athena (the same statue to be found in an early work by De Chirico, *The Departure of the Argonauts*). Some of Savinio's drawings feature this myth, mixed with chronicle. In De Chirico's album for his wife Raissa the geographical coordinates are set forth.
It is a childhood of strict studies: painting for Giorgio and music for Andrea. New horizons are opened by literature: Pinocchio, illustrated by Carlo Chiostri, the books of Jules Verne, which portray adventure in modern times (in his *Around the world in eighty days* a combination train-ship appears), the books on Greek Art, the book by Louis Figuier on the pre-historic world, which later inspired Savinio for his forests, settings for games and toys of childhood.
From this childhood derives a schizophrenic idea of an "indirect birth," a stateless destiny, and a perpetual journey (an Odyssey). It gives rise to a self-identification with the Argonauts who, from the port of Volos, set sail in quest of their golden fleece. And then, the similarities with Castor and Pollux, the Dioscuri who defended Jason in a mythological research.

2) The Revelation of Metaphysics
The years in Italy. Milan then Florence, then Andrea leaves for Paris. De Chirico in 1910 does a portrait of him in heroic pose, a photograph of which Savinio always keeps on his desk. On the same desk rest a souvenir statuette of Praxiteles' Hermes, the greek god who oversees not only Savinio's works, but those of his brother, with omnipresence and secret obscurity.
Giorgio discovers the profund melancholy of Italian towns; in Florence he produces his first painting, *Malinconia d'un pomeriggio d'autunno*. It is executed in the autumn of 1910 in Piazza Santa Croce. During a trip to Paris (July 1911) De Chirico stops off in Turin, center of the Risorgimento and the city which saw the "madness" of the brothers' beloved Nietzsche.
The book of their youth register their metaphysical anxieties: whether by Schopenhauer, by Nietzsche, or by Weininger. Their love for idealism, recollections of the past and mythology.
In Piazza Santa Croce, De Chirico sees both a Gothic church and a municipal monument, and understands that in order to break through his restless ego, he has to, within himself, go beyond what he sees with his physical eye. This is what is metaphysical. In 1919 he defines it thus: "The word 'metafisica' taken to pieces could result in another huge misunderstanding: 'metafisica' from the Greek 'la metà ta fusikà' (after physical things) could lead one to think that what one finds after physical things must make up a kind of nirvanic void. Sheer imbecility if one thinks that in space, distance does not exist, and that an unexplainable state called X can just as well be experienced by a painted, described or imagined object, as here and, especially in the object itself — an abstract entity (this is what happens in my art).

3) Cubist Paris
During the period that spanned from July 1911 to the summer of 1915 (when the war obliges them to enlist in the Italian army — even if only to have a nationality), Paris sees their dreams take form and then come true. De Chirico exhibits his works, obtains success and is discovered by a poet and dealer. Guillaume Apollinaire and Paul Guillaume will also figure among his brother's greatest friends. A change of name, Alberto Savinio (inspired from the writer Albert Savine), after his first concert in order to distinguish himself from his artistic brother. Apollinaire's role is fundamental in the years of *L'Esprit Nouveau*, which he theorized. Here we see his portrait by De Chirico in an engraving by Pierre Roy, showing him in the guise of Orpheus with the fish of the Revelation, as in his *Cortège d'Orphée*. *Les peintres cubistes* is the breviary of a period, while the *Poète assassiné* represents the premonitory end. (Savinio reviews this in Ferrara.)
His discovery is an image-poem that is closely related to the work of his artistic friends: the first "calligrammes" he gave as a present to the young poet and musician, Alberto Savinio. While the official and non-official exhibitions are in full swing — the Salon d'Automne and Salon des Indépendans — the young art dealer Paul Guillaume, backed by Apollinaire, makes a name for himself.
Time was short. At the end of the war the poet Appollinaire dies. De Chirico imortalized him in the obituary that appeared in *Ars Nova*; Savinio in turn remembered him in Le Corbusier's review *L'Esprit Nouveau*. Ten years later, an edition of *Calligrammes* with sixty-six lithographs by Giorgio De Chirico was published.
The passionate work of the two brothers is presented with its original documentation. De Chirico's designs and manuscripts (which belonged to Paul Eluard and were rediscovered in the Picasso foundation) offer a chain of original and disturbing images that strike an emotional chord.
Savinio's metaphysical music can be understood through his piano scores, but also through the published documentation which appears in two reviews: *Les Soirées di Paris*, run by Apollinaire and *291* run by Alfred Stieglitz in New York.

4) Ferrara, the Restless Muses
Even in a small provincial town, the Dioscuri manage to discover a myth. The town of a hundred marvels, as De Pisis described it, that according to Bruckhardt was the most modern town in Europe; they remained there for three years in military service. At Villa del Seminaro, a clinic for the mentally ill, they meet Carlo Carrà, who does some portraits of Savinio, the

Argonaut, and the two brothers as "Dioscuri." They never lose touch with Europe, and articles by Savinio and paintings by De Chirico appear in Parisian journals, and above all in *Dada*, Tristan Tzara's review which speaks out against all wars.

Right at the end of the war, Savinio's book *Hermaphrodito* is published by Edizioni della Voce: the dedication is "to Giorgio De Chirico". De Chirico exhibits the fruits of his work in Ferrara at the gallery of the Futurist Bragaglia: in the journal *Cronache di attualità* (here the copy sent to Tzara is on display), he expounds his ideas about painting in the article entitled *Noi metafisici*.

5) The Italian Interval

The years after the war are passed between Rome, Milan and Florence, and then they return to Paris. They are in the intellectual groups of *Valori Plastici* and *La Ronda*. They proclaim the return to technique, the "rappel à l'ordre," to neo-Classicism. De Chirico is in close contact with Massimo Bontempelli and exhibits in Germany with the *Valori Plastici* group, and then in Florence.

But there is also the revival of Courbet and his "magic Realism," as well as to Böcklin. The whole of Europe acknowledges him as a Master (including André Breton, Max Ernst, René Crevel and Paul Eluard).

At the end of 1924, the Dioscuri are in Paris where De Chirico has designed the sets for Pirandello's *La Jarre* with score by Casella. A year later, they meet again, as De Chirico paints the backdrop for *La morte di Niobe* by Savinio, a pantomime he wrote ten years earlier in Paris. In the Pirandello theater, they meet their future wives: Giorgio falls in love with Raissa, who becomes an archaeologist; and Alberto with Maria, an actress in Eleanor Duse's company.

The sources in their studies gain clarity. It is an art that attempts to be based on recollection, but indirectly, taking inspiration from the academic manuals and also those of Reinach. In these pages, we can find many prototypes of both Savinio's and De Chirico's works. These works, which today would be described as Pop, are in fact based on drawing, doubles and enigmatic mirror-images.

6) Surrealist Paris

When De Chirico returned to the promised city, he had in his pocket André Breton's address in Montmartre. The poet becomes his new 'Apollinaire'. De Chirico is acclaimed as being ahead of his times in all his shows and articles, at least for a certain period.

His image appears on the cover of the first issue of the magazine *La Révolution surréaliste*. Other Surrealist artists are close to the Dioscuri (Savinio has joined him in Paris in 1926). They design the frontispiece of two books of poetry for Roger Vitrac, and De Chirico gives his portrait to the poet for the small monograph issued in Paris. Savinio meanwhile has turned to painting.

Savinio's and De Chirico's works appear in the reviews *Les Feuilles Libres*, *Sélection* and *The Little Review*. Savinio announces the publication of his latest book with ten lithographs. Paul Eluard uses a drawing by Giorgio as a frontispiece.

In these years, the link between Metaphysics and Surrealism was strong. Breton in his *Anthologie de l'humour noir* consecrates their place in art (he exhibits this work with a dedication to Savinio); also Soupault remembers Savinio's role.

Savinio keeps on his desk a photograph of his brother by Man Ray.

Monographs on De Chirico's are released; the one by Waldemar George includes an etching of *Archeologi*; Cocteau's *Le mystère laic* presents two etchings of *Gladiatori*. De Chirico's copy bears two striking drawings by Cocteau.

Meanwhile, *Hebdomeros* is published. Even if the Surrealists have repudiated the painter, they warmly praise this book full of enigmatic paintings.

In the bookshop catalogues, Surrealist books by De Chirico and Savinio are included in the "must read" list.

In 1929, De Chirico works for Diaghilev's Ballets Russes, the dream of modernity that had filled them with passion in the first years in Paris. With the death of this last romantic hero, followed by the world-wide economic crisis, it seemed that an era had come to a close.

7) Italian Epilogue

"Non quando li prende / ma quando li rende / Parigi ci offende," is how the review *Il Selvaggio* greeted the Dioscuri upon their return to Italy.

Years of bitterness and mistrust; new relationships and voyages; their mother dies.

For Giorgio there was New York, for Alberto literary success. A new war, and then Alberto's work for the theatre and for 30 years De Chirico remains almost an exhile in his own country (detested by critics, he managed only to cause scandal).

Savinio leaves behind his Paris-style and embarks on a new pictorial style still full of mythology.

De Chirico changes his style again.

Close in spirit, the two brothers have grown apart in the ideal of the logic of life.

Savinio says, "It is there, in death, that my brother and I will be again what we were twenty or so years ago, when nothing separated us yet and together we had only one thought."

The day that Alberto died in 1952, Giorgio laid on his head a wreath of laurel. The new edition of *Hebdomeros*, published by the author, is dedicated to "the sacred memory of my brother, Alberto Savinio."

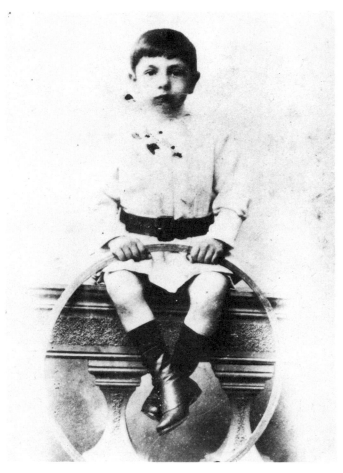

Giorgio De Chirico with his hoop, Athens

Metaphysics in Paris
The small copy of Praxiteles' Hermes that Alberto Savinio always kept at his desk. Savinio's *Introduction a une vie de Mercure*, published in French. Apollinaire in the guise of Orpheus with the fish (as Giorgio De Chirico envisioned him) in an engraving by Raoul Dufy. One of Giorgio De Chirico's drawings of 1913 which first belonged to Paul Eluard and later to Pablo Picasso (Paris, Musée Picasso).

Guillaume Apollinaire as seen by Alberto Savinio, and a page from *L'Esprit Nouveau*, 1926, with the photo that inspired Savinio in his portrait.

Ferrara. The barracks where De Chirico and Savinio were stationed. The journal *Dada*, to which De Chirico and Savinio contributed in 1917. Giorgio De Chirico's self-portrait with dedication to Filippo De Pisis.

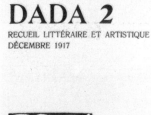

278

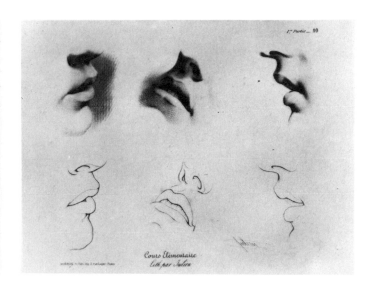

Neo-Classical Rome and Surrealist Paris
De Chirico with Mario Broglio,
founder of the review *Valori Plastici*.
Giorgio De Chirico's monograph on
Courbet, Edizioni Valori Plastici, 1924.
A page from Julian's manual, which
was the source of many of De Chirico's
and Savinio's images. Jean Cocteau's
preface to Alberto Savinio's exhibition
of 1927 in Paris. Giorgio De Chirico
throwing stones, photograph from
Raissa De Chirico's album. Roger
Vitrac's monograph, Paris 1927.

The Return to Italy
The "Italiens de Paris" exhibition,
Milan 1920. Savinio and De Chirico in
Maccari's caricature: "Non quando li
prende, ma quando li rende, Parigi ci
offende" (*Il Selvaggio*, 1933).

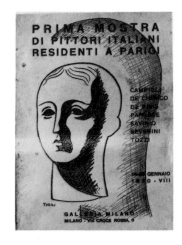

Giuseppe Pellizza da Volpedo
The Human Tide
(Fiumana)
1895-96
oil on canvas, 255 × 438 cm
Milan, Pinacoteca di Brera
Gift of Sprind Spa, 1986

283

Medardo Rosso
Laughing Woman
(Rieuse)
c. 1890
wax, 35 × 23 × 18 cm
Barzio, Museo Medardo Rosso

Medardo Rosso
Big Laughing Woman
(Grande Rieuse)
c. 1891
bronze, 61 × 68 × 22 cm
Florence, Galleria d'Arte Moderna di Palazzo Pitti

Medardo Rosso
Child in the Sun
(Bambino al sole)
c. 1892
plaster, 35 × 21 × 19 cm
Barzio, Museo Medardo Rosso

Medardo Rosso
Child in the Sun
(Bambino al sole)
c. 1892
wax, 37 × 21 × 19 cm
Milan, Private collection

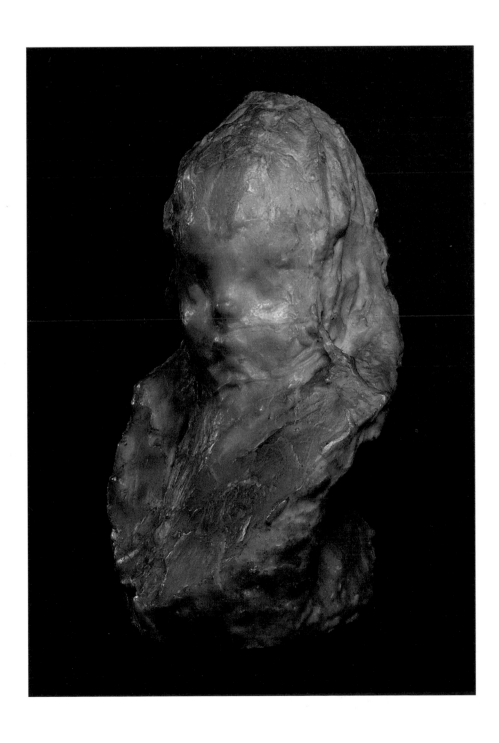

Medardo Rosso
Yvette Guilbert
undated
patinated plaster, 44 × 27.5 × 19.5 cm
Venice, Ca' Pesaro
Galleria Internazionale d'Arte Moderna

Medardo Rosso
Impression of a Boulevard or *The Veiled Lady*
(*Impression du boulevard* or *Femme à la voilette*)
c. 1893
wax, 60 × 59 × 25 cm
Salome and Eric Estorick Collection

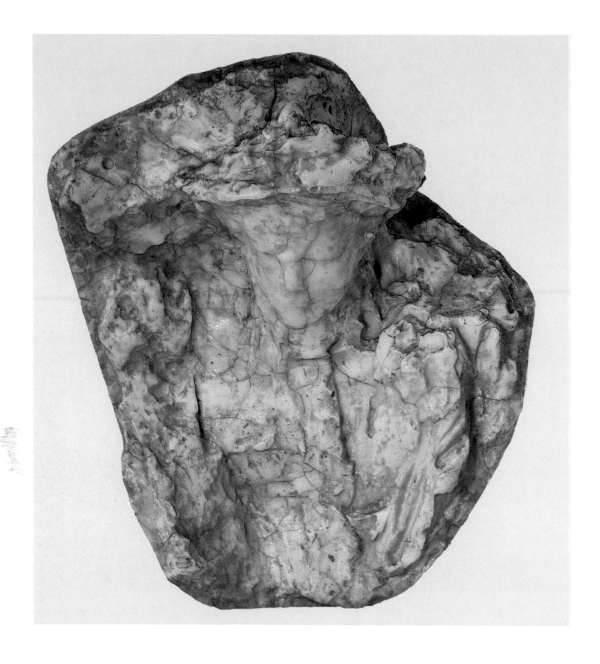

Medardo Rosso
The Concierge
(La portinaia)
c. 1893
plaster, 39.5 × 33.5 × 17.5 cm
Barzio, Museo Medardo Rosso

Medardo Rosso
Man Reading
(Uomo che legge)
c. 1894
wax, 29.5 × 30.5 × 19.5 cm
Barzio, Museo Medardo Rosso

Giacomo Balla
Portrait of the Artist's Mother
(Ritratto della madre)
1901
pastels and tempera on paper, 119 × 93 cm
Rome, Galleria Nazionale d'Arte Moderna
Gift of Luce and Elica Balla

Giacomo Balla
Bankruptcy
(Fallimento)
1902
oil on canvas, 116 × 160 cm
Cologne, Museum Ludwig

Giacomo Balla
Outdoor Portrait
(Ritratto all'aperto)
1903
oil on canvas, 154.5 × 113 cm
Rome, Galleria Nazionale d'Arte Moderna

Giacomo Balla
The Worker's Day
(La giornata dell'operaio)
1904
oil on paper, 100 × 135 cm
Private collection

Umberto Boccioni
Sculptor's Portrait
(Ritratto di scultore)
1907
oil on canvas, 102 × 124 cm
Genoa, Italia Assicurazioni Collection

Umberto Boccioni
Grandmother
(Nonna)
1905-06
pastels on cardboard, 124 × 79 cm
Venice, Cassa di Risparmio Collection

Umberto Boccioni
Three Women
(Tre donne)
1909-10
oil on canvas, 180 × 132 cm
Milan, Banca Commerciale Italiana S.p.A. Collection

Umberto Boccioni
Morning
(Mattino)
1909
oil on canvas, 60 × 55 cm
Private collection

Umberto Boccioni
Workshops at Porta Romana
(Officine a Porta Romana)
1909
oil on canvas, 75 × 145 cm
Milan, Banca Commerciale Italiana S.p.A. Collection

Rembrandt Bugatti
Camel Drinking
(Cammello all'abbeverata)
1901
bronze with black patina, Hébrard lost wax
41 × 47.5 × 24.5 cm
Paris, Alain Lesieutre Collection

Rembrandt Bugatti
Serpent
(Serpente)
undated
bronze, black patina, Hébrard lost wax, 20 × 53 cm
Paris, Alain Lesieutre Collection

Gino Rossi
Seascape – Douarnenez
(Marina – Douarnenez)
undated
oil on canvas, 46 × 64 cm
Venice, Ca' Pesaro
Galleria Internazionale d'Arte Moderna

Gino Rossi
The Little Parish Church
(La piccola parrocchia)
1908
oil on cardboard, 35 × 43 cm
Private collection

1909
1919

Giacomo Balla
Window in Düsseldorf
(Finestra di Düsseldorf)
1912
oil on wood, 28.5 × 35 cm
Private collection

Giacomo Balla
Girl × Balcony or *Girl Running on a Balcony*
(Bambina moltiplicato balcone
or *Bambina che corre sul balcone)*
1912
oil on canvas, 125 × 125 cm
Milan, Civico Museo d'Arte Contemporanea
Raccolta Grassi

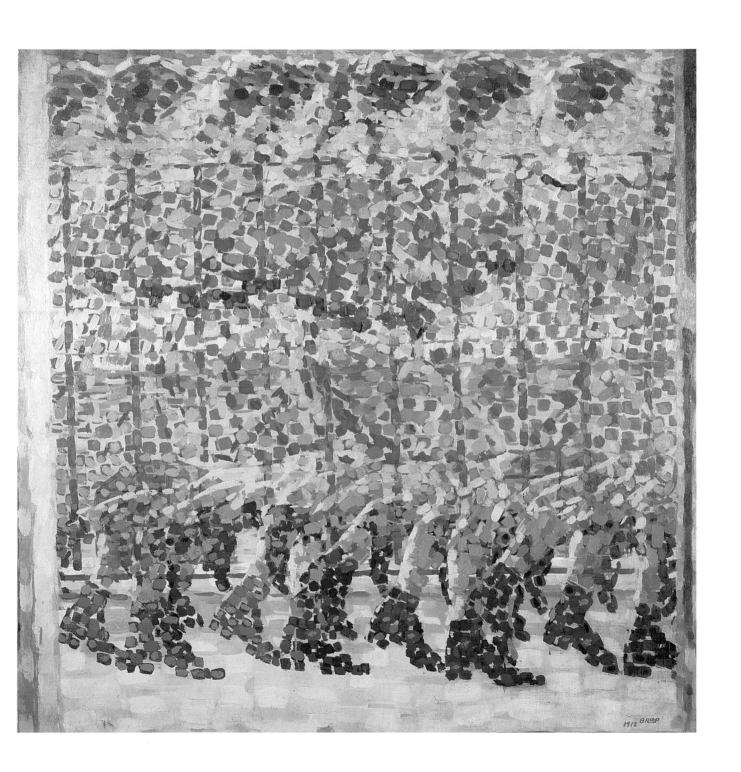

Giacomo Balla
The Hand of the Violinist or *Rhythms of the Violinist*
(La mano del violinista or *Ritmi del violinista)*
1912
oil on canvas, 52 × 75 cm
Salome and Eric Estorick Collection

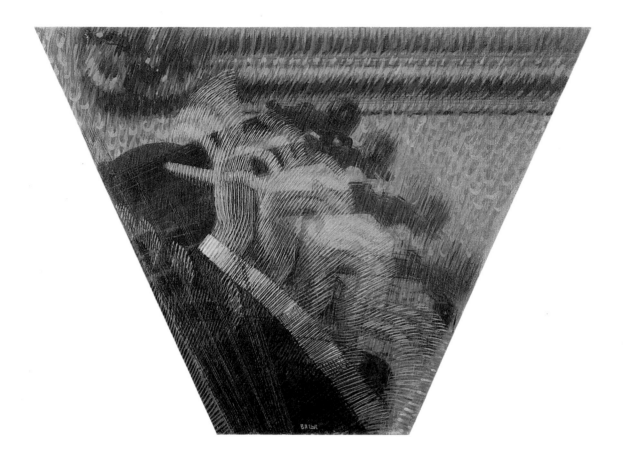

Giacomo Balla
Abstract Speed
(Velocità astratta)
1913
oil on canvas, 260 × 332 cm
Private collection

Umberto Boccioni
Modern Idol
(Idolo moderno)
1911
oil on wood, 60 × 58 cm
Salome and Eric Estorick Collection

Umberto Boccioni
The City Rises
(La città che sale)
1910-11
oil on canvas, 199.3 × 301 cm
New York, The Museum of Modern Art
Mrs Simon Guggenheim Fund, 1951

Umberto Boccioni
Antigraceful
(Antigrazioso)
1912
oil on canvas, 80 × 80 cm
Private collection

Umberto Boccioni
Horizontal Construction
(Costruzione orizzontale)
1912
oil on canvas, 95 × 95 cm
Munich, Bayerische Staatsgemäldesammlungen

Umberto Boccioni
Development of a Bottle in Space
(Sviluppo di una bottiglia nello spazio)
1912
bronze, 39.5 × 59.5 × 33 cm
Milan, Civico Museo d'Arte Contemporanea

Umberto Boccioni
Unique Forms of Continuity in Space
(Forme uniche di continuità nello spazio)
1913
bronze, 126 × 89 × 40 cm
Milan, Civico Museo d'Arte Contemporanea

Umberto Boccioni
The Two Friends
(Le due amiche)
1914-15
oil on canvas, 202 × 151.5 cm
Assitalia Collection
Le Assicurazioni d'Italia S.p.A.

Umberto Boccioni
Portrait of Maestro Ferruccio Busoni
(Ritratto del maestro Ferruccio Busoni)
1916
oil on canvas, 176 × 121 cm
Rome, Galleria Nazionale d'Arte Moderna

Carlo Carrà
Swimmers
(Nuotatrici)
1910
oil on canvas, 105.3 × 155.6 cm
Pittsburgh, The Carnegie Museum of Art
Gift of G. David Thompson, 1955

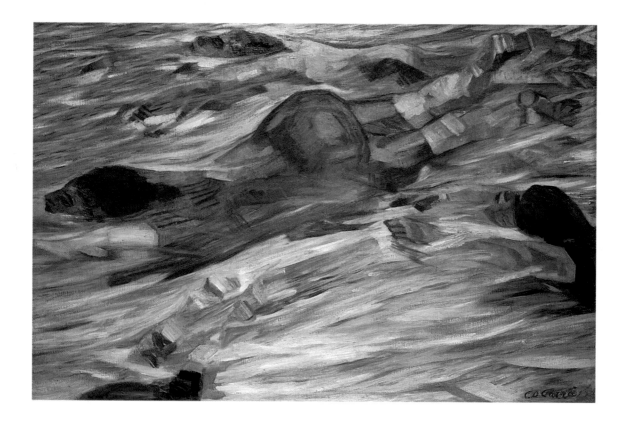

Carlo Carrà
Funeral of the Anarchist Galli
(Funerale dell'anarchico Galli)
1911
oil on canvas, 198.7 × 259.1 cm
New York, The Museum of Modern Art
Lillie P. Bliss Bequest, 1948

Carlo Carrà
Milan Station
(La stazione di Milano)
1910-11
oil on canvas, 50.5 × 54.5 cm
Stuttgart, Staatsgalerie

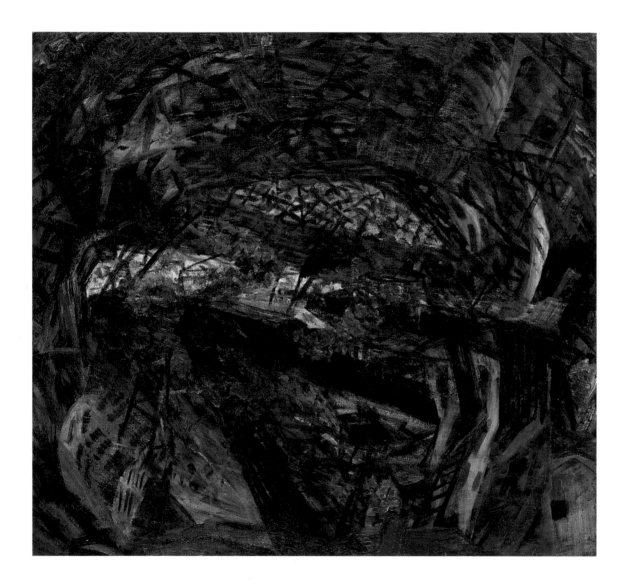

Carlo Carrà
Rhythms of Objects
(Ritmi di oggetti)
1911
oil on canvas, 51 × 66 cm
Milan, Pinacoteca di Brera
Gift of Emilio and Maria Jesi

Carlo Carrà
The Flask
(Il fiasco)
1915
collage and oil on cardboard, 39 × 31.5 cm
Milan, Private collection

Carlo Carrà
The Carriage
(La carrozzella)
1916
oil on canvas, 51.5 × 66 cm
Switzerland, Private collection

Carlo Carrà
Composition TA or *Still Life*
(*Composizione TA* o *Natura morta*)
1916
oil on canvas, 70 × 54 cm
Frankfurt, Städelsches Kunstinstitut
On loan from Private collection

Carlo Carrà
Metaphysical Still Life
(Natura morta metafisica)
1919
oil on canvas, 51 × 46 cm
Private collection

Carlo Carrà
The Metaphysical Muse
(La musa metafisica)
1917
oil on canvas, 90 × 66 cm
Milan, Pinacoteca di Brera
Gift of Emilio and Maria Jesi

Carlo Carrà
The Oval of the Apparitions
(*L'ovale delle apparizioni*)
1918
oil on canvas, 92 × 60 cm
Rome, Galleria Nazionale d'Arte Moderna

329

Giorgio De Chirico
Nude
(Nu aux cheveux noirs)
1911
oil on canvas, 71 × 56 cm
Private collection

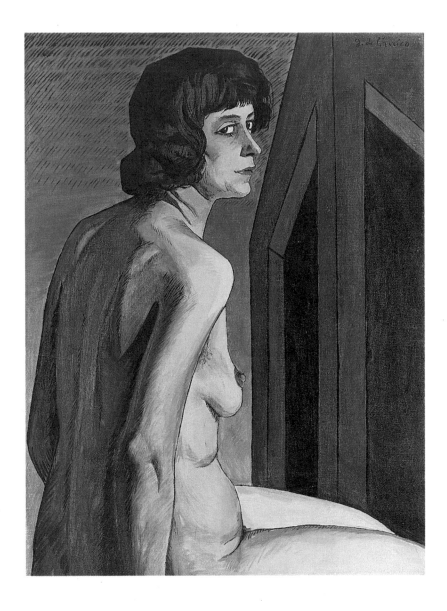

Giorgio De Chirico
Autumnal Meditation
(La Méditation automnale)
1912
oil on canvas, 55.7 × 70 cm
Private collection

Giorgio De Chirico
Melancholy
(Melanconia)
1912
oil on canvas, 80 × 63 cm
Salome and Eric Estorick Collection

Giorgio De Chirico
The Enigma of a Day
(L'énigme d'une journée)
1914
oil on canvas, 185.5 × 139.7 cm
New York, The Museum of Modern Art
James Thrall Soby Bequest, 1979

Giorgio De Chirico
The Enigma of Fate
(L'énigme de la fatalité)
1914
oil on canvas, 138 × 95.5 cm
Basel, Kunstmuseum
Emanuel Hoffmann Stiftung

Giorgio De Chirico
The Tower
(La torre)
c. 1913
oil on canvas, 115.5 × 45 cm
Zurich, Kunsthaus
Vereinigung Zürcher Kunstfreunde

Giorgio De Chirico
Ariadne
1913
oil on canvas, 134.6 × 179.7 cm
New York, The Metropolitan Museum of Art
On loan from private collection

Giorgio De Chirico
Gare Montparnasse - Parting Sadness
(Gare Montparnasse - La mélancolie du départ)
1914
oil on canvas, 140 × 184.5 cm
New York, The Museum of Modern Art
Gift of James Thrall Soby

Giorgio De Chirico
Premonitory Portrait of Guillaume Apollinaire
(Ritratto premonitore di Guillaume Apollinaire)
1914
oil on canvas, 81.5 × 65 cm
Paris, Musée national d'art moderne
Centre Georges Pompidou

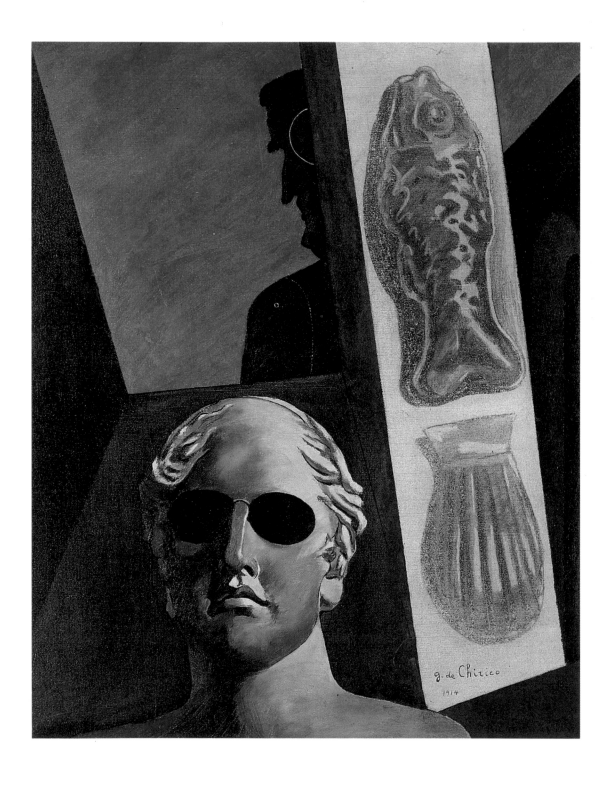

Giorgio De Chirico
The Child's Brain
(Le cerveau de l'enfant)
1914
oil on canvas, 80 × 65 cm
Stockholm, Moderna Museet

Giorgio De Chirico
The Astronomer – The Uneasiness of Life
(L'astronome – L'inquiétude de la vie)
c. 1915
oil on canvas, 41 × 33 cm
Houston, The Menil Collection

Giorgio De Chirico
The Melancholy of Leavetaking
(La mélancolie du départ)
1916-17
oil on canvas, 51.8 × 25.9 cm
London, The Trustees of the Tate Gallery

342

Giorgio De Chirico
Metaphysical Interior with Large Factory
(Interno metafisico con grande officina)
1916
oil on canvas, 96.3 × 73.8 cm
Stuttgart, Staatsgalerie

Giorgio De Chirico
The Revolt of the Wise Man
(La révolte du sage)
1916
oil on canvas, 67.3 × 59 cm
Salome and Eric Estorick Collection

Filippo De Pisis
The Fateful Hour
(L'ora fatale)
1919
tempera and collage on linen paper
32 × 22.5 cm
Milan, Private collection

Filippo De Pisis
Western Still Life
(Natura morta occidentale)
1919
mixed media and collage on cardboard
36 × 27 cm
Private collection

Alberto Magnelli
Still Life
(Natura morta)
1914
plaster, glass bottle, terracotta bowl
56.5 × 54 × 56.5 cm
Paris, Musée national d'art moderne
Centre Georges Pompidou
Gift of Susi Magnelli, 1978

Alberto Magnelli
The Globe and Lacerba
(Il mappamondo e Lacerba)
1914
oil on canvas, 100 × 75 cm
Meudon, Susi Magnelli Collection

Arturo Martini
The Friend of the Cypress Tree
(L'amica del cipresso)
1919
plaster, 62 × 60 × 30 cm
Verona, Private collection

Arturo Martini
A Man I Often Meet
(Uomo spesse volte incontrato)
1913
polychrome plaster, 119 × 64 × 32 cm
Venice, Ca' Pesaro
Galleria Internazionale d'Arte Moderna

Arturo Martini
Girl before Evening
(Fanciulla verso sera)
1919
plaster, 54 × 52 × 31 cm
Venice, Ca' Pesaro
Galleria Internazionale d'Arte Moderna

Arturo Martini
Girl's Head
(Testa di ragazza)
1920
plaster, 42 × 24 × 23 cm
Private collection

353

Amedeo Modigliani
Head
(Testa)
1911-13
calcareous stone, 63.5 × 15 × 21 cm
New York
Solomon R. Guggenheim Museum

Amedeo Modigliani
Crouching Nude
(Nu accroupi)
1916-17
oil on canvas, 114 × 74 cm
Antwerp, Koninklijk Museum
voor Schone Kunsten

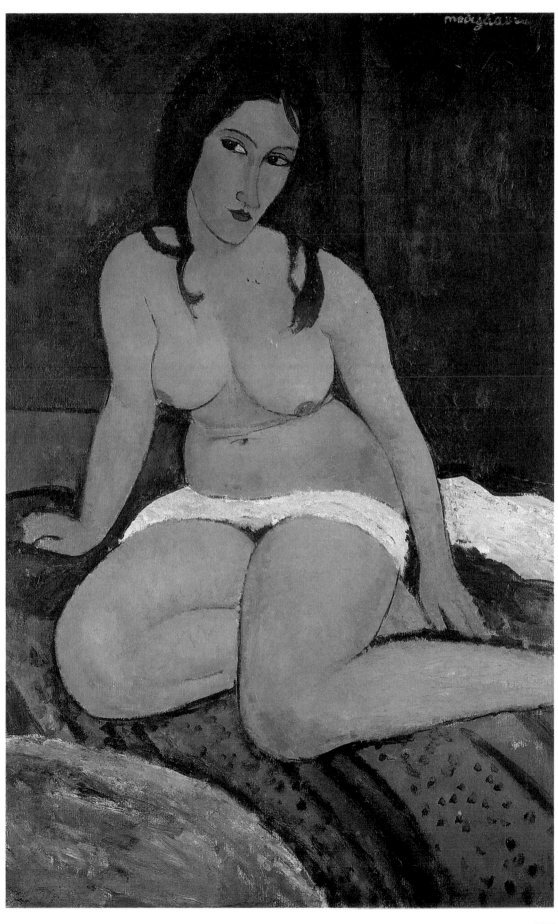

Amedeo Modigliani
Nude
(Nudo)
1917
oil on canvas, 73 × 117 cm
New York, Solomon R. Guggenheim Museum
Gift of Solomon R. Guggenheim, 1941

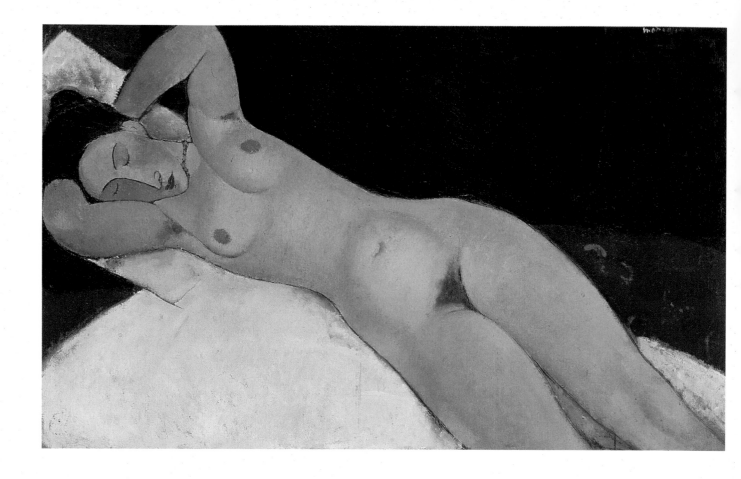

Amedeo Modigliani
Standing Figure
(Nu debout)
c. 1912
calcareous stone, 162.8 × 33.2 × 31.5 cm
Canberra, Australian National Gallery

Amedeo Modigliani
Large Nude
(Grand nu)
c. 1919
oil on canvas, 72.4 × 116.5 cm
New York, The Museum of Modern Art
Mrs. Simon Guggenheim Fund, 1950

Amedeo Modigliani
Head
(Testa)
1910-11
stone, 50 × 19.6 × 19 cm
Private collection

Amedeo Modigliani
Woman's Head
(Testa di donna)
1910-11
calcareous stone, 65 × 19 × 24 cm
Washington, National Gallery of Art
Chester Dale Collection, 1963

Amedeo Modigliani
Seated Nude in Shirt
(Nu assis à la chemise)
1917
oil on canvas, 92 × 67.5 cm
Villeneuve d'Ascq, Musée d'Art Moderne
Gift of Geneviève and Jean Masurel

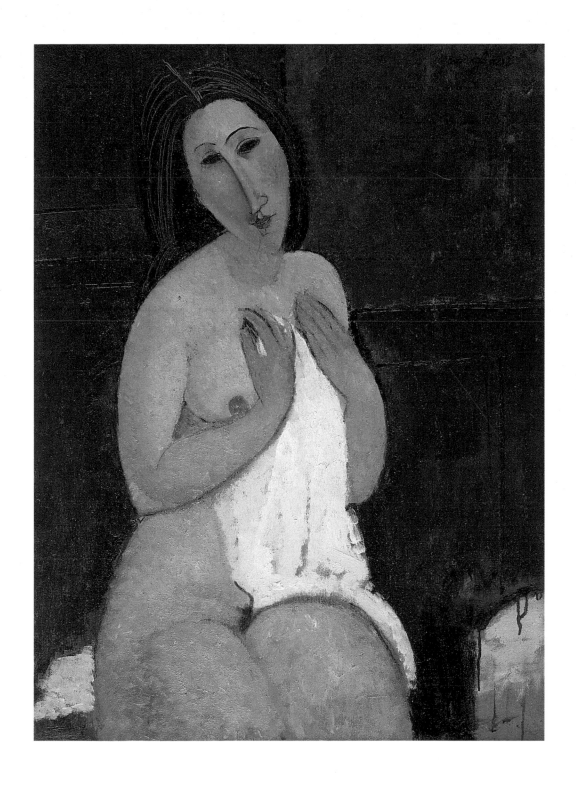

Amedeo Modigliani
Woman's Head
(Tête de femme)
1912
stone, 58 × 12 × 16 cm
Paris, Musée national d'art moderne
Centre Georges Pompidou, 1949

Critical References
Bibliography

Critical References

Nicoletta Boschiero

Afro (Basaldella)
Man with Pipe (Uomo con pipa), 1944
[p. 552]
Oil on canvas, 60 × 50 cm. Top right: Afro 44. Private collection.
Exhibitions: Rome 1946 no. 1; Udine 1947; Passariano 1978 no. 16; Spoleto 1987 no. 27.
Bibliography: Brandi 1977 no. 11; Crispolti 1984 p. 226 no. 198.

Afro (Basaldella)
Still Life (Natura morta), 1945
[p. 553]
Oil on canvas, 40 × 50 cm. Top right: Afro 45. Vicenza, Angelo Carlo Festa Collection.
Exhibitions: Trieste 1946; Spoleto 1987 no. 30.

Giacomo Balla
Portrait of the Artist's Mother (Ritratto della madre), 1901
[p. 292]
Pastels and tempera on paper, 119 × 93 cm. Rome, Galleria Nazionale d'Arte Moderna. Gift of Luce and Elica Balla.
Provenance: Rome, 1928; Turin 1963 no. 5; Rome 1971-72 no. 5; Milan 1973-1974 no. 15.
Bibliography: Drudi Gambillo-Fiori 1962 vol. II no. 1; Bellonzi-Fiori 1968 vol. II no. 1703 X 27; Dortch Dorazio 1970.
Reference: List 1982 no. 43.

Giacomo Balla
Bankrupt (Fallimento), 1902
[p. 293]
Oil on canvas, 116 × 160 cm. Bottom right: Balla 1902. Cologne, Museum Ludwig.
Provenance: Rome, Cosmelli.
Exhibitions: Rome 1904; Rome 1928; Rome 1951-52; Venice 1960; New York 1961, then Detroit 1961; Los Angeles 1962; Turin 1963 no. 10; Düsseldorf 1974 no. 15; Venice 1986 p. 25; London 1989 no. 4.
Bibliography: Nappi in *L'Italia Moderna* no. 13 July 1904; Roux in *Natura e Arte* 1903-04; Sapori in *La Gazzetta del Popolo* 3 February 1928; Severini 1946; Taylor 1961; Drudi Gambillo-Fiori 1962 vol. II no. 9; Calvesi in *L'Arte Moderna* vol. V 1967; Bellonzi-Fiori 1968 vol. II no. 1713 X 58; Dortch Dorazio 1970.
Reference: List 1982 no. 80.

Giacomo Balla
The Patients (I malati), 1903
[p. 294]
Oil on canvas, 175 × 115 cm. Bottom right: Balla 1903. Back: Prime cure elettriche del prof. Ghilarducci - L'uomo parte destra paralizzata, la donna nevrastenia - dipinto eseguito nell'ambulatorio sempre col vero - anno 1903 - Balla. Rome, Galleria Nazionale d'Arte Moderna. Gift of Luce and Elica Balla.
Provenance: Rome, Luce and Elica Balla.
Exhibitions: Rome 1909 no. 33; Paris 1909 no. 21; Rome 1928 no. 3; Rome 1929-30 no. 25; Turin 1963 no. 17; Rome 1971-72 no. 16.
Bibliography: Pica in *Emporium* vol. XXIX April 1909; De Fiori in *Caffaro* 19 March 1909; *L'Art décoratif* 1909; Randone (*Il Lupo delle Mura*) in *Cronache di Arte Educatrice* no. 6 1928; Costantini 1934; Drudi Gambillo-Fiori 1962 vol. II no. 5; Bellonzi-Fiori 1968 vol. II no. 1733 X 64.
Reference: List 1982 no. 123.

Giacomo Balla
Outdoor Portrait (Ritratto all'aperto), 1903
[p. 295]
Oil on canvas, 154.5 × 113 cm. Bottom right: Balla. Rome, Galleria Nazionale d'Arte

Moderna.
Provenance: Rome, Luce and Elica Balla.
Exhibitions: Rome 1903 no. 692; Paris 1960-61; Turin 1963 no. 13; Rome 1971-72 no. 10; Milan 1973-74 no. 6; Düsseldorf 1974 no. 16.
Bibliography: Drudi Gambillo-Fiori 1962 vol. II no. 11; Calvesi in *L'Arte Moderna* vol. II 1967; Bellonzi-Fiori 1968 vol. II no. 1701 X 33; Crispolti 1975.
Reference: List 1982 no. 82.

Giacomo Balla
The Worker's Day (La giornata dell'operaio), 1904
[p. 296]
Politico, oil on paper, 100 × 135 cm. Bottom center: Balla 1904. Private collection.
Provenance: Rome, Luce and Elica Balla.
Exhibitions: Rome 1907; Rome 1928 no. 5; Turin 1963 no. 22; Venice 1968 no. 1; Milan 1970 no. 106; Rome 1971-72 no. 18; Milan 1973-74 no. 25; Düsseldorf 1974 no. 17; Venice 1986 p. 26.
Bibliography: Marchi in *La Stirpe* March 1928; Dottori in *Oggi e domani* 30 January 1930; *Il Futurismo* 16 April 1933; Drudi Gambillo Fiori 1962 vol. II no. 10; Bellonzi-Fiori 1968 vol. II no. 1741 X 96; Dortch Dorazio 1970; Crispolti 1975.
Reference: List 1982 no. 89.

Giacomo Balla
Girl × Balcony or *Girl Running on a Balcony (Bambina moltiplicato balcone* or *Bambina che corre sul balcone)*, 1912
[p. 309]
Oil on canvas, 125 × 125 cm. Bottom right: Balla 1912; back: G.Balla 1912 via Oslavia 39 Roma. Milan, Civico Museo d'Arte Contemporanea.
Provenance: Milan, Grassi Collection.
Exhibitions: Rome 1913 no. 4; Rotterdam 1913 no. 28; Rome 1929; New York 1949 no. 26; Paris 1960-61; New York 1961 no. 5, then Detroit 1961, then Los Angeles 1962; Turin 1963 no. 49; Rome 1971-72 no. 32; Milan 1973-74; Düsseldorf 1974 no. 15; Venice 1986 p. 73; London 1989 no. 7.
Bibliography: Mastrigli in *La Vita* 23 February 1913; Prampolini in *L'Artista Moderno*, vol. XII 1913; Boccioni 1914; Taylor 1961; Drudi Gambillo-Fiori 1962 vol. II no. 37; Calvesi in *L'Arte Moderna* vol. V 1967; Bellonzi-Fiori 1968 vol. II no. 1836 X 219; Fagiolo 1970 no. 15; Dortch Dorazio 1970; Crispolti 1975.
Reference: List 1982 no. 290.

Giacomo Balla
Window in Düsseldorf (Finestra di Düsseldorf), 1912
[p. 308]
Oil on wood, 28.5 × 35 cm. Bottom right: Balla. Private collection.
Provenance: Rome, Luce and Elica Balla.
Exhibitions: Rome 1971-72 no. 28; Düsseldorf 1974 no. 19.
Bibliography: Fagiolo 1970 p. XIII; List in *Cahiers du Musée national d'art moderne* no. 5 September 1980.
Reference: List 1982 no. 251.

Giacomo Balla
The Hand of the Violinist or *Rhythms of the Violinist (La mano del violinista* or *Ritmi del violinista)*, 1912
[p. 310]
Oil on canvas, 52 × 75 cm. Bottom center: Balla. Salome and Eric Estorick Collection.
Exhibitions: Rome 1913 no. 2; Rotterdam 1913 no. 29; Berlin 1913, no. 31; New York 1961 no.

6, then Detroit 1961, then Los Angeles 1962; Rome 1971-72 no. 31; Paris 1972 no. 7; Düsseldorf 1974 no. 17; Venice 1986, p. 70; London 1989 no. 6.
Bibliography: Boccioni 1914; Petrucci in *Emporium* no. 312 December 1920; *Cahiers d'Art* 1950; Taylor 1961; Drudi Gambillo-Fiori 1962 vol. II no. 19; Calvesi in *L'Arte Moderna* vol. V 1967; Bellonzi-Fiori 1968 no. 1813 X 209; Fagiolo 1970 no. 16; Dortch Dorazio 1970; Damigella, 1971.
Reference: List 1982 no. 253.

Giacomo Balla
Abstract Speed (Velocità astratta), 1913
[p. 311]
Oil on canvas, 260 × 332 cm. Back: l'opera Marcia su Roma del 1922. Private collection.
Provenance: Rome Luce and Elica Balla.
Exhibitions: Rome 1914 no. 5; Rome 1968; Rome 1971-72 no. 38; Venice 1986, p. 77; London 1989, no. 12.
Bibliography: Boccioni 1914; Soffici 1914; *Il Futurismo* 16 April 1933; *Cahiers d'Art* 1950; Drudi Gambillo-Fiori 1962 vol. II no. 82; Dortch Dorazio 1970; Crispolti 1975.
Reference: List 1982 no. 293.

Giacomo Balla
Awakening of Spring (Risveglio di primavera), 1918
[p. 380]
Oil on canvas, 107 × 87 cm. Bottom left: Balla Futurista; back: Risveglio di Primavera, Balla 1918. Private collection.
Provenance: Rome, Pietro Campilli.
Exhibitions: Rome 1925 no. 3; New York 1925-26, then Boston 1926 no. 2; Turin 1963 no. 141; Rome 1971-72 no. 65; Paris 1972 no. 37.
Bibliography: Papini in *Emporium* 1925; Drudi Gambillo-Fiori 1962 vol. II no. 292.
Reference: List 1982 no. 556.

Giacomo Balla
The Spell is Broken (Si è rotto l'incanto), 1922
Oil on canvas, 106 × 75.5 cm. Bottom left: Balla Futurista. Rome, Private collection.
Exhibitions: Venice 1926, no. 6; Bologna 1927, no. 12; Milan 1927; Venice 1930; Zurich 1950 no. 11; Turin 1963 no. 184; Venice 1968 no. 41; Rome 1971-72 no. 73; Venice 1986 p. 316.
Bibliography: Prampolini in *Le Tre Venezie* suppl. May 1926; Fillia in *l'Impero* 20 May 1927; *Cahiers d'Art* 1950; Drudi Gambillo Fiori 1962 vol. II no. 335; Calvesi in *L'Arte Moderna* vol. V 1967; Fagiolo 1970 p. XXIX; Dortch Dorazio 1970.
Reference: List 1982 no. 686.

Giacomo Balla
Life's Arrows (Frecce della vita), 1928
[p. 381]
Oil on wood, 99 × 115 cm. Right: Futur Balla; back: Balla Futurista 1928; on upper edge of engraved frame: LE FRECCE DELLA VITA; bottom: LOTTE INSIDIE OSTACOLI; right: IDEALISMO ARTE; left: AMBIZIONE AMORE. Rome, Galleria Nazionale d'Arte Moderna. Gift of Luce and Elica Balla.
Provenance: Rome, Luce and Elica Balla.
Exhibitions: Rome 1928 no. 76; Rome 1931 no. 13; Turin 1963 no. 203; Venice 1968; Rome 1971-72 no. 79; Venice 1986 p. 317.
Bibliography: Biancale in *Il Popolo di Roma* 5 January 1929; Costantini 1934; *Cahiers d'Art* 1950; Drudi Gambillo-Fiori 1962 vol. II no. 388; Fagiolo 1970 p. XXIX; Dortch Dorazio 1970.
Reference: List 1982 no. 880.

Umberto Boccioni
Grandmother (Nonna), 1905-06
[p. 298]
Pastels on paper, 124 × 79 cm. Bottom right: U.Boccioni Rome 905-906. Venice, Cassa di Risparmio Collection.
Exhibitions: Rome 1906 no. 509; Venice 1910 no. 22; Milan 1916-17 no. 85; Venice 1958 no. 1; Milan 1973-74 no. 19; Milan 1982-83 no. 2.
Bibliography: *L'Adriatico* 16 July 1910; Argan-Calvesi 1953 p. 35; Taylor 1961 no. 2; Bruno 1969 no. 6; Calvesi-Coen 1983 no. 51.
Reference: Catalogue Verona 1985-86 no. 19.

Umberto Boccioni
Sculptor's Portrait (Ritratto di scultore), 1907
[p. 297]
Oil on canvas, 102 × 124 cm. Genoa, Italia Assicurazioni Collection.
Provenance: Milan, Marinotti.
Exhibitions: Milan 1916-17 no. 22; Venice 1958 no. 2 (*Ritratto dello scultore Brocchi* dated 1906); Venice 1960 p. 14 no. 14 (*Ritratto dello scultore Brocchi* dated 1907); New York 1961 no. 22 (*Ritratto dello scultore Brocchi*, dated 1907), then Detroit 1961, idem, then Los Angeles 1961-62; Verona 1985-86 no. 29, then Milan 1986, Venice 1986; New York 1988-89 no. 12.
Bibliography: Argan-Calvesi 1953 Plate 1 (*Ritratto dello scultore Brocchi*); Drudi Gambillo-Fiori 1962 no. 69 (*Ritratto dello scultore Ripamonti*); Fiori-Bellonzi 1968 no. 2247; Bruno 1969 Plate 27 (*Ritratto dello scultore Brocchi*).
Reference: Calvesi-Coen gen. cat. 1983 no. 250.

Umberto Boccioni
Morning (Mattino), 1909
[p. 300]
Oil on canvas, 60 × 55 cm. Bottom right: U.Boccioni. Private collection.
Provenance: Milan, Fanna.
Exhibitions: Milan 1909-10 no. 170; Venice 1910 no. 2; Milan 1916-17 no. 52; Milan 1924 no. 23 (*Sobborgo di Milano*); Venice 1966 p. 10 no. 16 (*Il mattino*); Milan 1982-83 no. 42 (*Il mattino*); Verona 1985-86 no. 65, then Milan 1986, then Venice 1986.
Bibliography: *La Perseveranza* 20 December 1909; *Il Secolo* 22 December 1909; Severini 1933 p. 354 (*Paesaggio suburbano*); Argan-Calvesi 1953 Plate 7; Drudi Gambillo-Fiori 1962 no. 88 (*Periferia*); Fiori-Bellonzi 1968 no. 2324; Bruno 1969 no. 93.
Reference: Calvesi-Coen gen. cat. 1983 no. 420.

Umberto Boccioni
Workshops at Porta Romana (Officine a Porta Romana), 1909
[p. 301]
Oil on canvas, 75 × 145 cm. Bottom right: U.Boccioni. Milan, Banca Commerciale Italiana S.p.A. Collection.
Provenance: Milan, Vico Baer.
Exhibitions: Milan 1916-17 no. 88; Milan 1973-74 no. 26; Düsseldorf 1974 no. 38; Milan 1982-83 no. 26; Venice 1986 p. 30; New York 1988-89 no. 38; London 1989 no. 14.
Bibliography: Carrà 1924 in *L'Ambrosiano* 13 March p. 3 (*Alle porte di Milano*); Argan-Calvesi 1953 Plate 5; Drudi Gambillo-Fiori 1962 vol. II no. 97 (*Periferia*); Ballo 1964 no. 120; Calvesi 1967 no. 13; Bruno 1969 no. 63.
Reference: Calvesi-Coen 1983 gen. cat. 1983 no. 423.

Umberto Boccioni
Three Women (Tre donne), 1909-10
[p. 299]
Oil on canvas, 180 × 132 cm. Bottom right:

U.Boccioni 1909-10. Milan, Banca Commerciale Italiana S.p.A. Collection.
Exhibitions: Milan 1910; Milan 1916-17 no. 55; Milan 1924 no. 30; Milan 1982-83 no. 48.
Bibliography: Teglio in *Il Panaro* 19 March 1911; Sarfatti in *Gli Avvenimenti* 24 September 1916 p. 12; *La Mostra Boccioni a Milano* in *Emporium* January 1917 p. 77; Argan-Calvesi 1953 no. 10; Drudi Gambillo Fiori 1962 no. 87; Calvesi in *L'Arte Moderna* 1967 p. 71; Bruno 1969 no. 102a; Calvesi-Coen 1983 no. 455.
Reference: Catalogue New York 1988-89 no. 41.

Umberto Boccioni
The City Rises (La città che sale), 1910-11
[p. 313]
Oil on canvas, 199.3 × 301 cm. Bottom right: U.Boccioni. New York, The Museum of Modern Art
Exhibitions: Milan 1911; Paris 1912 no. 6, then London 1912, then Berlin 1912, then Bruxelles 1912, idem; Milan 1916-17 no. 70; Milan 1933; New York 1961 no. 30, then Detroit 1961, then Los Angeles 1962; Venice 1986 p. 119; New York 1988-89 no. 50.
Bibliography: Barbantini in *L'Avvenire d'Italia* 19 May 1911; Soffici in *La Voce* 22 June 1911; Boccioni 1914 no. 6; Argan Calvesi 1953 Plate 15; Drudi Gambillo-Fiori 1962 vol. II no. 216; Ballo 1964 no. 346; Calvesi 1967 pp. 68-72; Bruno 1969 no. 119.
Reference: Calvesi-Coen gen. cat. 1983 no. 675.

Umberto Boccioni
Modern Idol (Idolo moderno), 1911
[p. 312]
Oil on wood, 60 × 58 cm. Bottom left: Boccioni. Salome and Eric Estorick Collection.
Provenance: London, Marlborough Gallery; Berlin, Barkard.
Exhibitions: Paris 1912 no. 8; London 1912, then Berlin 1912, then Bruxelles 1912 idem; Rotterdam 1913; New York 1961 no. 32, then Detroit 1961, then Los Angeles 1962; Venice 1986 p. 120; New York 1988-89, no. 55A; London 1989 no. 17.
Bibliography: Boccioni 1914 no. 8; Argan-Calvesi 1953 no. 17; Drudi Gambillo-Fiori 1962 vol. II no. 217; Ballo 1964 no. 383; Bruno 1969, no. 130a.
Reference: Calvesi-Coen gen. cat. 1983 no. 709.

Umberto Boccioni
Antigraceful (Antigrazioso), 1912
[p. 314]
Oil on canvas, 80 × 80 cm. Back: U.Boccioni. Private collection.
Provenance: Rome, Margherita Sarfatti.
Exhibitions: Rome 1913 no. 8; Rotterdam 1913 no. 8; Milan 1916-17 no,.60; Milan 1924 no. 9; Rome 1925 no. 11 (*Studio della madre* or *Antigrazioso*); Venice 1950 p. 58 no. 11; Venice 1966 p. 12 no. 73; Verona 1985-86 no. 76, then Milan 1986, then Venice 1986; Venice 1986 p. 131; New York 1988-89 no. 66; London 1989 no. 23.
Bibliography: Boccioni 1914; Soffici 1914; Sarfatti *Gli Avvenimenti* no. 39, 24 September 1916; Argan-Calvesi 1953 Plate 41; Drudi Gambillo-Fiori 1962 nos.348-387.
Reference: Calvesi-Coen gen. cat. 1983 no. 787

Umberto Boccioni
Horizontal Construction (Costruzione orrizontale), 1912
[p. 315]
Oil on canvas, 95 × 95 cm. Back: U.Boccioni. Munich, Bayerische Staatsgemäldesammlungen.

Critical References

Provenance: Milan, Toninelli.
Exhibitions: Rome 1913 no. 7; Rotterdam 1913 no. 7; Rome 1914 no. 12 (*Costruzione dinamica orizzontale*); Milan 1916-17 no. 32 (*Volumi o-rizzontali*); Rome 1925 no. 13 (*Volumi orizzontali*); Milan 1973-74 no. 161 (*Volumi orizzontali*); Düsseldorf 1974 no. 58; Venice 1986 p. 128; New York 1988-89 no. 59.
Bibliography: Sarfatti 1916 p. 15; Drudi Gambillo-Fiori 1962 vol. II no. 271; Ballo 1964 no. 460; Bruno 1969 no. 147a.
Reference: Calvesi-Coen gen. cat. 1983 no. 751.

Umberto Boccioni
Development of a Bottle in Space or *Force Lines of a Bottle in Space* (*Sviluppo di una bottiglia nello spazio* or *Linee e forza di una bottiglia nello spazio*), 1912
[p. 316]
Bronze, 39.5 × 59.5 × 33 cm. Milan, Civico Museo d'Arte Contemporanea (Inventory no. 5396).
Provenance: Turin, Ausonio Canavese.
Exhibitions: Zurich 1950; Milan 1979 1980; Rome 1980-81; Milan 1982-83.
Bibliography: Argan-Calvesi 1953 p. 20; Pirovano 1968 no. 55.
Reference: Calvesi-Coen gen. cat. 1983 no. 782.

Umberto Boccioni
Unique Forms of Continuity in Space (*Forme uniche di continuità nello spazio*), 1913
[p. 317]
Bronze, 125 × 89 × 40 cm. Milan, Civico Museo d'Arte Contemporanea (Inventory no. 5051).
Provenance: Rome, Filippo Tommaso Marinetti.
Exhibitions: Zurich 1950; Bruxelles 1973; Paris 1973; Düsseldorf 1974; Milan 1982-83; Frankfurt 1985.
Bibliography: Argan-Calvesi 1953 no. 58; Pirovano 1968 no. 57.
Reference: Calvesi-Coen gen. cat. 1983 no. 856.

Umberto Boccioni
The Two Friends (*Le due amiche*), 1914-15
[p. 318]
Oil on canvas, 202 × 151.5 cm. Bottom right: Boccioni. Assitalia Collection. Le Assicurazioni d'Italia S.p. A.
Provenance: Frankfurt, Luisa Hammershlag Ruberl; Milan, Galleria Philippe Daverio; Rome, Galleria La Medusa.
Exhibitions: Milan 1916-17 no. 77; Venice 1966 no. 287; Florence 1967 no. 379; New York 1988-89 no. 80A.
Bibliography: Argan-Calvesi 1953 Plate 67; Drudi Gambillo-Fiori 1962 no. 336; Ballo 1964 no. 596; Bruno 1969 no. 190.
Reference: Calvesi-Coen gen. cat. 1983 no. 923.

Umberto Boccioni
Portrait of Maestro Ferruccio Busoni (*Ritratto del maestro Ferruccio Busoni*), 1916
[p. 319]
Oil on canvas, 176 × 121 cm. Right, toward bottom: Boccioni 1916. Rome, Galleria Nazionale d'Arte Moderna.
Provenance: New York, Ferruccio Busoni.
Exhibitions: Milan 1916-17 no. 76 (*Grande ritratto del Maestro Busoni*); Milan 1933; Milan 1982-83 no. 43; New York 1988-89 no. 85
Bibliography: Severinin in *L'Esame artistico e letterario*, July 1933 p. 358; Argan-Calvesi 1953 fig.80; Drudi Gambillo-Fiori 1962 vol. II no. 402; Ballo 1964 no. 604; Bruno 1969 no. 198a.
Reference: Calvesi-Coen gen. cat. 1983 no. 946.

Massimo Campigli
Market of Women and Amphorae (*Marché des femmes et des pots*), 1929
[p. 382]
Oil on canvas, 220 × 160 cm. Bottom left: MAS-SIMO CAMPIGLI. Rome, Assitalia Collection. Le Assicurazioni d'Italia S.p. A.
Provenance: Paris, Galerie Jeanne Bucher; Rome, Giuditta Scalini; Prato, Galleria Farsetti.
Exhibitions; Paris 1929; Venice 1948; Venice 1954; Florence 1967 no. 815; Venice 1985 p. 33; London 1989 no. 140.
Bibliography: Kunstler in *Art et Décoration* May 1931 p. 138; Courthion 1938 Plate 6; Giani 1943 no. 3; Carrieri 1945 p42; de Grada 1969 p. 37.

Massimo Campigli
Women in the Sun (*Donne al sole*), 1931
[p. 383]
Oil on canvas, 81 × 60 cm. Bottom right: MAS-SIMO CAMPIGLI 1931. Bergamo, Private collection.
Provenance: Venice, Mario Ravagnani; Bologna, Galleria Marescalchi.
Exhibitions: Como 1946; Salsomaggiore 1949; Bern 1955; Milan 1967 no. 6; Ferrara 1979 no. 14; Bologna 1981 p. 33.
Bibliography: Courthion 1938 no. 14; Giani 1943 no. 20; Serafini 1972 no. 60.

Carlo Carrà
Swimmers (*Nuotatrici*), 1910
[p. 320]
Oil on canvas, 105.3 × 155.6 cm. Bottom right: C.D.Carrà. Pittsburgh, The Carnegie Museum of Art.
Provenance: Berlin, Borchardt.
Exhibitions: Paris 1912; London 1912; Bruxelles 1912; Venice 1986 p. 151; London 1989 no. 29.
Bibliography: Soffici 1928; Carrà 1943; Zervos 1950; Pacchioni 1959; Taylor 1961; Drudi Gambillo-Fiori 1962; Valsecchi 1962; Pierre 1966; Calvesi 1966; Bigongiari-Carrà, 1970 Plate II.
Reference: Carrà M. gen. cat. vol. I 1967-68 no. 4/10.

Carlo Carrà
Milan Station (*La stazione di Milano*), 1910-11
[p. 322]
Oil on canvas, 50.5 × 54.5 cm. Bottom left: C.D.Carrà. Stuttgart, Staatsgalerie.
Provenance: Berlin, Borchardt.
Exhibitions: Paris 1912 no. 21; London 1912 no. 21; Berlin 1912; Bruxelles 1912 no. 21; Amsterdam 1912; Berlin 1913 no. 14; Milan 1987 no. 12
Bibliography: Carrà 1943 p. 167; Carrieri 1961 p. 48; Calvesi 1967 in *L'Arte Moderna* vol. V p. 86; Martin 1968 p. 117; Bigongiari-Carrà 1970; Roche-Pezard 1983 p. 481.
Reference: Carrà M. gen. cat. vol. I 1967-68 no. 1/11.

Carlo Carrà
Funeral of the Anarchist Galli (*Funerale dell'anarchico Galli*), 1911
[p. 321]
Oil on canvas, 198.7 × 259.1 cm. Bottom left: C. Carrà. New York, Museum of Modern Art.
Provenance: Berlin, Borchardt; Amsterdam, P.Citroen.
Exhibitions: Paris 1912 no. 11; Berlin 1913 no. 6; Leipzig 1914; Venice 1950; Milan 1960; Paris 1973; Venice 1986 p. 153.
Bibliography: Longhi 1937 p. 19; Carrà 1943 p. 155; Pacchioni 1943 Plate 2; Taylor 1961 p. 31; Drudi Gambillo-Fiori 1962 p. 279; Valsecchi 1962 p. 8; Pierre 1966 p. 25; Calvesi 1966 p. 91; Calvesi in *L'Arte moderna* 1967 p. 89; Martin 1968 Plate 55; Bigongiari-Carrà 1970 Plate IV; Carrà 1978 p. 18; Roche-Pezard 1983 p. 481.
Reference: Carrà M. gen. cat. vol. I 1967-68 no. 8/11.

Carlo Carrà
Rhythms of Objects (*Ritmi di oggetti*), 1911
[p. 323]
Oil on canvas, 51 × 66 cm. Bottom left: C. Carrà 911. Milan, Pinacoteca di Brera. Gift of Emilio and Maria Jesi.
Provenance: Milan, Emilio Jesi.
Exhibitions: Rotterdam 1913; Rome 1914; Milan 1942; Bologna 1948; Venice 1958; Milan 1962; Ferrara 1977; Venice 1986 p. 623; Milan 1987 no. 15
Bibliography: Longhi in *La Voce* no. 15 1913; Longhi 1937 p. 9; Torriano 1942 Plate 1; Pacchioni 1945 p. 72; Taylor 1961 p. 76; Valsecchi 1962 p. 11; Drudi Gambillo-Fiori 1962 p. 277; Calvesi in *L'Arte Moderna* 1967 p. 89; Martin 1968 Plate 120; Bigongiari-Carrà 1970 Plate VII; Roche-Pezard 1983 p. 482.
Reference: Carrà M. gen. cat. vol. I 1967-68 no. 7/11.

Carlo Carrà
The Flask (*Il fiasco*), 1915
[p. 324]
Collage and oil on cardboard, 39 × 31.5 cm. Bottom right: C. Carrà 915. Private collection.
Provenance: Milan, Alberto Mazzotta.
Exhibitions: Milan 1917-18; Los Angeles 1970, then New York 1970; Ferrara 1977; Quargnento 1981; Verona 1981-82 p. 16; Milan 1987 no. 20.
Bibliography: Drudi Gambillo-Fiori 1962 p. 291; Bigongiari-Carrà 1970 no. 59; Roche-Pezard 1983 p. 455.
Reference: Carrà M. gen. cat. vol. I 1967-68 no. 4/15.

Carlo Carrà
The Carriage (*La carrozzella*), 1916
[p. 325]
Oil on canvas, 51.5 × 66 cm. Top left: C. Carrà 916. Private collection.
Provenance: Milan, Penazzo; Milan, Carlo Frua.
Exhibitions: Milan 1926; Milan 1942; Zurich 1950; Milan 1962 Plate 10; Iseo 1988 p. 99; Milan 1989 p. 4 (addenda).
Bibliography: *Valori Plastici* January-February 1921 between pp. 12 and 13; Sarfatti 1930; Bertocchi in *L'Italia Letteraria* 8 March 1931; Carrà 1943; Zervos 1950 p. 148; Pacchioni 1959; Valsecchi 1962; Bigongiari-Carrà 1970 Plate XVI-XVII (cover).
Reference: Carrà M. gen. cat. vol. I 1967-68 no. 1/16.

Carlo Carrà
Composition TA or *Still Life* (*Composizione TA* or *Natura morta*), 1916
[p. 326]
Oil on canvas, 70 × 54 cm. Top left: C. CARRÀ 16. Frankfurt, Städelsches Kunstinstitut, on loan from Private collection.
Provenance: Milan, Riccardo Jucker.
Exhibitions: Bologna 1948; Milan 1962; Iseo 1988, p. 103.
Bibliography: Zervos 1950; Raimondi in *Paragone* 1951; Ballo 1956; Valsecchi 1958; Pacchioni 1959; Bigongiari-Carrà 1970 Plate XVIII
Reference: Carrà M. gen. cat. vol. I 1967-68 no. 2/16.

Carlo Carrà
The Metaphysical Muse (La musa metafisica), 1917
[p. 328]
Oil on canvas, 90 × 66 cm. Bottom right: C. Carrà 917. Milan, Pinacoteca di Brera.
Provenance: Rome, Armando Spadini; Milan, Emilio Jesi.
Exhibitions: Milan 1917-18; Rome 1925; Milan 1962; Florence 1967; Berlin 1977; Venice 1979; Milan 1987 no. 22; Iseo 1988 p. 104.
Bibliography: *Valori Plastici* January-February 1921 between pp. 12 and 13; Cecchi in *L'Ambrosiano* 21 April 1925; Soffici 1928; Longhi 1937 Plate VI; Carrà 1943 p. 243; Valsecchi 1958; Pacchioni 1959 Plate 24; Valsecchi 1962 Plate VI; Carrà M. 1968 Plate 15; Bigongiari-Carrà 1970 Plate XXII; Calvesi 1982; Fossati 1982 p. 192.
Reference: Carrà M. gen. cat. 1967-68 vol. I no. 2/17.

Carlo Carrà
The Oval of the Apparitions (L'ovale delle apparizioni), 1918
[p. 329]
Oil on canvas, 92 × 60 cm. Bottom right: C. Carrà 918. Rome, Galleria Nazionale d'Arte Moderna.
Provenance: Zurich, Fleischmann; Milan, Riccardo Jucker.
Exhibitions: Rome 1918; Florence 1921; Milan 1926; Venice 1948; Zurich 1950; Milan 1962; Ferrara 1977 no. 77; Verona 1981-82 p. 16; Iseo 1988 p. 110.
Bibliography: Soffici 1928; Carrà 1943; Appollonio 1950; Zervos 1950; Valsecchi 1958; Pacchioni 1959; Valsecchi 1962; Bigongiari-Carrà 1970 Plate XXVII.
Reference: Carrà M. gen. cat. vol. I 1967-68 no. 1/18.

Carlo Carrà
Lot's Daughters (Le figlie di Loth), 1919
[p. 384]
Oil on canvas, 110 × 80 cm. Top right: C. CARRÀ 919. Private collection.
Provenance: Milan, Umberto Notari; Milan, Galleria del Milione; Milan, Galleria Annunciata; Turin, Galleria Gissi; Cortina d'Ampezzo, Carlo Larese.
Exhibitions: Bruxelles 1950 no. 22; Venice 1950 p. 71 no. 1 (dated 1915); Ferrara 1977 no. 12; Bologna 1980 vol. I, cover, between pp. 80 and 81; Paris 1980-81 pp. 77 and 519, then Berlin 1981 no. 88; Verona 1981 Plate 12; Verona 1988-89, then Milan 1989 no. 3; London 1989 no. 97.
Bibliography: *Valori Plastici* nos. XI-XII November-December 1919; Soffici 1928 Plate 3 (dated 1915); Longhi 1937 Plate III (dated 1915); Pacchioni 1945 p. 72 (dated 1915; II ed. 1959 Plate III); Fossati 1981 between pp. 194 and 195 no. 14; Calvesi 1982 p. 263; Barilli 1984 p. XXXVI Fig. 94; Fossati 1988 between pp. 72 and 73 no. 27.
Reference: Carrà M. gen. cat. vol. I 1967-68 no. 3/19.

Carlo Carrà
Metaphysical Still Life (Natura morta metafisica), 1919
[p. 327]
Oil on canvas, 51 × 46 cm. Top left: C. CARRÀ 19. Private collection.
Provenance: New York, Giuseppe Prezzolini; Milan, Emilio Jesi.
Exhibitions: Rome 1925; Milan 1926; Milan 1962; Florence 1967; Venice 1979; Verona 1981-82 p. 16; Tokyo 1982; Milan 1987 no. 24;

Iseo 1988 p. 111.
Bibliography: George 1932; Pacchioni 1959 Plate 29; Valsecchi 1962 p. 22; Carrà M. 1970 Plate XXIX; Carrà 1978 p. 188; Calvesi 1982 p. 125; Fossati 1982 p. 193.
Reference: Carrà M. gen. cat. col. I 1967-68 p. 1/9.

Carlo Carrà
The Engineer's Lover (L'amante dell'ingegnere), 1921
[p. 385]
Oil on canvas, 55 × 40 cm. Bottom right: C. CARRÀ / 921. Milan, Mattioli Collection.
Provenance: Milan, Mazzucotelli; Brescia, Pietro Feroldi.
Exhibitions: Turin 1923; Milan 1926; Milan 1935; Milan 1942; Venice 1948; New York 1949; Zurich 1950; Livorno 1959; Milan 1962; Iseo 1988 p. 111.
Bibliography: Soffici 1928; Bardi 1930; Sarfatti 1930; Longhi 1937; Torriano 1942; Piovene 1942; Repaci in *L'illustrazione italiana* 14 June 1942; Carrà 1943; Pacchioni 1945; Zervos 1950; Valsecchi 1958; Valsecchi 1962; Calvesi 1966; Bigongiari-Carrà 1970 Plate XXVIII.
Reference: Carrà M. gen. cat. vol. I 1967-68 no. 7/21.

Carlo Carrà
Saint Anne's Mill (Il mulino di Sant'Anna), 1921
[p. 387]
Oil on canvas, 91 × 69 cm. Bottom left: Carrà 921. Albinea, Reggio Emilia. Achille and Ida Maramotti Collection.
Provenance: Milan, Rino Valdameri; Varese, Gabbrielli Scalini.
Exhibitions: Milan 1942; Milan 1962; Milan 1987 no. 27.
Bibliography: Masciotta in *Letteratura* July-September 1941; Torriano 1942 Plate XII; Catalano 1945 Plate 3; Pacchioni 1959 Plate 32; Carrà M. 1968 Plate 39; Bigongiari-Carrà 1970 Plate XXXIII; Fossati 1981 Plate 34.
Reference: Carrà M. gen. cat. vol. I 1967-68 no. 4/21.

Carlo Carrà
The Pine Tree by the Sea (Il pino sul mare), 1921
[p. 386]
Oil on canvas, 68 × 52.5 cm. Bottom right: C. CARRÀ 921. Private collection.
Provenance: Rome, Alfredo Casella.
Exhibitions: Berlin 1921, then Hannover 1921 no. 4, then Hamburg 1921; Rome 1925 p. 32 no. 42; Milan 1942 p. 8 no. 42; Venice 1950 p. 72 no. 2; Rome 1955-56, cover, Plate 23; Milan 1962, cover, Plate 26; Rome 1972-73 p. 262 no. 54 and Plate 54; Paris 1980-81 p. 95 and p. 519, then Berlin 1981 no. 99; Milan 1987, cover, no. 25; Verona 1988-89 no. 4, then Milan 1989; London 1989 no. 96.
Bibliography: Worringer *Wissen und Leben* no. 18 10 November 1925 p. 1165 and p. 1169; Longhi 1937 Plate XI; Carrà 1943 p. 358; Zervos in *Cahiers d'Art I* 1950 p. 159; Fossati 1981 between pp. 194 and 195 no. 33; Fossati 1988 between pp. 72 and 73 no. 53.
Reference: Carrà M. gen. cat. vol. I 1967-68 no. 1/21.

Carlo Carrà
The House of Love (La casa dell'amore), 1922
[p. 389]
Oil on canvas, 90 × 70 cm. Top left: C. CARRÀ 922. Milan, Pinacoteca di Brera.
Provenance: Milan, Emilio Jesi.
Exhibitions: Rome 1925; Milan 1942; Milan 1962; Florence 1967; Paris 1980-81, then Berlin

1981; Milan 1987 no. 31; London 1989 no. 95.
Bibliography: Thovez in *Gazzetta del Popolo* 5 May 1922; Zervos 1950 p. 194; Pacchioni 1959 Plate 35; Valsecchi 1962 p. 4; Carrà 1968 Plate 39; Bigongiari-Carrà 1970 Plate XXXIV; Carrà 1978 p. 220.
Reference: Carrà M. gen. cat. 1967-68 no. 8/22.

Carlo Carrà
The Dioscuri (I dioscuri), 1922
[p. 390]
Oil on canvas, 52 × 67 cm. Top left: C. CARRÀ 922. Private collection.
Provenance: Stuttgart, Kaemerer.
Exhibitions: Milan 1962; Milan 1987 no. 33.
Bibliography: Thovez in *Gazzetta del Popolo* 5 May 1922; Sarfatti 1930 p. 152; Bigongiari-Carrà 1970 no. 101; Carrà 1978 p. 255.
Reference: Carrà M. gen. cat. vol. I 1967-68 no. 13/22.

Carlo Carrà
The Wait (L'attesa), 1926
[p. 388]
Oil on canvas, 95 × 100 cm. Bottom, toward right: C. CARRÀ 926. Private collection.
Provenance: Rome Alfredo Casella.
Exhibitions: Venice 1926 p. 32 no. 12 and Plate 163; Milan 1942 p. 7 no. 27; Milan 1962 Plate 37; Ferrara 1977 no. 21; Acqui Terme 1979 no. 9 and Plate 3; Bologna 1980 vol. I p. 83; Paris 1980-81, then Berlin 1981 no. 33; Verona 1981-82 Plate 23; Milan 1987 no. 46; Verona 1988-89 no. 5, then Milan 1989.
Bibliography: *Il Novecento italiano — Rassegna di pittura e scultura* no. 2 Summer 1926 Plate 20; Pica 1926 p. 30; Longhi 1937 Plate XV; Torriano 1942 p. 13; Zervos 1950 p. 196; Clair *Cahiers du Musée national d'art moderne* nos. 7-8 1981 no. 13; Calvesi 1982 p. 263.
Reference: Carrà M. gen. cat. vol. I 1967-68 no. 11/26.

Carlo Carrà
The Swimmers (I nuotatori), 1929
[p. 391]
Oil on canvas, 88 × 138 cm. Bottom right: C. CARRÀ 929. Milan, Private collection.
Provenance: Milan, Pallini; Milan, Scalvini.
Exhibitions: Milan 1933; Milan 1942; Milan 1962; Verona 1981-82 p. 16; London 1989 no. 99.
Bibliography: Bardi 1930; Rogers in *L'Italia Letteraria* 5 February 1933; Carrà 1943; Pacchioni 1959; Bigongiari-Carrà 1970 Plate LVII.
Reference: Carrà M. gen. cat. vol. I 1967-68 no. 8/29.

Felice Casorati
The Woman and the Suit of Armor (La donna e l'armatura), 1921.
[p. 392]
Tempera on canvas, 148.5 × 144 cm. Bottom left: F. CASORATI 1921. Turin, Museo Civico, Galleria d'Arte Moderna.
Provenance: Turin, Ettore de Fornaris.
Exhibitions: Venice 1952 no. 11; Turin 1964 no. 55; Florence 1976 no. 30; Paris 1980-81 p. 56; Ferrara 1981 no. 24; Turin 1985 no. 15 and cover.
Bibliography: Venturi in *Dedalo* September 1923 pp. 248-260; Giolli 1925 Plate 4; Guzzi 1931 p. 61; Galvano 1947 Plate V; Carluccio 1964 no. 214; Carluccio 1980 no. 33.

Felice Casorati
Midday (Meriggio), 1923
[p. 393]
Oil on canvas, 120 × 130 cm. Left center: F.

Critical References

CASORATI. Trieste, Civico Museo Revoltella. Galleria d'Arte Moderna.
Provenance: purchased at the Venice Biennale 1924.
Exhibitions: Venice 1924 no. 8 Plate 19; New York 1926 no. 16; Paris 1935 no. 35; Turin 1964 no. 59; Paris 1980-81 p. 55; Ferrara 1981 no. 27; Turin 1985 no. 19; London 1989 no. 114.
Bibliography: Venturi in *Dedalo* September 1923 pp. 242, 257 and 260; Giollio 1925 pp. 6-8; Sarfatti in *Rivista Illustrata* 15 ?? 1925 p. 30; Galvano 1947 Plate IX; Carluccio 1964 no. 48; Molesi 1970 Plate 39; Carluccio 1980 no. 46.

Felice Casorati
Platonic Conversation (Conversazione platonica), 1925
[p. 395]
Oil on wood, 78 × 100 cm. Bottom right: F. CASORATI. Private collection.
Provenance: Rome, Alfredo Casella.
Exhibitions: Milan 1926 no. 25; Geneva 1927 no. 18; Zurich 1927 no. 28; Pittsburgh 1927 no. 371; New York 1949 p. 128; Turin 1964 no. 78 and Plate 45; Ferrara 1981 no. 33 and Plate 15; Milan 1983 Plate 30; Turin 1985 no. 24; Verona 1988-89 no. 17, then Milan 1989.
Bibliography: Forbees in *The Arts* November 1927 pp. 265 and 269; Costantini 1934 p. 230; Carluccio 1964 no. 91; Fossati 1982 p. 221.

Felice Casorati
Raja, c.1925
[p. 394]
Tempera on wood, 120 × 100 cm. Bottom, toward right: F. CASORATI. Private collection.
Provenance: Turin, Galleria La Bussola.
Exhibitions: Venice 1925 Plate 2; Turin 1985 (not in catalogue); Verona 1988-89 no. 18, then Milan 1989.
Bibliography: Giolli 1925 Plate 24 (dated 1924); Carluccio 1964 no. 217 and Plate 217 (dated 1923); Carluccio 1980 no. 36 (dated 1923).

Giorgio De Chirico
Nude (Nu aux cheveux noirs), c. 1911
[p. 330]
Oil on canvas, 71 × 56 cm. Right, toward top: G. de Chirico. Private collection.
Provenance: Paris, Paul Guillaume; Brussels, René Gaffé; Milan, Galleria Levi.
Exhibitions: Paris 1926 no. 32; Berlin 1930 no. 2; London 1937 no. 2; London 1938 no. 1 *(Nude)*.
Bibliography: Soby 1955 no. 197; Bruni Sakraischik 1974 vol. V tome I no. 297; Fagiolo 1981 no. 20.
Reference: Fagiolo 1984 no. 37.

Giorgio De Chirico
Autumnal Meditation (La Méditation automnale), 1912
[p. 331]
Oil on canvas, 55.7 × 70 cm. Right toward bottom: Georgio de Chirico 1912. Private collection.
Provenance: Paris, Paul Guillaume; Paris, Mme André Peignot; New York, Joseph Slifka.
Exhibitions: Paris 1918 no. 15; Paris 1922 no. 34; New York 1982 Plate 11; Munich 1982-83 Plate 4, then Paris 1983.
Bibliography: Fagiolo 1981 no. 17; Bruni Sakraischik 1983 vol. VII tome I no. 386.
Reference: Fagiolo 1984 Plate VII.

Giorgio De Chirico
Melancholy (Melanconia), 1912

[p. 332]
Oil on canvas, 80 × 63 cm. Right, toward bottom: G. de Chirico 1912. Salome and Eric Estorick Collection.
Provenance: Brussels, René Gaffé; London, Peter Watson.
Exhibitions: Brussels 1934; London 1936 no. 54; London 1937 no. 1; New York 1982 Plate 12; Munich 1982-83 Plate 12; Paris 1983; London 1989 no. 42.
Bibliography: *Minotaure* no. 8 June 1936; Champigneulle 1939 p. 83; Soby 1941 no. 7; Soby 1955 no. 169; Bruni Sakraischik 1974 vol. IV tome I no. 257; Fagiolo 1981 no. 30.
Reference: Fagiolo 1984 no. 52.

Giorgio De Chirico
The Tower (La torre), c.1913
[p. 335]
Oil on canvas, 115.5 × 45 cm. Right, toward bottom: G. de Chirico. Zurich, Kunsthaus.
Provenance: Paris, Mouradran; Paris, Bernard Poissonnier.
Exhibitions: London 1936 no. 46; Paris 1937 no. 99; New York 1982 Plate 20; Munich 1982-83 Plate 9, then Paris 1983; London 1989 no. 43.
Bibliography: *Dictionnaire Biographique des Artistes Contemporains 1910-30* 1930 p. 291; Soby 1941 no. 5; Soby 1955 no. 172; Bruni Sakraischik 1971 vol. I tome I no. 7; Fagiolo 1981 no. 38.
Reference: Fagiolo 1984 no. 36.

Giorgio De Chirico
Ariadne (Ariadne o Piazza con Arianna), 1913
[p. 336]
Oil on canvas, 134.6 × 179.7 cm. Right, toward bottom: Georgio/G. de Chirico MCMXIII. New York, The Metropolitan Museum of Art.
Provenance: Paris, Jean Paulhan; Chicago, Samuel A. Marx.
Exhibitions: Rome 1965.
Bibliography: Soby 1955 no. 178; Fagiolo 1981 no. 29.
Reference: Fagiolo 1984 no. 26.

Giorgio De Chirico
The Child's Brain (Le cerveau de l'enfant), 1914
[p. 339]
Oil on canvas, 80 × 65 cm. Bottom left: G. de Chirico 1914. Stockholm, Moderna Museet.
Provenance: Paris, Paul Guillaume; Paris, André Breton.
Exhibitions: Geneva 1920-21 no. 40; Paris 1928; Brussels 1934 no. 23; New York 1936 no. 194; Paris 1960-61 no. 101; New York 1982 Plate 33; Munich 1982-83 Plate 20, then Paris 1983.
Bibliography: Peret in *Littérature* no. 4 September 1922 p. 24; Breton 1928 no. 26; Soby 1941 no. 230; Soby 1955 no. 193; Bruni Sakraischik 1972 vol. II tome I no. 106; Fagiolo 1981 no. 52.
Reference: Fagiolo 1984 no. 55 Plate XVII.

Giorgio De Chirico
The Enigma of Fate (L'énigme de la fatalité), 1914
[p. 334]
Oil on canvas, 138 × 95.5 cm. Basel, Kunstmuseum.
Exhibitions: New York 1982 no. 37; Munich 1982-83 no. 26, then Paris 1983; London 1989 no. 45.
Bibliography: *La révolution Surréaliste* no. 7 1926; Breton 1928; *London Bulletin* June 1938 p. 13 *(The Anxious Journey)*; Soby 1941 no. 39; Soby 1955 no. 198; Bruni Sakraischik 1971 vol. I tome I no. 16; Fagiolo 1981 no. 63.
Reference: Fagiolo 1984 no. 64.

Giorgio De Chirico
The Enigma of a Day (L'énigme d'une journée), 1914
[p. 333]
Oil on canvas, 185.5 × 139.7 cm. Bottom right: G. de Chirico 1914. New York, The Museum of Modern Art.
Provenance: Paris, Galerie Surréaliste; Paris, André Breton.
Exhibitions: Paris 1915 no. 684; New York 1935 no. 8; New York 1936 no. 19; New York 1982 Plate 29; Munich 1982-83 Plate 17, then Paris 1983.
Bibliography: Breton 1928 p. 23; *Le Surréalisme au service de la Révolution* no. 6 1933; Soby 1941 no. 27; Soby 1955 no. 189; Bruni Sakraischik 1971 vol. I tome I no. 20; Fagiolo 1981 no. 47.

Giorgio De Chirico
Gare Montparnasse — Parting Sadness (Gare Montparnasse — La mélancolie du départ), 1914
[p. 337]
Oil on canvas, 140 × 184.5 cm. Bottom left: G. de Chirico 1914. New York, The Museum of Modern Art.
Provenance: Paris, Pierre Loeb; New York, Matisse Gallery; New Canaan, James T. Soby.
Exhibitions: Lucerne 1935 no. 7; New York 1940 no. 8; New York 1943 no. 7; New York 1982 no. 19, then Paris 1982-83.
Bibliography: Zervos 1938; Soby 1941 no. 24; Soby 1955 no. 91; Bruni Sakraischik 1971 vol. I tome I no. 17; Fagiolo 1981 no. 45.
Reference: Fagiolo 1984 no. 46.

Giorgio De Chirico
Premonitory Portrait of Guillaume Apollinaire (Ritratto premonitore di Guillaume Apollinaire), 1914
[p. 338]
Oil on canvas, 81.5 × 65 cm. Bottom right: G. de Chirico 1914. Paris, Musée national d'art moderne, Centre Georges Pompidou.
Provenance: Paris, Paul Guillaume; Paris, Bernard Poissonnier.
Exhibitions: Paris 1934; Paris 1937 no. 37; Paris 1942; Rome 1981-82 no. 9; New York 1982 Plate 41; Munich 1982-83 Plate 28, then Paris 1983.
Bibliography: Diolé in *Les Expo* 30 March 1934; Soby 1955 no. 201; Bruni Sakraischik 1972 vol. II tome I no. 105; Fagiolo 1981 no. 54.
Reference: Fagiolo 1984 no. 56 Plate XIX.

Giorgio De Chirico
The Astronomer — The Uneasiness of Life (L'astronome — L'inquiétude de la vie), c.1915
[p. 341]
Oil on canvas, 41 × 33.2 cm. Bottom right: G. de Chirico. Private collection.
Provenance: Paris, Paul Guillaume; Paris, Jean de Hacebo.
Exhibitions: Houston 1955 no. 12; New York 1982 no. 51; Munich 1982-83 Plate 36, then Paris 1983.
Bibliography: *Sélection* 1929 p. 44; Ribemont-Dessaignes 1930; Soby 1955 no. 209; Fagiolo 1981 no. 80.
Reference: Fagiolo 1984 no. 84.

Giorgio De Chirico
Perspective with Toys (Prospettiva con giocattoli), c.1915
[p. 340]
Oil on canvas, 55 × 46 cm. Center bottom: G. de Chirico. Houston, The Menil Collection.
Provenance: Paris, Paul Guillaume; Paris, Jacques Doucet.

Exhibitions: Paris 1984.
Bibliography: *L'Illustration* 1930; *L'Œil* 1961 no. 19; Fagiolo 1981 no. 69; Calvesi in *Art Dossier* no. 28 October 1988.
Reference: Fagiolo 1984 no. 69.

Giorgio De Chirico
Metaphysical Interior with Large Factory (Interno metafisico con grande officina), 1916
[p. 343]
Oil on canvas, 96.3 × 73.8 cm. Center left: G. de Chirico, 1916. Stuttgart, Staatsgallerie.
Provenance: Milan, Carlo Frua de Angelis.
Exhibitions: Berlin 1921, then Hannover 1921, then Hamburg 1921; Milan 1939 no. 7; New York 1949 no. 34; Munich 1982-83 Plate 49, then Paris 1983; London 1989 no. 48.
Bibliography: *Valori Plastici* September-October 1920 between pp. 84 and 85; Ravegnani in *Corriere Padano* 5 November 1939; Bruni Sakraischik 1972 vol. II tome I no. 112.
Reference: Fagiolo 1984 no. 119.

Giorgio De Chirico
The Revolt of the Wise Man (La révolte du sage), 1916
[p. 344]
Oil on canvas, 67.3 × 59 cm. Bottom right: G. De Chirico, 1916. Salome and Eric Estorick Collection.
Provenance: Brussels, René Gaffé; London, Roland Penrose.
Exhibitions: Paris 1922; Paris 1926 no. 3; Venice 1948 no. 20; New York 1982 Plate 66; Munich 1982-83 Plate 48, then Paris 1983; London 1989 no. 51.
Bibliography: Ternovetz 1928; Bruni Sakraischik 1973 vol. III tome I no. 174.
Reference: Fagiolo 1984 no. 108.

Giorgio De Chirico
The Melancholy of Leavetaking (La mélancolie du départ), 1916-17
[p. 342]
Oil on canvas, 51.8 × 25.9 cm. Top right: G. de Chirico. London, The Tate Gallery.
Provenance: Brussels, René Gaffé; London, Roland Penrose.
Exhibitions: Paris 1926 no. 13; New York 1982 no. 62; Munich 1982-83 no. 44, then Paris 1983.
Bibliography: Bruni Sakraischik 1971 vol. I tome I no. 36.
Reference: Fagiolo 1984 no. 103 Plate XXVII.

Giorgio De Chirico
Roman Villa (Villa romana), 1922
[p. 396]
Tempera on canvas, 101.5 × 75.5 cm. Center of frame: G. de Chirico, 1922. Palino Inc.
Provenance: Mexico City, Bruno Pagliai.
Exhibitions: Florence 1922, no. 20; New York 1949 p. 55; Florence 1967 n.940; New York 1982 no. 82; Venice 1988-89 no. 36 Plate 35.
Bibliography: Courthion in *Sélection* VII 1929 p. 59; Pica 1967, 1944 Plate 10; Soby 1941 no. 139; Bruni Sakraischik 1974 vol. IV tome I no. 280.
Reference: Fagiolo 1984 no. 182 Plate XLIII.

Giorgio de Chirico
The Dream of the Poet Atenai (Il sogno del poeta Atenai), 1925
[p. 397]
Oil on masonite, 34.3 × 25.4 cm. Houston, The Menil Collection.
Provenance: Paris, Alexander Jolas; New York, Hugo Gallery.
Exhibitions: Houston 1955 no. 17; Washington 1983 no. 6.

Giorgio De Chirico
Two Horses on the Seashore (Due cavalli davanti al mare), 1926
[p. 401]
Oil on canvas, 100 × 81 cm. Top right: G. de Chirico, 1926. Private collection.
Provenance: Paris, Galerie L'Effort Moderne, no. 8701; Prato, Galleria d'Arte Moderna Farsetti.
Exhibitions: Milan (Fiera), 1985, p. 45.
Bibliography: *Bulletin de L'Effort Moderne*, no. 32, February 1927; Vitrac, 1927, p. 57; Baldacci-Fagiolo, 1982, no. 117.
Reference: cat. Verona, 1986-87, p. 126.

Giorgio De Chirico
The Prodigal Son (Il Figliuol prodigo), 1926
[p. 399]
Oil on canvas, 100 × 80 cm. Right, toward top: G. de Chirico/1926. Private collection.
Provenance: Paris, Galerie L'Effort Moderne; Florence, Giorgio Castelfranco; Milan, Galleria del Milione no. 1697; Turin, Galleria Gissi no. 1377.
Exhibitions: London, 1928 no. 22; Milan 1941 no. 17; Turin 1967-68 no. 151; Milan 1970 no. 73, then Hannover 1970; Venice 1988-89 no. 48 Plate 47; London 1989 no. 69.
Bibliography: Sitwell *Drawing and Design* no. 28 October 1928 p. 270; Lo Duca 1945 Plate XVII; Bruni Sakraischik 1972 vol. II tome I no. 135; Baldacci-Fagiolo 1982 Plate V no. 37.
Reference: cat. Verona 1986-87 p. 100.

Giorgio De Chirico
The Banks of the Thessaly (Le rive della Tessaglia), 1926
[p. 402]
Oil on canvas, 93 × 73 cm. Bottom left: G. de Chirico. Puos d'Alpago, Augusto Vallunga Collection.
Provenance: Paris, Galerie Renou et Colle; Los Angeles, Dalzell Hatfield Galleries; New York, Sotheby Parke-Bernet.
Exhibitions: Milan, 1985 no. 7; London 1989 no. 72.
Bibliography: Venturi 1947 pl.41; Bruni Sakraischik 1987 vol. VIII, tome I no. 503.

Giorgio De Chirico
Cruel Acts of Tenderness (Les Tendresses cruelles), 1926
[p. 398]
Pastels on papier velours, 100 × 80 cm. Toward center left: G. de Chirico. Private collection.
Provenance: Paris, Paul Guillaume; Paris, André Pieyre de Mandiargues.
Exhibitions: Paris 1926 no. 23; Milan 1971.
Bibliography: Vitrac 1927 no. 63; Raynal 1927 no. 101; George 1928 Plate IX.
Reference: Baldacci-Fagiolo 1982 no. 78.

Giorgio De Chirico
Female Nude in an Interior or *The Spirit of Domination (Nudo femminile in un interno* or *L'esprit de domination)*, 1927
[p. 403]
Oil on canvas, 89 × 116 cm.
Right toward center: G. de Chirico/1927. Milan, Private collection.
Provenance: Paris, Paul Guillaume; New York, E. A. Silbermann; New York, Perls Galleries; Milan, Galleria Philippe Daverio.
Exhibitions: Milan 1982 no. 4; Munich 1982-83 no. 83, then Paris 1983 no. 81, London 1989 no. 73.
Bibliography: Baldacci-Fagiolo 1982 p. 109 (part.) Plate XXI no. 65; Bruni Sakraischik

1983, vol. VII tome I no. 433.
Reference: cat. Verona 1986-87 p. 144.

Giorgio De Chirico
Furniture in the Valley (Meubles dans une vallée), 1927
[p. 406]
Oil on canvas, 100 × 135 cm. Bottom right: G. de Chirico. Verona, Galleria dello Scudo.
Provenance: Milan, Adriano Pallini.
Exhibitions: London 1989 no. 74.
Bibliography: *Bulletin de L'Effort Moderne* 1927 no. 38; George 1928 Plate XXII; Barbaroux-Giani 1940; Bruni Sakraischik 1971 vol. I tome I no. 77; Fagiolo-Baldacci 1982 Plate XXII and p. 530.

Giorgio De Chirico
Rearing Horses (Chevaux se cabrant), 1927-28
[p. 400]
Oil on canvas, 131 × 98 cm, Top left: G. de Chirico. Private collection.
Provenance: Paris, Léonce Rosenberg (no. 1043).
Exhibitions: London, 1928, no. 13.
Bibliography: Rutter 1928 no. 206; Sitwell in *Drawing and Design* no. 28 October 1928 no. 266; Lo Duca 1945 Plate XXVIII.
Reference: Baldacci-Fagiolo 1982 no. 143, Plate XXVI.

Giorgio De Chirico
Victory (La vittoria), 1928
[p. 404]
Oil on canvas, 160 × 240 cm. Top left: G. de Chirico. Milan, Private collection.
Provenance: Paris, Léonce Rosenberg; Milan, Galleria del Milione; Milan, Rino Valdameri.
Exhibitions: Milan, 1939, not in catalogue; Rome, 1942 no. 70 (*Il Trionfo*, dated 1927); Milan 1970 no. 87 (dated 1928); London 1989 no. 76.
Bibliography: George, *Formes*, no. 1 January 1930, between pp. 12 and 13; Lo Duca 1945 Plate XXXIII (*Il trionfatore* dated 1928); Bruni Sakraischik 1973 vol. III tome I no. 237 (dated 1928); Baldacci-Fagiolo 1982 p. 541 no. 216.
Reference: catalogue Milan 1987 p. 240.

Giorgio De Chirico
Battle of the Gladiators in the Room (Le Combat), 1928-29
[p. 405]
Oil on canvas, 160 × 240 cm. Center, toward right: G. de Chirico, Milan, Civico Museo d'Arte Contemporanea.
Provenance: Paris, Léonce Rosenberg; Milan, Antonio Boschi and Marieda di Stefano.
Exhibitions: Milan 1930 Plate 5 (part./not exhibited); Milan 1970 no. 88 (*La scuola dei gladiatori: il combattimento — The School for Gladiators: The Combat*), dated 1928); Venice 1979 no. 40 (*La scuola dei gladiatori*) dated 1928); Rome 1981-82 no. 63.
Bibliography: *Sélection* no. 8 1929 p. 74; George *Formes* no. 1 January 1930 between pp. 12 and 13; Lo Duca 1936 Plate XXV (*La Mischia*, dated 1928); Bruni Sakraischik 1973 vol. III tome I no. 236 (*La scuola dei gladiatori: il combattimento*, dated 1928); Baldacci-Fagiolo 1982 p. 541 no. 215.
Reference: cat. Milan 1987 p. 238.

Giorgio De Chirico
The Prodigal Son - Overture to the Dance (Il figliol prodigo - L'ouverture du bal), 1929
[p. 407]
Oil on canvas, 81 × 65 cm. Bottom right: G. de Chirico. Milan, Private collection.

737

Critical References

Provenance: Paris, Jean Bonjean; Milan, Galleria Milano.
Exhibitions: Cortina d'Ampezzo 1941; Madrid 1948.
Bibliography: Ribemont-Dessaignes 1930; Carrieri 1939 no. 61; Bruni Sakraischik 1987 vol. VIII no. 518.
Reference: Baldacci-Fagiolo 1982 no. 253.

Giorgio De Chirico
Visit to the Mysterious Baths (Visita ai bagni misteriosi), 1935
[p. 408]
Oil on canvas, 38 × 46 cm. Bottom right: G. de Chirico. Private collection.
Provenance: New York, Kleeman Galleries.
Exhibitions: Ume/lecké Besedy 1935 no. 29.
Bibliography: Fagiolo 1988, no. 122.

Giorgio De Chirico
The Mysterious Baths (Les bains mystérieux), 1934
[p. 409]
Oil on canvas, 36.6 × 26.6 cm. Bottom right: G. de Chirico. New York, Private collection.
Exhibitions: Milan 1970 no. 99; New York 1982 no. 95; Munich 1982-83 no. 91, then Paris 1983 no. 88.
Bibliography: Bruni Sakraischik 1973 vol. III tome II no. 217; Far-Porzio 1979 p. 294 no. 179 (dated 1935).

Fortunato Depero
The Toga and the Woodworm (La toga e il tarlo), 1914
[p. 411]
Varnished cardboard and wood, 58 × 54 × 10 cm. First cardboards, 1914. Trento, Museo Provinciale d'Arte (Inventory no. MPA 209).
Provenance: Rome, Emilio Villa.
Exhibitions: Trento 1914; Bassano 1970 no. 26 p. 237; Paris 1986 p. 46 no. 43; Rovereto 1988-89, then Düsseldorf 1989.
Bibliography: Passamani 1981 no. 38; Scudiero 1987 Plate 4.
References: Catalogue Rovereto 1988-89 no. I.6.

Fortunato Depero
Soldier-boy Hop Hop (Soldatino Hop Hop), 1917
[p. 410]
Varnished wood, 39 × 19 × 20 cm. Turin, Galleria Narciso.
Provenance: Trento, Bruno Mattedi.
Exhibitions: Rome 1969-70 no. 46 (*Marionetta soldatino Hop-Hop*); Bassano 1970 no. 94 p. 252; Turin 1974 no. 5.
Bibliography: Passamani 1981 no. 131.

Fortunato Depero
My "Plastic Dances" (Plastic Complex — Dancers) (I miei "Balli Plastici" (Complesso plastico — Ballerini), 1918
[p. 413]
Oil on canvas, 180 × 190 cm. Bottom left: Fortunato Depero. Private collection.
Provenance: Milan, Gianni Mattioli.
Exhibitions: Florence 1918 no. 113; Milan 1919 no. 53, then Genoa 1919 idem; Milan 1921 no. 84 (dated 1919), then Rome 1921; Monza 1923 p. 120 (*Automi?*); Turin 1969 no. 57; Bassano 1970 no. 159 Plate V; Rovereto 1988-89, then Düsseldorf 1989.
Bibliography: *Noi* nos.6-7-8 1924 p. 33 (*Scène-Décor*); in *Comoedia* no. 23 1 December 1925 p. 1198; *Theatre Magazine* March 1930 p. 43 (*I pupazzetti*); Depero 1940 p. 209; Depero 1947 between pp. 24 and 25 (*Plastic dances — new puppet theatre*); Passamani 1981 no. 147; Scudiero 1987 Plate 25.
Reference: Catalogue Rovereto 1988-89 no. 10.

Fortunato Depero
Rubber Jack-in-the-box Devils (Diavoli di cauccíù a scatto), 1919
[p. 412]
Oil on canvas, 125 × 110 cm. Bottom left: Depero/1919 - VIAREGGIO. Private collection.
Provenance: Pallanza, Fedele Azari; Milan, Gianni Mattioli.
Exhibitions: Milan 1919 no. 60 p. 11, then Genoa 1919 idem; Milan 1921 no. 85, then Rome 1921 idem; Florence 1967 p. XXI no. 39 (*Diavoli di cauccíù*); Bassano 1970 no. 180 Plate VI; Rovereto 1988-89 no. 14, then Düsseldorf 1989.
Bibliography: Depero 1940 p. 130 (*Diavoli di cauccíù*); Depero 1947 betwen pp. 32 and 33 (*India-rubber devils*); Giani 1951 Plates 14-15; Drudi Gambillo-Fiori 1962 vol. II p. 351 no. 6; Passamani 1981 no. 161; Scudiero 1987 Plate 29.
Reference: Catalogue Rovereto 1988-89 no. 14.

Filippo De Pisis
Western Still Life (Natura morta occidentale), 1919
[p. 345]
Mixed media and collage on cardboard, 36 × 27 cm. Bottom right: de Pisis/5 XII 19/Natura morta occidentale. Private collection.
Provenance: Paris, André Pieyre de Mandiargues.
Exhibitions: Verona 1969 no. 6; Venice 1979; Brugherio 1980 no. 7; Geneva 1980-81.
Bibliography: Ballo 1968 no. 36 and cover.

Filippo De Pisis
The Fateful Hour (L'ora fatale), 1919
[p. 345]
Tempera and collage on linen paper 32 × 22.5 cm. Bottom, toward center: De Pisis "L'ora fatale" 1100. Milan, Private collection.
Exhibitions: Verona 1969 no. 4; Brugherio 1980 no. 8; Milan 1983 p. 66; Venice 1983 p. 9; Comacchio 1986 no. 3.
Bibliography: Ballo 1968 no. 32.

Filippo De Pisis
Still Life with "Capricho" by Goya or *Still Life with Feather-duster (Natura morta con "Capriccio" di Goya o Natura morta con piumino)*, 1925
[p. 417]
Oil on canvas, 68.5 × 86.5 cm. Bottom right: DE PISIS, 925. Private collection.
Provenance: Milan, Antonio Mazzotta.
Exhibitions: Florence 1941 no. 3 Plate II; Ferrara 1951 no. 21; Rome 1955-56 p. 56 no. 33 (*Stanza con piumino*); Verona 1969 no. 48; Venice 1983 no. 22; Verona 1987-88 no. 2, then Rome 1988 idem; London 1989 no. 83.
Bibliography: Cavicchioli 1942 Plate 7; Raimondi 1944 Plate V (*Natura morta*); Castelfranco-Valsecchi 1956 Plate LXXVI; Ballo 1968 no. 178.

Filippo De Pisis
Still Life with Kingfisher (Natura morta con il martin pescatore), 1925
[p. 414]
Oil on cardboard, 47 × 73 cm. Bottom right: De Pisis/Ferrara 7 XII 925. Ferrara, Private collection.
Exhibitions: Ferrara 1973 p. 21; Verona 1978-79; Brugherio 1980 no. 14; Venice 1983 no. 23; Comacchio 1986 no. 13.

Filippo De Pisis
Sacred Fish (I pesci sacri), 1925
[p. 415]

Oil on canvas, 55 × 62.5 cm. Bottom right: DE PISIS-25. Milan, Pinacoteca di Brera.
Provenance: Milan, Emilio Jesi.
Exhibitions: Ferrara 1951 no. 16; Verona 1969 no. 45; Venice 1979; Bologna 1980 p. 405.
Bibliography: Raimondi 1952; Valsecchi 1956 no. 4; Ballo 1968 no. 181.

Filippo De Pisis
Marine Still Life with Lobster (Natura morta marina con Aragosta), 1926
[p. 416]
Oil on canvas, 56 × 88 cm. Bottom right: DE PISIS 26. Rome, Galleria dell'Oca.
Provenance: from the Artist.
Exhibitions: Ferrara 1951 no. 28; Verona 1969 no. 51; Venice 1983 no. 28; Verona 1987-88 no. 6, then Rome 1988 idem; London 1989 no. 84.
Bibliography: George 1928 Plate XII (*Nature morte marine*); Solmi 1931 Plate 6 (*Natura morta*); Brandi 1932 in *Dedalo* Issue V p. 402 (*La casa rosa*); Raimondi 1952 p. 34; Ballo 1968 no. 147.

Filippo De Pisis
The Large Shell (La grande conchiglia), 1927
[p. 418]
Oil on canvas, 55 × 42 cm. Bottom right: DE PISIS 27. Private collection.
Provenance: Milan, Cesare Tosi.
Exhibitions: Ferrara 1951 no. 40; Geneva 1965 no,42 (*Coquillage*, dated 1925-26); Verona 1969 no. 44 (dated 1925); Venice 1983 no. 27 (dated 1925); Verona 1987-88 no. 13, then Rome 1988.
Bibliography: Ballo 1968 no. 46 (dated 1925).

Filippo De Pisis
Still Life with Glass and Bread (Natura morta con bicchiere e pane), 1930
[p. 419]
Oil on canvas, 64 × 91 cm. Bottom right: de Pisis 30. Private collection.
Provenance: Milan, Antoinio Mazzotta.
Exhibitions: Venice 1956 no. 18; Verona 1969 no. 117; Brugherio 1980 no. 21; Venice 1983 no. 63; Comacchio 1986 no. 32.
Bibliography: Raimondi 1952 Plate VIII; Ballo 1968 no. 61.

Filippo De Pisis
Sacred Bread (Pane sacro), 1930
[p. 420]
Oil on canvas, 100 × 65 cm. Bottom right: de Pisis 30. Private collection.
Provenance: Milan, Galleria del Milione (no. 6489).
Exhibitions: Venice 1979 no. 89; Verona 1987-88 no. 25, then Rome 1988; London 1989 no. 85.
Bibliography: Ballo 1968 no. 58.

Filippo De Pisis
Little Nude on Tiger Skin (Nudino sulla pelle di tigre), 1931
[p. 421]
Oil on canvas, 60 × 91 cm. Bottom right: DE PISIS 31. Venice, Private collection.
Provenance: Venice, Carlo Cardazzo; Venice, Galleria del Cavallino (no. 1002).
Exhibitions: Rome 1941 no. 33 (*Il leone*); Ivrea 1954 no. 32 (*Nudino sulla pelle di leopardo*); Venice 1956 p. 73 no. 24; Verona 1969 no. 141; Venice 1983 no. 79 (*Nudino sulla pelle di tigre*); Verona 1987-88 no. 35, then Rome 1988.
Bibliography: Raimondi 1953 Plate 41 (*Nudino sulla pelle di leopardo*); Ballo 1968 no. 226 (*Nudo sulla pelle di tigre*); Bertelli-Briganti-Giuliano vol. IV 1986 p. 271 no. 33.

Nicolay Diulgheroff
Equilibrio Spirituale (Spiritual Balance), 1923
[p. 422]
Oil on canvas, 79 × 63 cm. Below center:
DIULGHEROFF. Turin, Galleria Narciso.
Exhibitions: Turin 1930 no. 14; Turin 1962 no.
87; Torre Pellice 1976 Plate 1; Turin 1982 Plate
1.
Bibliography: *Bollettino Belle Arti* no. 1 January-
February 1982.

Nicolay Diulgheroff
Donna alla finestra (Woman at the Window),
1927
[p. 423]
Oil on canvas, 65 × 80 cm. Below left:
DIULGHEROFF. Milan, Marco Beltchev Collection.
Exhibitions: Novara 1931 no. 8; Savona 1931
no. 10 bis (*Simultaneità di donna alla finestra*).

Fillia (Luigi Colombo)
Feminility (Femminilità), 1928
[p. 427]
Oil on canvas, 95 × 68 cm. Bottom right: FILLIA.
Turin, Antonio and Marina Forchino Collection.
Provenance: Turin, Federico Leumann; Turin,
Galleria Narciso.
Exhibitions: Milan 1929 no. 85?; Turin 1962
no. 8; Biella 1966 cover; Turin 1976 no. 7;
Milan 1986 no. 66.
Bibliography: *Notizie* January 1960 p. 27; Pierre
1967 p. 49.
Reference: Catalogue Cuneo 1988 no. 16.

Fillia (Luigi Colombo)
The Builder (Il costruttore), 1932
[p. 426]
Oil on cardboard, 65 × 50 cm. Bottom left:
FILLIA. Milan, Private collection.
Provenance: Turin, Germana Colombo Fillia.
Exhibitions: La Spezia 1932 (*Costruzione dello
spazio*); Genoa 1932 no. 2; Turin 1936 no. 445;
Turin 1962 no. 41; Paris 1982 no. 73.
Bibliography: Cabutti 1985 p. 73; Lista 1985 p.
75.
Reference: Catalogue Milan 1986 no. 167.

Lucio Fontana
Black Figures (Figure nere), 1931
[p. 432]
Colored terracotta, black and white, 41 ×
30 × 12.5 cm. On base, bottom right: Fontana
31. Milan, Teresita Fontana Collection.
Exhibitions: Turin 1970 no. 6 fig. 5; Milan
1971 no. 366; Milan 1972 (not in catalogue);
New York 1977 no. 3; Florence 1980 fig. 1;
Rimini 1982 no. 11; Munich 1983-84 no. 3,
then Darmstadt 1984; Paris 1987 p. 125, then
Barcelona 1988, then Amsterdam 1988, then
London 1988; London 1989 no. 122.
Bibliography: Ballo 1970 fig. 85; Crispolti 1971
fig. 7; Fossati 1971 fig. 43; Crispolti-Van der
Marck 1971 vol. I p. 26, vol. II p. 12.
Reference: Crispolti gen. cat. 1986 no. 31 SC 7.

Lucio Fontana
Scratched Tablet (Tavoletta graffitta), 1931
[p. 434]
Scratched and colored concrete, 23 × 29 cm.
Bottom right: L.Fontan (sic) 31. Turin, Private
collection.
Provenance: Turin, Galleria Il Ridotto; Turin,
Serafino Boschetti.
Exhibitions: Venice 1958 no. 2(?); Turin 1969
no. 2; Turin 1970 nop. 8; Milan 1971 no. 43;
Milan 1972 fig. 9; New York 1977 fig. 8; Mun-
ich 1983-84 no. 7, then Darmstadt 1984; Paris
1987 p. 131, then Barcelona 1988, then Amster-

dam 1988, then London 1988; London 1989 no.
123.
Bibliography: Tapié 1961; Ballo 1970 fig. 58;
Crispolti-Van der Marck 1974 vol. II p. 12.
Reference: Crispolti gen. cat. 1986 no. 31 SC
16.

Lucio Fontana
Girl's Head (Testa di ragazza), 1931
[p. 430]
Colored terracotta, gold, 38 × 32 × 15.5 cm.
Milan, Teresita Fontana Collection.
Provenance: Brescia, Pietro Ferodi.
Exhibitions: Milan 1933-34; Florence 1967 p.
377; Turin 1970 no. 2 fig. I; New York 1977
no. 6; Munich 1983-84 no. 5, then Darmstadt
1984; Paris 1987 p. 121, then Barcelona 1988,
then Amsterdam 1988, then London 1988; London 1989 no. 121.
Bibliography: Belli in *Quadrante* no. 9 January
1934 p. 45; Ballo 1970 p. 42 fig. 39; Crispolti
1971 fig. 14; Crispolti-Van der Marck 1974 vol.
II p. 12.
Reference: Crispolti gen. cat. 1986 no. 31 SC
12.

Lucio Fontana
Venus (Venere), 1931
[p. 433]
Terracotta and green tempera, 41 × 17 × 10 cm.
Bottom right: l.Fontana. Private collection.
Provenance: Milan, Giulia Veronesi.
Exhibitions: Turin 1981; Munich 1983-84 no.
2, then Darmstadt 1984.
Bibliography: Crispolti-Van der Marck 1974 vol.
II p. 12.
Reference: Crispolti gen. cat. 1984 no. 31 SC 6.

Lucio Fontana
Conversation (Conversazione), 1934
[p. 441]
Scratched and gilt bronze, 68 × 57 cm. Back:
l.Fontana/33. Milan, Private collection.
Exhibitions: Venice 1958 p. 21 no. 4; L'Aquila
1963 no. 102; Turin 1970 no. 13; Milan 1972
fig. 25; Brussels 1972 no. 3; Venice 1972 no.
14; New York 1977 fig. 15; Milan 1982 p. 635;
Rimini 1982 no. 7; Munich 1983-84 no. 9, then
Darmstadt 1984; Paris 1987 p. 141, then
Barcelona 1988, then Amsterdam 1988, then
London 1988.
Bibliography: Apollonio-Argan-Masciotta 1960;
Dorfles in *Aujourd'hui* no. 26 April 1960 p. 30;
Barilli 1968 Plate XXV; Crispolti-Van der
Marck 1974 vol. II p. 14.
Reference: Crispolti gen. cat. 1986 no. 24 SC
II.

Lucio Fontana
Women Sitting on Sofa (Donne sul sofà), 1934
[p. 429]
Colored plaster, pink and gold, 40 × 43 × 20 cm.
Rome, Giulio Carlo Argan Collection.
Reference: Crispolti gen. cat. 1986 no. 34 SC
II.

Lucio Fontana
Abstract Sculpture (Scultura astratta), 1934
[p. 437]
Colored plaster, black and white, 28 × 18 × 1
cm. Back: l. fontana/34-50. Milan, Teresita
Fontana Collection.
Exhibitions: Venice 1966 no. 18a; Paris 1970
no. 2; Turin 1970 no. 9 fig. 7; Milan 1972 fig.
20; Venice 1972 no. 13; New York 1977 fig. 19;
Florence 1980 fig. 5; Rimini 1982 no. 9; Paris
1987 p. /137, then Barcelona 1988, then
Amsterdam 1988, then London 1988; London
1989 no. 12

Bibliography: Ballo 1970 fig. 34; Crispolti-Van
der Marck 1974 vol. II p. 16;
Reference: Crispolti gen. cat. 1986 no. 34 SC
26.

Lucio Fontana
Abstract Sculpture (Scultura astratta), 1934
[p. 436]
Colored plaster, black and white, 41 × 23 × 1.8
cm. Milan, Giorgio Marconi Collection (201/
21).
Provenance: Rome, Galleria L'Obelisco; Rome,
Marlborough Galleria d'Arte.
Exhibitions: Perugia 1978; Munich 1983-84 no.
11 p. 38, then Darmstadt 1984; Paris 1987 p.
136, then Barcelona 1988, then Amsterdam
1988, then London 1988; London 1989 no. 125.
Bibliography: Carrieri 1950 p. 287 fig. 358;
Ballo 1970 fig. 65; Crispolti-Van der Marck
1974 vol. I p. 30, vol. II p. 16.
Reference: Crispolti gen. cat. 1986 no. 34 SC
24.

Lucio Fontana
Abstract Sculpture (Scultura astratta), 1934
[p. 438]
Colored metal, black, 62.5 × 50 × 7 cm. Turin,
Museo Civico; Galleria d'Arte Moderna.
Provenance: Rome, Marlborough Galleria
d'Arte.
Exhibitions: Ferrara 1960 p. 49 no. 88 fig. 88;
Venice p. 18 no. 17 fig. II, Florence 1967 no.
1577; Turin 1970 no. II fig. 9; Brussels 1972
no. 4; Milan 1972 p. 69 fig. 24; Venice 1972 no.
17; New York 1977 fig. 16; Rimini 1982 no. 10,
reproduction?; Munich 1983-84 no. 10, then
Darmstadt 1984; Paris 1987 p. 143, then
Barcelona 1988, then Amsterdam 1988, then
London; London 1989 no. 128.
Bibliography: Tapié 1961; Barilli 1968 Plate
XXIII; *Nac* no. 31 15 February 1970 p. 21;
Crispolti 1971 p. 53 fig. 54; Crispolti-Van der
Marck 1974 vol. II p. 16; Armellini 1980 p. 99
fig. 78.
Reference: Crispolti gen. cat. 1986 no. 34 SC
13.

Lucio Fontana
Abstract Sculpture (Scultura astratta), 1934
[p. 435]
White scratches on colored concrete, black and
white, 29 × 32 cm. Beatrice Monti della Corte
Collection.
Exhibitions: Milan 1972 no. 28; Venice 1972 p.
4 no. 18; Brussels 1972 no. 6; New York 1977
fig. 14; Florence 1980 no. 8; Milan 1982 p. 163
no. 2; Paris 1987 p. 135; Barcelona 1988, then
Amsterdam 1988, then London 1988; London
1989 no. 124.
Bibliography: Ballo 1970 p. 40 fig. 37; *Nac* no.
31 15 February 1970 p. 24; Crispolti-Van
Marck 1974 vol. II p. 14; Barilli 1984 Plate
XLV fig. 117.
Reference: Crispolti gen. cat. 1986 no. 24 SC 8.

Lucio Fontana
Abstract Sculpture (Scultura astratta), 1934
[p. 439]
Scratches on black painted plaster, pink and
white, 59 × 50 cm. Rome, Carla Panicali Collection.
Provenance: Rome, Marlborough Galleria
d'Arte
Exhibitions: Venice 1966 no. 16; Milan 1972
fig. 22; New York 1977 fig. 17; Milan 1982 no.
4; Paris 1987 p. 145; Barcelona 1988, then
Amsterdam 1988, then London 1988; London
1989 no. 127.
Bibliography: Barilli 1968 Plate XXII; Ballo

1970 fig. 33; Fossati 1971 fig. 56; Crispolti-Van der Marck 1974 vol. I p. 29, vol. II p. 16.
Reference: Crispolti gen. cat. 1986 no. 34 SC 17.

Lucio Fontana
Young Seated Woman (Signorina seduta), 1934
[p. 428]
Colored bronze, gold, black, red, 84 × 103 × 83 cm. Base: l.Fontana. Milan, Civico Museo d'Arte Contemporanea.
Provenance: Milan, Galleria del Milione; Bonn, Gustav Stein; Milan, Teresita Fontana.
Exhibitions: Milan 1972 no. 32; Brussels 1972 no. 5; New York 1977 no. 12; Rimini 1982 no. 20; Paris 1987 p. 117; Barcelona 1982 no. 20, then Amsterdam 1988, then London 1988; London 1989 no. 120.
Bibliography: Persico 1964 vol. I p. 192; Crispolti-Van der Marck 1974 vol. II p. 14; Folin-Quaranta 1977.
Reference: Crispolti gen. cat. 1986 no. 34 SC 1.

Lucio Fontana
Butterfly (Farfalla), 1935-36
[p. 442]
Colored, glazed ceramic, black and blue, 14.5 × 35.5 cm. Rome, Massimo Carpi Collection.
Provenance: Milan, Valdameri.
Bibliography: Zocchi 1946 fig. 14.
Reference: Crispolti gen. cat. 1986 no. 35-36 SC 12.

Lucio Fontana
Horses (Cavalli), 1938
[p. 440]
Colored ceramic, black, brown, reddish-brown and white, 38 × 62 × 47 cm. Beneath base: l. Fontana 38. Duisburg, Wilhelm-Lehmbruck-Museum, On permanent loan from Volker Feierabend.
Provenance: Milan, Renato Cardazzo; West Germany, Private collection.
Exhibitions: Milan 1977; Laveno 1980 p. 22; London 1989 no. 13a.
Bibliography: Zocchi 1946 fig. 16.
Reference: Crispolti gen. cat. 1986 no. 38 SC 13.

Lucio Fontana
Conch and Octopus (Conchiglia e polpo), 1938
[p. 443]
Ceramic, 13 × 45 × 23.5 cm. Beneath base: L. Fontana 38/M.G.A. Turin, Galleria Narciso.
Provenance: Milan, Domenico Tempestini.
Exhibitions: London 1989 no. 129.
Reference: Crispolti gen. cat. 1986 no. 38 SC 21.

Lucio Fontana
Portrait (Ritratto), 1938
[p. 431]
Polychrome mosaic, 34 × 33 × c.15 cm, Milan, Teresita Fontana Collection.
Exhibitions: Turin 1970 no. 18; Milan 1971 no. 606 (cover and poster); Rimini 1982 no. 19.
Bibliography: Crispolti 1971 p. 65 fig. 70; Crispolti-Van der Marck 1974 vol. I p. 18.
Reference: Crispolti gen. cat. 1986 no. 38 SC 5.

Renato Guttuso
Flight from Etna (Fuga dall'Etna), 1940
[p. 557]
Oil on canvas, 149.8 × 258.7 cm. Bottom right: Guttuso 40. Rome, Galleria Nazionale d'Arte Moderna.
Exhibitions: Milan 1940 no. 115; Bagheria 1962 no. 9; Parma 1963-64 no. 24 Plates 15-16-17;

Palermo 1971 no. 30; London 1989 no. 147.
Bibliography: Piovene in *Primato* no. 16 15 October 1940 pp. 19-20; Marchiori 1952 pp. 56-57; Morosini 1960 p. 6; Moravia-Grasso 1962 p. 47; *L'Arte Moderna* vol. VIII 1967 p. 258; Crispolti 1970 fig. 1; de Micheli 1970 pp. 34-35 Plate 1.
Reference: Crispolti gen. cat. 1984 no. 38-39/14.

Renato Guttuso
Crucifixion (Crocifissione), 1941
[p. 556]
Oil on canvas 200 × 200 cm. Bottom, toward right: Guttuso, Rome. Rome, Galleria Nazionale d'Arte Moderna.
Provenance: Genoa, Alberto Della Ragione.
Exhibitions: Bergamo 1942 no. 22; Milan 1959 no. 2; Parma 1963-64 Plate 25; Darmstadt 1967 no. 3; Berlin 1968 no. 43; Cologne 1968; Palermo 1971 no. 41; Paris 1971 no. 13; Geneva 1977-78 no. 121; Milan 1982 p. 51; London 1989 no. 148.
Bibliography: Costantini in *Illustrazione Italiana* no. 37 13 September 1942 pp. 284-285; De Grada 1952 fig. 13; Ballo 1956 p. 173; De Micheli in *L'Arte Moderna* vol. VIII p. 270; Crispolti 1970; Del Guercio 1980 p. 109.
Reference: Crispolti gen. cat. 1984 no. 40-41/25.

Leoncillo (Leonardi)
Natura morta con il domino (Still Life with Dominoes), 1943
[p. 560]
Gilded terracotta, 32.5 × 46 × 5 cm. Private Collection.
Exhibitions: Spoleto 1969 no. 11 Plate 7.

Leoncillo (Leonardi)
Natura morta con polipo (Still Life with Octopus), 1943
[p. 561]
Glazed terracotta, 36 × 30 × 21 cm. Rome, Fabio Sargentini Collection.
Provenance: Florence, Cesare Brandi.
Exhibitions: Venice 1954 p. 117 no. 50 (dated 1944); Spoleto 1969 no. 10 Plate 6; Bologna 1986 no. 205.

Leoncillo (Leonardi)
Madre romana uccisa dai tedeschi II (Roman Mother Killed by the Germans II), 1944
[p. 558]
Polychrome terracotta, 13 × 50 × 23.5 cm. Private Collection.
Exhibitions: Spoleto 1969 no. 14 Plate 10

Leoncillo (Leonardi)
Ritratto di Donata (Portrait of Donata), 1945
[p. 559]
Polychrome ceramics, 50 × 12 × 21 cm. Private Collection.
Exhibitions: Venice 1954 p. 118 no. 52 (dated 1945); Spoleto 1969 no. 12 Plate 8.

Osvaldo Licini
Archpittura, 1933
[p. 447]
Oil on canvas, 83 × 102 cm. Private collection.
Bibliography: *Cahiers d'Art* no. 10 1937 cover.

Osvaldo Licini
Composition no. 10, 1933
[p. 444]
Oil on canvas, 27 × 19.2 cm. Private collection.
Exhibitions: Milan 1935; Como 1936; Ivrea 1958 p. 57; Venice 1958; Venice 1966; Turin 1968-69 no. 57 Plate 32.

Bibliography: Ballo 1962 Plate 63.
Reference: Marchiori gen. cat. 1968 no. 00 Plate XIX

Osvaldo Licini
The Balance (Il bilico), 1934
[p. 445]
Oil on canvas, 90 × 68 cm. Milan, Pinacoteca di Brera.
Provenance: Milan, Emilio Jesi.
Exhibitions: Turin 1961 p. 89, then Milan 1961; Venice 1966.
Reference: Marchiori gen. cat. 1968 Plate XCI.

Osvaldo Licini
Mouth (Bocca), 1934
[p. 446]
Oil on canvas, 21.3 × 28.3 cm. Private collection.
Exhibitions: Ivrea 1958 p. 58; Venice 1966; Turin 1968-69 no. 65 Plate 51; Ferrara 1980 no. 45.
Bibliography: *Comunità* May-June 1958 p. 77; Ballo 1962 Plate 64.
Reference: Marchiori gen. cat. 1968 Plate XXIV.

Osvaldo Licini
Composition with Black and Blue Lines (Composizione linee nere e blu), 1935
[p. 448]
Oil on canvas, 17.5 × 82 cm. Ascoli Piceno, Caterina Hellstrom Riccitelli Collection.
Exhibitions: Rome 1959-60; Ancona 1960; Florence 1964; Turin 1968-69 n.77 Plate 48; Bologna 1969; Ferrara 1980 Plate 38; Ascoli Piceno 1986; Ascoli Piceno 1988 no. 33; London 1989 no. 132.
Bibliography: Marchiori 1960 Plate 10; Fossati 1971 Plate 37.
Reference: Marchiori gen. cat. 1968 Plate XCII.

Osvaldo Licini
Biting (Addentare), 1936
[p. 450]
Oil on canvas, 65.5 × 88.5 cm. Private collection.
Exhibitions: Ivrea 1958; Venice 1958; Ancona 1960; Venice 1966; Ferrara 1980 no. 52; London 1989 no. 131.
Reference: Marchiori gen. cat. 1968 Plate XXV.

Osvaldo Licini
Biting (Addentare su fondo grigio), 1936
[p. 449]
Oil on canvas, 66.5 × 90 cm. Ascoli Piceno, Caterina Hellstrom Riccitelli Collection.
Exhibitions: Rome 1959-60; Ancona 1960; Turin 1968-69 no. 72 Plate 52; Bologna 1969; Ferrara 1980 Plate 51; Ascoli Piceno 1986; Ascoli Piceno 1988 no. 39.
Bibliography: Dorfles in *Domus* May 1958; Marchiori 1960 Plate 9; Fossati 1971 Plate 41; Del Guercio 1980.
Reference: Marchiori 1968 gen. cat. no. XCIV.

Osvaldo Licini
Archipittura, 1937
[p. 451]
Oil on canvas, 81 × 10 cm. Private collection.
Exhibitions: Ivrea 1958 p. 56; Livorno 1958; Venice 1966; Turin 1968-69 no. 75 Plate 56.
Bibliography: Marchiori in *Corriere Padano* 9 October 1937; Sartoris in *Origini* no. 5-6 1941; Marchiori 1960 p. 184.
Reference: Marchiori gen. cat. 1968 Plate XXVIII.

Mario Mafai
Self-Portrait (Autoritratto), 1929
[p. 452]
Oil on wood, 63 × 52 cm. Top right: Mafai 1929. Private collection.
Exhibitions: Rome 1930 no. 18; Rome 1965 no. 2; Rome 1969 no. 11; Macerata 1986 no. VII; Milan 1988 no. 134.
Bibliography: De Libero in *Belvedere* April 1930; Martinelli 1967 Plate I and cover.

Mario Mafai
Women Hanging out the Wash (Donne che stendono i panni), 1933
[p. 453]
Oil on canvas, 144 × 116 cm. Bottom right: Mafai. Private collection.
Exhibitions: Rome 1935 no. 5; Rome 1945; Florence 1967 no. 1918; Rome 1969 no. 36; Rome 1984 p. 26; Macerata 1986 no. 21; Milan 1988 no. 62.
Bibliography: Martinelli 1967 no. 52; Fagiolo-Rivosecchi 1986 no. 7; Fagiolo 1986 p. 50.

Mario Mafai
Procession (Corteo), c. 1942
[p. 562]
Oil on canvas, 80.2 × 94.8 cm. Turin, Galleria Narciso.
Exhibitions: Turin 1985; Macerata 1986, no. 32.

Mario Mafai
Fantasy (Fantasia), c. 1942
[p. 563]
Oil on canvas, 112 × 142 cm. Private collection.
Exhibitions: Rome 1984 p. 31; Milan 1988 no. 101.

Mario Mafai
The Globe and Lacerba (Il mappamondo e Lacerba), 1914
[p. 347]
Oil on canvas, 100 × 75 cm. Meudon, Susi Magnelli Collection.
Bibliography: Descargues in *Plaisir de France* February 1971 p. 38.
Reference: Maisonnier gen. cat. 1975 no. 98.

Alberto Magnelli
Still Life (Natura Morta), 1914
[p. 346]
Assembly: plaster, bottle glass, and terracotta bowl, 56.5 × 54 × 56.5 cm. Paris, Musée national d'art moderne, Centre Georges Pompidou.
Bibliography: Ponente 1973 p. 27.

Alberto Magnelli
Stones (Pierres-Pietre), 1932
[p. 454]
Oil on canvas, 100 × 81 cm. Top left: Magnelli 32. Private collection.
Exhibitions: Brussels 1954 no. 38; Florence 1988 no. 19.
Bibliography: Ponente 1973 p. 53.
Reference: Maisonnier gen. cat. 1975 no. 387.

Alberto Magnelli
Stones no. 1 (Pierres no. 1 - Pietre n. 1), 1933
[p. 455]
Oil on canvas, 116 × 89 cm. Bottom right: Magnelli/33. Meudon, Susi Magnelli Collection.
Exhibitions: Brussels 1954 no. 39; Antibes 1955 no. 18; Florence 1963 no. 49; London 1989 no. 137.
Bibliography: Maisonnier gen. cat. 1975, no. 399.

Alberto Magnelli
Stones no. 31 on Blue Background (Pierres no. 31 sur fond bleu — Pietre n. 31 su fondo blu), 1934
[p. 456]
Oil on canvas, 130 × 170 cm. Bottom right: Magnelli 34. Meudon Susi Magnelli Collection.
Exhibitions: Brussels 1954, no. 43; Antibes 1955, no. 44; Zurich 1963, no. 60; Florence 1963 no. 58; Paris 1968 no. 55.
Bibliography: Fresnay 1969 no. 44; Ponente 1973 p. 56.
Reference: Maisonnier gen cat. 1975 no. 433.

Giacomo Manzù
Adam and Eve (Adamo ed Eva), 1929
[p. 564]
Bronze, 41 × 29 cm. Ardea, Amici di Giacomo Manzù Collection.
Exhibitions: Bergamo 1930; Milan 1930 no. 18.

Giacomo Manzù
Small Male Head (Piccola testa d'uomo), 1932-34
[p. 565]
Polychrome plaster, h. 19 cm. Florence City Council, Raccolta d'Arte Contemporanea Alberto Della Ragione.
Exhibitions: Milan 1988-89 no. 39.
Bibliography: Ragghianti 1957 p. 66.

Giacomo Manzù
Crucifixion (Crocefissione), 1940
[p. 564]
Bronze, 53 × 33 cm. Private collection.
Provenance: Rome, Riccardo Gualino.
Exhibitions: Milan 1941; Milan 1988-89 no. 61.
Bibliography: Ragghianti 1957 no. 31 (dated 1941).

Marino Marini
Gentleman on Horseback (Gentiluomo a cavallo), 1937
[p. 458]
Bronze, 156 × 130 × 86 cm. Rome, Camera dei Deputati Collection.
Exhibitions: Rome 1966 no. 10 fig.7; Venice 1983 Plate 26.
Bibliography: San Lazzaro 1970 p. 192; Azuma 1980 Plates 36-37.

Marino Marini
Young girl (Giovinetta), 1938
[p. 459]
Bronze, 153 × 27 × 43 cm. Pistoia, Fondazione Marino Marini.
Provenance: Milan, Pallini; Milan, Galleria del Milione.
Exhibitions: Lausanne 1947 no. 127; Rome 1966 no. 11; Venice 1983 no. 27.
Bibliography: De Pisis 1941 Plate 42-43; Vitali 1946 no. 1; Apollonio 1958 Plate 12-13; San Lazzaro 1970 p. 36; Azuma 1980 Plate 23-24.

Marino Marini
The Juggler (Il giocoliere), 1939
[p. 457]
Polychrome bronze, 170 × 62 × 40 cm. Florence Museo Marino Marini, Fondazione Marini San Pancrazio.
Exhibitions: Rome 1966 no. 12 (dated 1938); Venice 1983 no. 31.
Bibliography: San Lazzaro 1970 no. 93; Azuma 1980 no. 29.

Arturo Martini
A man I often meet (Uomo spesse volte incontrato), 1913
[p. 349]
Polychrome plaster, 119 × 64 × 32 cm. Venice, Ca' Pesaro, Galleria Internazionale d'Arte Moderna.
Provenance: Rome, Fiammetta Sarfatti Gaetani.
Exhibitions: Venice 1913 no. 114; Rome 1914 no. 24; Venice 1987-88 no. 11.
Bibliography: Perocco 1966 no. 42 fig.35-38.

Arturo Martini
The Friend of the Cypress Tree (L'amica del cipresso), 1919
[p. 348]
Plaster, 62 × 60 × 30 cm. Verona, Private collection.
Exhibitions: Verona 1919 Hall VI no. 18; Venice 1919 Hall II no. 47; Treviso 1967 no. 37; Venice 1987-88 no. 18.
Bibliography: Perocco 1966 no. 50 fig.41; Bellonzi 1974 no. 13.

Arturo Martini
Girl before Evening (Fanciulla verso sera), 1919
[p. 350]
Plaster, 54 × 52 × 31 cm. Venice, Ca' Pesaro, Galleria Internazionale d'Arte Moderna.
Provenance: Venice, Nino Barbantini.
Exhibitions: Verona 1919 Hall VI no. 19; Venice 1919 Hall II no. 48; Treviso 1967 no. 37; Venice 1987-88 no. 19.
Bibliography: Perocco 1966 no. 51 fig.42; Bellonzi 1974 no. 17

Arturo Martini
Girl's Head (Testa di ragazza), 1920
[p. 351]
Plaster, 42 × 24 × 23 cm. Private collection. On Left: Martini 1920.
Provenance: Venice, Mentasti Collection; Rome, Sarfatti Collection.
Exhibitions: Venice 1920 no. 39; Milan 1920 no. 7; Venice 1987-88 no. 20.
Bibliography: Bellonzi 1974 no. 20.

Arturo Martini
The Pisan Girl (La Pisana) 1929-30
[p. 462]
Patinated terracotta, 37 × 131 × 64 cm. Florence City Council, Raccolta d'Arte Contemporanea Alberto Della Ragione.
Provenance: Venice, Massimo Bontempelli; Alberto Della Ragione.
Exhibitions: Venice 1948 no. 5 (1928); London 1989 no. 113.
Bibliography: Bontempelli 1939 Plate VI; Scalia 1987 no. 6.

Arturo Martini
The Wife of the Sailor (La moglie del marinaio), 1930
[p. 463]
Terracotta, 46.8 × 21 × 22 cm. Florence, Private collection.
Provenance: Florence, Papi
Exhibitions: Treviso 1967 no. 79; Milan 1979.
Bibliography: Perocco 1966 no. 210 fig. 167-168; Bellonzi 1974 no. 52.

Arturo Martini
The Happy Wife (La Sposa felice), 1930
[p. 460]
Plaster, 234 × 100 cm. Private collection.
Provenance: Florence, Contini Bonacorsi; Florence, Papi.
Exhibitions: Rome 1931 no. 5; Paris 1935; Treviso 1967 no. 76; Florence 1967 no. 1178; Milan 1985 no. 31.
Bibliography: Venturi 1930; Lo Duca 1933 Plate XII; Bontempelli 1939 Plate VIII; Perocco 1966 no. 156-157; Bellonzi 1974 no. 48; Mazzotti 1979 Plate XVII.

Critical References

Arturo Martini
The Convalescent (La convalescente), 1932
[p. 461]
Teracotta, 100 × 100 × 49 cm. Genoa-Nervi, Galleria d'Arte Moderna.
Exhibitions: Milan 1933; Parma 1980.
Bibliography: Bontempelli 1939 Plate XVII; Perocco 1966 no. 246 fig.207.

Fausto Melotti
Little Theater, (Teatrino), 1930-31
[p. 464]
Colored terracotta, 38 × 32 × 11 cm. Milan, Melotti Collection.
Exhibitions: Milan 1979 no. 2; Rome 1983 no. 7; Milan 1987 no. 1; Matera 1987 no. 2.

Fausto Melotti
Sculpture no. 11 (Scultura n. 11), 1934
[p. 466]
Plaster, 80 × 70 × 14.5 cm. Milan, Melotti Collection.
Exhibitions: Turin 1935; Reggio Emilia 1968; Turin 1968; Milan 1969; Dortmund 1971; Turin 1972 Plate I; Venice 1972; Parma 1976; Milan 1979 no. 22; Matera 1987 no. 3; London 1989 no. 134.
Bibliography: Veronesi in *L'Arte Moderna* vol.VI 1967 p. 278; Fossati 1971 Plate 57; Drudi in *Data* no. 15 spring 1975; Hammacher 1975.

Fausto Melotti
Sculpture no. 12 (Scultura n. 12), 1934
[p. 469]
Plaster, 55 × 55 × 15 cm. Milan, Melotti Collection.
Exhibitions: Milan 1935 no. 7; Milan 1969; Dortmund 1971 Plate 11; Turin 1972 Plate 2; Venice 1972; Milan 1979 no. 23; Rome 1983 no. 3; London 1989 no. 133.
Bibliography: Sartoris 1935 *Abstraction-Création* no. 4 1935 p. 23; Fossati 1971 Plate 58; Hammacher 1975.

Fausto Melotti
Sculpture no. 15 (Scultura n. 15), 1935
[p. 467]
Plaster, 71.8 × 70 × 10 cm. Rome, Corrado Rava Collection.
Exhibitions: Milan 1935; Venice 1966 no. 43; Milan 1969; Dortmund 1971 Plate 59; Turin 1972 Plate 4; Trento 1977 no. 2; Milan 1979 no. 25.
Bibliography: Ballo in *Domus* no. 424 March 1965 p. 56; Fagiolo 1970 p. 97; Fossati 1971 Plate 60.

Fausto Melotti
Sculpture no. 16 (Scultura n. 16), 1935
[p. 470]
Plaster, 90 × 90 cm. Milan, Melotti Collection.
Exhibitions: Milan, 1935 (no. 16 or 17): Venice 1966 no. 41; Florence 1967 no. 1610; Milan 1969; Dortmund 1971; Turin 1972 no. 5; Parma 1976; Trento 1977 no. 3; Milan 1979 no. 28; Matera 1987 no. 7; London 1989 no. 135.
Bibliography: Veronesi in *L'Arte Moderna* vol.VI 1967 p. 278; Fagiolo 1970 p. 97; Pica in *Domus* May 1971 Plate 18; Fossati 1971 Plate 61; Hammacher 1975 p. 7.

Fausto Melotti
Sculpture no. 23 (Scultura n. 23), 1935
[p. 471]
Plaster 90 × 90 cm. Milan, Melotti Collection.
Exhibitions: L'Aquila 1963; Venice 1966 no. 44; Florence 1967 no. 1613; Milan 1969; Dortmund 1971 Plate 16; Turin 1972 Plate 9;

Parma 1976; Trento 1977 no. 6; Milan 1979 no. 29.
Bibliography: Fossati 1971 Plate 64; Hammacher 1975 p. 6.

Fausto Melotti
Sculpture no. 24 (Scultura n. 24), 1935
[p. 470]
Plaster 90 × 90 cm. Milan, Melotti Collection.
Exhibitions: L'Acquila 1963; Venice 1966 no. 45; Florence 1967 no. 1612; Milan 1969; Turin 1972 Plate 10; Parma 1976; Trento 1977 no. 7; Milan 1979 no. 30; London 1989 no. 136.
Bibliography: Fossati 1971 Plate 65; Hammacher 1975.

Fausto Melotti
Sculpture no. 25 (Scultura n. 25), 1935
[p. 468]
Plaster, 92 × 56 × 10 cm. Turin, Private collection.
Exhibitions: Milan, 1935 no. 20: Turin 1968; Milan 1969; Dortmund 1971 no. 6; Turin 1972 Plate 11; Venice 1972; Milan 1979 no. 31; Rome 1983.
Bibliography: *Bolletino Galleria del Milione* no. 40 1935; Fagiolo 1970 p. 97; Fossati 1971 Plate 66; Drudi in *Data* no. 15 spring 1975; Hammacher 1975.

Fausto Melotti
The Wise One (Il Sapiente), 1936
[p. 465]
Plaster, 225 × 55 × 31 cm. Private collection.
Exhibitions: Milan 1987.

Amedeo Modigliani
Woman's Head (Tête de femme), 1910-11
[p. 360]
Limestone, 65 × 19 × 24 cm. Washington, National Gallery of Art.
Provenance: New York, Chester Dale.
Exhibitions: Philadelphia 1943 no. 20; New York 1951 p. 22.
Bibliography: Werner 1962 fig. 38-39; Ceroni 1970 no. XVII; Roy 1985 p. 64-65; Castieu-Barrielle 1987 p. 82.

Amedeo Modigliani
Head (Tête), 1910-11
[p. 359]
Stone, 50 × 19.6 × 19 cm. Private collection.
Provenance: Paris, Leopold Zborowski; Paris, Galerie Mouradian-Vallotton; Paris Jacques Guérin.
Exhibitions: Paris 1981 no. 223, London 1989 no. 66.
Bibliography: Modigliani 1961 no. 69; Ceroni 1965 no. XIII; Ceroni-Cachin 1972 no. XIII. Reference: Lanthemann gen cat. 1970 no. 626.

Amedeo Modigliani
Head (Tête), 1911-13
[p. 354]
Limestone, 63.5 × 15 × 21 cm. New York Solomon R. Guggenheim Museum.
Provenance: London Augustus John; London Arthur Tooth; New York J. J. Klejman Gallery.
Exhibitions: London 1954 no. 27; Houston 1959; Hartford 1961; New York 1977-78 no. 100; London 1989 no. 67.
Bibliography: John 1952 p. 131; Ceroni 1965 no. XIII; Sichel 1967 pp. 212-213; Ceroni 1970 no. XXI; Hall 1984 no. 12; Roy 1985 p. 46. Reference: Lanthemann gen. cat. 1970 no. 625.

Amedeo Modigliani
Standing Figure (Nu debout - Donna in piedi), c. 1912

[p. 357]
Limestone, 162.8 × 33.2 × 31.5 cm. Canberra, Australian National Gallery.
Provenance: New York, Gustav Schindler.
Exhibitions: New York 1951 p. 23; New York 1954 no. 44; New York 1964 no. 1.
Bibliography: Werner 1962 no. 1; Ceroni 1970 no. XI; Hall 1984 Plate 13; Roy 1985 p. 61; Castieu-Barrielle 1987 p. 87.

Amedeo Modigliani
Woman's Head (Tête de femme - Testa di donna), 1912
[p. 362]
Stone, 58 × 12 × 16 cm. Paris, Musée national d'art moderne, Centre Georges Pompidou.
Exhibitions: Paris 1950 no. 105; Rome 1951-52.
Bibliography: Pfannstiel 1929 p. 82; Werner 1962 fig. 5-8; Ceroni 1965 no. XII; Roy 1985 p. 55; Castieu-Barrielle 1987 p. 93.

Amedeo Modigliani
Juan Gris c. 1915
[p. 352]
Oil on canvas, 55.8 × 38 cm. New York, The Metropolitan Museum of Art.
Provenance: New York, Adelaide Milton de Groot.
Exhibitions: Columbus 1958 no. 8, then New York 1958; Rome 1959 no. 8; Boston 1961 no. 8, then Los Angeles 1961; Tokyo 1968 no. 24, then Kyoto 1968; Paris 1975-76 no. 40; Tokyo 1979 no. 5, then Osaka 1979; Paris 1981 no. 28.
Bibliography: Pfannstiel 1956 no. 114; Ceroni 1965 no. 173; Ceroni 1970 no. 99; Hall 1984 no. 24. Reference: Lanthemann gen. cat. 1970 no. 108.

Amedeo Modigliani
Crouched Nude (Nu accroupi), 1916-17
[p. 355]
Oil on canvas, 114 × 74 cm. Top right: modigliani. Antwerp, Koniklijk Museum voor Schone Kunsten.
Exhibitions: Venice 1930; Brussels 1933; Basel 1934; Rome 1951-52; Milan 1958 no. 33.
Bibliography: Pfannstiel 1929 p. 105; Carrieri 1950 no. 101; Pfannstiel 1956 no. 139; Ceroni 1970 no. 188; Castieu-Barrielle 1987 p. 183.

Amedeo Modigliani
Nude (Nu) 1917
[p. 356]
Oil on canvas, 73 × 117 cm.
Bottom right: modigliani, back: Modigliani 3, Joseph Bara/Paris. New York, Solomon R. Guggenheim Museum.
Provenance: Paris, Leopold Zborowski; Paris, Galerie Bing et Cie; Paris, Félix Fénéon.
Exhibitions: Paris 1925; Paris 1926 no. 3104; New York 1959-60; New York 1977-78 no. 102.
Bibliography: George in *L'Amour de l'art* October 1925 p. 388; Salmon 1926 no. 18; Pfannstiel 1929 p. 108; Ceroni 1965 p. 18-19; Ceroni 1970 no. 186; Rudenstine 1976 no. 186. Reference: Lanthemann gen. cat. 1970 no. 214.

Amedeo Modigliani
Seated Nude in Shirt (Nu assis à la chemise — Nudo seduto con camicia), 1917
[p. 361]
Oil on canvas, 92 × 67.5 cm. Villeneuve d'Ascq, Musée d'Art Moderne.
Provenance: Paris, Leopold Zborowski; Paris, Roger Dutilleul; Paris, Jean et Geneviève Masurel.
Exhibitions: Paris 1945 no. 15; Marseille 1958

no. 27; Bordeaux 1964 no. 172; Tokyo 1968 no. 49, then Kyoto 1968; Paris 1981 no. 52.
Bibliography: San Lazzaro 1953 Plate 10; Pfannstiel 1956 no. 309; Ceroni-Cachin 1972 no. 191.
Reference: Lanthemann gen. cat. 1970 no. 162.

Amedeo Modigliani
Portrait of Dédie (Portrait de Dédie), 1918
[p. 353]
Oil on canvas, 92 × 60 cm. Top left: modigliani. Paris, Musée national d'art moderne, Centre Georges Pompidou.
Provenance: Paris André Lefèvre.
Exhibitions: Paris 1964 no. 23; Washington 1968, then New York 1968, then Boston 1968; Leningrad 1979 no. 26, then Moscow 1979; Paris 1981 no. 97.
Bibliography: Jaffé 1963 no. 25; Ceroni 1965 no. 214; Ceroni-Cachin 1972 no. 236; Zurcher 1980 no. 57; Castieu-Barrielle 1987 p. 203.
Reference: Lanthemann gen. cat. 1970 no. 282.

Amedeo Modigliani
Large Nude (Grand nu), c. 1919
[p. 358]
Oil on canvas, 72.4 × 116.5 cm. Bottom right: Modigliani. New York, The Museum of Modern Art.
Provenance: New York, Simon Guggenheim.
Exhibitions: New York 1929 no. 16; Brussels 1933 p. 30; Basel 1934 no. 4; New York 1949; New York 1951 p. 45.
Bibliography: Salmon 1926 no. 33; Pfannstiel 1929 p. 132; Venturi 1947 Plate XI; Pfannstiel 1956 no. 336; Ceroni 1970 no. 200 and Plates XLIV-XLV; Castieu-Barrielle 1987 p. 179.

Amedeo Modigliani
Jeanne Hébuterne in a Yellow Sweater (Jeanne Hébuterne en pullover jaune), 1918-19
[p. 363]
Oil on canvas, 100 × 65 cm. Top right: modigliani. New York, Solomon R. Guggenheim Museum.
Provenance: Paris, Galerie Bing et Cie; Paris, Félix Fénéon.
Exhibitions: Zurich 1927 no. 109; London 1957 no. 52, then The Hague 1957, then Helsinki 1957, then Rome 1957-58, then Cologne 1958, then Paris 1958; Milan 1960 no. 147; New York 1977-78 no. 103.
Bibliography: Pfannstiel 1929 p. 104; Pfannstiel 1956 no. 268; Ceroni 1970 no. 220; Rudenstine 1976 no. 189, Castieu-Barrielle 1987 p. 157.
Reference: Lanthemann gen. cat. 1970 no. 389.

Giorgio Morandi
Still Life with Watchcase (Natura morta con portaorologio), 1915
[p. 364]
Oil on canvas, 74.5 × 53 cm. Bottom right: Morandi 1915. Mattioli Collection.
Exhibitions: Florence 1953 no. 24; Siegen 1962 no. 1; Berne 1965 no. 11; Venice 1966 no. 6; Bologna 1966 no. 8; Washington 1967-68 no. 74, then Dallas, San Francisco, Detroit, Kansas City 1968, then Boston, New York 1969, then Brussels, Copenhagen 1969, then Hamburg 1970, then Madrid, Barcelona 1970-71, then Seville 1971; Milan 1971 no. 7; Rome 1973 no. 10; Bologna 1975 no. 2; Paris 1987 no. 6.
Bibliography: Marchiori 1960 Plate 41; Vitali 1964 Plate 14; Arcangeli 1964 no. 10; Brandi 1976 Plate 1.
Reference: Vitali gen. cat. no. 23.

Giorgio Morandi
Still Life (Natura morta), 1916

[p. 365]
Oil on canvas, 82.5 × 57.5 cm. Bottom right: Morandi 2.7.916. New York, The Museum of Modern Art.
Exhibitions: Rome 1939 no. 3; Venice 1948 no. 27; New York 1949 Plate 57; Milan 1960 no. 149; Washington 1963-64; Venice 1966 no. 8; Bologna 1966 no. 12; London 1970-71 no. 7; Milan 1971 no. 11; San Francisco 1981 no. 6 then New York 1981-82, then Des Moines 1982.
Bibliography: Beccaria 1939 Plate VIII; Brandi 1942 Plate VII; Brandi 1976 Plate 5.
Reference: Vitali gen. cat. 1977 no. 27.

Giorgio Morandi
Still life (Natura morta), 1916
[p. 367]
Oil on canvas, 60 × 54 cm. Bottom right: Morandi, back: Morandi 1916. Mattioli Collection.
Provenance: Brescia, Pietro Feroldi.
Exhibitions: Venice 1948 no. 29; Zurich 1950 no. 155; Naples 1964 Plate 151a; Berne 1965 no. 13; Venice 1966 no. 10; Bologna 1966 no. 10; Florence 1967 no. 1191; Washington 1967-68 no. 75, then Dallas, San Francisco, Detroit, Kansas City 1968, then Boston 1969, then Brussels, Copenhagen 1969, then Hamburg 1970; Madrid 1970; Barcelona 1970-71, then Seville 1971; Milan 1971 no. 9; Rome 1973 no. 12; Bologna 1975 no. 8; Paris 1987 no. 8.
Bibliography: Beccaria 1939 Plate VII; Castelfranchi-Valsecchi 1956 Plate XXXVI; Marchiori 1960 Plate 43; Vitali 1964 Plate 22; Arcangeli 1964 fig.11; Siblik 1965 Plate 6.
Reference: Vitali gen. cat. 1977 no. 28.

Giorgio Morandi
Roses (Rose) 1917
[p. 366)
Oil on canvas, 58 × 50 cm. Bottom right: Morandi 1917. Mattioli Collection.
Provenance: Milan, Carlo Frua Angeli; Milan, Galleria del Milione; Milan, Pallini.
Exhibitions: Rome 1939 no. 6; Catania 1949 no. 30, then Palermo 1949; Turin 1959 no. 31; Washington 1967-68 no. 79; then Dallas, San Francisco, Detroit, Kansas City 1968, then New York, 1969, then Brussels, Copenhagen 1969, then Hamburg 1970; Madrid, Barcelona 1970-71; then Kyoto, Tokyo 1972; Rome 1973 no. 16.
Bibliography: Beccaria 1939 Plate IX; Martini 1964 Plate IV; Vitali 1964 Plate 26.
Reference: Vitali gen. cat. 1977 no. 31.

Giorgio Morandi
Still Life (Natura morta), 1918
[p. 369]
Oil on canvas, 54 × 38 cm. Bottom center: 1918. Parma, Fondazione Magnani-Rocca.
Provenance: Rome, Rollino; Turin, Galleria Galatea; Milan, Emilio Jesi.
Exhibitions: Amsterdam 1961 no. 94; Berne 1965 no. 15; Florence 1967 no. 1194; Turin 1967-68 no. 65; Venice 1979 no. 71; London 1989 no. 55.
Bibliography: Brandi 1952 Plate XIII; Vitali 1964 Plate 29; Carrà 1968 Plate VII.
Reference: Vitali gen. cat. 1977 no. 36.

Giorgio Morandi
Still Life (Natura morta) 1918
[p. 368]
Oil on canvas, 68.5 × 72 cm. Bottom right: Morandi. Milan, Pinacoteca Nazionale di Brera (gift of Emilio and Maria Jesi).
Provenance: Rome, Mario Broglio; Genoa,

Alberto Della Ragione; Milan, Emilio Jesi.
Exhibitions: San Francisco 1939 no. 22; Venice 1948 no. 32; Zurich 1950 no. 159; Berne 1965 no. 18; Venice 1966 no. 12; Bologna 1966 no. 16; Florence 1967 no. 1193; Rome 1973 no. 20; Bologna 1975 no. 5; Madrid 1984-85, then Barcelona 1985; Bologna 1985-86 no. 22; Paris 1987 no. 10.
Bibliography: Brandi 1942 Plate XII; Apollonio 1950 Plate XIX; Marchiori 1960 Plate 44; Vitali 1964 Plate 36; Arcangeli 1964 fig.15; Carrà 1968 fig.185; Fossati 1988 no. 35.
Reference: Vitali gen. cat. 1977 no. 35.

Giorgio Morandi
Still Life (Natura morta), 1918
[p. 370]
Oil on canvas, 71 × 61 cm. Bottom center: Morandi 918. Leningrad, The Hermitage Museum.
Provenance: Moscow, Museum of Modern Art.
Exhibitions: Bologna 1966 no. 17; London 1970-71 no. 13; Paris 1971 no. 13; Leningrad 1973 no. 1; Leningrad 1989 no. 4, then Moscow 1989.
Bibliography: Vitali 1964 Plate 37; Arcangeli 1964 fig.12; Carrà 1968 fig. 187.
Reference: Vitali gen. cat. 1977 no. 37.

Giorgio Morandi
Still Life (Natura morta), 1919
[p. 371]
Oil on canvas, 56.5 × 47 cm. Top right: Morandi 919. Milan, Pinacoteca di Brera (gift of Emilio and Maria Jesi).
Provenance: Rome, Mario Broglio; Milan, Galleria Barbara; Milan, Emilio Jesi.
Exhibitions: Venice 1948 no. 34 or 36; Zurich 1950 no. 163; The Hague 1954 no. 11; Berne 1965 no. 19; Florence 1967 no. 1196; London 1970-71 Plate 8; Bologna 1975 no. 6; Ferrara 1978; Munich 1981; Bologna 1985-86 no. 23; Paris 1987 no. 11.
Bibliography: *Valori Plastici* 1921 no. IV; Beccaria 1939 Plate XIV; Brandi 1942 Plate XIII; Scheiwiller 1943 Plate IV; Marchiori 1960 Plate 47; Vitali 1964 Plate 40; Arcangeli 1964 fig. 18; Carrà 1968 fig. 189; Solmi-Vitali 1988 no. 11.
Reference: Vitali gen. cat. 1977 no. 44.

Giorgio Morandi
Still Life (Natura morta), 1919
[p. 472]
Oil on canvas, 53.5 × 57.5 cm. Top left: Morandi 919. Private collection.
Provenance: Milan, Galleria del Milione; Milan, Vigan Collection.
Exhibitions: Zurich 1950 no. 163/4; Milan 1967 no. 25; Rome 1973 no. 24; Bologna 1985-86 no. 24; Paris 1987 no. 9; Massa Carrara 1988 p. 25; London 1989 no. 56.
Bibliography: Ballo 1956 p. 43; Marchiori 1960 Plate 46; Fossati 1988 no. 33.
Reference: Vitali gen. cat. 1977 no. 45.

Giorgio Morandi
Still Life (Natura morta), 1921
[p. 473]
Oil on canvas, 44.7 × 52.8 cm. Bottom center: Morandi. Cologne, Museum Ludwig.
Provenance: Milan, Francesco Messina; Milan, Galleria Annunciata; Milan, Emilio Jesi.
Exhibitions: Rome 1939 no. 4; Madrid 1984-85 no. 8, then Barcelona 1985; London 1989 no. 88.
Bibliography: Siblik 1965 no. 26.
Reference: Vitali gen. cat. 1977 no. 65.

Critical References

Giorgio Morandi
Still Life with Yellow Cloth (Natura morta con drappo giallo), 1924
[p. 476]
Oil on canvas, 70.6 × 67.8 cm. Top center: Morandi. Private collection.
Provenance: Florence, Roberto Longhi.
Exhibitions: San Francisco 1939 no. 26; The Hague 1954 no. 21, then Rotterdam 1954, London 1954 no. 20; Venice 1966 no. 20; Bologna 1966 no. 25.
Bibliography: Vitali 1964 Plate 67; Martini 1964 Plate X.
Reference: Vitali gen cat. 1977 no. 101.

Giorgio Morandi
Still Life (Natura morta), 1925
[p. 474]
Oil on canvas, 51 × 57.5 cm. Top center: Morandi. Leningrad, The Hermitage Museum.
Provenance: Moscow Museum of Modern Art.
Exhibitions: Leningrad 1989 no. 12, then Moscow 1989.
Bibliography: Soffici in *L'Italiano* March 1932; Brandi 1942 Plate XXV; Vitali 1964 Plate 70.
Reference: Vitali gen. cat. 1977 no. 107.

Giorgio Morandi
Still Life (Natura morta), 1926
[p. 475]
Oil on canvas, 60 × 60 cm. Bottom center: Morandi. Florence City Council, Raccolta d'Arte Contemporanea Alberto Della Ragione.
Provenance: Genoa, Alberto Della Ragione.
Exhibitions: Rome 1939 no. 20; Florence 1967 no. 1210; Rome 1973 no. 36; Bologna 1975 no. 11; Bologna 1985-86 no. 36; London 1989 no. 89.
Bibliography: Soffici in *L'Italiano* March 1932 no. 10; Vitali 1964 Plate 74; Arcangeli 1964 fig. 26.
Reference: Vitali gen. cat. 1977 no. 114.

Giorgio Morandi
Landscape with Pink House (Paesaggio con casa rosa), 1928
[p. 477]
Oil on canvas, 61.5 × 47 cm. Rome, Camera dei Deputati Collection.
Provenance: Milan, Prospero Guarini; Milan Galleria del Milione; Milan, Galleria Toninelli.
Exhibitions: Rome 1973 no. 39.
Reference: Vitali gen. cat. 1977 no. 125.

Giorgio Morandi
Still Life (Natura morta), 1932
[p. 479]
Oil on canvas, 43 × 48 cm. Bottom center: Morandi 32. Private collection.
Provenance: Milan, Augusto Giovanardi; Milan, Galleria del Milione; Milan, Cesare Tosi.
Exhibitions: Milan 1949-50; Sao Paolo 1957; Milan 1962.
Bibliography: Vitali 1964 Plate 94; Arcangeli 1964 fig. 29.
Reference: Vitali gen. cat. 1977 no. 173.

Giorgio Morandi
Still Life (Natura morta), 1932
[p. 478]
Oil on canvas, 62.2 × 72 cm. Top left: Morandi/1932. Rome, Galleria Comunale d'Arte Moderna (lodged with the Galleria Nazionale d'Arte Moderna, Rome).
Exhibitions: Rome 1935 no. 9(?); Winterthur 1956 no. 17; Munich 1981 no. 17; Madrid 1984-85 no. 17, then Barcelona 1985; Helsinki 1988; Leningrad 1989 no. 15, then Moscow 1989.
Reference: Vitali gen. cat. 1977 no. 170.

Giorgio Morandi
Landscape (Paesaggio), 1936
[p. 480]
Oil on canvas, 63 × 65 cm. Bottom right: Morandi 1936. Florence City Council, Raccolta d'Arte Contemporanea Alberto Della Ragione.
Provenance: Genoa, Alberto Della Ragione.
Exhibitions: London 1970-71 no. 40; Paris 1971 no. 40; Milan 1971 no. 44; Rome 1972-73 no. 60.
Bibliography: Ragghianti-Valsecchi 1970 Plate 21.
Reference: Vitali gen. cat. 1977 no. 213.

Giorgio Morandi
Still Life of Purple Objects (Natura morta di oggetti in viola), 1937
[p. 481]
Oil on canvas, 62 × 76 cm. Private collection.
Provenance: Florence, Roberto Longhi.
Exhibitions: San Francisco 1939 no. 25; Sao Paolo 1951 no. 85; Venice 1966 no. 42; Bologna 1966 no. 53.
Bibliography: Vitali 1964 Plate 100; Boschetto 1971 Plate 142.
Reference: Vitali gen. cat. 1977 no. 222.

Giorgio Morandi
Still Life (Natura morta), 1940
[p. 482]
Oil on canvas, 35 × 63 cm. Bottom right: Morandi. Private collection.
Provenance: Rome, Scialoja; Turin, Galleria Gissi; Turin, Perona; Turin, Cerruti.
Exhibitions: Rome 1965-66 no. 13.
Reference: Vitali gen. cat. 1977 no. 257.

Giorgio Morandi
Still Life (Natura morta), 1941
[p. 483]
Oil on canvas, 26.5 × 41 cm. Back: Morandi 1941. Private collection.
Provenance: Brescia Pietro Feroldi; Milan, Gianni Mattioli.
Exhibitions: Milan 1942 no. 72; Ferrara 1978; Munich 1981 no. 35; Madrid 1984-85 no. 25, then Barcelona 1985.
Reference: Vitali gen. cat. 1977 no. 315.

Bruno Munari
Useless Machine (Macchina inutile), 1934
[p. 484]
Wood, squash rind, aluminium, 57 × 16 × 10 cm. Private collection.
Exhibitions: Novara 1986; Milan 1986-87 p. 30 (dated 1933).
Bibliography: Tanchis 1986 p. 34.

Bruno Munari
Tactile Table (Tavola tattile), 1938
[p. 485]
Various materials on bare wood, 122 × 13 × 3 cm. Novara, Private collection.
Exhibitions: Novara 1986; Milan 1986-87 pp. 34-35.
Bibliography: Tanchis 1986 pp. 110-111.

Giuseppe Pellizza da Volpedo
Human Tide (Fiumana), 1895-1896
[pp. 282-283]
Oil on canvas, 255 × 438 cm. Milan, Pinacoteca di Brera (gift of Sprind S.p.A., 1986). Provenance: Volpedo, Pellizza; Vigevano, Masera; Turin, Bertolotto; Turin, Plurinvest; Milan, Sprind.
Exhibitions: Rome 1920-21 no. 20; Turin 1939; Alessandria 1954 no. 81; Turin 1977 no. 3; Alessandria 1980-81 no. 44; Milan 1986 no. 116.

Bibliography: Sapori 1921 pp. 44-48; *Alexandria* 1937 p. 213; Fiori-Bellonzi 1968 vol. I pp. 185, 192, 198 and vol. II; Barilli in *L'Arte Illustrata* nn. 22-24 1969 pp. 29-30; Quinsac 1986 pp. 141-142 Plate 116.
Reference: Scotti gen. cat. 1986 no. 943.

Fausto Pirandello
Interior in the Morning (Interno di mattina), 1931
[p. 486]
Oil on canvas, 175 × 150 cm. Paris, Musée national d'art moderne, Centre Georges Pompidou.
Exhibitions: Rome 1932 Plate XXXIX; Rome 1951 no. 18; Rome 1959-60 no. 29; Rome 1965 no. 5 (dated 1932); Florence 1967 no. 2043; Rome 1976-77 Plate 19; London 1989 no. 141.
Bibliography: Lucchese in *La Fiera Letteraria* 11 March 1951; Neppi 1951; Venturi in *Commentari* January-March in *La Giustizia* March 1954 p. 52; Maltese 1960 p. 371.

Fausto Pirandello
Golden Rain (Pioggia d'oro), 1934
[p. 487]
Oil on wood, 100 × 130 cm. Private collection.
Provenance: Artist's collection.
Exhibitions: Rome 1935 no. 13; Rome 1951 no. 24; Rome 1959-60 no. 28; Rome 1965 no. 6; Florence 1967; Melbourne 1971; Rome 1976-77 Plate 23; London 1989 no. 142.
Bibliography: Neppi 1951; Marcheselli in *Gazzetta di Parma* 2 December 1975.

Enrico Prampolini
Encounter with Matter (Intervista con la materia), 1930
[p. 489]
Oil, enamel, galalith, and sponge on wood, 98 × 78.5 cm. Bottom right: PRAMPOLINI 930. Turin, Museo Civico Galleria d'Arte Moderna.
Provenance: Rome, Giorgio Franchetti.
Exhibitions: Venice 1930 (no. 74-79?); Milan 1956; Rome 1959; Rome 1961 no. 31; modena 1978; Rome 1980; Rome 1986 no. 10; London 1989 no. 119.
Bibliography: *Natura* February 1936 p. 24; Prampolini 1944 (dated 1927); Menna 1967 no. 85; Calvesi 1968 p. 45.

Enrico Prampolini
Encounter with Matter (Intervista con la materia), 1930
[p. 488]
Collage and mixed media on cardboard, 61 × 46.3 cm. Bottom left: PRAMPOLINI. Turin, Galleria Narciso.
Exhibitions: Turin 1985 Plate 54.
Bibliography: *Il Mondo* no. 36 9 September 1985 p. 48.

Enrico Prampolini
Encounter with Matter (Intervista con la materia), c.1930
[p. 490]
Multi-media on cardboard, 48.8 × 67.8 cm. Bottom right: PRAMPOLINI. Turin, Galleria Narciso.
Exhibitions: London 1971; Milan 1976; Turin 1985 Plate 55.
Bibliography: *Il Mondo* no. 36 9 September 1985 pp. 46-47.

Enrico Prampolini
Polimaterico (?), c.1930
[p. 491]
Multi-media on masonite, 60 × 55.5 cm. Bottom right: PRAMPOLINI. Albinea, Reggio Emilia, Ida and Achille Maramotti Collection.

Enrico Prampolini
Plastico-Marine State of Mind — Multi-Material Automatism B (Stato d'animo plastico marino — Automatismo polimaterico B), 1937
[p. 492]
Various materials on plaster, 32 × 41 cm. Back: PRAMPOLINI 1937. Modena, Galleria Fonte d'Abisso.
Exhibitions: Rome 1941; Venice 1942; Paris 1958; Rome 1962 no. 55; Modena 1985-86 no. 58.
Bibliography: Prampolini 1944; Menna 1967 no. 156.

Mario Radice
Composition C.F.O. 33, 1932-34
[p. 493]
Oil on canvas, 70 × 130 cm. Bottom left: Radice. Private collection.
Exhibitions: Florence 1967 no. 1622; Rome 1971 no. 1; Zurich 1976 Plate 10, then Rome 1976; Milan 1982 p. 166 no. 2 (dated 1934-36).

Antonietta Raphaël
Miriam asleep (Miriam che dorme), 1933-58
[p. 496]
Porphyry, 32 × 22 × 25 cm. Bottom right: Raphaël 933; Private collection.
Provenance: Artist's Collection.
Exhibitions: Milan 1984 no. 21; Milan 1985 no. 2; Milan 1988 no. 112.
Bibliography: Pinottini 1971 no. 2.

Antonietta Raphaël
Simona with comb (Simona con il pettine), 1935-48
[p. 497]
Fiesole stone, 52 × 36 × 33 cm. Private collection.
Provenance: Artist's Collection.
Exhibitions: Milan 1955; Rome 1955; Turin 1972; Milan 1985 no. 36; Milan 1988 no. 114.
Bibliography: Pinottini 1971 no. 4; D'Amico 1985 no. 3.

Antonietta Raphaël
Three sisters (Tre sorelle), 1936
[p. 495]
Concrete, 97 × 70 × 80 cm. Rome, Galleria Nazionale d'Arte Moderna.
Provenance: Artist's Collection.
Exhibitions: Rome 1937; Rome 1959-60; Turin 1960; Florence 1967; Rome 1978 p. 24; Milan 1982; Milan 1985 no. 6.
Bibliography: Pinottini 1971 no. 7.

Antonietta Raphaël
Simona singing (Simona che canta), 1938-39
[p. 494]
Terracotta, 32 × 22 × 25 cm. Private collection.
Provenance: Artist's Collection
Exhibitions: Rome 1951-52; Milan 1985 no. 16 and cover.
Bibliography: Dias in *l'Unità*, 22 July 1949; Pinottini 1971 no. 37.

Mauro Reggiani
Composition No.2, 1935
[p. 497]
Oil on wood, 54 × 64 cm. Private collection.
Exhibitions: Milan 1936; Venice 1966 no. 63; Modena 1967 no. 4; Turin 1973-74 no. 4; Prato 1980 p. 81 no. 8; Modena 1984 p. 81.
Bibliography: Fossati 1971 fig. 4.

Mauro Reggiani
Composition, 1936
[p. 496]
Oil on canvas, 55 × 65 cm. Savona, Anna and Vittorio Venturino Collection.

Provenance: Milan, Bernasconi-Porlezza.
Exhibitions: Milan 1936?; Prato 1980 p. 81; Modena 1984 no. 84.

Manlio Rho
Composition, 1933
[p. 498]
Oil on canvas board, 54 × 45 cm. Bottom left: Manlio Rho. Milan, Zita Vismara Collection.
Exhibitions: Venice 1966; Como 1966 Plate 1.

Manlio Rho
Composition 95 RDSA, 1940
[p. 501]
Oil on wood, 80 × 65 cm. Bottom left: MANLIO RHO. Private collection.
Exhibitions: Venice, 1940; Venice 1966; Milan 1966.
Bibliography: Sartoris 1941 fig. 59.

Ottone Rosai
Serenade (Serenata), 1920
[p. 502]
Oil on canvas, 68 × 44 cm. Signed in bottom right: ROSAI. Prato, Galleria d'Arte Moderna Farsetti.
Provenance: Florence, Piero Vallecchi; Florence, Galleria Michaud.
Exhibitions: Florence 1965-66; Milan 1971 Plate XIX.
Bibliography: Santini 1960 Plate 10; Valsecchi-Russoli-Cavallo 1968 p. 9; Fossati 1988 no. 46.
Reference: Cavallo 1973 no. 11/IV.

Ottone Rosai
Under the Pergola (Sotto la Pergola), 1922
[p. 503]
Oil on canvas, 84 × 87 cm. Bottom right: O. ROSAI 1922. Prato, Galleria d'Arte Moderna Farsetti.
Provenance: Milan, Galleria Bergamini.
Exhibitions: Ivrea 1957 no. 16; Florence 1960 no. 61; Florence 1964 no. 6; Florence 1967 no. 1286; Bologna 1985-86 no. 178.
Bibliography: Santini 1960 Plate 24.
Reference: Cavallo 1973 no. 18 Plate CLXI.

Ottone Rosai
Via Toscanella, 1922
[p. 504]
Oil on canvas, 65 × 54 cm. Bottom right: O. ROSAI 1922. Florence, Private collection.
Exhibitions: Rome 1922; Florence 1960 no. 47; Florence 1967 no. 1289; Turin 1983 Plate 18, then Rome 1983; Bologna 1985-86 no. 179.
Bibliography: *Il Nuovo Corriere* 28 April 1955; Santini 1960 Plate 17.

Gino Rossi
Seascape - Douarnenez (Marina - Douarnenez), undated
[p. 314]
Oil on canvas, 46 × 64 cm. Venice, Ca' Pesaro, Galleria Internazionale d'Arte Moderna.
Provenance: Venice, Nino Barbantini
Exhibitions: Venice 1911 no. 74; Venice 1913 no. 106 ; Venice 1948 no. 10; Rome 1956 no. 28; Venice 1958 no. 7; Verona 1971 p. 22; Verona 1983-84, no. 6, then Venice 1984.
Bibliography: Valeri *Le Tre Venezie* December 1933; Marchiori in *Emporium* May 1935 p. 284; Geiger Plate 24; Perocco 1965 p. 46 ff.
Reference: Menegazzi gen. cat. 1984 no. 6.

Gino Rossi
The Little Parish Church (La piccola parrochia), 1908
[p. 315]
Oil on cardboard, 35 × 43 cm. Bottom right:

Rossi. Private collection.
Provenance: Venice, Renza Soppelsa.
Exhibitions: Venice 1913 no. 108; Venice 1919 Plate IV; Venice 1948 no. 1; Rome 1956 no. 18; Verona 1983-84 then Venice 1984.
Bibliography: Candida in *Emporium* April 1943; Geiger 1949 no. VII; Apollonio 1950 p. 51; Perocco 1972 p. 136.
Reference: Menegazzi gen. cat. no. 15.

Medardo Rosso
Laughing Woman (Rieuse), c.1890
[p. 284]
Wax, 35 × 23 × 18 cm. Barzio Museo Medardo Rosso.
Exhibitions: Vienna 1905 p. 5; Rome 1911; Venice 1914 p. 87; Milan 1923 p. 25; Rome 1931 no. 149 no. 8; New York 1958-59 Plate 4-5; Alessandria 1979-80 no. 9; Frankfurt 1984 p. 19.
Bibliography: Sarfatti 1925 pp. 110-117; Papini 1940 Plate XVII; Barbantini 1950 pp. 37,38,42; Borghi 1950 p. 66; Scolari Barr 1963 pp. 9,34,35,38,43,46,65; Pirovano 1968 Plate 41.
Reference: cat. Milan 1979 no. 26.

Medardo Rosso
Large Laughing Woman (Grande Rieuse), 1891 (?)
[p. 285]
Bronze, 61 × 68 × 22 cm. Florence, Galleria d'Arte Moderna di Palazzo Pitti.
Exhibitions: Frankfurt 1984 no. 19.

Medardo Rosso
Child in the Sun (Bambino al sole), 1892
[p. 286]
Plaster, 35 × 21 × 19 cm. Bottom center, toward right: M.Rosso. Barzio, Museo Medardo Rosso.
Exhibitions: Vienna 1905 p. 6; Venice 1914 p. 87; Milan 1926 p. 21; Rome 1931 no. 17; Frankfurt 1984 no. 22.
Bibliography: Sarfatti 1925 p. 110; Papini 1940 Plate XXI; Barbantini 1950 p. 33; Borghi 1950 p. 66; Scolari Barr 1963 pp. 36,37,46,78; Pirovano 1968 Plate 43.
Reference: cat. Milan 1979 no. 29.

Medardo Rosso
Child in the Sun (Bambino al sole), c. 1892
[p. 287]
Wax, 37 × 21 × 19 cm. Private collection.
Provenance: Milan, Carlo Carrà.

Medardo Rosso
Impression of a Boulevard or The Veiled Lady (Impression de boulevard or Femme a la voilette), 1893
[p. 289]
Wax, 60 × 59 × 25 cm. Salome and Eric Estorick Collection.
Exhibitions: Frankfurt 1984 no. 24; London 1989 no. 1.

Medardo Rosso
The Concierge (La Portinaia), c.1893
[p. 290]
Plaster, 39.5 × 33.5 × 17.5 cm. Barzio, Museo Medardo Rosso.
Exhibitions: Vienna 1905 p. 6; Venice 1914 p. 86; Milan 1923 p. 25; Rome 1931 p. 150 no. 20; Florence 1984 no. 9.
Bibliography: Sarfatti 1925 pp. 107-108; Papini 1940 pp. 18-20; Barbantini 1950 pp. 22-24; Borghi 1950 p. 64; Scolari Barr 1963 pp. 9, 24, 25, 27-30, 64, 78; Pirovano 1968 Plate 39; Caramel-Pirovano 1975 no. 2223.
Reference: cat. Milan 1979 no. 13.

Critical References

Medardo Rosso
Man reading (Uomo che legge) c.1894
[p. 291]
Wax, 29.5 × 30.5 × 19.5 cm. Barzio, Museo
Medardo Rosso. Bottom right: M. Rosso.
Exhibitions: Venice 1914 p. 87; Milan 1923 p.
25; Milan 1926 p. 21; Rome 1931 p. 149 no. 1;
Florence 1984 no. 27.
Bibliography: Papini 1940 Plate XXVI; Bar-
bantini 1950 pp. 23,41; Borghi 1950 p. 68;
Scolari Barr 1963 pp. 9,43,45,65,73; Caramel-
Pirovano 1975 no. 2231.
Reference: cat. Milan 1979 no. 34.

Medardo Rosso
Yvette Guilbert
[p. 288]
Patinated bronze, 44 × 27.5 × 19.5 cm. Venice,
Ca' Pesaro - Galleria Internazionale d'Arte
Moderna.
Exhibitions: Venice 1914 p. 87; Rome 1931 p.
149 no. 4; Paris 1960-61 no. 606; Florence 1984
no. 28.
Bibliography: Sarfatti 1925 p. 110; Papini 1940
Plate XXVII; Barbantini 1950 p. 331; Borghi
1950 p. 68; Taylor 1961 p. 90; Scolari Barr
1963 no. 46; Pirovano 1968 Plate 45.
Reference: cat. Milan 1979.

Mino Rosso
The Woman Pianist (La Pianista), 1932
[p. 505]
Metal and lacquered wood, 73.5 × 50.5 × 41 cm.
Turin, Galleria Narciso.
Provenance: Turin, Cantatore.
Exhibitions: Venice 1932; Paris 1935; Milan
1951 p. 4; Turin 1962 no. 66; Turin 1976 no.
33.
Bibliography: *La Noche* 5 January 1934; *Paris
Soir* 2 April 1935; *Stile Futurista* nn.15-16
December 1935 Plate 66; Marchiori 1960 Plate
74; Crispolti 1969 Plate 159; Dragone 1976
Plate 123.

Luigi Russolo
The Revolt (La rivolta), 1911
[p. 373]
Oil on canvas, 150 × 230 cm. The Hague, Haags
Gemeentemuseum.
Exhibitions: Milan 1911; Paris 1912 no. 22;
London 1912 no. 22; Berlin 1912; Brussels
1912; Venice 1960; Venice 1968; Venice 1986
p. 206.

Luigi Russolo
*Plastic Synthesis of a Woman's Simultaneous
Movements (Sintesi plastica dei movimenti simul-
tanei di una donna)*, 1912
[p. 372]
Oil on canvas, 85 × 65 cm. Bottom right: L.
Russolo, 1913. Grenoble, Musée de Peinture et
de Sculpture.
Exhibitions: Rotterdam 1913 no. 25; Rome
1914; Paris 1929-30 no. 22; Venice 1960;
Venice 1968; Venice 1986 p. 209; London 1989
no. 32.

Giuseppe Santomaso
*Composition with Black Rope (Composizione con
cordone nero)*, 1941
[p. 566]
Oil on canvas, 38 × 62 cm. Bergamo, Mario Fi-
nazzi Collection.
Provenance: Artist's Collection.
Exhibitions: Cortina d'Ampezzo 1941; Venice
1954 no. 1; Milan 1986 no. 4.
Bibliography: Pallucchini in *Emporium* May
1942; Podestà in *Domus* no. 169 1942 p. 41;
Venturi 1958 p. 61.

Reference: Ponente-Alfieri gen. cat. 1975 no.
70.

Giuseppe Santomaso
*Still Life with Bucranium (Natura morta con
bucranio)*, 1941
[p. 566]
Oil on canvas, 55 × 141 cm. Private collection.
Provenance: Brescia, Scarampella Collection.
Exhibitions: Bergamo 1941; Milan 1986 no. 3.
Bibliography: Pallucchini in *Emporium* May
1942; Giani in *Cinema* no. 31 1950 p. 47;
Venturi 1958 p. 61; Ballo 1964 no. 361.
Reference: Ponente-Alfieri gen. cat. 1975 no.
68.

Giuseppe Santomaso
Still Life (Natura morta), 1941
[p. 567]
Oil on canvas, 51 × 70 cm. Florence, Galleria
Palazzo Vecchio.

Alberto Savinio
The Lost Ship (Le navire perdu), 1926-28
[p. 517]
Oil on canvas, 66 × 82 cm. Left toward center:
Savinio. Private collection.
Exhibitions: Milan 1976 Plate IV, then Brussels
1976; Rome 1978 no. 22; Ferrara 1980 no. 21;
London 1989 no. 79.
Bibliography: Briganti-Sciascia 1979 p. 87.

Alberto Savinio
Atlas (Atlante), 1927
[p. 506]
Oil on canvas, 71 ×91 cm. Bottom left: Savi-
nio/1927. Private collection.
Exhibitions: Milan 1976 no. 8, then Brussels
1976; Rome 1978 no. 13; Ferrara 1980 no. 12;
London 1989 no. 77.
Bibliography: Briganti-Sciascia 1979 p. 47.

Alberto Savinio
The Poet's Dream (Le rêve du poète), 1927
[p. 507]
Oil on canvas, 116 × 88.5 cm. Bottom right:
Savinio/1929. Private collection.
Exhibitions: Milan 1963 no. 13 (*Il Poeta*); Turin
1963 no. 5; L'Aquila 1968 no. A3; Milan 1976
Plate II, then Brussels 1976; Rome 1978 no. 14;
Bologna 1980 no. 80.
Bibliography: Briganti-Sciascia 1979 p. 49.

Alberto Savinio
The Shelter of Promises (La cité des promesses),
1928
[p. 509]
Oil on canvas, 97 × 146 cm. Prato, Galleria
d'Arte Moderna Farsetti.
Provenance: Paris, Léonce Rosenberg.

Alberto Savinio
The Isle of Charms (L'île des charmes), 1928
[p. 508]
Oil on canvas, 114 × 162 cm. Cortina d'Ampez-
zo, Collezione Regole d'Ampezzo, Galleria
Mario Rimoldi.
Provenienza: Paris, Léonce Rosenberg.
Exhibitions: Milan 1970, no. 42; Rome 1978
no. 20; Ferrara 1980 no. 18; London 1989 no.
78.
Bibliography: Cavallo-Vivarelli 1984 no. 15.

Alberto Savinio
Gladiators (Gladiatori), 1928
[p. 512]
Oil on canvas, 101 × 80 cm. Bottom left: Savi-
nio. Private collection.
Exhibitions: Milan 1976 Plate III, then Brussels

1976.
Bibliography: Briganti-Sciascia 1979 p. 71;
Cavallo-Vivarelli 1984 no. 18.

Alberto Savinio
The Southern Astrologer (L'astrologue méridien),
1929
[p. 511]
Oil on canvas, 65 × 81 cm. Bottom right: Savi-
nio/1929. Puos d'Alpago, Collezione Augusto
Vallunga.
Provenance: Paris, Petite Galerie; Milan.
Galleria Medea.
Exhibitions: Milan 1970 no. 43; New York
1987 pp. 100-101.

Alberto Savinio
Builders of Paradise (Bâtisseurs du paradis), 1929
[p. 510]
Oil on canvas, 73 × 91 cm. Bottom right: Savi-
nio 1929. Verona, Galleria dello Scudo.
Provenance: Venice, Semenzato.
Exhibitions: Milan 1930 p. 13; New York 1987
pp. 92-3; Milan 1988 no. 42.

Alberto Savinio
The Fall of the Angels (La chute des anges), 1929
[p. 513]
Oil on canvas, 116 × 88.5 cm. Bottom right:
Savinio 1929. Assitalia Le Assicurazioni d'Italia
SpA Collection.
Provenance: Paris, Jeanne Castel; New York,
Lanfear B Norrie; Rome, Galleria La Medusa.
Exhibitions: Paris 1932; Rome 1978 no. 35;
Venice 1985 p. 25.
Bibliography: Scheiwiller 1930 p. 77.

Alberto Savinio
The Faithful Spouse (La fidèle épouse), 1929
[p. 514]
Oil on canvas, 81 × 65 cm. Bottom right: Savi-
nio. Verona, Galleria dello Scudo.
Exhibitions: Milan 1970 no. 29; Milan 1976 no.
36, then Brussels 1976; London 1989 no. 80.
Bibliography: Briganti-Sciascia 1979 p. 111;
Fagiolo in *Art-forum* January 1983 p. 51.

Alberto Savinio
The Magi (I re magi), 1929
[p. 516]
Oil on canvas, 89 × 116 cm. Trento, Museo
Provinciale d'Arte Sezione Contemporanea,
Palazzo delle Albere.
Bibliography: in cat. Ferrara 1980 (among the
works not shown).

Alberto Savinio
Ulysees and Polyphemus (Ulysse et Polyphème),
1929
[p. 518]
Oil on canvas, 65 × 82 cm. Bottom left: Savi-
nio/1929. Cologne, Museum Ludwig.
Provenance: Bergamo, Galleria Lorenzelli.
Exhibitions: New York 1987 p. 98-99.

Alberto Savinio
Penelope, 1930
[p. 515]
Oil on canvas, 35 × 27 cm. Private collection.

Alberto Savinio
*The First Light in the World (La première lumière
du monde)*, 1930
[p. 519]
Oil on canvas, 65 × 82 cm. Private collection.
Provenance: Bergamo, Galleria Lorenzelli.

Scipione
The Octopus — Molluscs, Pierina arriving in a

large city (*La piovra — I molluschi, Pierina è arrivata in una grande città*), 1929
[p. 520]
Oil on wood, 60 × 71 cm. Macerata, Cassa di Risparmio della Provincia di Macerata Collection.
Provenance: Genoa, Della Lanterna Collection; Venice, Carlo Cardazzo; Rome, Mimì Pecci Blunt.
Exhibitions: Rome 1930; Milan 1941 no. 6; Rome 1941 no. 62; Milan 1950; Lausanne 1950 no. 135; Rome 1954 no. 14; Florence 1967 no. 2089; Macerata 1985 no. 11; London 1989 no. 145.
Bibliography: Marchiori 1939 Plate IV; Trombadori in *Primato* 1 May 1941; Apollonio 1945 no. VI; Ungaretti 1950 no. 50; Borghi 1960 p. 104; Mascherpa 1983 no. 10.
Reference: Fagiolo-Rivosecchi gen. cat. 1988 no. 33.

Scipione
The Apocalypse (L'Apocalisse), 1930
[p. 523]
Oil on wood, 65 × 78 cm. Turin, Museo Civico Galleria d'Arte Moderna (inv. no. 1105).
Provenance: acquired in 1935 at the II Quadriennale.
Exhibitions: Rome 31 no. 18; Rome 1935 no. 15; Venice 1948 no. 10; Macerata 1948 no. 8; Turin 1981.
Bibliography: Marchiori 1939 Plate XV; Nebbia 1941 p. 191.
Reference: Fagiolo-Rivosecchi gen. cat. 1988 no. 63.

Scipione
Piazza Navona, 1930
[p. 522]
Oil on wood, 80.5 × 78.5 cm. Rome, Galleria Nazionale d'Arte Moderna (inv. no. 5511).
Provenance: Rome, Margherita Caetani di Bassiano; New York, Nelson Rockefeller.
Exhibitions: Rome 1930; Rome 1935 no. 13; Venice 1948 no. 7; Macerata 1948 no. 6; New York p. 134; Macerata 1985 no. 26; London 1989 no. 143.
Bibliography: Callari 1935 Plate XXV; Marchiori 1939 Plate XIII and cover; Bertocchi in *Arte Mediterranea* July-August 1949; Carrieri 1950 Plate 268; Giannelli in *Le carte parlanti* 1950.
Reference: Fagiolo-Rivosecchi 1988 no. 55.

Scipione
Portrait of the Senior Cardinal Decano — Cardinal Vannutelli, (Ritratto del Cardinale Decano — Il Cardinale Vannutelli), 1930
[p. 521]
Oil on wood, 133.7 × 117.3 cm. Bottom left: Scipione 30. Rome, Galleria Comunale d'Arte Moderna (inv. AM 1081).
Provenance: Rome, Alberto Arduini.
Exhibitions: Venice 1930 no. 21; Rome 1930; Rome 1935 no. 11; Milan 1941 no. 12; Rome 1944 no. 28; Rome 1954 no. 30; Milan 1985; Macerata 1985 no. 17; London 1989 no. 144.
Bibliography: Nebbia 1930 p. 201; Venturi in *Belvedere* May-June 1930; Marchiori 1939 Plate X; Maltese in *Emporium* July-August 1948; Borghi 1960 p. 102; Argan 1970 p. 461.
Reference: Fagiolo-Rivosecchi gen. cat. 1988 no. 39.

Scipione
Road Leading to St Peter's (Strada che porta a San Pietro), 1930

[p. 524]
Oil on wood, 39 × 46 cm. Rome, Galleria Comunale d'Arte Moderna (inv. AM 973).
Provenance: Acquired from the I Quadriennale.
Exhibitions: Rome 1931 no. 19; Rome 1954 no. 23; Ferrara 1960 no. 225; Florence 1967 no. 2081; Macerata 1985 no. 23.
Bibliography: Marchiori 1939 p. 29; Bucarelli 1956 p. 233.
Reference: Fagiolo-Rivosecchi gen. cat. 1988 no. 57.

Gino Severini
The Pan-Pan at "Monico" (La Danse du Pan-Pan au "Monico"), 1911 (replica 1959-60)
[p. 375]
Oil on canvas, 280 × 400 cm. Paris, Musée national d'art moderne, Centre Georges Pompidou.
Provenance: Paris, Severini
Exhibitions: Rome 1961 no. 9; Paris 1967 no. 3; Düsseldorf 1974 no. 139; Florence 1983 no. 15.
Bibliography: Venturi 1961 Plate 4; De Sardi 1964 no. 110; Pacini 1966 no. 9.
Reference: Fonti gen. cat. 1988 no. 97A.

Gino Severini
Forms of a Dancer in the Light (Formes d'une danseuse dans la lumière), c.1913
[p. 376]
Oil on canvas, 71 × 56 cm. Bottom right: G. Severini. Private collection.
Provenance: Romana Ayala Severini.
Exhibitions: Rome 1961 no. 23; Rome 1965 no. 4; Paris 1967 no. 17; Rome 1972 no. 5; Milan 1973 no. 4; Paris 1973 no. 58.
Bibliography: Drudi Gambillo-Fiori 1962 vol.II no. 47; Pacini 1966 no. 21.
Reference: Fonti cat. gen. 1988 no. 172.

Gino Severini
Plastic Rhythm of 14 July (Ritmo plastico del 14 luglio), 1913
[p. 377]
Oil on canvas, 66 × 50 cm. Bottom right: G. Severini 1913. Rome, Collezione Gina Severini Franchina.
Exhibitions: Berlin 1913 no. 325; London 1914 no. 51; Rome 1914 no. 7; Paris 1929-30 no. 4; Rome 1945 no. 4; Zurich 1950 no. 85; Rome 1959 no. 13; Venice 1960 no. 124; Milan 1973 no. 6; Milan 1982-83 no. 11; Florence 1983 no. 35; Venice 1986 p. 232.
Bibliography: Zervos 1950 p. 176; Drudi Gambillo-Fiori 1962 vol II no. 52; Pacini 1966 Plate 20; Martin 1968 Plate 100.
Reference: Fonti gen. cat. 1988 no. 158.

Gino Severini
Red Cross Train Passing Through a Village (Train de la Croix Rouge traversant un village), 1915
[p. 374]
Oil on canvas, 89 × 116 cm. Back: Gino Severini 2/"Train de la Croix Rouge/traversant un village"/1915. New York, Solomon R. Guggenheim Museum.
Provenance: New York, Alfred Stieglitz; New York, Quinn; New York, Morton Neumann.
Exhibitions: Paris 1916 no. 6; New York 1917 no. 2 (*Toiles*); Rome 1982; Florence 1983 no. 43.
Bibliography: Caffin in *New York American* 12 March 1917; Martin 1968 Plate XV; Lukach in *Burlington Magazine*, April 1971, fig. 47.
Reference: Fonti gen. cat. 1988 no. 234.

Gino Severini
Motherhood (Maternità), 1916

[p. 525]
Oil on canvas, 92 × 65 cm. Bottom right: G. Severini 1916. Cortona. Museo dell'Accademia Etrusca.
Provenance: Rome, Severini.
Exhibitions: Amsterdam 1931 no. 14; Paris 1924; Venice 1936 no. 3; Rome 1961 no. 47; Paris 1967 no. 34; Bologna 1980 p. 62; Florence 1983 no. 68; Alessandria 1987 no. 5.
Bibliography: Albert-Birot in *Sic* no. 14 February 1917; Courthion 1930; Fierens 1936; Nicodemi 1940 p. 284; Severini 1946 pp. 249-250; Pacini 1966 no. 33; Calvesi in *L'Arte Moderna* vol.V 1967 p. 110.
Reference: Fonti gen. cat. 1988 no. 276.

Gino Severini
The Card Players (Les joueurs de cartes), 1924
[p. 526]
Oil on wood, 75.5 × 100 cm. Right, toward bottom: G. Severini. Verona, Galleria dello Scudo.
Provenance: Paris, Léone Rosenberg; Chicago, Frederic Clay Bartlett; Honolulu Museum of Fine Arts.
Exhibitions: Rome 1980, cover p. 60; Florence 1983 p. 116 and p. 178 no. 72; Bolzano 1987-88 p. 62 no. 32, then Genoa 1988, Munich 1988 no. 81; Verona 1988-89 no. 12, then Milan 1989.
Bibliography: *Bulletin de L'Effort Moderne* 1924; Roth 1925 Plate 16; Courthion 1930 Plate 20 (dated 1923); Courthion 1941 Plate XVIII (dated 1923); Carrà M., 1967 p. 357.
Reference: Fonti gen. cat. 1988 no. 413.

Gino Severini
Pierrot the Musician - Polichinelle with Guitar (Pierrot musicien - Polichinelle avec guitare), 1924
[p. 527]
Oil on canvas, 130 × 89 cm. Bottom right: G. Severini. Rotterdam, Museum Boymans-van Beuningen.
Provenance: Paris, Léonce Rosenberg.
Exhibitions: Amsterdam 1931 no. 34; Venice 1932 no. 37; Rome 1961 no. 86; Florence 1983 no. 73; Alessandria 1987 no. 29.
Bibliography: Cassou in *Dedalo* 1932 p. 895; Venturi 1961 no. 46; Pacini 1966 no. 48.
Reference: Fonti gen. cat. 1988 no. 414.

Mario Sironi
The Yellow Truck (Il camion giallo), 1919
[p. 528]
Collage, tempera and oil on linen paper, 89 × 63 cm. Private collection.
Exhibitions: Venice 1962 p. 24 no. 11; Milan 1973 fig. 21; Milan 1985 no. 23.
Bibliography Anzani-Caramel 1983 p. 149.
Reference: Bellonzi 1985 no. 21.

Mario Sironi
Synthesis of an Urban Landscape (Sintesi di paesaggio urbano), 1919
[p. 533]
Oil on canvas, 40 × 42 cm. Private collection.
Exhibitions: Milan 1985 no. 28; Düsseldorf 1988 no. 41.

Mario Sironi
Outskirts (Periferia), c. 1920
[p. 529]
Oil on linen paper, 98 × 72 cm. Milan, Private collection.
Provenance: Genoa, Galleria Genova; Genoa, Galleria Rotta.
Exhibitions: Milan 1973.

Critical References

Mario Sironi
Urban Landscape with Truck (Paesaggio urbano con camion), 1920-23
[p. 530]
Oil on canvas, 50 × 80 cm. Bottom right: Sironi. Private collection.
Provenance: Milan, Emilio Jesi.
Exhibitions: Venice 1962 p. 24 no. 17; Florence 1967 fig. 14; Paris 1980-81 p. 106; Verona 1982-83; Milan 1984 fig. 28; Milan 1985 no. 33; Düsseldorf 1988 no. 51; London 1989 no. 100.
Bibliography: Sarfatti 1925 p. 137; Morosini in *Paese Sera* 7 October 1969 p. 9; Sironi 1980 between pp. 96 and 97; *Arte* April 1985, cover.
Reference: Bellonzi 1985 no. 25.

Mario Sironi
Urban Landscape (Paesaggio urbano), 1922
[p. 531]
Oil on canvas, 56 × 76 cm. Bottom right and left: Sironi. Private collection.
Exhibitions: Venice 1962 no. 21; Milan 1973 fig. 37 (*Periferia*; Milan 1983 Plate 128; Milan 1985 no. 41; Düsseldorf 1988 no. 59.
Bibliography: Costantini 1934 p. 271; Anceschi 1944 Plate 14; Pica 1955 fig. 13; Valsecchi 1962 Plate 19.
Reference: Bellonzi 1985 no. 29.

Mario Sironi
Nude with Mirror (Nudo con lo specchio), 1923
[p. 534]
Oil on canvas, 96 × 72.5 cm. Bergamo, Private collection.
Exhibitions: Düsseldorf 1988 no. 89; London 1989 no. 104.

Mario Sironi
Urban Architectural Composition (Composizione architettonica urbana), c. 1923
Oil on canvas, 58 × 80.3 cm. Bottom left: SIRONI. Verona, Galleria dello Scudo.
Provenance: Milan, Galleria Philippe Daverio.
Exhibitions: Düsseldorf 1987 p. 59 no. O.61; Düsseldorf 1988 no. 44; Verona 1988-89 no. 24; London 1989 no. 102.

Mario Sironi
The Wayfarer (Il Viandante), c. 1923
[p. 539]
Oil on wood, 58 × 64 cm. Milan, Pinacoteca di Brera (gift of Emilio and Maria Jesi).
Exhibitions: Milan 1973 no. 36; Verona 1982-83 (dated 1920); Düsseldorf 1988 no. 75.
Bibliography: Anceschi 1944 Plate 18; Valsecchi 1962 no. 23.

Mario Sironi
The Pupil (L'Allieva), 1924
[p. 537]
Oil on canvas, 97 × 75 cm. Bottom left and right: SIRONI. Private collection.
Provenance: Milan, Brustio; Venice, Ferruccio Asta; Venice, Arturo Deana.
Exhibitions: Venice 1924 p. 78 no. 16; Rome 1931 p. 36 no. 19; Rome 1955-56 p. 58 no. 52 and Plate 112; Florence 1967 no. 1380; Milan 1973 p. 59 Plate 47; Bologna 1978 p. 345; Venice 1979 no. 93; Paris 1980-81 cover, then Berlin 1981; Milan 1985 no. 53; Düsseldorf 1988 no. 86; Verona 1988-89 no. 23, then Milan 1989.
Bibliography: Scheiwiller 1930 Plate XI; Costantini *Emporium* April 1934 p. 270; Giani 1942 Plate 127 (*La modella*; Pica 1955 Plate 16;

Valsecchi 1962 p. 19; De Grada 1972 Plate XII; Clair *Cahiers du Musée national d'art moderne* no. 7-8 1981 p. 182.
Reference: Bellonzi 1985 p. 56 no. 43.

Mario Sironi
The Neighborhood Belle (La Bella del Sestiere), 1924
[p. 536]
Oil on canvas, 80 × 70 cm. Private collection.
Exhibitions: Venice 1962 p. 24 no. 23 (*Donna del Sestiere*); Milan 1973 no. 46; Düsseldorf 1988 no. 78.
Bibliography: Anceschi 1944 Plate 61; Pica 1962 no. 18.
Reference: Bellonzi 1985 no. 44.

Mario Sironi
The White Horse and the Pier (Il cavallo bianco e il molo), 1924
[p. 535]
Oil on canvas, 44 × 56 cm. Private collection.
Exhibitions: Milan 1973 no. 33; Verona 1982-83; Düsseldorf 1988 no. 48; London 1989 no. 103.
Bibliography: Anceschi 1944 Plate 16.
Reference: Bellonzi 1985 no. 49.

Mario Sironi
Urban Landscape with Factory and Bridge (Paesaggio urbano con fabbrica e cavalcavia), 1926
[p. 538]
Tempera and oil on linen paper, 75 × 55 cm. Private collection.
Provenance: Milan, Palazzoli.
Exhibitions: Iseo 1988 pp. 32-33 and cover.

Mario Sironi
Melancholy (Malinconia), 1928
[p. 540]
Oil on linen paper, 81 × 60 cm. Milan, Civico Museo d'Arte Contemporanea.
Exhibitions:. Milan 1973 fig. 51; Bologna 1980 p. 122; Paris 1980-81 p. 100; Milan 1983 p. 68; Milan 1985 no. 75.
Bibliography: Scheiwiller 1930 Plate II; Costantini 1934 p. 270; Anceschi 1944 Plate 38 (*Donna seduta e paesaggio*); Sartoris 1946 Plate IX; Mascherpa-Valsecchi 1976 p. 144; Anzani-Caramel 1983 p. 170.
Reference: Bellonzi 1985 no. 57.

Mario Sironi
The Builders (I costruttori), 1929
[p. 543]
Oil on canvas, 100 × 70 cm. Milan. Civico Museo d'Arte Contemporanea, Boschi Collection.
Exhibitions: Milan 1973 fig. 84; Milan 1974 p. 57; Bologna 1980 p. 125; Milan 1985 no. 80; Düsseldorf 1988 no. 100.
Bibliography: Mascherpa 1976 p. 142; Caramel-Fiorio-Pirovano 1980 no. 166.
Reference: Bellonzi 1985 no. 72.

Mario Sironi
The Family (La Famiglia), 1929
[p. 541]
Oil on canvas, 167 × 210 cm. Private collection.
Provenance: Rome, Piacentini.
Exhibitions: Rome 1931; Venice 1932; Paris 1935; Venice 1962 p. 25 no. 40; Milan 1973; Sassari 1985, no. 24; Düsseldorf 1988 no. 107; London 1989 no. 109.
Bibliography: Castelfranco-Valsecchi 1956.
Reference: Bellonzi 1985 no. 71.

Mario Sironi
The Mountain Fairy (La Fata della montagna), 1929
[p. 542]
Oil on canvas, 100 × 90 cm. Milan, Civico Museo d'Arte Contemporanea, Boschi Collection.
Exhibitions: Rome 1955-56 fig. 5; Milan 1973 fig. 104; Milan 1974 p. 59; Milan 1985 no. 83; Düsseldorf 1988 no. 110.
Bibliography: Sironi 1980 p. 177; Caramel-Fiorio-Pirovano 1980 no. 1665.
Reference: Bellonzi 1985 no. 68.

Mario Sironi
Discourse: The Disciples (Colloquio: i discepoli), 1935-36
[p. 544]
Oil on linen paper, 178 × 155 cm. Rome, Collezione d'Arte Religiosa Moderna dei Musei Vaticani.
Exhibitions: Rome 1980.
Reference: Bellonzi 1985 no. 106.

Ardengo Soffici
Ines, 1920
[p. 545]
Oil on canvas, 200 × 100 cm. Private collection.
Exhibitions: Milan 1989 no. 3 (addenda).
Bibliography: *Valori Plastici* no. 5 May 1921 between pp. 96 and 97; Fossati 1981 no. 29.
Reference: Raimondi-Cavallo 1967 no. 241.

Atanasio Soldati
Composition, 1935
[p. 547]
Oil on canvas, 35 × 49 cm. Center and left, toward center: SOLDATI. Private collection.
Exhibitions: Turin 1969-70 Plate 36.

Atanasio Soldati
Composition, 1938
[p. 546]
Oil on canvas, 65 × 40 cm. Bottom right: SOLDATI. Milan, Zita Vismara Collection.
Provenance: Milan, Galleria Bergamini.
Exhibitions: Ivrea 1965 no. 19; Genoa 1966-67; Turin 1969-70 Plate 75; Parma 1970 no. 19.
Bibliography: Santini 1965 no. 103.

Emilio Vedova
Self-Portrait on Mirror on the Ground (Autoritratto sullo specchio a terra), 1937
[p. 569]
Oil on canvas, 70 × 60 cm. Venice, Artist's Collection.
Exhibitions: Verona 1961; Ferrara 1968; Venice 1984 no. 13.

Emilio Vedova
Saint Moisè, 1937-38
[p. 568]
Oil on linen paper, 50 × 35 cm. Venice, Artist's Collection.
Exhibitions: Venice 1984 no. 22; Milan 1985 p. 176 no. 1.

Emilio Vedova
The Burning of a Village (Incendio del villaggio), 1945
[p. 570]
Pastels and mixed media on linen paper, 100 × 70 cm. Venice, Artist's Collection.
Exhibitions: Warsaw 1958; Milan 1961; Madrid 1961, then Barcelona 1961; Verona 1961; Baden-Baden 1964-65; Ferrara 1968; Braun-

schweig 1981; Bologna 1983; Venice 1984 no. 30.

Emilio Vedòva
Assault on the Prisons (Assalto alle prigioni), 1945
[p. 571]
Pastels and mixed media on linen paper, 70 × 100 cm. Venice, Artist's Collection.
Exhibitions: Warsaw 1958; Milan 1961; Madrid 1961, then Barcelona 1961; Verona 1961; Livorno 1963; Baden-Baden 1964-65; Ferrara 1968; Braunschweig 1981; Venice 1984 no. 30.

Luigi Veronesi
Composition, 1936
[p. 548]
Tempera on paper, 35 × 50 cm. Bottom right: LUIGI VERONESI 1936. Turin, Civico Museo, Galleria d'Arte Moderna.
Exhibitions: Saint Paul de Vence 1970 cover.

Luigi Veronesi
Composition no. 51, 1938
[p. 549]
Tempera and photogram on paper, 60 × 80 cm. Bottom right: CLV 16. Artist's Collection.
Exhibitions: Parma 1975 no. 54; Milan 1982 p. 164 no. 4.

Afro (Basaldella)
Exhibitions
1946 Trieste, Galleria Trieste, *Pittura Moderna Italiana.*
1946 Rome, Galleria dello Zodiaco, *Afro*, December.
1947 Udine, *Mostra Triveneta del Ritratto*, September.
1978 Passariano, Villa Manin, *Afro 1912-1976*, 1 July-30 October.
1987 Spoleto, Palazzo Rosai Spada, *Afro fino al 1952*, organized by B. Mantura and P. Rosazza Ferraris.
Bibliography
C. Brandi, *Afro*, Rome 1977.
E. Crispolti, *I Basaldella*, Udine 1984.

Giacomo Balla
Exhibitions
1903 Rome, Società degli Amatori e Culturi di Belle Arti, *LXXIII Esposizione Internazionale di Belle Arti*, February-June.
1904 Rome, Società degli Amatori e Cultori di Belle Arti, *LXXIV Esposizione Internazionale di Belle Arti*, February-June.
1907 Rome, Società degli Amatori e Cultori di Belle Arti, *LXXXVII Esposizione Internazionale di Belle Arti*, February-June.
1909 Rome, Società degli Amatori e Cultori di Belle Arti, *LXXIX Esposizione Internazionale di Belle Arti*, February-June.
1913 Rome, Foyer del Teatro Costanzi, *Mostra Futurista*, 21 February-21 March.
1913 Rotterdam, Rotterdamsche Kunstkring, *Les Peintres et les Sculpteurs Futuristes Italiens*, 18 June-15 August.
1913 Berlin, Der Sturm, *I Deutscher Herbstsalon*, 20 September.
1925 Rome, Palazzo delle Esposizioni, *III Biennale Romana*, 1 March-30 June.
1925-1926 New York, *Exhibition of Modern Art*, December-January (then Boston, Museum of Fine Art).
1926 Venice, *XV Biennale Internazionale d'Arte*, April-October.
1927 Bologna, Casa del Fascio, *Grande Mostra di Pittura Futurista*, January.
1927 Milan, Galleria Pesaro, *Mostra di trentaquattro Pittori Futuristi*, November-December.
1928 Rome, Società degli Amatori e Cultori di Belle Arti, *XCIX Esposizione Internazionale di Belle Arti*, February-June.
1929-1930 Rome, Palazzo delle Esposizioni, *Mostra del Centenario della Società degli Amatori e Cultori di Belle Arti 1828-1929*, December-January.
1930 Venice, *XVII Biennale Internazionale d'Arte*, May-September.
1931 Rome, Palazzo delle Esposizioni, *I Quadriennale Nazionale d'Arte*, January-June.
1949 New York, The Museum of Modern Art, *Twentieth-Century Italian Art*, text by J.T. Soby and A.H. Barr jr., 28 June-18 September.
1950 Zürich, Kunsthaus, *Futurismo e Pittura Metafisica*, November-December.
1951-1952 Rome, Palazzo delle Esposizioni, *VI Quadriennale Nazionale d'Arte*, December-April.
1960 Venice, *XXX Biennale Internazionale d'Arte - Mostra storica del futurismo*, organized by G. Ballo, 18 June-16 October.
1960 Paris, Musèe National d'Art Moderne, *Les sources du XX Siècle - Les Arts en Europe de 1884-1914*, 4 November-23 January.
1961 New York, The Museum of Modern Art, *Futurism*, organized by J.C. Taylor, 31 May-5 September (then Detroit, The Detroit Institute of Arts, 18 October-19 December; Los Angeles, County Museum, 14 January-19 February 1962).
1963 Turin, Galleria Civica d'Arte Moderna, *Giacomo Balla*, April.
1968 Venice, *XXXIV Biennale Internazionale d'Arte. Quattro maestri del futurismo italiano*, July-September.
1970 Milan, Palazzo della Permanente, *Mostra del Divisionismo italiano*, March-April.
1971-1972 Rome, Galleria Nazionale d'Arte Moderna, *Giacomo Balla*, 23 December-23 February.
1972 Paris, Musée d'Art Moderne de la Ville de Paris, *Giacomo Balla*, 24 May-2 July.
1973-1974 Milan, Palazzo Reale, *Boccioni e il suo tempo*, texts by G. Ballo, F. Cachin-Nora, F. Russoli, L. De Maria, P. Quaglino, December-February.
1974 Düsseldorf, Städtische Kunsthalle, *Futurismus 1909-1917*, texts by J. Harten, M. Calvesi, F. Russoli, F.W. Heckermanns, R. Langer, 25 March-28 April.
1986 Venice, Palazzo Grassi, *Futurismo e Futurismi*, May-October.
1989 London, Royal Academy of Arts, *Italian Art in the 20th Century - Painting and Sculpture 1900-1988*, 14 January-9 April.
Bibliography
O. Roux, "La LXXIV Esposizione Internazionale di Belle Arti a Roma," in *Natura e Arte* 1903-1904.
S.A. Nappi, "Visitando l'Esposizione di Belle Arti. Giacomo il notturno," in *L'Italia Moderna*, no. 13, July 1904.
V. Pica, "L'Esposizione degli Amatori e Cultori di Belle Arti in Roma," in *Emporium*, Bergamo, April 1909.
M. De Fiori, "Balla," in *Caffaro*, Genoa, 19 May 1909.
"L'Art Decoratif," in *Salon d'Automne*, 1909.
F. Mastrigli, "La mostra futurista al Costanzi," in *La Vita*, Rome, 23 February 1913.
E. Prampolini, "Pittori Futuristi - Prima Esposizione Italiana in Roma," in *L'Artista Moderno*, Turin 1913.
U. Boccioni, *Pittura e scultura futuriste (Dinamismo plastico)*, Milan 1914.
A. Soffici, *Cubismo e Futurismo*, Florence 1914.
A. Petrucci, "Problemi d'arte contemporanea: il movimento in pittura," in *Emporium*, Bergamo, December 1920.
R. Papini, "Vecchio e nuovo nella Terza Biennale Romana," in *Emporium*, Bergamo 1925.
E. Prampolini, "I Futuristi Italiani alla XV Biennale Veneziana," in *Le Tre Venezie*, Venice, May 1926.
Fillia, "La pittura futurista alla Quadriennale di Torino," in *L'Impero*, Rome, 20 May 1927.
B. Randone, "Difendo Giacomo Balla," in *Cronache di Arte Educatrice*, no. 6, 1928.
F. Sapori, "L'Arte del maestro Giacomo Balla," in *La Gazzetta del Popolo*, Turin, 3 February 1928.
V. Marchi, "Giacomo Balla," in *La Stirpe*, Rome, March 1928.
M. Biancale, "Un arazzo di Balla," in *Il Popolo di Roma*, Rome, 5 January 1929.
G. Dottori, "Una visita alla Mostra," in *Oggi e Domani*, Rome, 30 January 1930.
V. Costantini, *Pittura Italiana Contemporanea*, Milan 1934.
G. Severini, *Tutta la vita di un pittore*, Milan 1946.
Cahiers d'Art, Paris, XXV, I, 1950.
M. Drudi Cambillo - T. Fiori, *Archivi del Futurismo*, Rome, vol. I, 1959, vol. II, 1962.
J.C. Taylor, *Futurism*, New York 1961.
M. Calvesi, "Il Futurismo," in *L'Arte Moderna*, vol. V, Milan 1967.
T. Fiori - F. Bellonzi, *Archivi del Divisionismo*, Rome 1968.
V. Dortch Dorazio, *Balla*, Venice 1970.

Critical References - Bibliography

M. Fagiolo, *Futur Balla*, Rome 1970.
A.M. Damigella, *Il Futurismo*, Catania 1971.
E. Crispolti, *Balla*, Rome 1975.
G. Lista, "Cubisme et cubo-futurisme," in *Cahiers du Musée national d'art moderne*, Paris 1980.
G. Lista, *Balla*, Modena 1982.

Umberto Boccioni
Exhibitions
1906 Rome, Società degli Amatori e Cultori di Belle Arti, *LXXVIII Esposizione Internazionale di Belle Arti*, February-March.
1909-1910 Milan, Famiglia artistica, *Esposizione annuale della Famiglia artistica*, 15 December-8 January.
1910 Venice, Palazzo Pesaro, *Mostra d'estate in Palazzo Pesaro a Venezia*, 16 July-20 October.
1911 Milan, ex Padiglione Ricordi, *Mostra d'arte libera - I Manifestazione collettiva dei futuristi*, spring.
1912 Paris, Galerie Bernheim-Jeune, *Les peintres futuristes italiens*, 5-24 February.
1912 London, The Sackville Gallery, *Exhibition of Works by the Italian Futurist Painters*, March.
1912 Berlin, Galerie Der Sturm, *Zweite Austellung: Die Futuristen*, 12 April-31 May.
1912 Brussels, Galerie Georges Giroux, *Les peintres futuristes italiens*, 20 May-1 June.
1913 Rome, Galleria Giosi, Ridotto del Teatro Costanzi, *I Esposizione di pittura futurista*, February.
1913 Rotterdam, Rotterdamsche Kunstkring, *Les Peintres et les Sculpteurs futuristes Italiens*, 18 May-15 June.
1914 Rome, Galleria Sprovieri, *Esposizione di pittura futurista: Balla, Boccioni, Carrà, Russolo, Severini, Soffici*, February-March.
1916-1917 Milan, Palazzo Cova, *Grande esposizione Boccioni*, 28 December-14 January.
1924 Milan, Bottega di poesia, *Umberto Boccioni*, organized by F.T. Marinetti, 10-21 March.
1925 Rome, Palazzo delle Esposizioni, *III Biennale romana - Mostra retrospettiva di Umberto Boccioni*, preface by F.T. Marinetti, 1 March-30 June.
1933 Milan, Civica Galleria d'Arte Moderna, *Mostra Boccioni*, summer.
1950 Venice, *XXV Biennale Internazionale d'Arte - Retrospettiva di Boccioni*, 8 June-15 October.
1950 Zürich, Kunsthaus, *Futurismo e Pittura Metafisica*, November-December.
1958 Venice, Ala Napoleonica, *Primi espositori di Ca' Pesaro 1908-1919*, organized by G. Perocco, 28 August-19 October.
1960 Venice, *XXX Biennale Internazionale d'Arte - Mostra storica del Futurismo*, organized by G. Ballo, 18 June-16 October.
1961 New York, The Museum of Modern Art, *Futurism*, organized by J.C. Taylor, 31 May-5 September (then Detroit, The Detroit Institute of Arts, 18 October-19 December; Los Angeles, County Museum, 14 January-19 February 1962).
1973 Paris, Musée National d'Art moderne, *Le Futurisme 1909-1916*, 19 September-19 November.
1973 Brussels, Musée Royaux d'Art et d'Histoire, *Sculptures italiennes contemporaines*.
1973-1974 Milan, Palazzo Reale, *Boccioni e il suo tempo*, texts by G. Ballo, F. Cachin-Nora, F. Russoli, L. De Maria, P. Quaglino, December-February.
1974 Düsseldorf, Städtische Kunsthalle, *Futurismus 1909-1917*, texts by J. Harten, M. Calvesi, F. Russoli, F.W. Heckermanns, R. Langer, 25 March-28 April.
1979-1980 Milan, Palazzo Reale, *Origini dell'Astrattismo - Verso altri orizzonti del reale*, organized by G. Ballo, 18 October-18 January.
1980-1981 Rome, Galleria Nazionale d'Arte Moderna, *Apollinaire e l'avanguardia*, 30 November-4 January.
1982-1983 Milan, Palazzo Reale, *Boccioni a Milano*, organized by G. Ballo, December-April.
1985 Frankfurt, Frankfurter Kunstverein, *Italienische Kunst 1900-1980*, 22 February-8 April.
1985-1986 Verona, Galleria dello Scudo, *Boccioni a Venezia*, 1 December-31 January (then Milan, Accademia di Brera, 27 February-6 April; Venice, Chiesa di S. Stae, 19 April-1 June).
1986 Venice, Palazzo Grassi, *Futurismo e Futurismi*, May-October.
1986 Venice, Palazzo Grassi, *Futurismo e Futurismi,* May-October.
1988-1989 New York, The Metropolitan Museum of Modern Art, *Boccioni*, 15 September-8 January.
1989 London, Royal Academy of Arts, *Italian Art in the 20th Century - Painting and Sculpture 1900-1988*, 14 January-9 April.
Bibliography
"L'esposizione alla Famiglia artista," in *La perseveranza*, Milan, 20 December 1909.
"L'esposizione alla Famiglia artistica," in *Il Secolo*, Milan, 22 December 1909.
"L'Adriatico," Venice, 16 July 1910.
A. Teglio, "Ritratti a penna - Umberto Boccioni," in *Il Panaro*, Modena, 19 March 1911.
N. Barbantini, "L'esposizione libera di Milano," in *L'Avvenire d'Italia*, Rome, 19 May 1911.
A. Soffici, "Arte libera e pittura futurista," in *La Voce*, Florence, 22 June 1911.
U. Boccioni, *Pittura e scultura futuriste (Dinamismo plastico)*, Milan 1914.
A. Soffici, *Cubismo e Futurismo*, Florence 1914.
M. Sarfatti, "L'opera di Umberto Boccioni," in *Gli Avvenimenti*, no. 39, MIlan, 24 September 1916.
"La mostra di Boccioni a Milano," in *Emporium*, Bergamo, January 1917.
C. Carrà, "Un pittore scomparso ma più vivo che mai - Boccioni e la sua opera," in *L'Ambrosiano*, Milan, 13 May 1924.
G. Severini, "Ricordi su Boccioni," in *L'Esame Artistico e Letterario*, no. 6, July 1933, pp. 345-360.
G.C. Argan-M. Calvesi, *Boccioni*, Rome 1953.
M. Drudi Gambillo-T. Fiori, *Archivi del Futurismo*, Rome, vol. I, 1959, vol. II, 1962.
J.C. Taylor, *The Graphic Work of Boccioni*, New York 1961.
G. Ballo, *Boccioni*, Milan 1964.
M. Calvesi, "Dinamismo e simultaneità nella poetica futurista," in *L'Arte Moderna*, vol. V, Milan 1967.
T. Fiori-B. Bellonzi, *Archivi del Divisionismo*, Rome 1968.
C. Pirovano, *Scultura italiana - Dal Neoclassicismo alle correnti contemporanee*, Milan 1968.
G. Bruno, *L'opera completa di Boccioni*, Milan 1969.
M. Calvesi-E. Coen, *Boccioni - L'opera completa*, Milan 1983.

Rembrandt Bugatti
Exhibitions
1904 Paris, Galerie Hébrard.
1955 Antwerp, Société Royale de Zoologie d'Antwerpen.
1973 Paris, Salon d'Automne.
1975 Paris, Galerie Paul Ambroise.
1988 Ferrara, Galleria Civica d'Arte Moderna, Palazzo dei Diamanti, *I Bugatti*, 3 July-10 October.
Bibliography
Carlo Rembrandt Ettore Jean Bugatti, texts by P. Dejean, Milan 1982.

Alberto Burri
Bibliography
C. Brandi, *Burri*, Rome 1963.

Massimo Campigli
Exhibitions
1929 Paris, Galerie Jeanne Bucher, *Massimo Campigli*.
1946 Como, Galleria Borromini.
1948 Venice, *XXIV Biennale Internazionale d'Arte*, text by C. Maltese, 29 May-30 September.
1949 Salsomaggiore, *Cinquant'anni di Pittura Italiana*.
1954 Venice, *XXVII Biennale Internazionale d'Arte*, June-October.
1955 Berne, Kunsthalle.
1967 Florence, Palazzo Strozzi, *Arte Moderna in Italia 1915-1935*, presentation by C. Ragghianti, 26 February-28 May.
1967 Milan, Palazzo Reale, *Mostra di Massimo Campigli*, organized by M.L. Mele, June.
1979 Ferrara, Galleria Civica d'Arte Moderna, Palazzo dei Diamanti, *Massimo Campigli*, 30 June-7 October.
1981 Bologna, Galleria Marescalchi, *Lo specchio di Giuditta*, October.
1985 Venice, Sima, *Il Novecento italiano nelle collezioni Assitalia*.
1989 London, Royal Academy of Arts, *Italian Art in the 20th Century - Painting and Sculpture 1900-1988*, 4 January-9 April.
Bibliography
C. Kunstler, "Le Motif antique dans la peinture moderne," in *Art et Décoration*, Paris, May 1931.
P. Courthion, "Massimo Campigli," in *Art Italien Moderne*, no. 6, Paris-Milan 1938.
G. Giani, *Campigli*, Milan 1943.
R. Carrieri, *Massimo Campigli*, Venice 1945.
R. De Grada, *Campigli*, Rome 1969.

Carlò Carrà
Exhibitions
1912 Paris, Galerie Bernheim-Jeune, *Les peintres futuristes italiens*, 5-4 February.
1912 London, The Sackville Gallery, *Exhibition of Works by the Italian Futurist Painters*, March.
1912 Berlin, Galerie Der Sturm, *Zweite Austellung: Die Futuristen*, 12 April-31 May.
1912 Brussels, Galerie Georges Giroux, *Les peintres futuristes italiens*, 20 May-1 June.
1912 Amsterdam, Galerie Andrestch, *Due Futuristen*, August.
1913 Rotterdam, Rotterdamsche Kunstkring, *Les Peintres et les Sculpteurs Futuristes Italiens*, 18 May-15 June.
1914 Leipzig, Galerie del Vecchio, *Carlo Carrà*.
1914 Rome, Galleria Sprovieri, *Esposizione di pittura futurista: Balla, Boccioni, Carrà, Russolo, Severini, Soffici*, February-March.
1917-1918 Milan, Galleria Chini, *Mostra personale del pittore futurista Carlo Carrà*, 18 December-10 January.
1918 Rome, Galleria L'Epoca.
1921 Florence, Palazzo delle Esposizioni, *La Fiorentina primaverile*, April-June.
1921 Berlin, Nationalgalerie, *Das junge Italien*, April (then Hannover, Kestner Gesellschaft, 22 May-19 June; then Hamburg).
1923 Turin, *Quadriennale di Belle Arti*.
1925 Rome, Palazzo delle Esposizioni, *III Biennale romana*, 1 March-30 June.
1926 Milan, Galleria Pesaro, *Mostra individuale dei pittori Carlo Carrà, Giorgio De Chirico e postuma di Rubaldo Merello*, February.
1926 Venice, *XV Biennale Internazionale d'Arte*, April-October.
1933 Milan, Galleria Pesaro, *Mostra di Carlo*

Carrà pittore, Romano Romanelli scultore, Ardengo Soffici pittore, January-February.
1935 Milan, Galleria del Milione, *Carlo Carrà in una mostra personale*, 28 November-12 December.
1942 Milan, Pinacoteca di Brera, *Mostra di Carrà*, 26 May-24 June.
1948 Bologna, Francesco Francia Associazione per le Arti, *Mostra personale del pittore Carlo Carrà*, 1-15 February.
1948 Venice, *XXIV Biennale Internazionale d'Arte*, text by C. Maltese, 29 May-30 September.
1949 New York, The Museum of Modern Art, *Twentieth-Century Italian Art*, text by J.T. Soby and A.H. Barr Jr., 28 June-18 September.
1950 Venice, *XXV Biennale Internazionale d'Arte*, 8 June-15 October.
1950 Brussels, Palais des Beaux-Arts, *Art italien contemporain*, 28 January-26 February.
1955-1956 Rome, Palazzo delle Esposizioni, *VII Quadriennale Nazionale d'Arte*, October-March.
1959 Livorno, Galleria Modigliani, *Carlo Carrà*.
1960 Milan, Palazzo Reale, *Arte italiana del XX secolo da collezioni americane*, 30 April-26 June.
1962 Milan, Palazzo Reale, *Mostra di Carlo Carrà*, April-May.
1967 Florence, Palazzo Strozzi, *Arte Moderna in Italia 1915-1935*, presentation by C. Ragghianti, 26 February-28 May.
1970 Los Angeles, Country Museum of Art, *The Cubist Epoch* (then New York, The Metropolitan Museum of Art).
1972-1973 Rome, Palazzo delle Esposizioni, *X Quadriennale Nazionale d'Arte*, November-May.
1973 Paris, Musée National d'Art Moderne, *Le Futurisme 1909-1916*, 19 September-19 November.
1977 Ferrara, Galleria Civica d'Arte Moderna, Palazzo dei Diamanti, *Carlo Carrà*, 2 July-9 October.
1977 Berlin, Schloß Charlottenburg, *Tendenzen der Zwanziger Jahre*, 14 August-16 October.
1979 Venice, Istituto di Cultura di Palazzo Grassi, *La pittura metafisica*, texts by G. Briganti and E. Coen, with the contribution of A. Orsini Baroni, May-September.
1979 Acqui Terme, Palazzo Liceo Saracco, *Carlo Carrà*, 28 July-5 September.
1980 Bologna, Galleria Comunale d'Arte Moderna, *La metafisica: gli anni Venti*, organized by R. Barilli and F. Solmi, May-August.
1980-1981 Paris, Musée National d'Art Moderne, Centre Georges Pompidou; *Les Réalismes 1919-1939*, organized by J. Clair, 17 December-20 April (then Berlin, Staatlische Kunsthalle, *Realismus - Zwischen Revolution und Reaktion 1919-1939*, 16 May-28 June).
1981 Quargnento, *Carlo Carrà 1881-1966 Mostra del centenario*, 3-18 October.
1981-1982 Verona, Galleria dello Scudo, *Carlo Carrà - Mostra antologica nel centenario della nascita*, 21 November-16 January.
1982 Tokyo, XVI International Biennial of Art, *One Hundred Years of Modern Italian Art 1880-1980*.
1986 Venice, Palazzo Grassi, *Futurismo e futurismi*, May-October.
1987 Milan, Palazzo Reale, *Carrà*, 8 April-28 May.
1988 Iseo, Sale dell'Arsenale, *Carlo Carrà - il primitivismo 1915-1919*, 23 April-20 June.
1988-1989 Verona, Galleria dello Scudo, *Realismo Magico - Pittura e Scultura in Italia 1919-1925*, 27 November-29 January (then Milan, Palazzo Reale, 16 February-2 April).
1989 London, Royal Academy of Arts, *Italian Art in the 20th Century - Painting and Sculpture 1900-1988*, 14 January-9 April.

Bibliography
R. Longhi, "Carrà," in *La Voce*, no. 15, Florence 1913.
Valori Plastici, nos. XI/XII, Rome, November-December 1919.
Valori Plastici, Rome, January-February 1921.
E. Thovez, "Carrà," in *Gazzetta del Popolo*, Turin, 5 May 1922.
E. Cecchi, "Carrà," in *L'Ambrosiano*, Milan, 21 April 1925.
W. Worringer, "Carlo Carrà's Pinie am Meer," in *Wissen und Leben*, Zürich, November 1925.
"Il Novecento italiano - Rassegna di Pittura e Scultura," Milan, no. 2, summer 1926.
V. Pica, *La XV Esposizione Internazionale d'Arte della città di Venezia 1926*, Milan 1926.
A. Soffici, *Carlo Carrà*, Milan 1928.
P.M. Bardi, *Carrà e Soffici*, Milan 1930.
M. Sarfatti, *Storia della pittura moderna*, Rome 1930.
N. Bertocchi, "Carlo Carrà," in *L'Italia letteraria*, Rome, 8 March 1931.
W. George, "Carlo Carrà," in *Formes*, no. 30, Paris 1932.
R. Longhi, *Carlo Carrà*, Milan, 1937.
M. Masciotta, *La pittura metafisica*, in *Letteratura*, Florence, July-September 1941.
G. Piovene, *La raccolta Feroldi*, Milan 1942.
L. Repaci, "Carlo Carrà," in *L'Illustrazione italiana*, Milan, 14 June 1942.
P. Torriano, *Carrà*, Milan 1942.
C. Carrà, *La mia vita*, Rome 1943.
S. Catalano, *Carlo Carrà*, Milan 1945.
G. Pacchioni, *Carlo Carrà*, Milan 1945.
U. Apollonio, *Pittura metafisica*, Venice 1950.
C. Zervos, *Cahiers d'art - Un demi-siècle d'art italien*, Paris 1950.
G. Raimondi, "La congiuntura metafisica Morandi-Carrà," in *Paragone*, no. 19, Florence, July 1951.
G. Ballo, *Pittori italiani dal futurismo ad oggi*, Rome 1956.
M. Valsecchi, *La pittura metafisica moderna*, Venice 1958.
M. Drudi Gambillo-T. Fiori, *Archivi del Futurismo*, Rome, vol. I, 1959, vol. II, 1962.
J.C. Taylor, *Futurism*, New York 1961.
M. Valsecchi, *Carrà*, Milan 1962.
J. Pierre, *Le futurisme e le dadaisme*, Lausanne 1966.
M. Calvesi, *Le due avanguardie*, Milan 1966.
M. Calvesi, "Dinamismo e simultaneità nella poetica futurista," in *L'Arte Moderna*, vol. V, Milan 1967.
M. Carrà, *Tutta l'opera pittorica*, Milan, 1967-1968.
M. Carrà, *Metafisica*, Milan 1968.
M.W. Martin, *Futurist Art and Theory 1909-1915*, Oxford 1968.
P. Bigongiari-M. Carrà, *Carrà 1910-1930*, Milan 1970.
C. Carrà, *Tutti gli scritti*, edited by M. Carrà, Milan 1978.
J. Clair, "Sous le signe de Saturne: notes sur l'allegorie de la Mélancolie dans l'art de l'entre deux guerres en Allemagne et en Italie," in *Cahiers du Musée national d'art moderne*, no. 7/8, Paris 1981.
P. Fossati, *Valori Plastici 1918-1922*, Turin 1981.
P. Fossati, "Pittura e scultura tra le due guerre," in *Storia dell'arte italiana. Il Novecento*, vol. 7, Turin 1982.
M. Calvesi, *La metafisica schiarita*, Milan 1982.
F. Roche-Pezard, *L'aventure futuriste 1909-1916*, Rome 1983.
R. Barilli, *L'arte contemporanea: da Cézanne alle ultime tendenze*, Milan 1984.
P. Fossati, *La "pittura metafisica,"* Turin 1988.

Felice Casorati
Exhibitions
1924 Venice, *XIV Biennale Internazionale d'Arte*, presentation by M. Sarfatti, spring-summer.
1925 Venice, Palazzo Pesaro, Opera Bevilacqua La Masa, *I Esposizione degli artisti di Ca' Pesaro al Lido*, July-September.
1926 Milan, Palazzo della Permanente, *Il Novecento italiano. I Mostra d'arte*, February-March.
1926 New York, Italy America Society, *Exhibition of Modern Italian Art*.
1927 Geneva, Musée Rath, *Exposition d'artistes italiens contemporains*, February.
1927 Zürich, Kunsthaus, *Italienische Maler*, March-May.
1927 Pittsburgh, Carnegie Institute, *26th International Exhibition of Paintings*, October-December.
1935 Paris, Jeu de Paume, *L'art italien des XIX et XX Siècles*, May-July.
1948 New York, House of Italian Handicraft, *Handicraft as a Fine Art in Italy*, spring.
1952 Venice, *XXVI Biennale Internazionale d'Arte*, May-September.
1964 Turin, Galleria Civica d'Arte Moderna, *Casorati*, April-May.
1976 Florence, Palazzo Strozzi, *Felice Casorati nell'opera di Gobetti*, December-March.
1980-1981 Paris, Musée National d'Art Moderne, Centre Georges Pompidou, *Les Réalismes 1919-1939*, organized by J. Clair, 17 December-20 April (then Berlin, Staatlische Kunsthalle, *Realismus - Zwischen Revolution und Reaktion 1919-1939*, 16 May-28 June.
1981 Ferrara, Galleria Civica d'Arte Moderna, Palazzo dei Diamanti, *Casorati*, July-October.
1983 Milan, Palazzo della Permanente, *Il Novecento italiano 1923-1933*, organized by R. Bossaglia, January-March.
1985 Turin, Accademia Albertina di Belle Arti, *Felice Casorati 1883-1963* organized by M.M. Lamberti and P. Fossati, 19 February-31 March.
1988-1989 Verona, Galleria dello Scudo, *Realismo Magico - Pittura e Scultura in Italia 1919-1925*, 27 November-29 January (then Milan, Palazzo Reale, 16 February-2 April).
1989 London, Royal Academy of Arts, *Italian Art in the 20th Century - Painting and Sculpture 1900-1988*, 14 January-9 April.

Bibliography
L. Venturi, "Il pittore Felice Casorati," in *Dedalo*, Milan, September 1923.
R. Giolli, *Felice Casorati*, Milan 1925.
M. Sarfatti, "Pittori d'oggi. Felice Casorati," in *Rivista illustrata del popolo d'Italia*, 15 March 1925.
W. Forbes, "The Carnegie International," in *The Arts*, New York, November 1927.
V. Guzzi, *Pittura italiana contemporanea*, Rome-Milan 1931.
V. Costantini, *Pittura italiana contemporanea*, Milan 1934.
A. Galvano, *Felice Casorati*, Milan 1947.
L. Carluccio, *Casorati*, Milan 1964.
S. Molesi, "Casorati," in *Catalogo della Galleria d'Arte Moderna del Civico Museo Revoltella*, Trieste 1971.
L. Carluccio, *Casorati*, Torino 1980.
P. Fossati, "Pittura e scultura tra le due guerre," in *Storia dell'arte italiana. Il Novecento*, vol. 7, Turin 1982.

Giorgio De Chirico
Exhibitions
1915 Paris, Galerie Paul Guillaume, *de Chirico*.
1920-1921 Geneva, *Exposition International d'Art Moderne*, 26 December-25 January.
1922 Paris, Galerie Paul Guillaume, *Giorgio de Chirico*, 21 March-1 April.

Critical References - Bibliography

1922 Florence, Palazzo delle Esposizioni al Parco di Sangallo, *La Fiorentina primaverile*, 8 April-31 July.
1926 Paris, Galerie Paul Guillaume, *Giorgio de Chirico*, text by A.C. Barnes, 4-15 June.
1928 London, Arthur Tooth and Sons Gallery, *First Exhibition in England of Paintings by Giorgio de Chirico*, text by T.W. Earp, 10 October-3 November.
1928 Paris, Galerie Surrealiste, *Oeuvres anciennes de Giorgio de Chirico*, 15 February-1 March.
1930 Milan, Galleria Milano, *Prima mostra di pittori italiani residenti a Parigi*, 14-26 January.
1930 New York, Demotte Galleries, *Paintings by Giorgio de Chirico*, 15 October-15 November.
1930 Berlin, Galerie Alfred Flechteim, *Giorgio de Chirico*, text by C. Einstein, 19 October-November.
1934 Brussels, Palais des Beaux-Arts, *Exposition Minotaure*, 12 May-3 June.
1935 Luzern, Kunstmuseum, *Thèse antithèse synthèse*, 24 February-31 March.
1935 New York, Pierre Matisse Gallery, *Giorgio De Chirico 1910-1918*, 16 November-15 December.
1935 Umelecke Besedy, Galery Skupiny, *De Chirico*, 15 April-5 May.
1936 London, New Burlington Galleries, *Surrealism. International Surrealist Exhibition*, 11 June-4 July.
1936 New York, Julien Levy Gallery, *Recent Paintings by Giorgio de Chirico*, text by A.C. Barnes, 28 October-17 November.
1937 London, Zwemmer Gallery, *De Chirico and Picasso*, June.
1937 Paris, Petit Palais, *Les Maîtres de l'Art Indépendant 1895-1937*, June-October.
1938 London, London Gallery, *The impact of machines*, July-August.
1938 London, Lefèvre Galleries, *New Painting by Giorgio de Chirico*, July.
1939 Milan, Galleria del Milione, *18 opere di pittura metafisica di Giorgio de Chirico dal 1912 al 1919*, 26 October-15 November.
1940 New York, Pierre Matisse Gallery, *Giorgio De Chirico - Exhibition of Early Paintings*, 22 October-23 November.
1941 Milan, Galleria del Milione, *De Chirico 1919-1926*, 5-26 March 1941.
1941 Cortina d'Ampezzo, Palazzo Municipale, *Prima mostra delle collezioni d'arte contemporanee*, 10-31 August.
1942 Rome, Galleria di Roma, *LI Mostra della Galleria di Roma con opere di R. Valdameri*, 27 January-10 February.
1943 New York, Art of this Century, *Masterworks of early de Chirico*, 5 November-6 November.
1948 Madrid, Museo Nacional de Arte Moderno, *Esposicion de arte italiano contemporaneo*, 1-30 May.
1948 Venice, *XXIV Biennale Internazionale d'Arte*, text by C. Maltese, 29 May-20 September.
1949 New York, The Museum of Modern Art, *Twentieth-Century Italian Art*, text by J.T. Soby and A.H. Barr Jr., 28 June-18 September.
1955 Houston, Museum of Fine Arts, *Chagall and De Chirico*, 3 April-1 May.
1960-1961 Paris, Musée National d'Art Moderne, *Les Sources du XX siècle. Les Arts en Europe de 1884 à 1914*, 4 November-23 January.
1965 Rome, *Capolavori nelle collezioni americane*.
1967 Florence, Palazzo Strozzi, *Arte Moderna in Italia 1915-1935*, presentation by C. Ragghianti, 26 February-28 May.
1967-1968 Turin, Galleria Civica d'Arte Moderna, *Le muse inquietanti - Maestri del Surreali-*

smo, text by L. Carluccio, November-January.
1970 Milan, Palazzo Reale, *Giorgio de Chirico*, April-May (then Hannover, Kestner Gesellschaft Hannover in der Orangerie Herrenhausen, 10 July-30 August).
1971 Milan, Galleria d'Arte Medea, *Giorgio de Chirico - L'immagine dell'infinito*, texts by R. Carrieri and L. Cavallo, 18 November-20 December.
1979 Venice, Istituto di Cultura di Palazzo Grassi, *La pittura metafisica*, texts by G. Briganti and E. Coen, with the contribution of A. Orsini Baroni, May-September.
1981-1982 Rome, Galleria Nazionale d'Arte Moderna, *Giorgio de Chirico, 1888-1978*, organized by P. Vivarelli, 11 November-3 January.
1982 New York, The Museum of Modern Art, *De Chirico*, texts by M. Fagiolo, J.M. Lukach, W. Rubin, M.W. Martin, W. Schmied, L. Rosenstock, April-June.
1982 Milan, Galleria Daverio, *Giorgio De Chirico - Parigi 1924-1930*, organized by M. Fagiolo, June-20 July.
1982-1983 Munich, Haus der Kunst, *Giorgio De Chirico der Metaphysiker*, organized by W. Rubin, W. Schmied and J. Clair, 17 November-30 January (then Paris, Centre Georges Pompidou, 24 February-25 April).
1984 Paris, Grand Palais, *La rime et la raison: les collections Ménil (Houston-New York)*, April-July.
1985 Milan, Fiera di Milano, *Internazionale d'arte contemporanea*, 25 May-2 June.
1986-1987 Verona, Galleria dello Scudo, *De Chirico anni Venti*, organized by M. Fagiolo, 14 December-31 January (then Milan, Palazzo Reale, 7 March-18 April).
1988-1989 Venice, Museo Correr, *De Chirico nel Centenario della nascita*, organized by M. Calvesi, 1 October-5 January.
1989 London, Royal Academy of Arts, *Italian Art in the 20th Century - Painting and Sculpture 1900-1988*, 14 January-9 April.

Bibliography
Valori Plastici, no. 7/8, Rome, July-August.
B. Peret, "Giorgio de Chirico," in *Littérature*, no. 4, Paris, September 1922.
La Revolution Surréaliste, no. 7, Paris 1926.
Bulletin de l'Effort Moderne, nos. 32/38, Paris, February-October.
M. Raynal, *Anthologie de la peinture en France de 1906 à nos jours*, Paris 1927.
R. Vitrac, *Giorgio de Chirico*, Paris 1927.
A. Breton, *Le surréalisme et la peinture*, Paris 1928.
W. George, *Giorgio De Chirico avec des fragments littéraires de l'artiste*, Paris 1928.
F. Rutter, "Giorgio De Chirico," in *Apollo*, London 1928.
O. Sitwell, "The Art of Chicago," in *Drawing and Design*, no. 28, London, October 1928.
B. Ternovetz, *Giorgio de Chirico*, Milan 1928.
P. Courthion, "L'art de Giorgio de Chirico," in *Sélection Chronique de la Vie Artistique*, no. 8, Antwerp, December 1929.
P. Courthion - A. Bardi - Giorgio De Chirico, "Giorgio de Chirico," in *Selection Chronique de la Vie Artistique*, no. 8, Antwerp, December 1929.
Dictionnaire biographique des Artistes Contemporaines 1910-1930, Paris 1930.
W. George, *Appels du Bas-Empire Giorgio de Chirico*, no. 1, Paris, January 1930.
G. Ribemont-Dessaignes, "Giorgio de Chirico," in *Documents: Archéologie, Beaux-Arts, Ethnographie, Variétes*, no. 6, Paris 1930.
P. Diolé, "Il souvenir d'Apollinaire," in *Les Expo*, 30 March 1934.
Minotaure, no. 8, June 1936.
G. Lo Duca, *Giorgio De Chirico*, Milan 1936.
C. Zervos, *Histoire de l'art contemporain*, Paris

1938.
Champigneulle, *L'inquietudine dans l'art d'aujourd'hui*, Paris 1939.
R. Carrieri, *Fantasia degli italiani*, Milan 1939.
V.E. Barbaroux - G. Giani, *Arte italiana contemporanea*, Milan 1940.
J.T. Soby, *The Early Chirico*, New York 1941.
A. Pica, *12 opere di Giorgio de Chirico*, Milan 1944.
G. Lo Duca, *Dipinti di Giorgio de Chirico (1912-1932)*, Milan 1945.
L. Venturi, *Pittura contemporanea*, Milan 1947;
J.T. Soby, *Giorgio de Chirico*, New York 1955.
L'oeil, 1961.
C. Bruni Sakraischik, *Giorgio de Chirico*, general catalogue, Milan 1971-1988.
Le surrealisme au service de la Révolution, Paris, no. 6, pp. 13-16 (1976 rep.).
I. Far-D. Porzio, *Conoscere de Chirico*, Milan 1979.
M. Fagiolo, *Giorgio de Chirico - Il tempo di Apollinaire, Paris 1911-1915*, Rome 1981.
P. Baldacci-M. Fagiolo, *Giorgio de Chirico - Parigi 1924-1929*, Milan 1982.
M. Fagiolo, *L'opera completa di Giorgio de Chirico 1908-1924*, Milan, 1984.
M. Fagiolo, *La vita di Giorgio de Chirico*, Turin 1988.
M. Calvesi, in *Art Dossier*, no. 28, October 1988.

Fortunato Depero
Exhibitions
1914 Trento, Palazzo della Filarmonica (*I esposizione di pittura futurista nel Trentino*), 21-29 July (interrupted).
1918 Florence, Florentina Ars-Palazzo Antinori, *Pittori d'oggi*, 17 October-15 November.
1919 Milan, Galleria Centrale d'Arte Moretti, *Grande Esposizione Nazionale Futurista*, organized by F.T. Marinetti, March (then Genoa, Galleria Moretti, April-May 1919).
1921 Milan, Galleria Centrale d'Arte Moretti, *Depero e la sua Casa d'Arte*, 20 January-20 February (then Rome, Galleria d'Arte Bragaglia, 15 March-15 April).
1923 Monza, Villa Reale, *I Mostra Internazionale delle Arti Decorative*, May-October.
1967 Florence, Palazzo Strozzi, *Arte Moderna in Italia 1915-1935*, presentation by C. Ragghianti, 26 February-28 May.
1969-1970 Rome, Galleria Obelisco, *Depero*, text by M. Fagiolo, December-January.
1970 Bassano, Palazzo Sturm, *Fortunato Depero 1892-1960*, organized by B. Passamani, July-September.
1974 Turin, Martano/Due, Galleria Martano, *Fortunato Depero* text by B. Passamani, 14 February-14 March.
1986 Paris, Musée National d'Art Moderne, Centre Georges Pompidou, *Qu'est-ce que la sculpture moderne?*, organized by M. Rowell, 3 July-13 October.
1988-1989 Rovereto, corso Rosmini 58, *Depero*, 12 November-14 January (then Düsseldorf, Kunsthalle, January-March).
Bibliography
Noi, nos. 6-7-8, 1924.
Comoedia, no. 23, 1 December 1925.
Theatre Magazine, New York, March 1930.
Fortunato Depero nelle opere e nella vita, Trento 1940.
So I think so I paint. Ideologies of an Italian self-made Painter, Trento 1947.
G. Giani, *Fortunato Depero futurista*, Milan 1951.
M. Drudi Gambillo-T. Fiori, *Archivi del Futurismo*, Rome, vol. I, 1958, vol. II, 1962.
B. Passamani, *Fortunato Depero*, Trento 1981.
M. Scudiero, *Fortunato Depero opere*, Trento 1987.

Filippo De Pisis
Exhibitions
1941 Rome, Galleria di Roma, *XLIII Mostra della Galleria di Roma con opere della raccolta di Carlo Cardazzo, Venezia*, text by G. Marchiori, April.
1941 Florence, Galleria Firenze, *Filippo de Pisis*, 20-31 December.
1951 Ferrara, Castello Estense, *Filippo de Pisis*, organized by G. Raimondi, June-July.
1954 Ivrea, Biblioteca Olivetti, *Figure e ritratti nell'opera di Filippo de Pisis*, text by G. Raimondi, 28 February-15 March.
1955-56 Rome, Palazzo delle Esposizioni, *VII Quadriennale Nazionale d'Arte*, November-April.
1956 Venice, *XXVIII Biennale Internazionale d'Arte*, 16 June-21 October.
1965 Geneva, Galerie Krugier & Cie, *De metaphisica*, text by G. Marchiori, 20 May-20 July.
1969 Verona, Galleria Civica d'Arte Moderna, Palazzo della Gran Guardia, *Mostra dell'opera pittorica e grafica di Filippo de Pisis*, organized by L. Magagnato, M. Malabotta and S. Zanotto, 12 July-21 September.
1973 Ferrara, Galleria Civica d'Arte Moderna, Palazzo dei Diamanti, *Filippo de Pisis*, organized by F. Farina, texts by G. Marchiori, A. Pieyre de Mandiargues and S. Zanotto, 1 July-30 September.
1978-1979 Verona, Galleria dello Scudo, *Filippo de Pisis*, texts by B. de Pisis, L, Magagnato, G. Perocco and M. Valsecchi, 25 November-7 January.
1979 Venice, Istituto di Cultura di Palazzo Grassi, *La pittura metafisica*, organized by G. Briganti and E. Coen, with the contribution of A. Orsini Baroni, May-September.
1980 Bologna, Galleria Comunale d'Arte Moderna, *La metafisica: gli anni Venti*, organized by R. Barilli and F. Solmi, May-August.
1980 Brugherio, Villa Favorita, *Omaggio a de Pisis - Mostra antologica nello studio del pittore a Villa Favorita*, organized by G. Ballo, 2 June-6 July.
1980-1981 Geneva, Marie-Louise Jeanneret Art Moderne, *Hommage à Filippo de Pisis*, 23 October-31 January.
1983 Venice, Palazzo Grassi, *De Pisis*, organized by G. Briganti, texts by D. Bonuglia, V. Brosio, B. de Pisis, C. Levi and N. Naldini, 3 September-20 November.
1986 Comacchio, Palazzo Bellini, *De Pisis*, organized by F. Farina and G. Gian Ferrari, 12 July-22 September.
1989 London, Royal Academy of Arts, *Italian Art in the 20th Century - Painting and Sculpture 1900-1988*, 14 January-9 April.
Bibliography
W. George, *Filippo de Pisis*, Paris 1928.
S. Solmi, *Filippo de Pisis*, Milan 1931.
C. Brandi, "Il pittore Filippo de Pisis," in *Dedalo*, Milan, May 1932.
G. Cavicchioli, *Filippo de Pisis*, Florence 1942.
G. Raimondi, *Filippo de Pisis*, Milan 1944.
G. Raimondi, *Filippo de Pisis*, Florence 1952.
M. Valsecchi, *Filippo de Pisis*, Milan 1956.
G. Castelfranco-M. Valsecchi, *Pittura e scultura italiana dal 1910 al 1930*, Rome 1956.
G. Ballo, *De Pisis*, Turin 1968.
C. Bertelli-G. Briganti-A. Giuliano, *Storia dell'arte italiana*, vol. IV, Milan 1986.

Nicolay Diulgheroff
Exhibitions
1930 Turin, Galleria Codebò.
1931 Novara, *Arte Futurista - Pittura Scultura*.
1931 Savona, *Mostra Futurista Savona*.
1962 Turin, Galleria Civica d'Arte Moderna, *Aspetti del Secondo Futurismo torinese*, 27 March-

4 April.
1976 Torre Pellice, XXVII Mostra d'Arte Contemporanea.
1981-1982 Turin, Galleria Narciso, *Ottanta anni di Diulgheroff futurista*, organized by M. Pinottini, 10 December- 9 January.
Bibliography
Bollettino *Le Belle Arti periodico d'informazione della Società Promotrice di Torino*, year II, no. January-February 1982.

Farfa
Exhibitions
1959 Milan, Galleria Blu, *Farfa il futurista*, February.
1962 Milan, Galleria Schwarz, *Farfa-opere futuriste (1919-1934)*, 10-30 November.
1963 L'Aquila, Castello Cinquecentesco, *Aspetti dell'Arte Contemporanea*, 28 July-6 October.
1967 Brescia, Galleria d'Arte Cavalletto, *Farfa il futurista*, 16-30 December.
1968 Turin, Galleria Narciso, *Farfa dal futurismo alla patafisica*, 12 March-16 April.
1988 Crevalcore, Centro Civico di Porta Modena, *Farfa*, 15 May-12 June.

Fillia
Exhibitions
1929 Milan, Galleria Pesaro, *Trentatre Artisti Futuristi*, 5-15 October.
1932 Genoa, Galleria Vitelli, *Mostra di Aeropittura, pittura e scultura futurista*, June.
1932 La Spezia, Casa d'Arte, *Aeropittura Arte Sacra Futurista*, 26 November.
1936 Turin, Palazzo della Promotrice, *VIII Esposizione Regionale del Sindacato di Belle Arti e 94ª Esposizione della Società Promotrice di Belle Arti*, May-June.
1962 Turin, Galleria Civica d'Arte Moderna, *Aspetti del secondo futurismo torinese*, organized by E. Crispolti and A. Calvano, 27 March-30 April.
1966 Biella, Galleria Narcico, *Fillia*, organized by M. Pinottini, 6 May-12 June.
1982 Paris, Musée d'Art Moderne de la Ville de Paris, *Léger et l'esprit moderne. Une alternative d'avantgarde à l'arta non-objectiv*, 17 March-6 June.
1988 Cuneo, San Francesco, *Fillia*, 14 May-30 June.
Bibliography
E. Crispolti-M. Drudi Gambillo, "Il Secondo Futurismo," in *Notizie*, no. 10, January 1960.
E. Crispolti, *Il Secondo Futurismo. Torino 1923-1935 5 pittori + 1 scultore*, Turin 1962.
J. Pierre, *Le Futurisme et le Dadaïsme*, Lausanne 1967.
L. Cabutti, "Quel secondo futurismo," in *Arte*, no. 152, Milan, May 1985.
G. Lista, *Le futurisme*, Paris 1985.

Lucio Fontana
Exhibitions
1933-34 Milan, Galleria del Milione, *La Collezione Pietro Feroldi in Brescia*, 23 December-8 January.
1958 Venice, *XXIX Biennale Internazionale d'Arte*, June-October.
1960 Ferrara, Casa Romei, *Rinnovamento dell'arte in Italia 1930-1945*, June-September.
1963 L'Aquila, Castello Cinquecentesco, *Aspetti dell'arte contemporanea omaggio a Cagli, omaggio a Fontana, omaggio a Quaroni*, 28 July-6 October.
1966 Venice, *XXXIII Biennale Internazionale d'Arte*, 18 June-16 October.
1967 Florence, Palazzo Strozzi, *Arte Moderna in Italia 1915-1935*, presentation by C. Ragghianti, 26 February-28 May.

1969 Turin, Martano/Due, Galleria Martano, *Lucio Fontana: Opere 1931-1968*, October-November.
1970 Paris, Musée d'Art Moderne de la Ville de Paris, *Lucio Fontana*, 10 June-6 September.
1970 Turin, Galleria Civica d'Arte Moderna, *Lucio Fontana*, 5 February-28 March.
1971 Milan, Museo Poldi Pezzoli, *Milano 70/70*, 28 April-10 June.
1972 Brussels, Palais des Beaux Arts, *Lucio Fontana*, 26 September-6 November.
1972 Milan, Palazzo Reale, *Lucio Fontana*, 19 April-31 July.
1972 Venice, *XXXVI Biennale Internazionale d'Arte*, 11 June-1 October.
1977 Milan, Centro Annunciata, *L'umano nella scultura italiana*, text by M. Carrà, from 19 February.
1977 New York, Solomon R. Guggenheim Museum, *Lucio Fontana 1899-1968: a retrospective*, 20 October-11 December.
1978 Perugia, Sagittario Galleria d'Arte, *Lucio Fontana*, September.
1980 Florence, Palazzo Pitti, *Fontana*, April-June.
1980 Laveno, Museo della Ceramica, Palazzo Perabò, *Terra & Terra*, 27 September-26 October.
1980 Turin, Martano/Due, Galleria Martano, *Astrattismo italiano tra le due guerre*, 10 November-10 December.
1982 Milan, Palazzo Reale, Galleria del Sagrato, ex Arengario, *Gli Anni Trenta: Arte e Cultura in Italia*, organized by R. Barilli, 27 January-23 May.
1982 Rimini, Sala Comunale d'Arte Contemporanea, *Lucio Fontana: mostra antologica*, 30 June-30 September.
1983-1984 Munich, Staatsgalerie moderner Kunst, *Lucio Fontana*, 16 December-12 February.
1987 Paris, Musée National d'Art Moderne, Centre Georges Pompidou, *Lucio Fontana*, October.
1989 London, Royal Academy of Arts, *Italian Art in the 20th Century - Painting and Sculpture 1900-1988*, 14 January-9 April.
Bibliography
C. Belli, "Una collezione di provincia," in *Quadrante*, no. 9, Milan, January, 1934, pp. 2-11.
J. Zocchi, *Lucio Fontana*, Buenos Aires 1946.
R. Carrieri, *Pittura e scultura d'avanguardia in Italia 1890-1950*, Milan 1950.
U. Apollonio-G.C. Argan-M. Masciotta, *Cinque scultori d'oggi: Moore, Fontana, Mastroianni, Mirko, Viani*, Turin 1960.
M. Tapié, *Devenir de Fontana*, Turin 1961.
E. Persico, *Tutte le opere 1923-1935*, edited by G. Veronesi, Milan 1964.
R. Barilli, "La scultura del Novecento," in *Capolavori della scultura*, no. 12, Milan 1968.
G. Ballo, *Fontana: idea per un ritratto*, Turin 1970.
Nac, no. 31, Milan, 15 February 1970.
E. Crispolti, *Omaggio a Fontana*, Rome 1971.
P. Fossati, *L'immagine sospesa*, Turin 1971.
E. Crispolti-J. van der Marck, *Lucio Fontana*, Brussels 1974.
A. Folin-M. Quaranta, *Le riviste giovanili del periodo fascista*, Treviso 1977.
G. Armellini, *Le immagini del fascismo nelle arti figurative*, Milan 1980.
R. Barilli, *L'arte contemporanea: da Cézanne alle ultime tendenze*, Milan 1984.
E. Crispolti, *Fontana*, general catalogue, Milan 1986.

Renato Guttuso
Exhibitions
1940 Milan, Palazzo della Permanente, *II Pre-*

Critical References - Bibliography

mio Bergamo, November-December.
1942 Bergamo, Palazzo della Regione, *IV Premio Bergamo*, September-October.
1959 Milan, Galleria del Milione, *Renato Guttuso*, presentation by F. Russoli, February.
1962 Bagheria, *La Sicilia nella pittura di Renato Guttuso*, presentation by C. Levi, October-November.
1963-1964 Parma, Palazzo della Pilotta, *Omaggio a Guttuso 1931-1963*, texts by M. Alicata, M. Azzolini, R. Carrieri, D. Cooper, A. Del Guercio, M. De Micheli, R. Hiepe, H. Honour, C. Levi, R. Longhi, M. Mida, E. Morlotti, P.P. Pasolini, G. Piovene, C. Quintavalle, J. Richardson, F. Russoli, L. Saba, M. Soldati, R. Tassi, G. Testori, A. Trombadori, E. Vittorini, December-January.
1967 Darmstadt, *Renato Guttuso*, texts by H.G. Sperlich and B. Krimmel, August-October.
1968 Berlin, *Italienische Kunst des XX Jahrhunderts* (then Cologne).
1971 Palermo, Palazzo dei Normanni, *Renato Guttuso*, texts by L. Sciascia, F. Russoli and F. Grasso, 13 February-14 March.
1971 Paris, Musée d'Art Moderne de la Ville de Paris, *Guttuso: opere di "Corrente" e opere recenti 1968-1971*, texts by P. Gaudibert, J. Lassaigne and A. Del Guercio, October.
1977-1978 Geneva, Musée Rath, *Du Futurisme au Spatialisme*, 7 October-15 January.
1982 Milan, Palazzo Reale, Galleria del Sagrato, ex Arengario, *Gli Anni Trenta: Arte e Cultura in Italia*, organized by R. Barilli, 27 January-23 May.
1989 London, Royal Academy of Art, *Italian Art in the 20th Century - Painting and Sculpture 1900-1988*, 14 January-9 April 1989.
Bibliography
G. Piovene, "Il II Premio Bergamo," in *Primato*, no. 16, 15 October 1940.
C. Costantini, "Gare pittoriche nel IV Premio Bergamo," in *L'illustrazione italiana*, no. 37, Milan, 13 September 1942.
R. De Grada, *Il movimento di "Corrente,"* Milan 1952.
G. Marchiori, *Guttuso*, Milan, 1952.
G. Ballo, *Pittori Italiani dal futurismo ad oggi*, Rome 1956.
D. Morosini, *Renato Guttuso*, Rome 1960.
A. Moravia-F. Grasso, *Guttuso*, Palermo 1962.
M. De Micheli, "L'arte di opposizione e d'impegno politico e sociale in Europa dall'inizio del '900 alla seconda Guerra Mondiale," in *L'arte Moderna*, vol. VIII, Milan 1967.
E. Crispolti, *Guttuso: La Crocifissione*, Rome 1970.
M. De Micheli, *Guttuso*, Sofia 1970.
A. Del Guercio, *La pittura del Novecento*, Turin 1980.

Leoncillo
Exhibitions
1954 Venice, *XXVII Biennale Internazionale d'Arte*, June-October.
1969 Spoleto, Chiostri di San Nicolò, *Leoncillo*, 8 July-8 September.
1985-1986 Bologna, Galleria Comunale d'Arte Moderna, *Morandi e il suo tempo*, organized by R.Barilli, 9 November-10 February.

Osvaldo Licini
Exhibitions
1935 Milan, Galleria del Milione, *Osvaldo Licini*.
1936 Como, Villa Olmo, *Mostra di pittura moderna italiana*, organized by A. Sartoris, 26 September-19 October.
1958 Venice, *XXXIX Biennale Internazionale d'Arte*, June-October.

1958 Livorno, Casa della Cultura, *Mostra di cinquanta artisti degli ultimi trent'anni*.
1958 Ivrea, Centro Culturale Olivetti, *Osvaldo Licini*, text by L. Dania.
1959-1960 Rome, Palazzo delle Esposizioni, *VIII Quadriennale Nazionale d'Arte*, December-April.
1960 Ancona, *Osvaldo Licini*, text by G. Marchiori.
1961 Turin, *Da Boldini a Pollock, Mostra della Moda, Stile, Costume Italia 1961*, texts by F. Russoli, L. Carluccio, M. Valsecchi (then Milan, Civico Padiglione d'Arte Contemporanea).
1964 Florence, Galleria Palazzo Libri, *Concretismo*.
1966 Venice, *XXXIII Biennale Internazionale d'Arte*, 18 June-16 October.
1968-1969 Turin, Galleria Civica d'Arte Moderna, *Osvaldo Licini*, texts by A. Passoni and Z. Birolli, October-January.
1969 Bologna, Palazzo dell'Archiginnasio, *Licini*.
1980 Ferrara, Galleria Civica d'Arte Moderna, Palazzo dei Diamanti, *Osvaldo Licini*, October-December.
1986 Ascoli Piceno, Galleria Civica d'Arte Contemporanea, *Arte astratta nelle Marche 1935-1985*, text by C. Melloni, May-June.
1989 London, Royal Academy of Arts, *Italian Art in the 20th Century - Painting and Sculpture 1900-1988*, 14 January-9 April.
Bibliography
G. Marchiori, "Breve storia della pittura astratta in Italia -Da Léger a Licini," in *Corriere Padano*, 9 October 1937.
Cahiers d'Art, no. 10, 1937.
A. Sartoris, "Osvaldo Licini archipittore," in *Origini*, nos. 5/6, Rome, March 1941.
G. Dorfles, "Osvaldo Licini," in *Domus*, Milan, May 1958.
P.C. Santini, "Considerazioni sulla pittura di Licini," in *Comunità*, Milan, May-June 1958.
G. Marchiori, *Licini, con 21 lettere inedite del pittore*, Rome 1960.
G. Marchiori, "Osvaldo Licini," in *Arte e artisti d'avanguardia in Italia (1910-1950)*, Milan 1960.
G. Ballo, *Vero falso nell'arte moderna*, Milan 1962.
G. Marchiori, *I cieli segreti di Osvaldo Licini*, Venice 1968.
P. Fossati, *L'immagine sospesa*, Turin 1971.
A. Del Guercio, *La pittura del Novecento*, Turin 1980.

Mario Mafai
Exhibitions
1930 Rome, Palazzo delle Esposizioni, *II mostra del Sindacato Fascista di Belle Arti*.
1935 Rome, Palazzo delle Esposiziozi, *II Quadriennale Internazionale d'arte*, February-July.
1945 Rome, Galleria del secolo, *Mario Mafai*.
1965-1966 Rome, Palazzo delle Esposizioni, *IX Quadriennale Nazionale d'Arte*, October-March.
1967 Florence, Palazzo Strozzi, *Arte Moderna in Italia 1915-1935*, presentation by C. Ragghianti, 26 February-28 May.
1969 Rome, Fondazione Premi Roma, *Mario Mafai*.
1984 Rome, Studio Sotis, *Mafai*.
1985 Turin, Galleria Narciso, *Mafai e Raphaël: una vita per l'arte*, text by M. Pinottini, 19 October-30 November.
2986 Macerata, Palazzo Ricci e Pinacoteca Comunale, *Mario Mafai*, 6 July-15 September.
1988 Milan, Palazzo Reale, *Scuola Romana - Artisti tra le due guerre*, organized by M. Fagiolo, 13 April-19 June.
Bibliography
L. De Libero, "'800 e '900 a Roma. La tradizio-

ne Mafai e Scipione," in *Belvedere*, Milan, April 1930.
V. Martinelli, *Mario Mafai*, Rome 1967.
M. Fagiolo-V. Rivosecchi, *Mafai*, Rome 1986.
M. Fagiolo, *Scuola Romana*, Rome 1986.

Alberto Magnelli
Exhibitions
1954 Brussels, Palais des Beaux-Arts, *Alberto Magnelli*, presentation by L. Degand, November.
1955 Antibes, Musée Grimaldi, *Alberto Magnelli, peinture, collages, 1914-1954*, presentation by A. Verdet.
1963 Zürich, Kunsthaus, *Alberto Magnelli*, text by R. Wehrli, J. Lassaigne and J. Arp, 4 May-3 June.
1963 Florence, Palazzo Strozzi, *Alberto Magnelli*, texts by F. Russoli, M. Mendes and J. Lassaigne.
1967 Paris, Musée National d'Art Moderne, *Magnelli*, text by B. Dorival, 28 February-21 April.
1989 London, Royal Academy of Arts, *Italian Art in the 20th Century - Painting and Sculpture 1900-1988*, 14 January-9 April.
Bibliography
D. Fresnay, *Peintres et sculptures - Leur monde*, Paris 1969.
Descargues, "Alberto Magnelli," in *Plaisir de France*, February 1971.
N. Ponente, *Alberto Magnelli*, Rome 1973.
A. Maisonnier, *Alberto Magnelli*, catalogue raisonné, Paris 1975.

Giacomo Manzù
Exhibitions
1930 Bergamo, Mostra del Sindacato Pittori.
1930 Milan, Galleria Milano, *C. Grassi, G. Manzù, G. Occhetti, G. Pancheri, A. Sassu, N. Strada*, 1-13 April.
1941 Milan, Galleria Barbaroux, *Giacomo Manzù*, February-March.
1988-1989 Milan, Palazzo Reale - Arengario - Museo del Duomo, *Manzù, mostra antologica*, 17 December-26 February.
Bibliography
C.L. Ragghianti, *Giacomo Manzù scultore*, Milan 1957.

Marino Marini
Exhibitions
1947 Lausanne, Musée cantonal des Beaux-Arts, *Quarante Ans d'Art Italien*, 15 February-15 March.
1966 Rome, Palazzo Venezia, *Marino Marini*, organized by G. Carandente, 10 March-10 June.
1983 Venice, Istituto di Cultura di Palazzo Grassi, *Marino Marini, sculture, pitture, disegni dal 1914 al 1977*, organized by M. De Micheli, 28 May-15 August.
Bibliography
F. De Pisis, *Marino Marini*, Milan 1941.
L. Vitali, *Marini*, Florence 1946.
U. Apollonio, *Marino Marini scultore*, Milan 1958.
G. di San Lazzaro, *Marino Marini. L'opera completa*, Milan 1970.
K. Azuma, *Marino Marini*, Turin 1980.

Arturo Martini
Exhibitions
1913 Venice, Palazzo Pesaro, *Esposizione Opera Opera Bevilacqua La Masa*.
1914 Rome, *II Mostra Internazionale della Secessione Romana*.
1919 Venice, Palazzo Pesaro, *Esposizione Opera Bevilacqua La Masa*.
1919 Verona, *Esposizione Cispadana di Belle Arti*.

1920 Venice, Galleria Geri-Boralevi, *Mostra degli Artisti dissidenti di Ca' Pesaro*, July-August.
1920 Milan, Galleria gli Ipogei, *Martini*, presentation by C. Carrà.
1931 Rome, Palazzo delle Esposizioni, *I Quadriennale Nazionale d'Arte*, January-June.
1933 Milan, Galleria Milano, *Martini*, February.
1935 Paris, Jeu de Paume, *Art italien des XIX et XX Siècles*, May-June.
1948 Venice, *XXIV Biennale Internazionale d'Arte*, text by C. Maltese, 29 May-30 September.
1967 Florence, Palazzo Strozzi, *Arte Moderna in Italia 1915-1935*, presentation by C. Ragghianti, 26 February-28 May.
1967 Treviso, ex Tempio di Santa Caterina, *Arturo Martini*, 10 October-12 November.
1979 Milan, Galleria Gianferrari, *Veri e falsi a confronto*.
1980 Parma, Galleria Nicoli, *Arturo Martini*.
1985 Milan, Palazzo Reale, *Arturo Martini*, organized by M. De Micheli, February-April.
1987-1988 Venice, Museo Correr, Ala Napoleonica, *Ca' Pesaro 1908-1920*, 19 December-28 February.
1989 London, Royal Academy of Arts, *Italian Art in the 20th Century - Painting and Sculpture 1900-1988*, 14 January-9 April.

Bibliography
L. Venturi, "Arturo Martini," in *L'arte*, Turin, November 1930.
G. Lo Duca, *Arturo Martini*, Milan 1933.
M. Bontempelli, *Arturo Martini*, Milan 1939.
G. Perocco, *Arturo Martini*, Venice 1966.
F. Bellonzi, *Arturo Martini*, Rome 1974.
G. Mazzotti, *Arturo Martini scultore del nostro tempo*, Treviso 1979.
F. Scalia, *Raccolta d'Arte Contemporanea Alberto della Ragione*, Florence 1987.

Fausto Melotti
Exhibitions
1935 Turin, Studio di Casorati e Paulucci, *Prima mostra collettiva d'arte astratta italiana*, March.
1935 Milan, Galleria del Milione, *Fausto Melotti*, 10-24 May.
1963 L'Aquila, Castello Cinquecentesco, *Aspetti dell'arte contemporanea, omaggio a Cagli, omaggio a Fontana, omaggio a Quaroni*, 28 July-16 October.
1966 Venice, *XXXIII Biennale Internazionale d'Arte - Aspetti del primo astrattismo italiano 1930-1940*, organized by N. Ponente, 18 June-16 October.
1967 Florence, Palazzo Strozzi, *Arte Moderna in Italia 1915-1935*, presentation by C. Ragghianti, 26 February-28 May.
1968 Reggio Emilia, Sala Comunale delle Esposizioni, *Fausto Melotti. Sculture, disegni e pitture 1933-1958*, 8 June-23 June.
1968 Turin, Galleria Notizie 1 e 2, *Melotti, profezia della scultura*, presentation by M. Fagiolo, 21 November-30 December.
1969 Milan, Galleria dell'Ariete, *Melotti*, 7-21 October.
1971 Dortmund, Museum am Ostwall, *Fausto Melotti*, presentation by G. Dorfles, 31 October-19 December.
1972 Turin, Galleria Civica d'Arte Moderna, *Melotti*, texts by A. Passoni, Z. Birolli and L. Mallè.
1972 Venice, *XXXVI Biennale Internazionale d'Arte*, 11 June-1 October.
1976 Parma, Palazzo della Pilotta, *Fausto Melotti*, presentation by M. Calvesi, 8 June-11 July.
1977 Trento, Castello del Buonconsiglio, *Sculture di Fausto Melotti dal 1935 al 1977*, 22 May-20 July.

1979 Milan, Palazzo Reale, *Fausto Melotti*, organized by C. Pirovano, 15 May-17 June.
1983 Rome, Galleria Nazionale d'Arte Moderna, *Melotti*, organized by B. Mantura, 28 April-30 June.
1987 Matera, Chiese Rupestri delle Virtù e San Nicola dei Greci, Palazzo Lanfranchi, *Fausto Melotti 1901-1986*, 6 June-15 September.
1987 Milan, Civico Padiglione d'Arte Contemporanea, *Melotti l'acrobata invisibile*, organized by M. Precerutti Garberi and G. Carandente, articles by Melotti edited by V. Scheiwiller, texts by M. Fagiolo, G. Dorfles, G. Zampa, Z. Birolli, F. Russoli, G. Drudi, A.M. Hammacher, G. Gualdoni and C. Belli, 12 March-27 April.
1989 London, Royal Academy of Arts, *Italian Art in the 20th Century - Painting and Sculpture 1900-1988*, 14 January-9 April.

Bibliography
A. Sartoris, *Gli elementi dell'architettura funzionale*, Milan 1935.
Abstraction création, no. 4, Paris 1935.
Bollettino della Galleria del Milione, no. 40, Milan 1935.
G. Ballo, *La linea dell'arte italiana, dal simbolismo alle opere moltiplicate*, Rome 1964.
G. Ballo, "La Galleria del Milione e il primo astrattismo italiano," in *Domus*, Milan 1965.
N. Ponente, *Aspetti del primo astrattismo italiano Milano-Como 1930-1940*, catalogue of the XXXIII Biennale di Venezia, Venice 1966.
C. Ragghianti, *Fausto Melotti*, catalogue of the exhibition "Arte Moderna in Italia 1915-1935," Florence, Palazzo Strozzi 1967.
G. Veronesi, "Razionalità e fantasia dell'arte astratta," in *L'Arte Moderna*, vol. VI, Milan 1967.
M. Fagiolo, *Progetti di Melotti 1932-1936*, Turin 1970.
P. Fossati, *L'immagine sospesa*, Turin 1971.
A. Pica, "Milano 70/70 (1915-1945)," in *Domus*, Milan, May 1971.
G. Drudi, "Fausto Melotti," in *Data*, Milan, April 1975.
A.M. Hammacher, *Melotti*, Milan 1975.

Amedeo Modigliani
Exhibitions
1925 Paris, Galerie Bing, *Modigliani*, October-November.
1926 Paris, Salon des Artistes Indépendants, *Retrospettiva di Modigliani*.
1927 Zürich, Kunsthaus, *Italienische Maler*, March-May.
1929 New York, De Hauke and Co., *Paintings by Amedeo Modigliani*, October-November.
1930 Venice, *XVII Biennale Internazionale d'Arte*, May-September.
1933 Brussels, Palais des Beaux-Arts, *Modigliani*, November.
1934 Basel, Kunsthalle, *Modigliani*, 7 January-4 February.
1943 Philadelphia, Museum of Art, *Paintings from the Chester Dale Collection*.
1945 Paris, Galerie Claude, *Modigliani et ses modèles*, 1-30 June.
1949 New York, The Museum of Modern Art, *Twentieth-Century Italian Art*, text by J.T. Soby and A.H. Barr Jr., 28 June-18 September.
1950 Paris, Musée National d'Art Moderne, *L'Art moderne italien*, May-June.
1951 New York, Museum of Modern Art, *New York Private Collections*, 26 June-12 September.
1951-1952 Rome, Palazzo delle Esposizioni, *VI Quadriennale Nazionale d'Arte*, December-April.
1954 London, Arthur Tooth and Sons Gallery, *Recent Acquisitions*, 15 November-18 December.
1954 New York, Valentin Gallery, *Sculpture and Sculptors, Drawings*.

1957-1958 London, Tate Gallery, *An exhibitions of paintings from the Solomon R. Guggenheim Museum, New York*, 16 April-26 May (then the Hague, Gemeentemuseum, 25 June-1 September; Helsinki, Ateneumin Taidekokoelmat, 27 September-20 October; Rome, Galleria Nazionale d'Arte Moderna, 5 December-8 January; Cologne, Wallraf-Richartz Museum, 26 January-26 March; Paris, Musée des Arts Décoratifs, 25 April-1 June).
1958 Columbus, Ohio, Gallery of Fine Arts, *The Adelaide Milton de Groot Collection*.
1958 New York, Perls Galleries, *Masterpieces from the Collection of Adelaide Milton de Groot*.
1958 Marseille, Musée Cantini, *Modigliani*, June-July.
1958 Milan, Palazzo Reale, *Amedeo Modigliani*, November-December.
1959 Houston, Contemporary Arts Museum, *Totems Not Taboo: An Exhibition of Primitive Art*, 26 February-29 March.
1959 Rome, Galleria Nazionale d'Arte Moderna, *Amedeo Modigliani*, January-February.
1959-1960, New York, Solomon R. Guggenheim Museum, *Inaugural Selection*, 21 October-19 June.
1960 Milan, Palazzo Reale, *Da Gauguin a Gorky*, April-June.
1961 Hartford, Wadsworth Atheneum, *Salute to Italy: 100 years of Italian Art 1861-1961*, 21 April-28 May.
1961 Boston, Museum of Fine Arts, *Modigliani: Paintings and Drawings*, January-February (then Los Angeles, County Museum, March-April).
1964 Bordeaux, Musée des Beaux-Arts, *La Femme et l'Artiste, de Bellini à Picasso*, May.
1964 Paris, Musée National d'Art Moderne, *La Collection André Lefèvre*, March-April.
1964 New York, Perls Galleries, *Modigliani*.
1968 Tokyo, Seibu Gallery, *Modigliani*, May-June (then Kyoto, National Museum of Modern Art, June-August).
1968 Washington, National Gallery of Art, *Painting in France 1900-1967* (then New York, Metropolitan Museum of Art; Boston, Museum of Fine Arts).
1975-1976 Paris, Musée Jacquemart-André, *Le Bateau-Lavoir, berceau de l'Artr moderne*, October-January.
1977-1988 New York, The Salomon R. Guggenheim Museum, *Forty Modern Masters: An Anniversary Show*, 16 December-5 February.
1979 Leningrad, Hermitage museum, *Peinture française 1909-1939* (then Moscow, Pushkin museum, 1 September-18 December).
1979 Tokyo, *Modigliani: Love and Nostalgia for Montparnasse*, 13 September-16 October (then Osaka, 25 October-6 November).
1981 Paris, Musée d'Art Moderne de la Ville de Paris, *Amedeo Modigliani 1884-1920*, 26 March-28 June.
1989 London, Royal Academy of Arts, *Italian Art in the 20th Century - Painting and Sculpture 1900-1988*, 14 January-9 April.

Bibliography
W. George, "Modigliani," in *L'Amour de l'Art*, VI, October 1925.
A. Salmon, *Modigliani, sa vie son oeuvre*, Paris 1926.
A. Pfannstiel, *Modigliani, preface de Louis Latourettes*, Paris 1929.
L. Venturi, *La pittura contemporanea*, Milan 1947.
R. Carrieri, *Modigliani*, Milan 1950.
A. John, *Chiaroscuro*, London 1952.
G. di San Lazzaro, *Modigliani*, Paris 1953.
A. Pfannstiel, *Modigliani et son oeuvre, étude critique et catalogue raisonné*, Paris 1956.
J. Modigliani, *Modigliani sans légende*, Paris 1961.

A. Werner, *Modigliani, le sculpteur*, Geneva 1962.
H.L.C. Jaffé, *La pittura del XX secolo*, Milan 1963.
A. Ceroni, *Amedeo Modigliani, dessins et sculptures*, Milan 1965.
P. Sichel, *Modigliani*, New York 1967.
J. Lanthemann, *Modigliani, 1884-1920. Catalogue raisonné, sa vie, son oeuvre complet, son art*, Barcelona 1970.
A. Ceroni, *I dipinti di Modigliani*, Milan 1970.
A. Ceroni-F. Cachin, *Tout l'ouvre peint de Modigliani*, Paris 1972.
Rudenstine, *Collection Catalogue*, New York 1976.
B. Zurcher, *Modigliani*, Paris 1980.
D. Hall, *Modigliani*, Oxford 1984.
C. Roy, *Modigliani*, Geneva 1985.
G. Castieu-Barrielle, *La vie et l'oeuvre de Amedeo Modigliani*, Paris 1987.

Giorgio Morandi
Exhibitions
1922 Florence, Palazzo delle Esposizioni al Parco di Sangallo, *La Fiorentina primaverile*, 8 April-31 July.
1935 Rome, Palazzo delle Esposizioni, *II Quadriennale Nazionale d'Arte*, February-July.
1939 Rome, Palazzo delle Esposizioni, *III Quadriennale Nazionale d'Arte*, February-July.
1939 San Francisco, Golden Gate, *Golden Gate International Exhibition of Contemporary Art*.
1942 Milan, Pinacoteca di Brera, *Mostra della collezione Pietro Feroldi*, 7-22 November.
1948 Venice, *XXIV Biennale Internazionale d'Arte*, text by C. Maltese, 29 May-30 September.
1949 Catania, *40 anni d'Arte italiana*, February-April (then Palermo).
1949 New York, The Museum of Modern Art, *Twentieth-Century Italian Art*, text by J.T. Soby and A.H. Barr Jr., 28 June-18 September.
1949-1950 Milan, Centro Annunciata, *Morandi*.
1950 Zürich, Kunsthaus, *Futurismo e Pittura Metafisica*, November-December.
1951 São Paulo, Museu de Arte Moderno, *I Bienal/Artistas italianos de hoje*, October-December.
1953 Florence, Palazzo Strozzi, *Arte moderna in una raccolta italiana*, April-May.
1954 The Hague, Gemeentemuseum, *Morandi*, 14 April-6 June (then Rotterdam).
1954 London, New Burlington Galleries, *Morandi*, 25 June-24 July.
1956 Winterthur, Kunstmuseum, *Giorgio Morandi/Giacomo Manzù*, 24 June-29 July.
1959 Turin, Galleria Civica d'Arte Moderna, *Capolavori d'Arte Moderna*, 31 October-8 December.
1960 Milan, Palazzo Reale, *Arte italiana del XX secolo da collezioni americane*, 30 April-26 June.
1961 Amsterdam, Stedelijk Museum, *Polariti és: The Dionysiac and the Apollonian in Art*, 22 August-8 September.
1962 Milan, Galleria Lorenzelli, *Maggini-Morandi*.
1962 Siegen, Haus seel am Markt, *Giorgio Morandi Rubenspreis 1962 der Stadt Siegen*, 27 October-17 November.
1963-1964 Washington, National Gallery of Art, *Paintings from the Museum of Modern Art, New York*, 16 December-1 March.
1964 Napoli, Palazzo Reale, *La natura morta italiana*, October-November.
1965 Bern, Kunsthalle, *Morandi*, 23 October-5 December.
1965-1966 Rome, Palazzo delle Esposizioni, *IX Quadriennale Nazionale d'Arte*, October-March.
1966 Venice, *XXXIII Biennale Internazionale d'Arte - Aspetti del primo astrattismo italiano 1930-1940*, organized by N. Ponente, 18 June-16 October.
1966 Bologna, Palazzo dell'Archiginnasio, *Morandi*, 30 October-15 December.
1967 Florence, Palazzo Strozzi, *Arte Moderna in Italia 1515-1935*, presentation by C. Ragghianti, 26 February-28 May.
1967 Milan, Palazzo della Permanente, *I Mostra d'arte moderna e trame contemporanee*, March.
1967-1969 Washington, The Phillis Collection, *Masters of Modern Italian Art from the Collection of Gianni Mattioli. Circulated by the International Exhibition Foundation*, text by F. Russoli, 30 November-14 January 1968 (then Dallas, Museum of Fine Arts, 1 February-3 March 1968; San Francisco, Museum of Art, 16 March-21 April 1968; Detroit Institute of Art, 19 June-21 July 1968; Kansas City, William Rockill Nelson Gallery of Art, 6 October-17 November 1968; Boston, Museum of Fine Arts, 23 January-23 February 1969; New York, Olivetti, 5 March-5 April).
1967-1968 Turin, Galleria Civica d'Arte Moderna, *Le muse inquietanti - Maestri del Surrealismo*, text by L. Carluccio, November-January.
1969-1971 Brussels, Palais des Beaux-Arts, *Maitres de l'Art moderne en Italie 1910-1935*, text by F. Russoli, 9 September-12 October 1969 (then Copenhagen, Louisiana-Museet, 8 November-14 December 1969; Hamburg, Hamburger Kunsthalle, 19 February-30 March 1970; Madrid, Museo Español de Arte Contemporaneo, November-December 1970; Barcelona, Palacio de la Virreina 1970, December 1970-January 1971; Seville, Museo de Arte Contemporaneo, January-February 1971).
1970-1971 London, Royal Academy of Art, *Morandi*, 5 December-17 January.
1971 Paris, Musée National d'Arte Moderne, *Morandi*, 9 February-12 April.
1971 Milan, Rotonda della Besana, *Morandi*, May-June.
1972-1973 Rome, Palazzo delle Esposizioni, *X Quadriennale Nazionale d'Arte*, November-May.
1973 Leningrad, Hermitage museum, *Morandi*, 17 April-10 May (then Moscow, Pushkin museum, 18 May-16 June).
1973 Rome, Galleria Nazionale d'Arte Moderna, *Morandi*, 18 May-22 July.
1975 Bologna, Galleria Comunale d'Arte Moderna, *Morandi*, May-June.
1978 Ferrara, Galleria Civica d'Arte Moderna, Palazzo dei Diamanti, *Morandi*, July-October.
1979 Venice, Istituto di Cultura di Palazzo Grassi, *La Pittura metafisica*, texts by G. Briganti and E. Coen, with the contribution of A. Orsini Baroni, May-September.
1981 Munich, Haus der Kunst, *Morandi*, June-September.
1981 San Francisco, Museum of Modern Art, *Morandi*, organized by Des Moines Art Center, 24 September-1 November (then New York, The Solomon R. Guggenheim Museum, 19 November 1981-17 January 1982; Des Moines, Des Moines Art Center, 1 February-14 March 1982).
1984-1985 Madrid, Sala de Exposiciones, Caja de Pensiones, *Morandi*, December-January (then Barcelona, Caja de Pensiones, February-March).
1985-1986 Bologna, Galleria Comunale d'Arte Moderna, *Morandi e il suo tempo*, organized by R. Barilli, 9 November-10 February.
1987 Paris, Hotel de Ville, *Morandi*, organized by the Galleria Comunale d'Arte Moderna di Bologna, June-August.
1988 Massa Carrara, Palazzo Ducale, *Morandi*, texts by G.C. Argan, F. Solmi and L. Vitali, 4 August-25 September.
1989 Leningrad, Hermitage museum, *Giorgio Morandi*, 21 January-19 February, (then Moscow, Central Picture Gallery, 1-26 March.
1989 London, Royal Academy of Arts, *Italian Art in thte 20th Century - Painting and Sculpture 1900-1988*, 14 January-9 April.
Bibliography
Valori plastici, III, Rome 1921.
A. Soffici, "Morandi," in *L'Italiano*, Bologna, March 1932.
A. Beccaria, *Giorgio Morandi*, Milan 1939.
C. Brandi, *Giorgio Morandi*, Florence 1942.
G. Scheiwiller, *Giorgio Morandi*, Turin 1943.
U. Apollonio, *Pittura metafisica*, Venice 1950.
E. Montù, *Capolavori dell'arte moderna italiana*, Milan 1950.
G. Ballo, *Pittori italiani dal futurismo a oggi*, Rome 1956.
G. Castelfranco-M. Valsecchi, *Pittura e scultura italiana dal 1910 al 1930*, Rome 1956.
G. Marchiori, *Arte e artisti d'avanguardia in Italia (1910-1950)*, Milan 1960.
A. Martini, *Giorgio Morandi*, Milan 1964.
L. Vitali, *Giorgio Morandi pittore*, Milan 1964.
F. Arcangeli, *Giorgio Morandi*, Milan 1964.
J. Siblik, *Giorgio Morandi*, Prague 1965.
M. Carrà, *Metafisica*, Milan 1968.
C.L. Ragghianti, M. Valsecchi (editors) *La raccolta Alberto Della Ragione*, Florence 1970.
A. Boschetto, *La collezione Roberto Longhi*, Florence 1971.
L. Vitali, *Morandi*, general catalogue, Milan 1977.
F. Solmi-L. Vitali, *Morandi*, New York 1988.
P. Fossati, *La (pittura metafisica)*, Turin 1988.

Bruno Munari
Exhibitions
1986 Novara, Galleria Uxa, *Bruno Munari*, 18 November-18 December.
1986-1987 Milan, Palazzo Reale, *Bruno Munari opere 1930-1986*, 11 December-1 March.
Bibliography
Tanchis, *Bruno Munari*, Milan 1986.

Giuseppe Pellizza da Volpedo
Exhibitions
1920-1921 Rome, *I Biennale romana*.
1939 Turin, Salone della Stampa, *G. Pellizza da Volpedo*, March.
1954 Alessandria, Pinacoteca Civica, *Giuseppe Pellizza da Volpedo*, 12 June-30 September.
1977 Turin, Foyer del Teatro Regio, *Pellizza per il Quarto Stato*.
1980-1981 Alessandria, Palazzo Cuttica, *Pellizza da Volpedo*, November-January.
1986 Milan, Palazzo della Permanente, *Pellizza da Volpedo, 1886-1986 La Permanente. Un secolo d'arte a Milano*, 9 June-14 September.
Bibliography
F. Sapori, "La prima mostra biennale d'arte in Roma," in *Emporium*, III, Bergamo, July 1921.
Alexandria, Alessandria, July 1937.
T. Fiori-F. Bellonzi, *Archivi del Divisionismo*, Rome 1968.
R. Barilli, "Aspetti del simbolismo italiano," in *Arte illustra*, nos. 22/24, Florence 1969.
A. Scotti, *Pellizza da Volpedo*, general catalogue, Milan 1986.

Fausto Pirandello
Exhibitions
1932 Rome, *III Mostra del Sindacato Regionale Fascista delle Belle Arti*, spring.
1935 Rome, Palazzo delle Esposizioni, *II Quadriennale di Roma*, February-May.
1951 Rome, Fondazione Premi (*I Retrospettiva - Palazzo Barberini*).
1959-1960 Rome, *VIII Quadriennale d'Arte Nazionale, Sguardo alla Giovane Scuola Romana*.

1965 Rome, Palazzo delle Esposizioni, *Rassegna di Arti Figurative di Roma e del Lazio*, April-May.
1967 Florence, Palazzo Strozzi, *Arte Moderna in Italia 1915-1935*, presentation by C.L. Ragghianti, 26 February-28 May.
1971 Melbourne, Canberra, Sydney, Brisbane, Adelaide, Perth, Hobart, Launceston, *Exhibition of Contemporary Italian Painting* in the Australian state galleries.
1976-1977 Rome, Galleria Nazionale d'Arte Moderna, *Fausto Pirandello*, 21 December-27 February.
1989 London, Royal Academy of Arts, *Italian Art in the 20th Century - Painting and Sculpture 1900-1988*, 14 January-9 April.
Bibliography
R. Lucchese, "Colori indimenticabili in Pirandello," in *La Fiera Letteraria*, Rome, 11 March 1951.
A. Neppi, "Realismo ed espressionismo di Fausto Pirandello," in *La Giustizia*, Rome, 11 March 1951.
L. Venturi, "Fausto Pirandello," in *Commentari*, Rome, January-March 1954.
C. Maltese, *Storia dell'arte in Italia 1785-1943*, Turin 1960.
T. Marcheselli, "L'umanità greve di Fausto Pirandello," in *Gazzetta di Parma*, Parma, 2 December 1975.

Enrico Prampolini
Exhibitions
1930 Venice, *XVII Biennale Internazionale d'Arte*, May-September.
1941 Rome, Galleria Roma, *Enrico Prampolini*.
1942 Venice, *XXIII Biennale Internazionale d'Arte*.
1956 Milan, Galleria Bompiani, *Rassegna d'Arte Astratta*.
1958 Paris, Galerie Denise René, *Enrico Prampolini*.
1959 Rome, Fondazione Premi Roma, *Mostra del Futurismo*.
1961 Rome, *Galleria Nazionale d'Arte Moderna, Enrica Prampolini 1894-1956*, presentation by P. Bucarelli.
1971 London, Annely Juda Gallery, *Non Objective World 1924-1939*, July-September.
1976 Milan, Galleria GianFerrari, *Verifica della situazione torinese dal 1920 al 1945*, March.
1978 Modena, Galleria Nazionale d'Arte Moderna, *Continuità all'avanguardia in Italia, Enrico Prampolini 1894-1978*, January-March.
1980 Rome, Galleria Nazionale d'Arte Moderna, *Arte astratta italiana 1909-1959*, 2 April-11 March.
1985 Turin, Galleria Narcico, *Futurismo a Torino*, organized by M. Pinottini, 30 April-15 June.
1985-1986 Modena, Galleria Fonte d'Abisso, *Prampolini 1913-1956*, organized by A.B. Oliva, 7 December-28 February.
1986 Rome, Galleria Sprovieri, *Arte astratta italiana dal Futurismo agli anni Trenta*.
1989 London, Royal Academy of Arts, *Italian Art in the 20th Century - Painting and Sculpture 1900-1988*, 14 January-9 April.
Bibliography
Natura, February 1936.
E. Prampolini, *Arte polimaterica*, Rome 1944.
F. Menna, *Prampolini*, Rome 1967.
Il Mondo, no. 36, 9 September 1985.
M. Calvesi, *Il Futurismo*, Milan 1968.

Mario Radice
Exhibitions
1967 Florence, Palazzo Strozzi, *Arte Moderna in Italia 1915-1935*, 26 February-28 May.
1971 Rome, Galleria d'Arte Marlborough, *Mario Radice*, October-November.

1976 Zürich, Marlborough Galerie AG, *Mario Radice*, 10 February-20 March (then Rome, Galleria Marlborough, 11 May-12 June 1976).
1982 Milan, Galleria del Sagrato, Palazzo Reale, ex Arengario, *Gli Anni Trenta Arte e Cultura in Italia*, organized by R. Barilli, 27 January-20 April.

Antonietta Raphaël
Exhibitions
1937 Rome, Mercati Traianei, *VII Mostra del Sindacato Fascista Belle Arti del Lazio*, April-June
1951-1952 Rome, Palazzo delle Esposizioni, *VI Quadriennale Nazionale d'Arte*, December-April.
1955 Milan, Galleria La Colonna, *A. Raphaël Mafai*, April.
1955 Rome, Galleria La Tartaruga, *A. Raphaël Mafai*, May.
1959-1960 Rome, Palazzo delle Esposizioni, *VIII Quadriennale Nazionale d'Arte*, December-April.
1960 Turin, Galleria Narciso, *Raphaël*, September.
1967 Florence, Palazzo Strozzi, *Arte Moderna in Italia 1915-1935*, presentation by C. Ragghianti, 26 February-28 May.
1972 Turin, Galleria Narciso, *Antonietta Raphaël Mafari*, April-May.
1978 Rome, Galleria Incontro d'Arte, *Raphaël. Scultura lingua viva*, February.
1982 Milan, Palazzo Reale, Galleria del Sagrato, ex Arengario, *Gli Anni Trenta: Arte e Cultura in Italia*, organized by R. Barilli, 27 January-23 May.
1984-1985 Milan, Galleria Daverio, *Roma tra espressionismo barocco e pittura tonale 1929-1943*, December-January.
1985 Milan, Civico Padiglione d'Arte Contemporanea, *Antonietta Raphaël*, summer.
1988 Milan, Palazzo Reale, *Scuola romana - Artisti tra le due guerre*, organized by M. Fagiolo, 13 April-19 June.
Bibliography
W. Dias, "Incontro con una scultrice," in *L'Unità*, Genoa, 22 July 1949.
M. Pinottini, *Scultura di Raphaël*, Milan 1971.

Mauro Reggiani
Exhibitions
1936 Milan, Galleria del Milione, *Reggiani*.
1966 Venice, *XXXIII Biennale internazionale d'Arte - Aspetti del primo astrattismo italiano 1930-1940*, organized by N. Ponente, 18 June-16 October.
1967 Modena, Galleria Comunale, *Mauro Reggiani*, organized by N. Ponente.
1973-1974 Turin, Galleria Civica d'Arte Moderna, *Mauro Reggiani*.
1980 Prato, Palazzo Novellucci, *Anni creativi al "Milione" 1932-1939*, texts by C. Belli, M. Cernuschi Ghiringhelli, A. Longatti, N. Ponente and G. Marchiori, 7 June-20 July.
1984 Modena Galleria Civica, *Mauro Reggiani*.
Bibliography
P. Fossati, *L'immagine sospesa*, Turin 1971.

Manlio Rho
Exhibitions
1940 Venice, *XXII Esposizione Biennale Internazionale d'Arte*, June-October.
1966 Venice, *XXXIII Biennale Internazionale d'Arte - Aspetti del primo astrattismo italiano 1930-1940*, organized by N. Ponente, 18 June-16 October.
1966 Como, Villa Olmo, *Manlio Rho*, June-July.
Bibliography
A. Sartoris, *Gli elementi dell'architettura funzionale*, Milan 1941.

Ottone Rosai
Exhibitions
1922 Rome, Galleria d'Arte Bragaglia, *Ottone Rosai*, presentation by A. Soffici, November.
1957 Ivrea, Centro Culturale Olivetti, *Ottone Rosai*, text by P.C. Santini, May.
1960 Florence, Palazzo Strozzi, *Ottone Rosai 1911-1957*, organized by P.C. Santini, May-June.
1964 Florence, Palazzo Strozzi, *Galleria Michaud alla II Mostra mercato nazionale d'arte contemporanea*, text by L. Cavallo, 21 March-9 April.
1965-1966 Florence, Galleria Michaud, *Gli omini di Rosai*, text by M. Masciotta.
1967 Florence, Palazzo Strozzi, *Arte Moderna in Italia*, presentation by C. Ragghianti, 26 February-28 May.
1971 Milan, Palazzo della Permanente, *Mostra di Pittori e Scultori che recitano a soggetto*, text by M. Carrà, March-May.
1983 Turin, Circolo degli artisti - Palazzo Graneri, *Ottone Rosai*, April-May (then Rome, Galleria Nazionale d'Arte Moderna).
1985-1986 Bologna, Galleria Comunale d'Arte Moderna, *Morandi e il suo tempo*, organized by R. Barilli, 9 November-10 February.
Bibliography
A.R., "Mostre d'Arte," in *Il Nuovo Corriere*, Florence, 28 April 1955.
P.C. Santini, *Rosai*, Florence 1960.
M. Valsecchi-F. Russoli-L. Cavallo, *Ottone Rosai*, Florence 1968.
L. Cavallo, *Ottone Rosai*, Milan 1973.
P. Fossati, *La (pittura metafisica)*, Turin 1988.

Gino Rossi
Exhibitions
1911 Venice, Palazzo Pesaro, *Esposizione Opera Bevilacqua La Masa*.
1913 Venice, Palazzo Pesaro, *Esposizione Opera Bevilacqua La Masa*.
1919 Venice, Palazzo Pesaro, *Esposizione Opera Bevilacqua La Masa*.
1948 Venice, *XXIV Biennale Internazionale d'Arte Iª retrospettiva*, text by C. Maltese, 29 May-30 September.
1956 Rome, Galleria Nazionale d'Arte Moderna, *Gino Rossi*.
1958 Venice, Palazzo Pesaro, *Primi espositori di Ca' Pesaro*, 28 August-19 October.
1971 Verona, Galleria Civica d'Arte Moderna, Palazzo della Gran Guardia, *Verona anni Venti*.
1983-1984 Verona, Galleria dello Scudo, *Gino Rossi* (then Venice, Ca' Vendramin Calergi), 20 November-31 January.
Bibliography
D. Valeri, "La Mostra d'Arte di Treviso," in *Le Tre Venezie* Decembre 1933.
G. Marchiori, "Pittori a Burano," in *Corriere Padano*, 2 January 1935.
Candida, "Una mostra di Gino Rossi," in *Emporium*, Bergamo, April 1943.
B. Geiger, *Gino Rossi pittore*, Venice 1949.
U. Apollonio, *Pittura italiana moderna (idee per una storia)*, Venice 1950.
G. Perocco, *Gli artisti del primo Novecento Italiano*, Turin 1965.
G. Perocco, *Origini dell'Arte Moderna a Venezia (1908-1920)*, Treviso 1972.
L. Menegazzi, *Gino Rossi*, general catalogue, Milan 1984.

Medardo Rosso
Exhibitions
1905 Vienna, Kunstsalon Artaria, *Medardo Rosso*, February.
1911 Rome, *Mostra Internazionale di Belle Arti*, April.
1914 Venice, *IX Esposizione Internazionale*

d'Arte della Città di Venezia, April-October.
1923 Milan, Bottega di Poesia, Medardo Rosso, March-April.
1926 Milan, Palazzo della Permanente, I Mostra del Novecento Italiano, preface by M. Sarfatti, February-March.
1931 Rome, Palazzo delle Esposizioni, I Quadriennale d'Arte Nazionale, January-June.
1958-1959 New York, Peridot Gallery, First Exhibition in American of Sculpture by Medardo Rosso, December-January.
1960-1961 Paris, Musée National d'Art Moderne, Les Sources du XX siècle - Les arts en Europe de 1884 à 1914, November-January.
1979 Milan, Palazzo della Permanente, Mostra di Medardo Rosso (1858-1928), January-March.
1979-1980 Alessandria, Palazzo Cuttica, Medardo Rosso, organized by L. Caramel, 21 December-31 January.
1984 Frankfurt, Kunstverein Steinernes Hans am Romerberg, Medardo Rosso, 20 January-11 March.
1989 London, Royal Academy of Arts, Italian Art in the 20th Century - Painting and Sculpture 1900-1988, 14 January-9 April.
Bibliography
M. Sarfatti, Segni colori e luci, Bologna 1925.
G. Papini, Medardo Rosso, Milan 1940.
N. Barbantini, Medardo Rosso, Venice 1950.
M. Borghi, Medardo Rosso, Milan 1950.
J.C. Taylor, Futurism, New York 1961.
M. Scolari Barr, Medardo Rosso, New York 1963.
C. Pirovano, Scultura italiana - Dal neoclassicismo alle correnti contemporanee, Milan 1968.
L. Caramel, C. Pirovano, Musei e Gallerie di Milano - Galleria d'Arte Moderna - Opere dell'Ottocento, Milan 1975.

Mino Rosso
Exhibitions
1932 Venice, XVIII Biennale di Venezia.
1935 Paris, Galerie Bernheim Jeune.
1962 Turin, Galleria Civica d'Arte Moderna, Aspetti del Secondo Futurismo torinese, 27 March-30 April.
1951 Milan, Galleria Bompiani.
1976 Turin, Galleria Narciso, Mino Rosso, 16 October-16 November.
Bibliography
La Noche, Barcelona, 5 January 1934.
Paris Soir, Paris, 2 April 1935.
Stile Futurista, year II, no. 15-16, December 1935.
G. Marchiori, Arte e artisti d'avanguardia dal 1910 al 1950, Milan 1960.
E. Crispolti, Il mito della macchina e altri temi del Futurismo, Trapani 1969.
A. Dragone in AA.VV. Torino 1920-1936. Società e cultura tra sviluppo industriale e capitalismo, Turin, 1976.

Luigi Russolo
Exhibitions
1911 Milan, I Esposizione d'Arte Libera.
1912 Paris, Galerie Bernheim Jeune, Les Peintres futuristes italiens, 5-24 February.
1912 London, The Sackville Gallery, Exhibition of Works by the Italian Futurist Painters, March.
1912 Berlin, Galerie Der Sturm, Zweite Austellung: Die Futuristen, 12 April-31 May.
1912 Brussels, Galerie George Giroux, 20 May-1 June.
1913 Rotterdam, Rotterdamsche Kunstkring, Les Peintres et les sculpteurs futuristes italiens, 18 May-15 June.
1914 Rome, Galleria Futurista Permanente Sprovieri, February-March.
1929-1930 Paris, Galerie 23, Peintres Futuristes

Italiens, 27 December-9 January.
1960 Venice, XXX Biennale di Venezia.
1968 Venice, XXXIV Biennale di Venezia.
1986 Venice, Palazzo Grassi, Futurismo & Futurism, April-October.
1989 London, Royal Academy of Arts, Italian Art in the 20th Century - Painting and Sculpture 1900-1988, 14 January-9 April.

Giuseppe Santomaso
Exhibitions
1941 Cortina d'Ampezzo, Palazzo Municipale, Prima mostra delle collezioni d'arte contemporanea, 10-31 August.
1954 Venice, XXVII Biennale Internazionale d'Arte, June-October.
1986 Milan, Palazzo Reale, Santomaso opere 1939/1986, 29 April-15 June.
Bibliography
R. Pallucchini, "Artisti contemporanei - Bepi Santomaso," in Emporium, Bergamo, May 1942.
A. Podestà, "Posizione di Santomaso," in Domus, Milan, no. 16, February 1942.
R. Giani, "Pittura e cinema a colori, Giuseppe Santomaso," in Cinema, Rome, 30 January 1950.
L. Venturi, Pittori italiani d'oggi, Rome 1958.
G. Ballo, La linea dell'arte italiana, dal simbolismo alle opere moltiplicate, Rome 1964.
N. Ponente-L. Alfieri, Santomaso, Venice 1975.

Alberto Savinio
Exhibitions
1930 Venice, XVII Biennale Internazionale d'Arte, May-September.
1930 Milan, Galleria Milano, Prima mostra di pittori italiani residenti a Parigi.
1932 Paris,? (cfr. W. George, 1932; the critic discusses animal-human metamorphoses in his review of an exhibition of that year).
1963 Milan, Galleria Levi, Alberto Savinio, 25 dipinti dal 1927 al 1931, February.
1963 Turin, Galleria Narciso, Savinio, 32 dipinti dal 1927 al 1930, presentation by E. Crispolti, April-May.
1968 L'Aquila, Castello Spagnolo, Alternative Attuali 3, presentation by E. Crispolti, July-September.
1970 Milan, Galleria d'Arte Medea, 44 opere di Alberto Savinio, presentation by F. Passoni, March-April.
1976 Milan, Palazzo Reale, Alberto Savinio, 1891-1952, June-July (then Brussels, Palais des Beaux Arts, 5 August-5 September).
1978 Rome, Palazzo delle Esposizioni, Alberto Savinio, 18 May-18 July.
1980 Ferrara, Galleria Civica d'Arte Moderna, Palazzo dei Diamanti, Alberto Savinio, 5 July-5 October.
1980 Bologna, Galleria Comunale d'Arte Moderna, La metafisica: gli anni Venti, organized by R. Barilli and F. Solmi, May-August.
1985 Venice, Sima, Il Novecento italiano nelle collezioni Assitalia.
1987 New York, Philippe Daverio Gallery, The Dioscuri Giorgio De Chirico and Alberto Savinio in Paris 1924-1931.
1988 Milan, Galleria Spazio Immagine, Savinio, 22 April-15 June.
1989 London, Royal Academy of Arts, Italian Art in the 20th Century - Painting and Sculpture 1900-1988, 14 January-9 April.
Bibliography
G. Scheiwiller, Art Italien Moderne, Paris 1930.
G. Briganti-L. Sciascia, Alberto Savinio, Milan 1979.
M. Fagiolo, "Biographical notes on metaphysical Argonaut - Alberto Savinio," in Art form, January 1983.
L. Cavallo-P. Vivarelli, Savinio disegni immaginati

1925-1932, Milan 1984.
Scipione
Exhibitions
1930 Venice, XVII Biennale Internazionale d'Arte, May-September.
1930 Rome, Galleria di Roma, Scipione e Mafai, 8-27 November.
1931 Rome, Palazzo delle Esposizioni, I Quadriennale Nazionale d'Arte, January-June.
1935 Rome, Palazzo delle Esposizioni, II Quadriennale Nazionale d'Arte, February-July.
1941 Milan, Pinacoteca di Brera, Mostra postuma a cura del centro di azione per le arti, text by A. Santangelo, 8-23 March.
1941 Rome, Galleria di Roma, La Collezione Cordazzo, April.
1944-1945 Rome, Galleria Nazionale d'Arte Moderna, Esposizione d'Arte Contemporanea.
1947 Lausanne, Musée cantonal des Beaux-Arts, Quarante Ans d'Art Italien, 15 February-15 March.
1948 Venice, XXIV Biennale Internazionale d'Arte, text by C. Maltese, 29 May-30 September.
1948 Macerata, Pinacoteca comunale, Scipione, text by M. Rivosecchi, 12-26 December.
1949 New York, The Museum of Modern Art, Twentieth-Century Italian Art, text by J.T. Soby and E.H. Barr Jr., 28 June-18 September.
1950 Milan, Centro Annunciata, Opere di Scipione, 25 March-7 April.
1954 Rome, Galleria Nazionale d'Arte Moderna, Mostra di Scipione, organized by P. Bucarelli, April.
1960 Ferrara, Casa Romei, Rinnovamento dell'arte in Italia 1930-1945, text by V. Guzzi, June-September.
1967 Florence, Palazzo Strozzi, Arte Moderna in Italia 1915-1935, critical references by G. Visentini, 26 February-28 May.
1981 Turin, Galleria Civica d'Arte Moderna, Materiali: Arte italiana 1920-1940 nelle collezioni della Galleria Civica d'Arte moderna di Torino, organized by L. Caramel.
1985 Milan, Palazzo Reale, Corrente, organized by R. De Grada.
1985 Macerata, Palazzo Ricci, Scipione 1904-1933, 6 July-15 September.
1989 London, Royal Academy of Arts, Italian Art in the 20th Century - Painting and Sculpture 1900-1988, 14 January-9 April.
Bibliography
U. Nebbia, XVII Esposizione Internazionale d'Arte, Venice 1930.
L. Venturi, "Venezia XVII," in Belvedere, Milan, May-June 1930.
F. Callari, II Quadriennale d'Arte Nazionale, Rome 1935.
G. Marchiori, Scipione, Milan 1939.
A. Trombadori, "La raccolta Cardazzo," in Primato, Rome, 2 May 1941.
U. Nebbia, La pittura del Novecento, Milan 1941.
U. Apollonio, Scipione, Venice 1945.
C. Maltese, "Scipione," Emporium, Bergamo, July-August 1948.
N. Bertocchi, "Piazza Navona," in Arte Mediterranea, Rome July-August 1949.
R. Carrieri, Pittura e scultura d'avanguardia in Italia 1890-1950, Milan 1950.
G. Ungaretti, Pittori italiani contemporanei, Bologna 1950.
S. Giannelli, "Scipione senso di una apparizione," in Le Carte Parlanti, Florence 1950.
P. Bucarelli, "La pittura di Scipione," in Scritti di Storia dell'arte in onore di L. Venturi, vol. II, Rome 1956.
M. Borghi, Da Mancini a Scipione, Rome 1960.
G.C. Argan, Storia dell'Arte Moderna, Florence 1970.
G. Mascherpa, in AA.VV., Palazzo Ricci a Mace-

rata, Macerata 1983.
M. Fagiolo-M. Rivosecchi, *Scipione vita e opere*, Turin 1988.

Gino Severini

Exhibitions
1913 Berlin, Erster Deutscher Herbstsalon, *I Sturm Ausstellung*.
1914 London, The Doré Galleries, *Exhibition of the Works of Italian Futurist Painters and Sculptors*.
1914 Rome, Galleria Sprovieri, *Esposizione di pittura futurista: Balla, Boccioni, Carrà, Russolo, Severini, Soffici*, February-March.
1916 Paris, Galerie Boutet de Monvel, *Ière Exposition Futuriste d'Art Plastique de la Guerre et d'autres oeuvres anterieures (Gino Severini)*.
1917 New York, Photo Secession Gallery, *Drawings, Pastels, Watercolors and Oils of Severini*.
1924 Paris, Salon d'Automne.
1929-1930 Paris, Galerie 23, *Peintres Futuristes Italiens*.
1931 Amsterdam, Huinck & Scherjon Kunstanded, *Gino Severini - Exposition retrospective*, text by J. Maritain.
1932 Venice, *XVIII Biennale Internazionale d'Arte*.
1936 Venice, *XX Biennale Internazionale d'Arte*, 1 June-30 September.
1945 Rome, Galleria in via del Tritone 123, *Présence: Gino Severini*.
1950 Zürich, Kunsthaus, *Futurismo e Pittura Metafisica*, November-December.
1959 Rome, Palazzo Barberini, *Il futurismo* (then Munich, 1960).
1960 Venice, *XXX Biennale Internazionale d'Arte - Mostra storica del futurismo*, organized by G. Ballo, 18 June-16 October.
1961 Rome, Palazzo Venezia, *Severini*, text by E. Lavagnino, with unpublished articles by G. Severini.
1965-1966 Rome, Palazzo delle Esposizioni, *IX Quadriennale Nazionale d'Arte*, October-March.
1967 Paris, Musée National d'Art Moderne, *Severini*, text by B. Dorival.
1972-1973 Rome, Palazzo delle Esposizioni, *X Quadriennale Nazionale d'Arte*, November-May.
1973 Paris, Musée National d'Art Moderne, *Le Futurisme 1909-1916*, 19 September-19 November.
1973 Milan, Centro Rizzoli, *Omaggio a Gino Severini*.
1974 Düsseldorf, Stadtische Kunsthalle, *Futurismus 1909-1917*, texts by J. Harte, M. Calvesi, F. Russoli, F.W. Heckermanns, R. Langer, 25 March-28 April.
1980 Rome, Galleria Giulia, *Gino Severini "Entre les deux guerres" 1919-1939*, texts by M. Fagiolo and E. Coen.
1980 Bologna, Galleria Comunale d'Arte Moderna, *La metafisica: gli anni Venti*, organized by R. Barilli and F. Solmi, May-August.
1982 Rome, Pinacoteca Capitolina, *Guggenheim Venezia - New York. Sessanta opere 1900-1950*.
1982-1983 Milan, Galleria Daverio, *Severini*, organized by M. Fagiolo and E. Coen.
1983 Florence, Palazzo Pitti, *Severini*, texts by G. Morales, R. Barilli, M. Fagiolo, P. Pacini, C. Cresti, S. Evangelisti, P. Marescalchi, 25 June-25 September.
1987 Alessandria, Palazzo Cuttica, *Gino Severini dal 1916 al 1936*, texts by U. Eco, M. Boidi-Sotis, M. Calvesi, M. Vescovo, H. Heijerman-Ton, D. Fonti.
1987-1988 Bolzano, Castel Marecchio, *Severini*, organized by G. Dorfles and P.L. Siena, 15 December-31 January (then Genoa, Villa Croce, 9 March-24 April).

1988 Munich, Haus der Kunst, *Mythos Italien - Wintermacken Deutschland*, organized by C. Schultz-Hoffmann, 24 March-29 May.
1988-1989 Verona, Galleria dello Scudo, *Realismo Magico - Pittura e Scultura in italia 1919-1925*, 27 November-29 January (then Milan, Palazzo Reale, 16 February-2 April).
1989 London, Royal Academy of Arts, *Italian Art in the 20th Century - Painting and Sculpture 1900-1988*, 14 January-9 April.

Bibliography
P. Albert-Birot, "Etc... peinture," in *Sic*, no. 14, Paris 1917.
C.H. Caffin, "Severini's Works seen at '291'," in *New York American*, 12 March 1917.
Bullettin de l'Effort Moderne, Paris 1924.
F. Roth, *Nach-Espressionismus*, Leipzig, 1925.
P. Courthion, *Gino Severini*, Milan 1930.
J. Cassou, "Il pittore Gino Severini," in *Dedalo*, Milan, November 1932.
P. Fierens, "Gino Severini," in *L'Urbe*, Milan-Paris, 20 October 1936.
G. Nicodemi, "Artisti contemporanei: Gino Severini," in *Emporium*, Bergamo, June 1940.
G. Severini, *Tutta la vita di un pittore. I Roma-Parigi*, Milan 1946.
C. Zervos-Benedetta-P. Buzzi-F. Pastonchi, "Le Futurisme. Un demi-siècle d'art italien," in *Cahiers d'Art*, XXV, I, Paris 1950.
M. Drudi Gambillo-T. Fiori, *Archivi del Futurismo*, Rome, vol. I, 1959, vol. II, 1962.
L. Venturi, *Gino Severini*, Rome 1961.
M.A. De Sardi, "Severini et le Futurisme," in *Jardin des Arts*, no. 110, January 1964.
P. Pacini, *Severini*, Florence 1966.
M. Calvesi, "Dinamismo e simultaneità nella poetica futurista," in *L'Arte Moderna*, vol. V, Milan 1967.
M. Carrà, *Al di fuori delle avanguardie*, Milan 1967.
M.W. Martin, *Futurist Art and Theory 1909-1915*, Oxford 1968.
J.M. Lukach, "Severini's 1917 Exhibition at Stieglitz's '291'," in *Burlington Magazine*, no. 817, April 1971.
D. Fonti, *Gino Severini*, catalogue raisonné, Milan 1988.

Mario Sironi

Exhibitions
1924 Venice, *XIV Biennale Internazionale d'Arte*, presentation by M. Sarfatti, spring-summer.
1931 Rome, Palazzo delle Esposizioni, *I Quadriennale Nazionale d'Arte*, January-June.
1932 Venice, *XVIII Biennale Internazionale d'Arte*.
1935 Paris, Jeu de Paume, *Art italien des XIX et XX Siècle*, May-June.
1955-1956 Rome, Palazzo delle Esposizioni, *VII Quadriennale Nazionale d'Arte*, October-March.
1962 Venice, *XXXI Biennale Internazionale d'Arte*, June-October.
1967 Florence, Palazzo Strozzi, *Arte Moderna in Italia 1915-1935*, presentation by C. Ragghianti, 28 February-28 May.
1969 Verona, Palazzo Corsini, *Sironi 1913-1961*, texts by C. Cagli and A. Gatto, October-December.
1973 Milan, Palazzo Reale, *Mario Sironi*, organized by R. De Grada, February-March.
1974 Milan, Palazzo Reale, *Cinquanta anni di pittura italiana nella collezione Boschi di Stefano*, presentation by M. Precerutti Garberi, M. Valsecchi and A. Boschi, May-September.
1978 Bologna, Galleria Comunale d'Arte Moderna, *La metafisica del quotidiano*, presentation by F. Solmi, June-September.
1979 Venice, Istituto di Cultura di Palazzo

Grassi, *La pittura metafisica*, texts by G. Briganti and E. Coen, with the contribution of A. Orsini Baroni, May-September.
1980 Bologna, Galleria Comunale d'Arte Moderna, *La metafisica: gli anni Venti*, organized by R. Barilli and F. Solmi, May-August.
1980-1981 Paris, Musée National d'Art Moderne, Centre Georges Pompidou, *Les Réalismes 1919-1939*, organized by J. Clair, 17 December-20 April (then Berlin, Staatlische Kunsthalle, *Realismus - Zwischen Revolution und Reaktion 1919-1939*, 16 May-28 June).
1980 Rome, Braccio di Carlo Magno, *Acquisizioni della collezione Vaticana d'arte religiosa*, presentation by C. Pietrangeli and M. Ferrazza, June-July.
1982-1983 Verona, Galleria dello Scudo, *Mario Sironi: 1905-1961*, texts by A. Pica, G. Perocco and G.L. Verzellesi, November-January.
1983 Milan, Palazzo della Permanente, *Il Novecento italiano 1923-1933*, organized by R. Bossaglia, January-March.
1984 Milan, Galleria Daverio, *Mario Sironi, metodo e tecnica*, organized by F. Meloni, text by A. Pica and P. Baldacci.
1985 Sassari, Padiglione dell'Artigianato Sardo, *Sironi, opere 1902-1960*, 26 October-24 November.
1985 Milan, Palazzo Reale, *Sironi 1885-1961*, 4 October-8 December.
1987 Düsseldorf, Städtische Kunsthalle, *Die Axt hat geblut... Europaïsche Konflikte der 30er Jahre in Erinnerung an die frühe Avantgarde*, October-December.
1988 Düsseldorf, Städtische Kunsthalle, *Mario Sironi*, 30 April-26 June.
1988 Iseo, Sale dell'Arsenale, *Sironi opere inedite*, 16 September-27 November.
1988-1989 Verona, Galleria dello Scudo, *Realismo Magico - Pittura e Scultura in Italia 1919-1925*, 27 November-29 January (then Milan, Palazzo Reale, 16 February-2 April).
1989 London, Royal Academy of Arts, *Italian Art in the 20th century - Painting and Sculpture 1900-1988*, 14 January-9 April.

Bibliography
M. Sarfatti, "Segni, colori e luci," in *Note d'Arte*, Bologna 1925.
G. Scheiwiller, *Mario Sironi*, Milan 1930.
V. Costantini, "Mario Sironi," in *Emporium*, no. 4, Bergamo, April 1934.
G. Giani, *Pittori italiani contemporanei*, Milan 1942.
L. Anceschi, *Mario Sironi*, Milan 1944.
A. Sartoris, *Mario Sironi*, Milan 1955.
A. Pica, *Mario Sironi*, Milan 1955.
G. Castelfranco-M. Valsecchi, *Pittura e scultura italiana dal 1910 al 1930*, Rome 1956.
A. Pica, *Mario Sironi*, Milan 1962.
M. Valsecchi, *Mario Sironi*, Rome 1962.
D. Morosini, *Il caso Sironi*, in *Paese Sera*, Rome, 7 October 1969.
R. De Grada, *Sironi*, Milan 1972.
G. Mascherpa-M. Valsecchi, *Arte moderna a Milano*, Milan 1976.
M. Sironi, *Scritti editi e inediti*, edited by E. Camesasca, Milan 1980.
L. Caramel-M. Fiorio-C. Pirovano, *Galleria d'Arte Moderna, Padiglione d'Arte Contemporanea - collezione Boschi*, Milan 1980.
J. Clair, "Sous le signe de Saturne: notes sur l'allegorie de la Mélancolie dans l'art de l'entre deux guerres en Allemagne et en Italie," in *Cahiers du Musée National d'Art Moderne*, no. 7/8, Paris 1981.
G. Anzani-L. Caramel, *Pittura moderna in Lombardia*, Milan 1983.
Arte, April 1985.
F. Bellonzi, *Sironi*, Milan 1985.

759

Critical References - Bibliography

Ardengo Soffici
Exhibitions
1989   Milan, Palazzo Reale, *Realismo magico - Pittura e scultura in Italia 1919-1925*, 15 February-2 April.
Bibliography
Valori Plastici, no. 5, May 1921.
G. Raimondi, L. Cavallo, *Ardengo Soffici*, Florence 1967.
P. Fossati, *Valori Plastici 1918-1922*, Turin 1981.

Anastasio Soldati
Exhibitions
1965   Ivrea, Centro Culturale Olivetti, *Soldati*, text by P.C. Santini, June.
1966-1967   Genoa, Galleria La Polena, *Soldati*, text by G. Beringheli.
1969-1970   Turin, Galleria Civica d'Arte Moderna, *Soldati*, texts by N. Ponente and L. Mallé, 6 November-6 January.
1970   Parma, Palazzo della Pilotta, *Soldati* organized by N. Ponente, 1-30 March.
Bibliography
P.C. Santini, *Anastasio Soldati*, Milan 1965.

Emilio Vedova
Exhibitions
1958   Warsaw, Zachenta museum, *Emilio Vedova*, September-October.
1961   Milan, Centro Annunciata, *Emilio Vedova*, spring.
1961   Milan, Galleria Blu, *Vedova*.
1961   Milan, Galleria Il Disegno, *Vedova*.
1961   Madrid, Ateneo, *Vedova*, texts by G.C. Argan. V. Aguilera Cerni, U. Apollonio, W. Haftmann, J. Leymarie, R. Zepinski, G. Marchiori, M. Pedrosa, May-June.
1961   Barcelona, Sala Gaspar, *Vedova*.
1961   Verona, Galleria Civica d'Arte Moderna, Palazzo della Gran Guardia, *Emilio Vedova*, texts by G.C. Argan, V. Aguilera Cerni, U. Apollonio, S. Branzi, M. Calvesi, W. Haftmann, Z. Kepinski, J. Leymarie, L. Magagnato, G. Marchiori, G. Mazzariol, N. Ponente, C.L. Ragghianti, F. Russoli, M. Valsecchi, L. Venturi, C. Vivaldi, 30 September-31 October.
1963   Livorno, Palazzo del Museo.
1964-1965   Baden-Baden, Staatliche Kunsthalle, *Vedova*.
1968   Ferrara, Galleria Civica d'Arte Moderna, Palazzo dei Diamanti, *Vedova. Presenze 1935-1968*, texts by G. Montana and E. Vedova, 22 September-17 November.
1981   Braunschweig, Kunstverein, *Emilio Vedova*.
1983   Bologna, Galleria Comunale d'Arte Moderna, *L'informale in Italia*, organized by R. Barilli and F. Solmi, June-September.
1984   Venice, Ala Napoleonica, Museo Correr, Magazzino del Sale, 266 alle Zattere, *Vedova 1935-1984*, organized by G. Celant and I. Giannelli, 12 May-30 September.
1985   Milan, Palazzo Reale, *Corrente: il Movimento d'Arte e Cultura d'opposizione*, 25 January-28 April.

Luigi Veronesi
Exhibitions
1970   Saint-Paul-de-Vence, Musée Municipal, *Exposition de Luigi Veronesi*, February-March.
1975   Parma, Sala delle Scuderie in Pilotta, *Luigi Veronesi*, 20 June-20 July.
1982   Milan, Galleria del Sagrato, Palazzo Reale, ex Arengario, *Gli anni Trenta - Arte e Cultura Italia*, 27 January-30 April.

Selected Bibliography

Nicoletta Boschiero

The following essential bibliography provides a short run through the most representative movements of the period 1900-1945. The texts, the articles and the catalogues, in chronological order, are of a general nature. For specific publications on individual artists see the section entitled "Critical References".

A. Soffici
Scoperte e massacri, Florence 1919.
Arte moderna italiana, series of monographs edited by G. Scheiwiller, Milan 1925 et seg.
M. Sarfatti
Storia della pittura moderna, Rome 1930.
G. Castelfranco
La Pittura moderna, 1860-1930, Florence 1934.
V. Costantini
Sculptura e pittura italiana contemporanea (1880-1926), Milan 1939.
V.E. Barbaroux, G. Giani
Arte italiana contemporanea, text by M. Bontempelli, Milan 1940.
U. Nebbia
La pittura del Novecento, Milan 1941.
G. Giani
Pittori italiani contemporanei, Milan 1942.
C. Carrà
Il rinnovamento delle arti in Italia, Milan 1945.
S. Cairola
Arte italiana del nostro tempo, Bergamo 1946.
U. Apollonio
Pittura moderna italiana, Venice 1950.
R. Carrieri
Pittura e scultura d'avanguardia in Italia, Milan 1950.
A. Soffici
Trenta artisti moderni italiani e stranieri, Florence 1950.
G. Castelfranco, M. Valsecchi
Pittura e scultura italiane dal 1910 al 1930, Rome 1956.
T. Sauvage
Pittura italiana del dopoguerra, Milan 1957.
R. Modesti
Pittura italiana contemporanea, Milan 1958.
M. De Micheli
Le avanguardie artistiche del '900, Milan 1959.
C. Maltese
Storia dell'arte in Italia (1785-1943), Turin 1960.
G. Marchiori
Arte e artisti d'avanguardia in Italia (1910-1950), Milan 1960.
G. Mazzariol
Pittura italiana contemporanea, Bergamo 1961.
G. Perocco
Artisti del primo Novecento italiano, Turin 1965.
R. Barilli
La scultura del Novecento, Milan 1968.
C. Pirovano
Scultura italiana del Neoclassicismo alle correnti contemporanee, Milan 1968.
F. Bellonzi
Pittura italiana: Il Novecento, Milan 1969.
G.C. Argan
L'arte moderna 1770/1970, Florence 1970.
F. Arcangeli
Dal Romanticismo all'Informale, Einaudi, Turin 1976.
C. Brandi
Scritti sull'arte contemporanea, Turin 1976.
A. Del Guercio
La pittura del Novecento, Turin 1980.
M. De Micheli
La Scultura del Novecento, Turin 1980.
P. Fossati
Pittura e scultura fra le due guerre, in AA.VV., *Il Novecento (Storia dell'arte italiana, 7)*, Turin 1982.
R. Barilli

L'arte contemporanea: da Cézanne alle ultime tendenze, Milan 1984.
Catalogue *Arte italiana dal 1910 ad oggi*, text by F. Bellonzi, München, Haus der Kunst, June 1957.
Catalogue *50 anni d'arte a Milano - Dal divisionismo ad oggi*, Milan, Palazzo della Permanente, 31 January-15 March 1959.
Catalogue *Arte Moderna in Italia 1915-1935*, edited by C.L. Ragghianti, Florence, Plazzo Strozzi, 1967.
Catalogue *Sculpteurs italiens*, text by F. Bellonzi, Paris, Musée d'Art Moderne de la Ville de Paris, 1968.
Catalogue *100 opere d'arte italiana dal Futurismo ad oggi*, Rome, Galleria Nazionale d'Arte Moderna, 20 December 1968-20 January 1969.
Catalogue *Métamorphose de l'Objet. Art et Anti-Art 1910-1970*, 22 April-6 June 1971.
Catalogue *Anni Trenta - Arte e cultura in Italia*, edited by R. Barilli, Milan, Palazzo Reale, 1982.
Catalogue *Italian Art in the 20th Century - Painting and Sculpture 1900-1988*, London, Royal Academy of Arts, 14 January-9 April 1989.

Divisionism

L. Guaita
La scienza dei colori e la pittura, Milan 1893
D. Tumiati
"Divisionismo. Tre artisti: Segantini, Pellizza da Vopedo, Morbelli," in *Il Marzocco*, no. 2, Florence, February 1896.
G. Pellizza da Volpedo
"Luce, pittura, divisionismo," in *La festa dell'Arte*, no. 1, Florence 1896.
A. Melani
"Pittura a puntini," in *Gazzetta di Venezia*, Venice 1903.
G. Mucchi
"Esperienze e contraddizioni del divisionismo," in *Realismo*, no. 3, Milan, September 1952.
M. Muraro
"Il Divisionismo," in *Emporium*, Bergamo, July-August 1952.
M. Valsecchi
"Breve scheda del divisionismo italiano," in *La Biennale di Venezia*, no. 9, July 1952.
F. Bellonzi
Il divisionismo nella pittura italiana, Milan 1967.
F. Bellonzi, T. Fiori
Archivi del divisionismo, Rome 1968.
A.P. Quinsac
La peinture divisionniste en Italie. Origines premiers développements 1880-1895, Paris 1972.
F. Bellonzi
Architettura, pittura, scultura dal neoclassicismo al Liberty, Rome 1973.
M. Poggialini Tominetti
"Un decennio di studi sul Divisionismo italiano," in *Arte Lombarda*, no. 50, 1978.
Catalogues of the Esposizione di Belle Arti, Società degli Amatori e Cultori from 1899 to 1914, Rome.
Catalogue I Biennale Romana, *Esposizione di Belle Arti nel Cinquantenario di Roma capitale*, Rome 1920-1921.
Catalogue XXVI Biennale Internazionale d'Arte, *Divisionismo in Francia e in Italia*, Venice 1952.
Catalogue *50 anni d'arte a Milano dal divisionismo ad oggi*, Milan, Palazzo della Permanente, 31 January-15 March 1959.
Catalogue *Mostra del divisionismo italiano*, texts by F. Bellonzi, P.L. De Vecchi, M. Rosci, R. De Grada, A.M. Brizio, Milan, Palazzo della Permanente, 1970.
A.M. Damigella, *Modernismo, simbolismo, divisionismo, arte sociale a Roma dal 1870 al 1911*, in the catalogue *Aspetti dell'Arte a Roma 1870-1914*, Rome 1972.

Catalogue *Arte e socialità in Italia dal realismo al simbolismo*, texts by F. Bellonzi, R. Bossaglia, M. Poggialini Tominetti, D. Bacile, Milan, Palazzo della Permanente, 1979

Futurism

G. Apollinaire
"Futurisme," in *Les Arts*, 31 May 1914, Paris.
A. Soffici
Cubismo e Futurismo, Florence 1914.
Ch. Zervos
"Le Futurisme," in *Cahiers d'Art*, 1938.
Ch. Zervos, Benedetta, P. Buzzi, F. Pastonchi
"Le Futurisme. Un demi-siècle d'art italien," special issue of *Cahiers d'Art*, XXV, 1950.
M. Drudi Gambillo and T. Fiori
Archivi del Futurismo, Rome 1958-1962.
E. Falqui
Bibliografie e iconografie del Futurismo, Florence 1959.
C. Ballo
Preistoria del futurismo, Milan 1960.
R. Carrieri
Il futurismo, Milan 1961.
E. Crispolti
Il Secondo Futurismo: 5 pittori + 1 scultore, Torino 1923-1938, Turin 1962.
J. Pierre
Il Futurismo e il Cubismo, Lausanne 1965.
M. Calvesi
Le due avanguardie, Milan 1966.
M. Calvesi
"I Futuristi e la simultaneità: Boccioni, Carrà, Russolo e Severini," in *L'Arte Moderna*, V, no. 39, Milan 1967.
M.W. Martin
Futurist Art and Theory 1909-1915, Oxford 1968.
F.T. Marinetti
Teoria e invenzione futurista, edited by L. De Maria, Milan 1968.
E. Crispolti
Il mito della macchina e altri temi del Futurismo, Trapani, 1969.
U. Apollonio
Futurismo, Milan 1970.
L. De Maria
Per conoscere Marinetti e il futurismo, Milan 1977.
C. Tisdall, A. Bozzolla
Futurism, London 1977.
L. De Maria
F.T. Marinetti - Teoria e invenzione futurista, Milan 1983.
F. Roche-Pézard
L'aventure futuriste 1909-1916, Paris-Rome 1983.
C. Salaris
Storia del futurismo. Libri giornali manifesti, Rome 1985.
E. Crispolti
Storia e critica del futurismo, Bari-Rome 1986.
Catalogue *Prima Esposizione Libera Futurista Internazionale*, Rome, Galleria Sprovieri, April-May 1914.
Catalogue III Biennale Romana, *Mostra Futurista di Balla Depero De Pistoris Dottori Marasco Prampolini Tato*, Rome, Palazzo delle esposizioni, March-June 1925.
Catalogue *Mostra di trentaquattro pittori futuristi*, Milan, Galleria Pesaro, 1927.
Catalogue, *Futurismo e pittura metafisica*, Zürich, Kunsthaus, November-December 1950.
Catalogue *Futurism: Balla Boccioni Carrà Russolo Severini*, text by G. Coquiot, New York, Sidney Janis Gallery, 1954.
Catalogue *Mostra del Futurismo*, Rome, Palazzo Barberini, 1959.
Catalogue *XXX Biennale Internazionale d'Arte. Mostra storica del Futurismo*, Venice 1960.
Catalogue *Futurism*, edited by J. Taylor, New York, The Museum of Modern Art, 31 May-5

Selected Bibliography

September 1961.
Catalogue *Aspetti del secondo futurismo torinese*, edited by E. Crispolti and A. Gavano, Turin, Galleria Civica d'Arte Moderna, 27 March-30 April 1962.
Catalogue *The Futurism*, New York, Albert Loeb and Krugier Gallery, 1968.
Catalogue *Filippo Tommaso Marinetti e il futurismo*, Milan, Palazzo Sormani, 11 February-8 March 1969.
Catalogue *Le Futurisme 1909-1916*, Paris, Musée National d'Art, 19 September-19 November 1973.
Catalogue *Boccioni e il suo tempo*, edited by G. Ballo, F. Cachin Nora, F. Russoli, Milan, Palazzo Reale, 1974.
Catalogue *Du futurisme au spatialisme*, Geneva, Musée Rath, 7 October 1977-15 January 1978.
Catalogue *Ricostruzione futurista dell'universo*, edited by E. Crispolti, Turin, Mole Antonelliana, June-October 1980.
Catalogue *Futurismo Futurismi*, edited by P. Hulten, G. Celant, S. Fauchereau, S. Zadora, Venice, Palazzo Grassi, 1986.

Metaphysical Art

C. Carrà
"La pittura metafisica," in *Il Popolo d'Italia*, 3 June 1918.
C. Carrà
Pittura metafisica, Florence 1919.
G. De Chirico
"Noi metafisici," in *Cronache di attualità*, 15 February 1919.
R. Longhi
"Al Dio ortopedico," *Il Tempo*, Rome 22 February 1919 (reprint in *Scritti giovanili 1912-1922*, Sansoni, Florence 1961).
G. De Chirico
"Sull'arte metafisica," in *Valori Plastici*, nos. 4-5, 1919.
F. Roth
Nach-Expressionismus - Magischer Realismus - Probleme der neuesten europäischen Malerei, Leipzig 1925.
P. Zanfrognini
Il problema spirituale della pittura d'oggi, Modena 1934.
F. De Pisis
"La così detta 'arte metafisica'," *Emporium*, Bergamo, November 1938.
M. Masciotta
"La pittura metafisica," in *Letteratura*, nos. 7-9, 1941.
J.T. Soby
"The scuola metafisica," in *Twentieth-Century Italian Art*, New York 1949.
U. Apollonio
Pittura metafisica, Venice 1950.
Arcangeli
"Sulla pittura metafisica," in *Vernice*, nos. 22-23, 1950.
Ch. Zervos
"Un demi siècle d'art italien," in *Cahiers d'art*, I, 1950 (ibid., G.A. Dell'Acqua, *La peinture métaphysique*).
G. Raimondi
"La pittura metafisica - De Chirico, Carrà, Morandi," in *Comunità*, Milan, December 1957.
M. Carrà
Metafisica, Milan 1968.
P. Waldberg
"La diffusione della metafisica e la sua influenza sul surrealismo," in *L'arte moderna*, Fabbri, Milan 1969.
P. Fossati
La pittura a programma - De Chirico metafisico, Venice-Padova 1973.
P. Fossati

Valori Plastici 1918-1922, Turin 1981.
F. Bellonzi, R. Assunto, G. Di Genova, E. Valeriani, F. Ulivi and others
La metafisica, Rome 1982.
M. Calvesi
La Metafisica schiarita, Milan 1982.
A.M. Andreoli
"Metafisica e dintorni," in *Il Verri*, nos. 26-27, 1983.
P. Fossati
La "pittura metafisica", Turin 1988.
Catalogue *Metafisica del quotidiano*, text by F. Solmi, Bologna, Galleria Comunale d'Arte Moderna, June-September 1977.
Catalogue *La pittura metafisica*, texts by G. Briganti, E. Coen, Venice, Istituto di Cultura di Palazzo Grassi, May-June 1979.
Catalogue *La metafisica: gli anni Venti*, edited by R. Barilli and F. Solmi, Bologna, Galleria d'Arte Moderna, May-August 1980.

Novecento

M. Sarfatti
Segni colori e luci, Bologna 1925.
R. Papini
"La mostra del Novecento," in *Emporium*, Bergamo, February 1926.
C. Tridenti
"La prima mostra del Novecento italiano - Primavera spirituale," in *Il Giornale d'Italia*, Rome, 16 February 1926.
E. Somaré
"Novecento," in *Il Novecento Italiano - Rassegna di Pittura e Scultura*, Milan, summer 1926.
M. Tozzi
"Le 'Novecento italiano'," in *Cahiers d'Art*, Paris, 5 May 1929.
A.F. Della Porta
Polemica sul "900", Milan 1930.
I. Cinti
"Gli equivoci del Novecento," in *Perseo*, Milan, 1 May 1933.
I. Cinti
"Gli equivoci del Novecento: Arte infantile," in *Perseo*, Milan, 15 November 1933.
M. Bontempelli
L'avventura novecentesca (1926-1938), Florence 1938.
U. Nebbia
La pittura del Novecento, Milan 1946.
R. Modesti
"Il Novecento," in *Pittura italiana contemporanea*, Milan 1958.
M. Carrà
"Tra le due guerre: il rapporto di cultura e realtà," in *L'arte moderna*, vol. IX, Milan 1967.
M. Rosci
"Il fascismo degli intellettuali," in AA.VV., *Arte e fascismo in Italia e in Germania*, Milan 1974.
Ph. Cannistraro
La fabbrica del consenso, Bari 1975.
F. Tempesti
Arte dell'Italia fascista, Milan 1976.
R. Bossaglia
Il Novecento italiano (with texts by Claudia Gian Ferrari and Marco Lorandi), Milan 1979.
G. Armellini
Le immagini del fascismo nelle arti figurative, Milan 1980.
P. Fossati
"Il Novecento," in *Storia dell'arte italiana*, Turin 1982.
R. Jacobbi
L'avventura del Novecento, Milan 1984.
Catalogue *La Fiorentina primaverile*, first national exposition of the work of art and its creation, Florence, Palazzo delle Esposizioni al Parco di San Gallo, April-July 1922.
Catalogue *I Mostra del Novecento italiano*, Milan,

Palazzo della Permanente, February-March 1926.
Catalogue *Les artistes italiens de Paris*, preface by W. George, Paris, Salon de l'Escalier, February-March 1928.
Catalogue *II Mostra del Novecento italiano*, Milan, Palazzo della Permanente, March-April 1929.
"Appels d'Italie," introduction by W. George, coordinated by M. Tozzi, in Cat. *XVII Esposizione biennale internazionale d'arte*, Venice 1930.
Catalogue *I Mostra di pittori italiani residenti a Parigi* (Campigli, De Chirico, De Pisis, Paresce, Savinio, Severini, Tozzi), Milan, Galleria Milano, January 1930.
Catalogue *La metafisica: gli anni Venti*, edited by R. Barilli and F. Solmi, Bologna, Galleria d'Arte moderna, May-August 1980.
Catalogue *Les réalismes 1919-1939*, Paris, Centre Georges Pompidou, December 1980-April 1981, Berlin Staatliche Kunsthalle, May-June 1981.
Catalogue *Il Novecento italiano 1923-1933*, edited by R. Bossaglia, Milan, Palazzo della Permanente, January-March 1983.
Catalogue *Dal ritorno all'ordine al richiamo della pittura - Continuità figurativa nella pittura italiana 1920-1987*, edited by B. Mantura and Pia Vivarelli, Oslo, Kunstnernes Hus, 6-23 February 1988.

Scuola romana

C. Maltese
"Mario Mafai da oltre vent'anni guida la famosa 'Scuola romana'," *L'Unità*, Rome, 15 March 1919.
G. Castelfranco, D. Durbé
La Scuola romana dal 1930 al 1945, De Luca, Rome 1960.
P. Scarpellini
"I quindici della Scuola romana," in *Il Ponte*, Florence, July 1960.
M. Carrà
Gli anni del ritorno all'ordine, Milan 1977.
V. Rivosecchi - A. Trombadori
Roma appena ieri, Rome 1986.
M. Fagiolo dell'Arco
Scuola romana - Pittura e scultura a Roma dal 1919 al 1943, text by A. Trombadori, with the collaboration of V. Rivosecchi and with the advice of N. Vespignani, Rome 1986.
Catalogue *VIII Quadriennale d'Arte*, La Scuola romana dal 1930 al 1945, Rome, Palazzo delle Esposizioni, December 1959-April 1960.
Catalogue *La Scuola romana*, edited by R. Lucchese, Rome, Galleria La Barcaccia, 11-25 April 1964.
Catalogue *Scipione, Mafai, Raphaël*, edited by L. Vinca Masini, Todi, Palazzo del Popolo, 1979.
Catalogue *Scuola romana. Pittori tra le due guerre*, edited by M. Fagiolo, Rome, Galleria Cembalo Borghese, 1983.
Catalogue *Roma tra Espressionismo barocco e pittura tonale 1929-1943*, Milan, Galleria Daverio, 1984.
Catalogue *Programma*, edited by M. Fagiolo, Turin, Studio Scuola romana, November-December 1986.
Catalogue *I volti della Scuola romana*, text by V. Sgarbi, Turin, Studio Scuola Romana, January-February 1987.
Catalogue *Natura morta*, texts by M. Fagiolo and M. Rosci, Turin, Studio Scuola Romana, 27 May-15 July 1987.
Catalogue *Scuola romana. Artisti tra le due guerre*, edited by M. Fagiolo and V. Rivosecchi, Milan, Palazzo Reale, 13 April-19 June 1988.
Catalogue *Le scuole romane - Sviluppi e continuità*, edited by G. Cortenova, Verona, Palazzo Forti, 9 April-15 June 1988.

Corrente

G. Piovene
"La mostra di Corrente," in *Corriere della sera*, Milan, 7 December 1939.
R. De Grada
Il movimento di Corrente, Milan, 1939.
M. De Micheli
"Il movimento di Corrente," in *Calendario del Popolo*, Milan 1950.
R. De Grada
Il Movimento di Corrente, Milan 1952.
M. De Micheli
"Storia di Corrente," in *Le Arti*, January-February 1960.
E. Gian Ferrari (editor)
"Corrente," in *Belvedere*, bulletin of the Galleria GianFerrari, Milan 1960. With articles by Treccani, De Grada, Valsecchi, Guttuso, Sassu, Ballo, Russoli, Anceschi, Marchiori, Vittorini, Testori, Biasion, Pallucchini, De Micheli, Vedova, Apollonio.
M. Valsecchi
Gli Artisti di Corrente, Milan 1963.
R. De Grada
Verifica di Corrente, Milan 1967.
A. Luzi
Corrente di Vita Giovanile (1938-40), Rome 1975.
V. Fagone
Introduzione a Corrente, gennaio 1938-maggio 1940, Macerata 1977.
G. Seveso
Da Corrente a oggi, Milan 1980.
AA.VV.
Omaggio a Corrente - Poesie, Quaderni di Poesia del gruppo Fara, Bergamo 1983.
Catalogue, *Rinnovamento dell'arte in Italia dal 1930 al 1945*, Ferrara, Casa Romei, June-September 1960.
Catalogue *Gli Artisti di Corrente*, Verona, Palazzo della Gran Guardia, July-August 1963.
Catalogue *Arte della resistenza in Europa*, edited by C. Gnudi, J. Cassou, M. De Micheli, Bologna, Museo Civico, 1965.
Catalogue *Trent'anni di Corrente*, edited by R. De Grada, Milan, Galleria Trentadue, 1967.
Catalogue *Corrente trent'anni dopo*, edited by R. De Grada, Ravenna, Galleria dell'Accademia Loggetta Lombardesca, 1971.
Catalogue *Milano 70/70 un secolo d'arte*, G.F. Bruno, "Da Boccioni a Corrente," Milan, Museo Poldi Pezzoli, April-June 1971.
Catalogue *Corrente. Cultura e società 1938-1942*, edited by E. Crispolti, V. Fagone, C. Ruju, Naples, Palazzo Reale, 1978.
Catalogue *Gli scultori di Corrente*, edited by Z. Birolli and R. De Grada, Milan 1979/80.
Catalogue *Gli Anni di Corrente*, exhibition document I Quaderni della Collezione civica d'arte, with texts G. Bergamaschi, S. Cherchi, R. De Graa, Pinerolo, 7-23 October 1983.
Catalogue *Corrente: il Movimento di Arte e Cultura di Opposizione 1930-1945*, Milan, Palazzo Reale, 25 January-28 April 1985.

Abstract Art

C. Belli
Kn, Milan 1935.
A. Sartoris
"Mostra a Villa Olmo e la sua eccezionale importanza artistica," *La Provincia*, Como, 4 October 1936.
M. Seuphor
L'Art abstrait, ses origines, ses premiers maîtres, Paris 1949.
M. Seuphor
Dictionnaire de la Peinture Abstraite, Paris 1957.
E. Crispolti
"Appunti per una storia del non figurativo in Ita-

lia," in *Ulisse*, Rome XXII, vol. 33, 1959.
G. Dorfles
Ultime tendenze dell'arte di oggi, Milan 1961.
C. Belloli
Proposta per un'evidenza dell'astrattismo italiano, Milan 1963.
M. Seuphor
La peinture abstraite, Paris 1962.
M. Valsecchi
"Cronologia de primo astrattismo italiano," *Le Arti*, Milan, 6 January 1966.
J. Lassaigne, F. Russoli
L'Arte Moderna. Il dopoguerra: dal naturalismo astratto all'informale, Milan 1967.
P. Fossati
L'immagine sospesa. Pittura e scultura astratta in Italia: 1934-1940, Turin 1971.
C. Belli
Lettera sulla nascita dell'astrattismo, Milan 1978.
G. Ballo
Origini dell'astrattismo, Milan 1980.
A. Sartoris
Lunga marcia dell'arie astratta in Italia, Milan 1980.
D. Vallier
L'arte astratta, Milan 1984.
D. Morosini
Arte degli anni difficili 1928-1944, Rome 1985.
Catalogue ""Prima mostra collettiva d'arte astratta italiana," Turin, Studio of Casorati and Paulucci, via Barolo 2, March 1935.
Catalogue *Pittura moderna italiana*, text by A. Sartoris, Como, September-October 1936.
Catalogue *Mostra arte astratta*, Turin, Politecnico, 1946.
Catalogue *Arte astratta italiana*, Rome, Galleria Nazionale d'Arte Moderna, 1948.
Catalogue *Arte astratta e concreta in Italia*, Rome, Galleria Nazionale d'Arte Moderna, 1950.
Catalogue *Arte astratta italiana - I primi astrattisti 1913-1940*, texts by C. Monnet, Perogalli, Milan, Galleria Bompiani, 1951.
Catalogue XXXIII Biennale Internazionale di Venezia, *Rassegna del primo astrattismo italiano*, texts by N. Ponente, Venice 1966.
Catalogue *Esperienze dell'astrattismo italiano 1930-1940*, text by M. Fagiolo, Turin, Galleria Notizie, February-March 1968.
Catalogue *Aspetti del primo astrattismo italiano*, text by L. Caramel, Monza, Palazzo Civico, 1969.
Catalogue *Origini dell'Astrattismo verso altri orizzonti del reale*, Milan, Palazzo Reale, 18 October 1979-18 January 1980.
Catalogue *Anni creativi al "Milione" 1932-1939*, Prato, Palazzo Novelucci, 1980.
Catalogue *Arte Astratta Italiana 1909-1959*, Rome, Galleria d'Arte Nazionale Moderna, 2 April-11 May 1980.
Catalogue *Astrattismo italiano tra le due guerre*, Turin, Galleria Martano, 10 November-10 December 1980.
Catalogue *Astratta*, edited by G. Cortenova and F. Menna, Verona, Palazzo Forti, 23 January-15 March 1988.

Index of names

Index of names

Index of names

Index of names

Index of names

Translators

Patrick Creagh
Wendy Dallas
Andrew Ellis
Silvia Hunte
Roberta Kedzierski
Geoffrey Land
Brian McDonald
Carol Rathman
Terry Rogers
Anthony Shugaar
Virginia Shuey
Shara Wassermann

Photo Credits

Franco Abbondanza, Milan
Pino Abbrescia, Rome
Agosto, Genoa
Aurelio Amendola, Pistoia
Archivi Musei Vaticani, Rome
Archivio fotografico Pininfarina, Cambiano
Archivio fotografico Scuola Romana, Rome
Archivio Storico delle arti contemporanee della Biennale, Venice
Graziano Arici, Venice
Myles Aronovitz, New York
Arte Fotografica, Milan
Muriel Assens, Villeneuve d'Ascq
Böhm, Venice
Cameraphoto, Venice
Giancarlo Campeggi, Milan
Luca Carrà, Milan
Centro Studi Anton Giulio Bragaglia, Rome
Centro Studi e Archivio della Comunicazione, Parma
A.C. Cooper, London
Tarcisio Dal Gal, Verona
Dardanelli, Florence
Giuseppe Dell'Aquila, Turin
Paola Depietri, Florence
Philippe R. Doumic, Paris
W. Dräyer, Zurich
Ursula Edelmann, Frankfurt/Main
Fasolo, Venice
Mario Finotti, Novara
Foto Ancillotti, Milan
Foto Bertolini, Milan
Foto Casali, Milan
Foto Electa, Milan
Foto Fabbri - Piero Baguzzi, Milan
Foto Giacomelli, Venice
Foto Giana, Como
Foto Perotti, Milan
Foto Vasari, Rome
Gabinetto fotografico nazionale, Rome
Giuseppe Gaeta, Neaples
Mario Gerardi, Rome
Giovara, Gallarate
Tom Haastsen, Oudeker
David Heald, New York
Paul Hester, Houston
Hickey & Robertson, Houston
Hans Hinz, Allschwil, Basel
Istituto Scala, Florence
Bernd Kirtz, Duisburg
Laboratorio fotointerpretazione e aerofotogrammetria, Rome
Domenico Lucchetti, Bergamo
B.P. Manusardi, Milan
Dante Mariotti, Macerata
Italo Martinero, Biella
Robert E. Mates, New York
The Metropolitan Museum of Art, New York
Miceat, Musée national d'art moderne, Paris
Herbert Michel, Zurich
Musée national d'art moderne, Paris
The Museum of Modern Art, New York
Massimo Napoli, Rome
National Gallery of Art, Washington
Daniele Paparelli, Perugia
Philadelphia Museum of Art, Philadelphia
Piccardo & Rosso, Savona
Vincenzo Pirozzi, Rome
Ferruccio Rampazzi, Turin
Saporetti, Milan
Oscar Savio, Rome
Giuseppe Schiavinotto, Rome
Mark Smith, Venice
Statens Konstmuseet, Stockholm
Jim Strong, New York
Studio Padovan, Turin
Studio Parlatini Pugnaghi, Modena
Studio 3, Milan
Tavanti, Arezzo
The Tate Gallery, London
Riccardo Toffoletti, Udine
La Triennale, Milan
Paolo Vandrasch, Milan
Janet Woodard, Houston

The following works: Carlo Carrà, *La casa dell'amore*, 1922; Umberto Boccioni, *Costruzione orizzontale*, 1912; Giorgio De Chirico, *Ariadne*, 1913; Arturo Martini, *La Convalescente*, 1932; Arturo Martini, *La veglia* o *L'attesa*, 1930-31, though reproduced in the catalogue, are not on display in the exhibition due to techicalities which arose at the last minute.